MW00575511

THE AWAKENING

EGO SVM VIA
VERITAS ET VITA

THE AWAKENING

A History of the Western Mind

AD 500 - 1700

CHARLES FREEMAN

An Apollo Book

For my daughter Cordelia

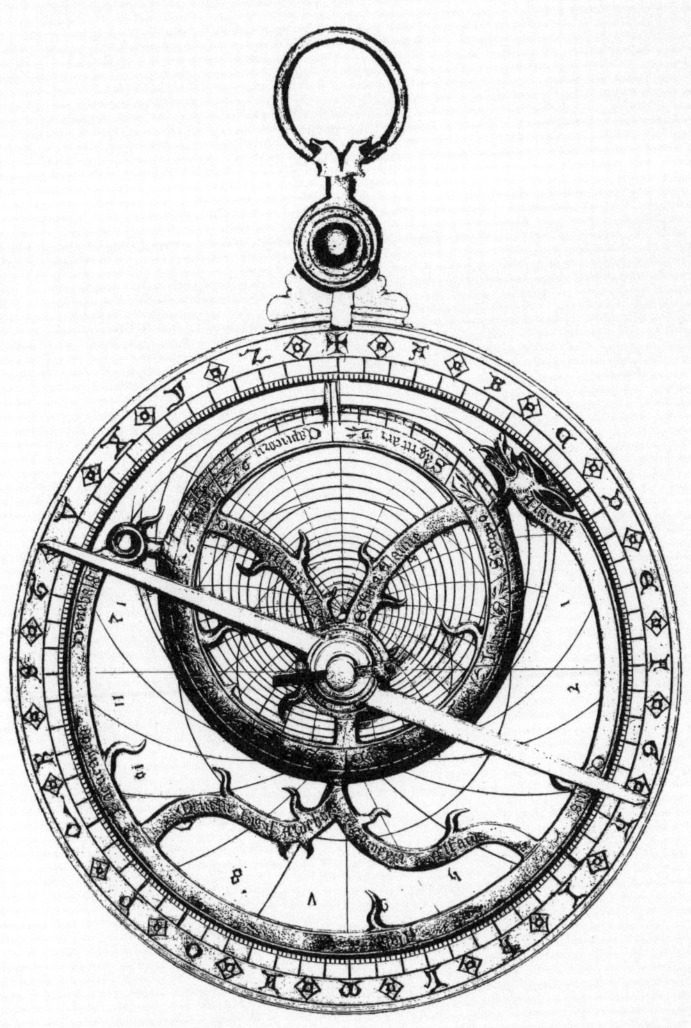

This is an Apollo book,
first published in the UK in 2020
by Head of Zeus Ltd

9 7 5 3 1 2 4 6 8

A catalogue record for this book is available from the British Library.

ISBN [HB]: 9781789545623
ISBN [E]: 9781789545647

Designed and typeset by Isambard Thomas at Corvo,
in Linotype Garamond and Didot

Printed and bound in Serbia by Publikum

Head of Zeus Ltd
First Floor East
5–8 Hardwick Street
London EC1R 4RG
www.headofzeus.com

Preface

The epithets 'barbarous' and 'civilized' occur so frequently in conversation and in books, that whoever employs his thoughts in contemplation of the manners and history of mankind will have occasion to consider, with some attention, both what ideas these words are commonly meant to convey, and in what sense they ought to be employed by the historian and moral philosopher.

James Dunbar, *Essay on the History of Mankind in Rude and Cultivated Ages* (1780)

The monastic foundation of the Chora in Istanbul, formerly the great Christian city of Constantinople, is a rare survival of a church with its original medieval decorations in what has been an Islamic city since 1453. Founded in the fourth century as a monastery of the Holy Saviour in the Fields, outside the walls built by Emperor Constantine (*chora* designates the open space around a city), it then became enclosed within the later, fifth-century, set of walls but never lost its name. It is famous today for its wonderful fourteenth-century mosaics and, in a fresco in a side chapel, a stunning portrayal of the resurrected Christ entering Limbo to release the souls there.

It was in 1295, just before the mosaics were created, that one Maximus Planudes, an erudite Byzantine Greek monk who was fascinated by the ancient world, tracked down in the library the one manuscript he was looking for, a copy of Claudius Ptolemy's *Geographike Hyphegesis* (*Guide to Drawing the Earth*).[1] The *Geographike* was one of the major intellectual achievements of the second century AD and its rediscovery proved a vital breakthrough. Ptolemy (*c.*AD 100–*c.*170), perhaps more famous for his great work on astronomy, the *Almagest*, had adopted the concepts of longitude and latitude from the Greek astronomer Hipparchus (*c.*190 BC–120 BC). He then used a text by the cartographer and mathematician Marinus of Tyre (*c.*AD 70–130) to provide the co-ordinates for no fewer than 8,000 locations, covering an area that extended from the Canary Islands in the west to what is now the Gulf of Thailand in the east, with maps setting them out. For these Ptolemy followed Hipparchus in dividing the Earth into 360 equal degrees, with the equator at 0 degrees and the imagined North Pole some 90 degrees latitude above it. The Canary Islands were designated by Ptolemy at 0 degrees longitude, with the total span of his locations 180 degrees to the east in distant Asia. Sadly, none of these maps have survived, but there was enough material in the text to recreate them. We still use Ptolemy's system today, bands of longitude and latitude equally spaced on the surface of a globe.* The rediscovery of the *Geographike* in the late thirteenth century, 1,000 years after it had been written down and presumed lost, was a seminal moment in the awakening of the western mind.

Planudes' was not the only copy of the *Geographike* to survive; another was known to the Arabs and had been translated into Arabic in the ninth century. It was used by the nobly born cartographer

* By a convention adopted in 1884, 0 degrees longitude – the so-called Prime Meridian – passes through Greenwich, in south-east London.

Muhammad al-Idrisi, who had been invited to join the cultured court of the Norman king of Sicily, Roger II, in about the year 1138. Al-Idrisi adopted Ptolemy's concepts of longitude and latitude to create seventy regional maps in which all the sections were drawn to the same scale, the first time this had been done. The maps were recognizably accurate in delineating the known world of Ptolemy even though, according to Arabic convention, north and south were reversed. (Most illustrations of al-Idrisi's maps follow the western convention of the north at the top.) They reflected the faith of its maker, so they showed the Arabian peninsula and Mecca at the centre and the text was in Arabic, but al-Idrisi used Greek, Latin and Arabic sources without discrimination. The open-minded Roger II took such an interest in the project that the volume containing the maps and accompanying text became known as the *Tabula Rogeriana* (*The Book of Roger*). Following the death of Roger – who had proved such an enthusiastic patron to al-Idrisi – in 1154, the climate of the times was hardly conducive to the dissemination of the work of the *Tabula*'s creator. With the crusades dominating the Christian imagination, an Islamic map of this date, even one produced at a 'European' court, was hardly likely to be welcomed. Al-Idrisi's pioneering work therefore remained little known in Europe. Yet it serves to highlight one of the major themes of this book: the Arabs were well ahead of the Europeans in intellectual life at least until the thirteenth century and they were to make a formidable contribution to the revival of 'western' learning.[2]

overleaf Al-Idrisi's 1154 map of the world as tabulated by Ptolemy is shown with the Arabic world at the top and Europe at the bottom.

The copy of Ptolemy found by Planudes proved more influential in Europe. The monk took his find to the Byzantine emperor Andronikos II Palaiologos, who was equally excited by the discovery. He soon had his finest copyists working on the manuscript and his best mathematicians plotting out the maps. Planudes added his own explanatory texts, translating the Greek numerals into the Arabic ones that we use today. Three copies of their atlases survive, in large folios with all the twenty-six maps Ptolemy had given co-ordinates for. Manuel Chrysoloras, a scholar from Constantinople, brought one copy to Florence when he initiated the teaching of Greek there in 1396. By 1410 the first Latin translation of the original Greek text had been made by one of Chrysoloras's students, the Tuscan Jacobus Angelus, who dedicated it to Pope Alexander V. For the humanists† the

† 'Humanism' in a fifteenth/sixteenth-century context does not mean a movement that rejected religion but refers to the study of the 'humanities', largely through classical texts (see Chapter 11).

IX.
VIII.
VII.
VI.
bahr al hozar

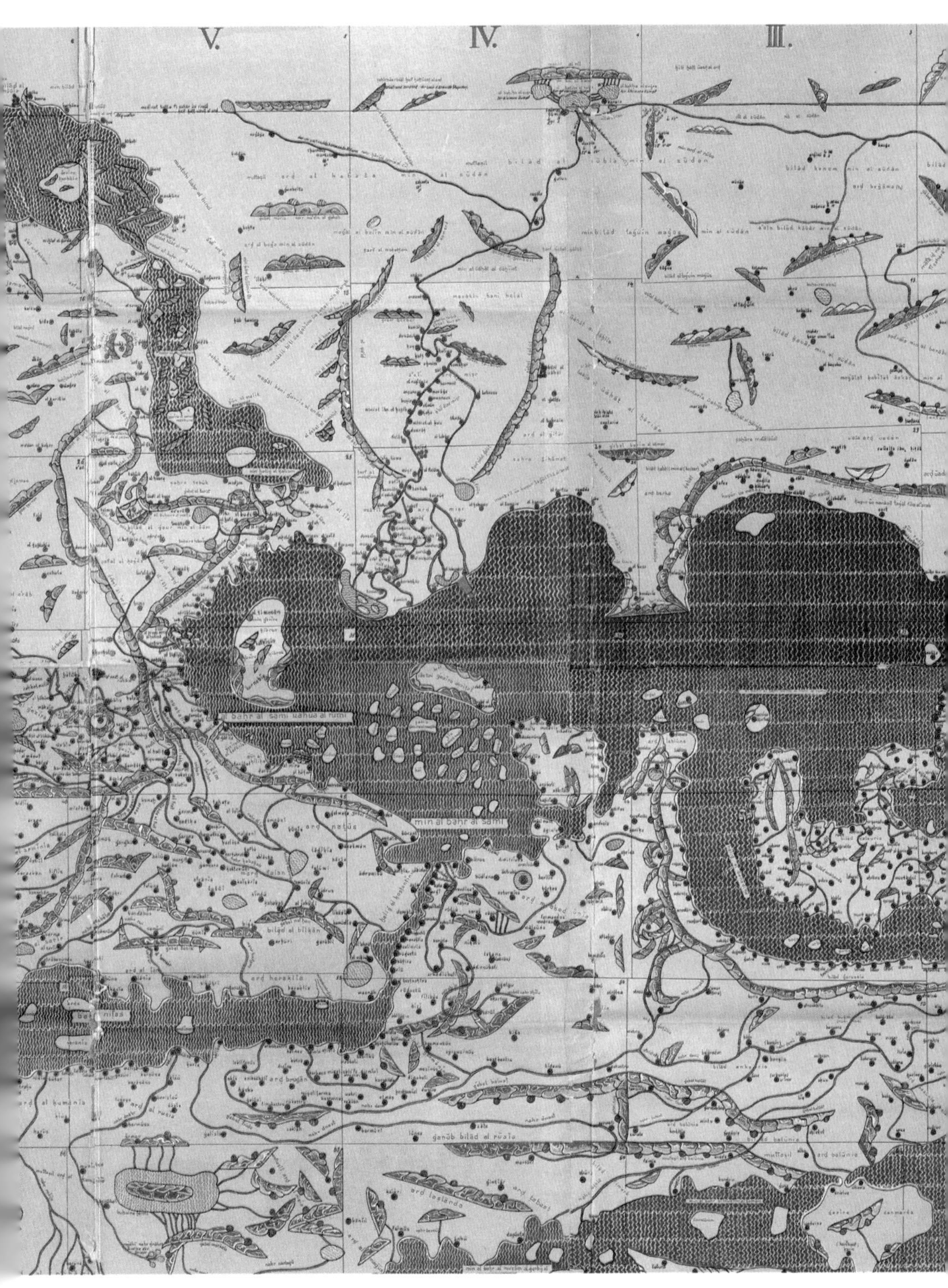
V.
IV.
III.
min al bahr al sami

Geographike became honoured as another window into the minds of the ancients and as a text that was clearly superior to its competitors. It gradually supplanted medieval conceptions of the geography of Europe, the Christian *mappae mundi* and the portolan charts that used compass bearings to plot the ports of the Mediterranean. By the end of the fifteenth century, the *Geographike* was still dominating the world of the cartographers. As knowledge of the Earth's land masses expanded, Ptolemy's findings could be adapted to fit these new discoveries. So while Ptolemy knew nothing of Scandinavia – the northernmost point in the *Geographike* was the semi-mythical island of 'Thule' at 63 degrees – his system could be used to incorporate the region in newly drawn maps.

Yet by 1520 Ptolemy was being challenged. While his longitude and latitudes remained essential, his inaccuracies were becoming apparent. He had provided locations only as far as 20 degrees south of the equator, leaving the south of Africa unplotted. It was not even known whether sea surrounded the continent. Only after the Cape of Good Hope had been rounded by Bartholemeu Dias in 1488 was the full extent of Africa appreciated and Ptolemy's system had to be adapted to include it. More dramatically, his sweep of locations stretched too far round the globe. This suggested that navigation across the undiscovered and uncharted section would be over a relatively short distance, with the possibility that a voyage to the west could reach eastern Asia without difficulty. Columbus had set off in 1492 with this misconception that was demolished by the unexpected discovery of the 'New World' of the Americas. These had to be fitted in once their long coastlines were surveyed. Ptolemy's sweep of locations across Eurasia had then to be compressed. When Magellan's sailors circumnavigated the world for the first time in 1521 this opened the way for a global map that went well beyond anything Ptolemy had envisaged.

The shift in perspective can be seen in the maps and accompanying texts of the period. A Florentine silk merchant, Gregorio Dati (1362–1435), had already compiled a series of maps based on Ptolemy – the *Sfera-Cosmographia* – but with information from his fellow merchants as additions. The early (manuscript) copies of the *Sfera* from the fifteenth century suggest that this was a popular text continually improved by the contributions of returning sailors.[3] Then there was the 1507 *Mondus Novus* (*New World*) of the Utrecht cartographer Johannes Ruysch (*c.*1460–1533). Little is known of Ruysch, but he had been to sea and had probably travelled along the coast of north America. While he used Ptolemaic principles for his meticulous world map, he had incorporated a great deal of extra information from his own travels and those of others, especially the Portuguese explorers of the later fifteenth century. The coastlines of Africa and much of the Americas are shown fairly accurately and the islands of Madagascar and Sri Lanka (formerly Ceylon) are in their correct positions. *Mondus Novus* was a 'scientific' project in so far as it left out the mythical lands of the medieval imagination shown on earlier maps.

By the end of the sixteenth century, the distinction between the land masses of the Earth as they really existed and those given locations by Ptolemy was well established. The extraordinary maps of Gerard Mercator (1512–94) and the wonderfully illustrated and accurate atlas (1570) of the Antwerp-based Abraham Ortelius that contained seventy maps of the known world represented considerable advances on the Ptolemaic model. Ptolemy was still honoured – Mercator helped compose a new edition of the *Geographike* (under its Latin name *Geographia*) as late as 1578 – but by now the experience of exploration had supplanted it. This was just at the time when another achievement of Ptolemy, the Earth-centred universe that he had made the core of his remarkable *Almagest*, was being challenged by followers of Copernicus; most notably, in the early 1600s, by Galileo. Writing in 1620, the English philosopher Francis Bacon complained that it would be wrong if 'the limits of our intellectual world were restricted to the narrow discoveries of the ancients'.[4] In a conflict between 'Ancients', those who believed that the classical texts were still authoritative, and 'Moderns', who believed they had been superseded by new inventions such as the printing press, Bacon proved a leading figure among the 'Moderns'. This transition, from one world view to another, from the reliance on the authority of ancient texts to what might loosely be called scientific knowledge, would prove another crucial moment in the awakening of the western mind.

The example of Ptolemy's *Geographike* illustrates the trajectory of this book. An ancient text, one of immense importance and sophistication, is rediscovered by both Arabs and Europeans. The Arabs exploit it most successfully some 300 years before the Europeans do. This becomes a common theme in the history of medieval thought. (In later chapters the many works and ideas transferred from the Arab world into Europe will be discussed in greater detail.) In this case Ptolemy provided a framework for the early mapmakers and the superiority of the *Geographike* allowed it to displace medieval charts. Yet as time went on, and exploration added new regions and continents to the known world, its inadequacies became obvious and what might be called 'scientific' thinking took over so that by the end of the sixteenth century accurate maps were being produced. This was part of a much wider intellectual revolution leading to the claim by the philosopher A. C. Grayling 'that the seventeenth century in Europe redirected the course of human history by changing humankind's perspective on the universe and itself'.[5] I will be more cautious than Grayling. Whether such a radical transformation in western thought can be supported must remain unanswered until my final chapter.

In traditional Eurocentric accounts the 'history of the western mind' would have been told as if there was some form of inevitability about the triumph of western, often Christian, values. Such a view has now been comprehensively questioned. The success of Europe often depended on the exploitation of others and there is a much greater critical appreciation of the contributions made by other civilizations – the Arab world, India and China, for instance – to western learning. Any attempt to define 'western civilization' philosophically soon becomes frustrated. By the end of the period covered by this book writers such as Michel de Montaigne, disturbed by the atrocities of the religious wars of his day, were wondering whether the 'savages' discovered in the New World of the Americas might not be more 'noble' than their European counterparts.* There was an accumulation of wealth, associated with urban life, the recovery of literacy and financial acumen in western Europe over the centuries following the collapse of the Roman empire, but the story is as much one of shifting cultural perspectives as of a steady march of 'progress'. As the conflict between 'Ancients' and 'Moderns' mentioned above suggests, the classical texts weave in and out of the story, sometimes stimulating new ideas and sometimes acting as defenders of conservative philosophies. The extraordinary contribution of 1,000 years of what can be truly called 'classical civilization' is fundamental to understanding the later history of Europe.

Claudius Ptolemy's works on astronomy and geography provided the foundation of any serious study of the universe until supplanted by 'scientific' replacements in the sixteenth century. In this engraving, dating from 1503, he partners Astronomy.

There is one component that, inevitably, forms the background to the narrative of European history and that is Christianity, manifested first in the Catholic Church of the medieval period, then in the major 'reformed' churches of the sixteenth century. It deserves the full treatment that will be given here. The story of Christianity has

* The term 'noble savage' was first used by the seventeenth-century English poet John Dryden but the concept is to be found earlier in the essays of Montaigne (1580). See below, p. 567.

Ptolemeus
Astronomia

to be set within the context of its earlier history. In my *The Closing of the Western Mind: The Rise of Faith and the Fall of Reason* (2002),[6] my aim was to explore what happened when Greek philosophy was confronted by Christianity, especially after the emperor Constantine (*c.*AD 272–337) had given the religion toleration and patronage and the emperor Theodosius (AD 347–95) had made it the state religion and banned all pagan cults. Constantine had attributed his victory over a fellow usurper Maxentius, at the battle of the Milvian Bridge in 312, to an apparition in the sky telling him to conquer through the cross. This apparent sign of divine support helped give legitimacy to Christian warfare (as discussed further, p. 41).

The first Christian emperors were confronted with the image of Christ, a revolutionary prophet whose suffering on the cross at the hands of a Roman governor had brought salvation to his followers. There had been intense and inconclusive discussion among the erudite Greek theologians over the relationship between divinity and humanity in the figure of Christ but both Constantine and Theodosius now proclaimed that he was 'one in substance' with God the Father in a Trinity of divine persons.

The Trinity was to become the core of orthodox Christian doctrine, in both Catholic and Protestant churches. After the Reformation, adherence to the doctrine was required for many public offices and even entry to the universities. So how did it become such an essential part of Christian belief? After all, for the first three hundred years of Christianity the dominant theology had been subordinationism, the belief that Jesus Christ was in some way subordinate and a later creation of his Father. A reading of the gospels of Matthew, Mark and Luke appeared to support this view. An alternative view, that Jesus had existed eternally as part of the Godhead, had certainly been elaborated, especially in the Latin west, but was not universally accepted.

The change came in 325 when the emperor Constantine had proclaimed in the Nicene Creed that God the Father and Jesus the Son were 'consubstantial', one in substance, with each other. Yet subordinationism remained strong. It was not until 380 when an emperor from the west, the Spanish general Theodosius, issued an edict aimed at the people of Constantinople in January 380, with the Holy Ghost now added to Father and Son. 'We shall believe in the single deity of the Father, Son and the Holy Ghost under the concept of equal majesty and of the Holy Trinity'. Anyone dissenting: 'we judge demented and insane' and they 'shall carry the infamy of heretical dogmas'.

At a time of crisis for the empire (Theodosius' predecessor Valens had been killed by the Goths in 379), it was understandable that Theodosius wished to bring theological debate to an end by insisting on a single doctrine, moreover one in which Christ was elevated from a man suffering at the hands of Roman authority to being eternally part of the Godhead. His tough approach worked. The emperor used his authority to call a council of supportive bishops to Constantinople in 381 to declare the Trinity the core of Christian faith. The harassing of the newly declared 'heretics' followed.

Traditional histories of Christian theology suggest that the Trinity was the only possible resolution of the debates that the Greek theologians had indulged in during the third and fourth centuries but the Trinity has proved hard to defend. *The Catechism of the Roman Catholic Church* (1994) refers to the doctrine as 'a mystery of faith, one of those mysteries that are hidden in God which can never be known unless they are revealed by God… God's inmost being as Holy Trinity is a mystery that is inaccessible to reason alone'. In short, the doctrine has to be accepted as an article of faith, not one that can be supported through reason.

The declaration of the Trinity shifted the focus away from a suffering human Christ. The transition can be seen in the iconography and texts that followed. The Crucifixion is downplayed. On the wooden panelled door of Santa Sabina in Rome of *c.*410, Christ is shown with his arms outstretched but with no cross behind him.* More remarkable was the transformation of Christ from one suffering at the hands of the Romans to one who was represented as Roman himself. As early as 390 he is shown as a Roman magistrate in the Church of Santa Pudenziana in Rome (and his beard marks him out as a typical pagan philosopher) and in the Archiepicopal Chapel in Ravenna of *c.*500 he is portrayed as a Roman warrior (see Frontispiece).

The fourth century, therefore, saw a momentous shift in the history of western thought, not least through a radical break with previous ethical traditions and the spirit of religious tolerance that Constantine had originally promised to maintain in the Edict of Milan of 313. All expressions of paganism including festivities such as the Olympic Games, now over 1,000 years old, were suppressed. Just as revolutionary was the transformation of Christianity itself as it was integrated into the structure of the empire. One motive of Constantine for endorsing Christianity may have been to use the support of the

* A renewed emphasis on the humanity and suffering of Christ on the cross comes only in the fourteenth century.

bishops in the fast-growing Christian communities of the cities. By the end of the century they played a full part in upholding the imperial hierarchy, even to the extent of maintaining secular authority in their dioceses.* The argument, found in some histories of Christianity, that the new religion encompassed a moral revolution that brought respect for the powerlessness, is hard to sustain after the fourth century. As Kyle Harper has shown in his *Slavery in the Late Roman World*, slavery was maintained in Christian households. There is no hint in political thought of the era, or for many centuries afterwards, that society should be reorganized in favour of those without power. Martin Luther condemned, rather than sided with, the peasant revolts of his day. While there was some recognition of the importance of charity for the poor, Christian society was, in fact, successfully integrated into the traditional Roman hierarchies.[7]

While I stressed in *The Closing of the Western Mind*, and in a subsequent book *AD 381*,[8] that the emperors played the leading role in imposing orthodox doctrine, I also argued that, far from Greek philosophy being suppressed by Christianity, Platonism, the dominant philosophical tradition of the fourth century, provided its intellectual backbone. Plato had taught that 'truths' existed beyond the material world and could only be grasped by a small elite who, as Plato had argued, had the right to impose them on the masses. (For a fuller discussion of Platonism, see pp. 31–2.) I argued that the church absorbed this philosophy. So this book starts with a religious tradition in which the truth is assumed to be found only within the church whose duty it is to defend it against all outsiders and any 'heretics' within. There is no salvation outside the church.† This had important repercussions in ethics. If you did not, for any reason, make an absolute commitment to Christ, you were condemned as an outsider.[9] So pagans, Jews and Muslims were considered beyond salvation and they were treated as outcasts from the fourth century onwards. In 1455 Pope Nicholas V recognized the right of the Portuguese to own African slaves. (See further the debates on how to deal with pagans in Chapter 22.) The recognition of political and social rights for non-believers took centuries to achieve in Europe, well beyond the period covered by this book.

There was the added problem of finding uniformity within the church. There were always new intellectual challenges that threatened

* Even today, as an enduring sign of the fourth-century revolution in Christianity, the twenty-six senior bishops of the Anglican church in England and Wales are guaranteed seats in the House of Lords and thus become part of the law-making process.

† This phrase, later adopted as dogma by the church, is traced back to Cyprian, bishop of Carthage, who was martyred there in 258.

traditional doctrines and it proved impossible to define clear principles under which heresies could be classified. Innovative thinking was discouraged. One of my main themes, to be explored especially in the theology of Abelard (Chapter 5) and Thomas Aquinas (Chapter 8), was how the use of logic and pagan philosophy, notably that of the empiricist Aristotle, could be reconciled with the doctrines of the church. For anyone interested in the history of thought, the problems inherent in introducing new thinking within an authoritarian structure are important issues in themselves. In this case they helped define the context for the relationship between medieval Christianity and a fast-changing secular world.

The early medieval church provided the context in which Latin was sustained and much learning was preserved in a language that was comprehensible across the intellectual elite. Yet from the fourth century onwards the church was privileged through its wealth, and conservative through its authoritarian structure. As will be seen in Chapter 3, the dominance of the theologian Augustine was also important in defining conservative 'Christian' attitudes. Nevertheless, expressions of Christianity were so diverse that it is often easier to talk of 'Christianities', even in the medieval period. Christianity would never have become embedded in rural societies where the vast majority of the population lived if it had not absorbed many pagan customs and legends. Local shrines and the patron saints of cities were often as important a focus for worshippers as the ministrations of an absentee bishop or far distant popes whose reigns were on average only five years in duration. Monks, by definition, withdrew from society, usually for life, and it was not until the thirteenth century that the orders of friars, notably the Dominicans and Franciscans, were commissioned by the pope as itinerant preachers.

There were consistent attempts to reform the church but it was on a model that required a return to the simpler ways of worship of the early apostles. This emphasis diverted attention from reforms that could respond to and integrate social change. The medieval church was certainly not the monolithic and overpowering force portrayed in more traditional histories and in many of its activities, the defence of the land and wealth of monasteries, for instance, was as secular in its ambitions as other landowners. Moreover, any link between papal pronouncements and changes in lay attitudes or behaviour is hard to establish, largely because the laity brought their own spiritual traditions and impulses into their religious life. This makes the definition of 'Christian values' in any one period elusive – there was never a chance of uniformity of belief when large parts of Europe had been under Roman rule for centuries, adopting the culture of the Roman elites, and others, such as Ireland, Germany and Scandinavia, had never experienced this culture at all.

I shall argue (in Chapter 16) that, by 1300, respect for the papacy was already diminished and it was further squandered by the residence of the popes in Avignon in the fourteenth century and then the Great Schism of 1378–1415. This was not without its advantages. The vacuum allowed local expressions of Christianity to flourish and the laity to take on new spiritual roles. A lay confraternity or a commercial guild could carry out charitable work in their communities much more successfully than the clergy, who would never have managed, for example, an effective distribution of funds across a city or the building of the dome of Florence's cathedral. As a result it can be argued that the reassertion of Christian dogmatism by the Protestant reformers was retrogressive. By providing authoritarian theological regimes which, in the 'reformed' churches, meant the destruction of shrines and the denigration of local saints, the Reformation stifled rather than encouraged spiritual expression. A rich Christian mythology which included many legends of the deeds of holy men and women and elaborated the gospel stories was suppressed. Furthermore, where you were born, or came to live, now defined the kind of Christian you were. Toleration of alternative Christianities was grudging, certainly in the period covered by this book. A fresh commitment by the reformers to the theology of Augustine, with his denigration of free will, discouraged optimism. It was hard to find peace of mind when Christian leaders, both Catholic and Protestant, insisted that their congregations should always be on the alert for occasions of sin. Apart from the well-established Augustinianism, theology becomes an unstable discipline, with scripture, tradition, faith and reason producing a wide variety of possible solutions to the definition of God and his purposes. Sadly, the differences all too often led to conflict. Diarmaid MacCulloch, an authority on Reformation Europe, has pessimistically argued that the result of the Reformation 'might indeed be viewed simply as two centuries of warfare'.[10]

It is also misleading to talk as if the Reformation led to the spread of a secularism that had been quiescent in the medieval period. It used to be argued that the year 1648, the end of the Thirty Years War, a war in which religion and nationalism combined in a devastating sequence of atrocities, saw a new start to relationships between the European states. Now there is a greater appreciation of how religion persisted as a powerful force across Europe, if never, with the variety of Christianities on offer, as a coherent one. I shall be cautious, for instance, in assuming that there was an effective relationship between the diverse expressions of Christianity and the many activities that can loosely be grouped together under the umbrella of science.* The two disciplines had such different aims that little meaningful can be said about the relationship (see Chapter 30). A conflict between science and religion can only be imagined if both were monolithic entities when clearly both were not. As will be seen (Chapter 31), a much more intense conflict can be seen between the philosophers of the seventeenth century and the Christian hierarchies, both political and ecclesiastical. Again Protestantism is often associated with the revival of reason. As will be seen (p. 526), this was not the intention of the reformers. Both Luther and Calvin denigrated reason. They preferred a more immediate emotional commitment to Christ.

In conclusion, it is worth stressing that this is a book rooted in personal experience. My first encounter with the Mediterranean came in 1966 when I was the so-called '*camerone* boy' for six months at the British School at Rome before I went up to Cambridge. I mended pottery, packed away Etruscan gold brooches and worked on digs outside Rome. In the decades since then, I have absorbed the story of 'the awakening' in a variety of ways, above all through nosing my way around the Mediterranean and writing and lecturing about it. As recently as May 2019 I led a study tour of Lazio, the area around Rome. This included Fossanova, the monastery where Thomas Aquinas died in 1274; Monte Cassino, where the great Abbot Desiderius presided over an influential scriptorium; and the astonishing thirteenth-century crypt in the cathedral at Anagni where Hippocrates and Galen are portrayed alongside references to Plato and the four elements within a programme that includes scenes from the Old and New Testament as well as the life of Anagni's patron saint St Magnus. I have tried to bring together all these experiences in a coherent form in the book that follows but those expecting a textbook approach will be disappointed. Within the narrative I have often dwelt on particular parts of the story that resonate for me, among them the Arena Chapel in Padua, the dome of Florence's cathedral (having climbed it a number of times!), the drawings of Leonardo da Vinci, the *studiolo* of Federico da Montefeltro in Urbino and the essays of Montaigne.

* The term 'science' in the sense that we use it today was not coined until the 1830s. 'Natural philosophy' was the preferred term until then.

Prologue

The Collapse of Learning

There rose up in various parts of the world all the barbarous people against Rome, whence there ensued after no long time not only the humiliation of so great an empire but the ruin of the whole, and above all of Rome itself, and with her were likewise ruined the most excellent craftsmen, sculptors, painters and architects.

Giorgio Vasari, *Lives of the Artists* (first published in 1550)

By the time I was fifteen, in the early 1960s, I had developed a passion for archaeology. So when the local museum, at Ipswich in Suffolk in the east of England, announced that they would be mounting a rescue dig of a Roman villa and would welcome volunteers, I joined in enthusiastically. The foundations of a new bungalow had uncovered the bathhouse of the villa, which needed digging out, so I got my hands dirty shovelling out the ashes from the boilers that had heated the water.

Like many of the villas of Roman Britain, this one had achieved its height of opulence in the fourth century. It was well placed on a low headland overlooking fertile land and the extent of its estate has since been established, with one of the boundary lines used even now as a farm track. Sadly, the funds needed to excavate the main part of the villa have never become available, and the ground where it is buried, which, since I still live in Suffolk, I drive past once or twice a week, remains untouched.

Happy as I was sifting through the ashes, I never imagined then that I must have been digging out the remains of the last fires of Roman Britain, a province of the empire since AD 43. The formal end of the empire in Britain is usually dated to 409 or 410 when the legions protecting the island from the raiding Angles and Saxons were withdrawn to the continent. Were these fires being lit as the last owners of the villa were packing up and about to flee or were they simply enjoying the comforts of a warm home, unaware that their way of life was threatened? The disintegration that followed is poorly documented but it was complete. Taxation ceased almost at once and nowhere else in the empire did conditions fall back so quickly to levels even lower than they had been when the Romans first arrived. So the ashes I dug out could be seen as a symbol of what was truly the end of civilization. Historians are cautious about using the words 'Dark Ages' – a term first coined by the humanist Petrarch in the fourteenth century – for the period that followed, but with the disappearance of literacy and the confusion brought by invading settlers, it is undeniable that life in fifth- and sixth-century England fades beyond the historical record.

If there was one single day that doomed the western Roman empire it was probably 31 December 406. The Rhine, so long a formidable boundary between the empire and Germany, had frozen and a large group of barbarians, including Vandals, Alans and Suebi, had poured across. In effect the border ceased to exist and the years that followed saw rival groups fragmenting the provinces of Gaul and then moving southwards into Spain and beyond. The legions in Britain were soon withdrawn to confront them, but the taxation that had funded the empire and the moral authority and confidence that had sustained it against the odds for so many centuries were diminished beyond repair. While there were Roman commanders, such as Flavius Aetius, 'the last of the Romans', who had some success in pushing back the tribes or playing one off against another, a fresh blow came with the successful invasion of north Africa by the Vandal leader Gaiseric. The great port city of Carthage fell in 439 and with it the resources of the fertile fields of the provinces of Mauretania on which Rome had come to depend to feed its citizens and sustain its armies. This was a strategic disaster. Even though the strongman Aetius managed to defeat Attila's Huns in 451, further disintegration was inevitable. In 455 Gaiseric sacked Rome and in 458 conquered Sicily, another fertile province, which had been part of the empire for seven hundred years. The last of the Roman emperors, Romulus Augustulus, abdicated in 476, bringing the Roman empire in the west to a formal end.

One man who lived through these years of turmoil was Sidonius Apollinaris, a Gallic aristocrat who documented the collapse of learning and Roman culture. Sidonius had been born about 431 into a family that already had a distinguished reputation; his grandfather had held the military post of Praetorian prefect of Gaul and his father that of prefect under the emperor Valentinian III. Sidonius himself married the daughter of Avitus, who was briefly emperor in the 450s, and composed a panegyric in honour of his father-in-law in Rome. Two more panegyrics followed for later emperors and Sidonius was appointed city prefect in 468, still a prestigious position even though the fabric of the city itself was deteriorating. In 469, however, he headed back to Gaul and then, having already converted to Christianity, became bishop of the town of Clermont.

overleaf Thomas Cole's painting *Destruction* (1836) depicts the sack of an imaginary city, suggestive of the Vandals' ransacking of Rome in AD 455.

There was no precedent for someone as distinguished as Sidonius becoming a bishop in Gaul, although many lesser nobles had taken this step as the best way of maintaining their status. There was, however, no lack of Christian commitment from Sidonius. Despite the loss of Clermont to the Visigoths in 475, he proved to be an effective and conscientious bishop. He was companionable and even flexible with the new rulers of Gaul, allowing Gothic troops to settle on his lands and visiting the emerging 'barbarian' kings. Yet he was haunted by

the decay and breakdown of the empire. He published many of his letters and his preoccupation with the loss of traditional culture shines through. By 'culture' he meant the literary heritage and the quality of Latin learning that he felt was intrinsic to the ethos of the Roman aristocracy. 'Since old grades of rank are now abolished which once distinguished the high from the low, in future culture must afford the sole criterion of nobility.'

So in 470 Sidonius laments, in a letter to one Hesperius, whom he has praised for his 'love of letters', that 'the numbers of the indifferent grow at such a rate that unless your little band can save the purity of the Latin tongue from the rust of sorry barbarisms we shall soon have to mourn its abolition and decease'.

Some years later a Roman general, Arbogast, wrote an elegant letter to Sidonius from northern Gaul. In response, he earns himself plaudits from the bishop:

> You have your conversation among barbarians, yet you permit no barbarism to pass your lips; in eloquence and valour you equal those ancient generals whose hand could wield the stylus no less skillfully than the sword... The Roman tongue is long banished from Belgium and the Rhine, but if its splendour has anywhere survived, it is surely with you; our jurisdiction is fallen into decay along the frontier, but while you live and preserve your eloquence, the Latin language stands unshaken.

A year later, in a letter to his scholarly correspondent Johannes, Johannes is told that

> it is your glory to have revived, supported and championed Literature... In this tempest of war which has wrecked the Roman power, you are the sole master in Gaul who has brought the Latin tongue safely into port... our contemporaries and our successors should all with one accord and fervent gratitude dedicate statues to you as a new Demosthenes or Cicero.

It was high praise indeed to place Johannes among the greatest of the Greek and Roman orators.

Literate though he was, no one pretends that Sidonius was a major intellectual. His writing is conventional, even stilted, but in his fears for the 'purity of the Latin tongue' he showed considerable foresight. A century later Gregory (539–94), the bishop of the major Christian city of Tours, home of the shrine of St Martin, undertook to write his *History of the Franks*. At that time, according to his preface to the work, 'many were lamenting and saying: "Woe to our day, since the pursuit of letters has perished from among us and no one can be found among the people who can set forth the deeds of the present on the written page."' Gregory sees learning and moral standards as going hand in hand. In the same preface he goes on to say: 'Humane learning is on the decline or rather is perishing altogether in the cities of Gaul where no distinction is made between good and evil, no bounds are set on the ferocity of peoples or the madness of princes.'

The world that Sidonius and Gregory of Tours were lamenting had a long and distinguished cultural history.[1] For 700 years Rome had been a major and, for most of this period, supreme Mediterranean power. The city had its own traditions. Some had been absorbed from the Etruscans but predominant was a deep-rooted republicanism following the overthrow of the Etruscan kings at the end of the sixth century BC. By the second century BC, however, these traditions had been challenged as Rome expanded into the eastern Mediterranean. A flood of new texts and treasures reached the Latin west from the much older and more sophisticated civilization of the Greeks. Among them were the epics of Homer which had been written down in the eighth century BC and had achieved iconic status, one that they retain to this day. By the sixth century, Greek philosophy had begun to probe the deeper problems of human existence. As in Rome, the overthrow of a 'tyrant' ruler in Athens in 510 BC gave a new boost to republicanism. By the fifth century the concept of *isonomia*, equal rights for all – although it extended only to male members of the citizenry and relied heavily on slavery – gave every Athenian citizen a right to speak in the Assembly and to be judged in the law courts. This was the genesis of Athenian democracy, in which the administration of the city was open to all its participating citizens.

Within this lively society, there were fervent debates over the nature of government and society, especially among the so-called Sophists, a group of intellectuals attracted to Athens by its cultural sophistication (note the origin of the word!) and role in seeing off the Persian invaders in 490 and 480 BC. Fundamental to sophistic thought was the distinction between the natural order of things, the underlying, unchanging parameters of existence (*phusis*) and convention (*nomos*). In Sophocles' play *Antigone* (*c.*441 BC), Antigone is determined to bury her brother against the dictates of the city ruler Cleon. She calls on ancient customs ('the unwritten, unalterable laws... they are not of yesterday or today, but everlasting, though where they come from none of us can tell') as having primacy over city law. Were these laws innate, or established through reason, or, when debated among theologians, determined by God? The concept of such a 'natural law' and its possible sources was to resonate throughout the period covered by this book.

The Sophists ranged widely, speculating about the nature and existence of the gods, the problems in using language and in finding certainty in knowledge. For the first time in the recorded history of the west the human mind self-consciously takes responsibility for determining truth; 'Man is the measure of all things', in the famous statement of the Sophist Protagoras. Antiphon, another Sophist, is seen by Siep Stuurman, a scholar of human rights, as articulating 'the first glimmerings of a universalist notion of common humanity grounded in a common human nature'.[2]

Then in the fourth century the two great strands of Greek philosophy, those of Plato (420s–*c.*348 BC) and Aristotle (384–322 BC), were formulated and caused a tension between those who believed the ultimate truths rest in this material world (Aristotle) and those, the Platonists, who saw them as beyond it. Here was the birth of political philosophy and the opposing views of Plato and Aristotle ensured that there would be vigorous debate over the essence of good government and the nature of ethics, the best way of living well. This tension spawned many other approaches to the fundamental questions of existence so that by the second century BC there were lively and competing schools of philosophy. Among them was Stoicism. The Stoics saw the world as a single enduring entity, a cosmos that moved forward in time under its own purpose. The Stoics provided some of the most profound explorations of the concept of natural law. Human beings were equally subject to the laws of the cosmos and there was earnest debate over how an individual should act: to foster the inexorable move forwards or to learn to accept the vagaries of fate. The application of Stoic ethics to the whole of humankind, although seldom realized in practice by individual Stoics, was another step forward in the conception of a universal humanity.

By the time that the Romans confronted the Greek world the original city-states (Athens, Sparta and a host of others) had become part of the so-called Hellenistic kingdoms, ruled by the successors of Alexander the Great (356–323 BC). The Hellenistic age (conventionally dated to 330–30 BC) was a period of flamboyant display and exuberant architecture and sculpture. In Alexandria there were extraordinary achievements by the scientists who plotted the stars (as Ptolemy did), measured the size of the Earth and explored the natural world around them. This was the age of Euclid (active *c.*300 BC), Archimedes (*c.*287–212 BC), of the mathematical proof and the application of mathematics to the natural world. The work of the geometrician Apollonius of Perga (active *c.*200 BC) on conic sections taxes mathematicians to this day. Hipparchus spotted the precession of the equinoxes that make the Earth a moving observation platform and, even more remarkably, calculated the speed of the movements. Eratosthenes of Cyrene (*c.*276–194 BC) measured the circumference of the Earth with reasonable accuracy. Scholars are still trying to work out the intricate technology of the Antikythera Mechanism (so-called from the Greek island near where it was recovered on the western edge of the Aegean Sea) of *c.*150–100 BC, which appears to have been an advanced astronomical calculating machine.[3] The 'Atomists', a school founded by Democritus (*c.*460–370 BC), discussed the nature of matter, arguing that there were particles, invisible to the naked eye, which were constantly rearranging themselves in new forms. The idea was picked up by the Roman Lucretius (98–*c.*55 BC) whose *De rerum natura* idolized the natural world as thriving independently of any divine force and lambasted those who inflicted cruelty in the name of the gods (see p. 482). Hippocrates (*c.*460–370 BC) and his successors created medical schools where observation, even if not understanding, of the human body was carefully recorded. The Greeks spoke and argued well. Skill in rhetoric was seen as the supreme accomplishment of the educated elite.

The Romans could hardly avoid this, even though their culture traditionally valued a life of action above one of contemplation. By the first century BC the Roman elite expected to speak Greek, collect Greek statues and be at home with the work of the major Greek intellectuals. Cicero (106–43 BC), who studied rhetoric in Rhodes, was able to adapt Greek philosophy for a Roman audience, Virgil (70–19 BC) produced his own 'Homeric' epic, the *Aeneid*, the poet Horace (65–8 BC) was profoundly influenced by Greek models. By the first century AD Rome had become an empire, its republican traditions supplanted through the political genius of the emperor Augustus (r.27 BC–AD 14). The relationship between Greek and Roman prospered. The philosopher Seneca (*c.*4 BC–AD 65) showed how the Greek philosophy of Stoicism fitted closely with the Roman mind. Plutarch (AD 46–120), a Greek well versed in Roman history, was able to compare prominent men of both cultures in his famous *Lives*. Most of his sources have been lost but a good idea of the vast body of works available for study can be seen in the analysis of the texts known by the physician Galen (AD 129–*c.*216). There are 2,500 quotations in Galen's works from the Hippocratic texts alone. Meanwhile, the Romans were developing their own skills, notably in administration and architecture. The body of Roman law, eventually gathered together by the emperor Justinian in the sixth century (see pp. 142–3), was a formidable achievement and eagerly grasped by the city-states of northern Italy when it was rediscovered in the eleventh century. In Rome, the Pantheon, with one of the largest domes of antiquity, still stands, its concrete as firm as ever despite the stresses it has endured. Another survivor, the Pont du Gard, part of a 30-mile Roman aqueduct, runs over the River Gardon at a height of 330 feet. The fall of water over the entire length of the aqueduct is less than 42 feet. Remarkably, the stonework of the bridge is held up solely through its own weight; there is no cement involved. Nor were the Romans without reflection. The historian Tacitus (AD *c.*55–after 117), suspicious of the imperial absolutism that had destroyed republicanism, is able to imagine that the spread of imperialism was not always welcomed by those who were conquered and that the 'barbarian' tribes, notably those in Germany, deserved respect.

Enough has been said to show that a vast cultural tradition, which by the fifth century AD stretched back in various forms for well over 1,000 years, provided an indispensable heritage for the later history of Europe. Much of this heritage was to be lost in the devastation of the collapse of the empire but what survived was considered of a much higher authority than anything else available. In many ways, it would prove more influential, especially among the European cultural elites, than Christianity, as it was receptive to a much broader spectrum of sources than the authoritarian church – with its intransigence over the discussion of doctrine – could endorse. Above all, the Greeks, and less volubly the Romans, had initiated the concept of free debate over alternative ways of organizing a state or city or defining moral imperatives in a way that was to prove highly attractive as intellectual life revived in the centuries following the fall of the Roman empire. In a fragment of text attributed to the fifth-century BC playwright Euripides, the commitment to learning by the Greeks is applauded: 'Blessed is he who learns how to engage in inquiry, with no impulse to harm his countrymen or to pursue wrongful actions, but perceives the order of immortal and ageless nature, how it is structured.' Such an approach took time to reappear, and that is why I will give its reassertion a central place in this book. It is unlikely that cultural progress would ever have been made in Europe if there had not been the reconciliation between the church and classical culture that I detail in later chapters. As the preface has suggested, it was not until the sixteenth century that the authority of ancient texts was effectively challenged by the rebirth of scientific thinking. My immediate question is, how many of the classical texts could be saved in a world where the survival of texts depended on accurate copying and the luck of preservation? This is the subject of the next chapter.

The Saving of the Texts 500 - 750

This activity is a pious one unequalled in merit, by any other which men's hands can perform. For the fingers rejoice in writing, the eyes in seeing, and the mind at examining the meaning of God's mystical words.

Rabanus Maurus[1]

It would be many centuries before material culture grew much beyond subsistence level in post-Roman Europe. This meant that the fragments of literature surviving from the classical world needed to be preserved if the cultural heritage was to be saved. This chapter explores the individuals who made this possible but stresses how fragile were the links between one generation of scribes and the next. It is also important to emphasize that there was never a revival of 'philosophy' and learning in the form in which they had existed in the classical world, but a distinct and fresh relationship between the surviving texts and the new context of a Christian society.

If Sidonius Apollinaris could hardly be called an intellectual, the same could not be said for Anicus Manlius Severinus Boethius, born in 480 just after the official fall of the western empire.[2] The Anicii, a major aristocratic family, were his kinsmen and his other names suggest connections to families that had held the consulship, by now a largely honorary position but one reflecting the prestige of the holder. The city of Rome had continued to appoint them even after the fall of the western empire. Boethius' wife, Rusticana, was the daughter of Symmachus, from another noble family, who had been consul in 485. These families were now all Christian. While Boethius would be sucked into political affairs and forced to spend time managing large estates, his priority was academic study. By his twenties he was being addressed as 'your wisdom' and described as the 'most learned of men'. His Greek was so polished, at a time when most Romans knew little of it, that it is assumed he had been sent to study at Athens, Alexandria or one of the other cultural centres of the Greek world. Boethius' mission now became to translate the work of the great Greek writers into Latin before they drifted out of the Roman consciousness. Among his early translations were works by Pythagoras, Ptolemy, Euclid and Archimedes. These provided material for what Boethius called the *quadrivium*, a curriculum that was made up of four subjects: arithmetic, astronomy, geometry and music. Boethius' texts on music and arithmetic were to become popular in the medieval universities. The *quadrivium* was integrated with three other foundational subjects, the *trivium*, made up of grammar, rhetoric and dialectic (or logic). These seven liberal arts, formerly taught as individual subjects in Roman education, had been enunciated as a complete course of study for the first time by one Martianus Capella in the early fifth century. In his *De nuptiis Philologiae et Mercuri* (*On the Marriage of Philology and Mercury*) the seven arts are presented as a wedding gift to Philology by the gods of Mount Olympus. Later commentators suggested that Philology stood for 'reason and wisdom' and Mercury for 'facility of speech'.[3] Their marriage provided a powerful combination of skills. Despite the obscurity of Martianus, his curriculum was taken up by Boethius and others and, although they were not Christian texts, would later provide the core curriculum of Europe's medieval universities.

Boethius then conceived a massive project: not only to translate the entire known works of Aristotle and Plato, but also to show how they could be reconciled with each other. As later scholars were to find, this was a daunting task. Aristotle had laid the foundations for the coherent study of the natural world, both in works of theory and logic, and in compilations of the observed behaviour of living organisms. Among the works Boethius is known to have translated are the *Categories*, which delineate the way that objects can be defined, according, for instance, to their substance, quantity or quality, and the *Prior Analytics*, a major work on deductive reasoning. He also continued one well-established tradition, of writing commentaries on Aristotle from what were often poorly organized texts, possibly even notes taken from the philosopher's lectures. Before the transmission of Aristotle's texts from the Arab world (which is dealt with in Chapters 7 and 8), Boethius' works were to provide much of the foundation for the teaching of logic by such scholars as the great Abelard (whose life and teachings will be explored in Chapter 5).

Plato, who had been Aristotle's teacher in fourth-century BC Athens before the latter had set out on his own distinct philosophical path, had a very different conception of the natural world.[4] He believed it was a volatile place of which very little could be said for certain, and that it was futile to indulge in painstaking accumulation of empirical evidence when so much was in flux. For Plato, the ultimate reality was, instead, an unchanging set of Ideas or Forms, such as Beauty and Justice, which could be reached through the exercise of reason, but only by an elite cadre of thinkers. As a result, many of Plato's works are set in the form of dialogues in which the starring role is given to the philosopher Socrates, who attacks conventional wisdoms to show that they have no rational underpinning. His disputants are forced to recognize that truth cannot be found in this material world but must be searched for beyond it. The elite who had grasped the ultimate realities through many years of rational thinking had the right to impose their findings on the rest of society. In his best-known work, *The Republic*, probably written around 375 BC, Plato denounces democracy, so setting up an enduring debate over the best form of government.*

By the time of Boethius there was relatively little direct study of the natural world and Aristotle's empiricism was in abeyance. Plato had fared very differently; not only had the tradition of Platonism been carried forward by the so-called Neoplatonist philosophers, such as the third-century AD thinker Plotinus, but Christians had found much to absorb from Platonism to complement or even to inspire their own evolving theology. It suited the church to believe that there was an ultimate reality, God, now seen as part of the divine Trinity of Father, Son and Holy Spirit, whose nature could only be understood by a few who had the right to enforce it on others. It becomes impossible to understand Christian theology without recognizing that its authority came from Platonism. St Augustine of Hippo, the dominant voice of the Latin Church Fathers, in particular, had been deeply influenced by the philosophy of Plotinus.[5]

Boethius' life was to be cut short after he had completed a limited number of Aristotle's texts and it can never be known whether he would have forged a reconciliation between the two philosophers. Unlike many committed Christians, Boethius had no inhibitions about studying these 'pagan' authors alongside his Christianity. Among his works are a number of theological tracts, the so-called *Opuscula Sacra*, one of which was a straightforward statement of Christian doctrine. Yet, from the philosophical point of view Boethius remained a Platonist, happy to reconcile Plotinus' 'The One' with the Christian God. His most famous work, *The Consolation of Philosophy*, which was to be copied from edition to edition in the Middle Ages, appeared as a traditional exploration of Platonism without any mention of Christianity.[6]

The context in which Boethius wrote *The Consolation* was a tragic one. In 522, when he was in his early forties, Boethius had the pleasure of seeing his young sons jointly appointed to consulships, the high point, he recorded, of his entire life,† but he was then summoned from Rome to Ravenna to serve as the *Magister officiorum* ('master of the offices'), the senior civil servant, in the Ostrogothic government of Theodoric which ruled over much of Italy at that time. Boethius had had links with Theodoric's court before, through his fellow administrator Cassiodorus, but this was a rare example of Theodoric using a Roman of such high status in his administration. But there was

* Plato was condemned as an enemy of 'the open society' by the twentieth-century philosopher Karl Popper in his classic *The Open Society and its Enemies* (1945).

† Aristocratic fathers often paid for their young sons to be appointed to a consulship, as appears to be the case with Boethius.

soon to be trouble. Boethius was an outsider whose continuing links to the Roman senate raised suspicions and it may also have been that his commitment to philosophy was seen as subversive. More damagingly, it seems that he may have become tangled up with plotting surrounding the succession of the seventy-year-old Theodoric, who lacked an adult son. Whatever the truth of the matter, he was accused of treason, thrown into prison in 524 and executed, probably in 526.

In *The Consolation of Philosophy*, which was written in the months he lay in prison, an elderly woman appears to Boethius. She represents Philosophy, here presented as the source of all moral virtue. In a dialogue with the woman, Boethius complains that he is a good man, dedicated to the application of wisdom to competent government but brought down by an evil king and his unscrupulous counsellors. There is much discussion of the contrast between Fortune, quick to change from good to bad, and the stability of Plato's philosophy, which envisages an unchanging certainty beyond the material world. In a mixture of prose and verse *The Consolation* offers a variety of approaches to the nature of wisdom but Boethius also presents himself as the proud representative of philosophy in a society that is abandoning it. He calls on Philosophy to acknowledge his status, but there is a tension between her desire to point to an immaterial world reached through death and his own determination to remain on earth.

It has often been said that there is little consolation in *The Consolation*. It is a complex but original work and in the final book Boethius wrestles with what has become a major theological quandary: how can an all-knowing 'One' or God, who can see how an individual will behave before he or she is born, still allow that individual the space to exercise free will? The Arabic philosophers were as challenged by the issue as were the Christians but the latter had the added problem that Augustine had decreed that humans were so burdened by original sin (see p. 72) that their freedom to act was restrained. The debate over how far there was freedom to determine one's own destiny raged through the Middle Ages and into the theologies of the Reformation. Medieval commentators would use *The Consolation* as part of their own debate of the issue. The discussions began early. Some 90 per cent of the manuscripts of *The Consolation* written before 1100 have glosses, or explanatory comments, added to them. Many hundreds of further commentaries on *The Consolation* were produced during the Middle Ages and it was read in schools, universities and the princely courts by both clergy and laity. While it was commonly accepted that there was nothing in the text that conflicted with Christianity, it inspired much critical thought on how far philosophy, in this case Platonism, could be reconciled with theological orthodoxy. *The Consolation* also seems to have acted like a balm, assuring readers that philosophy might have the answers.

Boethius' contemporary, Cassiodorus, was born in the mid-480s in what is now Calabria, in southern Italy.[7] Cassiodorus also came from the Roman elite but his roots were not as grand as those of Boethius. His father had acquiesced in the Ostrogothic takeover of Italy by Theodoric and served him as governor of Sicily. This had given Cassiodorus access to service as a junior official in Theodoric's administration. He was soon known for his ability to draft official edicts, letters and documents – the *Variae*, as they became known – in an elegant traditional style, often with erudite digressions for his recipients. In short, the *Variae* gave respectability to the regime, masking the reality of a disintegrating world outside the court. Among the letters are requests to Boethius on subjects as varied as establishing the relationship between gold and bronze coins and recommendations for a harpist. The two men should have been natural allies but there is nothing in Cassiodorus' writing

to suggest he opposed Boethius' imprisonment. Indeed, following Boethius' execution, he stepped into his place as *Magister officiorum*. Cassiodorus outlived Theodoric and served as Praetorian prefect for Italy during the regency of Theodoric's ten-year-old son, Athalaric. After Athalaric's death in 534 Cassiodorus left for Constantinople, where he was to spend some fifteen years – there are reports that suggest his family may have originally come from the Greek east. Meanwhile, the armies of the Byzantine emperor Justinian were doggedly trying to reconquer Italy for the empire, one side-effect of their campaign being the elimination of much of the remaining senatorial elite of Rome by the Ostrogoths. Ravenna fell to Byzantium in 540 and remained under rule from the east for another 200 years.

The years in the east drew Cassiodorus into religion. Like most 'barbarians', Theodoric was an Arian Christian, a believer in the subordinate nature of Christ. While this had been declared a heresy for Roman Christians in the fourth century, the 'barbarian' tribes had been converted to earlier

Boethius talks with 'Philosophy', while the Wheel of Fortune mirrors his own fate; fifteenth-century illumination of *The Consolation of Philosophy*.

subordinationist traditions. It might well have been guilt over his compromises with Theodoric's regime that acted as the catalyst for Cassiodorus' greater commitment to orthodox Christianity. He wrote tracts on the soul and, in what was to become the most widely copied of his works, on the psalms. Eventually, in his sixties, he returned to his birthplace in southern Italy to set up the monastery of Vivarium on the shores of the Ionian Sea. This might have been intended as a place to enjoy a quiet retirement but Cassiodorus lived well into his nineties and under his supervision Vivarium became a major centre for the copying of texts.

Even before he had left for the east Cassiodorus had attempted to set up a library of Greek and Latin texts for use in Christian schooling in Rome. How far he imported books from the east (with scholars to translate them) and how far he was able to accumulate his library within Italy is unknown, but he accumulated a good selection of the scriptures, scriptural commentaries, histories and grammars as well as Greek texts. The monastery employed the services of three named monks able to translate Greek into Latin. It is not known whether Vivarium was run under a formal monastic rule, such as had been instituted by Benedict of Nursia for his foundation of Monte Cassino in 529, but there is no doubt that it was expected by its founder to be a place of disciplined religious activity and observance.

Cassiodorus' hopes for his community were set out in his *Institutiones*, 'a handbook for the Christian scholar', a work he revised over the years. The first volume deals with the practical requirements of finding, preserving and copying texts. Cassiodorus lists the major books of scripture contained in the library at Vivarium – the full Bible, with both New and Old Testaments in Jerome's Latin translation, the Vulgate, and commentaries on them. He is careful to explain the authority of various commentators. Augustine scores high marks but the third-century Greek theologian Origen is treated with some ambivalence. No one could doubt Origen's brilliance but on some subjects, such as eternal punishment and free will, he had already been declared heretical. Cassiodorus seems to have marked the passages where he was not to be followed. Other books mentioned as available in his library include some histories and other religious works by those theologians whom Cassiodorus favoured: Augustine; Jerome; Ambrose, the formidable bishop of Milan; and Cyprian, bishop of Carthage, who had been martyred there in 258. The few secular writers who are recorded include writers on the universe (the famous astronomer and geographer Ptolemy), agriculture and medicine – primarily practical handbooks rather than works of literature. Cassiodorus frequently mentioned books he hoped to acquire.

The second volume of the *Institutiones* is an extended treatment of the seven liberal arts. Cassiodorus follows the influential *De doctrina christiana* (*On Christian Teaching*) of Augustine in stressing that the main purpose of secular knowledge is to understand the scriptures more fully.* In his earlier work on the psalms he had even suggested that the liberal arts had a scriptural origin. Now he sets them out in detail, dwelling especially on the methods of argument used in the art of dialectic, so that his monks can approach the many books that they have been dealing with in an organized manner. The *Institutiones* was yet another work that helped implant the seven liberal arts into the medieval curriculum. The stress on dialectic rather than the traditional rhetoric favoured by the Roman elite was an important intellectual shift for a world in which monastic life was becoming influential.

Traditionally, Cassiodorus has been applauded as a major conduit between the classical and medieval worlds. For instance, in 1886 when the distinguished historian of the early Middle Ages, Thomas Hodgkin, introduced a translation of the *Variae*, he claimed that 'the great merit of Cassiodorus, that which shows his deep insight into the needs of his age and entitles him to the eternal gratitude of Europe, was his determination to utilize the vast leisure of the convent for this preservation of divine and human learning and for its transmission to later ages'.[8] So far as 'transmission' is concerned this seems an exaggeration. Cassiodorus' aim appears rather to provide a corpus of works for the education of his own community – scriptures, commentaries on them and ancillary handbooks. More recent assessments, such as that by James O'Donnell in a detailed and authoritative life of Cassiodorus,[9] stress his lack of interest in secular works unless they were of direct religious use. The greatest literary minds of Latin antiquity, Virgil and Cicero, are missing. Although Cassiodorus was inspirational and resourceful in building his community, O'Donnell sees no sign that he had any missionary belief in saving the culture of the classical world for its own sake. Apart from some composite histories of the church since the conversion of Constantine in 312 and a *computus*, a calculation of the dates for the Christian calendar, based on the year 562, the Vivarium produced no original works. The community at Vivarium disappeared soon after Cassiodorus' death and the library was dispersed. A late work of Cassiodorus, *De orthographia* (*On orthography*; *c.*580),[10] is so

* Augustine's *De doctrina christiana* became one of the most influential guides to interpreting the Bible.

detailed in setting out the rules of copying and the errors to avoid that it suggests that by then Cassiodorus, now in his nineties, had become deeply frustrated with the incompetence of his scribes. Yet, as will be seen later in this chapter, one of its books, the *Codex Grandior*, a complete edition of the Bible (a pandect, as these are known), was to have an influential afterlife.

The account of the liberal arts in the second book of the *Institutiones* proved more immediately influential in early seventh-century Spain. Here the Arian Visigoths had established an unstable government within a much larger community of Romans. At the end of the sixth century a Visigothic king, Reccared (r.586–601), converted to Catholicism and established a close relationship between the monarchy and the church that healed many of the ethnic differences between Visigoths and the native Iberians. Just before Reccared died in 601, a new bishop of Seville had been appointed. Isidore remained in office for another thirty-five years, dying in 635. He proved to be a committed scholar with a breadth of knowledge of the Latin texts that were still available to him. The works he produced included reviews of scripture, lists of heresies, studies of liturgy and lives of the Christian fathers. Yet Isidore's most influential work was his vast and discursive *Etymologies*, most of which was written in the 620s. While much of the work is concerned with the derivation of words, as its title suggests, it is also an encyclopaedia set out in twenty books, ranging from discussion of the seven liberal arts (Books 1–3) to legal systems, the church, languages, the Earth, animals, stones and metals and even shipbuilding.[11] In short, there is an attempt to impose order on knowledge but it is an arbitrary one. The text is a rag-bag of texts and fragments of classics, 'packed with information and misinformation on every topic from angels to the parts of a saddle… an uncritical parade of absurd bric-a-brac', in one scholarly assessment.[12] Isidore's account of the liberal arts is clear and informative and in the book on astronomy he distinguishes between astronomy and astrology, which he considers superstitious. What, on the other hand, are we to make of his view that Gaul is named after the Greek word *gala*, meaning 'milk', because its people are white, or that wine (*vinum*) is so-called because it replenishes the veins (*vena*) with blood?

The eighth-century *Codex Amiatinus* purports to show Cassiodorus at work with a cupboard of codices behind him.

One of Isidore's disciples claimed that 'in him antiquity reclaimed something for itself'.[13] It is true that the *Etymologies* contain extracts from ancient authors that might otherwise have been lost, but these do not appear to have been drawn from the original texts, rather from sources that had already been selected for secondary works. Isidore quotes directly from Cassiodorus' *Institutiones* from a few decades earlier, but of the works of ancient 'pagan' authors only Pliny's *Natural History*, which was a similar compilation from the Roman world, and the grammar of the fourth-century scholar Donatus appear to have been available in full. The only Christian authors to whom we can be sure Isidore had direct access were the querulous scholar Jerome, translator of the scriptures, and Augustine. Other sources, represented by 475 quotations from some 200 authors, appear to be picked at random to fill in the needs of the text.

Yet the *Etymologies* caught on. Within a few decades copies were to be found in almost every monastic library and today over 1,000 manuscripts of it survive. With the invention of printing, new editions

were soon to appear. It is considered second only to the Bible as the most widely read book of the Middle Ages. Isidore even appears among those in Paradise in Dante's *Divine Comedy*. This adulation is partly because Isidore wrote simple and comprehensible Latin but largely because the *Etymologies* appeared to offer an authoritative survey of the sum of human knowledge. This adulation was disastrous on two levels. Firstly, it helped preserve a wide variety of myths about many different subjects for almost 1,000 years; secondly – and more crucially – it was assumed that the classical works drawn on in the book did not need to be preserved and so hundreds of surviving texts were never recopied. There was much scurrilous comment when Pope John Paul II seriously proposed in 2000 that St Isidore, as he was by then,* should become the patron saint of the internet. Isidore's promulgation of false material seemed to make the Polish pope's suggestion entirely appropriate, even if not in the sense that he intended.

Gradually, Latin was being preserved as the language of scholarship, administration, law and commercial transactions. Thanks to the breadth of Rome's imperial reach, Latin was the only viable language for written communication across western Europe. In Anglo-Saxon Britain, however, where Latin had largely vanished, it was by now a foreign language, and likewise in Ireland, which had never been part of the Roman empire. In Italy, the Iberian peninsula and Gaul, the original parts of the Roman empire, the modern Romance languages developed, and Latin became the preserve of a privileged elite. The church, of course, played a prominent part in spreading Latin as a written language and in keeping up standards, especially in the monasteries. As far back as the sixth century the Rule of St Benedict required daily readings to the monks and this would have been from Latin texts.

The monastery that was to become the intellectual capital of Christian Europe in the early eighth century was in the Anglo-Saxon kingdom of Northumbria in the north-east of England. At the Synod of Whitby in 664, the Northumbrian church had pledged its allegiance to Rome by adopting the Roman rather than Celtic calendar for Easter. Ten years later, in 674, a prominent Northumbrian noble, Benedict Biscop, was granted land at Wearmouth (on the River Wear) by King Ecgfrith to found a monastery. Growing archaeological evidence from Anglo-Saxon England has shown that in the seventh-century monasteries often emerged on what originally had been royal settlements.[14] Biscop had already taken vows at the island monastery

* Isidore was canonized in 653, less than twenty years after his death.

of Lérins, off the coast of Provence in southern France, so he was ready to supervise the building of this and another nearby monastery at Jarrow (on the river Tyne) and preside over both houses. He already had books, vestments and craftsmen in stone and glass gathered from numerous trips to Rome and the continent. By 685 both houses were ready to welcome monks.

As this example suggests, monasteries depended on royal or aristocratic patronage. They needed land from which to support themselves and their monks and in return the patrons received prayers for their own safety, the success of their armies and the peace of their regimes. None of this would have been possible if rulers had not been able to reconcile Christianity with their own political aims. One has to return to that crucial moment in 313 when Constantine, the emperor of the west, granted toleration and patronage to Christianity through his Edict of Milan (jointly signed with Licinius, the emperor in the east). While scholars still argue over his motivations, Constantine's later account of the catalyst for his conversion,[15] the appearance of a cross in the sky, accompanied by the Latin words *In hoc signo vinces* ('By this sign, conquer'), before the vital battle for the city of Rome, had legitimized warfare as a means of spreading Christianity. A few decades later, Ambrose, bishop of Milan (339–97), claimed that 'no military eagles, no flight of birds here lead the van of our army, but Thy Name, Lord Jesus, and Thy worship'.[16] One of the extraordinary paradoxes of the evolving Christian societies was the adulation of a man crucified by Roman soldiers as an inspiration for those same soldiers in battle. The mosaic in the Archiespiscopal Chapel in Ravenna of *c.*500 that shows Christ dressed as a Roman warrior fitted well with Old Testament texts where there were numerous references to a vengeful god inflicting defeat on his enemies. The Ravenna mosaic shows Christ crushing a lion and an adder, a clear reference to Psalm 91. The New Testament Epistle to the Ephesians, although its traditional attribution to Paul himself is doubted, contains powerful martial symbolism in chapter 6 (verse 11), as in the words 'Put on the full armour of God' and 'the breastplate of righteousness'. While King Oswald of Northumbria (r.634–42), was saintly in his personal life, he called on God to help him in battle and when he died fighting the pagan Mercians at the Battle of Maserfield, the site of his death became a place of pilgrimage and a cult honouring him spread across Europe.† The magnificent hoard of seventh-century Anglo-Saxon gold and silver metalwork found by a metal detectorist at

† Some years ago I was surprised to find a shrine to Oswald in a small village in the Italian Alps.

quando .i. in leua .ii. in dextera quando .ii. in leua .iii. in dextera quando .iii. in leua. Et cetera usque ad .viiii. Porro .x. cum dicis leuam medio pectori supinam adpones digitis tantum ad collum erectis. .xx. cum dicis eandem pectori expansam late superpones. .xxx. cum dicis eandem pronam sed erectam pollice cartilagini medii pectoris inmittes. .xl. cum dicis eandem in umbilico erectam supinabis. .l. cum dicis eiusdem pronae sed erecto pollice umbilico inpones. .lx. cum dicis eadem prona femur leuum desuper conprehendes. .lxx. cum dicis eandem supinam femori superpones. .lxxx. cum dicis eandem pronam femori superpones. .xc. cum dicis eadem lumbos apprehendes pollice ad inguina uerso. At uero .c. et .cc. et cetera usque ad .dcccc. eodem quo diximus ordine in dextera corporis parte conplebis. Decies autem centena milia cum dicis ambas sibi manus insertis inuicem digitis inplicabis. Hic igitur numerus ut manifestius elucerct subdere depingere studuimus.

Hammerwich, Staffordshire, in 2009 largely comprised martial objects that included part of a religious shrine designed to be carried into battle. It bore the inscription from the Book of Numbers 10:35: 'Rise up, Lord, and let thine enemies be scattered, and let them that hate thee flee before thee.' When Pippin, the father of Charlemagne, embarked on a devastating campaign of conquest in Aquitaine in the 760s, the pope, Paul I (r.757–67), wrote to Pippin's sons: 'May the almighty Lord grant you victories from heaven and subject all barbarian nations beneath your feet.'[17] It is impossible to understand the nature of Christian kingship, the conquests of Charlemagne and the later crusades without stressing the prominence of this martial tradition.

Military valour was, of course, only one element in Christian kingship. Ancient traditions from the kingdoms of the Middle East recorded in the Old Testament described the just king who listens to his subjects and upholds the rights of the poor against the rich. In 601 Pope Gregory wrote to King Ethelbert of Kent exhorting him to 'strengthen the morals of your subjects by outstanding purity of life, by encouraging them, terrifying, enticing and correcting them, and by showing them an example of good works'. An ideology of Christian kingship became established.[18] Yet always among the attributes of a good monarch was his right to defend his kingdom. Without this Christianity and monarchy would never have been able to co-exist in the volatile societies and cultural groups of the first millennium, and without this co-existence the spread of monasteries with their insistent need for resources would never have taken place.

Illustrations from Bede's *On the Reckoning of Time* show finger counting: units and tens on the left hand, hundreds and thousands on the right. Larger numbers are indicated by touching parts of the body.

Yet there was an issue here that would be confronted by the Protestant reformers 1,000 years later. Jesus and the apostle Paul and their immediate successors established a model for Christian teaching by living in society and addressing their audiences face to face, even to the point of being judged and executed by them. This was the inspiration for the missionaries who were to be a vital part of the spread of Christianity in the first millennium. In contrast, monastic life had no scriptural backing. Jesus' withdrawal into the wilderness (described in Matthew 4:1–11 and Luke 4:1–3) lasted only forty days: there was no precedent for lifelong exclusion from society. The first monasteries, many of which appeared in the Egyptian desert in the fourth century, were, in fact, set up by bishops attempting to keep itinerant and often unruly ascetics under control by encouraging them to settle as hermits or in communities. While it took some 200 years for more formal institutions to evolve, first in the Greek church and later in the Latin, they soon became a prominent part of the Christian landscape.[19] Medieval monasticism was the supreme act of self-denial, the closest an individual could come to imitating the self sacrifice of Christ. Symbolically, the foundation by Benedict of a monastery high up on Monte Cassino in central Italy in 529, some 500 years after the Crucifixion, is seen as the birth of western monasticism.

Monasteries were largely independent of outside supervision, in most cases following a rule that laid out the principles by which each community lived. Celibacy and a commitment to individual poverty was mandatory for all members of the monastic community, and seclusion – at least within the confines of the monastic buildings – for many, unless their abbot had given them permission to travel. The cloister which allowed monks to exercise in the open air while maintaining their seclusion appears in the eighth century. It provided the most harmonious of monastic interiors for centuries to come. The most influential of the Rules in the west was the one drawn up by St Benedict which was championed by Pope Gregory the Great in his *Dialogues*. This gave authority to a presiding abbot and established models for community living, based on prayer, study and work. At Jarrow-Wearmouth, Benedict's Rule appears to have been well known but was used only as guidance. By the tenth century it had been adopted throughout Europe.

As is revealed by the records of monks who later became prominent churchmen – or even popes – there were opportunities for escaping monastic seclusion. Benedict Biscop is known to have made six journeys to Rome and back. There is something moving about these lone travellers covering long distances on foot or horseback over the decaying network of Roman roads. While written sources of these pilgrimages are rare, it is surprising how much interaction there was between widely separated communities. Even the insular Anglo-Saxon kingdoms of England were in constant contact with the continent. Given that so many early manuscripts were written in the native styles of itinerant scribes or copied directly from foreign scripts, one of the challenges for scholars is finding where they were originally created. The script of the *Codex Amiatinus*, described below and written in Northumbria, deceived early scholars into believing that it had been composed in Italy. The great Old English epic *Beowulf* was set in Denmark.

Biscop is recorded as having brought back many sacred books for his library, not only from Rome but from surviving manuscripts in France. We know the identity of one of these – the *Codex Grandior* from Cassiodorus' library at Vivarium. The *Codex* was a pandect in Jerome's fourth-century Latin translation, the Vulgate. However, it was not the final version. Jerome had translated the Old Testament from a Greek translation of the original Hebrew, the Septuagint. He had later completed a further translation directly from the Hebrew, to which Biscop also had access. Once back in Northumbria, the *Codex* was used as the basis for copying out three Vulgates now from Jerome's final translation. Two of these are lost, but there is one extraordinary survival, a copy that was taken from Jarrow-Wearmouth back to Rome 'as a gift to St Peter' by Biscop's successor as abbot, Ceolfrith, in the early eighth century. Ceolfrith died on the way and it appears that the *Codex* never reached Rome. Instead, it ended up in the Abbazia di San Salvatore in Tuscany, possibly because, after Ceolfrith's death, his companions continued towards Rome but faltered on the way and left it there for safekeeping. The *Codex Amiatinus*, so called from Monte Amiata, where the Abbazia was situated, is the earliest surviving copy of the entire Vulgate. Study of the *Codex* shows that some of Cassiodorus' original text and illustrations were directly copied, so establishing the link to Vivarium.[20]

The great libraries of Greece and Rome had relied on papyrus rolls, a comparatively cheap way of preserving texts, but papyrus was becoming rare in Europe. The trading of the material north of the Alps seems to have ended in the late seventh century just as the monasteries at Jarrow and Wearmouth were being founded, even though the Vatican was to have supplies as late as the eleventh century. So parchment, made from the prepared skin of calves, sheep or goats, had replaced it. Close examination of the *Codex Amiatinus* has isolated seven different hands. It is estimated that these seven scribes must have laboured for some ten years to complete the 1,030 leaves or folios of the volume, which would have required the skins of some 515 calves. Clearly, a monastic scriptorium, where copying took place lit by openings in the roof, could only have flourished if it had large pastures to draw on. Only the wealthiest of monasteries would have been able to support a library and scriptorium. Books were prestige objects in themselves and were expensive. Abbot Ceolfrith is recorded as having exchanged eight 'hides' of land, enough to support eight households, for a single manuscript, albeit one of 'miraculous workmanship'. With such demands on resources, it was inevitable that the texts needed for worship and Christian study would take precedence. A romanticized view of monks dutifully copying out the works of classical authors is still common but it is hard to see why they should have given secular texts any priority, other than for utilitarian reasons, when parchment was so valuable.

* * *

In 680 a seven-year-old boy entered the monastery at Wearmouth; he was to be based there until his death in 735. A feature of early medieval society was parents giving their children to monasteries as 'oblates' dedicated to the religious life – often to be secluded there for life. The practice was a common one, and was intended to prevent the splitting up of aristocratic estates between sons. The Wearmouth oblate is never known to have travelled outside the north of England, but Bede, later to be dubbed 'the Venerable', was to become famous throughout Europe for his scholarship.[21] He had access to what was probably the best library in England and among the best in Europe, with an estimated 200 texts, and he embarked with alacrity on a study of its works. As he wrote in the conclusion to his masterwork, *Historia ecclesiastica gentis Anglorum* (*The Ecclesiastical History of the English People*): 'It has always been my delight to learn or to teach or to write.'[22] Yet, beyond the pattern of existence followed by a contemplative dedicated to the rituals of a monastic community, virtually nothing is known of Bede's daily life. He does seem to have been devastated, however, when Abbot Ceolfrith departed for Rome with the *Codex Amiatinus* in 716, never to return. He had other frustrations. In a censorious letter written in 735, a few months before he died, to Egbert, an incoming bishop of York, he inveighed against bishops and clergy who abused their power or neglected their duties.[23] Many of the clergy were never proficient enough in Latin to fulfil their spiritual obligations and Bede records how he has to translate Latin for them, even that of a staple text such as the Apostles' Creed.

The Ecclesiastical History is by far the best known of Bede's works, but he wrote more than forty others, which scholars have studied more closely over the past thirty years. Like Cassiodorus before him, Bede gave priority to the study and interpretation of scripture. There are commentaries on the gospels and on several books of the Old Testament and even a commentary on Augustine's commentary on the letters of the apostle Paul. While these works of exegesis are hard to follow, we can nonetheless learn much about Bede's views from his remarks in them. One of the most fascinating findings from an analysis of his works as a whole is his growing disillusionment with Isidore of Seville. He starts off dependent on the Spanish bishop as a source but by the end of his life he is profoundly critical of his work. Bede said that he did not want 'children learning what is not true, and losing their labour on this [the *Etymologies*] when I am gone'.[24] When he does use Isidore, he strips out any mention of classical sources, using only Christian ones.

Bede's interests extended beyond the theological. Living next to an estuary and overlooking the sea, he was aware of the tides and the degree to which they were influenced by the moon. Even so, his main preoccupation was with the liturgical year and he became obsessed with correlating the rhythms of the natural world with the church's calendar. It was as a by-product of this objective that he learned as much as he could about natural phenomena. He was even prepared to rework the chronology of the world, placing the birth of Christ at 3,952 years after the Creation. In the last of the three works he wrote on the subject, *The Reckoning of Time* (*c*.721–5), he wove the movements of the sun and the planets into an elaborate chronology in an attempt to fix the date of Easter, a *computus*. *The Reckoning* confirms that the Greek discovery, possibly by Pythagoras as early as the sixth century BC, that the Earth is a sphere (acknowledged also by Isidore) had been carried over into the medieval world. It is particularly valuable in that it appears to record the actual lessons that Bede taught to the younger monks.[25] Their content was elementary compared to the great scientific figures of the past, Ptolemy, Hipparchus or Archimedes, but in his *The Beginnings of Western Science* the American historian David Lindberg acknowledged that Bede 'restated and preserved existing scientific knowledge in an age when the study of nature was a marginal activity'. He 'powerfully influenced what Europeans knew about nature and how Europeans thought about nature'.[26]

The Ecclesiastical History had a moral purpose. In its preface, dedicated to Ceolwulf, who had become king of Northumbria in 729, Bede sets it out clearly:

> Should history tell of good men and their good estate, the thoughtful listener is spurred on to imitate the good; should it record the evil ends of wicked men, no less the devout and earnest reader is kindled to eschew what is harmful and perverse, and himself with greater care pursue those things which he has learned to be good and pleasing in the sight of God.

He goes on to claim the academic high ground by listing his sources. He is trying to be as reliable as he can be. His model was the *Historia Ecclesiae*, by the fourth-century historian Eusebius, which told the story of the Christian church from the earliest times as a march towards the salvation of the world. Bede was to use his sources and contacts to tell the story of England after the Roman invasion of Julius Caesar, but concentrating its progress towards Christianization from the conversion of Ethelbert, king of Kent, and his subjects in 597 by the monk Augustine, to his own day. High points of Bede's narrative include the reign of the Northumbrian martyr-king Oswald and the Synod of Whitby (664), which linked Northumbria firmly to the Roman papacy. *The Ecclesiastical History* is remarkable for its drive and coherence even if Bede had only limited access to sources for much of England, the west in particular. In comparison with the brief annals of earlier medieval historians, he provides a narrative that is often gripping in its dramatic evolution.[27] Of course, the assumed end point of the narrative, the triumph of Roman (as opposed to Celtic) Christianity, is made clear from the start and, as was conventional in medieval religious narratives, Bede includes accounts of miracles to help his story on its way, but there was no other work of early medieval historiography that could equal it. *The Ecclesiastical History* remains the best contemporary source for the history of the Anglo-Saxon world. Its renown spread far: Bede was widely revered by the Carolingians and it has been suggested that as many manuscripts of the *History* were to be found in continental libraries as in England. In a typical monastic library of the twelfth century they were ranked equal in status to those of the Church Fathers.[28]

However, the quality of learning and the preservation of texts were still precarious in the eighth century. Some 500 manuscripts dating from before 750 survive from what had been Roman Gaul and so it is possible to make a survey of them. They used a wide variety of scripts, selecting different forms of letters and elaborate calligraphy that was not always easy to read: 'Most writing is in undistinguished scripts, crude uncials or minuscules rich in ligatures which made the shape of any letter vary greatly… Spelling is confused.'[29] As a result the scribes often made mistakes in copying that were then passed on to each new copy. The written Latin was itself often obscure. The sixth-century historian Gregory of Tours, for instance, developed his own case endings and idiosyncratic spellings in the Latin of his *History of the Franks*. Later scribes tried to correct these, making Gregory's original meaning uncertain. In other instances, the text took second place to the work of illumination. Christopher de Hamel, the authority on these early manuscripts, notes that even the wondrous Book of Kells, an illuminated set of the four gospels dating from about 800, is 'a poor and degraded witness to the Gospel text'.[30] While the script is clear and regular, the text itself is a mixture of Jerome's Vulgate 'contaminated' with older Latin versions some of which seemed to be drawn from the childhood memories of the scribes. These 'insular' gospel texts, which were created in a monastery in Britain or Ireland and are superb artistic achievements, show variations in the way they present the Latin translations of the original Greek. They were prestige objects, designed for veneration as such rather than for textual study.

Meanwhile, spoken Latin began to diverge from the Latin of the elite, and the church had to recognize this. The Council of Tours of 813 ordered the clergy to give their sermons not in formal Latin but in a language their congregations could understand (*lingua rustica* as against *lingua Romana*). Scholars regard this as the moment when the French language was born as the older language deteriorated. The traditions of copying manuscripts were fading out by the eighth century. The demands of military expenditure led to the selling of monastic lands by their patrons so that monasteries closed down, with the monks dispersed and the scriptoria left empty. In the words of the Carolingian scholar Giles Brown:

> Few resources remained for the production of books. Charters and diplomas attest that the standard of written Latin had sunk to an alarming level. Against this background, and with so few indications that manuscripts continued to be copied and new works composed, it would seem unwise to place much emphasis on the continuity of learning and cultural activity over this period.[31]

It is often forgotten how precarious the survival of 'western civilization' had become in the eighth century. Would there be anybody who could save it? This is the subject of the next chapter.

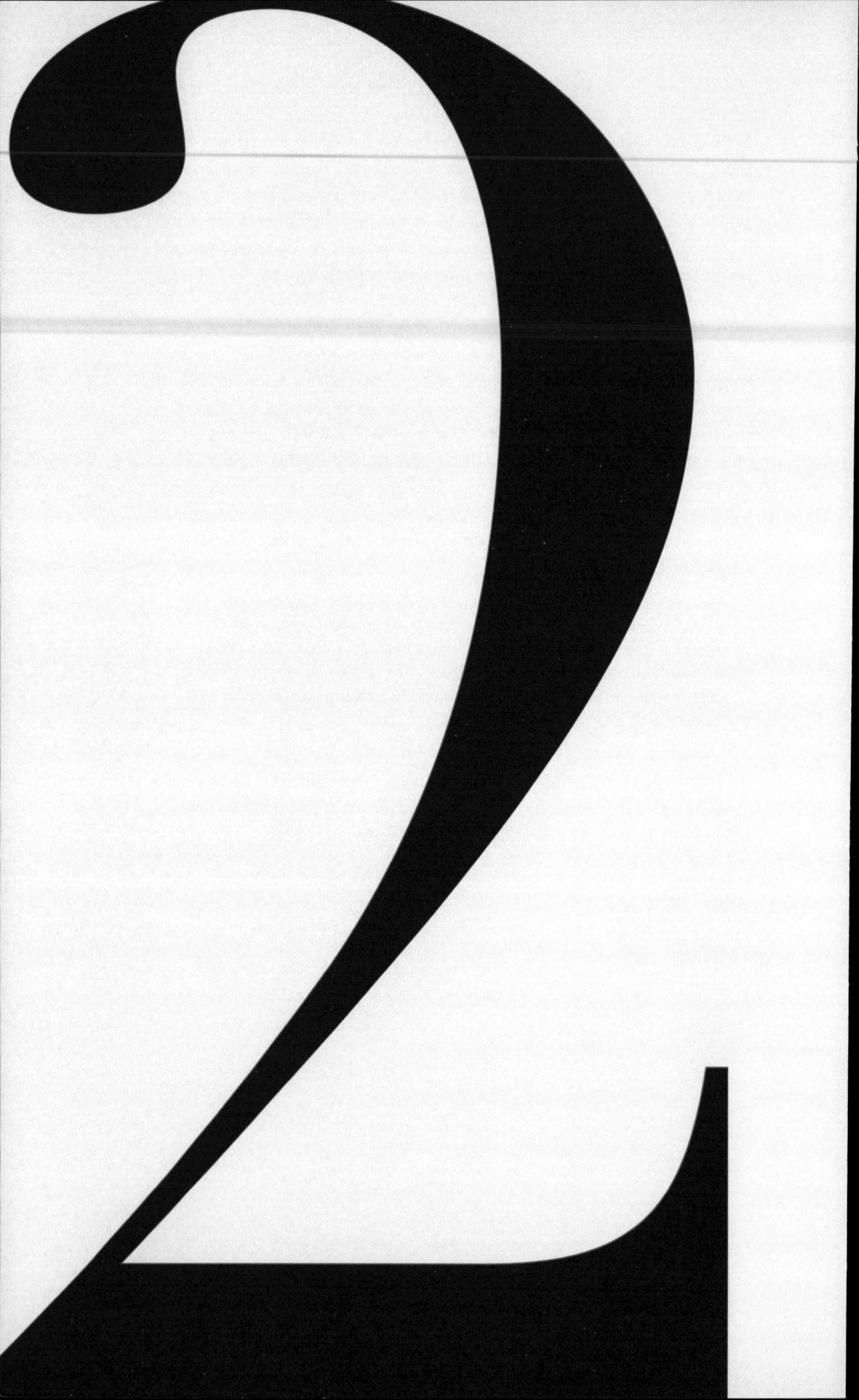

Charlemagne Restores the Discipline of Learning

He was so eloquent, indeed, that he might have passed for a teacher of eloquence. He most zealously cultivated the liberal arts, held those who taught them in great esteem, and conferred great honors upon them… The King spent much time and labour with Alcuin, a man of Saxon extraction, who was the greatest scholar of the day, studying rhetoric, dialectics, and especially astronomy; he learned to reckon, and used to investigate the motions of the heavenly bodies most curiously,

From Einhard, *Vita Karoli*[1]

It was purely fortuitous that a few years after Bede's death western Europe was to be transformed by the rise of an empire that had the resources and determination to consolidate and expand scholarship and save it from extinction. The Merovingian dynasty had ruled over Francia for generations, but it had been supplanted from within the royal household by Charles Martel, its chief administrator (or 'mayor of the palace'), in the 720s. Charles had thrown back the Arab advance into Europe at the Battle of Poitiers in 732 and his son Pippin was recognized by the papacy as the lawful king of Francia after Charles's death in 741. When Pippin died in 768, his two sons, Charles and Carloman, succeeded him. On Carloman's death in 771, Charles, later Carolus Magnus or Charlemagne, as he was to become known, became sole ruler. Physically imposing (as his surviving bones confirm), gregarious, eloquent and with a will of iron, Charlemagne was soon set on the expansion of his kingdom.[2]

The first opportunity came from across the Alps. The Lombards had spread across northern Italy in the sixth century, and by the eighth century they were expanding further, capturing Ravenna from the Byzantines in 751. Now the papal states, which covered much of central Italy, were under threat and the pope, Adrian I (r.772–97), asked Charlemagne for help. In a swift campaign Charlemagne crossed the Alps, captured the Lombard capital at Pavia and proclaimed himself *rex Langobardorum*, so earning himself the title 'protector of Rome'. Charlemagne's successors were to claim suzerainty over northern Italy for centuries to come.

Charlemagne haunted the later European imagination; Albrecht Dürer's painting dates from 1512.

However, north of the Alps, the Saxons, still unconverted to Christianity, took their chance to raid into Francia. Charlemagne responded with a determination 'to overwhelm in war the infidel and faithless Saxon people and to continue until they either had been defeated and subjugated to Christianity or were completely annihilated'.[3] So began a series of brutal campaigns. Mass deportations and the massacres of prisoners were commonplace. As the Saxons were divided among themselves, identifying themselves according to individual *gens* or clan, they would prove exceptionally difficult to subdue. The defeat of one *gens* was not conclusive, as another could always arise in revolt. Once a campaign had been finished, Charlemagne would hold a great assembly; the first was at Paderborn in 777, where victory would be

karolus
magnus
Annis · 14 ·

proclaimed at a mass baptism of captured Saxons. In the early 780s the *Capitulatio de partibus Saxoniae* (*Ordinances concerning Saxony*) decreed that the refusal to baptize would be met with the death penalty, as would destruction of churches and attempts to undermine Christianity. When Saxony finally became part of Charlemagne's empire, thirty years after his first campaigns, its traditional society had been shattered. The annals are replete with Latin words of destruction, *vastare*, *devastare*, *incendere*, suggesting the widespread ravaging of land and burning of buildings. Large estates, owned by king, church or nobles, filled the vacuum. Later conquests of Charlemagne took him into northern Spain, where he suffered a humiliating defeat in the Pyrenees when his troops were ambushed by Basques,* eastwards through Bavaria, into Hungary (where the pagan Avars provided immense booty after their defeat) and even down the eastern coastline of the Adriatic (now Croatia). These campaigns were less destructive, but by the 790s Charlemagne had established a vast empire that could claim equality with the Byzantine empire to the east. It irked him that the Byzantines – who had suffered immense losses after the Arab invasions of their territory in the seventh and eighth centuries – still treated him as if he were a barbarian.

Having shown himself to be a robust destroyer of paganism in the name of the church, it was now that Charlemagne consolidated his relationship with the papacy. When Adrian's successor as pope, Leo III, came into conflict with the Roman aristocracy (the accounts suggest that he was ambushed and brutally beaten up), he had every reason to call upon 'the protector of Rome' for help. On Christmas Day 800, Charlemagne was anointed as 'Emperor of the Romans' by Leo in St Peter's Basilica.† Here was the revival of ancient imperial traditions that saw the emperor receiving his sacral power from Rome, if now from the pope rather than from the senate. (One account tells how Charles 'was saluted by the pope in the customary manner of ancient emperors, and the name of *patricius* was abandoned and he was called emperor and *augustus*'.) The Byzantines were infuriated at being dislodged from their role as successors of the Roman empire and feared a further expansion of Charlemagne into territories they still held in southern Italy, but there was very little they could do to protest. The empress Irene, who had come to power in the Byzantine capital

* The popular medieval epic of Roland was based on this defeat at the Roncevaux Pass in August 778 where Roland, Charlemagne's protector of his borders, was killed.

† The circular 'imperial' porphyry stone on which tradition says he was crowned is still to be seen inside the atrium of St Peter's in Rome. Nelson, *King and Emperor*, recounts the ceremony, pp. 380–5.

Constantinople through the murder of her own son, had discredited herself and could be ignored. The imperial throne was, in effect, vacant. While the popes had claimed supremacy over all Christians, west and east, the relationship between the Latin and Greek churches now broke down, and by 1054 the Greeks were in schism with the western church. The sack of Constantinople by the Fourth Crusade in 1204 is still remembered by Greek Orthodox Christians as a dastardly betrayal of the earliest Christian communities by an upstart Latin church.

In the introduction to her study of Charlemagne, Rosamond McKitterick explores the way in which he has been represented by later generations.[4] His early recognition (by a poet of his day) as 'father of Europe' still has resonance and an adulatory biography of 814, soon after his death, the *Vita Karoli*, confirmed him as 'the most splendid and greatest of all men'.[5] Einhard, the *Vita*'s author, was a palace official who had risen through his own talents and become an intimate of his subject. In his presentation of Charlemagne he harked back to the Roman emperors of the past who were both conquerors of Rome's enemies and protectors of their people. Einhard even adopted the style of the first-century AD historian Suetonius (69–*c.*122), famous for his lives of the Caesars, to shape his narrative. While Charlemagne was known to have been promiscuous (nineteen known children are credited to him, five from concubines), Einhard praises him for his good character, family life and friendliness with his subordinates. Learning was of great importance to Einhard and naturally he highlights Charlemagne's erudition. Yet the emperor differed markedly from most of his Roman predecessors in being a Christian, and moreover one dependent on papal patronage for his title and authority. Once he had stabilized his conquests, the creation of a Christian society became Charlemagne's dominant objective and his extraordinary energy was focused on achieving it. The exercise of his secular power in creating an efficient administrative framework is impossible to separate from the imposition of his religious programme.

While Charlemagne may not have been a fluent reader (Einhard tells us that he had to take lessons in grammar), he was well acquainted with Augustine's *City of God* (in which Augustine compares the secular city with the celestial one) and believed that a distinct Christian society could be created on the model of 'the heavenly city' that Augustine had described there. To make sure that every one of his subjects was under the eye of the church, Charlemagne created a hierarchy of archbishops, bishops and parishes that covered the whole empire. He summoned synods to discuss church affairs and insisted that the clergy came to assemblies to hear his demands. Circulars known as capitularies – from the 'chapters' with which they were set out – were promulgated through his territories by *missi*, envoys who were deployed to enforce them through the local counts and bishops. The authority on medieval sainthood and spirituality, André Vauchez, has termed Charlemagne's empire a 'liturgical civilization'. By 381 he had recruited Alcuin of York to his court – 'the most learned man in the entire world', as Einhard described him, and a fine teacher. Alcuin, a deeply religious man, helped set the tone of the Carolingian regime. In his *De rhetorica* (794) he writes that 'religion is an attribution of justice to give everyone his due. The worship of God, the laws of humanity, and the principle of equity in all of life, are preserved in this virtue.'[6]

By now, however, there were many clergy and monks who were simply not well enough educated or fluent in Latin to sustain the liturgy. Charlemagne and his advisers spotted the problem. 'Letters have often been sent to us in these last years from certain monasteries – in most of these writings their sentiments were sound but their language was uncouth. Because of their neglect of learning their unskilled tongues could not express it without fault,' records one circular of 784.[7] In 786 Charlemagne lamented that learning had been lost, 'destroyed by the sloth of our forefathers', that many texts had been corrupted by careless copying, and that there needed to be a revival of the 'liberal arts'.[8] The sources talk of *sermones inculti* and *lingua inerudita* ('uncouth sermons' and 'crude language').

The policy most associated with Charlemagne, *correctio*, envisaged that central power could be exercised more effectively through an educated society.[9] The *Admonitio Generalis* of 789 laid down a demanding programme of Christianization in which the clergy were subjected to an ambitious programme of reform and education.[10] 'Let the clergy join and associate to themselves not only children of servile condition but also the sons of free men. And let schools be established in which boys may learn to read.' The *Admonitio* recognizes that many texts were corrupted: 'Correct carefully the Psalms, the chant, the calendar, the grammars in each monastery and bishopric, and the catholic books, because often some desire to pray to God properly, but they pray badly because of the incorrect books.'[11] There was a particular emphasis on the importance of preaching. The fact that thirty-two copies of the *Admonitio* still survive attests to the efficiency and outreach of the imperial administration.

Extraordinary to relate, it seems that Charlemagne might not have been able to write. 'He used to keep tablets and blanks in bed under his pillow, that at leisure hours he might accustom his hand to form the letters; however, as he did not begin his efforts in due season, but late in life, they met with ill success', records Einhard.[12] In order to carry out his programme of reform, the emperor assembled an impressive array of scholars: Alcuin from York, Clement Scotus II from Ireland, the Italians Peter of Pisa and Paulinus of Aquileia, and even a Visigoth, Theodulf of Orléans. Together, they made the Carolingian courts centres of literacy and intellectual debate. For Charlemagne's officials literacy became a requirement for any form of advancement and it also became a mark of the cultivated courtier. One later source, Hincmar of Rheims (806–82), defined Charlemagne's court not in terms of its buildings but rather of its rational and learned members. The revival of 'the liberal arts' demanded by Charlemagne can be seen in the adoption, probably through the influence of Alcuin, of the seven subjects that Boethius, Cassiodorus and Isidore of Seville had championed. Martianus Capella's *De nociis* was intensely studied despite its pagan mythology, and this embedded 'the arts' still further into the medieval curriculum. (Charlemagne insisted that both his sons and daughters studied these liberal arts.) Alcuin wrote elementary school texts for young scholars; *De rhetorica*, for instance, is an exploration of dialectical reasoning in the shape of a dialogue between Alcuin and Charlemagne. By stressing the importance of rhetoric in public life it preserved one of the most important skills of the Roman elite. Yet the pre-eminent subject was grammar, the *Ars Minor* and *Ars Major* of the fourth-century Donatus the most popular text. As Donatus assumed a knowledge of Latin, commentaries had to be provided to ease students into the work.

The vast majority of written sources from Charlemagne's reign have vanished, but enough manuscripts survive to show that there was a prodigious programme of sending out of texts, of the gospels and epistles, for instance, as well as other favoured works for specific groups, including Augustine's *City of God*, Pope Gregory's *Pastoral Care* and the Rule of Benedict. The scriptorium in Tours produced two Bibles per year and a preface by Alcuin stresses the care to be taken in reading the word of God so its full benefit will be absorbed by the congregation.

The texts produced by court illuminators and copyists remain a major legacy of Charlemagne's court culture. It used to be thought that these specialists were centred on Aachen, the glittering capital of his last years (now in western Germany, close to the border with France), but the comparatively late development of this palace complex suggests that there may have been several schools of scribes.[13] Charlemagne was clearly the inspiration. The most important outcome was a concentra-

OMNIA ET PROPTER VOLUNTATEM
PERPETUI DECORIS STRUCTURA
STABILI FUNDAMINE

tion on correct written Latin (Charlemagne was said to speak it well, even if he could not write it). For Alcuin, as an Anglo-Saxon, Latin was a foreign language but he composed a text that set out the conventions of the Latin of the great orator Cicero, already seen as the benchmark for correctness. (Einhard had also adopted Ciceronian Latin for his biography.) Alcuin also appears to have been behind the development of what is known as Carolingian minuscule, a script that was easy to read (with spaces between words) and comparatively fast to write, and which became the uniform medium for copying texts. Larger, majuscule, letters were retained for headings and one feature of the script involved the use of different majuscule and minuscule fonts to highlight the start of a new text. This again made it easier for preachers to pause and understand the moment when they could conclude a reading and start afresh. The majuscules became increasingly elaborate, one of the glories for readers of the surviving texts. By 800 Carolingian minuscule had spread from the imperial copyists throughout France; it was taken up by the scriptoria of the great monasteries and then spread as far as Anglo-Saxon England. According to one estimate, some 50,000 copies had been produced in minuscule by 900, of which 7,000 survive.[14]

Many of the works of classical authors that might have been lost were revived as exemplars. Reconstructions of Charlemagne's imperial library suggest that among the codices were many speeches of Cicero, extracts from Virgil's *Aeneid* and *Georgics* (an eighth of the total text in an illustrated manuscript now in the Vatican Library), the histories of Sallust, Lucan on the civil wars of the Roman republic, the satires of Juvenal and 500 lines of the poet Horace in addition to works on grammar.[15] By the year 900 texts by as many as seventy different classical writers had been copied and many others must have been present in Charlemagne's libraries. Ermenrich, the scholarly bishop of Passau in the late ninth century, knew of works by Lucretius, Virgil, Horace and Ovid. Classical survivals not otherwise recorded but copied in the eighth and ninth centuries were still being discovered in monasteries by the humanists 600 years later. Many Renaissance scholars assumed that they were Roman originals and the script was adopted by early printers in tribute. In short, the Carolingian renaissance, as it can justly be called, was crucial in creating copies of texts that survive and are the basis of modern editions. The act of accurate copying in itself created a tradition of scholarly precision. One outstanding contributor here was Lupus, abbot of the monastery at Ferrières (*c.*805–62). Lupus was aware of

Charlemagne's sumptuous chapel at Aachen, built in the late eighth century, was modelled on the Church of San Vitale in Ravenna.

how easily texts became corrupted when copied, so he went out of his way to get as many examples of each text as possible so that he could assemble an authoritative copy. In this respect he was a forerunner of the humanist scholarship of the fifteenth century.[16]

Of course, the majority of surviving texts were religious works, many of them sumptuous productions. The earliest illuminated manuscript to survive from the Carolingian court is the Godescalc Evangelistary of 781–3, a wonderful volume of gospel readings compiled under the supervision of a Frankish scribe, Godescalc. As befits a 'renaissance' text, it draws on many earlier styles, from the Celtic traditions of illumination to the Byzantine.* Another beautifully illustrated Carolingian text, the Dagulf Psalter, now in the Imperial Library in Vienna, was written in gold and appears to have been a gift from Charlemagne to the pope. These treasures are not only magnificent in themselves, the texts have been quarried for a deeper understanding of Charlemagne's own religious preferences for the liturgies that were performed in the opulent chapel at Aachen.

Charlemagne was avid for knowledge and some records survive of his 'lessons' with Alcuin, as noted in the opening quotation for this chapter. These must reflect the tone of discussion among the court scholars. The sources suggest that there was a buzz of intellectual debate, not least on theological issues. The historian Chris Wickham has even argued that 'the importance of intellectuals for the political practice of the ninth-century West was as great as or greater than it would ever be again in the Middle Ages'.[17] There were question-and-answer sessions following the dialectical method of Socrates and Plato. Debates took place on astronomy, the meaning of time (using Bede's *The Reckoning of Time*) and the uses of rhetoric, even if, under the influence of Augustine's *De doctrina christiana*, knowledge was always subordinated to understanding of the scriptures. One of the surviving texts is a picture book of the constellations, the *Aratea*, named after its original author, the third-century BC Greek astronomer, Aratus of Soli, which has come down to us in a ninth-century copy of a fourth-century AD original. The *Aratea* has an extraordinary illustration of the cosmos in which the sun, the moon, Mars, Jupiter and Saturn are shown circling the Earth but Mercury and Venus are circling the sun. It was an idea

A rare fourth-century text of Virgil's *Aeneid*. Dido, queen of Carthage, offers a sacrifice in front of the temple of Juno, goddess of marriage, in the hope that her lover Aeneas will stay with her. Note the uncial text with majuscule (capital) letters and no separation of words.

* It is now in the Bibliothèque nationale in Paris. An evangelistary contains only selections of the gospels.

DIDO

QUONIAMQUIDEM
MULTICONATISUNT
ORDINARENARRA
TIONEMQUAEIN
INNOBISCOMPLE
TAESUNT·RERUM
SICUTTRADIDERUNT
NOBISQUIABINI
TIOIPSIUIDERUNT
ETMINISTRIFUE
RUNT·SERMONIS·
UISUMESTETMIHI
ADSECUTOAPRIN
CIPIOOMNIA
DILIGENTEREXOR
DINETIBISCRIBE
REOPTIMETHEO
PHILE
UTCOGNOSCASEORUM
UERBORUMDEQUI
BUSERUDITUSES
UERITATEM
FUITINDIEBUSHERO
DISREGISIUDAEAE
SACERDOSQUIDAM

NOMINEZACHARI
ASDEUICEABIA
ETUXORILLI·DEFI
LIABAARON
ETNOMENEIUSELI
SABETH·
ERANTAUTEMIUSTI
AMBOANTEDM
INCEDENTESINOM
NIB·MANDATISET
IUSTIFICATIONIB
DNISINEQUAE
RELLA
ETNONERATILLIS
FILIUS·
EOQUODESSETELI
SABETH·STERILIS
ETAMBO PROCES
SISSENTINDIE
BUSSUIS
FACTUMESTAUTEM
CUMSACERDOTIO
FUNGERETURZA
CHARIASINORDINE
UICISSUAEANTEDM

to be revived in the sixteenth century by Tycho Brahe.[18] While there is some record of tensions over whether such 'pagan' texts should be used, most of Charlemagne's scholars accepted their relevance. They used excerpts of Pliny the Elder's *Natural History* to explain astronomy. Thirty-eight manuscripts of the *Natural History* dating from the ninth to the twelfth centuries survive, which suggests that the debates spread to other centres of learning. Music and verse were other areas that were enthusiastically patronized.[19] The famous plan drawn up for a new monastery at St Gall (now in Switzerland) in the early ninth century shows that elementary concepts of proportion and geometry were understood in this period.[20]

An analysis of book lists from eighth- and ninth-century libraries is an excellent way of charting the progress of monastic learning.[21] The origins of many monasteries are not well documented but it is clear that a few major foundations received substantial patronage from Carolingian royalty or leading aristocrats. Without it they could hardly have maintained scriptoria working full time with the necessary supply of animal skins to make parchment. In contrast the majority of foundations had hardly any books at all. Libraries in the first half of the eighth century did not catalogue their books separately from their other possessions and the earliest lists suggest that they arranged them either by the chronological order in which the books had arrived or with special treasures appearing first. So the library at Würzburg placed a venerated Acts of the Apostles, once used by Bede, top of its list of thirty-six books. By the early ninth century there are clear signs of the emergence of a formal system of classification. At the Benedictine abbey of Reichenau on Lake Constance, the scriptures are placed first followed by commentaries on them, notably by Augustine, Jerome or Gregory. Josephus' histories (*History of The Jewish War* and *Antiquities of the Jews*) come next and then there is a section of law codes. These include the Roman emperor Theodosius II's famous code of 438 but also laws from 'barbarian' codes and those promulgated by Charlemagne. There is a medical section, another for books on the liturgy and then a section for grammars and schoolbooks. Within each section the authors are arranged in chronological order and each volume is listed by name. The library of the Benedictine Abbey

previous pages
The evangelist Luke depicted in the gospels brought to Britain by the Benedictine monk Augustine in 596 as a prelude to the island's conversion to Christianity. A reader to a congregation would pause at the end of each section of the uncial text.

By the late eighth century, as seen in the wonderful Book of Kells (top), opening letters have become an elaborate feature of the text, and the text itself is precise and easily legible.

In the Grandval Bible (bottom), of *c.*830–40, the introduction to *Exodus* exemplifies the transition from majuscule to 'Carolingian' minuscule letters, which are much easier to write.

MATHEUS
atthessicutprimus poni
tur inordine
hocevangelium iniudea primus scripsit cuius
vocatio addm ex publicanis actibus fuit

HAECSUNT Cap. I.
NOMINA
FILIORU
ISRAHEL
QUIINGRES
SISUNTIN II
AEGYPTU
CUMIACOB
SINGULI
CUMDOMI
BUS SUIS
INTROIE
RUNT
Ruben. symeon. leui. iuda. issachar. zabulon
etbeniamin. danetnepthalim. gad etaser
Erantigiturommnesanimaeeorum quaeegres
saesuntdefemoreiacob. septuaginta quinque

of St Gall, which is not far from Reichenau, and which collaborated closely with its neighbour in matters of book production, reveals a sophisticated approach to bibliographical organization – with detailed records of books lost, those sent away to be copied and those placed separately in the monastery schoolroom. There is even a 'wants' list. By the end of the ninth century the library at St Gall possessed some 395 separate works in 264 codices. The library catalogue of 830 for the enormously wealthy royal monastery at Lorsch (in south-central Germany), where Carolingian minuscule may have been developed, contains a description of the contents of each volume. The history section of the library boasts works by Josephus, Eusebius, Bede and the Roman historian Livy. Its collection of classical texts includes works by the Roman orator Cicero. By the tenth century Lorsch was acknowledged as one of the finest libraries of the Christian world and the Lorsch Gospels, composed during the reign of Charlemagne but now, alas, broken up, survive as testament to the quality of its scribes.*

Charlemagne died in 814. The traditional view expressed by German historians of the late 1940s, but translated into English only in the 1960s, that Charlemagne's empire was already in decline in the early ninth century, has been revised. The emperor's energy seems to have been intact until the final months of his life and there is enough evidence to show that he was actively involved in administration in these last years. Even though his empire broke up in the following decades, much of his legacy continued in the shape of patronage for monasteries from his successors. Yet it remains instructive to place the libraries of early medieval Europe within a wider cultural context. Looking back to tenth-century Cordoba, the seventeenth-century Moroccan author Ai-Maqqari wrote that the library of the Khalif Al-Hakem was said to have some 400,000 volumes and that there were in the city 'many other libraries in the hands of wealthy individuals, where the studious could dive into the fathomless sea of knowledge and bring up its inestimable pearls'.[22] In comparison with the Arab cultures of southern Spain and the southern and eastern Mediterranean, western Europe remained a backwater. And it was not just the Islamic societies of the south and east that were culturally ahead of their northern European counterparts. Peter Brown, who has done more than any other recent scholar to chart the history of early Christianity, notes how the library of the White Monastery at Sohag on the middle Nile, 'with its thousand carefully produced parchment volumes, dwarfed the libraries of Dark Age Western Europe' long after

* The Gospels are now divided between the Batthyaneum Library in Romania, the Vatican Museum and the Victoria and Albert Museum, London.

the Muslim conquests.[23] Even so, Rosamond McKitterick, a leading authority on Carolingian scholarship, emphasizes the consolidation of the position of Latin, the secure access that it provided to the classical world and knowledge of antiquity, and its role for centuries to come as a common tongue, especially for intellectual debate. Of 1,300 surviving texts produced or owned in England before 1100, only 200 have any Old English in them at all. Poetry is the sole form of literature that survives in the vernacular.[24] In short, 'the Carolingians imparted to future generations... the conviction that the past not only mattered but was a priceless hoard of treasure to be guarded, conserved, augmented, enriched and passed on'.[25] As Alcuin lay dying in 804, he addressed his 'little cell' at Aachen: 'In you the gentle voices of teachers could be heard expounding with hallowed lips the books of Wisdom.'[26] Among all the bloodshed and forced conversions of the reign, a tradition of scholarship had been preserved.

The Carolingian 'renaissance' in learning depended on one secular ruler and his chosen scholars using Christianity as a medium through which the preservation of texts and the stimulation of elementary education could take place. As yet the church itself, despite having a number of texts – predominantly those by Augustine and Pope Gregory the Great – that were influential, had failed to act as a coherent force for the dissemination of learning. Local traditions of Christianity existed alongside wealthy monasteries that were subject to secular rulers or magnates. In fact, the Christian communities were torn between conformity and local expressions of spirituality. As such, how well placed were they to become agents for the broadening of the western mind?

Conformity and Diversity in the Christian Communities of the Late First Millennium

Put on the whole armour of God, that you may be able to stand against the wiles of the devil. For we are not contending against flesh and blood, but against the principalities, against the powers, against the world rulers of the present darkness, against the spiritual forces of wickedness in the heavenly places…

St John Cassian (AD 360–425)[1]

In his *Western Society and the Church in the Middle Ages* (1970), the eminent historian Richard Southern described the medieval church 'as the most elaborate and thorough integrated system of religious thought and practice the world has ever seen'.[2] Such a sweeping assessment has long been superseded by the findings of more recent scholarship. Southern envisaged a quiescent society onto which a system of thought could be successfully imposed so that dissent and diversity were eliminated. As will be seen, this completely ignores the intellectual and religious vitality of medieval Europe and the dissensions within the medieval church. Spiritual feelings could be, and were, expressed in a myriad of different ways. Even in the Carolingian period there was earnest debate between theologians over unresolved issues such as predestination, the relationship of Christ to God the Father, the nature of the soul, the validity of icons and relics, and the reality of evil.[3] The finest philosopher of the age, the Irish-born Eriugena (*c.*815–*c.*877), battled with the question of free will and determinism at a sophisticated level. In the centuries to come there would be an increasing preoccupation with 'heresies', however hard these proved to define. At the same time, the absolute barriers that existed between clergy in the parishes, secluded monks and the mass of the faithful makes it hard to see 'religious thought and practice' as 'integrated'.

While there is a common assumption that 'western civilization' rests on Christian values, discovering what these values were is elusive not least because early medieval Europe was characterized by a wide range of spiritual allegiances. As the opening quotation in this chapter shows, Christian societies emerged in a world haunted by malign forces. In the troubled times that followed the collapse of the western Roman empire, when living standards were low and havoc arising from the migration of peoples all too common,* the power of Christianity as a focus for salvation from disruptions cannot be overestimated. To many the church was primarily a bulwark against the demonic terrors that lurked in dark corners. There were supportive biblical sources. Even today Anglican evensong may include the comforting Psalm 91: 'You will not fear the terror of night, nor the arrow that flies by day, nor the pestilence that stalks in the darkness, nor the plague that destroys at midday.'

By 1000 there were two major tensions within western Christianity that were to persist throughout the medieval period. The first was

* Witness the desperate accounts of Viking raids on English monasteries.

between local Christianities and papal authority. Europe was simply too extensive, its local cultures too vibrant and their secular rulers too ambitious for papal authority to shape, let alone transform, religious attitudes. The cultural history of those regions that had been part of the Roman empire, often for centuries, was very different from those that had not. As a result there were always lively varieties of local Christian tradition that were disturbing to the hierarchy, not least among them the many shrines that attracted thousands of pilgrims.[4] The second tension was between the wealth of the church, shown most blatantly in its independent monasteries, and its proclaimed ideals. While there were many clergy who enjoyed access to enormous resources and privileges, others were deeply offended by this apparent betrayal of the teachings of Christ. Ecclesiastical reformers railed against the corruption of the church and the laxity and ignorance of its clergy. Their success would depend on papal support or the charisma of individual reformers, but ultimately the conservatism of the church proved too strong and its authoritarian structure remained intact until the Reformation (and, for Catholics, lasts to this day). As will be seen in Chapter 16, many Christians had detached their religious lives from the institutional church long before the sixteenth century.

Ever since the banning of pagan cults by the emperor Theodosius in 390, Christianity had proclaimed itself as the only true faith. This isolated Jews, despite the appropriation in the second century of what had been the (Jewish) Hebrew Scriptures, in Christian terms the Old Testament, for scriptural inspiration. By 1000 there were common features of Christian allegiance, baptism into the community, of course, the Eucharist and eventually another five sacraments that became integrated in the life of the church in the Middle Ages.† Worship centred on the liturgy of the Mass, which was in Latin accompanied by a sermon in the vernacular.

It was assumed, perhaps too easily, that the Christian knew what he or she had to believe.[5] While the early Christians had supported the Jewish version of Genesis that told of God creating order from pre-existing material, in the second century the doctrine of an act of creation, *ex nihilo*, 'from nothing', by an elevated supreme God replaced it. This development was to prove of some importance when theologians attempted to reconcile it with Greek philosophy.‡

† The other five sacraments of the Catholic Church are Confirmation, Penance (Confession of Sins), Matrimony, the Anointing of the Sick and Holy Orders, the process by which a man is dedicated to the priesthood.

‡ Aristotle, for instance, believed that the world had existed eternally (see Chapter 8, p. 190).

Originally, the first two humans, Adam and Eve, had lived in Paradise but had been expelled by God for their sin. According to the theologian Augustine (354–430), bishop of Hippo in North Africa, this 'original' sin had been transmitted from generation to generation by sexual intercourse, so tarnishing the sexual act. Every individual was therefore a diminished form of the original couple created by God. The qualities that God had given to Adam and Eve had been forever depreciated. This was in dramatic contrast to the Greek conception, most fully explored in the works of Aristotle, that human beings were freely able to achieve *eudaimonia*, a state of flourishing in which the ability to think rationally was predominant. It would take a long time, probably not until the Aristotelian theology of Thomas Aquinas (see Chapter 8, pp. 194–202), for intellectual confidence to return.

Many years later, the Son of God, Jesus Christ, had come down to earth and acted as a redeemer through his sacrifice on the cross. He had founded the church with its promise of salvation for troubled humanity. Following bitter debates in the fourth century, the emperor Theodosius had proclaimed the doctrine of the Trinity, that God the Father, Jesus Christ the Son and the Holy Spirit were united as three

The conversion of St Augustine in a garden in Milan after many months of doubt in 386 was a crucial moment in the history of western Christianity. The artist Fra Angelico painted this in *c.*1430.

distinct persons in one. At the Council of Constantinople in 381 this had been endorsed by the church and all other formulations of the relationship between the three declared heretical.[6] The complete banning of all pagan cults in the empire followed in the 390s and Jews were also gradually excluded from public life.

This was just the moment when Augustine was emerging as the figure who would do most to define Latin Christianity.[7] Although he had a Christian mother, Augustine had come to Christianity via a tortuous route, brilliantly explored in his famous *Confessions*, one of the finest self-searching autobiographies in western literature. His mind was expansive and probing, his sermons compelling (not least because he had been the city orator in Milan before his conversion) and there are many who still find him inexhaustible as a theological inspiration. He relied heavily on Plato, or more especially the third-century Platonic philosopher Plotinus, for his concept of God, in Plotinus' terms 'the One'. This God dominated Augustine's imagination – there was no escaping his presence.

Despite his inspiration from Plotinus, Augustine was always an original thinker, building his distinctive theology from his inner feelings.

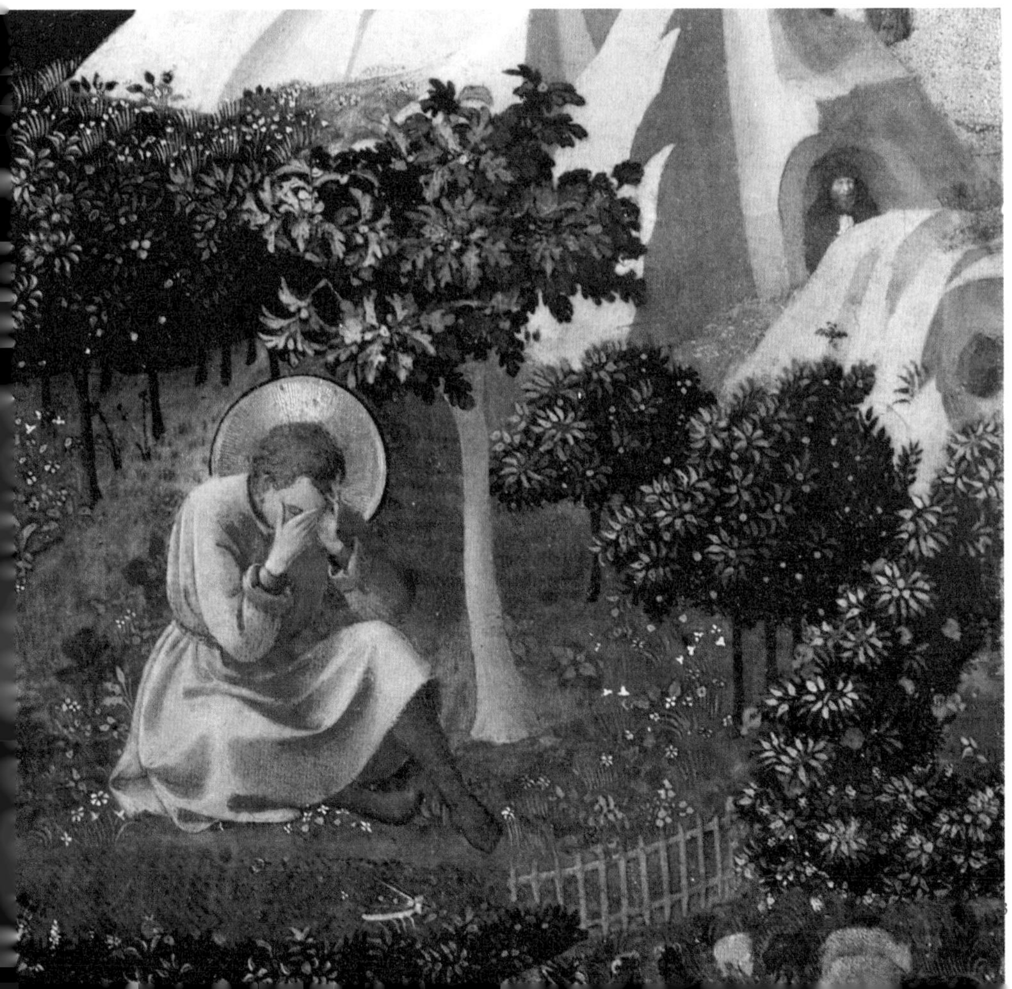

Perhaps it would not be until Descartes in the seventeenth century that a philosopher would rely so heavily on his own existence as a basis for establishing truth. As such he was far removed from the tradition of public theological controversy that the Greeks had indulged in for three centuries. He could not even read the gospels and the letters of Paul in the original Greek, let alone master the subtleties of the debates that had followed.[8] When he embarked on a study of that most central Christian doctrine of all, the Trinity, it is extraordinary that he found 'things for me to read on this subject [the Trinity] have not been widely circulated in Latin – perhaps because they do not exist, or they cannot be found or I at least have trouble finding them'.[9] Such a vivid illustration of the continuing isolation of the Latin from the more sophisticated Greek intellectual world did not deter Augustine from composing his own treatise, *De trinitate*, over the next twenty years. Crucially (for future Augustinian philosophers), he argued that God had placed knowledge of the Trinity in the human mind and this truth could be accessed through contemplation. Apparently unaware of the promulgation of the revised Nicene Creed at the Council of Constantinople in 381, which talked of the procession of the Spirit from God the Father, Augustine unilaterally insisted that the Holy Spirit processed not only from the Father but also from the Son (*filioque*, 'and the Son').[10] Once the Nicene-Constantinopolitan Creed *without* the *filioque* had been confirmed as inviolable by the Greeks at the Council of Ephesus in 431 (a year after Augustine's death) and *filioque* had been added to Latin translations of the creed from the sixth century, a major theological divergence between east and west was inevitable. Eventually, in 1024, to the dismay of the Greeks, Pope Benedict VIII officially added *filioque* to the creed and it was one element in the complete breakdown of relations in the schism of 1054 that lasts to this day.[11] A revival of the rich Greek theological tradition in the Latin west had to wait until Erasmus in the sixteenth century (see Chapter 16, pp. 392–8).

In his *Confessions*, Augustine records his feelings of helplessness and his frustration that language could not express the ultimate realities that he hoped to grasp. Eventually, he comes to accept that he must wait on the will of a punitive God who has absolute power over his creation. However much those feelings of helplessness originated in Augustine's own mind, they were now extended to define the fate of humanity as a whole. As a result of the 'original sin' of Adam and Eve, no one could be guaranteed salvation. It depended utterly on the grace of God but this could be received through the sacraments administered by the church.

A major debate, which was played out in the so-called Pelagian controversy in Augustine's own lifetime, raged on over whether individuals were indeed helpless, not even able to achieve salvation through good works and a life of piety. Pelagius, who was probably born in Britain, argued for the freedom to be able to choose and find one's own path to salvation, but his views were crushed in Rome after a campaign against him by Augustine.[12] Among the accusations that Augustine made against Pelagius was that he had drawn on Greek theology, an indication that Augustine now believed that Latin Christianity was superior to the much older and more sophisticated theological traditions of the east. It was one more element in the narrowing of theological debate and the development of distinctive Greek and Latin theological traditions. In the final chapters of his magisterial *The City of God* Augustine has a free hand to argue relentlessly that hell is the destination for those to whom a merciless God will not offer his grace.

The rigour of Augustine's views risked threatening the concept of moral responsibility as they gave no incentive for good behaviour. He and, notably, the Protestant reformers who followed him, were ambivalent over whether good works were an essential part of Christian living. This was clearly unsatisfactory. The debate on free will continued throughout the Middle Ages with some theologians arguing that it was possible for individual effort to overcome sin and others that God could himself make some individuals more receptive to receiving grace.[13] There was eventually a compromise that accepted that sinners still had the freedom of will to act, to accept or reject the grace of God when it was offered to them. For those who rejected the offer of grace, however, their 'original sin' condemned them to eternal suffering in hell, the fate, Augustine had preached, for the majority of humanity.

No one denies the theological brilliance of Augustine but, to the extent that he reigned supreme, Latin theology would never be a freely evolving collegiate enterprise as it had been in the combative philosophical world of Greece before AD 381 (the date when debate was silenced by imperial decree and the Council of Constantinople). Surprisingly, his writings say relatively little about the figure of Jesus Christ; his preference is for the letters of Paul, with telling effect. The New Testament scholar Paula Fredriksen has gone so far as to argue that 'much of Western Christian thought can be seen as one long response to Augustine's Paul'.[14] By the Carolingian period, 'opinions of him [Augustine] can verge on idolatry' and even Latin translations of Aristotle's *Categories* were attributed to his authorship. One reason why

Augustine became so firmly embedded was that there was no Latin theologian of comparable stature for another six and a half centuries, in fact until Anselm, archbishop of Canterbury (1093–1109) put forward his logical arguments for the existence of God. (The most brilliant of the ninth-century theologians, Eriugena, was later declared heretical.) Even the Protestant reformers were to be in thrall to Augustine's distinctive understanding of the omnipotence of God and his unrequited anger at the sin of Adam and Eve. Augustine's profound influence will weave in and out of the rest of this book, not least in his view that *curiositas*, the desire of an individual to seek worldly knowledge, risked undermining the need to contemplate the divine.[15]

If human beings are inherently sinful, as Augustine taught, there had to be definition of what was sinful and what was not. St John Cassian, who is credited with bringing the ideals and practices of eastern monasticism to the west, outlined eight vices in his influential *Institutes*, among them any expression of sexuality.[16] In the Irish church, the clergy used *Penitentials*, handbooks that listed sins and the correct penance for each one. Crucially, as Augustine had already argued, the inner mind became accessible to God. 'Let us consider how severe a judge is coming; who will judge not only our evil deeds but our every thought,' preached Pope Gregory the Great.[17] This was a psychological transformation of enormous importance. Nothing was invisible to God. Furthermore, the church itself defined what was sinful or not. The opportunities to manipulate its control over its congregations were magnified. No ancient religion had enjoyed this power and its appearance marks a revolutionary development in the history of European thought. The Christian was required to live in a permanent state of alert, something unknown in the classical world. Discussing 'The Theme of the Bible' in his study of the scriptures, John Barton highlights the Christian story as a drama, describing the Bible as 'a story about a disaster [the Fall of Man] followed by a rescue mission [of Christ]'.[18]

It is worth imagining what Latin theology would have been like if, at that moment of spiritual crisis in a garden in Milan that he describes at the end of Book 8 of the *Confessions*, Augustine had drawn back from conversion. His somewhat confused concept of God is displayed in the *Confessions*:

> You were always present, angry and merciful at once, strewing the pangs of bitterness over all my lawless pleasures to look for others unalloyed by pain… you teach us by inflicting pain, you smite that you may heal and you kill us so that we may not die away from you.[19]

What would have filled the void? Would the power of God and his judgement have been quite so dominant and intrusive an influence in the history of European thought as it became? Was it healthy to allow one man, however brilliant, who could not even read the New Testament in the original, to define western theology in such a profound way? One cannot understand much of what follows in the history of European thought without realizing that, in the fourth and early fifth centuries, there were possible patterns of Christian living that were not chosen.

The central ethical problem of Christianity might be seen as how to deal with those not of the faith. While the apostle Paul may have talked of there being 'neither Greek nor Jew, slave or free, nor male or female' (Galatians 3:28), this was only relevant *within* Christianity, after all had become 'one in Christ Jesus'. Christ demanded commitment and it was accepted that those left outside needed to be coerced, with different levels of persuasion, into salvation. Throughout this book, we will come across the various ways in which Christians defined and dealt with those who had not made this commitment. Moreover, it was assumed that those who were outsiders would suffer eternal agonizing punishment in hell. The comparison can be made with the classical Greek world and those philosophies such as Stoicism that talked of a universal humanity and contemplated a much less fraught relationship between the spiritual and material worlds.

* * *

Yet this monolithic portrayal of Christianity was hardly the whole picture. The ways in which communities had become Christian and how this Christianity fitted with previous beliefs varied greatly. This is recognized by more recent scholarship and is neatly reflected in the title of volume 3 of the *Cambridge History of Christianity: Early Medieval Christianities c.600–c.1100*. By 1000 there were many within the original boundaries of the Roman empire who had been Latin-speaking Christians over several centuries. In Ireland, on the other hand, a distinctive Celtic Christianity was an import to an island that had never been Roman. After the mission of St Patrick in the fifth century, it spread slowly and peacefully from community to community. For the Irish Latin was a foreign language, although many clergy developed a taste for the literature of the Church Fathers. In mainland Britain a small Christian community disappeared along with Roman rule after 400 and Christianity only reappeared 200 years later with the mission of the monk Augustine to King Ethelbert of Kent in 597. Bede tells us that 10,000 of Ethelbert's subjects converted with him, but they could hardly have grasped what the change in allegiance meant.[20] A more deep-rooted Christianity spread across the Anglo-Saxon kingdoms in the seventh century, at first in the north through Irish missionaries, but, according to Bede, the Anglo-Saxons distanced themselves from the Celts. On the European mainland, in Germany – which like Ireland was never part of the empire – Christianity was forced brutally on the Saxons by Charlemagne. The traumatic experience of the coming of the faith must have lingered in their collective memory. Further north, Denmark was nominally Christian by 1000, as were Bohemia, Poland and Hungary to the east. The Baltic crusades, unleashed by the Teutonic Knights, were to come later. In southern Italy and Sicily, Latin Christianity imposed itself from the eleventh century through its Norman rulers over the Greek and Muslim communities that had settled there over many centuries. In Spain too there was a regaining of territory from Islam after the Arab conquests of the eighth century, notably through the capture of Toledo, the original capital of the Visigothic kingdom, in 1085. The memories of conquest and conversion were to shape Spanish attitudes to the newly discovered peoples of the Americas in the sixteenth century (see Chapter 22).

A baptismal font, in this case dating from the Norman period, symbolizes the consolidation of spiritual life in the parish churches.

Local populations continued to follow traditional pre-Christian practices that were absorbed within their new beliefs. As one scholar of Christian Ireland has put it: 'After Christianity arrived the pagan deities retreated underground, but the magic taboos and prescriptions which had determined the actions of the pagan heroes were handed on to Christian kings.'[21] Many 'holy men' of Ireland appeared to have lived before Christianity had ever reached the island. This seems typical of other communities. Edward Gibbon, writing in the eighteenth century with typical Enlightenment hauteur, was dismissive: 'To the invincible band of genuine and primitive martyrs, they [the clergy] added myriads of imaginary heroes, who had never existed, except in the fancies of crafty or credulous legendaries.'[22] Yet it was just this structure gave Christianity a flexibility that allowed it to adapt to the various pagan cultures it encountered. In *The Rise of Magic in Early Modern Europe*, Valerie Flint showed how certain magical practices were 'baptized' to make them acceptable within Christian belief, so 'swallowing up the religious core of paganism', as another scholar has put it.[23] At one extreme the Danes were said to have acknowledged

Christ but continued to worship their pagan gods as before. English weekdays include Woden's day and Thor's day while 'Easter' derives from an Anglo-Saxon goddess Eostre. As Bede noted in his *The Reckoning of Time*, 'they now designate that Paschal season by her name, calling the joys of the new rite by the time-honoured name of the old observance'.[24] The extraordinary ecclesiastical headdress, the earliest surviving one known, found among the Staffordshire hoard, echoes those of pagan Roman priests. In his *Antibarborum Liber* (*Against the Barbarians*), the humanist Desiderius Erasmus was later to claim that Christianity would have been diminished without the inventions of the pagans. Erasmus specifically highlights Latin and writing.*

Local Christianities were made more vibrant by their celebration of local saints. Holy men and women were always troubling to those around them and so it helped when they were safely dead. The belief that their bones could resonate with spiritual power took hold in the Christian world in the fourth century. The saints, however they came to be designated as such by those left behind, were close to God in heaven and could intercede for those who prayed to them or visited their shrines. The patronage of the shrines that held their bodies flourished on the initiative of local bishops and monasteries, with the achievements of many saints manipulated to serve the ambitions of their patrons. St Martin is revered as the compassionate Roman soldier who cut up his cloak to give half of it to a beggar. After his death at Candes on the River Loire in 397, his body was taken upriver and buried at Tours. His place of burial became a major pilgrimage site, publicized to that end by Bishop Gregory, the historian we met in the Prologue. Each community could champion its own, whether a Christian king killed in battle, such as Oswald of Northumbria, or a pioneering bishop, such as St Martial, a third-century bishop of Limoges, whose shrine became one of the richest pilgrimage destinations in Europe. Rulers were prominent supporters of those saints who could

* Erasmus's *Antibarborum Liber* was an early work, probably composed between 1489 and 1495 when Erasmus was in his early twenties. One of the arguments that Erasmus put forward for the worth of the pagan world was that the extent of the Roman empire allowed Christianity to spread more easily.

enhance their religious status. The collaboration between Louis VII of France and Suger, abbot of St Denis, the shrine of the first bishop of Paris, resulted in a complete rebuilding of the monastery church in the 1140s (and incidentally the birth of Gothic architecture which could more easily accommodate crowds) and the proclamation that St Denis was the patron saint of France and his church the burial place of the royal family as it had been since the Merovingians. Charlemagne had established a similar royal shrine at Aachen, as had Edward the Confessor at Westminster Abbey (completed 1065), where his body still lies and where English monarchs are still crowned. The sacral power of kings offered an alternative – and arguably more influential – religious focus to that of the popes.

The spread of Christianity on the ground is most easily traced through the appearances of churches, some established by bishops with a baptismal font, others founded by local landowners. It took some time before these became the centres of an ordered system of parishes; in fact, it was not until the Fourth Lateran Council of 1215 that the required duties for parish priests were formalized and, amazingly, not until the sixteenth century and the canons of the Council of Trent that there was a standardized system of education for the clergy. In 1000

most churches were still very poor and their buildings rudimentary but the imposition of tithes, a tax of produce given to the church by the laity, and local patronage allowed many to prosper. It helped that the churches gradually became the focus for social gatherings, baptisms, marriages and funerals (and the burials that followed).

Monasteries were particularly well endowed in comparison. By the year 1000 there were hundreds of them. The wealthiest enjoyed vast estates given to them by royal or aristocratic founders that were added to by local benefactors. In the Carolingian period in the ninth century the Abbey of Saint Germain-des-Prés had properties dotted over a 7,700-square-mile area around Paris. Even peasants would make contributions of land. Nearly 900 charters recording transactions from small landowners survive for the monastery of St Gall in the 200 years from 720. In England, the Domesday Book of 1087 suggests that one-sixth of total annual revenue for the kingdom came from monastic lands. The monastery founded at Cluny in Burgundy by William I, duke of Aquitaine, in 909 is especially well documented. By 1049 there are records of some 3,000 transactions and a vast array of estates, forests, mills and saltpans. The income was transferred into building the largest church in Europe to serve as the mother house of the Cluniac Order. Yet, despite its size, it only had places for sixty monks. While Cluny followed the Benedictine rule, which normally required each house to be independent, it was unique in that the mother house controlled a 'congregation' of priories, as they were known, whose lesser houses were scattered across Europe. The Cluniac monasteries were fiercely independent. Their founding charter required that no lay or religious authority should have any control over them. They were to be subject only to the pope but even he could not interfere with their property without the consent of the monks. The forcefulness and wealth of the Cluniac monasteries aroused much resentment from their competitors.

Pilgrims crowd into the shrine of Edward the Confessor in Westminster Abbey; from an illustrated Life, written in the mid-thirteenth century.

The records suggest that the faithful gave land to monasteries for reasons of piety (often with specific contributions for poor relief), to secure legal or economic support or give thanks for assistance. A burial place and commemorative masses also bound local notables to a favoured monastery. In this sense they were surrogates, allowing populations to hive off their spiritual needs to those dedicated to prayer. The consequences were twofold. Firstly, monasteries developed as wealthy representatives of local communities, and many were

REGALI
1. Porta major Monasterij
2. Atrium Ecclesiæ.
3. Regalis Basilica.
4. Sacrarium
5. Claustrum paruum B.M.
6.
7.
8.
9.
PAX

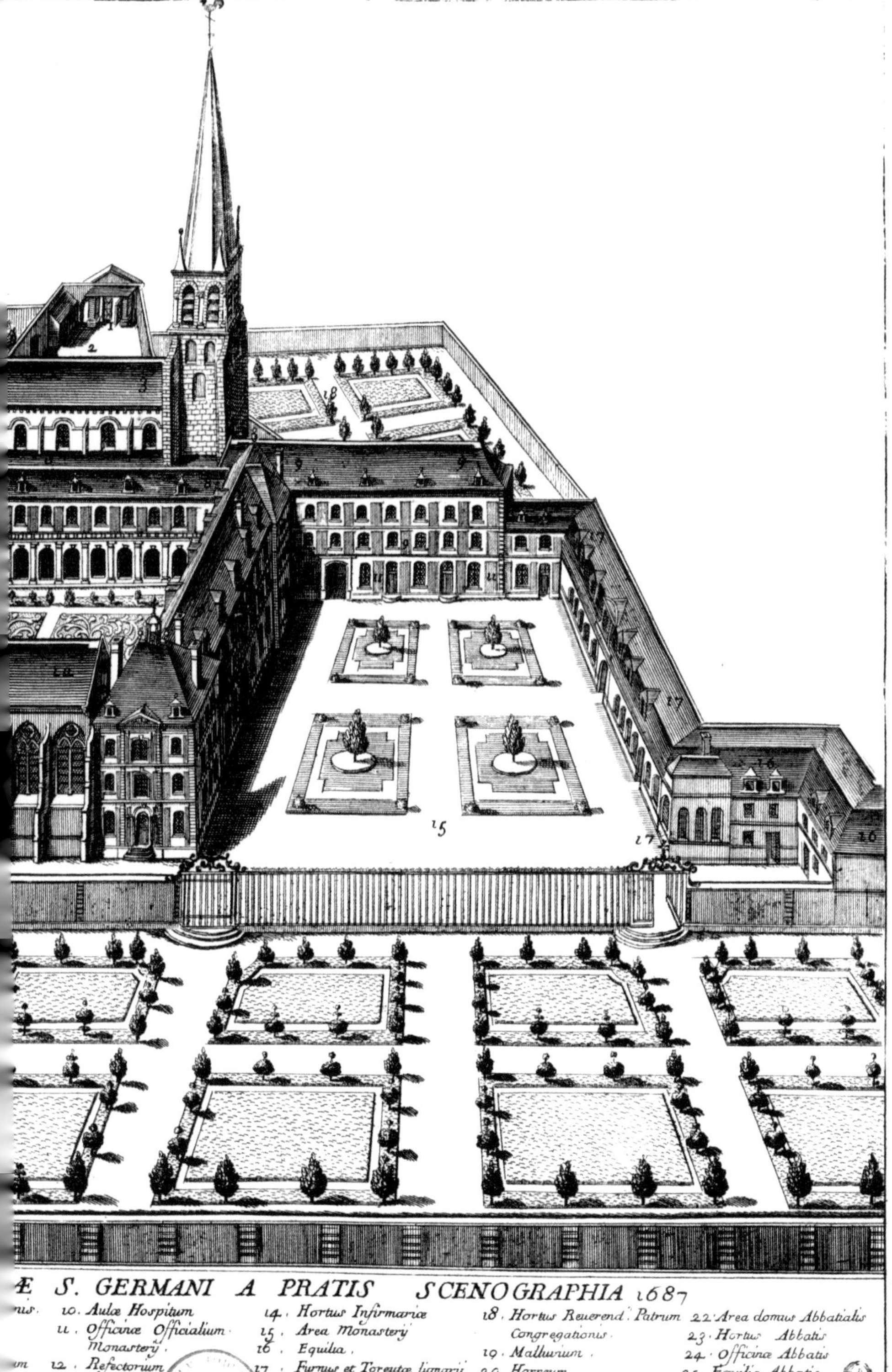

Æ S. GERMANI A PRATIS SCENOGRAPHIA 1687

nis. 10. Aulæ Hospitum
11. Officinæ Officialium Monasterij.
um 12. Refectorium
13. Infirmaria
14. Hortus Infirmariæ
15. Area Monasterij
16. Equilia.
17. Furnus et Toreutæ lignarij Officina &c.
18. Hortus Reuerend. Patrum Congregationis.
19. Malluvium.
20. Horreum.
21. Domus Abbatialis.
22. Area domus Abbatialis
23. Hortus Abbatis
24. Officinæ Abbatis
25. Equilia Abbatis

powerful enough to defy the local authorities, both spiritual and secular. Secondly, wealth was diverted away from landowners, large and small, and so undermined the vitality of the agricultural economy. The larger landowners had their revenge at the expense of the smaller. Chris Wickham describes the years 800–1000 as ones in which the peasants were 'caged', subjected to the feudal lords, both clerical and secular.[25] The monks might have dedicated themselves to a life of poverty but, as numerous documents show, the abbots, custodians of their wealth, fought bitterly to keep their properties and had no inhibitions about calling on their patron saints to support them. In one dispute of the 1340s, St Edmund, a martyred Christian king of East Anglia, whose shrine was in the vast Benedictine abbey of Bury St Edmunds in the east of England, miraculously intervened to support the independence of the abbey against the attempts by William Bateman, the bishop of Norwich (1344–55), to bring it under his control and even destroyed the papers of legal opponents who threatened its lands.[26] While it is true that some monasteries used the vastness of their estates to reorganize agricultural production and engage in trade, the profits did not return to the community as a whole. Grand monastic buildings, and the oil and candles to light them, rich vestments, opulent reliquaries and, of course, books and the flocks needed to create them, absorbed the surplus. As the medieval period developed, the church poured resources into the building of cathedrals, churches and monasteries and into the art with which to decorate them. Today, of course, they are admired, rightly so, as quintessential achievements of medieval Europe but at the time reformers were troubled by their opulent presence. The majestic gatehouse of the abbey at Bury St Edmunds was sacked by the townspeople in 1327.

previous pages The Abbey of Saint Germain-des-Prés owned vast estates around Paris in the ninth century. This later depiction shows its splendour before it was largely destroyed in the French Revolution.

Any assessment of the church in the Middle Ages has therefore to distinguish between the church as a wealthy institution, which through its very presence had a major social and economic impact on the society around it, and the church as the means through which religious belief was expressed and imposed. As Jesus had lived a life of poverty and rejected materialism, there was a contradiction here that runs through the history of Christianity. (Not that the poor were neglected; it is worth mentioning a decree of Pope Gelasius I (r.492–6) which decreed that out of a church's income, a quarter should be devoted to the bishop and his household, a quarter to the clergy, a quarter to the upkeep of churches and the remaining quarter to the poor.)

While Catholic philosophers such as Charles Taylor in his *A Secular Age*[27] bemoan the loss of an all-encompassing spiritual dimension to society after 1500, it is impossible not to discern secular motives in, say, the management of monastic estates or the diversion of funds to the families of popes. Even if the boundaries between secular and spiritual remain hard to define, secularism, in terms of worldly ambition and an obsession with material goods, pervaded the medieval church. It was one of the complaints of the humanist Petrarch, a member of the papal court at Avignon, that his age, the fourteenth century, was consumed by a lust for wealth (see p. 371). As we shall see, it is very hard to see medieval society as being as socially and theologically stable as Taylor assumes.

Yet throughout the medieval period there were attempts at reforming the institution in the name of the ideals of the gospels. Notable among the eleventh-century reformers was Peter Damian (1007–72), a monk at Fonte Avellana in central Italy, who raged against the corruption and laxity of both monks and bishops. Even the laity, in the shape of the Pataria of Milan, a religious movement that drew support from the trading community, joined in the fight for reform. Their targets were wealthy magnates, both in the church and aristocracy, and they aroused bitter resistance from their opponents. Those clergy who had wives or concubines were especially incensed at the demand that they should be celibate. Popes sympathetic to reform had to intervene to calm the unrest that swept Milan. This is another reason why Richard Southern's assessment is outdated. Such conflicts as these made 'an integrated system of thought and practice' impossible. In so far as there was antagonism between those who clung to the institutions, teachings and wealth of the church as the manifestation of God's power and those who believed that the materialism of the church destroyed true spirituality and the hope of salvation, the church could never be stable. There is intense scholarly debate over how far the general population might even be called Christian by 1000, so pervasive were the other spiritual forces that acted on their imaginations and rituals. As the Latin Vulgate was treated as a sacred text which could not be translated into the vernacular, the laity was even deprived of a direct relationship with the scriptures. Yet from the eleventh century the church made a determined effort to create uniformity under the leadership of the popes. This is the subject of the next chapter.

Authority and Dissent in the Medieval Church, 1000 - 1250

That the Roman church was founded by God alone. That the Roman pontiff alone can with right be called universal. That he alone can depose or reinstate bishops. That in a council his legate is above all bishops and can pass sentence of deposition against them. That we ought not to remain in the same house with those excommunicated by him. That it may be permitted to him to depose emperors. That the Roman church has never erred, nor will err to all eternity, the Scripture bearing witness.

from *Dictatus Papae*
(*The Dictates of the Pope*), 1075[1]

There were immense, probably insuperable, challenges involved in bringing early medieval Christianity into any kind of order. The monasteries were largely beyond papal control as the Benedictine rule that most of them had adopted insisted on the independence of each abbot. In many cases it was local royalty that was the most effective patron. The only way leadership of Christendom as a whole could be imposed was through the papacy acting through the bishops. Between 1050 and 1250, the papacy attempted to create a Europe-wide Christian civilization within which there were possibilities that a renewed and sustained tradition of learning might prosper.

Playing on their unbroken link, pope by pope, to St Peter, whom tradition and early veneration of a shrine placed in Rome rather than Jerusalem, Antioch or Alexandria, the popes claimed supremacy over all Christians, east and west. However, Rome was isolated from Europe for much of this period, its aqueducts cut and its diminished population huddled in the curve of the River Tiber. The only pope, other than the apostle Peter, whose authority was respected across the ages was Pope Gregory the Great, who ruled (590–604) at a time when Rome itself had shrunk to a shadow of its original power. His texts on pastoral care and his *Dialogues* were, as has been seen, staples of every eleventh-century monastic library. The reason behind the rare dedication of an English church to Pope Gregory in the village of Rendlesham in Suffolk, close to where I am writing, only became clear very recently when excavations showed that the village was the site of a major Anglo-Saxon royal settlement which was trading across Europe by the sixth century. Presumably, it was shortly afterwards that Gregory, a contemporary of the settlement, was adopted as its patron saint and survives as such to this day.[2]

The lack of papal authority allowed secular rulers, among whom Charlemagne was pre-eminent, to be the driving forces in setting up monasteries and royal shrines. By 1000, in fact, the papacy had become little more than the plaything of the Roman aristocracy and the German emperors. Between 850 and 1050 the average reign of a pope was only four years. A thousand years after its founding, the fragile institutional edifice of the Roman church seemed in danger of collapse. Then in 1046, Henry III, the Holy Roman Emperor, the title now held by the rulers of the German Salian dynasty, came to Rome to be crowned in the tradition of Charlemagne. Henry, a devout man, was so disgusted by the corruption of the city that he intervened to depose and appoint popes himself, most of them fellow Germans. In a sense he was too successful, as one of his appointees, a distant cousin of his from Alsace, consecrated in 1049 as Pope Leo IX, immediately began asserting his own authority. It helped that as an outsider, with his own coterie of enthusiastic reformers, he could operate free of the politics of Rome.

Leo's targets were threefold. First was the practice of simony, the buying of church offices;[3] second was the sexual laxity of the clergy, many of whom lived with concubines; and third was the power that lay rulers had assumed in appointing and investing bishops. In a breach with convention, Leo left Rome and took to the road back north to France and Germany. There was a dramatic moment in the cathedral of Reims when the pope stood before the relics of St Remigius, the bishop who had baptized the Merovingian Clovis, the first Catholic king of all France, and demanded of the assembled bishops that they individually confess whether they had bought their offices or not. There was consternation; most were stunned into silence and some deposed. Leo's decision in 1054 to formalize the breach between Latin Christianity and the Greek Orthodox Church that remains to this day highlighted the determination and capacity of a pope to act decisively. His papacy was characterized by a new concentration on effective administration. In these years the Donation of Constantine, a document later discovered to have been forged in the eighth century (see Chapter 12, p. 294), which claimed that the emperor Constantine had transferred his temporal power to the popes, became a prominent manifestation of papal propaganda. In 1059 the laity, including the emperor, was excluded from the election of the pope, the power now being reserved to the cardinals, as it still is. One cardinal, Hildebrand of Sovana (now in southern Tuscany), a man of humble background, was already a key figure in the move.

Nothing, however, could have prepared western Europe for the astonishing *Dictatus Papae* of 1075 issued by Hildebrand, now Pope Gregory VII (1073–85). Like his namesake in the sixth century, Gregory believed that times were dire, the Last Judgement at hand. He shared earlier concerns at the corruption of Christian communities, especially the practice of simony: 'I find hardly any bishops who conform to the law either in their appointment or in their way of life, and who rule the Christian people in the love of Christ and not for worldly ambition.'[4] His response to this bleak assessment of his compromised church was the assertion of papal absolutism. While there had been hints of this trend in the records of popes such as Leo IX, these were now taken to an extreme. The *Dictatus* decreed that the Roman church, founded by God alone, could never be in error and would remain so for eternity. The church was represented on earth by the papacy, which had supreme power not only over bishops but even over emperors to the extent of having the power to depose them. The pope alone could make new laws 'according to the needs of the time' and anyone who disagreed with the Roman church should be declared *infidelis*, 'unrighteous', as a later pope put it. In an age when oath-taking was sacrosanct, the pope could absolve anyone from their oaths of fealty to 'unjust men', a shift that offended traditional canon law. The Donation of Constantine was written into the papal record but even here Gregory claimed that the emperor had never had the right to the temporal powers he had apparently transferred to the popes. This was incompatible with the notion of sacral kingship that had, in practice, been such a feature of Christian societies in the first millennium. Up to now the emperors had included 'vicar of Christ' among their titles.[5]

The mid-1070s saw the start of the so-called Investiture Controversy, which began with a confrontation between Gregory and Emperor Henry IV, Henry III's son, then only twenty-five years old. While the relative powers of emperor and pope in northern Italy remained, and were to remain, unclear, Henry acted unwisely and provocatively in condemning Gregory as a 'false monk' and asserting his right in 1075 to appoint a new archbishop of Milan, the honoured see of Ambrose (340–97), the formidable bulwark of orthodox Catholicism in the late fourth century. Within a year Gregory had excommunicated him and Henry found his own position weakened when several German rulers supported the pope. There was a temporary reconciliation in 1077 when a penitent Henry humbled himself before Gregory at Canossa in northern Italy, waiting three days in a January blizzard before the castle gate was opened to him and the excommunication lifted. Even so, and perhaps inevitably, the troubled relationship continued. Gregory infuriated many by insisting that any clergy who had bought their offices or were married should be shunned by the laity, a stance that led to Henry accusing the pope of showing contempt for his own bishops. Gregory was eventually driven from Rome and died in the care of Norman knights in 1085. A new pope backed by Henry (Victor III, formerly Desiderius, abbot of the great Benedictine monastery on Monte Cassino) took his place. It was only in 1122 at the Concordat of Worms that a pope and emperor, successors to the original antagonists, agreed on a formula that reduced the power of the emperors to invest their own choice of bishops.

Gregory's assertion of papal power depended on an idealistic view of the early church where the clergy were chaste, resistant to 'the foul pollution of contaminating lust', and free of the temptations of wealth. His crucial innovation lay in accepting that the church could be restored to health by human effort. There were always new abuses to be confronted and the pope adopted the right to define and suppress them on an ad hoc basis. In practice Gregory used his power flexibly, working through those he knew who would be sympathetic to his claims and exploiting populist anti-clericalism, yet he had shifted the focus of power within Europe towards the papacy and so to the exclusion of secular powers. This was no less than a revolution. It was confirmed by Gregory's obsession with the control of church property, the right to which he claimed Constantine had given the church through his Donation.

So could the church ever be stabilized in such a way as to bring benefits to Europe? The fundamental weakness of the papacy continued to be the short reigns of individual popes. Between January 1045 and the election of Leo IX just four years later, there had been six popes. Between 1118 and 1198, there were fifteen popes, each with an average reign of just over five years. In the thirteenth century the average was about the same, with no fewer than thirteen popes between 1252 and 1296. When elected, their position was precarious even in Rome, a city riven by the squabbles of its noble families, each seeking control of the papacy to further its ambitions. Between 1100 and 1304, a legitimate pope ruled within Rome for only 82 years in comparison to 122 years spent outside (often in a residence in the papal territories). So unless a young pope with energy and administrative skills was elected and enjoyed a long reign, there was little chance that the church would ever be run effectively under papal leadership.

One result was that the Roman Curia, the ministers who actually ran the papal court in Rome, consolidated their own institutional power as they took advantage of the rapid turnover of popes. Their authority was boosted by the development of canon law, the law as defined by the church to regulate its own affairs. Canon law was based less on the commandments or precedents set by the Old or New Testaments than on Roman law and the subsequent proclamations of popes. The rediscovery, in about 1070, of the great *Digest* of Roman law compiled by the emperor Justinian in the sixth century was enormously important as a provider of sources and precedents, especially in respect of personal relationships, marriage, adultery, divorce and wills, all of which now were claimed to be the responsibility of the church. Some eighty years later, the *Digest* was quarried by Gratian, a monk apparently working in

Bologna, for a vast (4,000-chapter) collection of texts from Roman law, church councils, the scriptures and papal judgements. The so-called *Decretum Gratiani* became authoritative, but Gratian's achievement lay not simply in bringing together so many sources into a coherent whole. His compilation, whose fuller title was *Concordia Discordantum Canonum* (*Harmony between Discordant Rules of Law*), encouraged debate on how various legal sources could be reconciled. Moreover, it reinforced the notion that there could be a single legal system covering the world of Christendom in the same way that the original Roman law had covered the entirety of the empire. Written in 1150, within twenty years the *Decretum* seems to have spread throughout Europe, even if its size meant that its contents were often passed on through *summae*, or textbook summaries, of which there were many by 1200. Unfortunately, canon law became overwhelming in its complexity. A thirteenth-century legal scholar, Johannes Teutonicus, produced a vast commentary on the body of canon law, and there was an endless succession of papal decrees and pronouncements. The conglomeration of legal texts meant that by 1300 it would take a student many years to master them.

The *Decretum* of Gratian was the standard compilation of canon law. An illuminated manuscript of the *Decretum* from the late fourteenth century shows the pope of the day in council.

Yet the consolidation of canon law, as well as being an important element in the creation of a universal church, was a stabilizing force for good – even if its sovereign administrator, the Curia, became a byword for corruption. 'Blessed are the wealthy for theirs is the court of Rome,' as an apocryphal Beatitude put it. The Curia developed an elaborate system of fees – it was said that a fee had to be paid even to discover the scale of fees. Denunciations of its abuses became a common theme of medieval literature. The *Treatise of Garcia of Toledo*, of about 1100, for instance, is a satirical account of the visit of an archbishop of Toledo to Rome with relics of Saints Silver and Gold, which he intends to present to a 'shrine of Saint Cupidity'. The papal court is portrayed as luxurious and dissolute. When the theologian Peter Abelard faced accusations of heresy (see Chapter 5), and attempted to appeal – unsuccessfully as it turned out – to Rome, he was warned: 'Have you never heard of the avarice and filth of the Romans? Who could ever satisfy with money the gaping hole of such harlots?' Two centuries later the humanist Francesco Petrarch, referring to the Curia that had moved with the popes to Avignon where he worked, described, in words that hardly need translating, the *inextricabile curie labyrinthum*.

Incipit concordia discordantium ca
nonum ac primum de iure constitu
tionis nature et humane.
HVMANVM
genus duobus
regitur. natu
rali uidelicet i
ure et moribus.
Ius naturale est
quod in lege et in euangelio contine
tur, quo quisque iubetur alii facere quod si
bi uult fieri. et prohibetur alii inferre
quod sibi nolit fieri. Unde Christus in euangelio.
Omnia quecumque uultis ut faciant
uobis homines et uos eadem facite illis.
hec est enim lex et prophete. Unde Ysidorus in
V. libro ethimologiarum ait. Diui
ne leges nature, humane moribus
Omnes le constant:
ges aut diuine sunt
aut humane. diuine
natura. humane moribus
constant. ideoque hec discrepant. quoniam a
lie aliis gentibus placent. fas lex diui
na est. ius est lex humana. ut in sint per
agrum alienum fas est, ius non est. Ex
uerbis huius auctoritatis euidenter datur intel
ligi in quo differant inter se lex diuina
et humana. cum omne quod fas est nomine

While weak and remote leadership under short-lived popes remained the most significant obstacle to effective reform – and matters would only get worse with the exile of the papacy to Avignon (1309–76) and the Great Schism of 1378–1417 – there were other barriers to overcome. The problem facing almost every religious movement is that their inspiration and teachings come from the past. Reformers such as Peter Damian looked back to a golden age of the apostles selflessly spreading the news of salvation. It was one thing to fight materialism and attempt to introduce a more ascetic way of life, as a new monastic order, the Cistercians, did in the early twelfth century by retreating from society in a well-publicized reaction to the luxury of the Cluniac foundations. Many of their monasteries were in isolated valleys or moors (though here too careful management of large estates led to the accumulation of vast wealth, as at Rievaulx and Fountains Abbey in Yorkshire). It was quite another to deal with the rapid social and economic changes in medieval society that became pervasive after 1200. The rise of new secular rulers, some of whom, such as the Holy Roman Emperor Frederick II (1194–1250), were aggressive in their opposition to the church, the emergence of new ideas (many of which would challenge traditional Catholic theology), and the growth of towns with their own religious identities and patron saints, ensured that the church would always be on the defensive.

Meanwhile, an extraordinary diversion of religious energy was taking place, which had major implications for the medieval church. One of the papal policies that Gregory VII had developed further was the right of Christians to use warfare in the cause of their religion. Augustine had spelled out the conditions for a just Christian war, among them the need for the least possible violence. As we have seen, the right to go to war, especially when there were pagans to bring to salvation, had become an accepted attribute of Christian kingship. Gregory moved beyond this by arguing that the use of war could be sanctified in the defence of the church, and that the dangers endured were enough to earn absolution for the participants. A favourite biblical text of his came from the Old Testament prophet Jeremiah 48:10: 'Cursed be he who keepeth back his sword from blood.' Of course, in line with Gregory's insistence on papal absolutism it was left to the papacy to decide what was a suitable war or not. The only attempt Gregory made, in 1074, to launch a crusade in support of the Greek Orthodox Church (who, despite the schism of 1054, were still considered 'brothers in Christ') failed completely.*

In 1088 a protégé of Gregory, the French-born Odo of Châtillon, became Pope Urban II. It was a moment when the emperor, Henry IV, was in the ascendant and Urban could not even enter Rome, where Henry's choice of pope resided. It was natural that, in retaliation, Urban would look for support from his own class, the French nobility, in effect the knights. These were an unstable group, obsessed with their own honour and personal feuds with their fellows, but this was Urban's world and his reception as he travelled through France showed that he was at home in it. He began putting together a plan, to find a cause that could unite the knights, draw on his predecessor Gregory's expanded concept of a just war, and assert his authority under the name of a Christianity dedicated to the elimination of its enemies. In March 1095, a renewed request for help from the Byzantine empire against Seljuk Turkish expansion gave him his chance.

On 27 November 1095, Urban addressed a large assembly of knights and clergy at Clermont in the Auvergne. He painted a picture of Muslim desecration of Jerusalem, a sacred place that rightfully belonged to the Christians, but he went further than this in echoing Gregory's assertion that participation in war would lead to the remission of sins. By now an Augustinian obsession with sinfulness and the certainty of hellfire dominated the imagination of the laity. Knights were especially vulnerable to feelings of guilt and sinfulness as their way of life often involved the commission of acts of unjustified violence. Urban elaborated his appeal by describing the expedition to Jerusalem as a pilgrimage, in effect encouraging anyone, knight or not, to join in. His carefully planned strategy, which was endorsed by impassioned preachers throughout western Europe, was boosted by an abundant harvest in 1096 that suggested God was giving divine support to the enterprise. Thousands flocked to the cause.[6]

Urban had co-ordinated the response largely for his own political ends but he had unleashed forces that no one, least of all a pope, could control. A variety of groups, some of them lay, some of them knights accompanied by unarmed women and children, set out. Not surprisingly, the First Crusade was a ramshackle affair beset by tensions between rival groups of knights. It was fortuitous that a weak response by the Muslims, who had themselves been quarrelling over rights to

* Scholars are reassessing how conclusive was the schism at this point. It certainly became absolute after the sacking of Constantinople by Latin Christians led by the Venetians in the Fourth Crusade of 1204.

The Siege of Antioch (1097–8) during the First Crusade, from an illuminated manuscript of crusader chronicles illustrated by Jean Colombe, *c.*1475.

the city, allowed the disorganized crusaders to finally reach Jerusalem itself in 1099, where they massacred its inhabitants and gloried in the recapture of the Holy Sepulchre, nearly 400 years after its loss to Islam.

Possession of the city set an unhappy precedent. Jerusalem now had to be defended, but holding a territory so far from mainland Europe against counter-attack was impossible. The conquered territories were soon being eroded. A Second Crusade (1145–9) to regain land lost was a disaster and only emboldened the Muslims when they realized that the crusaders were not invincible. Jerusalem was lost to the Ayyubid sultan Saladin in 1187, a Third Crusade (1189–92) disintegrated through the squabbling of the crusaders, despite having recaptured Acre and Jaffa, and the notorious Fourth Crusade (1202–4) never reached the Holy Land at all (see further p. 100). The Fifth Crusade (1217–21) ended in disaster although the Sixth (1227–9), led by Emperor Frederick II, did regain control of the city, this time through effective diplomacy. Christian rule lasted only until 1244. The Seventh Crusade (1249–50), though well planned and led by the French king, Louis IX, ended with the king himself being taken prisoner. Once ransomed Louis tried yet again but died of typhoid fever in the Eighth Crusade in 1271 (so earning himself sainthood). The last toehold of Latin Christendom in the east, the port of Acre, was lost in 1291.

It was one of the paradoxes of these unhappy expeditions that, in the words of a foremost scholar of the period, Jonathan Riley-Smith, 'crusading thrived on disaster' in that each setback gave rise to more impassioned pleas to save what was precariously held or had been lost.[7] The resources consumed by the crusades were enormous. The cost of Louis's failed Seventh Crusade, including his ransom, came to six times his kingdom's annual income. In his 'Summing-Up' at the end of his magisterial *History of the Crusades* (in three volumes, 1951–4), the historian Steven Runciman described 'the whole crusading movement as a vast fiasco'.*[8] He noted how incipient cultural and intellectual contacts between Islam and the Byzantine empire were destroyed, a fact surely of some enduring relevance. After the sacking of Constantinople in 1204 and the establishing of a short-lived Latin empire in the east, the schism between the eastern and western churches moved beyond any hope of repair and remains so to this day. By reversing the original Christian model of Christ who had died without offering any form of resistance but who had attained glory, the church had sunk into a moral quagmire.

* One of Runciman's scholarly friends once asked him why he had 'wasted' so many years on researching such 'a fiasco', but it seems that telling a good story drove him on.

Yet it remained possible for a forceful reforming pope to emerge. Such a man was the Roman Lotario del Conti di Segni, who was only thirty-seven when he became Pope Innocent III in 1198. Innocent had enormous energy and a sharp and profound mind, was well schooled – as by this time were many of his clerical contemporaries – in canon law, and possessed a determination to exert papal authority over both secular and sacred alike. He could draw on a formidable treatise by the austere Cistercian Bernard of Clairvaux, *De Consideratione* (of *c.*1150), which preached that it was the duty of the papacy to assert its supremacy relentlessly. At his consecration as pope, Innocent chose a text from the prophet Jeremiah (1:10): 'See, I have set you this day over nations and over kingdoms, to pluck up and to break down, to destroy and to overthrow, to build and to plant.' The pope, he claimed on another occasion, is 'set between God and man, lower than God but higher than man... judges all and is judged by no one'. There was much talk of the pope's *plenitudo potestatis* ('plenitude of power'), which placed him above the law. This absolutist outlook was set within a profoundly pessimistic assessment of the human condition that Innocent had expounded before he became pope in his *De Miseria Humanae Conditionis* (*On the Wretchedness of the Human Condition*). The survival of some 700 manuscript copies suggests that it appealed to a wide audience.

Innocent's initiatives were partly political, namely to consolidate the power of the papal states as a bulwark against the pretensions of the Holy Roman Emperors in the north while ensuring that they did not assume power in southern Italy and Sicily as well. This did not work out well for the papacy in that the small boy whom Innocent championed as ruler of southern Italy and Sicily grew up to be the formidable Frederick II, the *stupor mundi* or 'wonder of the world'. Innocent's successor, Honorius III, eventually crowned Frederick as Holy Roman Emperor in 1220, but he would trample on the privileges of the church, and his delay in setting out on a promised crusade (the Sixth) would earn him excommunication by Pope Gregory IX in 1227. (The only time that Jerusalem was restored to Christian control through diplomacy rather than force was by a man who was excommunicate at the time!) Frederick labelled the pope an Anti-Christ, assailed the corruption of the Curia and challenged the right of the papacy to exert power over secular rulers.[9] While few rulers had the arrogance and opportunity to challenge the papacy as resolutely as did Frederick, it was a moment that showed that papal absolutism had to compromise with the reality of independent-minded secular rulers.

The ideology of sacrifice in the service of Christ, with heavenly bliss awaiting the fallen, had reached a new intensity in the twelfth century. Bernard of Clairvaux had taken the initiative. His *De laude nove militiae* (*In Praise of the New Knightly Order*) created the myth of the pure and heroic warrior dedicated only to Christ. 'The knight of Christ, I say, kills with an untroubled mind, dies with an even less troubled one… a Christian glories in the death of a pagan, since Christ is glorified.'[10] Innocent III showed he was of the same mind when he called for yet another crusade, the Fourth, to the Holy Land. His naivety was soon exposed when the crusaders, impelled by financial difficulties, helped the Venetians to recapture the Catholic city of Zara (on the Adriatic coast of what is now Croatia) in 1202, and then, having entangled themselves in the internal politics of the Byzantine empire, proceeded to Constantinople, which they sacked in 1204. This attack by Christians on Christians was at first condemned by Innocent and then glossed over as a just punishment for those who were now heretics. Vast numbers of relics, including the whole bodies of saints, were extracted from the city's shrines to boost the large collections already on display in Europe.

A fourteenth-century miniature showing Pope Innocent III excommunicating the Cathars and French knights massacring them.

Louis IX spent half of his annual income on purchasing the crown of thorns from Christ's Passion. He installed it in the magnificent Sainte-Chapelle he built for it in Paris. When there were complaints that the wood of the crown looked suspiciously fresh, this was taken as a sign not of possibly recent construction but of its evergreen authenticity.[11]

Innocent's conception of a crusade extended to any enemy of the church. It was given a new lease of life by a resounding Christian success in another theatre of war. This was the crushing defeat, at Las Navas de Tolosa in 1212, of a Muslim Almohad army by the Castilian king Alfonso VIII, assisted by the other Christian kings of the Iberian peninsula. Las Navas de Tolosa was a critical turning point in the Christian reconquest of Spain from the Muslim Almohads. Here was evidence that God favoured his own and might do so again. In 1213 Innocent set in hand meticulous planning for yet another crusade to the east. In his decree *Ad liberandum* (*To Free the Holy Land*) promulgated at the Fourth Lateran Council in 1215, he made it clear that this was to be more firmly under the control of the church. There was to be a larger financial levy on clerical incomes, a ban of any commerce with the Muslims so as to weaken their economies, and the crusaders were to leave from ports in southern Italy that were directly subject to the

pope. Innocent was to die before the crusade could start, in 1217, and it achieved little.

The church could hardly condemn those who championed the ideal of poverty but it was a question of whether it had the flexibility needed to appreciate their potential contribution. One Christian group, the Cathars, who appear to have spread from the east, were already well embedded in southern France and northern Italy and by now beyond the control of the Roman church. The Cathars were dualists who believed the material world was evil, but that the human soul was good. The Cathar elite, the *perfecti* ('pure ones'), were leaders or teachers who lived lives of austerity, sexual renunciation and frugality, while their ordinary followers, or *credentes* ('believers'), were not expected to adopt such austere lifestyles. The Cathars formed a separate church that stood outside Catholicism and rejected its sacraments (and the payment of tithes). Their strength came from their shared sense of community. Despite their esoteric beliefs, they were widely tolerated among both rich and poor alike, especially in southern France.

The Albigensian Crusade (so-called from the town of Albi in the Languedoc, which was a Cathar centre) was launched by Innocent in 1208 after a legate he had sent there had been murdered. The crusade, to which Innocent gave the same privileges as those to the east, was led by aristocrats from northern France and was as much about controlling land as combatting heresy. It was a brutal affair with widespread massacres of Cathars, including a reported 9,000 burned in the cathedral at Béziers, where there was no attempt to distinguish between heretics and faithful. (Arnaud Amaury, the papal legate, is alleged to have uttered the words: 'Kill them. For the Lord knows who are his own.'[12]) Following the suppression of the Cathars and their local supporters, the king of France, Philip II Augustus, extended his authority into the region.

An early biographer of Francis describes how Christ appeared as a seraphim and transmitted the *stigmata*, the wounds of Christ, onto him. This painting of the event is attributed to Giotto, *c.*1300.

The challenge for the popes lay in recognizing whether or not a commitment to gospel teaching by a spiritual rebel would undermine its authority. In two celebrated cases Innocent III licensed outsiders to found orders that were to transform the nature of the church's relationship with the faithful. The first was Dominic de Guzmán, a monk from a small town in Castile whose ascetic lifestyle and effectiveness as a preacher among the Cathars brought him to the attention of the pope. In one of his most visionary moves, Innocent created an order for Dominic's followers (in fact they adopted the rules of another order,

T. 1669.

that of St Augustine) that left them as canons, rather than monks, with a mission to preach in the cities whose shifting and expanding populations had made them especially vulnerable to heresies. The contrast with the wealthy cloistered monasteries, many of which were now in decline, was stark.[13] Members of the new order could be moved around and pick up a living from charitable gifts wherever they settled.

The Dominicans made a commitment to study a central part of their mission and so provided many of the leading scholars of the thirteenth century whose achievements in reinvigorating the intellectual life of the church will be discussed in Chapter 8. They also assumed control of the Inquisition, the body formally authorized by the pope to root out heresy. The need to find resources for study and their role as authority figures in the church hierarchy meant that their initial commitment to poverty lost its force. A study of Dominican houses shows that they were most prominent in large wealthy cities, especially those with universities such as Paris, Orléans and Bologna. Dominic himself is buried at Bologna.

The other major religious figure of the age was Francis, from the Umbrian town of Assisi. After a period as a soldier, Francis renounced his wealthy background, discarded his fine clothes and took on the role of preacher. He might well have been condemned as heretical but he was lucky in that, once again, Innocent was sufficiently convinced by his sincerity to license him to preach and found the Friars Minor for his incipient movement (1209). Francis, *il Poverello*, and his followers were more openly committed to poverty than the Dominicans. Francis insisted that his friars should disregard possessions and throw themselves on the charity of those they met. 'The brothers should consider it a privilege to live with the outcasts of the world, the sick, the weak, the poor lepers and the beggars of the road.' Learning was classed among the possessions, since it 'robs many people of their gentle characters'.[14] Francis' personal impact came from the harmony he appeared to establish between his poverty and his evangelical zeal. He was soon the stuff of legend, credited with having received the stigmata, the five wounds of Christ, direct from heaven. This gave him an authority like none other. How much closer could one get to Christ than this?* There are gruelling accounts of the excruciating infirmities he experienced later in his life when he still wonders whether he is suffering enough to deserve salvation. His asceticism resonated. The

Saint Dominic oversees the burning of heretical books in a fifteenth-century painting by Pedro Berruguete. One theologically orthodox book escapes the flames and floats upwards.

* The Italian mystic Padre Pio (1887–1968) claimed also to have received the stigmata.

movement grew fast, there were already 1,000 friars by 1221, numbers far greater than the otherworldly Francis could cope with. It took some time before there was a settled Franciscan rule. It was Bonaventure (see Chapter 8, pp. 191–2) who brought order to the movement. There were 30,000 friars by 1300.

There is no more vivid evidence of the stagnation of religious life in the cities by the thirteenth century than the success of the mendicant orders. The church had failed to respond to the growth of the cities. In northern Italy, as will be seen in Chapter 6, the bishops had wielded political control but they had been edged aside by elected magistrates. There was a religious hunger waiting to be fed. The strength of the mendicants lay in their flexibility: they could travel wherever they were needed and preach in an open space or in any church that welcomed them. They were much quicker to adapt to the needs of the new classes that were emerging as wealth and trade spread through the cities. Franciscan intellectuals such as Peter Olivi (1248–98) developed ingenious ways of avoiding the bans on charging interest. They were soon building their own churches. As will be seen, there were theological tensions between Franciscans and Dominicans and in many parts of France and Germany the secular clergy bitterly resented their intrusions (there was a famous confrontation in the 1250s over teaching posts at the University of Paris) while their readiness to support the merchant classes led to charges of hypocrisy.[15] Impassioned preaching can also get out of hand – the case of the Dominican Savonarola in Florence will be covered in Chapter 16. However, as a visible presence in the cities and themselves espousing poverty, the mendicants played an important part in what has been described as 'a reconquest of urban society'.[16]

In April 1213 Innocent called a new council to meet in the pope's Lateran Palace in Rome – the Fourth Lateran Council. The council was well advertised and eventually some 500 bishops and 900 other clergy gathered in the city in November 1215. Naturally, Innocent had taken the initiative in drafting the canons that they were to address, and they were substantial in range and content. It was an important moment, no less than 'the first major attempt to systemize religious practice' according to one scholarly assessment, a reminder of how resistant the variety of local Christianities remained to central authority.[17]

The council began with a general 'confession of faith' that confirmed that there was no salvation for any member of the human race outside the church. This declaration, with its significant ethical connotations, remained in force for centuries and would make reconciliation with other expressions of Christianity (and, of course, pagans, Muslims and Jews) impossible. In the same confession the doctrine of transubstantiation, the belief that the consecration of the bread and wine by a priest resulted in a complete change in its substance, to become the body and blood of Christ, was defined. With the bread and wine appearing to be exactly the same as before, this was a significant assertion of faith over empiricism. Already with the banning of vernacular translations of the scriptures, so that they could only be heard in the Latin Vulgate of Jerome, now given authoritative status, the laity was being excluded from the sacred mysteries of the consecration. To limit the proliferation of shrines to local 'saints', the church took control of the process. Sainthood, and thus confirmation that the candidate had been received into heaven, could only be officially proclaimed by the Vatican after a long process of examination, a system that is still largely in place today.*

Then followed canons on heresy. Innocent had already equated heresy with the secular offence of treason. Now he went much further, making an absolute distinction between orthodoxy and heresy. Crucially, heresy was nowhere defined as such but it was assumed to be persistent, with all heretics, 'whatever names they may go under', part of the same conspiracy and united in their pride. It was the public expression of heresy, here seen as 'pride', that rankled. Innocent used this canon, the third, to strengthen his control over secular authorities by requiring them to take the initiative in confronting heretics and making them subject to excommunication if they did not. The pope could even remove them from their lands and allocate these to 'Catholics'. Meanwhile, those who participated in the expulsion of heretics would enjoy the same 'crusader' privileges as those who went to the aid of the Holy Land. From now on, any new movement of thought was vulnerable. Later in the century the Oxford scholastic theologian Robert Grosseteste contributed his own definition of heresy as 'an opinion chosen by human beings, created by human reason [*sic*], founded on the Scriptures [!], contrary to the teachings of the Church, publicly avowed and obstinately defended'.[18] As a prominent scholar of medieval heresy, Gordon Leff, has noted: 'The road to heresy was paved with piety.' And it was often a matter of chance whether a reformer was condemned or idolized.

Other canons dealt with more effective supervision of the morals and behaviour of the clergy through annual provincial councils, and

* This did not prevent local veneration continuing. St Zita, a devout serving girl, died in Lucca in 1272 and a popular cult developed around her body, but it was not until 1696 that she was canonized as the patron saint of all servants.

better education for the poor through the appointment of teachers to the cathedrals, a demand that had been made at an earlier council in 1179 but which had never been enforced. Pastoral care was emphasized and a doctor who visited the sick was to call a priest to the bedside before he ministered himself. By now the clergy were expected to be celibate and they gradually became subject to special laws and restrictions, given a sacred status that separated them from their fellow human beings. This was achieved through investing in them the exclusive right to administer the sacraments, which would have valid force even if the clergyman himself was in a state of sin. In 1264 Pope Urban IV instituted the feast of Corpus Christi ('the body of Christ'), a day on which the consecrated host was carried by the clergy in public procession as if it were a relic that they themselves had the exclusive right to create. The rise of primogeniture, and hence the exclusion of younger sons from the inheritance of wealth, provided the recruits for both monasteries and parishes. Yet the cost of depriving the Catholic clergy of family life was to prove, to this day, to be a heavy one and can be seen as another of the ways in which the church as an institution cut itself off from mainstream society.

Prominent was the council's requirement that the faithful had to take communion once a year and also make a confession. This was, as one medievalist has described it, 'perhaps the most important legislative act in the history of the Church'.[19] The dialogue between confessor and sinner forced the individual to search his or her own conscience, discuss the nature of their intentions and so the extent to which they should take personal responsibility for their guilt. The distinguished German historian Johannes Fried argues that 'the history of the psyche and human attitudes, and hence the entire history of the West, was profoundly affected by this change'.[20] This may be too sweeping an assessment and assumes that the medieval mind was ready to be so subservient. Even so, taking personal responsibility for one's guilt was only part of the impact of the church's teaching on the probability of damnation at the Last Judgement. (Imaginative frescos depicting the latter in graphic detail were traditionally positioned over the west doors of churches, thereby making congregations aware of the penalties awaiting the unrepentant sinner as they departed.) The emphasis on guilt, tied as it was to the fear of eternal suffering for the sinner, was easy to exploit against the vulnerable.

One result was to give impetus to the concept of indulgences. It was assumed that the suffering of Christ had been so great as to leave a 'Treasury of Merit' with a surplus that could be used to release a sinner from the effects of his or her acknowledged and forgiven sins, including the remission of time that might be spent in purgatory. Indulgences originally involved some form of onerous act, such as a pilgrimage, but later they could be bought for cash, the scandal that gave rise to Martin Luther's protest against the church and so to the Reformation (see Chapter 23). Innocent did not live to supervise the outcome of his reforms but they were more influential than those of any council of the Middle Ages in establishing the model of an authoritarian and exclusive church that refused to allow any dissent. The Fourth Lateran Council was to be the high point of what can be seen as an imperial papacy.

Despite the success of the Fourth Lateran Council, the papacy never proved able to offer consistent leadership; its decline as an effective institution set in over the next century and as later chapters will show, lack of respect for the church was ubiquitous among the intellectual elite. The method of papal election was too vulnerable to factional pressures, popes when elected did not usually live long and they never managed to confront the corruption of the Curia (a state of affairs that persists to the present day). Papal absolutism was never fully accepted, although the campaign for an alternative method of decision-making, the use of church councils as in the early church, was also to fail in the fifteenth century (see pp. 373–4). The clergy had emerged as a celibate caste who had access to immense wealth. While much of this was diverted into building and art, and enjoyed as such, not least by later generations, it can be questioned whether this accorded with the primary message of the gospels. (It is hardly surprising that one of the main aims of the Protestant reformers was to return to simplicity in decoration, ritual and worship.) The mendicant orders did, however, bring new energy into religious life and had some success in recreating the apostolic mission of the early church.

The next challenge related to the emergence of new ideas. Would the church be able to find a way of coping with them and developing them intellectually, or would faith remain resistant to reason?

Abelard and the Battle for Reason

What king or philosopher could equal your name? What kingdom or city or village did not long to see you? Who did not rush to set eyes on you when you appeared in public, and crane their necks after you? What married woman, what young girl, did not desire you in absence and was not set on fire in your presence? What queen, what great and powerful lady, did not envy me my joys and my bed?

From a letter of Héloïse
to her lover, Abelard[1]

We have explored why the twelfth-century papacy was singularly unfitted to the task of uniting Christendom and to channelling its way of thinking in new directions. It is important, however, to look at the question of an awakening of the western mind at a level below the papacy, within the life of the church and its scholars. This chapter is concerned with the experiences and legacy of Peter Abelard, one of the most important philosophers of the Middle Ages, even though in the popular imagination his turbulent relationship with his beloved Heloise has tended to overshadow his intellectual achievements. He himself concurred with the assessment that he was the finest logician of his time, perhaps even the best since Aristotle.[2]

The Middle Ages has been dubbed 'an Age of Reason', one in which intellectuals, lawyers and merchants used reason or logical thinking in a variety of contexts to explore the problems of theology, the development of legal concepts and the effective planning of commercial ventures (and even, as Christopher Tyerman argues in his *How to Plan a Crusade*, crusades).[3] It is also known as 'an Age of Faith'. These two 'Ages' could co-exist as it was a common belief, held across the theological and philosophical spectrum, that the cosmos had been rationally ordered by God and so the effective use of reason would only reinforce what was believed through faith. Anselm (1033–1109), archbishop of Canterbury from 1093 to his death, and the leading theologian of the eleventh century, had argued that if one began to believe through faith then one could find rational arguments in support. He is remembered for the phrase *fides quarens intellectum* ('faith seeks understanding'). He also claimed that he had said nothing that could not be found in the works of Augustine, so boosting the authority of the theologian still further.[4]

Until the rise of independent universities in the twelfth century, the church had a monopoly on education.[5] As a result of Charlemagne's reforms it had adopted the classical curriculum of the seven liberal arts. A course of higher education would begin with grammar, rhetoric and logic or dialectic (the *trivium*), then proceed to geometry, arithmetic, astronomy and music (the *quadrivium*). The *quadrivium* emphasized the importance of order and harmony – the order of the stars was well known from ancient sources but they were worth studying as they were so close to heaven and their regular movements a prefiguring of what might be found there. In a tradition that went back to classical Greece, music was seen as bringing harmony to body and soul. It was believed to exist on a higher plane in the heavenly spheres beyond the human consciousness – a belief beautifully expressed by Shakespeare in the loving exchange between Lorenzo and Jessica in his *The Merchant of Venice*. The monastic chant had already been given notation by Guido of Arezzo (991–after 1033) and his system gradually replaced learning through memory and persists to this day as the framework through which western music has been passed on.[6]

The subjects of the *quadrivium* had been championed by 'the most learned man of the tenth century',[7] Gerbert from the Cluniac monastery of Aurillac. Gerbert (*c.*945–1003) had spent some time in northern Spain, where he came across Arabic science. When he was summoned to be tutor to the future German emperor Otto II (955–83), he brought his learning with him. At the German court, he found the subjects of the *quadrivium* to be more highly valued than they were in Italy or France. Gerbert is known for works on music, arithmetic and geometry but in practical terms his best-known achievement was to introduce the astrolabe to Europe, so allowing more careful astronomical calculations. He clearly loved nosing around in monastic libraries and he found several dialogues of Cicero that might otherwise have disappeared. Alongside such scholarly attainments, his career in the church culminated in his election as Pope Sylvester II in 999. He is the only mathematician ever to have held the office.

However, Gerbert was an isolated figure, and after his death the *quadrivium* became much less influential than the *trivium*. Seven hundred years after the fall of the Roman empire there were still too few texts to teach from. It was only in the mid-twelfth century that such important works as Euclid's *Elements* and Ptolemy's *Almagest* became available in comprehensible Latin translations. At the time of Abelard, earlier in the century, these works were not available, which is why the focus in this chapter is on the *trivium*.[8]

It was only once the three components of the *trivium* had been mastered that one could continue to the next level and follow a course in theology, medicine or canon law. Since Charlemagne, there had been an important shift in the places where learning took place. Already at the beginning of the ninth century, it was decreed that education in the monasteries was restricted to those entering them, while those following the liberal arts met in schools based in the cathedrals. (In practice some wealthy monasteries maintained schools for secular students on their boundaries with the outside world.) One of the most important effects of this was to lead to rivalry between cathedral schools, with individual 'masters' vying with each other to attract students and to gain extra prestige when these later achieved high office in the church. It was a highly competitive world with bitter rivalries and denunciations between masters.

The growth of administration and the recovery of Roman law led to literacy spreading beyond a small, largely clerical elite, and with it a demand for all kinds of literature. This period has been termed 'the twelfth-century renaissance' even though, unlike the better-known Renaissance of the fifteenth century, this 'renaissance' was not recognized as a 'rebirth' at the time. It was only defined as such by the scholar Charles Haskins 700 years later, in 1927.[9] Classical Latin was still dominant in both noble and clerical life – it was to be another century before any substantial works of vernacular literature appeared (in French and then in Italian) – and a well-educated person would have been expected to write and speak Latin with precision. The twelfth and thirteenth centuries are known for the quality of letter-writing, *ars dictaminis*, based on Cicero's advice on setting out a subject, and poetry, *ars poetriae*. A native of Amiens, Richard of Fournival, compiled a *Biblionomia* (*c.*1250) in which he attractively set out the genres available as if they were different plots in a garden. Yet there was always a logjam in the dissemination of popular texts, owing to the time spent copying every text by hand. Experts on the transmission of texts have found that, 300 years after Charlemagne, the quality of copying declines in this period and corruptions creep in which are then repeated by the next scribe. Inevitably, many scribes simply did not have the learning to understand fully the Latin texts they were writing out, making mistakes more likely.

The story of Abelard and Héloïse has resonated through the ages. The lovers are portrayed here in an illustration from the *Roman de la Rose*, a popular French poem about romantic love.

Despite the achievements of the scribes of the first millennium, what remained of the classical authors, especially those who had originally written in Greek, a language now almost unknown in the west, was limited. Students of grammar used a fourth-century author, Donatus, as their authority. In rhetoric there was a single work of Cicero and fragments of the *Institutes of Oratory* of the orator Quintilian (*c.*AD 35–100). Although a full copy of the original text was not discovered until 1416, this was a thoughtful analysis of approaches to the education of boys from elementary schooling upwards. Quintilian made the point, one which was readily accepted by medieval teachers, that the study of literature could help with the formation of character.

When Abelard was teaching logic in his schools he used a total of no more than seven texts: two by Aristotle, four by Boethius and one, a short pamphlet by Porphyry, the biographer of Plotinus, that

Et par esperiment le prouvent
Et quant en amours fame prise
Tu le savras bien atemise
Comment heloys labbesse
Entendit pierres abailart

Pierres abailart le confesse
Qui suer heloys labbesse
Du paraclit qui fu sa fame
Acorder ne se vouloit mie

commented on Aristotle's *Categories*. The *Categories* (as taught through the Latin translation of Boethius) was especially important as it contained the rules for classifying language, clarifying the distinctions between nouns, verbs and statements of affirmation and negation. However, it went much further than this. If one takes an object or substance, a human being or a tree, for instance, then there are various ways of categorizing it in terms of quantity, its special qualities, its relation to other objects, its relationship to time, and so on. Being forced to analyse in this way was an excellent way of introducing a student to logic.

Abelard (b.1079) was a Breton by birth, from a minor noble family. From an early age he rejected his conventional background and set upon his own path of intellectual discovery. So he entered the schools, gravitating towards Paris, the city whose schools and masters were the most prestigious. He arrived there in 1100 and naturally chose the school of one of the most respected teachers, William of Champeaux. However, Abelard's boundless self-confidence and readiness to challenge his teachers (he was particularly vindictive about William) meant that he infuriated those in authority as much as he enthused those students who heard him. He drifted between schools, studentships and minor teaching posts for several years. It was a long and tortuous process before he could call himself 'master', the title given to those who had distinguished themselves through their learning, teaching and moral behaviour.

It was probably in 1114, when he was about thirty-five, that Abelard finally became master at the cathedral school at Notre Dame in the centre of Paris. He found lodgings at the house of a canon of the cathedral, Fulbert, who had a niece, Heloise. Her education was already advanced, the quality of her written Latin was outstanding, so she was probably in her twenties when they met in about 1117; but the connection of two highly intelligent minds soon became one of sexual passion and a pregnancy ensued.

After the baby had been born in Abelard's native Brittany, and left in the care of his sister, the pair returned to Paris and married on the insistence of Fulbert. It was highly unusual, but not forbidden, for someone of Abelard's clerical status to marry and would certainly have prevented him progressing higher in the church hierarchy.[10] Heloise appears to have appreciated this – she recognized that philosophy required a dedication that was incompatible with family life and denied that they had been married at all. However, when Abelard returned her to the convent where she had been educated this was seen by Fulbert as a rejection so humiliating for his family's honour that it deserved retaliation. He therefore arranged for Abelard to be castrated. In his autobiographical *Historia Calamitatum* (*The Story of My Misfortunes*), written in about 1130 to an unknown monk, Abelard tells how it was the shame and humiliation of the assault that hurt more than the physical pain. The *Historia* seems to have been known to Heloise and other readers and it is best seen as part of Abelard's persistent desire to be noticed.[11]

The perpetrators of this mutilation were arrested and themselves castrated and blinded. To escape an escalating feud, Abelard withdrew to the safe haven of a monastery, no less than the royal foundation at St Denis, and for the rest of his life he was a monk. He insisted that Heloise take the veil at the same time at the convent where he had placed her. This was a rejection that she resented bitterly, as her famous letters to Abelard show. She told him of her smouldering lust for him, and that thoughts of their earlier lovemaking even overcame her at Mass. 'In my case, the pleasures of love which we shared have been too sweet – they cannot displease me and can scarcely shift from my memory.' Such was her passion, she told him, that she would happily follow him to hell and that even a respectable marriage would not have supplanted her desire to be his whore. Yet, she complained, he was only preoccupied with himself and his 'misfortunes'.[12]

Heloise's letters still astonish us for their balance between desperation for a lost love and an emotional understanding of the inevitability of their separation:

> God knows I never sought anything in you, except yourself. I wanted simply you, nothing of yours. I looked for no marriage-bond, no marriage portion, and it was not my own pleasures and wishes I sought to gratify but yours… I believed that the more I humbled myself on your account, the more gratitude I should win from you, and also the less damage I should do to the brightness of your reputation… Tell me one thing if you can. Why, after our entry into religion, which was your decision alone, have I been so neglected and forgotten by you that I have neither a word from you when you are here to give me strength… I will tell you what I think and indeed everyone suspects. It was desire, not affection that bound you to me, the flame of lust rather than love. So when the end came to what you desired, any show of feeling you used to make went with it.[13]

Abelard's replies seem ham-fisted and evasive; he is ever the logician: 'I have decided to answer you on each point in turn, not so much in self-justification as for your own enlightenment and encouragement…'[14]

Even though she made the best of her fate, first as prioress, then as abbess of her convent, Heloise's exclusion marks an important moment in the shutting up of women's voices. An outstanding intellect was silenced. Abelard may have come to appreciate this, but only when it was too late to rescue Heloise. In his later works, he repeatedly dwells on the equality of women, stressing, in an age where celibate clerics were denouncing women as temptresses, that Christ had always associated with both sexes, not least in giving Mary Magdalene special prominence as the one who passed on news of his Resurrection to the apostles (John 20:1–3). But other, narrower, perceptions of women would prove dominant over the coming centuries. The return of Aristotle's texts to the west would designate women as passive recipients of male semen that contained the whole embryo. Such thinking, in conjunction with the pervasive influence of religious texts, would exclude women from joining universities as full members until the twentieth century.

Abelard had already made a name for himself as a logician, teaching the logic element of the *trivium*. This did not involve mathematical logic but dialectical reasoning, the application of the rules that were used to distinguish valid arguments from false ones. The logicians were confident in their ability to attain truth and to use dialectic, the use of opposing statements as had been pioneered in Plato's dialogues, as a means of developing a more profound understanding of other issues. And no logician was more confident than Abelard. Dialectic was 'an instrument of order in a chaotic world'. It was 'the discipline of disciplines: it teaches how to teach, and how to learn; reason itself comes to the fore in it and reveals its nature and purpose'. It was a method endorsed by Augustine and so given authority for Christian teachers. 'From the eminence of his speculation Abelard saw the road of dialectic running straight to the City of God.'[15]

Abelard might have followed many traditional teachers in confining his lectures to the exposition of selected passages of scriptures, using reason only when it led to the 'right' answers. This was the approach adopted, to brilliant effect, by Anselm, famous for his arguments for the existence of God. Abelard, in contrast, revelled in disputation, the posing of questions that demanded an answer to the contradictions embedded in them. He followed where the argument led, irrespective of whether it ended with the orthodox theological solutions, although he cleverly used texts from Augustine to support his approach. This was much in the spirit of Aristotle, who had always accepted that any conventional knowledge was challengeable through logic or new empirical evidence. Abelard's openness, expressed in a flamboyant and even aggressive way, was irresistible to his students who crowded into the restricted spaces where teaching took place.

After the traumatic and sobering experience of his castration, Abelard's thinking developed new depths. His teaching appears to have become less frenetic since his authority, as the only man who was said to understand Aristotle's works on logic, for instance, was assured. At first his studies were helped by the rich resources of the library at St Denis and it was here that he appears to have begun his famous *Sic et Non* (*Yes and No*). *Sic et Non* is a remarkable collection of quotations from the Church Fathers (for which a well-stocked library would have been essential). If the Church Fathers were the arbiters of theological truth, then their texts had a sacred purpose. In *Sic et Non* Abelard hit on the original – if provocative – idea of quoting the Church Fathers on specific theological issues, some 158 of them, so that one could see that they often contradicted each other. Although Abelard stated that much could be resolved by a careful analysis of the language of different texts, it was inevitable that readers would be unsettled by this presentation of opposing views. Abelard did not seem to care – doubting was healthy in itself. As he put it in the Prologue to *Sic et Non*: 'For it is from doubt that we arrive at questioning and in a state of questioning we arrive at the truth.' He went on to suggest that anyone, not just experienced theologians, could grapple with the issues of logic in Christian doctrine. This was bound to offend conservatives who argued that doctrine was coherent and beyond challenge, especially by the ordinary faithful. Even if the importance of this approach was not grasped at the time, Abelard's championing of doubt was an important moment in the awakening of the western mind. Progress in knowledge is impossible if conventional thinking is never doubted.

As might be expected, the restless Abelard was soon on the move again, expelled from St Denis in 1121 for questioning the authenticity of its patron saint. A new work, *Theologia*, was denounced as heretical in the same year. The word 'theology', from the Greek 'reasoning about God', was relatively new and Abelard aroused suspicion for his claim that its purpose was to use reason to lead towards an understanding of God. This seems uncontroversial now but there was an alternative view, put forward by Anselm of Canterbury, that it was only through *starting* from belief that one could 'understand'. 'I believe that unless I believe I shall not understand,' as he put it in his *Proslogion*.[16] Abelard was arguing the opposite. He aroused further suspicion by venturing towards an 'understanding' of the most complex doctrine of all, that of the Trinity. With his typical arrogance, he assumed that he would solve the 'mystery' of the Trinity more completely than anyone else. This involved much that was controversial. Abelard claimed that God the Father alone had omnipotence, while the orthodox approach was that all three persons of the Trinity were equally powerful. He accorded Christ the Son the quality of wisdom and the Holy Spirit the quality of goodness, again making a distinction between the three persons that the orthodox would not accept. Again he appeared to believe that the reasoning behind his position was so obvious that anyone, even the pagan Greeks and Romans, could grasp it through straightforward logic. This infuriated those who wished to keep theological questions above the minds of the faithful. In the case of the Trinity, this was a sensible move. The doctrine has always resisted any explanation through reason – even today the Catholic catechism refers to it as a 'mystery'.*

One of the most remarkable features of Abelard's thinking was his tolerance for pagans. Augustine had discussed the issue but had taught that even the apparent virtues of pagans were false in that they were not specifically directed towards God. The possibilities for pagans to be saved through the grace of God were therefore slim. In fact, Augustine was building on earlier statements – the third-century bishop of Carthage, Cyprian, had coined the phrase *Extra Ecclesiam Nulla Salus* ('There is no salvation outside the Church'). Abelard argued in contrast that it had been possible for pagans to reach a rational understanding of God through natural law and thus if they lived virtuous lives they might well be saved. In a response to a theological question sent to him by Heloise towards the end of his life, he wrote:

> It accords with piety and reason that whoever, recognizing by natural law God as the creator and rewarder of all, adhere to him with such zeal that they strive in no way to offend him through consent which is the proper name for sin: such people, we judge, should by no means be damned.[17]

But this tentative move towards tolerance was to be quickly frustrated, as the Fourth Lateran Council reaffirmed the original doctrine. It was not until the pagans of the Americas were discovered that the issue became live again.

Following a spat with a former teacher, Roscelin, Abelard's ideas became public and the papal legate to France, Cardinal Cono, summoned him to a council at Soissons. By now the church was trying to define and suppress heresy, a procedure that was to develop into the

* 'The mystery of the Most Holy Trinity is the central mystery of Christian faith and life. God alone can make it known to us by revealing himself as Father, Son and Holy Spirit.' Article 261 of the Catechism of the Catholic Church.

Inquisition. Yet, as was noted in the last chapter, what could be defined as heresy was bound to be fluid in a developing intellectual climate and there was a risk that the legate and the pope might make judgements that they would later regret. Cono played safe by condemning the *Theologia* without even reading it, on the grounds that Abelard was publicly raising questions and encouraging debate on issues that were already closed. Copies were ordered to be burned, although we know that Abelard concealed one that he later used for further development of his ideas. The condemnation of Abelard's *Theologia*, by a German outsider to France, was not as devastating as it might have seemed – discussions of the importance of reasoning had become commonplace and the many cross-currents of French religious politics meant that Abelard still had his supporters.

Yet, after this condemnation Abelard spent three years as a hermit at a new foundation, the Paraclete (Holy Spirit), endowed for him by a noble admirer in the Champagne region. Here, despite its solitude, he gathered a few students around him before returning to his native Brittany as abbot of the monastery of St Gildas in about 1131. This was a period when the church authorities were trying to bring order to often corrupt monasteries and by now Abelard was seen as a Parisian 'outsider' representing this movement. His relationships with the monks became so bad that he feared that they might kill him. It was not until 1133 that he eventually found a safe haven as master at another Paris school, Mont Sainte-Geneviève. He survived here until his second condemnation as a heretic, in 1140, by Pope Innocent II following the Council of Sens, which will be described below. Hereafter, he was given shelter in one of Cluny's priories by an admirer, Cluny's abbot, Peter the Venerable, until his death in 1142.

Across these years Abelard had continued his work. As no original manuscript of his survives, it has not been easy to date his surviving texts or place them in order. One of the most important of Abelard's contributions, put forward in *Scito Te Ipsum* (*Know Yourself*), was his understanding of the role of intention in ethics. An act in itself might appear to be evil, but Abelard argues that it is not a sin unless it has been premeditated as such. This approach could have startling effects. The medieval church was weighed down by the belief that in crucifying Jesus, the Jews had in effect killed God and were thus collectively guilty of deicide. Abelard, however, argued that if they had thought they were behaving in good faith, they had no intention of committing evil and so were absolved of their terrible sin. While his approach had no immediate impact, Abelard was laying the foundations of a concept that was in direct contradiction of Augustine's view that free will was subverted by the original sin of Adam and Eve. He repudiated Augustine's notorious claim that babies who had died before they had been baptized would burn in hell.

The philosophical debate that simmered throughout the Middle Ages and which Abelard could not avoid was that of universals. The problem had already been argued over with immense sophistication by Plato, Aristotle and Boethius as well as many of the Church Fathers. From early in his career, Abelard was preoccupied with the many philosophical quandaries the issue raised and his work on it is considered one of his greatest achievements. What follows can only be a gross simplification of the issues.[18]

We see a garden full of a variety of rose bushes, each bush and each rose, of course, an individual. Yet is there an entity that transcends this, a universal rose to which each separate bud or bloom belongs? One might equally talk, for instance, of individual human beings and something called 'humanity' which transcends them. One party, the Nominalists, argued that 'humanity' was just a collective name (with no existence other than this) for a group of individual human beings. Their rivals, the Realists, who drew heavily on Platonic philosophy with its Forms or Ideas that existed as 'realities' beyond the world of the senses, believed in a universal rose or 'humanity' as having an existence distinct from the individuals within it. The issue was fraught because of the central importance for the church of the doctrine of the Trinity, which, as seen, frustrated rational attempts to explain it. The Nominalists might be accused of the heresy of believing in the distinct personalities of Father, Son and Holy Spirit, at the expense of the Universal, the Trinity, that transcended them. If 'Trinity' was no more than a name, then the doctrine lost its potency. Abelard worked out his own middle way, although one closer to Nominalism than Realism, which became known as Conceptualism. The words 'rose' or 'humanity' do not have an existence in themselves but are imagined terms against which a particular individual rose or human being might be assessed. One approach was to argue that God had conceived of humanity before he had created Adam. His concept of 'humanity' was beyond human understanding but this did not preclude logicians from exploring what his original conception may have been. One could only ground one's understanding of 'humanity' from individuals and work from there to build up a concept of 'humanity' which would always be limited and usually particular to the individual thinker. Bearing in mind that, at this time, several races were yet to be encountered by

Europeans, Abelard was right to argue that our conception of 'humanity' was, at any one moment, provisional. So 'humanity' or 'rose' remained a name or concept, one whose meaning could be explored, but not as a coherent entity. Abelard's work was an important step in the move away from Realism.

Abelard would always have had as many enemies as admirers but, in the last ten years of his life, one figure took it upon himself to confront him and succeed in a final condemnation of the philosopher as a heretic. Bernard of Clairvaux was the most powerful of the early Cistercians, founding abbot at the Cistercian monastery of Clairvaux in 1115, and inspiration for many more. He acted as the moral compass for his age. His faith, expressed in eloquent sermons, was austere and uncompromising. The Catholic Church had defined what the faithful should believe and there was no place for using reasoning to support or question this. Bernard drew on an ancient strand of Latin theology. As far back as the second century the earliest 'Latin' theologian, Tertullian, from Carthage in North Africa, had asked the question 'What has Jerusalem to do with Athens, the Church with the Academy, the Christian with the heretic?... Away with all attempts to produce a mottled Christianity of Stoic, Platonic, and dialectic composition. We want no curious disputation after possessing Christ Jesus, no inquisition after enjoying the gospel.'[19] Instead, one should simply be receptive to God's word, a view that was often repeated by the Church Fathers. Gregory the Great's saying that 'Faith has no merit for which human reason offers proof'[20] suggested that praise should be given to those who do *not* question, a view that has persisted in the Catholic Church throughout its history. Intrusion into faith was, in Bernard's graphic phrase, simply 'tearing out the guts of God's secrets' and in a specific condemnation of Abelard, he protested, 'Let him who scanned the Heavens go down into the depths of Hell'. Offering his mind directly to the heavens, Bernard valued the Virgin Mary as an intercessor with Christ and even reported that once when he was ill a statue of the Virgin came alive and offered her breasts for him to suck healing milk.[21]

There was no way that Bernard's theology could be reconciled with Abelard's. In his *The Dialogue of a Philosopher with a Jew and a Christian* (to be discussed below) Abelard stressed how an unthinking reliance on 'faith' led to the stagnation of knowledge:

> With faith – the area in which the threat of error is most dangerous – there is no progress... no one is allowed to investigate what should be believed among one's own people, or to escape punishment for raising

doubts about what is said by everyone… People profess themselves to believe what they admit they cannot understand, as if faith consisted in uttering words rather than in mental understanding.[22]

This was controversial enough, but Abelard had made himself vulnerable through his own speculations on key issues of Christian doctrine such as the Trinity. Not without some justification, Bernard mocked Abelard for his arrogance in claiming that he, Abelard, knew secrets of God that had not been entrusted to anyone else.

Bernard's detestation of Abelard was as much a matter of temperament as it was of theology. Bernard loathed what he saw as Abelard's showmanship and the way that he appeared to revel in spreading doubt about the most sacred of mysteries. It is a reminder too that being declared a heretic involved more than theological error; it was the presumption of persisting in error by publicly spreading one's errors, 'the deadly sin of pride', as Gregory the Great had defined it, that was an important element of the accusation.[23] Bernard had no time for the nuances of theology, but he knew that he could use language without scruple to ridicule Abelard for his arrogance. He was never one to mince his words and he had often won earlier campaigns against his enemies through the sheer power of his invective. He was not the first nor the last campaigner to understand that the constant repetition of malicious slander, however unjustified, often achieves the destruction of its object.

The final resting place of Abelard and Héloïse in Père Lachaise cemetery, Paris, in a mid-nineteenth-century French print.

It is not clear exactly how Bernard persuaded a church council that was to be held at Sens, in Burgundy, in 1140 to take on the issue of Abelard's 'heresies'. He, or collaborators, had worked their way through Abelard's works and produced nineteen texts that they claimed to be heretical. Among them was the passage on the Trinity from *Theologia* that claimed that 'the Father is full power, the Son some power, the Holy Spirit no power'. Although he was now in his sixties, Abelard retaliated by challenging Bernard to debate these texts with him at the council. Bernard knew that he would easily have been outmanoeuvred by the greatest logician of his day and he hit on the plan of arriving the day before the council opened and successfully persuading the bishops (when they were still at dinner, and, one report suggests, rather drunken) that these texts were indeed heretical. His hope seems to have been to avoid getting bogged down in theological issues but to launch – with his customary eloquence – a personal attack on Abelard on the next, opening, day, which would swing the assembled clergy into a condemnation.

The plan failed. Abelard arrived on the first morning but refused to respond to the charges. He insisted instead that he was appealing directly to the pope, Innocent II. This was possibly tactical on Abelard's part, since by not replying he would avoid condemning himself, but there is also evidence that he was in ill health. For whatever reason, proceedings were stopped and his direct appeal to Rome was allowed. Bernard had no alternative but to send his own letter of condemnation to Rome, a letter that was venomous in its content. Abelard decided to go to Rome in person.

This now became an issue of who had influence with whom. There were so many factions in Rome that it was unclear how the Curia would react. What seems to have decided the issue was the report from the bishops at Sens, that Abelard was indeed heretical and his works and teaching should be banned to stop their contagion spreading. Almost immediately Pope Innocent II declared Abelard's texts as 'pernicious doctrines and other perverse doctrines contrary to the Catholic faith'. He imposed perpetual silence on Abelard and the excommunication of any who persisted as his followers. Abelard was to be shut up in a religious house and his books burned.

It was lucky that Abelard had a friend and admirer in Peter the Venerable, abbot of the great monastery at Cluny. Peter claimed that he had come across Abelard passing on his way to Rome and had taken him in. Although his contacts must have told him of Abelard's condemnation, Peter feigned that he did not know of them but assured the pope that Abelard was under his supervision and that his behaviour was exemplary. Peter was highly influential and his monastery was under the special protection of the papacy. Indeed, there is some evidence that Abelard may have been absolved by the pope before his death in May 1142. This was certainly the impression given in a glowing letter the hospitable Peter wrote to Heloise, who was now abbess of the Paraclete, when he sent her Abelard's body. A legend describes how, when Heloise herself died some twenty years later, Abelard's tomb was opened and the corpse revived to embrace her body as it was laid beside his. After many vicissitudes their bodies now lie together in the Père Lachaise cemetery in Paris.

Abelard was undoubtedly a charismatic and a brilliant thinker but also arrogant, high-handed with Heloise, and seemingly unaware of how provocative his use of logic was to conservative theologians. He was so carried away with his own brilliance that he did not seem to care. He considered the attacks on him to be unfair, as the highlighting of his life in terms of 'misfortunes' makes clear. Yet his intellectual achievements were major ones. He was far ahead of his time in reviving the spirit of Aristotle, if only from a limited number of texts, and emphasizing the importance of doubt as a stepping-stone to knowledge. He was fearless in exploring the most complex of issues, as in the universals debate. He trespassed into the texts of the hallowed Church Fathers, suggesting that they might not be as authoritative as they seemed. In short he showed that individualism was possible even in a hierarchical society. Yet this was not a world where there could be freedom of thought. While Abelard lived in a period when the church did not have a formal way of dealing with dissent, he came up against a well-established tradition of the acceptance of 'faith' as unchallengeable. Once he had aroused the anger of the unscrupulous Bernard he was doomed.

In addition, Abelard left one particularly important legacy. His *Sic et Non* had established the concept of the disputation. A master would put up a student to defend a thesis, then a student would stand up to critique it. Once they had finished, the teacher would elaborate on the merits of each argument. This made learning more creative. Students did not have to sit down and be bored by the exposition of a teacher, they could become involved. The approach was taken up by the theologian known as Peter the Lombard, from his birthplace in northern Italy (*c.*1095). Peter learned his law at Bologna, then gravitated towards Paris, where he taught at Notre Dame (he may even have been a pupil of Abelard) and began writing his theological work, *The Sentences*, completed probably about 1155. Like *Sic et Non* this drew extensively on the works of the Church Fathers and on biblical references gleaned from Gratian's *Decretum*, but the discussions are presented in the same way as Abelard's disputations. *The Sentences* ranges over the whole field of theology and was important in creating a systematic approach, dividing up the subject matter into manageable sections. Inevitably, there were those who challenged elements of such an ambitious and innovative work but Pope Innocent III, confronted by Lombard's critics, declared the work to be orthodox and by the thirteenth century it was widely used as a textbook, mastery of which was needed for examinations. It was the standard work for budding theologians well into the sixteenth century, its longevity as a standard text evidence in itself of the difficulties in allowing creative evolution in theology.

One work of Abelard's needs further discussion: *The Dialogue of a Philosopher with a Jew and a Christian*.[24] There is no agreement on when it was written, although it was probably between 1125 and 1133. The *Dialogue* contains two separate parts: the 'Philosopher' debates first with a Jew and then, separately, with a Christian, asking each one central questions about their respective faiths, such as the nature of the ultimate good. In the dialogue with the Christian, Abelard, as might be expected, seems more concerned with asserting the importance of a philosophical approach to Christian doctrine and ethics. Christianity, he asserts, is a rational religion. What stands out in the dialogue with the Jew is the readiness of the Philosopher to listen to the Jew and to accept that his beliefs are part of his upbringing. Abelard teases out many of the underlying issues, of Jewish law, for instance. While critical of the law, he sympathizes with the practical problems Jews have in living in a Christian society.

Abelard's tolerant approach to Judaism was very rare for his time. Anti-Semitism was already rife in medieval Europe. In the First Crusade (1095–99), the rabble of crusaders massacred entire communities of Jews in the Rhineland as they passed through and there are similar reports from the Second Crusade (1145–9). It was as if the new prominence of Jerusalem in the popular imagination highlighted the role of the Jews in Christ's death and so legitimized the slaughter of their descendants. Just two years after Abelard's death, the dead body of a boy apprentice, William of Norwich, was discovered in that town in eastern England. Without any evidence to back up the claim, it was assumed that he had been crucified by Jews. William was acclaimed a saint and, alongside the cult that grew up around him, a myth that Jews sacrificed children spread across Europe. The institutional church also tightened its control over Jews. The Third Lateran Council of 1179 banned Christians from acting as servants in Jewish households under pain of excommunication, and privileged Christians above Jews in the law courts. The Fourth Lateran Council of 1215 was even harsher. Jews were to be distinguished by their dress and on Passion Sunday and the last three days of Holy Week were banned from public places. They were not allowed to hold public office 'since it is absurd that a blasphemer of Christ exercise authority over Christians'. Abelard's more reflective voice was lost within the swamp of prejudice but his readiness to uphold tolerance deserves to be remembered. He also grasped that knowledge is not static. As the 'Philosopher' in the *Dialogue* notes: 'Human understanding increases as the years pass and one age succeeds another.'

In 1159, just seventeen years after Abelard's death, there appeared an impressive defence of the *trivium*, especially the art of dialectic, by one of his former pupils, John of Salisbury, later bishop of Chartres. The *Metalogicon* (*On Behalf of the Arts of Words and Reasoning*) consolidated the works of Aristotle on logic as the core of the *trivium* and emphasized their importance as the first step to understanding the wisdom of God. While his knowledge of the classical authors remained very limited, John clearly saw them as an inspiration equal to that of the theologians, and in this sense he is often seen as a precursor of the humanists of the fourteenth century and beyond. Like them he found much to inspire him in what he had read of Cicero. He is also important as a critic of the aridity of much logical thinking and realized that often one has to be satisfied with no more than probable explanations for many phenomena. John held that the evidence of the senses ranks with faith and reason as a source of knowledge, so opening up the possibility that so-called 'truths' may not be as absolute as proclaimed. It implies as well that diverse views must be respected. John's *Policraticus* (*The Statesman*) provides examples where wisdom lies in the freedom to express one's views clearly: 'The practice of liberty displeases only those who live in the manner of slaves.'[25] There are broader aims to education as well. As John puts it in the *Metalogicon*: 'Any profession of philosophy whatsoever is valueless and deceitful if it does not manifest itself in the cultivation of virtue and the conduct of our lives.' The later humanists of the Italian Renaissance were dismissive of the 'eloquence' of both Abelard and John of Salisbury, but they deserve better.[26] Lacking the arrogance of Abelard and respected by his contemporaries, John merits recognition as one of those who eloquently bridged the classical and Christian worlds of knowledge before it became part of the cultural mainstream to do so.

The Cry of *Libertas*: the Rebirth of the City-State

The first praise of cities should furnish the dignity of the founder and it should include praise of distinguished men and also gods, just as Athens is said to have been established by Athena... The second [theme of praise] concerns the form of fortifications and the site, which is either inland or maritime and in the mountains or in the plain. The third concerns the fertility of the lands, the bountifulness of the springs, the habits of the inhabitants. Then concerning its ornaments or its good fortune, whether things had developed unaided or had occurred by virtue, weapons and warfare. We shall also praise it if that city has many noble men, by whose glory it shall provide light for the whole world.

From *De Laudibus Urbium*
(*Of the Praise of Cities*),
eighth-century Lombard text[1]

The roots of any effective challenge to the powerful position of the church lay elsewhere, in the slowly emerging trading cities of northern Italy. It would be wrong to over-emphasize the role of trade in the European economy at the beginning of the second millennium. For centuries the continent was to depend on surplus from land for its wealth, and here there was progress. The population was growing. By 1050 there are records of woodland being cleared, marshes being drained and horse-drawn ploughs improving yields. In contrast, the trading cities of the Mediterranean remained little more than parasites on the burgeoning economies of the Arab world.

Archaeological evidence is gradually adding to our understanding of the revival of trading networks. For many years the so-called Pirenne thesis dominated the scholarship. The Belgian historian Henri Pirenne (1862–1935) argued, notably in his posthumous *Mahomet et Charlemagne*,[2] that while trade between western Europe and Byzantium continued after the fall of the western empire, it was the rise of Islam that destroyed Mediterranean trade and forced alternative strategies, which included the authoritarian responses of Charlemagne. In a magisterial study, *The Origins of the European Economy, Communications and Commerce, AD 300–900*,[3] the economic historian Michael McCormick has turned this thesis on its head. He charts the *decline* of Mediterranean trade as taking place in the seventh century and ascribes its *revival* to the new contacts with the Arab economies forged in the eighth and ninth centuries. He draws on an extraordinary range of sources – many of which, such as Arab coinage and the import of relics from the east, have never been properly analysed – to suggest a mass of private traders from east and west peddling high-value goods. He is particularly good on the evidence of travelling people (he has analysed documentary evidence for 669 of them!) but perhaps his most important finding is the extent to which slaves from northern Europe provided one of the staples of European exports. Among his conclusions is a fascinating and not unjustified claim:

> The world that Charlemagne knew first hand was peopled not only by Franks, Alamannians, and Saxons, by Danes, Anglo-Saxons, Lombards and Visigoths, but by Venetians, Arabs, Jews, Byzantines and Slavs. Perhaps never again in its history would Europe be so culturally open, in so many directions, in so many ways.[4]

The other side of the story, the importance of the Arabs as traders, has been less well told. Fernand Braudel, in his famous history of the Mediterranean, hardly mentions them at all. The pioneer here is the French historian Christophe Picard, notably in his *The Sea of the Caliphs*.[5] Overcoming a paucity of sources, Picard establishes that despite conflicts between rival caliphs, the Arabs were well established across the southern Mediterranean by the eighth century and were a significant force by the tenth. They welcomed the early traders of northern Italy and recruited Greeks as their sea captains. In short, there was much more creative interaction between Christians, Arabs and, from the extensive evidence of the Genizah Archive from Cairo, of Jewish traders.* The amount of Islamic iconography to be seen in the churches of the Amalfi coast whose communities were trading with Islam from the ninth century is surprising. The eleventh-century cathedral of Salerno, for instance, has contributions from three civilizations: a courtyard that is heavily Islamic and a (Latin) Romanesque portal which surrounds bronze doors from Byzantine Constantinople. Picard echoes McCormick in recognizing the Islamic contribution to opening the Mediterranean to a world that encompassed not only Europe but the Sahara, Asia and the Indian Ocean. He notes that the first Arabic descriptions of the Mediterranean come from Baghdad and Iran, both far inland from the sea.[6] As will be seen, the Arab contribution, both cultural and economic, to the reawakening of the western mind is considerable.

Venice was indeed the first city to grow rich from the revival of Mediterranean trade. The earliest reference to mercantile capital in medieval Europe (in this case expressed as wealth tied up in ships) is found in 829 in the will of the Venetian doge (originally *dux*, 'leader'), Justinian Partecipacius. Unlike Venice's rivals on the Italian mainland the city had no Roman past. Founded only in the sixth century by refugees fleeing the Lombard invasions into northern Italy, its isolated and precarious position on a marshy lagoon forced its inhabitants to be creative with their energies and outward looking in their search for wealth. Originally subject to the Byzantine empire, Venice naturally looked to the east and its merchants had soon mastered the tricky currents of the Adriatic, one of the most treacherous inner seas of the Mediterranean. The Venetians tapped into what were much more sophisticated trading networks. Constantinople, the Holy Land and

* The Genizah Archive is a collection of 193,000 medieval Jewish manuscripts preserved in storage in Cairo after being discarded. It was transferred to Cambridge University Library in the 1890s, where it remains.

Islamic Egypt were centres of trade; slaves brought across the Alpine trade routes (to which Venice had easy access) one way; gold, spices and relics the other. The legendary stealing of the body of the evangelist St Mark from Alexandria in 828 gave a new impetus to the identity of the city and its centre moved from the island of Torcello, with its haunting, but now isolated, 'cathedral', to another spit of land, alongside what is now the basin of St Mark, where the basilica that housed the relics of the evangelist was completed in the eleventh century. Grand though the domed St Mark's was – it is said to have been copied from the now-vanished church of the Holy Apostles in Constantinople – it was no more than the doges' private chapel.

The popes had frowned on Christian trade with Islam and Leo V (813–20) had banned the Venetians from trading in Syria or Egypt. The Venetians, in response, developed a healthy disregard for such pronouncements. *Veneziani, poi Cristiani* ('We are Venetians first and only then Christians') was a favourite slogan. Venice's skill in making good trade deals led to the bypassing of the church's restrictions on usury. The standard interest rate on loans, 20 per cent in the twelfth century, was passed off as 'an old Venetian custom'. It was said that the relics had given a sign when they arrived in Venice that they did not want to be subject to the patriarch of Venice, whose cathedral was always at some distance from St Mark's.* St Mark's became the centre of religious life in Venice and the rituals that surrounded the parades

* From the fifteenth century, the seat of the patriarch's diocese was the Church of San Pietro di Castello on the island of that same name, at the far eastern end of the city.

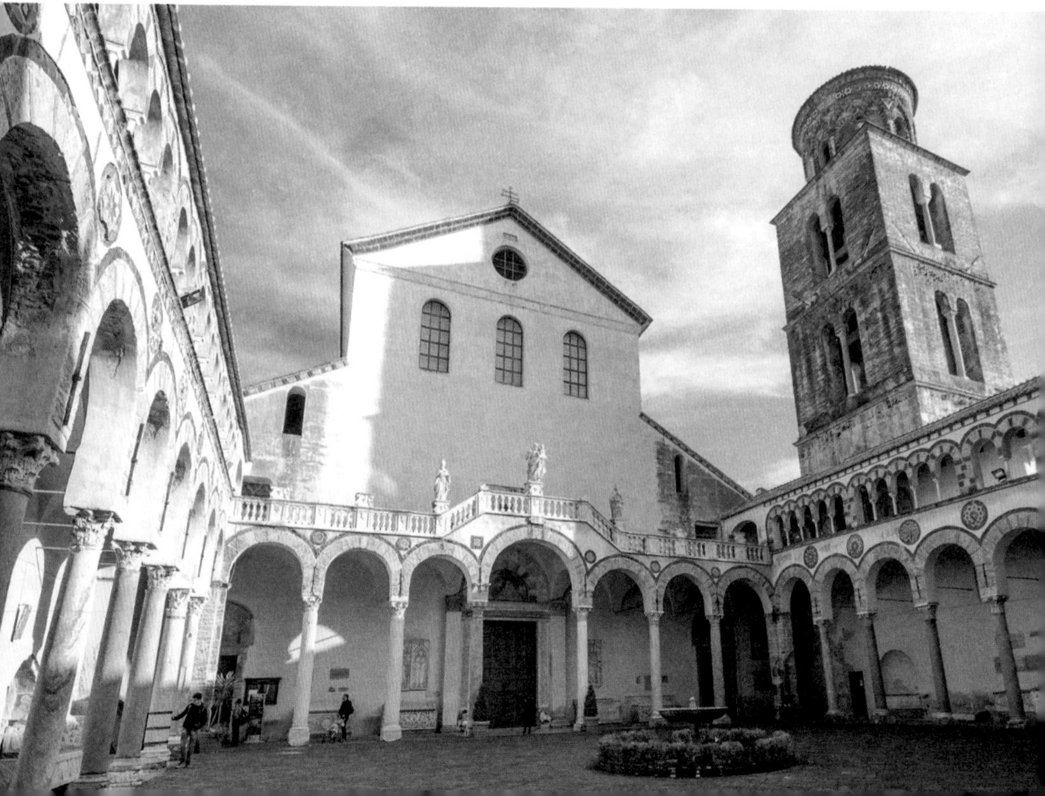

of Mark's relics around the impressive square that fronted the basilica were always community ones. There were elaborate rituals when a pope visited Venice to ensure that doge and pope respected each other's authority without submitting to it.

It was not only in creating a distance between the city and the 'official' church that Venice was a pioneer. The reach of the Byzantine empire westwards was faltering by the eighth century and by 1082 Venice had become independent. The very conditions in which the city originated fostered collegiate enterprise. The unstable mudflats could only be built on if piles were driven deep into the ground and expansion was only possible when the citizens worked together to reclaim land. There had to be laws for clearing out waste, keeping the waterways that were the 'streets' of the city clear, and making sure that fresh water supplies from wells were available. In 1291, following a number of fires, the glassmakers were moved by the government onto the island of Murano (where they are still to be found). The relative power of the community as against the wealthier families could be seen in the way they were never allowed to encroach on the large communal space of the Piazza (whose size, observers have noted, echoed the courtyard of the Great Umayyad Mosque in Damascus, one of Venice's trading partners). The nobles would show off their wealth, accumulated from trade and commerce rather than from feudal estates, in palaces. The nineteenth-century aesthete John Ruskin wrote of the contrast between Venice's opulence and more sombre architecture elsewhere: 'While the burghers and barons of the north were building their dark streets and grisly castles of oak and sandstone, the merchants of Venice were covering their palaces with porphyry and gold.'[7] The doge was officially the city's ruler but he was elected and his power limited by a number of councils, these restricted to noble families, so Venice was always *La Serenissima*, 'the most serene' republic (and lasted as such until 1797). So was created the myth, brilliantly portrayed in the Venetian cardinal Gasparo Contarini's *De magistratibus et republica Venetorum* (*On the Officials and the Republic of Venice*) of 1536, that Venice was the ideal republic in which even the city's merchants put the welfare of the city before their own commercial interests for over 1,000 years of history.

Salerno Cathedral, southern Italy. The doors were made in Constantinople, the porch is Romanesque and the upper colonnade (right) is Islamic in style. By the eleventh century merchants from throughout the Mediterranean were trading with the Amalfi coast and leaving their imprint.

Venice's position far up in the north of the Adriatic left other ports on the western coast of Italy free to build their own trading networks. Genoa and Pisa were the most prominent. Thanks to its position at the

A medieval depiction of fourteenth-century Venice reveals the city to be already flourishing. Note that the famous four horses are already in place on St Mark's Basilica (upper left-hand corner).

ïole de la graunt Ermenie de perse.

mouth of the River Arno, Pisa, originally a base for the Roman imperial navy, had been able to defend itself more successfully from raids than many other cities of northern Italy and had taken the initiative against the spread of Islam and the pirates threatening the emergence of trade routes. In the eleventh century Pisa clashed with Genoa, which had also developed a large navy. Initially, Pisa gained the upper hand by winning control over Sardinia (home to large flocks of sheep, grain and saltpans) and Corsica. The intense rivalry between the two cities persisted but when Pope Urban II launched the First Crusade to the Holy Land in 1095, both were prosperous enough to provide large fleets for the enterprise.

A visit to Pisa today shows how successful the city was. In this early period extrovert display was focused on the creation of ecclesiastical buildings. The wonderful complex that still stands to the north of the River Arno was inaugurated by the Romanesque cathedral, founded in 1063 and partially funded by loot from a raid on the (then) Muslim-held city of Palermo in Sicily. The victories that financed it were recorded on the fabric and it was further embellished over the following century during which it was joined by the free-standing baptistery and then by a bell tower that famously began leaning during its construction. There was an imaginative use of bands of black and white marbles. The extensive use of columns throughout shows that memories of the classical past were still powerful and Nicola Pisano's pulpit in the baptistery (1260) consciously echoes Roman relief sculpture, not least in a nude representation of Hercules as Fortitude. Europe's classical heritage was already weaving its way in and out of every aspect of culture. Pisano's achievement was applauded in the inscription that accompanied his work: 'May so greatly gifted a hand be praised as it deserves.' Individual excellence was being noticed, a significant development. With the late additions of the Camposanto, a burial ground for which earth was brought specially from the Holy Land, these buildings show just how much wealth was now flowing into the city.

So it is perhaps not surprising that Pisa is the first city to be recorded as having instituted annually elected magistrates, consuls, in an echo of the Roman past, in 1085. Their status was enhanced when the archbishop of Pisa, Bishop Daiberto, travelled with the First Crusade and became the first Latin patriarch of Jerusalem. He was now an absentee. The earliest record of a trade agreement, between Pisa and the Byzantine empire – which is made by the consuls without any reference at all to the archbishop – dates from 1111. Shortly afterwards the consuls are shown in charge of justice and warfare. Chris Wickham, writing of the emergence of communal government in Pisa in this period, notes how a few families monopolized the magistracies and, unlike other cities, did not have to challenge the powers of local aristocratic landowners.[8]

It is understandable that the newly rich classes were soon clamouring for greater power within the cities. By the late eleventh century there was a growing number of disputes between the bishops and the local communities. They are poorly recorded but in Cremona, a city on the plain of the River Po with a prosperous agricultural base, merchants (*negotiatores*) came into conflict with the local bishop over his right to collect dues on river goods. As early as the 990s, the merchants had persuaded the emperor to intervene and grant them, rather than the bishop, the toll rights, thus inflaming a crisis that simmered throughout the next century. In the 1030s the bishop was expelled from the city. The emperor ordered the merchants to allow him to return but it becomes clear in the documents of the 1090s that by then his political authority was only nominal and that a 'commune' had appeared.[9] This is just at the same time (1085) as Emperor Henry IV allowed Pisa to elect its own magistrates.

These assertions of communal independence emerged from a tangled web of conflicting powers and authorities in northern Italy. The emperors, relying on Charlemagne's conquest of the Lombards, claimed that they were ultimately sovereign and that they were owed the allegiances of the cities, but their territories were remote from Italy. As the structure of the Lombard kingdom atrophied in the ninth and tenth centuries, the grip of the emperors loosened. The challenge of the popes over the rights to investiture weakened their hold still further. They were forced to 'pay' for allegiance by granting the cities' privileges. It was Emperor Henry IV who had acknowledged the right of the Pisans to elect their own magistrates in return for their support.

overleaf Work began on Pisa's great ecclesiastical complex (the Piazza dei Miracoli) in the 1060s.

Yet by the closing decades of the eleventh century, the Investiture Controversy had stimulated intense debate over the relative rights of secular and religious authorities. For the first time since the fall of the Roman empire both sides to the debate began to write down and codify laws in the hope of giving them extra authority. This was just the moment when papal bulls such as *Dictatus Papae* were being issued from Rome and other canonical texts by teachers such as Ivo of Chartres

(1040–1115) were becoming available.* While the law governing the church or empire was essentially authoritarian, bolstering the perceived rights of either party to control its subjects, in northern Italy it was grasped that law could be used as a means of asserting rights *against* traditional authorities and so an ancient republican concept of the freedom of a community to run its own affairs, *libertas*, was reborn.

Where was this law to come from? The vacuum left by the collapse of the Roman empire had been filled in the west since 500 by Germanic laws and by Lombard law in northern Italy, but these were inadequate for a revived urban prosperity, especially with the rise of commercial disputes that called for a revised law of contract. Some fragments of Roman law remained, partly as recorded in Isidore of Seville's *Etymologies*, but its principles were little understood and they were not comprehensive enough to create a code. Fortuitously, in the eleventh century the great law code of the emperor Justinian was rediscovered. The code, which dates from the first half of the sixth century, was a magnificent administrative achievement and brought together centuries of sophisticated thinking on legal issues. By the late Roman empire, it had become very difficult to assess the relative status of imperial decrees, imperial responses to legal questions and the opinions of jurists. All could be raised in court as valid precedents. By consolidating these opinions and decrees and uniting them as the will of the emperor, Justinian avoided this confusion while boosting his own authority. He was well served by a highly efficient civil servant, Tribonian, who masterminded this ambitious project in just four years, between 528 and 532. The whole is known as the *Corpus Iuris Civilis* and it was made up of three parts. First was the *Codex Justinianus*, which brought together all the imperial decrees in a single volume so that they were immediately accessible to a court. Then came the *Digest*, a compilation of the opinions of jurists on Roman law. It condensed 3 million words of judgements into 1 million and the final text was proclaimed to be authoritative and unchallengeable but could be supplemented by later judgements. Finally, to help students master this enormous body of law, a third volume, the *Institutes*, served as a textbook.[10]

The *Codex* had first been published in Latin and so could be read

* St Ivo is remembered for his *Decretum*, a treatise on canon law that stressed the importance of caritas, 'love', rather than punishment in the exercise of the law. His works were available to Abelard and influential in the latter's theology.

by educated minds in the west.† Some memory of its content seems to have survived but there is no known reference to it by anyone after 680. Then in 1070 a copy of the *Digest* turned up in Bologna, the ancient city on the old Roman Via Emilia in northern Italy. It had apparently travelled from Constantinople in the sixth century to Byzantine southern Italy and from there to the great Benedictine monastery at Monte Cassino. Under Abbot Desiderius (1058–87), later Pope Victor III, this monastery had become the most important copying centre in Europe for classical texts. Without its efforts we may never have known of the works of the great Roman historian Tacitus or the novel *The Golden Ass* by Apuleius, among other important Roman works. It was probably here that the monks copied out the original manuscript, adding parts of another copy of the *Digest* that has now been lost. Finally, the amalgamated text arrived in Bologna, which city was developing as a centre for the study of law.

In short, the discovery of Justinian's texts, above all the *Digest*, caused an explosion of interest in Roman law just when a comprehensive model was urgently needed.[11] The code was especially important in supporting the right to private property. As Cicero had written in his *De Officiis*: 'The man in administrative office must make it his first care that everyone shall have what belongs to him and that private citizens suffer no invasion of their property rights by act of the state.'[12] The code reinforced this principle and the reappearance of the *Digest* was one of the great moments in the reawakening of the western mind, not least in affirming the principle of individual rights.

The centre for the study of the Code of Justinian remained Bologna.[13] Some early teachers of the subject are known by name. Irnerius, for instance, was teaching in the first quarter of the twelfth century having given legal advice to Emperor Henry V in his disputes with the papacy (and been excommunicated in 1119 as a result). He founded a school of glossators: jurists, who, using the original Roman texts, adapted them to meet the needs of the evolving city communes. The 'glosses' were commentaries written in the margins of the original text. One group of four Bolognese glossators: found advising Emperor Frederick Barbarossa in 1158, were particularly famous and they already show the different approaches to interpreting law. Among them Bulgarus favoured a strict interpretation of the original texts, while his colleague Martinus was prepared to interpret the law of the *Corpus*

† Latin was used as the language of administration throughout the empire, hence its use for the code. It was only in the seventh century that the Byzantine court adopted Greek as its administrative language.

a. Proseneticis. diri dicitur ... nunc dicitur personarum. accursius. ac.
a. Proseneticis. l. salariis quod datur proseneticis. ut ff. de proseneticis. l. i. sec.
Et hic nichil inique. ac. an in impensam ... ut ff. ... propter
b. Nichil fraudis. i. turpitudinis ... ut ff. de edil. edicto ...
c. Arris. hec eadem pignora vocantur. ut i. ti. l. i. ac.
f. Conditionem. pena eorum ... parte cessante. accursius. accursius.
g. Consulta persona. id est venerit osculum. l. uso ... iure tamen ... ut i. e. ti. si a sponso cum mittetur. ergo hec cum pena ... ut i. e. ti. l. cum veterem. ac.
h. Supervenit. tunc ei annuitur. annis. ac.
i. Ad nuptias. ad alia que iure recusare non poterit. ut ff. e. ti. l. i. ac.
k. Firmum. hoc ita ... ratione vel paterno eius quod pacifici. et quod tutor ... que sie non obstat. ff. de iu. o. l. tutis. ac.
l. Definitum. vel destinatum vel definitum ... nisi puella iure recusaret. sicut in tutore et. ut ff. de confir. tu. l. utilitate. ac.
m. Defensore. i. tutore vel curatore. ac.

Codicis domini iustiniani repetite prelectionis. Explicit liber iiii. Incipit quintus de sponsalibus et arris sponsaliciis et prosoneticis. rubrica.

Alii desponsate renuntiare conditioni ac nubere alii non prohibetur.

Imperator. Si is qui puellam suis nuptiis pactus est intra biennium exequi nuptias in eadem provincia degens supersederit eiusque spatii fine decurso in alterius postea coniunctionem puella pervenerit: nichil fraudis ei sit que nuptias maturando vota sua diutius ludi non passa est.

Imperator. Arris sponsaliorum nomine datis. sive ea sponsus vel sponsa decesserit: que data sunt iubemus restitui. nisi causam ut nuptie non celebrarentur: defuncta persona iam prebuit.

Imperator. Si pater pactum de filie nuptiis inierit et humana sorte consumptus ad vota non potuerit pervenire: id inter sponsum et sponsam firmum ratumque permaneat quod patri decebit. Et si ... nichilque permittatur libero momenti quod cum defensore a ad quem minoris commodi ... pertinebit. decebitur arras fuisse transactum. Proximum quidem est enim ut contra patriam voluntatem redempti forsitan tutoris aut curatoris admittatur arbitrium cum plerumque ipsius femine ad nuptias commodi propria ... matrimonium laborare consilium.

Imperator. Mulier iuris sui constituta arrarum sponsaliorum nomine usque ad duplum teneatur. id est in id quod accepit et aliud tantundem. nec amplius si post completum xxv. annum vel post impetratam veniam etatis atque in competenti iudicio comprobatam ... huiusmodi arras susceperit. In simplum autem. id est tantummodo in id quod accepit si minoris etatis est. sive virgo sive vidua sit. sive per se sive per tutorem aut curatorem vel aliam personam easdem arras accepit. Pater vero vel mater legittime etatis constituti sive simul sive separatim arras pro filia susceperint. in duplum autem vel pater avus vel proavus ... pronepote vel pronepte in duplum tantummodo convenient teneri. Que ita custodiri censemus. sive pro sponsalibus vel ... aut aliam causam legibus vel ... constitutionibus ... futurum nuptiarum contrahere prohibetur: tamen quasi nullo facto ... ne cum easdem arras ... tantummodo reddi consequentes precipimus.

Imperator. Hisque quoque adicimus ut si legibus prohibite non sint future nuptie post arras autem sponsalitias sponsa coniugium sponsi propter turpem vel impudicam conversationem aut religionis vel secte diversitatem recusaverit vel eo quod coitum ex quo spes sobolis oritur facere non potuerit vel ob aliam iustam excusationem cum si quid ... probatum fuerit ...

n. Commoda. s. peculiaria tunc datur ... ad autem ... mo. ... cum in coniunctione ergo puelle non querit consilium tutoris. si ipsius puelle ... ut ... de nuptiis. l. in coniunctione. ac. ... ff. de ritu nupt. l. sciendum ... alie ... si puelle ... cum ... coniunctio ... ut i. de nupt. l. i. ac.
o. Femine. ... tutori vel curatori ... ac.
p. Multi ... et plenis annis ut nuptie non celebrentur.
q. Quod accepit. ... ergo ipso iure vel si minor ... restituitur. ac.
r. Per tutorem. quia qui per alium ... accursius. ac. ac.
s. ... curatorem ... ac.

a. Proximum. quia ... turpis ... vel ... ac.
u. Conditionem. ut quia filia senatoris ... vidua ... ut ff. de ritu nupt. l. lege. ac.
x. ... ac.
y. Constitutionibus. ut in tutoribus et curatoribus. ut ... ac.

z. ... ac.
b. Religionis. quia non ... ac.
c. Secte. quia paterius est. ac.
d. Facere. ... ac.
h. ... per ... duplo ... ut ... ac.

more flexibly, advocating fairness or equity as the context in which justice should be administered. Crucially, the study of law was linked to the *trivium*. The glossators treated every text, even the clauses within them, as equally valid and used dialectic to resolve apparent differences. Gradually, the main texts and principles, known as brocards, for each legal issue were consolidated so that litigants knew where to start. The systematic application of logic to law was an important moment in the history of European thought.

After a century of creative collaboration, the most famous of the jurists, Accursius (1182–1263), put together thousands of glosses (100,000 according to one estimate) made by his predecessors into the *Glossa Ordinaria sive Magistralis* (commonly translated as the *Great Gloss*). By sorting through the extraordinary breadth of earlier opinion, Accursius was able to spot inconsistencies and contradictions and he was not afraid to offer solutions to them. As a result the *Great Gloss* acted as a definitive source of Roman law and was honoured as such by his contemporaries. Accursius still lies within a grand tomb in the churchyard of San Francesco in Bologna.

The church had always used pieces of Roman law but these existed alongside a mixture of other sources: the Bible, opinions of the Church Fathers, decisions of church councils and papal decrees. In about 1150, as has been seen, Gratian brought order to the muddle in his *Decretum*. When there were gaps, Gratian accepted that civil law would fill them. The civil lawyers, now confident of the authority of their work, looked down at first on this separate branch of law, canon law, and the two systems developed side by side. However, with its enforcement in the ecclesiastical courts, canon law soon enjoyed parity of esteem. By the end of the thirteenth century, with the incorporation of papal decrees, it was as authoritative in its sphere as civil law. Civil law dealt with the common good of man on earth, canon law with sin and salvation. In many cases, family law, crimes such as perjury and murder, the two overlapped and many lawyers were qualified in both.

The discovery of Justinian's sixth-century law code was a vital moment. Here, *c.*1275, the original text is surrounded by a mass of glosses as it was reinterpreted by lawyers for the city-states of northern Italy.

By now a development of great importance had taken place in the city. There was a strong demand for those who could argue logically from the foundations of Roman law. In the absence of restrictions on travel within Europe (for those who could manage the now-disintegrated Roman road system), students interested in mastering law were attracted to the schools of Bologna. Individuals who were already in clerical orders could claim the protection of the church, but those who were not found themselves very vulnerable. In Bologna the vulnerability was intensified as the city council refused to give citizenship to outsiders. One reason for this was the fear that bright law students would stay and practise in the city and threaten the increasingly lucrative business of the established law teachers. Among other restrictions, students were held responsible for paying the debts of their fellows who had left the city. In retaliation, perhaps as early as the late eleventh century (the traditional founding date is 1088), the students had organized themselves into a distinct community, a *universitas*. (The latter term was used from the thirteenth century; in the twelfth century the term *studium generale* was used.)

Very little is known of how this pioneering community was formalized. The first definitive records come from 1155 when the four glossators met with Frederick Barbarossa and asked for his protection for the emerging institution. In his *Authentica habita* of 1158, an imperial decree on the model of those issued by Justinian, the emperor responded by recognizing the teaching body and the rights of 'travelling students' to seek protection from either ecclesiastical courts or their own teachers. The requirement to share debts also disappeared. With this legal protection in place the relationship between teacher and taught, each dependent on each other, developed fast, mainly in forbidding the teachers to leave the city to set up elsewhere. The 'travelling students' could not be controlled in this way and the city began granting them privileges to ensure they remained.

Once the concept of a university, with its students and teachers operating as a distinct legal institution, had been accepted it spread fast throughout Europe. This development is the subject of the next chapter; here we are more concerned with how law was used in the emerging communes of northern Italy. The word 'commune' is a general one, but it encompasses a wide variety of independent city governments.

The celebrated nineteenth-century French historian Ernest Renan (1823–92) suggested that Italy never experienced the Middle Ages at all. The fall of the Roman empire was followed by the rebirth of classical civilization in exactly the same places where it had fallen into decay. But this suggestion of continuity is too sweeping. The inland cities of northern Italy were, in the tenth century, shadows of what they had been in Roman times but there were spaces, often the city forum, and buildings, some as large as the amphitheatre in Verona, that survived as footprints of a proud past when they had the right to govern themselves within the Roman empire. Here were memories that could be revived.

With the ports of Venice, Pisa and Genoa gathering strength, wealth was beginning to seep inland and the population of the emerging cities on the fertile plains of the Po and Arno were busy formulating their political and legal identity.

Their economies were benefiting from the comparative ease with which staples, such as grain and salt, could travel across the plains but underpinning the new prosperity was the continuing growth in trade. Venice, Genoa and Pisa had become rivals for the most lucrative commodities in the Byzantine empire and, despite opposition from the church, the Arab states of the eastern Mediterranean. Another coastline, centring on Amalfi in southern Italy, is dotted with churches whose decoration echoes Islamic themes. The technology of ships developed so that by the second half of the twelfth century the seas could be crossed even in winter. But a more sophisticated way of financing these endeavours was required. In Genoa, a body known as the *compagna communis** emerged through which a particular project, the building of a crusader fleet, for instance, could be sustained over several years. The origins of *commenda*, a mechanism that allowed investors to gather the capital for a voyage, to appoint a captain with full discretion to take what opportunities he could, and to define a procedure for dividing the profits if he returned successfully, are obscure, although some scholars see similar practices among the Arab traders. Of course, many voyages ended in failure and the more canny investors are found spreading their bets across different enterprises. The principle of insurance became accepted and the first banks developed as institutions for creating credit for this commerce. Credit was vital not least because it implied that sufficient trust had been built up between lenders and borrowers. As the profits extended from the coast inland, they stimulated new industries. Florence, for instance, exploited its natural advantage on the River Arno, using it for access to the sea via Pisa and for its rushing waters to create a fabulously lucrative cloth industry with the raw materials being bought in from northern Europe, a new focus for trade. The fields around where I am writing in Suffolk, in eastern England, were once grazed by sheep whose wool was shipped off to Italy and the profits were ploughed back into the fine medieval churches that still stand in the towns and villages nearby.

At first the cities' political recovery was thwarted by the most powerful ruler within northern Italy, the formidable Matilda of Tuscany, who held vast territories in the region. Matilda had supported

* *Compagna* literally means 'those breaking bread together'.

the popes against the emperors in the Investiture Controversy but in 1111, towards the end of her life, she was reconciled with Emperor Henry V and appointed his vice-regent. When she died in 1115, she gave freedom to many of the cities that had been in her territories. This left the ruling bishops increasingly vulnerable and over the next decades more communes emerged.[14]

Records are still sparse. One of the most notable is a relief from the church dedicated to the fourth-century patron saint of Verona, St Zeno, in which a group of mounted knights and an assembled crowd on foot hold a banner with an inscription that implies that it is given to the people of the city by the bishop acting on behalf of Zeno. It is dated to *c.*1135 and there is a documentary mention of a commune government in Verona at the same time. A few years later an account survives from the German historian Otto of Freising, who accompanied his nephew Emperor Frederick I Barbarossa (so named for his red beard; he was the grandfather of Frederick II) to northern Italy in the 1140s. He was shocked by the breach in tradition that had, unlike anywhere else in Europe, led to magistrates being elected rather than chosen by local magnates or bishops. By his time Milan, Arezzo, Lucca, Bologna and Siena were among the Italian cities that had appointed them, often for a year at a time, and allowed the participation of assemblies, some of them consisting of *il popolo*, the citizen body as a whole. 'Practically the entire land is divided among the cities,' notes Otto disapprovingly and 'scarcely any noble or great man can be found in all the surrounding territory who does not acknowledge the authority of his city… they [the cities] are so desirous of liberty that they are governed by [elected] consuls rather than rulers.'[15] This was, for Otto, no less than a subversion of the traditional hierarchies whose authority derived from inheritance and obligations from a submissive peasantry.

The lawyers of these cities had needed to do some creative thinking. The Code of Justinian had accepted the absolute power of the emperor, and Frederick Barbarossa found lawyers who backed him on this. One Bologna lawyer, Azo (*c.*1150–1230), developed an alternative argument, namely that an emperor had no greater power than to state what is lawful. Ultimately, an emperor's authority, his *iurisdictio*, came from the people. This had long been accepted in principle but it had been argued that once given it could not be revoked. Azo and his fellow jurists drew on ancient traditions of 'natural law', a law that could be appreciated through reasoning or the practice of communities and nations. In Azo's formulation it included the right to property and the upholding of contracts and other pacts. Azo came to a conclusion 'momentous for political theory'[16] that the emperor did not have greater power than 'the people' as a whole to abrogate these rights. So, it followed, the magistrates of a city had the power to make their own laws.

By 1265 the appearance of Aristotle's *Politics* in a Latin translation reasserted, for the first time since antiquity, the ideal of the city-state, the highest state of being, whose primary aim was to achieve the common good.[17] *Politics* analysed a wide range of ways of managing a city, from dictatorship to democracy. Aristotle argued that it was natural to want to work together. His instinct was for some form of popular involvement in government so long as it was orientated towards men of virtue and he assessed the means by which this could be achieved. He was particularly concerned with ways of avoiding dictatorship, and this is why his work was so influential for those attempting to define the independence of a city or state. He was also realistic about the importance of accumulating wealth to sustain the city's activities and grandeur. If there was a surplus, he argued, it could always be given to the poor for the ethical reason that one had a duty to the community as a whole. This ideal fitted well with the collegiality that was developing in government, universities and guilds and supported Christian ideals of giving to the poor. Plato's *Republic*, in contrast, denigrated any kind of rule by the masses and restricted government to an elite who would impose an austere and ordered state on those considered less able to participate.

Yet, whatever the jurists of Bologna might say, ultimately authority depended on whoever had the force to impose it. Frederick Barbarossa invaded northern Italy five times in a desperate attempt to assert his sovereignty. On the fifth incursion the Lombard League of 1167–83 brought together most of the Italian cities into an alliance that defeated the imperial forces at the Battle of Legnano in 1176. At the Peace of Constance of 1183 the formal language of the treaty masked a humiliating climbdown by the emperor and the recognition of the freedom of the cities. It was a triumph for their emerging forms of government and many cities integrated the terms of the peace into their constitutions. In his *The Italian City-State*, Philip Jones sees this as the moment of transition from a city dominated by ecclesiastical buildings (as in Pisa) to one in which the *palazzo pubblico* takes prominence, an important development in the rise of secular government.[18]

The scattered sources add up to a composite picture of a typical commune. The magistrates, or 'consuls', were elected every year and there might be as many as twenty of them in the larger cities. They were concerned not only with managing the fabric and security of the city but the surrounding countryside, the *contado*. Control of food supplies was essential and many of the merchants came in fact from the local landed families. Popular assemblies play some part in major decisions, of peace and war, or changes in government. Such assemblies were already held to elect bishops so it was hardly an innovation to call the people together to make major political decisions. The problem was that as population grew in the larger towns, the assemblies became hard to manage and so there are records of smaller councils representing *il popolo* or a specific post of *capitano del popolo* being set up.

The duties of a consul can be seen from a surviving oath from Pisa of 1162 where a consul promises to dedicate himself to the prosperity of his city 'on land, on the sea, in all places, in peace and war'. He goes on to say he will respect the archbishop and his clergy and maintain their churches as well as the bridges (over the River Arno) and 'the new walls'.[19] The reference to walls highlights one of the most important architectural developments of the period – many resources were diverted to building the walls not only as a means of defence but to show off the pride of the city. All the larger cities, Bergamo, Bologna, Brescia, Cremona, Milan, channelled their resources into building walls. By the end of the thirteenth century Pisa was onto its second extended circuit, and Florence its third. At the same time the commune government would build its own *palazzo pubblico* and, as a sign of its distancing from the authority of the church, it would be distinct from the city's cathedral, often, as in the case of Venice, with its own 'communal' relics. A typical palazzo had an open portico under which merchants could meet, but as time passed palazzi became more imposing, with

accommodation for the magistrates, large council chambers, their walls decorated with the exploits of the city, and even the city prison (as in Siena). One of the most powerful symbols of the independent city is its *carroccio*, or war chariot, a cumbersome cart that carried the city's standard and was taken under close guard onto the battlefield. To lose one was a humiliation.

The rise of communal government meant that there had to be statutes to establish the duties of the consuls and people and to define who was or was not a citizen, and what was expected of them. So in 1157, the citizens of Genoa agreed under oath to attend the assemblies and fulfil military obligations as well as not to give any help to merchants who were not local to the city. The 'rules' were drawn up by the lawyers, the *jurisperiti*, who have remained a prominent feature of Italian life ever since. Typically, the *jurisperiti* had been trained in Bologna and so could draw on the enormous range of Roman and canon law that was now collected and taught there. 'Without the twelfth century florescence of legal studies in Bologna, city statutes would not have been the great achievement that they are', as one scholar puts it.[20] Chris Wickham's study of Pisa shows the lawyers emerging as the city managers, with no wealth or status other than their legal training.[21] By 1200 Roman law reigned supreme and older traditions of Germanic law had become obsolete. The statutes evolved as new challenges arose, the vital grain supplies had to be protected, prices controlled so that there was not disorder, roads kept clear for transport, borders defined and manned against invasion. When there was a dispute between cities, Justinian's *Digest* was acknowledged as the authority to be consulted. One can also see another aspect of *libertas* in the growing recognition of personal rights, security of life and property and of citizenship. Here again Roman law provided exemplars from which the glossators could develop appropriate laws.

The Palazzo Pubblico in Siena, a symbol of the growing confidence of commune governments in northern Italy in the thirteenth century.

Among those Pisans posted abroad to help maintain relationships with foreign markets was one Guiglielmo Bonacci, sent in the 1170s to the port of Bugia, in today's Algeria, to liaise with the Berbers. He took his son Leonardo, still then a child, with him. Known as Filius Bonnaci, 'the son of Bonacci', his name was corrupted to Fibonacci and it has stuck.[22] Fibonacci is still known for the sequence of numbers that bears his name, in which each number is the sum of the two preceding numbers. (Leonardo's calculation was based on the rate of growth of a hypothetical and idealized rabbit population from an original newly born pair.) The resulting numbers reappear in all kinds of natural situations, including the number of petals on flowers.

Fibonacci must have grown up mastering Arabic, as he describes conversations with Egyptian and Syrian merchants. He soon grasped their methods of doing business calculation that derived from the Hindu-Arabic numeral systems – using single figures for numbers one to nine but also incorporating a zero – was far superior to the Roman numerals used by the Italians. In 1202 he published a mammoth 600-page manuscript, the *Liber Abaci* (*Book of Calculation*). It was the first time that the system had been spelled out fully and aimed directly at Italian merchants. Everything from how to divide profits and measure land to dealing in currency exchange was covered with a myriad examples to show how each kind of calculation could be made.

No copies of the 1202 manuscript survive, but copies of the second edition of 1228 are still extant. Fibonacci also wrote another large volume on geometry. By this time, he was famous. He was once summoned to meet Emperor Frederick II at his court in Naples. (While lord of territories in Germany as well as Sicily and southern Italy, Frederick preferred to live in the south, where he had spent his childhood.) It is said that Frederick set Fibonacci three problems, which the mathematician proceeded to solve without difficulty. He wrote up the answers in his *Liber quadratorum* (*The Book of Squares*) of 1225, a work that has helped confirm him as the finest mathematician of the Middle Ages. As a copy of the full *Liber Abaci* would have been both prohibitively expensive and unwieldy to carry, it is assumed that it was made available in a more compact version that travelling merchants would actually have used. However, no copies of such an edition are known. Later writers certainly referred to Fibonacci as if he was the man who introduced arithmetic and algebra to Europe. He is especially important in reinforcing the place of logical thinking in everyday commercial life. He died in 1250.

It is easy to romanticize these crucial developments in the awakening of the western mind. Despite their shared resistance to the emperor in the Lombard League, the city-states of northern Italy frequently waged war with one another over territory or access to trade routes. A persistent struggle between Genoa, its wealth boosted by trade across the Alps, and Pisa ended only in 1284 when the Genoans destroyed the Pisan fleet at the Battle of Meloria, after which Pisa never recovered. While the resources absorbed by the struggle allowed Venice a free rein to expand its trade in the east, endless small-scale wars drained the smaller cities of their resources.

The cities also struggled to achieve internal stability. By the twelfth century there was intense competition among noble families as well as rivalries between the new classes of merchants, lawyers, artisans and 'the people' themselves.* The relationships between them were bound to be volatile as wealth and population grew. Guilds representing different industries and crafts agitated for separate representation. 'The people' called for the removal of all privileges based on birth and class. The church remained powerful. It collected tithes and other taxes, had developed its own courts to enforce canon law, and through its councils laid down the standards of Christian behaviour. It had retained authority through its championing the cities against the emperor at the time of the invasion of Frederick Barbarossa. Yet there were also supporters of the emperors who hoped for their protection, as the lawyers of Bologna had done. Rival factions emerged, the Guelphs for supporters of the church, the Ghibellines for the emperors.[23] How these complex relationships played out in one city, Florence, will be explored in Chapters 12 and 13.

An ingenious political solution in times of disruption was the appointment of a *podesta*. Typically, the *podesta* was an outsider to the city called in at times of unrest to take charge of justice and defence for a fixed period, often six months or a year. One was appointed in Genoa, a city notorious for its political instability, in 1190 'because of the envy of many men who excessively desire to possess the office of consul, many civil discords and odious conspiracies have greatly risen up in the city'.[24] The *podesta* would bring his own retinue, including judges, lawyers and troops, and would be given an official residence away from the traditional seats of government so that he could keep his distance from the rival factions. In Florence it was the fortress-like Bargello that was allocated to his use. Naturally, the *podesta* tended to come from the noble class and would often be picked for his military skills so that he could galvanize the defence of the city or lead an expedition against a neighbouring city if required.

The appointment of a *podesta* involved, of course, a reversal of the move towards a city government that ruled with the acquiescence of its citizens and it can be seen as an attempt by the noble class to use a surrogate to retain control. It marked a trend that was to become prominent in the northern Italian cities by the thirteenth century, to

* The symbol of aristocratic status was the tower, with each family trying to outdo its rivals in height. Many still remain in the small town of San Gimignano in Tuscany, which had grown rich from its position on the pilgrim route, the Via Francigena, from northern Europe to Rome.

have a single ruler or ruling family in charge of the city. These were the *signori*, or 'lords'. Sometimes a *podesta* would have his period of rule extended indefinitely and so power gradually consolidated in his hands. In contrast, the rule of an outsider with absolute powers might stimulate a leading citizen, perhaps a *capitano del popolo*, to use popular support to gain power and retain it for himself and the next generation of his family. The rise of the *signori*, who provided some of the most famous ruling families of the later Middle Ages, marks a new phase in city government and in many cities led to courts that became centres of learning and patronage. This did not mean, however, that the ideals of *libertas* were lost. The integration of Roman law, which had given rights to citizens in the empire, could not be reversed and so a popular consciousness, based on values outside those of Christendom, became embedded in urban life. The mastery of Latin opened up a vast world of resources from the surviving texts, notable among them Cicero's *De Officiis* on the obligations of citizens (see earlier p. 143 and accompanying endnote).

It would be wrong, of course, to assume that northern Italy was the only place where ideals of liberty were expressed. In Plantagenet England a constitutional conflict between the barons and King John resulted in the remarkable Magna Carta of 1215, which is still recognized today in English law as a fundamental statement of liberty from arbitrary rule. Its original Latin title, *Magna Carta Libertatum* ('The Great Charter of Liberties'), proclaims its purpose. The personal and political freedoms it listed applied not only to the barons but to all freeborn men and to cities, notably London. There were now to be limits on royal authority, extraordinary taxes were only to be raised with the approval of 'the general council of the kingdom' (the word *parliamentum* appears for the first time only in 1237), and the barons would be able to supervise the actions of the king. One of its most famous articles, Clause 39, stated that 'no free man shall be seized, or imprisoned, or dispossessed, or outlawed, or exiled or injured in any way... except

Aristotle's *Politics* was translated into Latin in 1264 and became enormously influential as a guide to republican politics. Ambrogio Lorenzetti's *The Effects of Good Government in the City* (1338–9) in the Palazzo Pubblico, Siena, celebrates the benefits of stability.

by the lawful judgement of his peers or by the law of the land'. Rights of the individual to inheritance and chattels were also protected.

Pope Innocent III was still alive at the time Magna Carta was promulgated. In 1213, to resolve a long-running dispute between crown and papacy, John had surrendered his kingdom in fief to the pope, and in exercise of his supreme authority and in support of John, Innocent moved to condemn the charter. 'The charter with all its undertakings and guarantees we declare to be null and void of all authority forever.'[25] It is a sign of the shifting relationship between church and state that his condemnation was ignored and John's son, Henry III, renewed Magna Carta's provisions. In 1235 the lawyer Henry de Bracton published his *De legibus e consuetudinibus Angliae* (*On the Laws and Customs of England*). Although Bracton relied heavily on the Roman law now being taught at Bologna, this was also a statement of English common law, the accepted conventions by which the country should be governed.* By now it was firmly accepted that the power of the king should be limited. 'As the vicar and servant of God, the king may do nothing on Earth except that what he is permitted to do by law... and which following the counsel of the magistrates has been deemed to be lawful and just,' as Bracton put it.[26] In 1264 an English parliament, consisting of barons, knights, the leading clergy and representatives of the cities, met for the first time and to this day parliament has acted as a counterpart to royal power (or, as it has become, the 'prerogative' now exercised by the British prime minister).

Much overlooked is the sister charter to Magna Carta, the *Carta de Foresta* (Charter of the Forest) of 1217.[27] At a time when royalty and the aristocracy were trying to close off access to forests and commons, this charter enshrined the right of the 'common man' to share in the resources of common land, to graze his animals there, and to gather wood and – specifically in one clause – honey in forests. While the term 'man' is freely used in the charter, many of the tasks covered would actually have been carried out by women and children, and their traditional rights would also be protected. The charter was well known in the seventeenth century and often cited alongside Magna Carta, but its importance was lost as forests became less prominent. However, its principles were taken up by Thomas Paine in his *Rights of Man* (1791) and were influential in declarations that human rights were available for all. Geraldine van Bueren, a contemporary scholar of human rights, has argued that the Charter of the Forest provides the basis on which

* Bracton's work survived as authoritative until the eighteenth century and was relied on by parliamentarians in the seventeenth century in their struggle against the crown.

shared rights of all to public resources are still accepted today within the United Kingdom and other jurisdictions.

The developments described in this chapter show that new forces in Europe were gradually eroding the church as an institution with supreme power. This was partly due, of course, to the failure of the popes to exert a consistent authority or to supervise a papal court that was free of corruption. This does not mean that people became any less Catholic. It was rather that Catholicism incorporated a healthy scepticism of any church authority. Within the cities vast amounts were still spent by lay patrons on constructing churches, as much for political advantage as for the saving of their souls, while lay confraternities of believers, many of them with charitable ambitions, became more widespread. The Dominicans and Franciscans, with their immediate contact with the people, became a feature of everyday life but increasingly governments, whether of nations or cities, wanted to run their own affairs and there was a growing reluctance to allow the church to intervene.

The sophisticated manner in which communal organizations, oligarchic communes, guilds, universities and confraternities developed in the city-states of northern Italy is one of the most significant aspects of the Middle Ages. Again and again the statutes of guilds and confraternities stress the obligation of their members to sustain each other, to offer 'fraternal assistance in necessity of whatever kind… hospitality towards strangers when passing through the town… comfort in the case of debility', as one guild statute from Verona puts it.[28] Those not meeting their commitments would be ostracized. While cultural narratives talk of the emergence of 'the individual', something that has proved impossible to pinpoint at any one moment in European history, collegiality was far more important in fostering and sustaining change. It deserves to be explored in one of its most enduring forms, the university.

Success and Failure within the Medieval University

Since, beyond enjoying the infinite benefits that the study of letters has bestowed upon you, your city is famous above all others because of her *studium* and her name is proclaimed throughout the whole world, you should not only stop punishing the scholars, but should, in fact, shower honours on them, being aware that they have singled out your city as their place of study, which was humble before but now surpasses nearly all the cities of the region because of the riches they have brought to her.

Pope Honorius III defends the rights of students at Bologna against 'the people' of the city in a papal bull of 1220[1]

A sophisticated system of education for the elite was vital if the church, courts or cities were to be effectively administered. There were good precedents from the Roman world. In the first century AD, the orator Quintilian had defined the steps through which a Roman boy would develop the art of memory, learn Homer (in the original Greek) and Virgil, progress through a range of other texts and finally study and practise the art of rhetoric. This would be the final stage for many, as it equipped the students for public life in politics or the law courts and it was as much an education in moral behaviour as the accumulation of skills. Quintilian was suspicious of pure philosophy. He accepted that his students had to think philosophically but, like many Romans, he thought the Greeks spent too much time arguing about minutiae and insoluble philosophical problems. Yet the best Greek minds were extraordinarily productive. They could pass from one school of philosophy to another and so engage in intellectual debates that would range across the disciplines, from science to literature.[2] A few outstanding minds could progress further, to carry out innovative work in one of the many subject areas that the Greeks had pioneered: mathematics, astronomy, history, geography, medicine, physics and philosophy. This wealth of learning, or what survived of it, was now returning to Europe via the Arab intellectuals who had translated and commented on the texts that had survived.

No one pretends that the medieval university matched the formidable achievements of the scholars of the classical world. As will be seen, its curriculum and teaching methods were too narrow for that. The same texts were taught century after century and the concept of intellectual progress was unrecognized, certainly until the sixteenth century. While the Greeks had argued within their own language, the medieval scholars had to rely on what were at first weak translations of the originals. The Greeks were orientated towards understanding the natural world and they could explore this freely without having to worry about offending any religious authority. The medieval university had to reconcile the curriculum with Christian doctrine. Although the *idea* of the university was to prove influential, as an institution the medieval university was conservative, more concerned with a ritualized accumulation of knowledge than the asking of probing questions. By the end of the fourteenth century, the universities were losing their cultural impact. After that, the most impressive breakthroughs in intellectual life tended to take place in other cultural and economic contexts. By the eighteenth century more universities were closing than opening. It is only in the nineteenth century, and then in Germany, that universities revived after long centuries of slumber to take the prominent part in intellectual life that they enjoy today.

As we saw in the last chapter, the law schools in the prosperous city of Bologna saw the advantage of setting up their own identity as a *universitas*. This does not mean, of course, that higher forms of learning did not exist in other contexts. The most famous after the eighth century were the Islamic schools, notably in Baghdad, Cairo and, in Spain, Cordoba. They all had their libraries, schools and observatories, a far greater array of resources than anything to be found in Europe, and it has been argued that the similarities between these colleges and the universities that were appearing in Europe were marked, in their methods of teaching (lectures and disputations), the status of teachers and the subordination of the liberal arts to theology, law and medicine.[3]

The texts studied in the Islamic schools were those of the Greek scientists and philosophers that they revered and preserved. Under the tolerant rule of the caliphs, often seen as the last great empire of the ancient world, Baghdad welcomed scholars from Syria and Persia. Between 750 and 900 they translated most of the known works of Aristotle into Arabic. Aristotle was particularly valuable because he looked at a question from all angles and emphasized that issues were up for discussion that could only be resolved through reason. This led to sophisticated debates on the relationships between philosophy and theology and an awareness of the key issues in ethics and the sciences. Ibn Sina, known in the west as Avicenna (980–1037) was an intellectual superstar.[4] Persian in origin but writing in Arabic, Avicenna benefited from the magnificent library of the sultan of Bokhara (in what is now Uzbekistan) and was, according to his own precocious assessment (shades of Abelard!), at home with all the main fields of learning by the age of twenty. His chosen expertise was as a physician and he compiled his comprehensive *Canon Medicinae* using a synthesis of writings from the sophisticated texts of the Greeks, those of Hippocrates, 'the father of medicine' (*c.*460–*c.*370 BC), Galen (*c.*AD 130–*c.*210), who combined logic and observation of patients to an exceptional degree, and Aristotle in his various works on biology. With typical bravado, Avicenna described medicine as 'not one of the difficult sciences'.[5] After the *Canon* reached the west in the twelfth century, it was seized upon as authoritative and remained influential for centuries to come. His *Metaphysics*, which arrived in the west at much the same time, was a massive commentary on the works of Aristotle that reinterpreted

them to present a coherent system of Avicenna's own making. In the words of the contemporary scholar Peter Adamson: 'Avicenna went out of his way to be innovative, deliberately overthrowing centuries of tradition to forge a new and distinctive philosophy.'[6] This was an essential step forward if the scattered and heterogeneous works of the great Greek philosopher were to be at all comprehensible, but Avicenna went beyond Aristotle in providing original arguments for the nature of the existence of God. This made his works relevant for some western theologians but infuriated others who felt that Aristotle's texts were too authoritative to be tampered with.

Aristotle's authority was further enhanced by Ibn Rushd, known in the west as Averroes (1126–98), from Cordoba, in Muslim Spain, where he practised as a judge.[7] He was also the court physician to the Almohad caliphate, but his real passion was philosophy. Like Abelard, he came

under pressure from conservative theologians for his insistence that theology and philosophy could be used equally as alternative and perhaps divergent approaches to finding the truth (what Averroes termed the 'double truth'). There was always the fear, and it would return in the Paris schools of theology, that philosophy, based on pagan Greek sources, would overthrow theological orthodoxy (whether Muslim, Jewish or Christian), but Averroes, like Abelard, did not believe that it should do so. He admired Avicenna but felt that he had been too radical in diverting from Aristotle's original works. These were the gold standard, 'the highest truth, since his spirit was the highest point of the human spirit – it is justly said that he was created and delivered to us by the providence of God, so that we may come

Boethius remained an influential figure throughout the Middle Ages, not least for his texts on music and arithmetic. Here Philosophy introduces the Seven Liberal Arts to the late Roman polymath in a French illuminated manuscript of *c.*1460.

to know everything that can be known'.[8] So Averroes downplayed the importance of religious statements and his admirers in the Christian west, the so-called 'Latin Averroists' (see pp. 199–200), would get into trouble for following him. He struggled on with his immense and detailed commentaries on Aristotle, providing both short summaries and extended discussion of each work he covered. While Averroes had little influence in his own society, his commentaries would, in due course, find their way to the west, where they had a major impact on those hungry for knowledge. It would be Averroes' commentaries, translated into Latin, that would be the sources used, albeit cautiously, by the most prominent Christian intellectuals of the thirteenth century, among them Albertus Magnus (Albert the Great) and Thomas Aquinas.

Another major thinker of the age was the Jewish theologian Moses Maimonides (1138–1204), president of the Jewish community in Cairo and author of the *Guide for the Perplexed*, a work that was much admired by Thomas Aquinas and later by the philosophers of the seventeenth century as they battled to comprehend the nature of God. Together, Arabs, Jews and Christians shared their intellectual interests through the expanding trade networks. In southern Italy there remained substantial Greek and Arab communities after the Normans had emerged as rulers in the twelfth century. The courts of King Roger II (r.1130–54) and his successor William I (r.1154–66) in Sicily welcomed all faiths. While the rich tradition of Greek theology had vanished from the Latin world, one still finds, in the magnificent cathedral at Cefalù in Sicily built by Roger, mosaics of the Latin theologians, Pope Gregory, Augustine and Ambrose, facing the Greeks, Basil of Caesarea, John Chrysostom and Gregory of Nazianzus, across the choir. The results of this cultural openness were fruitful. Sicilian poetry was well known to Dante, who even considered writing the *Divine Comedy* in Sicilian dialect.[9] Translations into Latin of Ptolemy's *Optics*, Aristotle's *Meteorology*, two of Plato's dialogues (the *Meno* and *Phaedo*, although in 'nearly unintelligible versions')[10] and, directly from the Greek, Ptolemy's *Almagest* ('The Greatest', from an Arabic corruption of the Greek), his extraordinary survey of astronomy, all came out of Sicily. And as has been seen, it was at the court of Roger II of Sicily that Ptolemy's *Geographike* was to be transformed into maps by the Arab cartographer al-Sharif al-Idrisi.

Ptolemy's *Almagest* was so wide-ranging in its use of mathematical arguments, for the breadth of its ideas and the comprehensiveness of its results that it became the dominant text in its field and the works of many earlier Greek astronomers were discarded. Challenging enough in the original, few would be able to grasp its breadth in translations (and there is little evidence that it was widely read) but its introduction contained significant philosophical statements. Ptolemy meditated on the precariousness of knowledge: theological truth can only be guesswork 'because of its completely invisible and ungraspable nature', a good discussion point, while physics is equally guesswork because 'of the unstable and unclear nature of the matter'. 'Only mathematics can provide sure and unshakeable knowledge, provided one approaches it rigorously.'[11] Ptolemy's emphasis on mathematics was to be displaced during the Middle Ages by Aristotle's focus on logic but by the seventeenth century it would triumph. Further afield the merchant colonies in Constantinople had access to surviving texts of Greek works that could be translated directly into Latin. This was another of the conduits through which Aristotle entered Europe.

After the Christian capture of Toledo in 1085, Arab, Jewish and Christian scholars mingled with each other there too. The most important 'western' translator from Arabic here was Gerard of Cremona, who translated Ptolemy's *Almagest*, this time from the Arabic (it appears that he did not know of the Sicilian translation). In mathematics, the leading figure of this period was Adelard, from the English city of Bath. Adelard travelled extensively in the Mediterranean Basin, through Islamic Spain and Sicily as far east as Syria and Palestine, and was fascinated by the mathematics and astronomical calculations collected by the Arabs. He was responsible for the first Latin translation of all fifteen books of Euclid's seminal *Elements* and for introducing Arabic numerals to the west. He put together his findings from Arabic scientific texts to produce his *Quaestiones Naturales* of *c.*1125. It was influential as an introductory text in the period before Aristotle's texts on the same issues became better known.

There were also important developments in the recovery of ancient medicine. One famous work, the *De Materia Medica* of the first-century AD Greek Dioscorides, had never been forgotten. A finely illustrated sixth-century manuscript of it still survives.* Dioscorides had researched some 600 plants and assessed the medicinal potential of each. It was to be centuries before his findings were to be challenged (see Chapter 19, pp. 442–6). The most prominent centre for the teaching of medicine was Salerno, in southern Italy, a school whose origin is unknown but may date back to the ninth century. There were still elements of Greek learning here, but the earliest reports suggest its teachers were men of practical medical skills depending as much on folklore as on science.[12]

* After extraordinary journeys around the Mediterranean over the centuries, it is now in the Imperial Library in Vienna.

Even so, the eleventh century produced influential translations of the Hippocratic texts and, most important of all for future learning, of the works of Galen, which had survived in large quantities. Galen was an agnostic but he had said enough about the possibility of a supreme God existing for him to be acceptable to Christians. Translations of his works brought back into western medicine the science of physiology and records of observations of the human body, as well as the doctrine of the four humours, which Aristotle had pioneered and Galen had adopted. This doctrine, which saw the lack of balance between the humours as the cause of illness, was to prove dominant for centuries to come. Blood-letting was among its more questionable practices.

The monks of Monte Cassino produced copies of medical works for the nearby school at Salerno, but by the beginning of the twelfth century Montpellier in southern France was emerging as the leading medieval centre for the study of medicine. After Avicenna's major work on medicine had been translated here, Montpellier won out over Salerno through having a more comprehensive textbook for its teachers and students. Medieval Salerno never became a university, while Montpellier was recognized as a *universitas*, a community of 'physicians, teachers and other disciples', in 1220.

Henry of Germany delivering a lecture at Bologna in 1360. The back rows do not seem to be paying much attention!

The term *universitas* could apply to a wide variety of 'communities', so in this case we are talking of a specific *universitas magistrorum et scholarium*, 'an institutional structure which was completely new, without any real precedent and with an exceptional historical destiny'.[13] It was within a *universitas* that the rediscovered learning could be integrated into western academic life as part of the curriculum for the qualification known as the *licentium docendi*.

There was no single route by which universities became established – a traditional view that they were the creation of the church does not fit their individual histories. They depended on an emerging class of students avid for knowledge and for a qualification that would allow them to serve in courts, communes or the church. This was the result of the proliferation of employment opportunities for the educated. The administration of royal courts was becoming more sophisticated. In England, for example, after 1300 the privileges of the nobility were only valid if they were recorded in writing and for this a legal training was required. For clerics a degree in theology or canon law was a stepping-stone to higher church posts. For aspiring lawyers and physicians possession of a degree ensured their entry into a knowledge-based

profession (although in medicine, physicians did not require a degree in order to practise).

This was also the age when hospitals began to appear in large towns. The apostle Bartholemew had become a patron of medicine after his supposed relics had been placed alongside an ancient medical centre in Rome. A hospital in his name was founded in London in 1133.* In Paris, a long-established foundation, the Hôtel-Dieu, served the same purpose. New religious orders sprang up to serve them: the Brothers of the Holy Ghost, founded in Montpellier for the care of the infirm by lay people, had eighty-four hospitals throughout Europe by 1200.

* It is still known affectionately as Barts and, at the time of writing, has just been given new life with a £1.1 billion refit.

An echo of student voices can be found in the *Carmina Burana*, one of the most fascinating manuscripts of the early thirteenth century.[14] It is largely a collection of love and drinking songs, some serious and touching, others more ribald and raunchy.* The classical and biblical allusions suggest an educated clientele who nevertheless knew how to enjoy themselves at the local taverns even if the hopes of lovemaking with beautiful women of the kind who appear in the songs must often have remained fantasies. Here are the experiences of the wandering students of the twelfth and thirteenth centuries, who were now prepared to travel in order to get the learning they needed. 'No wild landscapes, no steep crags nor valley gorges, no road filled with dangers or harassed by bandits' were enough to keep them from reaching the schools in Paris, as one twelfth-century source put it.[15] Most already had some form of clerical status and in Latin they had a universal language. They found that the centres of learning were those cities whose masters were most renowned and where there was easy access to new texts. It was also in those cities that accommodation could be found and so a mutual dependency between landlords and students became an important element of a city economy, as noted in my opening quotation.

In Bologna it was the students themselves who took the initiative in demanding high standards, even fining their teachers for poor performances or unpunctuality. While the documentary evidence is fragmentary, the earliest use (in 1215) of the word 'university' relating directly to Bologna describes, in fact, two 'universities', one representing Italian students and one of those from abroad (*ultramontanes*, 'from across the mountains [the Alps]'). The demands of foreign students in Bologna made to the emperor in 1158 (as described in the last chapter) is good evidence that a valued system of teaching had been in place in the city much earlier. A decree from the city of 1245 saw the students guaranteed equal rights with those of the citizen body. The formal statutes of the universities date from 1252 when it was confirmed that it was the students who made the contracts with their teachers and set out the curriculum in law that they wished to follow. In 1260 a third university teaching the seven arts and medicine was recognized in Bologna, independent of the law schools. While one could study canon law at Bologna, there was no school of theology until much later, in 1364.[16]

The example of Bologna shows there was no blueprint for creating a university. It involved a set of pragmatic responses in which students

* The German composer Carl Orff created a cantata based on the medieval songs in the 1930s.

(here the driving force) and teachers were eventually recognized as making up a 'community' with distinct rights. A formal process through which a qualification was awarded, usually the *licentium docendi*, was vital as this gave the graduating student the right to teach anywhere he chose. This became a standard feature of any university and, as most students had some form of clerical status, papal recognition of the right to award the *licentium* became essential.

In contrast to Bologna, Paris was a *universitas* where the masters took the initiative.[17] As seen in Chapter 5, the city had evolved its cathedral schools, the most prestigious of which was Notre Dame, where Abelard had taught and where Peter Lombard (of the *Sentences*) was later master. This was predominantly a school of theology but it competed for students with two other major cathedral schools in the city and all three also had courses in the liberal arts whose students made up the bulk of the academic community. As the teachers were supported by the cathedrals they were not as dependent on fees from students as those in Bologna, but they were worried by the attempts of the church authorities to control what they taught and threatened by the appearance of rival schools in a city that was becoming a magnet for aspiring students. Paradoxically, in view of the masters' hope of achieving independence, it was Pope Alexander III (r.1159–81), stung by the initiative of Frederick Barbarossa, his imperial rival in northern Italy, who spotted the potential for giving status and protection to the teachers of the three cathedral schools. In a series of decrees Alexander accepted the responsibility of the church to pay for the teachers but also gave them the power to award *licentia docendi*. Crucially, in 1200, the church extended its power by persuading the French king, Philip II Augustus, to agree that students could only be tried in ecclesiastical courts rather than those of the city authorities. While, as is the case also with Bologna, there are many gaps in the Paris record, by the early thirteenth century students and masters are referred to as a united community, truly a *universitas*.

The 'masters', established by statute as the university's authorities, included those who had finished their study of the seven arts and were about to embark on courses of theology (or less often in Paris law or medicine). Each of the three original schools kept its own identity, but the university was governed collectively by the masters and there was an agreed teaching syllabus and examination system for each level. This led to a lively institution as the masters of arts vastly outnumbered the masters of theology – in the late thirteenth century 120 teachers of the arts were listed as against fifteen masters of theology, a reminder that the structure and curriculum of a medieval university education was based on classical rather than Christian foundations. While traditional histories talk of the overwhelming influence of the church in the Middle Ages, it is important to recognize that students gathered their knowledge largely from classical texts.

The chancellor was the senior official of the school of Notre Dame and he had held the right to award the *licentia docendi*. He now had to share the privilege with the other masters and here was a source of tension. There were further problems in asserting the independence of the university. The popes were worried by the growth of law as a secular subject that would rival theology and in 1219 Pope Honorius III, despite upholding and extending the privileges of the university, forbade the teaching of civil law. Another threat was the arrival of texts of Aristotle. His *Metaphysics* and *Physics* were banned in 1205, although the ban appears to have been ignored and by the 1250s all of his works formed part of the curriculum. The popes found themselves opposed by the local bishops of Paris, who saw it as their responsibility to control heretical teaching. In 1215 a legate sent by Innocent III (who had studied theology at Paris as a young man) elbowed aside the bishop by granting new statutes to the university. A papal bull of 1231 issued by Pope Gregory IX extended the privileges of the university while proclaiming that the pope was confident it would be 'the home of truth'. Despite its beginnings, the popes had hopes of adopting the University of Paris as their own. Pope Alexander IV (r.1254–61), for instance, championed the university as the best means of spreading the faith. 'Misshapen in the congenital blindness of its ignorance, humanity regains its vision and beauty in Paris, through the acknowledging of the true light that radiates from the theology there.'[18]

The background to another early university, Oxford, is even more obscure than Paris or Bologna.[19] The city had no known cathedral school and was not even a bishopric. There were other English schools, in Winchester, Hereford and London, that appear more popular and in the early twelfth century many English students were choosing to study in Paris. Yet in the early twelfth century there are records of a master in theology (Theobald of Étampes) in Oxford with as many as a hundred students under his care. An important development came in the 1160s during the conflict between King Henry II and his archbishop Thomas Becket. Becket had left for France with many clergy and Henry feared he would attract others; he ordered all English students to come home. By the end of the century Oxford seems to have been full of them, and there were also students coming from overseas. There is no record, however, of the Oxford masters being able to award degrees.

Oxford had no single specialism and there were schools of law, theology and medicine. The university seems to have been well established by 1209, but after a fracas between the town and the emerging university that led to the hanging of two students, the university was temporarily closed and many students left for another nascent centre of learning, Cambridge, which survived when Oxford reopened in 1214. Oxford was within the diocese of Lincoln and the bishop delegated any powers he might have had over the award of degrees or jurisdiction over students to a chancellor, elected by the masters from one of their own. Like Oxford, Cambridge did not have a bishop and so its institutions could evolve independently of the church supervision. This left the way open for initiatives from King Henry III. A royal charter of 1231 awarded Cambridge the privilege of enforcing its own discipline and in 1233 the pope recognized the right of Cambridge graduates to teach anywhere in Christendom. Oxford also received a royal charter from Henry but not until 1248, and it never received papal approval of the right of its graduates to teach elsewhere.

By 1215 the concept of an academic community was accepted but universities were not easy to establish, even with outside protection from the pope, king or emperor. There are several instances of students breaking away from Bologna to set up new universities elsewhere, but only one of these was successful – the University of Padua, which was founded in 1222 by 1,000 departing Bolognese students. Padua has a particular importance in the history of universities as it was incorporated into Venetian territory (it was named officially as the University of Venice in 1407) and so benefited from the more secular culture of that city. As a result, after the Reformation Protestant students – among them the Englishman William Harvey, who was the first physician to systematically describe the circulation of the blood – were able to study there.

In contrast to the student-inspired universities of northern Italy, the earliest state university was set up by Frederick II, the grandson of Frederick Barbarossa, in Naples in 1224. When he had arrived in his kingdom Frederick had faced strong opposition from the local barons and he was determined to impose his own centralized rule (as he did in 1231 through the Constitutions of Melfi – or *Liber Augustalis* – which introduced many aspects of Roman law). For this he needed trained bureaucrats and so the university emerged primarily as a school of law. Its autonomy was limited. Frederick forbade his subjects to study elsewhere (Bologna was the obvious rival) and those students already abroad had to return home. Medicine continued to be taught at nearby Salerno, but the school there was in decline and a separate college of medicine was recognized in Naples by the early fifteenth century. Frederick insisted that physicians followed a practical course in medicine before they could treat patients. It was another royal initiative that established the first university in Spain, at Salamanca, a twelfth-century cathedral school that was recognized as a university by King Alfonso X of Castile in 1254, with the pope of the day endorsing the foundation a year later.* The process of a city or a ruler founding a university, whose status as such was then confirmed by the pope, became especially common in the fourteenth century.

Looking ahead through the thirteenth century, there was a gradual rise in the number of students coming to the universities, but one must not overestimate their spread. There were only twelve functioning universities in Europe by 1300 and although many more were founded in the fourteenth and fifteenth centuries (there were thirty by 1400 and thirty-four more founded in the fifteenth century), most of these attracted only a local clientele and mediocre teachers. Only Paris, Bologna and Oxford maintained their prestige on a European level. With Paris and Oxford, one of the most fruitful and enduring developments of the thirteenth century was the rise of colleges – the word here used of a body of colleagues rather than a set of buildings. In Paris, in 1255, one Robert de Sorbon founded a house for theologians in the Latin Quarter of the city (that is, the area of Paris where the Latin of the students had become dominant). He was given two more houses by the king and in 1270 a set of statutes established the Sorbonne as a collegiate body, although restricted to those teaching or studying theology. Then it acquired its own prior, who would help scholars with their studies. Next a library and an *aula*, a teaching hall, appeared. The success of the Sorbonne rested on it not being a monastery: no vows had to be taken and fellows could come and go as long as their personal lives, academic studies and relationships with their colleagues were in good order.

Oxford followed suit. The first 'colleges' were small religious foundations that housed poorer students, but after 1250 the advantages of a separate institution with its own fellows, library and lodgings became increasingly attractive. At a time when student numbers were growing and many newcomers would have been without roots or contacts, they provided a home. So in Oxford we find University College founded

* There is a claim that the true date of foundation of Salamanca is earlier, in 1217.

in 1249, Balliol (1263), Merton College (1264), and then in Cambridge the first college, Peterhouse (1284). By the fourteenth century colleges in these two universities had become much more substantial, with kings or prominent ecclesiastics their founders. Oxford and Cambridge successfully resisted the foundation of any other English university, even in London, until the nineteenth century.

The universities were remarkably consistent in the way they organized their studies. This had the advantage that students could move from one to another and find similar courses, but the disadvantage that innovation in the curriculum was discouraged. Students would start young, they would often only be fifteen or sixteen when they began six (Paris) or seven (Oxford) years' study of the seven liberal arts. The only entry requirement was enough understanding of Latin to follow the courses (this would have required at least six years of pre-university education) but they would also have to be able to support themselves. A first examination, giving the status of *baccalaureus*, came after four years when the candidate had to provide a certificate of good attendance and be subjected to an oral examination. If successful, he was now able to teach the earlier part of the course before completing another examination two years on to give him the status of 'master' and the right to teach the arts anywhere. These two years of preliminary teaching were a valuable part of the process.

As noted in the chapter on Abelard, in the early part of the twelfth century the *trivium*, the teaching of grammar, rhetoric and logic, was more important than the *quadrivium*, arithmetic, geometry, astronomy and music, which suffered from the lack of texts. Yet the emphasis within the three *trivium* subjects varied from university to university. In Paris, logic predominated and was subservient to theology; in the universities, such as Bologna, where law was supreme, rhetoric was favoured as a subject that had practical use for fledgling lawyers. Even then it lacked the status and prestige of mastering civil or canon law.

The different emphases between universities highlight one of the weaknesses of the system, namely that the seven liberal arts did not have any coherence one with the other. They were not underpinned by any overriding logical or philosophical theory of knowledge. Even in the classical world this had been recognized as a problem, but the seven arts had achieved a sacred status and were resistant to being reformed. As will be seen in the next chapter, this was one reason why the works of Aristotle would be seized upon as filling the void. His works on logic and those by Boethius continued to be the main text for that part of the course but Aristotle's *Posterior Analytics*, first known in Latin in the 1220s, brought more depth to the subject by bringing in a theory of scientific demonstration. In grammar, two classical works, one by Donatus, the other by Priscian, *c.*500, who had been based in Constantinople and therefore had a wider range of sources to draw on, remained the basic texts for centuries.

The new texts were more relevant to the *quadrivium*, although sources seldom tell us what exactly was being taught. The sixth-century Boethius was still vital for music (*De institutione musica*) and arithmetic (his *Arithmetica*, supplemented by Euclid's *Elements*). The Englishman John Holywood, better known as John of Sacrobosco, who was active at the University of Paris in the first half of the thirteenth century, drew on Arabic texts for his *Algorismus*. This influential work introduced vulgar fractions, the system of Hindu-Arabic numerals and some mathematical backing for astronomy. In geometry Euclid's *Elements* was a crucial text, but it was within this discipline that a genuinely new subject, optics, was developed by scholars such as Robert Grosseteste and Roger Bacon in Oxford in the thirteenth century (see Chapter 9, p. 223). Mathematics played virtually no part in the curriculum. In his wide-ranging study *The First Universities*, Olaf Pedersen notes how the revised Paris syllabus of 1366 required no more than attendance of a total of 100 hours in lectures on mathematics and astronomy over six years. Surviving commentaries suggest that many students struggled with the basic rules of multiplications and long division.[20]

A page from an edition of Ptolemy's famous *Almagest* (1490), showing some of his star locations.

Astronomy had been an obsession with the Greeks, with extraordinary results, such as the recognition by Hipparchus (*c.*190–*c.*120 BC) of the precession of the equinoxes or the highly sophisticated star charts of Ptolemy (with 1,022 stars). Ptolemy's *Almagest* in translation was well beyond the grasp of the typical student, who had to make do with a watered-down version of Ptolemy in the anonymous text *Theorica planetarium*. This gave no more than a competent introduction to this scientific genius. A fundamental and unresolved problem was the clash between an Aristotelian perception of the cosmos made up of a number of concentric spheres fitting neatly together (so that there was no void between them) and Ptolemy's observations of planets moving in epicycles. (This contrast and the resolution to it will be explored further in Chapter 29.)

Sacrobosco's *De sphaera mundi* (*On the Sphere of the World*) continued to be taught as the standard introduction to astronomy for centuries. Galileo was still using it (although in a much expanded version by

							longitudo S	g	m	latitudo g	m	partes celi	magnitudo	complexiones
Que est sub concavitate pedis dextri	1	1	34	2	23	0	3	12	5	55	10	me	4	
Que est super extremitatem pedis sinistri	0	18	44	2	9	40	3	28	45	53	45	me	3	
Que est super extremitatem caude	0	10	44	2	2	10	2	21	15	50	40	me	3	

Earum 18 stellarum in magnitudine prima est una
in .3. 5 in quarta 5 in 5 septem

Que sunt circa canem et non sunt in forma					g		S	g	m	g	m			
Que est parte septentrionis a vertice capitis canis	0	28	4	2	19	30	3	8	35	38	15	me	4	
Longior. E que sunt quasi essent super lineam rectam sub duabus	0	18	34	2	10	0	2	29	5	61	30		4	
Que est declinior ad septentrionem pedibus	0	19	54	2	11	20	3	0	25	58	45		4	
Que est declinior harum ad austrionem	0	21	34	2	13	0	3	2	5	57	0		4	
Reliqua. E et est longior ea ad austrionem	0	22	44	2	14	10	3	3	45	55	30		4	
...ius trium que sunt super lineam rectam eo quod sequitur occidente	0	6	34	1	28	0	2	17	5	55	30	me	4	
Media earum a. e.	0	8	54	2	0	20	2	19	25	57	40		4	
Sequens trium	0	10	54	2	2	20	2	21	25	59	30		4	
Sequens .2. lucidarum que sunt sub istis tribus	0	7	34	1	29	0	2	18	5	59	30		2	
Antecedens earum	0	4	34	1	26	0	2	15	5	57	40		2	
Reliqua et est declivior ad meridiem ea que est ante ipsam	0	0	44	1	22	10	2	11	15	59	20	me	4	

Earum .11. stellarum in magnitudine .2. sunt .2. in .4. 9

Stellatio Anticanis et est ex ithere algomeisa
Alstenne ptolemeus

							S	g	m	g	m			
Que est in collario	1	4	4	2	24	30	3	14	35	14	0	me	4	
Lucidior stellis posterior et dicitur pechion Procyon et est algomeysa	1	7	44	4	29	10	3	19	15	16	10	me	1	

Earum .2. stellarum in magnitudine prima est .1. et in .4. .1.

Stellatio puppis et dicitur argo

					g		S	g	m	g	m			
Australis duarum que sunt super extremitatem	1	18	54	3	10	20	3	29	25	42	30	me	5	
Sequens earum	1	22	54	3	14	20	4	3	25	43	20		3	
Declinior .2. communicantium que sunt super scutum	1	17	24	3	8	50	3	27	55	45	0	me	4	
Declinior earum ad meridiem	1	17	14	3	8	40	3	28	45	46	0		4	
Antecedens illas duas	1	13	54	3	5	20	3	24	25	45	30	me	4	

Complementum puppis

					g									
Lucida que est in medio scuti	1	14	54	3	6	20	3	25	25	41	15	me	4	
Antecedens trium que sunt sub scuto	1	13	54	3	5	20	3	24	25	49	30		4	
Sequens earum	1	17	54	3	9	20	3	28	25	49	30		4	
Media earum	1	17	4	3	8	30	3	28	35	49	15		4	
Que est in extremo canthel	1	22	34	3	14	0	4	3	5	49	40	me	4	
Septentrionalis .2. que sunt in gubernaculo canthel	1	12	34	3	4	0	3	23	5	53	0		4	
Declinior earum ad meridiem	1	12	34	3	4	0	3	23	5	58	40		3	
Septentrionalis .2. que sunt in rostro canthel	1	18	44	3	10	10	3	29	15	55	30		5	
Antecedens trium sequentium illam	1	20	44	3	12	10	4	1	15	58	40		5	
Media earum	1	21	14	3	13	40	4	2	45	57	15	me	4	

Christoph Clavius, 1571) when he taught at the University of Padua some 450 years later, and the final edition appeared as late as 1633. Even though it drew on Ptolemy's *Almagest*, *De sphaera* is considered a dull and unsophisticated work and it is not clear how it achieved the elevated and enduring status that it was given. The text said little about what was perhaps the most important subject in astronomy, planetary motions. In short, it was 'hopelessly inadequate', in one recent scholarly assessment.[21] In editions from before 1500, *De sphaera* perpetuated Aristotle's claim that the waters occupied a different sphere from the Earth and that the only way the land ('earth') could be revealed was by holding back the seas. Ships were therefore believed to travel uphill when they left land.*[22] Generally, astronomy was stagnant, certainly in terms of observation of the stars. As the German mathematician and astronomer Johannes Müller, better known as Regiomontanus, put it in 1463: 'I cannot but wonder at the indolence of the typical astronomers of our age who, just like credulous women, receive as something divine and immutable whatever they come across in books.'[23]

Astronomy was also linked to astrology. Since it was believed that the heavens influenced the progression of disease, the movements of the stars had to be understood by those going on to study medicine. Chaucer's physician in *The Canterbury Tales* was 'grounded in astronomy'. The medical faculty at the University of Paris attributed the outbreak of the Black Death to a malign conjunction of the planets Saturn, Jupiter and Mars, at 1 p.m. on 20 March 1345. Since it was evident that the moon influenced the tides, as the varying heat of the sun did the seasons, it was understandable that scholars wished to go further and to link specific conjunctions of stars or the appearances of comets to world events. Here was a challenge for theologians. If the star over Bethlehem or the sign of the cross above Constantine as he prepared to do battle with his rival Maxentius outside Rome were to be taken as portents, then what other planetary movements might be messages from God? Yet astrology might suggest that the fate of human beings was influenced by the movements of the stars rather than by God. The ever-influential Augustine had condemned astrological predictions for this very reason, as had Isidore of Seville in his *Etymologies*. As a result the promotion of astrology could result in a condemnation for heresy – as appears to have happened to the English scholar Roger Bacon (see p. 226).

* The term 'high seas' remains as a reflection of this. The two-spheres theory was incompatible with belief in the rotation of the Earth, as so long as the spheres remained distinct the Earth sphere would have had to move under the water sphere.

What was lacking in medieval astronomy was any practical approach in the sense of requiring individual observations of the changing stars and a method of recording them. While the Arabic astronomers had had their own observatories, the earliest purpose-built observatory in Christendom was that of Tycho Brahe on the then-Danish island of Hven in 1580. (By that date universities had been largely bypassed as centres of new learning; technical progress in applying astronomical instruments was driven by seafarers rather than university academics.) Astronomers relied very heavily on Arabic tables of observations (and the later thirteenth-century Alfonsine Tables, named after Alfonso X of Castile), which had to be adapted for use in western Europe. In effect the subject was stagnant until shaken up by the remarkable *De Revolutionibus* of Copernicus in 1543 and the more accurate observations of Tycho Brahe (see pp. 653–9).

The limited and derivative texts were not given their best chance by the method of teaching, known as scholasticism. Teaching of the arts began with lectures based on the set textbooks, and surviving accounts suggest that many teachers clung rigidly to these. Some of the lectures of Thomas Aquinas survive. In one the designated hour is taken up with a consideration of Aristotle's text on the composition of the heavens, some 500 words, to which Aquinas added 2,900 words of commentary. One twelfth-century scholar, Hugh of St Victor, commented sarcastically on what was possible. 'The first word [of a text] has hardly been dealt with after three lectures. This is not teaching: it is a demonstration of ostentatious learning.'[24] Some lecturers spoke fast and there was not time to take notes; others seem to have done little more than give dictation, a dull approach but useful when manuscripts were so expensive. Other teachers chose to question the text, opening up the minds of students to other possible ways of interpreting issues and becoming aware of unanswered problems. While this meant that mastery of the texts themselves was limited, it did suggest that learning could progress beyond the mere assimilation of texts. The 'ordinary' lectures were the core of the curriculum but there were other courses, such as the 'cursory' lectures that were given by the less experienced teachers that could range more freely over topics not dealt with in set texts.

Every week the students also had to attend disputations. As we saw in the chapter on Abelard, the use of dialectic was integral to the *trivium* courses on logic so it was not unfamiliar for students. The teacher would set a topic (in one case, recorded from the Sorbonne in 1344, the topics were advertised for the year ahead) and appoint one student, who normally had completed the first four years of his course, to argue for it and one to argue against. Once the arguments were exhausted, the teacher would then intervene to give his own responses to the arguments for and against and formulate a solution. The reports on these disputations could be published by the teacher. Thomas Aquinas, for instance, published three collections of the disputations over which he presided.

This approach could suggest that there was always a right answer, already fixed in the mind of the teacher. In his authoritative *The Classical Heritage and its Beneficiaries*, R. R. Bolgar expressed his cynicism. He notes how 'objections' were raised against a thesis: 'These objections mostly consisted of an unassailable major followed by a misleading minor premise whose implications had then to be separated out or distinguished, the incorrect rejected and the correct shown to be in harmony with accepted doctrine.' This made scholastic theology 'practically unanswerable by the methods open to Aristotelian logic... By the thirteenth century the new logic was no longer a danger.'[25] So effective debate was neutralized. 'Reasoning', such as it was within this system, did not have any lasting impact on the creation of knowledge. Equally frustrating was the elaboration of a scholastic language that became so intricate and formal, 'impersonal in style, specialized and limited in vocabulary, abounding in abstract formulae, and somewhat rigid in the structure of its argumentation', that it obstructed any innovatory approaches.[26]

Furthermore, Latin in itself was not an ideal medium for representing the subtleties of the original Greek. As even Cicero, a man whose Greek was excellent from his own study in Greece, had found in the first century BC, translating texts from works that, if in Greek, were much more sophisticated than anything existing in the Latin world was challenging and Cicero had to coin new terms to convey his meaning. Few medieval translators were so scholarly. Even such a learned man as John of Salisbury, who was trying to translate the works of Pseudo-Dionysius from the Greek original, noted that 'in Greek one finds certain compounds by which things are designated elegantly and to the point. Latin must inelegantly, ineptly, and occasionally quite inadequately paraphrase the one word with two or more expressions.'*[27] In their authoritative survey of how classical texts were transmitted to the west, L. D. Reynolds and N. G. Wilson note how 'as a rule medi-

* Pseudo-Dionysius was a text dating from *c.*500 AD which was believed to be an original text by Dionysius, the disciple of the apostle Paul. The original attribution, which was not challenged until the fifteenth century, gave it enormous authority in the early Middle Ages. Pseudo-Dionysius is a profoundly mystical work, important for its formulation of 'negative theology', an understanding of God in terms of what he is not.

eval translations were made word for word, and quite often the translator was out of his depth when dealing with technicalities or the finer points of idiom'.[28] One wonders how many students really grasped the meaning of what they were reading from what were originally quite sophisticated texts.

Accommodating translations from the Greek and Arabic into the framework of the classical arts curriculum without offending Christian doctrine meant the creation of a mass of abstract neologisms. So one could take the Latin verb *existere*, which originally meant 'to stand out' or 'emerge', and use it as the base for translating a variety of Greek words for 'being' or 'becoming'. Derivative forms followed as philosophical thought developed during the medieval period and more sophisticated definitions were required, so that we find *existentia*, *existentialis* and *existentialitas*. Inevitably, this meant that there was a growing divergence between scholastic Latin and the purer forms found in the classical authors.[29]

A more imaginative approach to learning was through the *quaestiones quodlibetales*, debates that took place during Advent and Lent. Here a student could ask the organizer any question he wanted and after a period of preparation the debate was booked to fill a whole day. This meant that all kinds of issues could be raised, many of them nothing to do with the academic curriculum, and discussed in full. They ranged from the serious to the light-hearted. So we find such questions as whether a bishop who had been raised from the dead (as was not unrecorded in a world of daily miracles) would be able to return to his office or whether a child born with two heads needed to be baptized once or twice. It is from these debates that some absurd examples have been taken to ridicule – unfairly – the medieval university as a whole. Thomas Aquinas, the finest mind of his age, was asked by his students to grapple with the problem of whether it was better for a crusader to die on his outward journey to the Holy Land rather than on his return.

The same methods were used for the more advanced courses after the appropriate examinations had been completed for the master of arts. These courses were only for a dedicated elite. The doctorate in medicine required another five or six years' study, law seven or eight years beyond the arts course and theology at least eight more years. So a lawyer starting with the liberal arts class at fifteen might finish at twenty-two and then only receive his doctorate in law at thirty. In the gravediggers' scene in Shakespeare's *Hamlet*, it appears that Hamlet, studying (presumably law rather than theology or medicine) at Wittenberg, must indeed be thirty (although many literary commentators dispute this), leading to speculation as to how those long years of study must have affected his character. Obviously, only those with wealth to back them, like a Danish prince, could spend such a long time studying.* Yet the rewards were great. A quarter of the masters in theology in Paris in the thirteenth century went on to become bishops or cardinals.

It was the failure to develop any system by which new ideas could be integrated that made university learning relatively limited. Texts tended to develop their own authority that became embedded in the curriculum. Traditionally, theology had been taught as a series of questions on biblical texts but, as has been seen, Abelard established more searching methods of exploring the issues in his *Sic et Non* and his *Theologia*. His systematic approach to ordering the key concepts was followed up by another master of the cathedral school of Notre Dame, Peter Lombard. Lombard's *Sentences* now became the textbook for the theological schools after it had been given official recognition as such at the Fourth Lateran Council (1215). In his prologue to the *Sentences* Peter describes it 'folding up in a brief volume the statements of the Fathers, together with the testimonies to them, so that the seeker should not need to open numbers of books, this abridged collection offers him what he was seeking without effort'. In short, this was a typical textbook, competent, thorough and unimaginative, and apparently designed to excuse further study. It was safe to use it alongside the Bible. In fact it was claimed, by the chancellor of the University of Paris, Jean Gerson, in the early fifteenth century, that the *Sentences* had superseded the Bible.[30] It also reinforced the dominance of Augustine in Latin theology. The *Sentences* included 1,000 texts from Augustine, making up four-fifths of the whole work.[31] Augustine was also represented in the teaching of the seven arts, by his manual *De doctrina christiana*, which laid down that secular knowledge was relevant only in so far as it informed a more profound understanding of the scriptures.

In medicine, Dioscorides' *Materia Medica* and Avicenna's *Canon* were important, along with shorter selections of Galen and the Hippocratic writings. As Galen's huge corpus (some of it not translated even today) began to appear, his influence increased. One authority on medieval medicine, Nancy Siraisi, notes that 'what was conveyed to students was usually a Galenism that was at once simplified in the sense

* One reason for clerical absenteeism was that a scholar would be given a living that would support him while he was away studying at university.

that it was shorn of Galen's polemical context, breadth of knowledge of ancient medicine and attention to anatomical and clinical detail'.[32] For the first time, however, with the work of de Liuzzi, there was a return to dissection of the human body, last heard of in Alexandria about AD 200. De Luizzi's first dissection, of an executed female criminal, took place in Bologna in 1315 and it was followed by publication of his *Anathomia corporis humani* (*The Anatomy of the Human Body*) in 1316. This became a standard text, set within the curriculum for the next 200 years and unfortunately considered so authoritative that deviations from it were unacceptable. Galen had posited a mass of blood vessels around the brain. Some animals did have such a mass but not humans. Even though they had never been there Liuzzi felt impelled to include them, such was the authority of Galen. It was not until 1502 that Berengario, a lecturer in surgery at Bologna, noted, in lectures on Liuzzi's *Anathomia*, that they did not exist. So only in a limited way can one talk here of the rebirth of medical science, let alone any advance. The figures alone for completed degrees are instructive. Between 1400 and 1415, Bologna, one of the main centres for medicine, awarded sixty-six doctorates marking the completion of the course, only one of them in surgery; Turin awarded only thirteen in thirty-six years. One estimate is that only one in ten students completed the course.[33] A physician with a degree might enjoy greater prestige, but there is no evidence that he would be a better doctor than his colleagues without one. In 1527 the physician and alchemist Paracelsus was to make the point by publicly burning the *Canon* of Avicenna, by now a key text in the university curriculum, and telling medical students to leave 'that bare knowledge which their schools teach' and learn instead 'off old women, Egyptians and such-like persons, for they have greater experience in such things than all the Academicians'.[34]

In law there was little chance to study outside Roman law, for which Justinian's law code remained the basic text, as did Gratian's *Decretum* for canon law. Yet in the middle of the fourteenth century, conservative Bologna was surpassed by the University of Perugia (founded in 1308). This was largely due to one man, Bartolus da Sassoferrato (1313–57), whose commentary on the *Codex* of Justinian was so thorough that it was accepted by many legal systems as authoritative for any legal issues not covered by the original text or by Accursius' glosses on it. It was the urgency with which conflicts between the city-states of northern Italy needed to be resolved that gave Bartolus his prestige. They had varied law codes and traditions, some of which depended largely on customary law stretching back over centuries. There are some 400

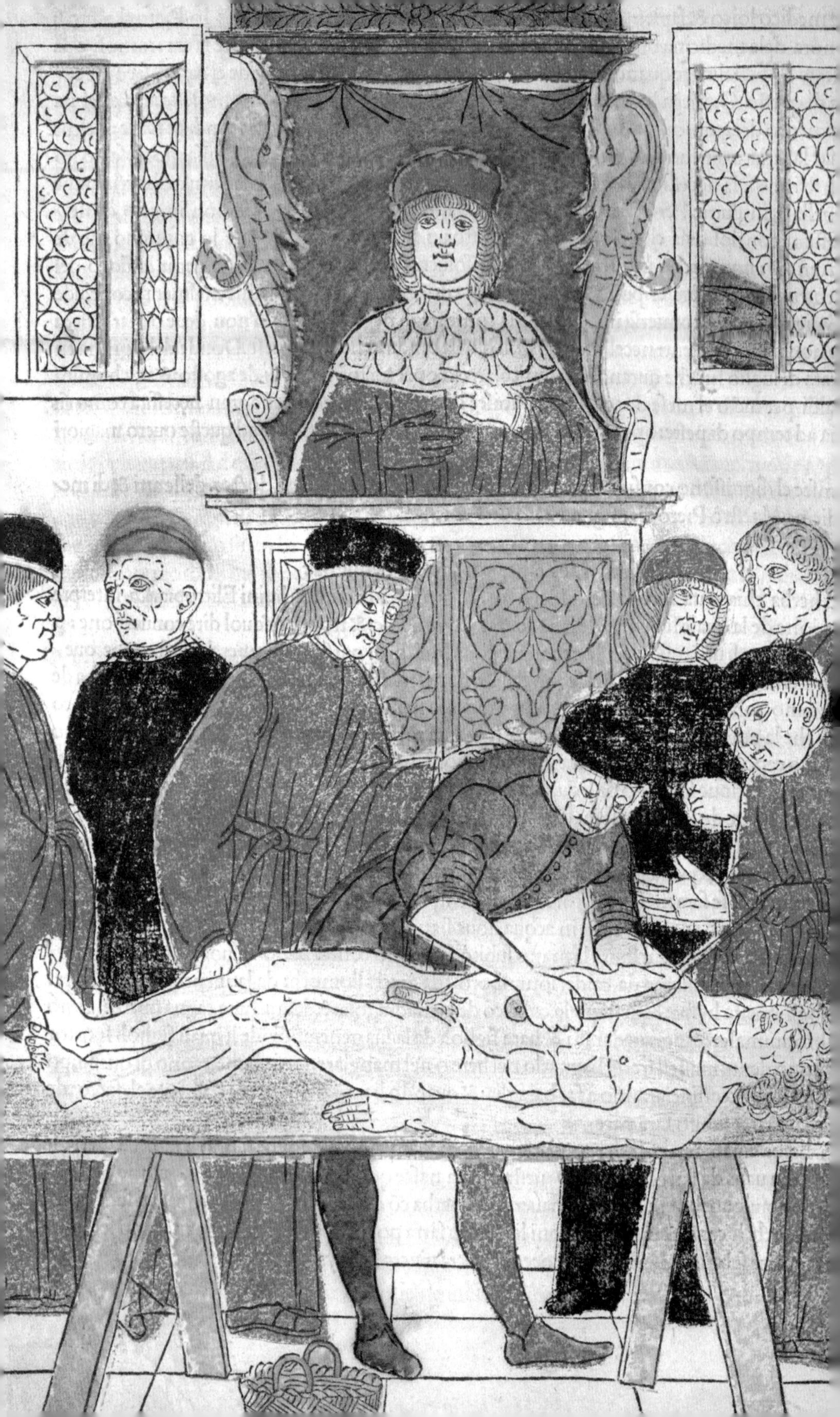

surviving *consilia*, legal opinions given by Bartolus to judges who had asked for guidance. Often when Roman law proved too rigid, Bartolus showed how it could be modified by using customary law to find a more practicable solution. One of his most influential works was on rivers, which often acted as a border between two city-states. Using mathematical examples from Euclid and from geometry, he provided ways of marking out territories even when a riverbed, was dry, as often happened in Italy in the summer heat. He also thought deeply about the relative powers of various bodies within city-states and their relationship with the emperor. In short, this is a rare example of how a university could be used as a base for intellectual innovation. It was said that in every lecture he made a reference to a case that he had recently experienced.

A major problem was the difficulty of adding new subjects to the curriculum. Despite the impetus given by the arrival of Aristotle's texts, there was no place in the medieval university for zoology, botany or geology. Albert the Great, whom we will discuss in detail in the next chapter, was a lone voice in arguing for the further accumulation of observations as a source for knowledge. There was no history and little study of classical texts in their own right. 'Classical studies survived and advanced and were successfully adapted to new tastes and conditions, but in a context in which they were never really emancipated, could never really catch fire', is one judicious assessment.[35] There was not even any teaching of Greek until later in the period, despite the immense riches available in that language and the advantage of studying original texts. Politics, ethics and economy all had major relevance but could not be squeezed into the straitjacket of the seven arts. The mechanical arts, where technology and commerce were adding new pressures for change, were excluded from the syllabus. A text of 1250 by the Dominican Robert Kilwardby, who taught at Oxford, lists what might have been studied in an expanded curriculum: it includes shipbuilding and commerce, engineering, architecture and textiles. Arguably, their exclusion was to leave them as second-class subjects, unsuitable for the 'educated' classes, well into the twentieth century.

Mondino de Luizzi wrote up a report of his dissection of a woman in 1316 and this, full of inaccuracies, became authoritative. The text was incorporated into a later textbook of medicine from 1493, shown here.

So while the concept of the university was of great importance and one that could be replicated throughout Europe, one must be cautious in seeing it as an engine of intellectual progress. By the fifteenth century the universities had come increasingly under the control of local rulers and so more authoritarian.[36] Bologna, once a student-led foundation, had become dominated by an alliance of the masters and the church. In Oxford, the threat of Lollardy meant that all students had to take an oath not to support this and other heresies (see p. 385). In his magisterial study *Medieval Philosophy*, John Marenbon notes how 'intellectually there is little in the fifteenth century universities, outside the field of logic, to compare with the innovative thinking of the fourteenth century. Rather than tackling problems, masters in the universities tended to put themselves behind one of the great philosophers of the previous two centuries.' He notes how the important philosophers of the fifteenth century such as Marsilio Ficino (see pp. 336–41) tended to work outside the universities.[37] It is telling that even the prosperous and well-educated citizens of Florence had only a small and undistinguished university. Christopher Celenza, a scholar of Italian humanism, notes that this may, in fact, be one reason why the Florentines were so ready to adopt new ideas.[38]

Typically, the universities had become more of a vehicle for advancement in courts, city republics and, predominantly, the church than centres of intellectual excellence. They remained attractive to those who wished to progress socially upwards and there are good cases of those from the artisan or peasant class who became important clerics. Some 60 per cent of students at New College, Oxford, were, in fact, the sons of small landowners. Jean Gerson (1363–1429), who ended up as chancellor of the University of Paris and a leading theologian at the Council of Constance (1414–18), was from a peasant background. In contrast, very few places in the universities of southern France or at New College were taken up by the nobility in the fifteenth century. This class did not need degrees to maintain their status.[39]

Dynamic advances in knowledge came from the highly educated men of the Italian city-states, who had learned the much more accessible Latin from classical sources. For these individuals, practical success in politics, sailing ships, assessing land and winning cases in the law courts was more important than long years closeted away at a leading university studying increasingly intricate texts. So the vast *Liber Abaci* by Fibonacci, the Pisan 'man of numbers', which appeared in 1202, was much more influential in providing the mathematics needed for trading calculations than anything to be found in a university. It is also telling that in England, perhaps the most centralized administration in Europe in the fourteenth century, aspiring lawyers were bypassing Oxford and Cambridge and studying instead at the Inns of Court in London.*

* The (four) Inns of Court emerged in the fourteenth century as institutions where secular lawyers could train. They remain central to the training of barristers to this day.

For all the undoubted limitations of the medieval universities, it was possible for some of the best minds of the period to use the universities as a base in which to complete important works in theology and natural philosophy, even if these were not absorbed within the curriculum. Indeed, the years 1250 to 1350 were a hotbed of theological and philosophical debate, to which we will next turn our attention.

Medieval Philosophy: A Reawakening or a Dead End?

We must bear in mind that there are two kinds of sciences. There are some which proceed from principles known by the natural lights of the intellect, such as arithmetic and geometry and the like. There are also some which proceed from principles known by the light of a higher science: thus the science of optics proceeds from principles established by geometry and music from principles established by arithmetic. So it is that sacred doctrine is a science because it proceeds from principles made known by the light of a higher science, namely the science of God and the blessed.

Thomas Aquinas, *Summa theologiae*[1]

No one denies that the Greeks were pioneers of western philosophy. It would be impossible to study the subject without following the great names that established the discipline from the sixth century BC onwards. Yet can one talk of medieval philosophy as a continuation of that same tradition, or is it more appropriate to talk simply of theology? In 1997 a large number of distinguished scholars met in Erfurt, Germany, to discuss just this question and after many days of earnest discussion failed to resolve the issue.[2] What can be said, however, is that no significant intellectual of the period was able to create a philosophy, in the classical Greek tradition, that did not include a belief in a single creator God whose powers over the lives of individuals and over the natural world itself were pervasive. Could medieval 'philosophy' ever find a niche that isolated itself from those powers?[3] The answer lies partly in the classical, and thus pagan, texts that were being rediscovered and in the extent to which they could be reconciled with Christian theology.

The Greeks had set high standards in mathematics, science and philosophy, and those who came across their works in medieval Europe were awed by them. The last chapter revealed the hunger for translations and commentaries in Latin either from the original Greek or, at second hand, through Arabic translations from the Greek. Naturally, much of the original sense was lost in these transmissions – Latin lacking the linguistic subtlety of the original Greek – but the breadth, the sheer richness of the material, and the attempts to explain natural phenomena and the methodology needed to do so were so superior to anything else available that western thought would have atrophied without their input.

Several ancient Greek thinkers were already known in medieval Europe through their works: Ptolemy's *Almagest*, Euclid's *Elements*, medical texts by Hippocrates, Galen and Dioscorides. The Irish philosopher Eriugena, a rare Greek speaker from the ninth century, had passed on the works of Greek Platonist Christians such as Gregory of Nyssa and, above all, Pseudo-Dionysius, probably a Syrian monk writing about AD 500, whom many wrongly believed to be the very Dionysius who had been converted by Paul in the first century AD. Pseudo-Dionysius contributed a mystical conception of God in which he was so far removed from human understanding that he could best be described by what he was not (the so-called negative or apophatic theology). Yet it was the pagan Aristotle who was the intellectually dominant influence on medieval thought. Aristotle's explanatory power and his ability to offer a comprehensive system through which to analyse the natural world were compelling. 'The philosopher', as he became known, had no rivals.

Aristotle had arrived from northern Greece to study at Plato's Academy as a seventeen-year-old in 367 BC.[4] He stayed there until 347 BC, gradually developing his own way of thinking, which moved well away from Plato's preoccupation with a 'real' immaterial state of being towards the empirical study of the natural world. 'There is something awesome in all natural things,' he once told his students when they showed disgust over a mound of decomposing cuttlefish that he had assembled for them to study. 'One should approach research on animals of whatever type without hesitation. For inherent in each of them is something natural and beautiful… The purpose for which each has come together, or come into being, deserves its place among what is beautiful.'[5]

This was the inspiration for his work, which covered the whole spectrum of the natural world, from political systems (as in his *Politics* already discussed) to pioneering works on zoology and biology that rested on acute observation of living things. His *History of Animals* includes some 500 different species, many of them examined closely through dissection. Aristotle pondered how to classify and distinguish between living organisms: where does a sea anemone fit between animals and plants?[6] Watching how an organism, an egg within a chicken, for instance, grows and then hatches, he reflected on the features that make a chicken a chicken – rather than something else – when it emerged from its shell. This led him on to deeper thoughts on the essence of living things, the importance of a 'soul' in providing a force that nourishes us towards some form of higher existence. For human beings this was the use of the reasoning mind to achieve *eudaimonia*, or 'flourishing'. Crucially, and in contrast to Plato and Christian thought, the soul died with the individual. Whether it then continued to exist in any form remained unclear, although some commentators assumed that there was a universal entity into which it was absorbed. From here, Aristotle explored ethics; his *Nicomachian Ethics* is one of his finest works. Again he is concerned as to how human beings can live effectively in the real world, mastering underlying moral codes that are reinforced in an individual through repetition, but knowing when to adapt them to changing circumstances.

Aristotle's works on logic were also revolutionary. His *Prior Analytics* is seen as the first time in history where the nature of logic is investigated in what might be seen as a scientific way. The *Posterior Analytics* defines the first principles from which one can demonstrate that knowledge is valid, and so provides the basis for scientific knowledge. These two works are often placed alongside the *Categories* in a body of Aristotle's works known as the *Organon*. Then there is his cosmology, an attempt to understand the universe as a whole. Aristotle observed the regularity of the movements of the planets and searched for the force that had set everything in motion. Nothing moves unless there is something that initiates the move. Here Aristotle postulated the idea of the 'unmoved mover', a supreme force that has no emotional relationship with the world other than being its first cause. Its existence is eternal – there is no moment of beginning for the universe. However, Aristotle believed that the physics of the world beyond the moon, where the planets stay in place, and those relating to Earth itself below the moon, where they fall downwards, were distinct, the celestial and the terrestrial regions were composed of different materials. While the Earth was made up of four elements, air, fire, water and earth, each with its own sphere, a view that had its roots in earlier Greek philosophy, Aristotle added a fifth, aether, which filled the celestial region. This distinction, between the make-up of Earth and that of space, was challenged by a brilliant sixth-century philosopher, Philoponus from Alexandria, but it was not until the seventeenth century that it was effectively shown to be false and that all matter followed the same laws. Aristotle's thoughts on the ultimate nature of things are included in his *Metaphysics*.* Following researches along the coastline of Asia Minor, and a spell, perhaps legendary, of acting as tutor to the young Alexander the Great, Aristotle returned to Athens to teach in the school he had founded there, the Lyceum, until his death in 322.

The problem with Aristotle's works is that many were recorded only in rough form, perhaps even as notes taken down as he was lecturing. This is why so many leading intellectuals provided commentaries, in an attempt to explain what Aristotle really meant. Those by the great Arabic philosophers, Avicenna and Averroes, have already been mentioned.

Aristotle's texts on natural philosophy began to arrive in Paris at the beginning of the thirteenth century, 1,600 years after they had been composed. By 1200 Avicenna's expansive commentaries were available, and by 1230 the more rigorous translations of Averroes. Only from the 1260s onwards, at the request of Thomas Aquinas, were the more

* The word comes from this work being placed after (Greek *meta*) Aristotle's study of *Physics* in a sequence of his works.

sophisticated translations of Aristotle, directly from the Greek, rather than through Arabic, completed by the Fleming William of Moerbeke, whom Aquinas trusted above his competitors. Aristotle was, of course, an empiricist and an independent philosopher whose 'God', a.k.a. the unmoved mover, had nothing to do with the God envisaged by the church. Christians believed in a moment of creation *ex nihilo*, 'from nothing'. The church taught that, following the Creation, God could also intervene to change the order of the heavens; they were not fixed as Aristotle taught. In fact, miracles happened on a daily basis. In his *De anima* (*On the Soul*), Aristotle described the soul as an intrinsic part of a living creature, as dependent on it as the image on the metal is for a coin. An individual soul did not survive death; certainly, the soul did not live on in any way that it could suffer the tortures of damnation or experience the bliss of salvation. Instead, Aristotle talked of an 'intellective soul' that was shared by all human beings. How could he be integrated within a Christian curriculum? It did not seem possible.

In 1228, in a letter to the University of Paris, Pope Gregory IX challenged those who placed philosophy and reason (i.e. Aristotle) above faith. Theology could only be taught if no *scientia*, then translated as 'philosophical knowledge', was involved. In 1231 the pope, while accepting the independence of the masters after they had gone on strike, repeated his ban on Aristotle's works of natural philosophy but, perhaps aware of how far things had gone, he added the words 'before they had been examined and purged of error'. The Dominicans, still conscious of how much they depended on the papacy for their survival, fell into line and preached sermons ridiculing those who could not part from Aristotle and who persisted in substituting 'brass' for 'the true gold' of orthodox theology. These got nowhere. The university masters stood by their independence and the pope was bypassed. The translations and commentaries on Aristotle by Avicenna and Averroes were being taught in the university by the 1240s and by 1255 a list of set books for the arts included no fewer than nineteen texts by Aristotle, including his *Physics*, *Metaphysics*, *Nicomachian Ethics* and *De anima*. The church had failed to suppress new currents of thinking.

Inevitably, there were those who fought against this stream of new teaching texts. The most revered was the Franciscan Bonaventure (1217–74), who had begun teaching in Paris in 1257, the same year as he became general of the Franciscan order. Bonaventure was a conservative, heavily influenced by Augustine and, through Augustine, Plato. In fact, he has been seen as the champion of medieval Augustinianism. He rejected Aristotle's view that the world had existed eternally, that there was one common intellectual soul, and that there was no life after death. While, despite these issues, Bonaventure admired Aristotle, he rated Plato much higher as a source of wisdom. Moreover, if one accepted Augustine's doctrine of original sin, it followed that human beings had been handicapped in their capacity to understand the natural world. Plato's Ideas, which were still known through Plotinus, were recast by Bonaventure as the 'eternal reasons' of God and it was the duty of the theologian to find these 'reasons'. Unfortunately, the 'fall of man' had diminished the intellect's ability to think rationally. Full understanding was impossible until one came face to face with God after death. Despite this, something might be achieved before then. Bonaventure's best-known book, *The Journey of the Mind to God*, imagined an ascent in mystical terms very similar to the same ascent as described by Augustine, a gradual unfolding of the joys of closeness to the divine presence. This emotional relationship with God was central to Bonaventure's theology. 'The best way to know God is through the experience of sweetness; this is more perfect, excellent and delightful than through rational enquiry.'[7] One should start with the examination of the 'shadows' and 'vestiges' of God's creation shown in the material world and then, since human beings were also part of creation, through inner contemplation (again there are shades of Augustine here). Finally, one must transcend the temporal world to pass into the eternal, a mystical experience. Bonaventure always placed faith, as found in the 'truths' of the scriptures, as predominant over reason but this does not mean that he had no place for reason. He used logical arguments, for instance, to challenge Aristotle's conception that the world had existed eternally. Yet overall he was reluctant to use philosophy to understand what he firmly believed was impossible for a human to grasp. In doing so, he set in place a tradition that would find itself in opposition to the Dominicans, who were much more receptive to philosophy and, as we shall see with Thomas Aquinas, especially the philosophy of Aristotle. This tension was to persist in the orders' respective approaches to medieval philosophy.

So it was that while Bonaventure was dismissing Aristotle as misguided, the philosopher was championed by the Bavarian Dominican Albert 'the Great' (Albertus Magnus), who had been introduced to Aristotle during his early studies at the University of Padua. Albert (1200–80) taught theology at Paris for three years, between 1245 and 1248, before being appointed head of a new *studium generale* set up by his order in Cologne. His life was extraordinarily active as he was responsible for supervising the affairs of the growing number of Dominican houses but somehow he found time to complete a prodigious amount of research. Central to his approach was his argument for a complete separation of the paths of philosophy and theology as a means of finding truth. The truths specific to theology were based on the revelations of the scriptures and the Church Fathers. Here Augustine still reigned supreme. In contrast Aristotle had used experimentation and inductive and deductive reasoning to reach conclusions that Albert argued did not trespass in any way on theology: 'The fundamental principles of theology do not fit those of philosophy, because they are founded on revelation and inspiration, not on reason, and so we cannot discuss them in philosophy.'[8] And Albert had this to say in a commentary on Aristotle's *Ethics*: 'Theological contemplation contemplates through a light infused by God, but the philosopher contemplates through an acquired disposition of wisdom.' The two philosophies were linked, however, in that Albert believed that when God acted he did not do so through sudden unnatural interventions but through the observable causation of natural events. Albert had exposed the philosophical chasm between those who believed knowledge was achieved through inner thoughts and those who relied on the evidence on the senses working on the external world, a chasm he hoped could be bridged. He was careful, however, never to present unresolvable contradictions between the two. 'What is divinely taught to us by faith cannot be contrary to what we are endowed with by nature. One or the other would have to be false, and since we have both of them from God, he would be the cause of our error which is impossible.'[9]

Albert worked through all Aristotle's works, making them accessible (in Latin) to the general reader. While he did not accept uncritically everything Aristotle said, he was happy to see him as an authority within the scope of his works and, unlike those scholars who concentrated on the works of logic, he mastered and accepted what Aristotle had written about living things, plants and animals, astronomy and geography. Albert appreciated that Aristotle represented a tradition of knowledge that would evolve with time and he backed up his knowledge of the texts with his own observations and experimentation, filling in gaps that Aristotle had left. His massive *On Animals*, which includes material from Aristotle, earlier medieval commentators and his own studies, extends even to discussions of nutrition and embryology based on his own observations. Having heard a story that ostriches ate iron, he attempted unsuccessfully to feed them with the metal, but reported that they were prepared to eat gravel instead! In short, the scale of Albert's investigations and interests was breathtaking and there are major challenges even today in assembling the whole body of his works (one edition is in thirty-eight volumes). In the judgement of the historian of medieval science David Lindberg, Albert was 'the best biologist of the entire Middle Ages'.[10] By introducing the empirical works of Aristotle into the curriculum, he initiated the possibility of a scientific approach to the natural world that, in this case, did not threaten religious belief. In comparison with the Oxford scientists, Robert Grosseteste and Roger Bacon, who will be covered in the next chapter, Albert did well to separate the study of the natural world from theology. Albert had his followers in Germany but as yet there was no impetus for the cumulative advance of scientific knowledge (as there had been among, say, the astronomers and mathematicians of the Hellenistic period in Greece).

While Albert was admired for the breadth of his knowledge, the church was hesitant in honouring a man who was so focused on understanding the natural world rather than the divine. Despite his genius, and his refusal to let Aristotle challenge Christian teaching, Albert was not even formally made one of the thirty-two Doctors of the Church and canonized until 1931. Only in 1948 did Pope Pius XII declare him the patron saint of scientists. For many years he was more famous for his role as the teacher of the most brilliant and prominent Dominican of all.

* * *

Thomas Aquinas (born *c.*1225) came from a noble family in southern Italy and he began to study the arts course at the new University of Naples.[11] It was here that he first came across the works of Aristotle. Then, to the horror of his family, he decided to become a Dominican, still a socially unacceptable choice for someone of his background. The more respectable Benedictines stayed at prayer and worked in wealthy monasteries (such as Monte Cassino, where Aquinas had his early education); the Dominicans were, in comparison, a scruffy lot, out on the streets and dependent on charitable handouts. Aquinas, however, had spotted their commitment to learning. Determined to make his own path, he went on from Naples to study at Paris, where he came under the tutelage of Albert and travelled with him to Cologne. Back in Paris in 1252 and studying for a mastership in theology, he had to teach Peter Lombard's *Sentences* and his first important work was a commentary on the book. This was a standard procedure for an up-and-coming theologian, but Aquinas had shifted the focus. Normally,

Augustine would be the main source of supporting quotations and indeed Aquinas quoted him 1,000 times – but then also included double the number of quotations from Aristotle. In contrast to Bonaventure, he was to integrate philosophy with theology, rather than making it a subordinate accessory. The French philosopher Étienne Gilson has a neat phrase for it: 'Thomas changed the water of philosophy into the wine of theology.'[12]

Aquinas achieved his mastership in 1256 and stayed on in Paris teaching for three years. He was, however, already deep into Aristotle's empiricism but it was his breadth and independence of thought that was now becoming prominent. Between 1259 and 1265, he compiled his first major work, the *Summa contra Gentiles*, a defence of the Christian faith. However, aimed as it was at an audience of Jews and Muslims, it did not rely on biblical sources for the foundations of its arguments, but solely on reason. So the first book of the *Summa* describes how reason, rather than biblical revelation, can be used to prove the existence of God.

Aquinas's arguments, clearly inspired by Aristotle, insist that the material world matters. Here he breaks ranks with the Platonists such as Augustine who see it as unstable and corrupting of the soul that reaches out towards God. Aquinas argued that surely God would not have created a world that was in opposition to him. His very nature would ensure that anything he created must be good and, following Aristotle, Aquinas argues that fundamentally there is an underlying stability to material things. There is no possibility of fully understanding the nature of an infinite God with our finite minds but at least a careful examination of his creation will help illuminate that nature. Aquinas's view that 'nothing exists in reason which has not come through the senses' is one that Aristotle would have endorsed with enthusiasm and Augustine, who believed that God acts primarily through the inner mind, would have rejected. This was also a rejection of Anselm of Canterbury's view that it is the mental concept of God's existence that underpins arguments that support that very existence. Even though merely a pagan, Aristotle had established a method of reasoning and exploring the natural world that his follower Aquinas could adapt to find Christian truth. It was a dramatic breakthrough and opened up new theological pathways that ran separately from Augustinian dogma. As the scholar Olaf Pedersen has noted: 'Thomas exploded what had formerly been an intellectual ghetto of Christian thought within the confines of Christianity, admitting that all people and ages are potential contributors to the growth of knowledge.'[13] Yet, for Aquinas, this knowledge was always subordinated to the truths of Christianity. He was always first and foremost a theologian and saw his extensive commentaries on the scriptures as more important than those on Aristotle or other Greek philosophers.

By 1268 Aquinas was in Italy, teaching at a Dominican institute attached to the lovely fifth-century Church of Santa Sabina on the Aventine hill in Rome. (Aquinas, like Albert the Great, was peripatetic, as was expected of the mendicant orders. Both men's studies took place largely outside the universities.) Aristotle continued to fascinate him and his study of Aristotle's work on the soul, *De anima*, brought him up against the conflict between Aristotle and Christian teaching. The Platonists had seen the soul as individual to each human being, but the most important element was the capacity of the soul to live on as a separate entity after death. As already seen, Aristotle argued that the soul was what gave life to a body; it could not be detached from it and died with it. Aquinas, as a good Christian, could not believe that. He had to accept that, ultimately, something of an individual human was raised at the Last Judgement. His arguments for some form of continuity of the soul after death are, in the words of one prominent Aquinas scholar, Denys Turner, 'complex, technical, and variously presented in different texts'.[14] He comes up with a solution that describes the soul as 'intellectual', by which he means that it is a reasoning force that exists independently of bodily organs and so can survive.

The problem that all Aquinas students have to face is whether he could always use the brilliance of his mind to find ways of reconciling Aristotle with Christian teaching rather than accepting that Aristotle may simply have been working within a different context of thought from the Christian, which had evolved independently many centuries after his death. The historical and social contexts in which each school of thought had emerged were so distinct that there was no philosophical reason why they should relate to each other. Aquinas, awed by the brilliant insights of 'the Philosopher', made the daring assumption that they could be reconciled and be used to reinforce the individual's understanding of the natural world. In this he went further than his mentor, Albert, who had rigorously separated philosophy and theology. Inevitably, there were difficulties. There were occasions when Aquinas had to turn to faith, notably in accepting the 'truth' of the Trinity. When faced with Aristotle's arguments for the eternity of the world, he concentrated on showing that the issue could never be proved one way or the other* but the act of Creation, like the Trinity, had to be accepted as an article of faith. As Aquinas argued, there was absolutely no need for God to have created the world. He could have existed perfectly happily without it.

By definition, articles of faith were beliefs that could not be proved by reason. Abelard had exposed some of the philosophical problems that arose as a result of having doctrines that every Christian had to give assent to even if there were no supporting proofs for them (see p. 123). Aquinas argued that because, in his view, the existence of God *could* be proved (as he did through setting out five detailed arguments in his *Summa theologiae*), then the existence was not an article of faith, rather *a preamble to faith*. In contrast there were other beliefs, the Trinity for instance, the Incarnation or clauses in the Nicene Creed (Aquinas listed fourteen of these) that could *not* be proved to be true. They could only be grasped through an act of faith. The Church taught that Christians should simply acquiesce in them without questioning. Aquinas accepted that not everyone would be able to focus on theological understanding and that, for many, faith in, say, the Creation was simply impossible to grasp in any intellectually coherent way. However, he insisted that theologians had a duty to consistently meditate on articles of faith so that they could be kept alive for believers. How could this be done? Aquinas, once again following Aristotle, argued that every human being had been endowed with a natural will or impulse to seek virtue and the theologian could join this with the intellect to make an effective search for divine truths. God or the Holy Spirit could respond by offering grace in the cause of understanding. Eventually, some apprehension of these truths would be reached through contemplation. 'Contemplation pertains to the simple act of gazing on the truth.' So either through the grace of God or the activity of the Holy Spirit articles of faith are communicated to those whose will is focused on finding them. What is important to achieve full understanding is consistency in contemplation as that ensures that faith becomes a living part of the seeker's life. So one of Aquinas's definitions of faith is: 'a habit of mind by which eternal life begins in us, making the understanding assent to things that are not seen.'[15] As he put it in his great hymn the *Pange Lingua*, two verses of which are sung in the ceremony of Benediction:† 'Faith, our outward sense befriending, makes our inward

* In this he differed from Bonaventure, who had argued that the notion of the eternity of the world could be proved to be false.

† Benediction is a Catholic ceremony in which the consecrated host is venerated by displaying it before the congregation.

vision clear.' There is the assumption, of course, that contemplation will lead inevitably to an acceptance of the Trinity or clauses of the Nicene Creed, or whatever the church has decreed are articles of faith, and not any other alternative formulation of Christian doctrine. The articles of faith exist eternally and can be accessed by the contemplative mind, as against those theological truths, such as the existence of God, that can be proved through reason. Yet, for Aquinas, there was no incompatibility between those truths accessed through reason and those through faith. He believed that they reinforced each other to form a coherent theology.

Aquinas's greatest work was his vast *Summa theologiae*, some 2 million words of it (the first printed copies ran to four volumes). Rather than a university textbook, this is a training manual for those entering the Dominican order. With extraordinary confidence, Aquinas set out each proposition that he wished to discuss and began the debate by listing the objections to the stand he would eventually take. In placing the points for and against each proposition, he had to go through the philosophical argument in depth, not only 'proving' his point but showing a valid means of doing so. Of course, there were areas, such as the eternity of the world, where he had to leave the philosophical question open and fall back on revelation, but the influence of Aristotle still predominates. This can be seen in his adoption of Aristotle's view that the highest state of being lies in using reason to achieve virtuous living. This is easy to translate into a Christian context, where the greatest happiness lies in the contemplation of the essence of God, essentially what Aquinas called 'a beatific vision'. Yet Aquinas, as a good Dominican, goes further in arguing that Christians, and above all his Dominican students, have a duty to spread the fruits of his contemplation through preaching and teaching. This marriage of contemplation with an active expression of the love of God was to be extolled by the poet Dante at the culmination of his *Divine Comedy* (see Chapter 10, p. 249).

Aquinas made important contributions to the philosophy of ethics, drawing on a breadth of sources, not only Christian but Greek and Jewish. He adopts elements of Aristotle's ethics in arguing that it is possible through reason and common sense to find a 'natural' ethics, one that accords with the search for human virtue. The idea of a natural law was deep rooted in classical philosophy, especially in Stoicism and, most influentially in medieval and humanist Europe, in the works of Cicero. As we have seen, it was already being used by the jurists of the time as a justification for limiting the power of princes, but it was

Aquinas who embedded the concept in Christian thought by assuming that an 'eternal law' had been founded by God. Natural law was that part of the eternal law that human beings could understand for themselves through active reasoning. For Aquinas the law included the need for preservation of oneself, the importance of family life and values of living within a community that allowed each member to flourish (there was a strong influence from Aristotle's *Politics* here). Aquinas did not adopt the pessimism of Augustine in seeing human beings as helpless without the grace of God. Rather, they had the possibility of turning themselves towards God through the use of their reasoning powers. Yet understanding natural law involved conscious effort. While believing in original sin, Aquinas differed from Augustine in asserting that it had not damaged the intellect or the ability to reason.* It was the duty of the Christian to strengthen the power of reason through the exercise of virtues such as prudence, the use of judgement in order to assess correct moral responses, and contemplation. Insofar as there was a natural impulse for human beings to reach towards goodness/God, wrongdoing might therefore be the result of faulty reasoning rather than the deliberate exercise of the human will to thwart God's commands. Yet there was always the fear that the process of reasoning would be subverted by allowing emotions to take control. As Aquinas put it in the *Summa*: 'The passions of the soul, in so far as they are contrary to the order of reason, incline us to sin: but in so far as they are controlled by reason, they pertain to virtue.' The concept of a natural law accessible through reason left problems. Were the concepts of natural law immutable, as might be suggested if it could be understood through reason? Or could an omnipotent God subvert them at will, as the philosopher Duns Scotus would later argue?

In 1268 Aquinas returned to Paris to find that a number of the arts teachers had gone further than he had, in preferring Aristotle's views on the soul and the eternity of the world over orthodox Christianity. The two most prominent were masters of arts, Siger of Brabant and Boethius of Dacia. They relied so heavily on the Islamic Averroes' adulation of Aristotle that they are known as the Latin Averroists. While they accepted Christian teaching, their support for Aristotelian philosophy as a means of finding the truth was so enthusiastic that it was as if they were ignoring theology. So they argued that God could not do something that Aristotle had shown to be physically impossible. One example was that God could not move the cosmos in a straight line as this would

* Augustine had specifically argued that original sin had damaged the power to think rationally.

leave a vacuum, and Aristotle had taught (erroneously, as would later be discovered) that a vacuum could not exist. This contrasted with the orthodox Christian view that God could do *anything* short of a logical contradiction. He could hardly be constrained by what the pagan Aristotle believed to be the nature of the material world. They also questioned whether the soul was of a material that could actually suffer in hellfire. The Averroists' approach was clearly unacceptable to the authorities, and to Aquinas himself who, in a final burst of intellectual activity, wrote several counter-attacks. The major criticism was that it assumed Averroes' 'double truth', the possibility that the truth found through empiricism was equal to the truth of revelation, even if they came to different conclusions. As Aquinas's mentor Albert had argued, it was impossible for there to be a contradiction between the two.

This time it was the bishop of Paris, Stephen Tempier, who launched a condemnation of thirteen apparently heretical theses of the Latin Averroists. More strident condemnation was to come in 1277 when Tempier, under pressure from Pope John XXI, and, understandably, the Franciscans, issued a list of 219 statements that were considered to be fallacious or heretical and the teaching of which by the masters of arts would lead to excommunication. These included the disputed elements of Aristotle such as the eternity of the world and his dismissal of the immortality of the soul, as well as the more adventuresome claims of the Averroists, that philosophers have the right to take reason wherever it goes and that one can never say a statement is valid if it has no more than authority to sustain it. Prominent among the targets of papal censure were any claims that God's power was limited to what Aristotle had claimed was the natural order of things. God could create anything new, even several worlds if he wanted to. Several statements came close to condemning Aquinas, so placing his authority in doubt.

Albert the Great, as seen in a thirteenth-century manuscript of his text *De Natura Rerum* (*On the Nature of Things*).

Tempier's list had no coherence, 'knocked together in great haste without order or design by a commission whose competence in philosophy was not very striking', as one scholar has put it.[16] Ultimately, it was to have the opposite effect to the one intended. Rather than quelling debate it stimulated all kinds of responses with different consequences. If God had the power to act as he wanted, then one could never depend on there being an unchanging order to the cosmos and there would be little point in trying to find the laws of the universe. This would make scientific investigation, in the sense that it is understood today, impossible. On the other hand, one could take the approach that God knew what he was doing in creating the universe as he willed it to be and one could count on his consistency. This could spark a curiosity over the way he had conceived his creation. Although there is little evidence that this was the case during the medieval period it may have been one element in encouraging scientific experimentation in the seventeenth century. Yet one of the finest scholars of medieval philosophy, Étienne Gilson, saw the condemnations of 1277 as a turning point, the moment when the theologians rejected reason as a means of finding theological truth: 'The condemnation of 1277 is a landmark in the history of medieval philosophy and theology… Instead of carrying on its effort to conquer philosophy by renovating it, scholasticism acted on the defensive. At that very moment, its golden age came to an end.'[17]

Not everyone in Paris was to be quelled by Tempier. The Averroist response is found in a riposte by one of the Paris masters of arts, James of Douai: 'Though philosophy is the great perfection of man, philosophers are oppressed nowadays… And the fact that philosophers are thus oppressed keeps many from practising philosophy.' Another voice, that of Godfrey of Fontaines, a master of theology, defended

the independence of the university. Godfrey was asked a quodlibetal question over whether a master could overrule a bishop if he believed him to be in error. Godfrey replied that he could: different opinions about a theological issue were often justified. In an echo of Abelard, Godfrey argued: 'For it is thanks to the diverse opinions that cultured and learned men hold concerning such questions, through various discussions taking one side or the other so as to find the truth, that truth is best discovered.' Hence it is wrong to impede such discussions. Godfrey then lays into 'the ignorance and simplicity of those prelates' who claim that certain beliefs are erroneous when they are clearly not. Thus did a master uphold the independence of his university from external control, a moment to be remembered.[18]

Three months before his death in 1274, Aquinas suddenly stopped writing. The *Summa* was never finished. Albert was still, in his late seventies or possibly early eighties, alive to hear the devastating news of his most brilliant pupil's death at the Cistercian abbey of Fossanova, south of Rome. Yet at the time it was difficult to appreciate what Aquinas had achieved. There were too many swirling theological currents, from Bonaventure, who died just four months after Aquinas, through Albert and Aquinas to the Latin Averroists, all taking different approaches to Aristotle. Rivalry between Dominicans and Franciscans, each supporting their own, added to the confusion. In 1282 the Franciscan order officially endorsed a text listing 118 of Aquinas's views that needed 'correction'. In just over two years there were four major retaliatory replies by Dominicans. As always with theological controversies, it was hard to find any objective standards by which to assess innovations.

It was fifty years before Pope John XXII set in motion the canonization of Aquinas, a process rendered difficult by the lack of any reported miracles associated with the Dominican friar.* Eventually, the pope had to propose that each section of the *Summa* was in itself a miracle. In 1323 Aquinas was declared to be a saint and two years later the ban on teaching his work was lifted in Paris. Oxford, which had adopted some of the same condemnations, never formally lifted the ban but Thomism, as the theology of Aquinas came to be known, was widely taught there by the end of the thirteenth century. The Dominicans were not slow in recognizing him as their intellectual superstar. In the Spanish Chapel in the convent of the Dominican Church of Santa Maria Novella in Florence there is a wonderful fresco by Andrea da Firenze that shows Aquinas presiding over the entire

* Thomas Becket, killed on the orders of a secular ruler, Henry II, and who had died four years before Aquinas was canonized within two years of his death.

range of human knowledge, both Christian and classical (1366). This was despite Augustine, supported by the Franciscans, regaining his predominance in theology. Only in 1879 did Pope Leo XIII declare that Aquinas was the intellectual champion of orthodox Catholic theology and he was now firmly established, in Catholic circles at least, with a status he has not lost.

Aristotle could not be removed from the university curriculum and, in fact, he became so embedded in it that the innovatory nature of his empirical approach to the natural world was hardly recognized. His works on botany, zoology and geology that had been such an important part of his active study found no place in the arts curriculum. Given the impossibility of reading Aristotle outside of a Christian context, one that taught the absolute power of God and the possibility of new knowledge arriving through divine revelation, full appreciation of the intellectual range of Aristotelian thought was unachievable during this period. The medieval church had, in effect, been forced to accept an uneasy philosophical compromise between two ways of thinking. Albert had found a way of giving Aristotle's philosophy an independent status but the Latin Averroists had gone too far and had been condemned for seeming to place Aristotle above the teachings of the church.

What was left in the mainstream of medieval philosophy were a number of alternative slipstreams. After the condemnations of 1277, new currents appeared in the works of two important philosopher/theologians, Duns Scotus and William of Ockham. Even though both were working within a Christian framework, they disagreed with each other and with Thomas Aquinas on fundamental issues. Many of these issues were so complex and so difficult to resolve that they created room for extremely sophisticated debate between these brilliant thinkers. But herein lay danger: power still lay with the church hierarchy, and the possibility of condemnation for heresy was very real. Abelard had discovered this, as we have seen, and so would William of Ockham.

overleaf
The central figure of this fresco from 1366 in the convent of Santa Maria Novella in Florence is Thomas Aquinas holding the Book of Wisdom. He presides over the world of learning, both contemporary and classical. See Appendix I (p. 742) for further elaboration.

Very little is known of Duns Scotus. He appears to have been born in the Scottish village of Duns in 1265 and to have joined a Franciscan house in Scotland. He then spent many years studying theology at Oxford before moving to Paris where he is found lecturing on the *Sentences*. In the conflict between Pope Boniface VIII and the French monarchy, which we will look at in Chapter 16 (see pp. 368–9), he and

S IOB PROPHETA

many of his fellow Franciscans supported the pope and were forced to leave Paris. Readmitted to the university a year later, he eventually achieved his doctorate but was again forced to leave Paris for reasons unknown and died suddenly in Cologne in 1308.

If one wants to breathe the rarified air of late medieval philosophy, then Scotus is the philosophers' philosopher, responsible for what some scholars believe to be the most complex arguments known for the existence of God. It had been a major feat of scholarship to bring together his papers as his sudden death left them in disorder. Many documents would later be wrongly attributed to him. Two commentaries on the *Sentences*, one made in Oxford and one in Paris, illustrate the core of his thinking and show that he was more at home within the bounds of university theology than those, such as Albert and Aquinas, who had spent many years preaching outside them. He was renowned for his ability to coin complex Latin neologisms, among which are *perseitas*, meaning 'in-itself-ness', and *anitas*, meaning 'whetherness'. The acuteness of his mind and his ability to create nuanced metaphysical distinctions make him impossible to summarize with any clarity, especially as he was often diverted by challenges to his arguments. Here I shall endeavour to show how he positioned himself against Aquinas and began to cast doubt also on the value of Aristotle.

Scotus felt that Aquinas had gone much too far in relying on Aristotle as a means of exploring theological issues. In this he agreed with his fellow Franciscan Bonaventure, and Augustine before him, that the Fall of Man had diminished human capacity to learn from the natural world. By assuming that the intellect of Adam and Eve had remained intact for later generations, Aquinas had been too optimistic. As Scotus put it graphically, Adam and Eve would have seen it in full sunlight, their fallen descendants as if evening darkness was beginning to set in. Of course, observation of the natural world had some intrinsic value, but it was limited compared to knowledge gained through the direct revelation of God and abstract philosophical reasoning.

Scotus disagreed with Aquinas's view, heavily dependent on Aristotle, that the world is fundamentally stable, operating under natural causes. So while Aquinas and Albert might accept that there are natural causes of earthquakes and that it is the warmth of the sun and the provision of water that causes plants to grow, Scotus argued instead that God had infinite power and thus absolute knowledge of all possible truths in every possible world. Yet he also had a divine will, and it was through this that he could choose between the infinite possibilities of creation and implement them. The world we see now is the one he has chosen to create; but he *could* have created it in a different way. God would be able to cause an earthquake or have a plant grow without a sun to warm it. He could even have created a number of parallel universes. This idea would open up new directions in theological thinking, not least because it raised the possibility that there might be other human beings of which we know nothing (a valid point when Europeans had still not learned of the Americas) or even a universe where the Fall of Man had never taken place. Duns Scotus argued therefore that Aquinas, by concentrating so heavily on the world as seen by Aristotle – who had no conception of the world being other than it is – might have given us only a limited idea of God's creation, potential or otherwise.

It followed that one could not talk of a natural law that would exist eternally. God could subvert that law at any time. This meant that Aquinas's hope that one could live comfortably within an unchanging moral law that could be discerned through reason could not be sustained. Scotus found biblical sources to back his own approach. For instance, it would seem to be in accordance with natural law not to kill an innocent human being (one of the examples that Aquinas had given), but by ordering Abraham to kill Isaac God was clearly prepared to dispense with this law for a specific purpose. While Aquinas had argued that wrongdoing is the result of defective understanding of the natural law, Scotus argued that God can command what he wills and it is only through revelation, rather than through reason, that one can discern what he wills. Wrongdoing is the deliberate act of the human will to thwart the ascertainable commands of God.

Scotus introduced the idea that rather than looking at the natural world to reason about the nature of God, as Aquinas suggested, one should undertake a more abstract approach. Here he developed ideas that Avicenna had put forward. So when one looks at, say, a horse, one is both aware of that particular horse but also of the 'horsiness' which it represents. One can make what Scotus called a 'formal distinction' between these two ways of seeing the same object, between the actual horse and the concept of 'horsiness' of which it forms a part. For Scotus, the concept of, in this instance, 'horsiness' is innate to an individual and a superior way of knowing, although it could, of course, be given added depth by looking at a wider range of horses. The understanding of 'horsiness' would be exercised through using a different and superior form of cognition ('abstractive cognition' in some accounts) from that used when learning about the specific horse in front of one ('intellectual' or 'intuitive' cognition). Duns Scotus believed 'abstractive cognition' to be superior as it could be applied to objects that one could not see, such as angels, and it would also be retained in the soul after death. This for Duns Scotus is the real business of metaphysics and, in the great debate over universals (see p. 122), it put him firmly in the Realist camp. Even if it was not easy to fully grasp, there was a (Platonic) Idea or Form of 'horsiness' that encompassed everything about those horses to be seen on earth. 'Formal distinction' could also be used of God. He has a divine nature but he also has omnipotence and omniscience. One could say that these are indivisible, the one totally fused with the other, but Scotus suggests that these other attributes should be 'formally distinguished' from the divine nature, even though they are found in the one-person God. This helped him to explain the Trinity, where there can be formal distinctions between Father, Son and Holy Spirit despite their unity.

One of Duns Scotus's most radical concepts was that of univocity. When Aquinas had said that 'God is good', this was only as an analogy. The nature of divine goodness would necessarily be of a different nature from goodness in the material world. Aquinas was using the term 'goodness' as an aid to understanding but without actually explaining what a 'goodness' specific to God consists of. For Duns Scotus the word 'good' applied to God would have exactly the same meaning as if it were used of a human being – the term used was 'univocal', of one voice. So when one talks of the essence of 'being', a key Aristotelian concept, one would include within it both the finite 'beings' of the material world and the infinite beyond it. The language applied to either 'being' has the same meaning. Scotus then goes on to prove philosophically the existence of an infinite being. Here he moved back towards Anselm's proofs of the existence of God, which rely on conceiving what might be the being of which there can be none greater. In fact, Scotus claimed to have improved on Anselm by introducing the concept of the *possibility* of God's existence, as the first efficient cause of all that there is, the final cause of all things and the most excellent of all beings, which he then shows to be the *only* possibility.

Duns Scotus opened up new ways of exploring the nature and existence of God that challenged those of Aquinas and, by implication, Aristotle. He shifted the focus back onto the absolute power of God to do what he wills and so demoted the view that God had set the world in motion and allowed it to take its own course. However, Aristotle, and following him Aquinas, would prove to be right over natural cause and effect, especially as the status of miracles declined. This is perhaps one reason why, with the rising authority of science over the past 150 years, Aquinas has become the Catholic philosophical superstar. In the short term, on the other hand, the philosophy of Scotus proved very attractive and the 'Subtle Doctor' (*Doctor Subtilis*), as he came to be known, was probably more influential than Aquinas among the theologians of the fourteenth and fifteenth centuries. The intellectual tension of the period was, however, heightened when Scotus was challenged by another major philosopher of the next generation, William of Ockham.

William of Ockham (a village in Surrey) joined the Franciscans in about 1302, while still a young boy. He arrived to study at Oxford about 1310 and by the end of the decade was teaching theology there, writing the expected commentary on the *Sentences*. Aggressively brilliant, and like Abelard always insistent on following his own logic, he was impossible to work with. He criticized the influential work of Scotus, thus annoying his fellow Franciscans, and he fell out with the university chancellor, who was a champion of Aquinas. So he left Oxford without completing his doctorate and settled down to write and teach in the provincial house in London. Here he developed his campaign against Scotus as well as writing his more important work, the *Summa logicae*, a textbook on logic. Perhaps unsurprisingly he was an ardent support of free will. He argued that the mere experience of our freedom to choose was enough to make the case.

Ockham's most substantial disagreement with Scotus was in the universals debate. Scotus had been a Realist, assuming that there were universal concepts that could be appreciated by the reasoning mind, through 'abstractive cognition'. Ockham was a Nominalist; that is, he believed that words such as 'humanity' were merely mental images or names. They had no independent reality. Rather, each thing was particular to itself and one could spot this either by observing the thing or, if it was simply a concept, using reason to distinguish one concept from another. (For the 'universals' debate, see p. 122.) So two human beings might have a relationship with each other but there was nothing beyond that relationship of which they were both part. But Ockham insisted that one must not make unnecessary distinctions. He criticized Aristotle for doing just that, by having so many different categories of an object in his work on the subject (see p. 116). He actually reduced the ten categories suggested by Aristotle down to just two, substances and qualities, as the other eight categories could be explained through these two, and, in line with other philosophers of his time, he began to formulate the relationship between objects in mathematical terms, thus moving beyond Aristotle's original definition of the relationships.

It followed that one should always limit explanations to their basics.

Earlier philosophers had made the same point but it was such an integral part of Ockham's philosophy that it has become known as Ockham's Razor, the shaving away of unnecessary elements to an argument.* Ockham argued that you must always give a reason for everything you suggest except when it is self-evident, can be known through experience or is found in the scriptures. So convoluted language must be pruned back, and the same goes for unnecessary distinctions between concepts. This led Ockham to challenge Scotus's 'formal distinctions' of the attributes of God. God's omnipotence or his omniscience were so intrinsic to his nature that they could not be separated out from it, as Scotus and, earlier, Aquinas had suggested. There was a divine simplicity. In fact, Ockham argued that it is impossible to use reason to describe the existence of God. We can have no experience of God in the way that we can experience material objects. God's existence as a single force was a matter of faith alone. It was even impossible to establish rationally that there was only one primary cause. Here Ockham broke with earlier traditions, notably those of Anselm and Aquinas, which taught that God could be understood through pure reasoning (Anselm) or direct experience of his creation (Aquinas).

One of the most influential contributions of Augustine to the scholastic philosophers was his argument that all human minds contained within them an appreciation of the Trinity. This approach would support the idea of a universal, here the Trinity, which all minds were capable of grasping. Ockham accepted that it was natural to imagine universals in the sense of having a general idea of what 'horsiness' or 'humanity' might be, but he argued that this was no more than an act of thinking, an item in an individual person's mental history, based on some awareness that horses or humans exist.[19] So while you may have a concept of what 'horsiness' or 'humanity' is, this is not because there is such a concept somewhere out there but because you have developed one unique to yourself based on the variety of horses or humans you may have seen or can imagine. Each horse or human remains a distinct horse or human and each understanding of 'horsiness' is unique to the individual. Here Ockham would agree with Abelard but, in his elaboration of the concept of 'mental language', he takes the argument in his *Summa logicae* to far greater philosophical depths than Abelard ever did.

Nominalism had important implications for the nature of faith. If one followed Aquinas and the Realists one could believe that it was a

* The term 'Razor' to describe Ockham's methodology was first used only in the nineteenth century. The principle is sometimes referred to as the 'law of parsimony'.

matter of grasping some eternal truths. However, the Nominalists such as Ockham denied that there were such truths, universals, to be found and so the only way of understanding God was through faith. The will of God was absolute, there was no innate tendency to reach towards his divinity in the way that Aquinas had suggested. One could do no more than attempt to understand the will of God.

Ockham was close to Scotus, but distant from Aquinas, in arguing that God has the absolute power to do anything short of a logical contradiction, but he suggested that God would normally act in accordance with the order he had created. However, he has the freedom to act otherwise and Ockham adduces the example of God ordering the murder of Isaac. God is also left free to effect miracles as and when he decides and even the church has no more validity than as the instrument that he has chosen to effect his relationship with humanity. It has therefore no right to call itself infallible. (This would give Ockham the courage to declare a pope heretical; see below.) Ockham adds a new twist in that he suggested that God might also act through the human senses so that he could make us 'see' something that did not in fact exist. Aquinas had argued that a 'good' God would never deceive us in this way. He would always act in accordance with what is good and for this reason what could be seen could be trusted as real. Ockham was challenging this. Is what we see actually real or could we be deceived? Certainly, God had the power to deceive us and it is possible to conceive of situations where he might do so.

All this was stimulating but deeply unsettling for the conservative Franciscans and in 1324 Ockham found himself summoned to Avignon to face a papal commission investigating suspected heresies, among them support for Pelagianism (see p. 75) within his commentary on the *Sentences*. The procedures dragged on and he was never convicted. While he was in Avignon, a controversy arose over the correct approach to poverty for the Franciscan order. It was acknowledged that the order could not own anything – this had been the stricture of St Francis himself (based on Matthew 19). However, it had been agreed within the order that they could *use* property without actually owning it. In 1322 this had been denounced by the Avignon pope John XXII as a fudge; even Christ and his apostles had owned things and it was God's will that the church should own its wealth. Ockham took the Franciscan side, accepting that use of property was justified but ownership was not. Ownership was retained by whoever donated possessions and they had a right (here was an important recognition of rights) to take it back at any time. However, in an intemperate outburst Ockham condemned the pope's response to the extent of declaring him heretical. About to be declared heretical himself in response, he fled Avignon in 1328 and took refuge with the sympathetic emperor Ludwig of Bavaria, whose own claim to be emperor had been opposed by the pope. One result of John XXII's ruling was that the alliance between the Franciscans and the papacy, so powerful in the thirteenth century, was broken.

In his final years, Ockham, by now formally a heretic and in exile, composed works that condemned the absolutism of the papacy, arguing instead for the power of councils to restrain and even depose popes. At a time when the church was struggling to maintain its authority, Ockham was offering theological challenges to its status but he spoke too of the importance of freedom of speech other than in matters of theology: 'Purely philosophical assertions should not be condemned or forbidden by anyone, because in connection with such assertions anyone at all ought to be free to say freely what pleases him.'[20] Likewise, while he favoured monarchy as the most stable form of government, the 'people' retained the right to get rid of a tyrannical ruler. Here he was a forerunner of John Locke. He would have opposed the divine right of kings that was promulgated by the Stuart kings in Britain in the seventeenth century. Ockham died in 1349, probably a victim of the Black Death.

Enough has been said here to show that minds of the highest quality were grappling with these complex theological issues. The problem remains as to where this would all lead. The field was now split between followers of Aquinas, Scotus and Ockham in addition to a mass of lesser-known figures, while there was a pervading division between Neoplatonists, those still following Augustine, and Aristotelians such as Aquinas. It was Ockham who described his contemporaries as 'tearing to pieces, like barking dogs, every view dissenting from their own dogmas'.[21] As the humanists were later to complain, it was hard to see how there could be any form of resolution of their conflicting approaches. There was, for instance, no agreed response to Ockham. He never set out to be a reformer; rather, he was primarily interested in seeing where his mind led him. Despite being at first banned in Paris (he remained excommunicate at the time of his death), it was perhaps a mark of his originality that he inspired a range of reactions. Some highlighted his insistence on faith and even mysticism (and this strand of his thinking was indeed to reappear among Protestants); others argued that his focus on God's absolute power left too much uncertainty. If God could exercise his power at will, where did that leave the church, the priesthood and the sacraments? Were they eternal expressions of his grace or not? Again, how could one establish scientific knowledge if God could use his power to subvert the natural order? Yet, the way that Ockham ordered knowledge and argued for simplicity has persuaded others that he was 'one of the initiators of the modern notion of science as an ordered body of knowledge'.[22] His nominalism proved attractive to German theologians but was opposed by the reformers John Wyclif and Jan Hus, who were both committed Realists. Ultimately, Ockham fell foul of the reality that any innovative thinking at this period risked being counted as heresy.

The already febrile debates of the age were further intensified by the historic rivalries between the Franciscans and Dominicans. Étienne Gilson concludes his history of medieval philosophy as follows:

> Every one of the great doctrinal innovations which took place in theology as well as in philosophy perpetuated itself throughout the following centuries. The doctrines accumulated by the successive masters, backed by their Orders, exploited by their schools and continually distorted in the heat of endless controversies, finally created what cannot be described otherwise than doctrinal confusion.[23]

By 1400 even theologians such as Jean Gerson were fed up with the rarified controversies of scholasticism that diverted attention from everyday contact with those in need of compassion. Gerson's student Nicholas of Clémanges (*c.*1363–1437) berated intellectuals for living in ivory towers, being lazy and formulating ideas that had no relationship with reality (an attitude to 'intellectuals' not completely dead today).[24]

In short, there was no unity to medieval philosophy. The relative weight that was given to theology and to pure philosophy ran along a spectrum, from Augustine and Bonaventure through Aquinas to the Averroists who saw philosophy as totally independent of religious belief. Ockham would join them in this respect. It was only centuries later, after the successful rise of science had brought new perspectives, that the church was able to stand back from the unresolved controversies of the thirteenth and fourteenth centuries to declare the winners: Albert the Great, now the patron saint of scientists, and his pupil Thomas Aquinas, the great Catholic philosopher.

In my earlier book *The Closing of the Western Mind*, the main part of which ended in AD 600, I included a chapter on 'Thomas Aquinas and the Restoration of Reason', in which I stated that 'Thomas Aquinas revived the Aristotelian approach to knowing things so successfully that he unwittingly laid the foundations of the scientific revolution that was to transform western thought'. This was clearly overstated, but insofar as Aquinas accepted that the world operated under consistent natural laws, which allows it to be open to scientific explanation, it is not completely unjustified. He had made a small step towards the secularization of knowledge.[25] (For those who believed in miracles – and, in the medieval world, these were believed to be an everyday manifestation of God's presence – there were no secure foundations from which to create scientific certainty.) It was the achievement of Aquinas that he succeeded in allowing a pagan philosopher to be integrated into western theology when less intellectually imaginative theologians might have excluded him. There is no doubting that as a work of sheer intellectual quality, Thomas Aquinas's *Summa* must have a place as one of the greater achievements of western philosophy, a classic that left Peter Lombard's *Sentences* in the shade. Here is the accolade given to Thomas by Pope Paul VI in 1974:

> Thomas possessed supremely the courage of the truth, a freedom of spirit in confronting new problems, the intellectual honesty of those who allow Christianity to be contaminated neither by secular philosophy nor by a prejudiced rejection of it. He passed therefore into the history of Christian thought as a pioneer of the new path of philosophy and universal culture… With all the brilliance of his prophetic intuition, he gave to the new encounter of faith and reason a reconciliation between the secularity of the world and the radicality of the Gospel.[26]

In conclusion, we could say that these debates had played some part in a reawakening of the western mind, notably through their sophisticated use of reason to make philosophical distinctions and explore different ways of describing the relationship between God and the natural world. There are modern philosophers who still find insights of importance, especially in logic, ethics and metaphysics, in medieval philosophy. The Scottish philosopher Alasdair Macintyre (b.1929) has championed Thomas Aquinas for his theory of moral virtues, which he believes should be reasserted in modern-day communities.[27] It was the failure to provide a means through which the subject itself could be carried forward in a coherent way that was a hindrance, and gradually intellectual life developed new contexts in which philosophy could be practised. Macintyre laments a dearth of Catholic philosophy before its revival in the late nineteenth century.

Fundamentally, the church was desperate to establish authoritative teachings that it could defend against future attack and so had no interest in encouraging speculation. Theological discourse would always be confined within the language and orthodoxies of a hierarchical system. As one historian of medieval thought has put it: 'The medieval church stubbornly resisted all forms of true secular autonomy, whether the independent study of philosophy apart from theology or the independent operation of secular political power apart from church oversight and freedom to interfere.'[28] Aquinas had, brilliantly, reconciled two systems of philosophy that had originated in contexts many centuries apart, but had he made any breakthroughs, other than for Catholics, at a more fundamental philosophical level? The problem of finding an agreed means of understanding God, through experience of his creation, through reason, through intuition or through faith, appeared intractable.

The Glimmerings of a Scientific Revival, 1200–1350

There, when introduced by wonderful teaching in the art through the nine figures of the Indians, knowledge of this art above other ones so much pleased me, and I so much believed in it, that I learned through much study and practices of disputation what was studied in it, with its various methods, in Egypt, Greece, Sicily and Provence, to which places I afterwards traveled in the course of business… Binding myself more strictly to this method, studying more carefully in it, adding some things from my own thinking, and introducing some things from the subtleties of Euclid's art of geometry, I laboured to compose as intelligibly as I could the main features of this book.

Liber abbaci of Fibonacci[1]

There is a legend that the English Franciscan friar Roger Bacon (1220–92), whose study of optics will be explored below, invented spectacles. He was certainly aware of how lenses could magnify but whether he was able, in his secluded laboratory, to create lenses that would be used specifically for reading is unknown. In fact, the first definite references come in the late thirteenth century, from Venice (where a decree of 1300 refers to *vitreos ab oculis ad legendum*, a 'glass for reading from the eyes') and Florence. In Venice, of course, the glassworkers of Murano were experts in their fields but there was work of a high technical quality elsewhere among the wealthy cities of northern Italy, so the reference, by a monk, Giordano da Pisa, in Florence to spectacles as an example of human ingenuity is not unbelievable. Preaching in 1305, Giordano dates the invention to some twenty years earlier.

It is instructive to contrast the medieval texts on natural philosophy and mathematics originating from the universities – which depended on original Greek, Arabic and, as can be seen from the opening quotation, Indian sources – and the associated commentaries on these – with the practical manifestations of science that were appearing in the cities. While Paris had always been the university of Aristotle and his relationship with theology, Oxford tended towards Platonism. Plato had argued that the beginning of any search for the ultimate meaning of things lay in mathematics so it was perhaps natural that the English university took a particular interest in the subject, whereas Paris, as the curriculum of 1366 stated, hardly bothered with it (see p. 174). Without a bishop in attendance, Oxford was also a university where there was more freedom to reflect on the natural world without the threat of ecclesiastical intrusion. Even when the chancellor, the Dominican Robert Kilwardby (later to be archbishop of Canterbury), followed Paris in setting out theses that could not be taught in the theology faculty, there were only thirty of them, mainly attacks on specific theses of Thomas Aquinas, and the penalty was not total excommunication from the church, as in Paris, but simply exclusion from teaching at the university.* This did not mean, of course, that the Oxford natural philosophers were not religious – even conservatively so, in that many clung to teachings that predated Aquinas. The first important

* This did not last. By the end of the thirteenth century, the university teachers themselves had adopted much of Aquinas's theology. See Brockliss, *The University of Oxford: A History*, pp. 96–7.

natural philosopher from Oxford, Robert Grosseteste (*c.*1175–1253), for instance, would never have known of Aquinas's work.

Much is unknown about Grosseteste's early career, but it is believed that after an earlier period studying in Paris he taught at Oxford between 1225 and 1230 and even became chancellor of the university before retiring to the Franciscan provincial house in the city as a lecturer there.[2] He then re-emerged as bishop of Lincoln five years later, a position that allowed him some, if limited, supervisory rights over the university, which fell within his diocese. This was just when new texts of Aristotle were beginning to appear and Grosseteste was one of the first English scholars to learn Greek so that he could translate both theological works and those of Aristotle. His commentary on Aristotle's *Posterior Analytics*, probably from the 1220s, is the earliest Latin one known. It soon became integrated into the teaching of logic. He also produced the first complete Latin translation of Aristotle's *Nicomachean Ethics*, an enormously influential work still held in high regard as one of the foundation texts of ethical theory and practice to this day. Grosseteste must have had a strong personality: in the early 1250s he openly criticized Pope Innocent IV for his lack of pastoral care for the church.

Despite his interest in Aristotle, Grosseteste was cautious about adopting his works. He hit out at 'moderns who, with amazing blindness and presumption, try to make Aristotle the heretic into a catholic'.[3] He remained conservative in his religious beliefs – his works contain a strong Augustinian flavour – but he showed considerable imagination in marrying theology to the study of the natural world in a way that would not have been possible if he had remained in Paris during the 1220s. Grosseteste was fascinated by light. God himself is light (and it is through his light that we can discover the truth about him). Light spread through the universe at the moment of creation from the Earth itself, where it achieves its densest form and gives energy to living things, to the outermost spheres of heaven. While this makes it hard to distinguish light as a metaphysical force from its practical use as a means of finding empirical truths in the material world, this did not deter Grosseteste from carrying out his own observations. He realized that the colours of rainbows were caused by light being refracted through a 'lens' of drops of water and from here he examined actual lenses, observing that light transmitted through them could lead to heat or magnification. He was one of the first to refute the Aristotelian idea that water and earth occupied different spheres, the water being held back to allow the land to emerge. Instead, earth and water were joined in one sphere, a view that was not fully accepted until the fifteenth- and sixteenth-century 'discovery' of the New World made Aristotle's theory redundant.

There is much scholarly dispute over the extent to which Grosseteste actually carried out experiments or merely provided theories on the basis of what he had read from, mainly, Arabic sources. Yet while Grosseteste's 'science' was primarily a means of better understanding the nature of God (in that the light that infused the natural world is a direct manifestation of God's creation), one can see in him some glimmering beginnings of scientific enquiry. Crucially, Grosseteste asserted the importance of mathematics, notably in a treatise *De lineis, angulis et figuris* (*On Lines, Angles and Figures*), in which he said that 'all causes of natural effects must be expressed by means of lines, angles and figures, for otherwise it is impossible to grasp their explanation'.[4] The implication was that, as Plato had argued, starting with mathematical models it was possible to ascend to higher states of knowing. In particular he argued that so far as the definition of natural phenomena were concerned, mathematics offered greater accuracy than Aristotelian logic. In this Grosseteste was well ahead of his time.

In the earliest known representation of spectacles (1352), Cardinal Nicholas of Rouen reads a text through an eye lens.

The most important follower of Grosseteste's was Roger Bacon, who was born in Somerset, England, in about 1220. Bacon was a lonely, introspective man, clearly brilliant in many ways in his mastery of languages (especially Greek but also Hebrew and Arabic, of which he produced the earliest Latin grammars) and breadth of knowledge but very intolerant of any intellectual rivals. His appreciation of the age of Aristotle and his successors both in Greece and the Arab world is evident in his supposition, undoubtedly a correct one, that academic standards were higher in earlier societies than in his own day. The Dominican Albert, a contemporary of Bacon's when the two men were teaching in Paris, was one of his targets. It was monstrous, said Bacon, that Albert was seen as an equal to Aristotle, Avicenna and Averroes and referred to as 'the Great'. His antagonism was misguided as Albert, in fact, shared his enthusiasm for observation and experiment, but Bacon was never one for collaboration and collegiality. He accused even Aquinas of 'a childish vanity and a voluminous superfluity'.[5] The most positive result of his invective was that it gave him an incentive to follow his own intellectual instincts with greater determination. Otherwise, it confirmed him as an awkward eccentric whose impact as a philosopher among his contemporaries was far less than it might have been.

Bacon was not, at first, a member of either mendicant order but, like Grosseteste, theologically he was a conservative, arguing that theology should be based on the scriptures rather than on Peter Lombard's *Sentences*. While he was fascinated by Aristotle, he felt that the philosopher's works should not intrude into the closed world of theology. Here Bacon followed Augustine in that he believed that all scientific knowledge should be subordinated to the 'nod and command' of theology. In contrast to Albert the Great (see p. 192), he was unable to separate philosophy from theology and see the natural world on its own terms. Philosophy alone led to 'the blindness of hell and therefore by itself it must be darkness and mist'.[6] This did not deter him from grasping with alacrity the opportunities offered by the new natural philosophies. In fact, he proposed a programme of radical reform in the university curriculum, placing mathematics above traditional logic, and introducing languages, optics, moral philosophy, experimental science and alchemy, all, of course, subordinate to theology.

Bacon knew of Grosseteste's works, notably from having access to his library, and may have met him in Lincoln. He developed many of Grosseteste's insights, benefiting from access to the most searching of the Arabic works on optics, that of Ibn al-Haytham (*c*.956–*c*.1040) or, as he is known in the west, Alhazen. Alhazen's major study on optics, the seven-volume *Book of Optics* (composed 1011–21), had been translated into Latin as *De aspectibus* in the early thirteenth century.[7]

The natural philosophers of the thirteenth century focused on God 'the geometer' creating the universe, whose harmonious workings could be revealed to the human mind. This image dates from *c*.1220.

The Greeks had been fascinated by the problems of light and vision. Inevitably, in such a lively intellectual climate, conflicting theories had emerged. Aristotle had argued that a perceived object produces an alteration in the organism, the eye, that receives it. This was known as the *intromission* theory: the agent responsible for vision enters the eye from the outside. One explanation for this was put forward by the Greek Atomists,* who suggested that a thin layer of atoms left the surface of the perceived object and then entered the eye. This did nothing to explain how the eye received, absorbed and interpreted the object. In contrast the mathematician Euclid approached the problem from *within* the eye. He claimed that the eye sent out rays that would meet together as a cone and when the tip of the cone met an object the rays interpreted its shape, size and location and transmitted this

* The Atomists were a Greek school founded in the fifth century BC by Leucippus and his student Democritus. As their name suggests, they believed all matter could be broken down into small particles.

back to the eye. This was the *extramission* theory. Further depth to the understanding of vision had been provided by the physician Galen, who had examined the structure of the eye and recognized the crystalline lens, its most powerful lens. Alhazen favoured the intromission theory. He noted, for instance, that if one looks directly at the sun one's eyes are burned, suggesting that something is indeed emanating from the sun. Yet he also adopted the concept of the cone from Euclid, reversed it to fit with his intromission theory, and produced a new synthesis of optics from these traditional sources.

Suppose one is looking at an iron rod. There are, according to the intromission theory, a mass of rays coming from it, from across its length, and in all directions. A small range of these rays, emanating from one end of the rod to the other, will reach the eye perpendicularly and pass through the curved surface of the eye. (The theory supposes that a ray hitting the curve of the eye perpendicularly will have more power than one entering from an angle and so will predominate in the ensuing image of the rod.) As the eye is a convex curve, these perpendicular rays must bend inwards to meet at a point, of a cone, within the eye. Noting the observations of Galen, Alhazen suggests that this is after they have passed through the crystalline lens. From the tip of the cone, the rays then head onwards into the eye as parallel lines and finally the optic nerve processes them to produce a clear image. Alhazen had managed to combine the extramission and intromission theories while finding a place for Galen's observations of the lens. In short, as the historian of science David Lindberg puts it, 'he was able to arrive at a comprehensive synthesis [of the opposing Greek theories] capable of explaining optical phenomena and vision with a precision and scope unprecedented in the history of the discipline'. *De aspectibus* was the achievement of a genius. In his *The Dialogue of Civilizations in the Birth of Modern Science*, Arun Bala argues that Alhazen's work in marrying mathematics to what the eye can see remained influential from the thirteenth century as far as the researches of Galileo and Newton in the seventeenth.[8]

Grosseteste had known of Alhazen's work and had developed it by positing that the eye processed knowledge of what it could see beyond just recording it. So a man approaching with a knife would be processed to see whether he offered a threat or not. In other words, there was a process of evaluating images which, Grosseteste argued, took place within the brain.[9] He also suggested that rays could be transmitted both into and out of the eye, so formulating a composite of the extramission and intromission theories. Roger Bacon followed him here. He agreed with Alhazen that the intromission theory was primary, something entered the eye to create an image, but he also believed that something from the eye was emitted outwards to 'enoble' the objects seen.

Bacon was to go further. He developed Alhazen and the work of Grosseteste on two fronts. The first was to use mathematics to portray how the rays that formed vision might be expressed through geometrical models. He compared the impact of rays on plane, convex and concave surfaces. His *Perspectiva* (1267) contained fifty-one diagrams to illustrate his arguments. This was an important moment: it showed that mathematics could be used to take forward scientific understanding and it was central to Bacon's programme of curriculum reform. He went beyond optics to show how mathematics informed every other discipline, the position of places on Earth, the movement of the stars, the workings of a calendar and the physical sciences. While Bacon was never a pioneering mathematician in his own right, he did much to consolidate mathematics as an important tool in the search for knowledge.

The second front involved actual examination of natural phenomena. In this Bacon drew on both Greek authorities, Aristotle, Euclid, Ptolemy and Galen, as well as their Arab interpreters. Scholars disagree as to how far he managed to integrate the observations and theories of all these past masters and then make scientific advances of his own. He does seem to have carried out some original experimentation, establishing the focal distances of lens and proving that the speed of light is finite, for instance. Bacon was the first to calculate that the maximum elevation of the rainbow is 42 degrees.* He was understandably fascinated by the way that a rainbow moved as an observer walked towards or away from it and this informed his work on lenses. Yet he followed Augustine in arguing that all experience was an illumination from God. 'All wisdom has been given by one God, to one world, for one purpose, namely salvation.'[10]

Moving between Paris and Oxford (which he made his base between 1247 and 1257), Bacon began to lose touch with reality as he made ever more extravagant claims for what science could achieve, especially in the fields of alchemy and astrology. Gossip about a man who spent years closeted away with his experiments made it inevitable that he would develop a reputation for possessing secret knowledge. There were rumours that he had created a 'brazen head' that could answer

* This was confirmed mathematically by Descartes in the seventeenth century.

any question that it was asked. It is telling that when optics arrived in the Oxford curriculum, it was not directly through Bacon's work but through the Polish physicist Witelo's massive *Perspectiva* (composed 1270–8), which, while influenced by Bacon, still depended heavily on Alhazen.

It was perhaps to gain some security that Bacon eventually joined the Franciscans in 1257 (at a time when Bonaventure was head of the order). He was soon in trouble. He expected to be funded for his research, was irritated by restrictions on what he could write without the approval of his fellow friars and attempted to communicate directly with a sympathetic pope, Clement IV, who died before the relationship could be consolidated. It was in his *Opus Maius*, the work sent to the pope, that he decried the ignorance of the age and the conservatism of the academic curriculum, and put forward his own proposals for reform. His immediate objective was to consolidate learning under the umbrella of theology with the ultimate aim of creating a truly Christian society that would spread throughout the globe. He had an enthusiasm for Christian missions.

How far it was Bacon's abrasive personality that led to his later troubles is unclear. In 1278 he was condemned by the minister general of the Franciscans, possibly for his views on astrology, that the stars could define the future of an individual. This had been one of the propositions condemned by Stephen Tempier just the year before. Later reports claim that he was imprisoned by his order for much of the rest of his life, although this may have been no more than a restriction on his teaching and movements. He was still working on mathematics when he died in old age in Oxford in 1292.

For many, especially in the sixteenth and seventeenth centuries, Roger Bacon was a lone genius, a man ahead of his time, who was unjustly neglected and condemned by his contemporaries. It was typical that the medieval Voynich manuscript, a mysterious codex written in an unknown script, was linked by one seventeenth-century source, since discredited, to Bacon. Undoubtedly, he conceived of many later developments: manned flight, divers reaching the ocean depths and boats driven by machinery.* Deeper research has shown that Bacon was more dependent on Grosseteste, Alhazen, and natural philosophers in Paris than was originally realized. There were other thirteenth-century figures such as Peter of Maricourt in Paris whose work on magnets combined experimentation with mathematical calculation and who may have been a direct influence on William Gilbert's work on magnetism (see pp. 650–1). Scholarly evaluations of Bacon's contribution to science are still evolving as his works are explored in more detail, but he certainly deserves the accolade as one of the most imaginative and far-ranging minds of his time.

* * *

The new emphasis on mathematics was an important riposte to Aristotle, who had distinguished the qualities of an object from the quantity. In Aristotle's view mathematics and empirical knowledge should be kept separate (a view followed in most of his works but disowned by him in his *Physics*). There were already challenges to this idea, not least from Ptolemy (see pp. 164–5). As already noted, in comparison with Paris's attachment to Aristotle, Oxford had favoured Platonism with its emphasis on making mathematical logic the first step towards moving towards the ultimate truths. A group of logicians at Merton College in Oxford – the Oxford Calculators, as they became known – working between 1325 and 1350, took the idea further.[11] As the best mathematician among them, Thomas Bradwardine, put it:

Roger Bacon conducting an experiment, in an engraving from 1617. Many later thinkers considered *Doctor Mirabilis* to be the founder of modern empirical science.

> It is mathematics which reveals every genuine truth, for it knows every hidden secret and bears the key to every subtlety of letters; whoever has the effrontery to study physics while neglecting mathematics should know from the start that he will never make his entry through the portals of wisdom.[12]

* These speculations take up a section of the *Opus Maius*.

He was right; physics is impossible without mathematics. One of Bradwardine's insights was to recognize that Aristotle had been wrong in suggesting that the circular movement of the planets was of a different kind from the movement of an object in a straight line. Bradwardine thus conceived the idea that there could be one unified mathematical explanation that encompassed the heavens and the Earth, an important step forward in the history of science.*

Bradwardine and his colleagues began developing mathematical representations of velocity, the study of objects in motion. Naturally, one important measure is a mathematical one and easy to calculate: how far the object will travel in a set period of time – say miles in an hour – if it is moving at a uniform speed. So a uniform speed of 20 miles an hour will result in a distance of 20 miles. Yet suppose that the speed is not uniform. Take a hawk, for instance. It might well be flying at a uniform speed until it sees its prey, at which point it will accelerate. If the speed of the acceleration is known and the period of time over which it takes place, then it would be possible to calculate the total distance travelled in, say, an hour. The Calculators developed a theorem that shows that a body that accelerates at a uniform rate covers the same distance in a set period of time as if it moved with a uniform speed equal to its average speed over that time. This became known as 'the Merton rule' or the 'mean-speed theorem'. Suppose again you have an object that is accelerating at a uniform rate over a set period of time. How far would it have travelled in the first half of that time compared to the distance in the second half? The answer is that the distance in the second half of the time period is three times the distance of the first half.

The Calculators did not actually carry out experiments to see if their theorems worked, but news of these calculations travelled fast. In Paris Nicholas Oresme (1320–82), one of the most important mathematicians of the age, constructed elegant geometrical models to illustrate the Oxford Calculators' theorems. Oresme also suggested that there was no reason why the Earth should not revolve on its own axis, with the stars and planets remaining stationary. This contradicted what Aristotle had said, but Oresme argued that it made for a much simpler act of creation. He rejected the arguments that there would be a continual rush of wind, that an object thrown into the air would

* Bradwardine was a man of worldly achievements as well as intellectual ones. As confessor to Edward III he accompanied that king on his French campaigns and preached a victory sermon after the Battle of Crécy. He was briefly archbishop of Canterbury before succumbing to the Black Death in 1349.

come down at a distance as the world moved round, and that scripture suggested it was the heavens that moved. In the end, good Catholic that he was (he became a bishop and was taken into the court of the French king Charles V), Oresme settled for the traditional cosmology but he had identified an important issue and in the long term he would be proved right.

It was also in Paris that a new theory to explain impetus was conceived.[13] In his *Physics*, Aristotle had struggled to explain how a thrown object continued to move once it had left the hand of the thrower. He implied that the air moved as well, coming in behind the object to push it on further. This idea of a continuing *external* force was not convincing. Already in the sixth century AD the Alexandrian philosopher John Philoponus had suggested that the force of the throw somehow added something *internally* to the object that gave it the power to go on moving. One suggested analogy that supported Philoponus was the way in which plants appeared to grow from within themselves.

In Paris in the mid-fourteenth century a master of arts at the university, John Buridan (*c.*1300–*c.*1360), took up the problem. He immediately spotted the flaw in Aristotle's theory. Take two lances, one with only the front end pointed, the second with both ends pointed so making it difficult for any external force to propel it through the air from behind. Yet he showed how both travelled an equal distance when thrown with equal force. As a result he conceived the idea of impetus, which he assumed was passed on to the object by the force that put it in motion. Where Buridan went further than Philoponus was in relating the distance travelled to the original force of the throw and the weight of the object. Buridan also noted that when impetus ran out the object did not drop directly to the ground. He posited instead that its weight as it fell gave it extra – but diminishing – impetus to allow it to go on moving for a certain distance. And Buridan achieved another important insight: he realized that there must be some kind of resistance within the air at terrestrial level that prevented the object from continuing in perpetual motion. Yet if one looked beyond the Earth to the heavens, the planets seemed to be in constant movement. One explanation was that God had given them a perpetual source of impetus when he created them, another that there was no form of resistance slowing them down. It was not until gravitational pull was recognized in the seventeenth century that the second explanation was confirmed. Buridan was not rejecting Aristotle as a philosopher – indeed, much of his work consisted of commentary on the major

Aristotelian texts – but he was part of a movement that was challenging individual elements of Aristotle's ideas. This movement was to gather pace in the sixteenth century, although it was to prove difficult to isolate criticisms of Aristotle's own works from the scholastic straitjacket in which they had become embedded in the university curriculum.

Buridan's intellectual interests were wide-ranging. Although a cleric, he never joined one of the orders and confined his teaching to the courses in the arts. This kept him well clear of the often bitter debates over theology and allowed him to develop his ideas without having to reconcile them with Christian doctrine. His major work, the *Summulae de dialectica*, was a rethinking of Aristotle's works on logic. It was neglected for many years, and it is only recently that logicians have come to appreciate its importance in dealing with issues that are still relevant

areas of debate in the subject today. Whether Buridan left an enduring legacy in science is more debatable. The Frenchman Pierre Duhem (1861–1916), a physicist and historian of medieval science, argued that Buridan was an important link between the natural philosophers of the Middle Ages and the so-called Scientific Revolution of the seventeenth century, especially through Galileo.[14] More recent assessments disagree. In John Heilbron's exhaustive list of those whose writings 'engaged' Galileo, Buridan's name is nowhere to be found, and nor is Oresme's. Sacrobosco, whose work *De Sphaera* was taught in an extended edition by Galileo, is the only medieval natural philosopher included.[15]

This lack of contact seems to be generally true of medieval university 'science'. As so many of Aristotle's works on the natural sciences and the methodology, in his *Prior* and *Posterior Analytics*, for instance, needed to explore the natural world had been integrated into the arts curriculum, one might have hoped they would have made the universities a hotbed of scientific enterprise. But with Paris choosing to concentrate on theology and Bologna on law, it was left to Oxford to carry out any pioneering work. However, the church was still powerful. In one scholarly assessment of medieval Oxford, 'intellectual curiosity and creativity had to be held in check in order that the church's spiritual and material power was not threatened by an institution that was there principally there to enhance its authority'.[16] It is right to be cautious about the achievements of medieval science in the universities in so far as they were subject to the 'nod and command' of theology. A traditional view that the medieval church actually fostered science has long been discredited, but so long as it was seen as a handmaid to theology the exploration of the natural world could be tolerated. Unless 'natural philosophy' was separated from theology so that it could develop as an independent discipline, as Albert the Great had argued it should, the findings of these university scholars would be limited.[17]

Alhazen's *Book of Optics* was incorporated in the *Optica Thesaurus* of 1572. This illustration shows a number of experiments using light and refraction, including Archimedes setting fire to Greek ships with a lens.

* * *

There was far more practical scientific achievement in northern Italy – and not only in the invention of spectacles. This was a society in which the wealth and the ebullience of both merchants and communal governments were having a dramatic effect on the urban and commercial landscape. Building techniques, stonemasonry, glassmaking, land surveying were all improving. Technology allowed greater mastery of the seas, notably through the compass and better ship design. Guilds kept up high standards in every field of manufacture. For textiles the introduction of the treadle loom in about 1000, from its origins weaving silk in China, revolutionized weaving. Speeds were three times what they had been and the use of rollers allowed longer cloths to be made.* The sumptuous costumes of sitters for Renaissance portraits show just how sophisticated cloth manufacture and design had become. In his *The Italian City-State*, Philip Jones notes other developments in technical fields, 'notably of statistics, mensuration, and mathematics, by precocious experiments and conversancy with musters and census, cadestral surveying and scientific cartography'.[18] It has already been noted that the man regarded as 'the greatest of medieval mathematicians', Leonardo of Pisa, Fibonacci, learned directly from the Arabs and Indians rather than through a university (see pp. 151–2) and was able to provide handbooks that underpinned commercial negotiations. In his *Reason and Society in the Middle Ages*, Alexander Murray charts the arrival of mathematical calculation in the cities of northern Italy. He takes the example of the *Cronica* of Giovanni Villani (1347), which we will encounter later, setting out the statistics of life in Florence: 'It never waits on much of a pretext [for Villani] to break out in a numerical rash – whether for a grain price, a military figure, a rate of tax or sum of income and expenditure related to some individual or project.'[19]

At the highest level of technical achievement, it is worth exploring the extraordinary *Astrarium*, an astronomical clock created in Padua by the mechanical engineer Giovanni Dondi (*c.*1330–88) between 1348 and 1364.[20] Giovanni's father had already built a clock for a tower in Padua and his son inherited his skills. The *Astrarium* was essentially the product of high-level craftsmanship – there is no record that Giovanni had anything to do with the University of Padua, although he is known to have used the *Theorica planetarum*, the standard – if limited – textbook on astronomy, as one of his sources, alongside works by Aristotle and Avicenna.

The *Astrarium* contained an extraordinarily complex mechanism that was designed to illustrate astronomy and the movements of the planets to observers. The Alfonsine Tables of 1272 (see p. 177) were recalibrated to fit the time in Padua. The clock's seven faces each showed the position of a planet, including the moon, and their

* One of the many reasons that we know that the Shroud of Turin is medieval is that the breadth and length of the cloth are typical of a treadle loom.

movements encompassed the epicycles of the planets that Ptolemy had proposed in his *Almagest*.† Below the seven faces was a twenty-four-hour dial and a drum that showed the major feast days of the church. There were calendars that indicated the saints' days and the names of the months and even the length of daylight for each of the 365 days. Dondi recognized that this would result in inaccuracies over time, but there was a mechanism for creating ten-minute intervals or stopping the clock entirely for adjustments. All this needed 107 gear wheels and pinions that Dondi constructed by hand and fitted together without screws. For horologists this is the earliest documented example of a verge and foliot escapement (the mechanism that allows the clock to advance at regular intervals or 'ticks'). The clock, wrote one of Dondi's contemporaries, Giovanni Manzini of Pavia, 'is full of artifice, worked on and perfected by your hands and carved with a skill never attained by the expert hand of any craftsman. I conclude that there was never invented an artifice so excellent and marvellous and of such genius.' The clock was presented by its maker to the duke of Milan but it vanished at the end of the fifteenth century, possibly because no one had the technical skills to keep it running. There are certainly reports that it was simply too ambitious to function correctly. Luckily, Dondi had compiled a detailed description of his work with illustrations, so that it has been possible to reconstruct the clock. It would be interesting to compare the *Astrarium* with the Antikythera Mechanism that had been designed for much the same function some 1,500 years earlier.

In short, the *Astrarium* was one of a number of technological innovations that appeared alongside the steady revival of the European economy after 1100. While in the universities there was no incentive other than natural curiosity to stimulate practical science, in the cities the lure of profit drove technological innovation across a wide range of crafts and industries. It was an essential part of a revolution that was as much cultural as economic and which will form the subject of the following chapters.

† Only six planets were known in the fourteenth century: Mercury, Venus, Earth, Mars, Jupiter and Saturn. Uranus would not be discovered until 1781.

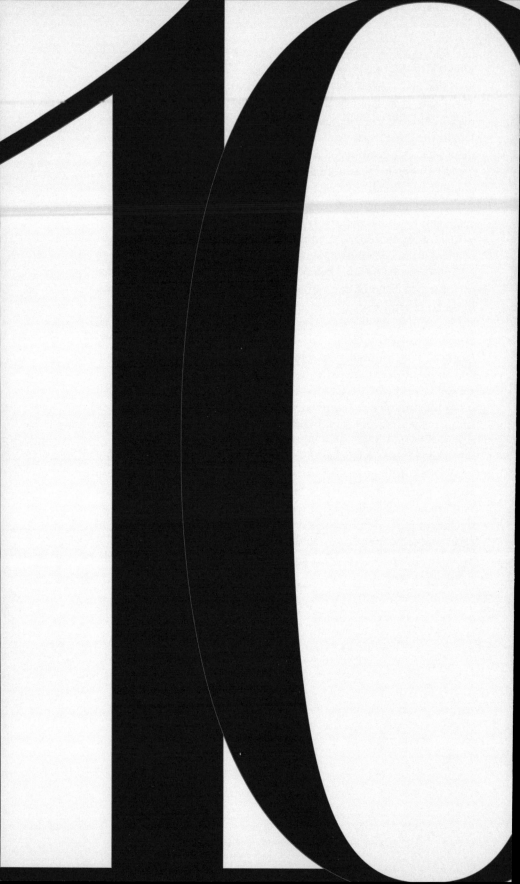

Dante, Marsilius and Boccaccio and their Worlds

I' fui nato e cresciuto
Sovra 'l bel fiume d'Arno a la gran villa.

I was born and raised
in the great city on the lovely River Arno.

The Divine Comedy,
Inferno, canto xxiii,
by Dante Alighieri, 1320

La gran villa, 'the great city' was, of course, Florence, and the writer of the words was the greatest of the medieval poets, Dante Alighieri. In a world of conflict and instability, the cut-throat politics of thirteenth-century Florence saw Dante driven into exile from his beloved city in 1302. He was to remain in exile for nineteen years before his death in Ravenna. Memories of the city, and above all those of Beatrice, a girl whose beauty he had glimpsed in a few meetings, in a church, at a wedding reception, but who, already married, had died young, haunted him for the rest of his life.[1]

Florence, *Florentia*, 'the place of flowers', had been a prosperous Roman colony, founded, according to tradition, by Julius Caesar in the days when Rome was still a republic. It had grown rich from exploiting the river crossing of the Via Cassia that ran northwards from Rome. The grid of the Roman streets can still be traced and the prestige of a republican Roman past was to inspire the imagination of its citizens. The economic boom that the city enjoyed in the fourteenth century would be accompanied by an extraordinary outburst of creative energy and thought.

Florence was among the cities given its freedom in 1115 on the death of Countess Matilda, but its medieval revival was delayed by its remoteness from the coast.[2] Its fortune lay in the narrowing of the River Arno, which provided a rush of water that would prove ideal for washing and fulling wool (beating cloth to rid it of impurities). Alas, this also made it very vulnerable to flooding.* Despite this, by the thirteenth century the city was expanding fast and the search for raw wool led its merchants and their financial supporters northwards into Europe, to Flanders and England. Labour from the surrounding countryside was plentiful and soon a wide range of crafts was flourishing. The treadle loom, Chinese in origin and known in Europe from about AD 1000, had revolutionized weaving speeds and by the early fourteenth century there were between 200 and 300 firms involved in the production of wool with an estimated workforce of 10,000 artisans, one in six of the male workforce, producing a total of 100,000 bolts of cloth. A further 10,000 bolts of finished cloth were imported each year to be dyed and resold. The Florentine merchants were ruthless in searching out new markets and setting out the international infrastructure needed to sustain the flow of raw materials back to Tuscany. As one Pisan, Fra Giordano, noted in 1303, the merchants 'did nothing day or night but

* The most recent flood in November 1966 was devastating.

think and calculate'. The florin, first minted in 1252, with the head of John the Baptist, patron saint of the city, on it, became the most stable currency in Europe.

Dante, drawing on the experiences of his ancestor Cacciaguida, whom he meets in Paradise in the *Divine Comedy*, idealized the city of a century before his time as a haven of peace. In fact, Florence had been ravaged by competing aristocratic factions, each with their own neighbourhood and towers.† While Florence's *contado*, its surrounding countryside, spread as smaller communities were absorbed, expansion encouraged counter-attacks by Florence's neighbours, Milan, Pisa, Lucca or Siena. A devastating defeat by Siena at Montaperti in 1260 is traditionally remembered in the taunts of Sienese supporters when they meet Florence's football team. None of this impeded the rapid growth of the city. The population tripled between 1200 and 1300 to 120,000 and in 1284 construction of a new set of walls, eight times the length of the old ones, was begun. It would be fifty years before they were finished and by this time they would enclose two of the great new churches of the city, those of the mendicant orders, the Franciscans at Santa Croce (rebuilt from 1294) and the Dominicans at the (rare for Tuscany) Gothic Santa Maria Novella, where building had begun in 1246.‡

The thirteenth century saw an escalating struggle between the magnates and a *popolo* that emerged as merchants and entrepreneurs grew rich and demanded participation in political life. A similar struggle was enacted, with a variety of outcomes, in many of the cities of northern Italy. Attempts were made to create constitutions that would bring peace between different factions. Prominent in the ideology of these constitutions was an idealized vision of the Roman republic. There was also an emphasis on Justice, portrayed as a female figure with a sword (to deal with wrongdoers) in one hand, and a scales in the other. It was a symbol of the way in which civic power was replacing more ancient traditions of inter-family feuds.

overleaf A famous painting of Dante by Domenico di Michelino *c.* 1465 shows the Inferno on the left, Purgatory in the centre and Heaven above the celestial spheres, as envisaged by Aristotle. Note the fine view of fifteenth-century Florence.

Florence appeared to have found a stable government under the Ordinances of Justice, first promulgated in 1293, then revised in 1295, a sophisticated attempt at creating a flexible oligarchy. In its preamble

† The towers were partly defensive, but also acted to show off the status of the aristocratic owner.

‡ Sensibly, in view of the tensions between the two orders, they were located at opposite ends of the city.

LASCIATE OGNI
SPERANZA VOC
HENTRATE

ELMEZODE
LCHAMINO
DINOSTRA
VITA MIRI
TROVAPE
RVNA SEL
VA SCVRA
CHE LADIRI
TTA VIAER
ASMARIT
VRA QVE
SILVAGGI

'justice' was defined according to Roman law as 'the constant and perpetual desire to ensure to each his own right', a reminder of how Roman law acted to promote liberty and a 'right'.[3] This constitution depended on the guilds that played such an important part in fostering the economic success of Florence.[4] The seven larger ones represented the city's main industries, the Lana all those involved in the manufacture of wool, the Calimala those who imported cloth, the Cambio the bankers, the guild of Por Santa Maria the silk weavers. There were also important guilds of the notaries and lawyers and another for the doctors and apothecaries. Another fifty guilds represented less important interests, among them bakers, shoemakers and builders.

Under the Ordinances, eight priors were to be chosen from the twenty-one largest guilds, balanced so that each district of the city was represented. Each prior only held office for two months – short terms of office were, according to the ever-influential Aristotle, a mark of democracy – but there was also a *gonfaloniere di giustizia*, the presiding official with a militia of 1,000 men to keep order on the streets. The nine were known collectively as the *signoria* and were given an imposing palazzo, dei Priori (now the Palazzo Vecchio), symbolically in an area cleared by the demolition of the strongholds of an expelled magnate family. It was perhaps inevitable, however, that tensions in this vibrant and expanding city would continue. It was as a result of infighting between the Ghibellines, those who looked to the emperor for protection, and the Guelphs, those who hoped for papal support, that Dante – a member of a Guelph faction – had been expelled.

The Florentine guilds were an important element in the republican government and another example of that collegiality that was such a feature of the Middle Ages. Each guild was recognized as a *universitas* and so had its own legal identity. It could govern its affairs, binding its members to strict codes of conduct. The guilds set standards of work and ensured that redress could be sought by customers, not least those from outside the city, who could ask for their cases to be adjudicated by the guild in cases of fraud or shoddy goods. One of the practical ways in which the guilds integrated themselves into the life of the city was through taking on responsibility for care of Florence's fabric. The hard-headed businessmen of the guilds knew how to supervise workers, draw up contracts and keep large projects moving. The Calimala maintained and embellished the much-venerated city baptistery, dedicated to John the Baptist. The Calimala were also responsible for two hospitals and the Franciscan Basilica of Santa Croce. The Lana, the wool guild, oversaw building works in the cathedral. This was a vast project, especially after the decision was made in the 1330s to make the building even larger – in fact the largest church of its time, to fit a congregation of 30,000. Meanwhile, the guild of silk weavers, the Por Santa Maria, looked after the convent of San Marco and the city's granary, the Orsanmichele, famed for its miracle-working statue of the Virgin Mary.

As Florence developed its own republican identity, there was a determined effort to break up the aristocratic strongholds that had previously divided the city into rival territories. Demolition opened up public spaces that could be exploited and so Florence, like other Italian cities of the day, became a city where display was encouraged. The guilds and the religious confraternities could show off their relics and banners in processions. Visiting preachers could speak to large congregations. The citizens would hold their own communal processions, notably on each 24 June, the feast day of John the Baptist. They could host the welcome of visiting dignitaries as in 1439 when, with great flamboyance, Cosimo de' Medici welcomed the Byzantine emperor John VIII and Pope Eugenius IV to a council in Florence. In tumultuous times, protesting crowds could gather in the Piazza della Signoria or could be summoned there at times of crisis by the city bell. The dramatic use of these spaces allowed a flourishing of political and social life that was beyond the control of any elite.

The chronicler of Florence in the first half of the fourteenth century was Giovanni Villani (1280–1348). While Villani was a man of his time in seeing the hand of God in the unfolding of everyday events, and relied too uncritically on legend for the early history of Florence, he is important for providing a statistical analysis of his city. As we have seen (p. 232) he simply loved numbers. The figures for textiles production given above are based on his own assessments. His chronicle is especially valuable for his calculations of the number of children in education. These are extraordinary for those who see the fourteenth century as an age of mass illiteracy or education as being the prerogative of the church. In Florence in the 1330s thousands of children from families below those of the elite went to school. Villani counted 8–10,000 girls and boys who were receiving education between the ages of six and eleven, possibly 70 per cent of the age group, although he does not give comparative figures for each sex. This schooling would enable them to read vernacular texts and provide them with the foundations for the study of Latin. This high rate of attendance is confirmed by documentary evidence from a century later, the *Catasto* of 1427, that showed that 80 per cent of heads of household were able to complete a fiscal declaration listing their belongings.

After primary school boys continued their education. Villani found between 1,000 and 1,200 in the abacus schools which taught commercial arithmetic and the other skills needed to be a merchant or run a shop. About half as many chose the more academic route in schools where they studied logic and Latin. Most teachers came from the notary class that was growing steadily in the early fourteenth century (880 notaries are recorded in Florence in 1338). Notaries were junior to the well-qualified jurists, with whom they shared a guild, but they were trained to draw up contracts, wills and other legal documents. Some wrote letters for the government; others were attached to an institution such as a hospital or a guild. They knew Latin well and so many supplemented their income by teaching and it was through them that bright Florentine boys were introduced to Roman texts and so to models of Roman politics, history, rhetoric and moral philosophy. For many notaries the Roman past and the quality of its Latin was an essential foundation of a proper education and here lies the genesis of humanism, the subject of the next chapter.

Florence was not the only Italian city to have high standards of education – many other cities placed teachers on a public payroll in the fourteenth century.[5] As a result, virtually everyone employed in a trade or craft possessed qualifications. Some of them had even acquired a knowledge of the cultures of the past, something that would have been impossible in a conventional university curriculum. So it is hardly surprising that Dante was well educated even though his family background was modest. When his father died, he left a small house in a respectable part of the city, two farms and a cottage, 'sufficient wealth to live honourably', as one contemporary put it, but no more than this. Although nothing is known about Dante's schooling, later in his life his Latin was good. Dante tells us that he was taught by the humanist Brunetto Latini, whom he will encounter in the seventh circle of hell in the *Divine Comedy*, suffering with the sodomites. While Dante does not show the intense interest in classical texts that the committed humanists would show, the broad scope of his reading makes him their equal.

In his *De vulgari eloquentia* (*On Eloquence in the Vernacular*), written in Latin in 1304, Dante sets out the arguments for the use of the vernacular, especially in the writing of poetry that needs to reach an audience that does not know Latin. Overshadowed by the *Divine Comedy*, it is a paean to Dante's native Tuscan tongue, which he hopes can be restored to equality with Latin. This cherishing of a vernacular language was part of a growing trend. As well as Tuscan Italian, French was in the process of acquiring a rich literary heritage, and Middle

English and a standard written version of Spanish would gather strength over the course of the fourteenth century. It has even been suggested that the use of the vernacular was a deliberate riposte to the supremacy of Latin in clerical circles.[6] With original works being written in the vernacular as well as translations from the Latin, a much wider reading audience was being catered for, the reader usually 'performing' a text before an audience. (Here was the birth of the audiobook!) Dante himself had been writing poetry in the vernacular well before his exile. His *La Vita Nuova* (*The New Life*), a set of love poems, was composed for a circle of fellow poets in Florence but it was innovative in style in the way it aligned physical attraction to the ideal woman, Beatrice, with spiritual introspection. In this he was rejecting the more earthy style of the Provençal poets who had been influential in Italy up to then. All this is recreated on the grandest of scales in Dante's masterpiece, one of the great works of world literature, not least as the founding text of European realism, the *Divine Comedy*.[7]

Dante was not an academic recluse; he had been engaged in the politics of his native city, deeply hurt by his exile and the dependence on patrons that had resulted, and enraged by the corrupt politics that had poisoned relationships in his own and other Italian cities. He particularly resented the intrusions of the church into politics. These emotions were to infuse the *Divine Comedy*, composed in exile between 1308 and 1320. Yet rather than write about his own civic society, Dante was inspired to place his poetry within the landscape of the afterworld. The settings here would give him full scope to explore his profound feelings about the unsettled society he saw around him *in pro del mondo che mal vive* ('for the benefit of the world that lives badly').

overleaf The French artist Gustave Doré's illustrations for Dante's *Inferno* (1861) were a sensation and helped embed the *Divine Comedy* in the popular imagination.

Originally, as Dante explains in a letter to one of his patrons, the Veronese Cangrande della Scala, he called his poem a 'comedy' in that, unlike 'tragedy' that starts well and ends badly, this poem starts badly, in hell, and ends well, in Paradise. It was an early biographer of Dante, Giovanni Boccaccio, who added the word 'Divine' and this has stuck, appearing as the title in early printed editions by the sixteenth century.

The *Divine Comedy* begins when Dante, himself the narrator, is thirty-five and at the mid-point of his life (and thus in 1300). In a dark wood, which stands for humanity in a state of sin, he meets the Roman poet Virgil, who will be his guide. The nod back to the classical world has a specific resonance for the Christian Middle Ages. Virgil had written in his Fourth *Eclogue* (*c.*40 BC) of the birth of a boy who

would usher in a golden age. In Dante's time this was regarded as a prophecy of the birth of Jesus, thus endowing Virgil with a form of 'Christian' legitimacy.* And the presence of the Roman poet implies another link between classical and medieval times. Virgil's great work the *Aeneid* describes the many hardships that Rome endured before reaching of the peace of the empire under the first emperor, Augustus. Many Christians believed that the stability of the empire was put in place by God so that Christianity could be born there and spread. The *Divine Comedy* tells too of an arduous journey towards a peaceful end.

Dante, no classical hero but one who could be seen as an everyman figure, moves through three realms, hell (the Inferno), then Purgatory, where Virgil leaves him, and finally Paradise, where his beloved Beatrice introduces him to the serenity of the divine love of God.[8] Before entering hell, Dante and Virgil pass through Limbo, where those who died without knowing Christ wait 'without hope but with desire'. Here are the great classical poets, Homer, Horace, Ovid and Lucan, the historian of the civil war that led up to the empire, who come out to welcome Virgil and, to the delight of Dante, include him in their company. He now has his longed-for status, among the greatest poets of antiquity. Next in Limbo are the philosophers, Socrates, Plato and Aristotle, Cicero, Dioscorides, Euclid, Ptolemy, Hippocrates, Galen, Avicenna and Averroes – a roll-call of those pagan intellectuals who resonated with the educated fourteenth-century mind.

Thomas Aquinas provides much of the theological framework for Dante's journey. Once in hell Dante relies on Aquinas's hierarchy of sin, in which sin is seen as a misuse of the rational mind that should seek out God but which turns away from him. Like Aquinas, Dante assumes that the committed rational mind is active in the pursuit of virtue and that it is therefore sinful to stand by when evil is being perpetrated or to allow oneself to become one of the *tristi* ('sullen ones'), who betray their rational nature by not relating to society at all. This is why these individuals are to be found in hell.

Hell shapes downwards in nine concentric circles, an upper Inferno of five circles and a lower one of four. The uppermost category of hell contains those who reject God through the diversions of lust and gluttony. The gluttons must perpetually swallow sludge in a ghastly re-enactment of their vice. Their punishment is eternal but not as agonizing as those the pilgrims will meet next. Things become darker and more horrific as Dante descends deeper into hell, through chasms, rocks and

* Scholars have argued this child was, in fact, the longed-for child of Mark Antony and Octavia the Younger.

lakes, encountering notorious figures from the past, including some he has known himself in the political turmoil of the Guelph–Ghibelline conflict. In fact, Florentines and Tuscans make up more than half of the souls encountered. Further down, in an inner circle beyond the River Styx, are those who are malicious in intent, those who have committed violence, fraud or who betrayed either their fellow humans or – worst of all – God himself, and thus deserving of greater torments. Among them are those who commit what Thomas Aquinas and, following him, Dante, consider sins against the natural order of things, including sodomy. The damned include those who have affronted God through their own sins of pride, such as Emperor Frederick II, who was still under excommunication when he died in 1250. There is even a pope, Nicholas III (r.1277–80), punished for the sin of simony. Nicholas mistakes Dante for the latter's bête noire, Boniface VIII, the dissolute pope whom Dante blamed for his exile and whose arrival in hell was expected imminently. Specific punishments are designed for each kind of sinner and relate to the sins they have committed. Those who spread discord, a sin that Dante especially abhorred, are ripped open; astrologers who have claimed to see the future have their heads bent round so they can only see backwards; corruption in public office merits being plunged into boiling pitch; traitors are buried head down in ice. Dante becomes emotionally involved with their suffering as, with the help of Virgil, he stumbles from one layer of hell to another, the barrenness and iciness increasing with each stage of the descent. Brutus and Cassius, the assassins of Julius Caesar, are close to the bottom, reflecting Dante's own condemnation of republican revolt. In the final depths is Lucifer himself, described very much as Dante would have seen him portrayed in a mosaic that dominated the baptistery in his native Florence, but here encased in ice.

Once they have passed Lucifer, Virgil and Dante move through to Purgatory, a mountain set on an island. Purgatory had been defined by Pope Gregory the Great as the imprisonment by sinners in 'mansions' until they are purged and able to continue to heaven. Salvation will eventually be assured. Repentance, even on one's deathbed, could save a sinner from hell, and if one reached Purgatory it was believed that the aid of prayer and indulgences on earth could shorten one's sentence there. Yet the doctrine had little support from scripture or tradition. It was only in 1274 that a church council, at Lyons, confirmed that prayers from earth could help a soul in purgatory on its way. Dante's imaginative portrayal of Purgatory, on a mountain with the souls ascending upwards and becoming lighter as their sins dropped away, was therefore a revelation. Many readers of the *Divine Comedy* never progress beyond the Inferno, but the poem is meaningless if they stop there. Some of Dante's best writing is in the cantos that follow.

The ascent is through the seven deadly sins, each one being met by its corresponding virtue, pride by humility, envy by pity, and so on. The sinner is punished on the way but also has the opportunity to reflect on his or her sin and, crucially, become open to the possibility of being released by a glimmering appreciation of divine love. In Purgatory Dante implies that the suffering is welcomed as the inevitable accompaniment of healing.

Virgil has now left Dante. As a pagan he cannot proceed further, but he has been replaced by the beloved Beatrice, who appears in the chariot of the church. She embodies theological wisdom, the highest state of being, *eudaimonia*, as taught by Aristotle in the pagan world and Aquinas in the Christian. It is the first time in western literature that a woman has been given this prominent and all-encompassing role. Beatrice has by now been dead for twenty-five years, but Dante assumes that she has been watching over him on earth and guiding him towards salvation. Now that he is purged, she can lead him into Paradise. Here the blessed all live in a state of bliss, but once again there are gradations to their happiness. Dante adopts the Aristotelian conception of the universe as a series of concentric spheres, each one complete in itself with no void between one and the next. Each has its own planet and the inhabitants of each reflect the qualities associated with it. So those who have died on crusade and thus have earned the promised immediate salvation are found in the circle of Mars, the god of war. They move through a growing awareness of God's works, to an appreciation of the truth of Christian doctrine, then to a complete understanding of God's love. These stages break up the final ascent and so allow Dante to meditate as he continues inwards towards the light. Those he meets become brighter as he does so and the lovely Beatrice herself becomes more radiant.

Towards the end of his life, 1317, Dante had settled in Ravenna, then a small city but one in which he seems to have found happiness, with his two sons and daughter who were able to join him in the first house he had owned since his exile.* It was in Ravenna that Dante finished Purgatory and completed Paradise, and it was here that he would die. The imposing sixth-century mosaic of the Christian emperor Justinian in the Church of San Vitale would have been as prominent then as it

* Marco Santagata, in his recent biography *Dante: The Story of his Life*, argues (pp. 332–4) that Dante's wife was also reunited with him.

still is now, so it is little wonder that Dante encounters Justinian, in the sphere of Mercury.

Moving further upwards, towards the core of Paradise, Dante comes across the theologians, Thomas Aquinas, Bonaventure, Benedict, St Francis and St Dominic. Boethius, Isidore of Seville, Bede, Gratian, Peter Lombard and Albert the Great are also among their number, a roll-call of the most important Christian thinkers that few would challenge today. More surprising is the presence here of the Averroist Siger of Brabant. While Thomas Aquinas vehemently rejected Siger's teachings in Paris, here he actually introduces him to Dante. Commentators assume that despite his Averroism, Dante respects Siger for his intellectual integrity. Augustine is to be found closer to the sun but Dante gives him little more than a mention.

As he meets these major figures of Catholic teaching, Dante hears their laments on how far the church has fallen from its ideal, particularly with the corruption of the monasteries. Beatrice too launches into a condemnation of the church, its incompetent preachers and its dissolute popes, notably Boniface VIII and his successor Clement V. Finally arriving at the Circle of the Fixed Stars, Dante has a vision of Christ and it is the austere Bernard of Clairvaux (none other than the scourge of Peter Abelard) who now appears to show him the Virgin Mary. Yet it is at this moment, when Dante appears to have reached the most intense realization of the nature of divine love, that St Peter intervenes with a powerful tirade against his successors who have degraded the office of the papacy. In the final cantos of the poem Dante has a vision of the Light of God that brings the human and spiritual worlds together. In a fuller understanding of the essence of God and his creation, Dante has at last found peace.

The *Divine Comedy* is, of course, deeply rooted in Catholic theology, primarily that of Thomas Aquinas. It is also a superb work of literature, notable for its relentless probing into the nature of good and evil, the ultimate ends of life and the supremacy of spiritual values. Virtually every theological issue of the day is touched upon and Dante's own emotions, from disgust to exultation, are expressed. There are many moving moments when Virgil tries to comfort him in face of the horrors that they encounter in hell. Poetically, the sense of order and evolution towards its end and the vivid nature of Dante's writing and insights mean that the journey, even in Paradise, is never dull. It also offers an early insight into the future development of western Christianity after 1300 in revealing a growing distinction between spirituality and the church hierarchy that seems to have abandoned it.

Dated to some time after 1308 is Dante's *De monarchia* (*On Monarchy*), a work written in Latin.[9] Haunted by the unrest that was pervading northern Italy, his own city not least, Dante was preoccupied with finding some way of ensuring peace, both for the individual and for the community. His answer was rooted in his hatred for the papacy of Boniface VIII, who had died in 1303. While he was happy for one purpose of life to be salvation in the next world, he argued that it was wrong for the church to exert political authority in this one. The role of the pope was to act as adviser to the emperors in a spiritual rather than a temporal sense. Surprisingly, perhaps, Dante argues that only the emperor can provide the security under which liberty can flourish and disputes between cities resolved. Of course, this view was not popular with those cities trying to be free of both church and emperor. It was also hopelessly idealistic, in that it depended on an emperor who was prepared to exercise the benign overlordship that Dante required of him. *De monarchia* was the precursor of more sophisticated studies of the role of the church in political affairs, but its anti-papal bias ensured that it would be placed on the first papal Index of Prohibited Books in 1559.* It would remain there, forbidden for Catholics to read, until 1891.

Dante's critical approach to the power of the church was developed in the most important and certainly the most original political document of the fourteenth century, the *Defensor Pacis* (*The Defender of Peace*) of Marsilius of Padua (1324).[10] The son of a lawyer, Marsilius was born in Padua about 1280 and it appears that he studied medicine at the university there before transferring to Paris. His approach to political theory owes much to the theories of the Greek physician Galen, which stressed the importance of balance among the four humours for a healthy life.[11] Like most of his contemporaries Marsilius revered Aristotle and must have come across his *Politics*, which had been translated for the first time in 1264. Not much else is known about his early life, but in the second part of his *Defensor Pacis*,† he attacks the pretensions of the church in exercising any kind of legal or political power. His anger may have been aroused by the attempts of Pope Boniface VIII to exclude all clergy from local taxes, and the accompanying papal threat of excommunication of any ruler who continued to collect them. Marsilius's opposition to Boniface's actions

* This was an official list of books that Roman Catholics were forbidden to read, on the grounds of their being contrary to Catholic faith or morals. It was not abolished until 1966.

† The first part is devoted to exploring theories of government.

was shared by most of his Parisian colleagues, especially after the pope and the French king Philip IV the Fair confronted each other on the issue (in the 1290s and 1300s; see pp. 368–9). Marsilius's response was a radical one: he went back to the New Testament to stress that Christ himself had ordered that what was Caesar's should only be rendered to Caesar. He also argued that the apostle Paul, in chapter 13 of his Letter to the Romans, had written that everyone, including the clergy, should submit themselves to secular courts. It followed that the apostles and their successors could not claim any right to judge others. The proper function of the priesthood was the education and preparation of souls for eternal life.

Marsilius continues with an analysis of the papal *plenitudo potestatis*,‡ as claimed, for instance, by Innocent III. He argues against the concept of papal monarchy, preferring a conciliarist approach in which the executive power of the church should rest with the whole community of Christians. He notes that it was only later in the history of the church that bishops were given any kind of secular power. As an example, the influential Council of Nicaea (325) had been called and presided over by the emperor Constantine, not the pope or senior bishops. Instead, the determination of doctrine and any form of coercive authority must be placed in the hands of the secular rulers of the city republics. The attempts of the popes to assert their authority in northern Italy must therefore be resisted by anyone who claims to be a *Defensor Pacis*, 'a defender of the peace'. Marsilius assumed the continuing importance of religion in the community, as Aristotle did in his *Politics*, but demanded that it be brought under the control of the state.

Surveying the condition of Italy, Marsilius, like Dante, sees it as one of anarchy, with rulers tyrannizing the city-states. Italy itself is 'battered on all sides because of strife and almost destroyed, so that it can be easily invaded by anyone who wants to seize it'.[12] Marsilius's preoccupation is therefore with devising a system of government that brings peace. Disorder arises from rival groups of magistrates and elite families fighting with each other for control of the city. There must therefore be a unified magistracy, a co-ordinated government that does not allow contending centres of power to arise. The only way this can be achieved, argues Marsilius, is through a ruler who has the support of the people as a whole. In contrast to those, such as Thomas Aquinas, who believed that the people should hand over authority to a ruler and

‡ The 'fullness of power' claimed by the medieval popes, giving them jurisdiction over both secular and religious institutions.

have no further involvement in government, Marsilius argues for no more than a delegation of power achieved through the election of a ruler. And this power can always be reclaimed. The elected ruler should be controlled by law so that he cannot act on his own whim but only within a legal structure. One of Marsilius's underlying concerns was that rulers needed to be wise and moderate – and the best way of achieving this was continuous supervision by the political community. Here Marsilius draws on Aristotle's *Politics*: 'The fewer things the rulers control, the longer every government must endure for [the rulers] become less despotic, they are more moderate in their ways and are less hated by their subjects.'[13] Faced with the traditional anti-democratic argument that the masses cannot be trusted to elect a wise ruler, Marsilius argues that other than the very poor, who have no stake in society, and a few others of 'vicious' temperament, most citizens would take their responsibilities seriously:

> The universal multitude of the citizens as a body… gathered together, can more fully perceive and will what is just and advantageous for the community than any of these parts by itself, however prudent it may be… the laws thus made will be better observed nor will anyone have any protest to make against them.[14]

Here Marsilius went further than Aristotle, who, while sympathetic to popular involvement in government, distrusted unrestrained democracy. Marsilius, however, rejects 'natural' hierarchies, in particular the concept that good birth is related to the ability to govern.

Within the next few years many of Marsilius's ideas were supported by the lawyer Bartolus da Sassoferrato, whose contributions to law-making were discussed earlier (p. 181). Bartolus was as concerned as Marsilius was with the internecine disputes between and within the Italian cities. The two agreed that the sovereignty of the people can never be alienated and that religion should be kept separate from politics. This approach was to prove especially fruitful. In their own time it provided a riposte to those who wished to retain the authority of the church over secular rulers. Not since the era of the Roman empire had anyone reflected as probingly and effectively as this on the ways in which the citizenry (though only males) as a whole could be involved in government. The influence of Aristotle, with his emphasis on the harmonious order of the city through the collective, and natural, will of the citizens to achieve civil happiness, is clear.

When the *Defensor Pacis* was published in 1324, Marsilius attempted to remain anonymous. But the secret of his authorship leaked out and Pope John XXII, resident in Avignon, condemned the *Defensor* as heretical without even bothering to read it. Copies were publicly burned in 1327. Like William of Ockham, Marsilius was forced to flee to the court of Ludwig of Bavaria, who was soon to become the legitimate emperor. He remained attached to the court for the rest of his life, dying in 1342. Marsilius's belief in involvement of the people in the election, and continued supervision, of their rulers as a means of ensuring the best form of government constitutes a critical staging-post in the evolution of political thought. It would have continuing relevance as new approaches to democracy emerged in the nineteenth century.

* * *

Despite Dante's hopes and Marsilius's prescriptions, Florence was no more settled in the fourteenth century than it had been in the thirteenth. The century started with a great fire that ravaged much of the city centre (1304). In 1333 a massive flood swept away all the city's bridges.* Then the Bardi and Peruzzi family banks, which had lent heavily to the English king Edward III, were driven into bankruptcy when the king defaulted on the debt, and this failure rippled through Florence's economy. Just two years later, in 1348, the Black Death ravaged the city, killing perhaps half of its inhabitants, the chronicler Giovanni Villani among them. Wars against imperial forces or neighbouring communes ate into civic resources.

In the 1350s, after the shock of the plague, the mood of the city shifted. Many have seen the transition through the comparison between Dante's *Divine Comedy* and the first major piece of vernacular prose, the *Decameron*, from another Florentine, Giovanni Boccaccio (1313–75). Boccaccio, the son of a member of the Bardi banking company, was sent as a young man to head the bank's office in Naples. Frustrated by the demands of banking, he turned for several years to the study of canon law in Naples before realizing that it was literature he loved above all. A visit to what was believed to be the tomb of Virgil in Naples is said to have been the catalyst,† but Boccaccio was equally drawn to contemporary literature. He idolized Dante and wrote a biography of the poet. Back in Florence – and 'rather fat and corpulent' according to one account – he proved an energetic networker, mingling his literary

* A replacement, the Ponte Vecchio, constructed in 1345, survives today.

† The 'tomb' is still intact today.

activities with a variety of administrative posts and diplomatic missions as a member of the cultural elite. The influence of Petrarch (see p. 271), nine years his elder, whom he met in Florence in 1350, and swapped manuscripts with, was pervasive and acknowledged by Boccaccio as such. In broad terms Boccaccio can be called a humanist (see the next chapter), in that he idealized classical texts, defended the use of pagan poetry and compiled a guide to classical mythology, *Genealogia Deorum Gentilium* (*The Genealogy of Pagan Gods*).[15] This covered an enormous range of material from both Latin and Greek – and even Arabic – sources and explored the relationships between different cultures across time.*

Yet Boccaccio was also innovative. One of his works, the novel *Elegia di Madonna Fiammetta* (*The Elegy of the Lady Fiammetta*), tells of the tortuous relationship of the heroine Fiammetta with her unfaithful lover, a first-person confessional kiss-and-tell that has been described as 'the first modern psychological novel'.[16] His unpublished work *De Canaria* contains an early description of the native peoples of the Canary Islands – which Portuguese mariners had reached in the fourteenth

* Boccaccio was horrified when visiting the monastery at Monte Cassino to find that the monks had been cutting up old manuscripts.

Boccaccio's *Decameron* had enormous appeal for the middle classes and became a popular theme for the *cassoni* or decorated marriage chests of Florentine households. This example dates from 1420.

century – from accounts that had been passed on to him. *De mulieribus claris* (*Concerning Famous Women*) (1361–2) is the first known set of biographies of famous women in western literature and was dedicated to a Neapolitan countess, Andrea Acciaiuoli. Surveying the extraordinary breadth of his works, Boccaccio comes across as a brilliant but manipulative narrator, adept at using different styles in both Latin or Italian when it suited his aims. Yet it is the 100 tales of the *Decameron* that have earned Boccaccio his fame.

The *Decameron* begins with a gruelling account of the Black Death in Florence. One morning, having attended a service in the Dominican Church of Santa Maria Novella, seven women, aged between eighteen and twenty-seven, decide they should find a rural retreat in which to shelter while the plague rages. Despite their taking the initiative for what follows, they agree that they need men to chaperone the enterprise. Accompanied by three men, all of whom are attracted to one or other of the group, they set off for a comfortable villa just outside the city. Once settled in, they decide, again on the initiative of one of the women, that each will tell a story on each of ten days, amounting to

100 in total. Each day will have its own theme, whether of love that ends tragically (one day), or happily (the next). Many of the tales in the *Decameron* were drawn from the oral traditions of the Florentine streets and taken together they explore the totality of human experience. Seventy of the stories are narrated by women (but of course through the authorial voice of a man), giving a significant important new perspective to the work. The setting that Boccaccio has chosen, the villa – a secular retreat – also allows him to create a relaxed atmosphere far removed from the turmoil of the city. There is no Inferno here.

The women are socially confident, virtuous but at ease with their male companions. Despite the horror unfolding back in the city, the pace is relaxed. On arrival 'the merry company sauntered slowly through the garden, conversing on pleasant topics, weaving fair garlands for each other from the leaves of various trees, and singing songs of love'.[17] There is good food; some of the women can play instruments and there is even a chessboard and other games. The women go off to bathe together in a neighbouring lake. They are quite happy to enjoy the more bawdy of the stories that show women taking as much pleasure in sex as men. Boccaccio has moved on from a world where illicit sex will result in eternal condemnation. For him it is an end worth pursuing for those couples in love with each other, even if they are not married. The aristocratic Ghismonda, the heroine of the first story of the fourth day, takes the initiative in seeking out a lover from a lower class, enjoys mutual pleasure in their lovemaking and defends her right to do so when confronted by her father. (It ends in tragedy, however – her lover dies in prison and she commits suicide.) Unwanted pregnancies abound: in the opening story of the third day, a gardener pretends to be dumb and thereby contrives to sleep with all of the nuns in a convent – each of whom believes he is incapable of revealing their scandalous secret. In the process he fathers 'a number of nunlets and monklets'.

In the tenth and final story to be told on the third day, an innocent fourteen-year-old girl in search of God is told by the Christians in her home town, Gafsa, that she should distance herself as far as possible from worldly things. She thus sets off into the desert. Here she comes across a hermit who decides to test himself against temptation by asking her to stay. His will fails and he manipulates her into believing that having sex with him would bring the devil, as manifested in his erection, under control. The sex is so frequent that the hermit, whose diet is meagre, is soon exhausted, but his partner is not. 'I can certainly see what those worthy men in Gafsa meant when they said that serving God was so agreeable,' she says. When she returns home, she recounts her adventures to the women of Gafsa, who soon spread her story around town, but they assure her that the man who wishes to marry her will continue to help her serve God in the way to which she has become accustomed.

The *Decameron* is not a polemic against religion – the women are portrayed as attending church services during the week – but it is certainly anti-clerical. In one story, set in Paris, a Jew is put under pressure by a merchant friend to convert to Christianity. He gives way, but says that before he is baptized he needs to visit Rome to observe the way the pope and his cardinals live. His merchant friend is horrified at the prospect but the Jew is adamant that he must go. In Rome he finds a papal court full of greed and sexual corruption. On his return, he still insists that he wishes to convert as the Holy Ghost must be protecting the church when 'your pontiff and the others too are doing their level best to reduce the Christian religion to nought and drive it from the face of the earth'. The two friends then go off together to Notre Dame for the baptism.

In another story, set in a convent in Lombardy, an abbess in her chamber is told that one of her nuns is entertaining a lover. She gets out of bed, intending to put on her veil before going off to confront the sinner. However, the abbess herself has a lover in her bed – a priest! – and she inadvertently puts his discarded breeches on her head instead of her veil. When, unaware of her mistake, she assembles her nuns in order to denounce the sinner, she is ridiculed and forced to confess that she also has succumbed to the temptations of the flesh. The young nun is allowed to keep her lover. Yet another, similarly scurrilous, tale tells of how a friar comes to collect offerings for St Anthony, promising his rural congregation that the saint will protect their crops and animals if they contribute. Later, he also promises that he will show them the relic he has gained in the Holy Land, a feather left from the wing of the angel Gabriel at the moment of the Annunciation. While the friar is away, however, two mischievous young men replace the feather with a few coals. On his return the quick-thinking friar explains that his relic boxes have become mixed up and that these are in fact the coals left over from the roasting of St Lawrence. The congregation rush forward to be touched by them and their offerings are the largest he has ever received.

The *Decameron* has always divided critics (including those who wish to expunge its eroticism), yet its appeal remains across the centuries. Boccaccio might be seen as playing with his readers, offering some possible versions of how the sexes present themselves to each other when classes mix together, sexually and socially, without inhibition in settings that are spread across the cultures of Europe and the Mediterranean. In this he was innovative. We know from the *ricordanze*, memoirs of the lives of well-to-do families which appear in their thousands in Florence from Boccaccio's time,[18] that there had been a shift from hard-headed mercantilism and property dealing towards a more family-centred culture. Records of the emotional bonds between members, their marriages, births and deaths and their thoughts about raising their children, reveal that this was a more socially fluid society that took pride in the family as the core of civilized living. Although Boccaccio's depiction of it is often sharp and unflattering, one can understand why the *Decameron* proved so popular among this elite group. He responded to their need for entertainment and caught the mood of the times, refining the oral culture of the streets for the literate classes.

Predominant among the three writers portrayed in this chapter is a healthy lack of respect for the institutional church. It was impossible for them, and the intellectual elite in general, to ignore its failure to live up to its ideals. By 1300 this had begun to have its effect. As will be seen in Chapter 16, the laity increasingly developed their own forms of Christian activity and were often much more effective than the clergy at carrying out charitable projects. It was, for instance, the citizens of Florence who took the initiative in running their churches during the 'War of the Eight Saints', 1375–8, against the papacy. The collapse of traditional church authority is an important feature of the period 1300–1550.

Dante and Boccaccio are known to students of Italian literature as two of the *tre corone*, 'the three crowned ones', who initiated the rich tradition of Italian vernacular texts. The founding text for this adulation was Giannozzo Manetti's *Lives of Three Illustrious Florentine Poets* (1440) where the third of the 'crowned ones', the poet Petrarch, appears between Dante and Boccaccio. And it is to Petrarch that we will turn next.

11

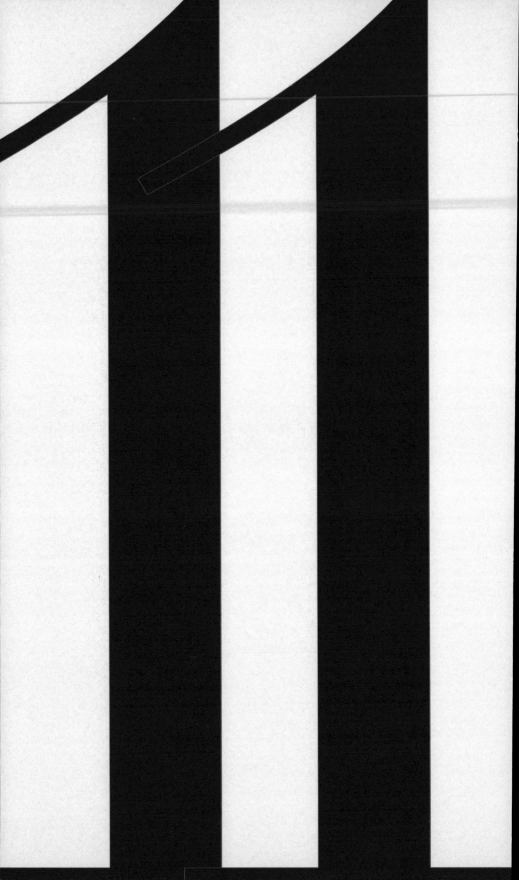

Humanism and the Challenge to the Scholastics

Giotto was a man of such outstanding genius that there was nothing in the whole of creation that he could not depict with his stylus, pen or brush. And so faithful did he remain to Nature (who is the mother and the motive force of all created things) that whatever he depicted had the appearance, not of a reproduction, but of the thing itself, so that one often finds, with the works of Giotto, that people's eyes are deceived and they mistake the picture for the real thing.

Giovanni Boccaccio, *Decameron*[1]

It is now nearly sixty years since my father first shared the fresco cycle of Giotto di Bordone in the Arena Chapel in Padua with me. We had a copy of Bernard Berenson's *Italian Painters of the Renaissance*[2] at home and, like Berenson, who enthused over what he called 'the tactile value' of the frescos, my father saw them as part of a revival of emotive art after the comparative sterility of the Byzantine era.

I must have visited the chapel for the first time myself when I was about twenty but the most powerful experience came many years later. I was showing the chapel to a group of historians and, with a new system in place that allowed only twenty-five visitors at a time, I was allowed to be alone for a few minutes after one part of my large group had left and the next had not yet arrived. I concentrated on two frescos that occupy the side walls of the chapel; one scene depicts the moment when Judas kisses Jesus in the garden of Gethsemane while the second, facing the first across the aisle, shows Mary and the women weeping over the dead body of Jesus. The colours are rich. Deep blue skies, green leaves, costumes in blue, red and yellow. Christ is always shown with a golden halo, as are those ministering to his dead body with angels hovering above in their own contortions of grief.[3]

The Arena Chapel is on the site of the original Roman arena in Padua where the Scrovegni family palace stood. The commission itself was unusual, perhaps the first in medieval Europe by a private citizen. Enrico Scrovegni paid for the decoration of his private chapel in expiation, it was said, for the sins of his father, Reginaldo, who had been a notorious usurer – so notorious, in fact, that he is found in Dante's Hell.

Fresco painting is very much cheaper than mosaic. One record for an apse mosaic (in Pisa cathedral) suggests that eighteen mosaicists laboured for ten months without even finishing their work. The skill of creating frescos was well known in antiquity. First, a thin layer of wet plaster was applied to a dried plaster base, onto which an outline of the painting to come, the *sinopia*, was drawn, and then paint – the creation of which from various pigments was a craft in itself – was applied to the wet plaster. It was the fusion of the two as the plaster dried that created the permanent artwork and part of the skill lay in predicting the changes in colour that would take place as the plaster dried. The artist had to work quickly; he might have just seven or eight hours – a *giornata*, or day's work – to complete one section, and if he made a mistake he would have to scrape off the added plaster layer and start again. If well preserved, frescos can last for centuries, but they are vulnerable to damp and pollution. Hence the very special conditions in which the Arena Chapel is kept. It is because of the sea mists of Venice, which have made it impossible to preserve frescos there, that canvas and oil paint became the preferred medium for that city's artists.

Giotto was born in a village outside Florence in about 1266. One story, narrated in Giorgio Vasari's *Lives of the Artists*,[4] tells of how, after his ability was recognized by Florence's leading painter Cimabue from drawings he had made on rocks, the young Giotto was then taken into his workshop. It appears that Giotto and assistants may have been responsible for some of the frescos of the life of St Francis in the Upper Church at Assisi, although there is much scholarly controversy over the attributions. Completed in the 1290s, seventy years after Francis's death, the frescos provide the image of Francis that has endured: his love of the poor, his preaching to the birds and his receiving of the stigmata, the wounds of Christ. Even if Giotto's contribution was limited, he may have learned much from his fellow painters, not least in placing the humanity of his subject as the core of the painting.

The Arena Chapel is dedicated to the Virgin of the Annunciation, and the angel Gabriel and Mary face each other across the upper register of the triumphal arch that leads into the choir. The body of the chapel has three fresco cycles. The uppermost recounts the life of the Virgin. Although they have no scriptural support, the difficulties Mary's parents, Anna and Joachim, have in conceiving a child, Mary's birth and her reception into the Temple before her betrothal to Joseph were all well-known stories. They draw on early Christian texts such as the second-century Proto-Evangelium (or Gospel) of James and the thirteenth-century *Legenda Aurea* (*Golden Legend*) of Jacobus de Varagine, a famous sequence of the lives of the saints,[5] and were often illustrated as the cult of the Virgin Mary flourished in the Middle Ages. (It is worth emphasizing how many of the narratives that medieval Christians would have absorbed from these frescos had no scriptural backing.) The second register details the childhood of Christ, his ministry and his betrayal by Judas. The final cycle depicts the Passion, the Crucifixion and the Resurrection, ending with the coming of the Holy Spirit to the apostles at Pentecost. A Last Judgement fills the west wall. Enrico Scrovegni is shown here, optimistically presenting a model of his church to the Virgin Mary.

Giotto is celebrated for having broken away from the static conventions of Byzantine art where the spirituality of the figures transcends their humanity. His figures are as if drawn from life, they have depth and solidity to them and they fit snugly into the spaces that Giotto has allocated for them rather than being shown as detached from any natural setting. Giotto has a genius for focusing on the most intense moment of an emotional drama but never without a simplicity that moves by its understatement. It was perhaps for this reason that I chose the scenes that I did as I stood in the centre of this great artistic creation.

Once Giotto's breakthrough had taken place, there could be no turning back. Emotion, natural settings even for religious scenes and the beginnings of perspective were to develop from this revolution in art. Some have seen this moment as the birth of the individual, a feature of the Renaissance that was emphasized by the Swiss historian Jacob Burckhardt in his *The Civilization of the Renaissance in Italy*,[6] although it is difficult to link Giotto's realism directly to changes in society. Yet the revolution was recognized. By the time Dante was writing the *Divine Comedy* just a few years later he relates how Giotto has pushed Cimabue into obscurity.[7] The humanist Petrarch, who owned a *Virgin and Child* by Giotto, wrote that while the ignorant might not recognize its beauty, no one who had any knowledge of the arts could fail to be astounded by it.[8] As seen above, Giotto was a hero to Boccaccio, who believed that the artist had restored to light an ancient tradition of art that had been 'buried beneath the blunders of those who aimed to bring visual delight to the ignorant rather than intellectual satisfaction to the wise'.[9] Some decades later, Lorenzo Ghiberti, the creator of the famous bronze doors of the Florence baptistery (see p. 301), acknowledged Giotto as 'the inventor and discoverer of much learning that had been buried some six hundred years'.[10] In their acknowledgement of the value of rediscovery of the lost learning of the past, Ghiberti's words give clear expression to the idea of a reawakening of the western mind. This fitted well with the philosophy of humanism, a movement that was gathering strength within the intellectual circles of northern Italy.

The drama and colour of the frescos in Giotto's Arena Chapel are shown in his *Kiss of Judas*. The focus on the central figures is, as his contemporaries recognized, revolutionary.

Giotto was, of course, a Florentine and, after working in Padua and Assisi, he returned to his native city to spend much of the remainder of his life there. In the Franciscan Church of Santa Croce he created a new cycle of scenes from the life of Francis for the chapel of the Bardi banking family (shortly before they went bankrupt) and there are other works attributed to him, in the neighbouring Peruzzi Chapel, for instance, even if the documentation for most of his works is very

sparse. By 1334, towards the end of his life, he was appointed *Magnus Magister*, the official in charge of building works in Florence, notably those of the great cathedral now rising in the centre of the city. He designed the *campanile*, the bell tower, and even though he died before it was finished and the design was changed, it provides even more evidence of the breadth of his genius. After his death in 1337 Giotto is said to have been buried under the original chapel to an early virgin martyr, Santa Reparata, to whom the cathedral is dedicated.

* * *

But we need to return to Padua, the home of the Arena Chapel. This prosperous city enjoyed a favourable position in the fertile Po Valley with good access to the sea. Unlike many cities of the north, it had maintained its prosperity through Byzantine and Lombard times. In 1222 it boosted its independence and status through the foundation of its university where, like Bologna, the students took the initiative in defining the curriculum. There was a strong emphasis on law and medicine – in fact, the university split into two institutions in 1399, each concentrating on just one of these. By the fourteenth century the university was developing a reputation for classical scholarship, what became known as humanism.*

Traditionally, humanism has been described as an intellectual style that manifested itself in an alternative approach to education, rooted in the intense study of classical texts – at first only those in Latin, but later those in Greek. The mastery of these was assumed to lead to independent and cultivated minds.[11] The contrast with the scholasticism of the universities was marked. The humanist curriculum was broader, and included poetry, history, moral philosophy and rhetoric. It drew heavily on those texts copied in Charlemagne's time or recopied over the next three centuries, many of which were discovered in the fourteenth and fifteenth centuries. There was immense and shared excitement over each new find. It was expected that the learning acquired from study of these texts would be put on public display – humanists were therefore expected to be able to speak and write well. One was judged by the quality and elegance of one's Latin. One cannot read the humanist texts without recognizing their confidence and the freedom to discuss issues that were narrowly defined by the university curriculum.

* The term 'humanist' was coined only in the nineteenth century, although the phrase *studia humanitatis* had been used in the first century BC by the orator Cicero (106–43 BC) as a reflection of his belief in the value of the humanities.

In recent scholarship, the term 'humanism' has been treated in a more nuanced way. A traditional view that saw it in opposition to the church is being modified to show that it would be accommodated quite comfortably with established religion. Late medieval Christianity was surprisingly porous, in that new intellectual movements could be absorbed so long as they did not directly challenge the authority or doctrine of the church. Many intellectuals had already sought out posts in the religious hierarchy and they could retain these while keeping their fascination with classical scholarship. A letter survives from the Florentine humanist Poggio Bracciolini (1380–1459) in which he hopes for a canonry in faraway Bordeaux which will give him the income needed to sustain his freedom to travel and study. The omnipresence of the church in late medieval life did not stop the humanists, including Petrarch, the subject of much of this chapter, from openly criticizing its corruptions.

The humanists placed a strong emphasis on what was known as *virtu*. It is not easy to pin down what was meant by the term. An expected response would be to tie it to moral goodness, but it could be used much more flexibly to denote the skills through which one individual maintained his superiority over another. In the early Middle Ages *virtu* had embraced the idea of valour in conflict. Christians emphasized the spiritual aspects of the term, even lauding withdrawal from society as an example of *virtu*, while, in contrast, the classical precedents emphasized an active role in political life, preferably in a republic. The humanist Petrarch saw *virtu* in Cicero's creative prose, while a biographer of the fifteenth-century Florentine architect Filippo Brunelleschi used the term to celebrate the architect's technical expertise, not least in his ability to find ways through obstacles. In short, *virtu* had the flexibility to be used creatively across a wide range of contexts, Christian, classical and contemporary. Gradually, it became associated with an aristocratic elitism. The Italian scholar Guido Ruggiero puts it well when he describes *virtu* as 'placing a greater emphasis on self-display and self-fashioning and *sprezzatura* (the ability to accomplish great things effortlessly) and fostering a greater suspicion of a growing range of activities associated with work that would come to be seen as debasing'.[12] One of the criticisms of the humanists is that they turn their back on scientific exploration, preferring instead to concentrate on higher things. By the sixteenth century they risked being laughed

overleaf Giorgione's *Three Philosophers* of 1509 pays tribute to the classical philosopher (Aristotle?), an Arabic interpreter and a contemporary figure who may be contemplating a cave such as Plato depicted in *The Republic*.

at for the pursuit of arcane learning for its own sake by poets such as Pietro Aretino (1492–1556).

The model for the humanists' own writing was the sophisticated use of Latin of the Roman orator and politician Cicero. The exercise of *virtu* could certainly be used to describe Cicero's life in public service. He had grown up in the tumultuous later years of the Roman republic and he was unique in getting to the top as a result of his devastatingly effective forensic oratory rather than through military prowess.[13] Petrarch referred to him as *Romani eloquii summe parens* ('the supreme father of Roman eloquence'). Pushed this way and that as the political currents turned, Cicero's frustrations were expressed in his letters to his cultivated friend Atticus, but he also composed works of philosophy that used Greek texts as the basis for sober meditations on contemporary life. His luck finally ran out in 43 BC when he was judicially murdered in the turmoil following the death of Julius Caesar. Cicero remains one of the founding fathers of European liberal humanism and a fitting mentor for the humanists, whose achievements were to go beyond an uncritical reverence for texts to understanding the lives of those who wrote them and the contexts of the language they used. The exposed public life of Cicero provided an ideal that contrasted with the ascetic seclusion of the monks, which had traditionally been seen as the highest form of living.

The forerunners of humanism were to be found in Padua.[14] There was a small circle of intellectuals here led, typically for the time, by lawyers, prominent among whom were Lovato Lovati (1241–1309), a judge, and Albertino Mussato (1261–1329), a notary who had also acted as an ambassador for the city. Both were searching around for classical texts and composing their own works in Latin. They had been especially influenced by the first-century AD tragedies of Seneca, the Roman Stoic philosopher and dramatist. Mussato's own tragedy *Ecerinus* is recognized as the first secular play since Roman times. In 1274, during building work in the city, a sarcophagus was unearthed. It actually dated from late antiquity but the enthusiastic Lovati seized upon it as the sarcophagus of Antenor, a refugee from Troy and the legendary founder of Padua, the Roman *Patavinum*. Ten years later the sarcophagus was given an arched and columned surround and inscriptions from classical authors such as Virgil, who was the source for the legend, placed above it.*

The most celebrated Roman citizen of *Patavinum* was the historian Livy (*c.*60 BC–AD 17) and so when an inscription was unearthed at the

* It is still to be seen today in Padua's Piazza Antenore.

end of the century that referred to one T. Livius, it was assumed by the credulous Lovati that this was the burial place of the great man. Relics from the find were carried in procession to the centre of the city just as if they had been those of a saint and embedded in the wall of the Church of Santa Giustina. Yet the learning of the Paduan scholars was rudimentary. They knew, of course, the medieval Latin of their times but, as the inscription over the tomb of Antenor showed, their classical Latin was weak and a closer reading of the Livy inscription would have shown them that it referred to a freed slave with a similar name.

There are several moments when one might argue that the incipient humanism of Padua was transformed into a more sophisticated movement, but the following is the one that is most compelling, not least because it confirms the relationship between humanism and Christian belief. On 26 April 1336, Francesco Petrarca (1304–74) – known in English as Petrarch – a minor canon connected to the papal administration at Avignon, made an arduous ascent of Mont Ventoux, near Avignon, with his younger brother.[15] His inspiration came from a passage from Livy, his favourite Roman historian, parts of whose *History of Rome* he would collect from surviving fragments. This passage told how Philip of Macedon, the father of Alexander the Great, had climbed a mountain in Thessaly from where he had been able to see two seas. Yet, despite this inspiration from a classical source, Petrarch saw his ascent primarily as a spiritual journey, as he recounted in a letter to his old confessor, an Augustinian monk named Dionisio da Borgo San Sepolcro.

When, after taking several false paths, Petrarch had finally reached the summit, he was overcome with the magnificence of the view, southwards across the Alps towards Italy and westwards to the mountains around Lyons. He reflected that all he had read from the classical authors about Mounts Athos and Olympus in Greece seemed much more credible and his view of the Alps brought to mind the celebrated crossing of Hannibal into Italy. However, his thoughts soon returned to the spiritual impact of the ascent. He had with him a copy of the *Confessions* of St Augustine that Dionisio had given him, and he turned to Book 10, where a sentence leapt out at him: 'And men go about to wonder at the heights of the mountains, and the mighty waves of the sea, and the wide sweep of rivers, and the circuit of the ocean, and the revolution of the stars, but they themselves they consider not.'[16] It had a dramatic impact:

Ytala p̄claros tellus alis alma poetas.
Sz tibi grecoz dedit hic attingere metas.
Servius altiloqui retegens archana maronis.
Ut pateant ducibz pastoribz atqz colonis.

> I was abashed, and, asking my brother (who was anxious to hear more), not to annoy me, I closed the book, angry with myself that I should still be admiring earthly things, who might long ago have learned from even the pagan philosophers that nothing is wonderful but the soul, which, when great itself, finds nothing great outside itself.

He believed that God had directed him to that passage and, as he and his brother made their descent in the gathering darkness, he became preoccupied with his own sinfulness.

This letter brilliantly catches a moment of transition. Petrarch describes how 'at first, owing to the unaccustomed quality of the air and the effect of the great sweep of view spread out before me, I stood like one dazed'. The aesthetic impact of the natural world laid out before him was overwhelming, but all such experience remained subject to the demands of God. Petrarch never lost his love of nature and would retreat to the countryside around Avignon to escape from the corrosive atmosphere of the papal court.

Of course, Petrarch may have exaggerated the spiritual impact of the experience to satisfy his confessor (and some scholars have even suggested he had never made the ascent other than in his imagination), but he remained strongly religious, as his work in the papal administration in Avignon attests. Yet he was also obsessed by the classical texts that he spent much of his time discovering in monastic libraries where they lay hidden. As a later admirer, Leonardo Bruni, the chancellor of Florence, put it, Petrarch was 'the first with a talent sufficient to recognize and call back to light the antique elegance of the lost and extinguished style'.[17] The letters of Cicero to Atticus, his friend in Athens, which he tracked down in Verona, were perhaps, for later generations, his greatest find as they gave an intimate portrait of the politics of the late Roman republic by one who was at the centre of events as well as a model for precise Latin prose.

The artist Simone Martini completed this frontispiece to Petrarch's collection of Virgil's texts in 1338. It shows the Roman poet, an important figure for the humanists, reclining in a bucolic landscape.

The breadth of Petrarch's aesthetic experience ensured that he did not see knowledge as the study of a fixed body of theology or the works of Aristotle, but as a continuous process leading to more profound truths. Petrarch had been trained in dialectic by his law studies, first at Montpellier and then Bologna, but he noted its sterility and inadequacy as a way of making intellectual progress. These were seven wasted years. Petrarch talks, in his later tract *On his Own Ignorance and That of Others*, of 'the crazy and clamourous set of Scholastics'. He can accept the greatness of Aristotle, but

I snarl at the stupid Aristotelians, who day by day in every single word they speak do not cease to hammer into the heads of others Aristotle whom they know by name only... His brilliance has stunned many bleary and weak eyes and made many a man fall into the ditches of error.[18]

Petrarch's ambition was to understand how to live a life of *virtu* and he saw the traditional university curricula, not only of Aristotle but of medicine and law, as irrelevant for his purpose. Petrarch lamented the neglect of other great writers. He had been introduced by his father to Latin literature and found it to be a much more fascinating subject for study. He proved to be an obsessive and profoundly engaged reader. As an orthodox Catholic he believed that there were truths that lay at a far deeper level than reason but, unlike many of the scholastic theologians, he did not fear breaking out of structures erected by medieval logic to find them. Essential to his studies was his belief that the classical virtues, of *pietas*, *virtus*, *caritas* and *humanitas*, were compatible with Christian living. *On his Own Ignorance* is a fine example of how an admiration for the works and style of Cicero can be reconciled with Christian teaching.

A miniature of 1503 showing Petrarch presenting his book 'Remedies for Fortune Fair and Foul' to Louis XII of France.

Petrarch never overcame his detestation of the scholastic obsession with Aristotle. He was responsible for coining the term 'Dark Ages' to describe the medieval period he believed he was still living in following the extinction of the 'light' of classical antiquity. Several of his works dwell on how the moral corruption of his age allowed a lust for wealth to transcend spiritual values. He believed he was restoring the light and continuously harked back in his writings to the superiority of Rome, even to the extent of wishing to recreate Italy as a single state.[19] So can this be called a 'renaissance'? In fact, the term was only coined in 1855 by the French historian Jules Michelet. In an excellent introduction to the issue Guido Ruggiero suggests that 'the term that would fit most closely for someone like Petrarch or Dante would be the Latin term *renovatio* or "renewal", as both men, along with many of their contemporaries, were fascinated with the idea of renewing the Roman world and the days of the first Christians.'[20] It would only be in the fifteenth century that humanists such as Leonardo Bruni talked explicitly of a *rinascita*, 'a rebirth' (see Chapter 12, p. 281, 291).

Petrarch had a gift for friendship, was a brilliant conversationalist and was as much at ease with fellow scholars as with great men of state. He met with emperors, popes and kings and, inspired by Cicero, was

an avid letter writer. In fact, the letter became the preferred method of humanist communication – a letter did not need to be long but it was enough to show off the elegant style and originality of the writer. Petrarch championed tolerance, echoing ancient beliefs when he noted that 'many can be forced to confess, but not to believe. No liberty is greater than the liberty to think. As I claim it for myself, so I do not deny it for others... I am unwilling to be the judge of the human conscience which is something hidden and deep.'[21] This acceptance of intellectual diversity was an important moment in Renaissance thought. It ensured that humanism was never a homogenous movement; rather, it opened up intense debates on 'the condition of man'.

It is in his writings that the intellectual versatility of Petrarch can be best explored. His epic poem *Africa* in Latin hexameters described the exploits of the Roman general Scipio Africanus, victor over Hannibal in the third century BC. This was followed by the accolade of 'poet laureate', awarded – for the first time since antiquity – to him in Rome, on the Capitoline Hill, in 1341. His sonnets and songs, *Canzoniere*, addressed to his idealized woman, one Laura, his own Beatrice, like Dante's married and unattainable, provided models for lyric poetry for future generations.* The *Canzoniere* were published for the first time in 1470, soon after the birth of printing. Thirty-four different editions would appear by 1500, with 167 to follow in the next century. Petrarch's status as a poet would open doors for him at courts throughout Italy. He was particularly excited to have discovered Cicero's speech *Pro Archia* in which the orator had defended a poet, Archias, and in the process the art of poetry itself.

Petrarch remained a traveller, endlessly searching out new documents in monasteries and libraries as far north as the Netherlands while his visits to Rome brought him face to face with the material evidence of the empire. A famous letter describes his thoughts on ancient Rome as he sat perched high up on the ruins of the Baths of Diocletian. In 1347 he was enthralled, rather naively so, by the uprising in Rome of the volatile, self-styled 'tribune of the people'† Cola di Rienzo in 1347 and the possibility, short-lived as it turned out, that ancient republican values of liberty might be restored. Even though he maintained his positions in the papal administration in Avignon, Petrarch was furious with the popes for abandoning 'the eternal city'.

Petrarch embodied many of the conflicts that were to pervade the humanist tradition. There remained tensions between his spirituality

* Laura was to die young in the Black Death.

† The tribunes were elected Roman officials who represented the people's rights.

and his sensuality (while unable, as a cleric, to marry, he fathered two children), between the secular philosophies of his favourite pagan authors and the works of Augustine. He hated the corruptions of the papacy but remained a recipient of papal patronage in Avignon. While admiring Cicero as a stylist and philosopher, he was troubled by the compromises and traumas of the great orator's public life, especially when he had come across the prevarications and doubts expressed in the letters to Atticus. Like those who followed him, he emphasized the intellectual rather than political achievements of the leading Greeks and Romans. Petrarch partially resolved these tensions through endless reworkings of his thoughts. His *Canzoniere* are full of self-searching and in this sense make him a modern spirit. His *Secretum* is a series of dialogues with no less a person than St Augustine, in which he explores the conflict between his desire for fame and the Christian demands that he should withdraw to contemplate and reject the attractions of physical love. He eventually appears to have learned how to balance solitude and contemplation with intense periods of activity.[22]

Petrarch spent his last years in Venice, where his daughter had married. He warmed to the city and promised that in return for the house they granted him he would leave Venice his library. Yet he became involved in a bitter dispute with a group of young men who proclaimed that the Arab philosopher Averroes was greater than the apostle Paul and Augustine. Petrarch was always sensitive to any perceived attack on his literary achievements and preferences. It was now that he wrote his tract *On His Own Ignorance*, lamenting the sterility of Aristotelian studies in the universities, and withdrew his promise of leaving his books to Venice. The library presumably went with him when he returned to live out his final years in the small town of Arquà, near Padua. He was found dead there, on 18 July 1374, his head lying on a copy of Virgil. Boccaccio was one of his closest friends and it is moving to find that in his will Petrarch left him fifty gold florins, 'for a winter coat for his studies and night-time scholarly work'.[23] His library never survived intact.

Petrarch has been highlighted here even if much modern scholarship is more cautious in assessing his contribution as 'the father of humanism'. While the most influential nineteenth-century study of the Renaissance, Jacob Burckhardt's *The Civilization of the Renaissance in Italy* (1860), argued that humanism involved a complete break with the past, when 'man became a *spiritual individual* [my emphasis] and recognized himself as such', in contrast to an assumed collective identity in the Middle Ages, Petrarch's identification with Augustine suggests

otherwise. While we will encounter in later chapters new ways in which individuals could express themselves – the portrait is often cited as the classic case for the emergence of 'individuals' – society as a whole remained hierarchical through the period termed the Renaissance.

In the fourteenth century knowledge and adoption of the ideas and language of the classical world still remained at a rudimentary stage. Classical Latin contended with two rivals, the scholastic Latin of the universities, now increasingly irrelevant as a means of providing accessible knowledge, and the Latin of commerce and government, mastered in the schools of the Italian cities. This version of Latin had the advantage of being able to evolve to reflect the fast-changing social and commercial scene. In taking classical Latin as the model, humanism was being consciously elitist.* It was this sense of superiority over their fellows, especially when the humanists linked their learning to the cultivation of *virtu*, that gave them their appeal. They like to term themselves *ingeniosi*, in reflection of their high level of wit and culture.

The elegant Latin of the humanists became embedded both as the language of scholarship and the mark of a gentleman. As Leon Battista Alberti, perhaps the most versatile of the humanists, put it: 'If there is anything which goes beautifully with gentility or which gives the greatest distinction to human life or adds grace, authority and name to a family, it is surely Latin letters, without which no one can be reputed to possess gentility.'[24] Over the fifteenth century there was a gradual adoption of Ciceronian Latin by lawyers and bureaucrats for government documents even as the vernacular took over in the streets and harbours. The adoption was marked by a return to scripts taken from classical inscriptions and manuscripts (often from the Carolingian period) that contrasted with the more decorative and less tractable scripts of scholastic texts. The association of humanism with elitism was also attractive to popes of the fifteenth century, notably Nicholas V, Pius II (who was renowned for his oratory) and Sixtus IV (of the Sistine Chapel and the elegant Ponte Sisto over the Tiber) who made the papal court as intellectually cultivated as any in Europe. In contrast Pius's successor, Paul II (r.1464–71), was ridiculed by the courtiers for his poor Latin and rejection of humanist scholarship.

In due course we will examine how humanism would fuel scholarly enterprises through Europe. But first the particular contribution of Florence to humanism needs to be explored.

A delightful study of Cicero as a boy reading, by the fifteenth-century artist Vincenzo Foppo. It reflects the humanists' fascination with Cicero as a master of prose and eloquence.

* There had been a precedent, in the second century AD, when educated Greeks started reusing the classical Greek of Athens, from 600 years earlier, instead of the common Greek, *koine*, of the streets.

The Exuberance of Florentine Humanism

Today we see our Leonardo [Bruni] of Arezzo sent into the world as the father and ornament of letters, the resplendent life of Latin elegance, to restore the sweetness of the Latin language to mankind... Anyone of intelligence thanks God for being born in these times, in which the excellent arts of the mind flourish more than at any other time in the last thousand years. It has pleased Him who rules everything to give a long and most tranquil peace to our humble Italy: that being so, it certainly can be seen that from these first revivals will follow marvellous fruits, ripe to correct, with time, the most obvious errors of the most valuable branches of learning.

Matteo Palmieri,
Della vita civile (*On Civic Life*), 1432[1]

If humanism was to be anything more than the poring over of classical documents by a scholarly elite, it had to grasp the imagination of a society and express itself not only in texts but in art and politics. Humanism spread throughout the cities and courts of northern Italy, and then later north of the Alps, but Florence has traditionally been seen as the centre of civic humanism, humanism integrated within the ethos of the civic community.

Florence's love of republican liberty was honed by the persistent need to assert itself against its rivals. Sixty per cent of its population died in the Black Death and there are horrific accounts of the shoving of bodies into mass burial pits, layer upon layer 'like a lasagne', as one report put it.[2] After the recovery from this trauma, conflict with Florence's neighbours and rivals – Milan, Siena, Pisa and Lucca – resumed.

Perhaps most surprising was a war with the papacy fought between 1375 and 1378.[3] This was unexpected because the papal party, the Guelphs, had, despite their factions, held power in the city for 100 years and Florentine bankers had handled the popes' money. But this conflict helped define Florence's identity and showed the growing isolation of the papacy. The war arose from Pope Gregory XI's determination to regain control of the papal states after the popes had returned from their residence in Avignon. Rumours abounded that Gregory was hoping to occupy some of Florence's territories and in response Florence allied itself with Milan, traditionally a Ghibelline city and often a feared rival. War broke out in 1375. The city's senior bureaucrat, chancellor Coluccio Salutati,* then began fomenting unrest in the major cities of the papal states, Bologna, Perugia, Orvieto, by crafting the conflict in ideological terms. He proved to be a master of the formal letter-writing that characterized the relationships between Renaissance city-states.† In letters that have been described by the Milanese 'tyrant', Giangaleazzo Visconti, as having the impact of 'a thousand Florentine horsemen', he urged these cities to throw off the 'tyranny' of papal monarchy and embrace the 'republican liberty' of Florence. Merchants and guildsmen, he told them, are natural lovers of freedom. They 'desire peace in which to practice their studies and arts, they love equality among citizens and do not glory in the nobility of family or blood'.[4]

* The chancellor ran the city government and represented it on formal occasions through his letters or speeches.

† The art of letter-writing was known as *ars dictaminis*, a skill for any aspiring bureaucrat to master.

This provocative campaign led to Gregory placing an interdict on the city: there were to be no religious services of any kind and Florentines would be subject to arrest anywhere they were to be found. This ban soon faltered, the French going so far as to defy the papal decree and offering protection to Florence's merchants.

What is remarkable is the Florentine response to the interdict. The citizens simply took over the religious ceremonies for themselves, exulting in processions, packed church services and anti-papal hysteria. The committee that ran the war named themselves 'the Eight Saints', as if they somehow represented a more authentic form of Christianity than the papacy. Houses of leading Guelphs, the papal party, were sacked. Meanwhile, in order to finance the war the city began confiscating and selling church property on a scale not known anywhere else before the Reformation. It was only with the death of Gregory in March 1378 that peace talks could begin with his successor, Urban VI. The Great Schism that followed meant that the indemnities that Florence agreed to pay in restitution for destroying church property were weakly enforced, and in the long term Florence had gained much more effective control of its religious institutions. This was a trend that would be seen throughout Europe after 1400 as papal power atrophied and the laity asserted themselves as participants in creating their own religious identities. (It will be explored further in Chapter 16.)

overleaf A view of Florence in the fifteenth century by Francesco Rosselli, emphasizing the dominance of the cathedral dome and Giotto's *campanile*. Note too the imposing Palazzo dei Priori to the right of the cathedral.

In the aftermath of the war, there was a dramatic expression of radical ideas and action by the Ciompi, the unskilled woolworkers.‡[5] It began as what appeared to be a typical power struggle between the ruling factions of the city. (For Florence's system of government, see pp. 237–40.) By now the eight priors were largely selected from the major guilds that were themselves dominated by the most powerful families of the city. When Salvestro de' Medici, a cousin of the famous family, was elected *gonfaloniere* in May 1378, he suggested restoring the Ordinances of Justice of 1293 to the original participation of the twenty-one guilds (fourteen minor guilds alongside the seven major ones).

The proposal attracted enormous support and sparked mass meetings of artisans and workers, who put forward their own coherent programme of reform. The shortage of workers after the Black Death had led to a rise in wages, but records show increasing pressure on incomes

‡ The name *ciompi* appears to come from the French *Compar*, a greeting meaning 'friend' or 'ally', as a prefix to 'Join me for a drink'.

FIESOLE

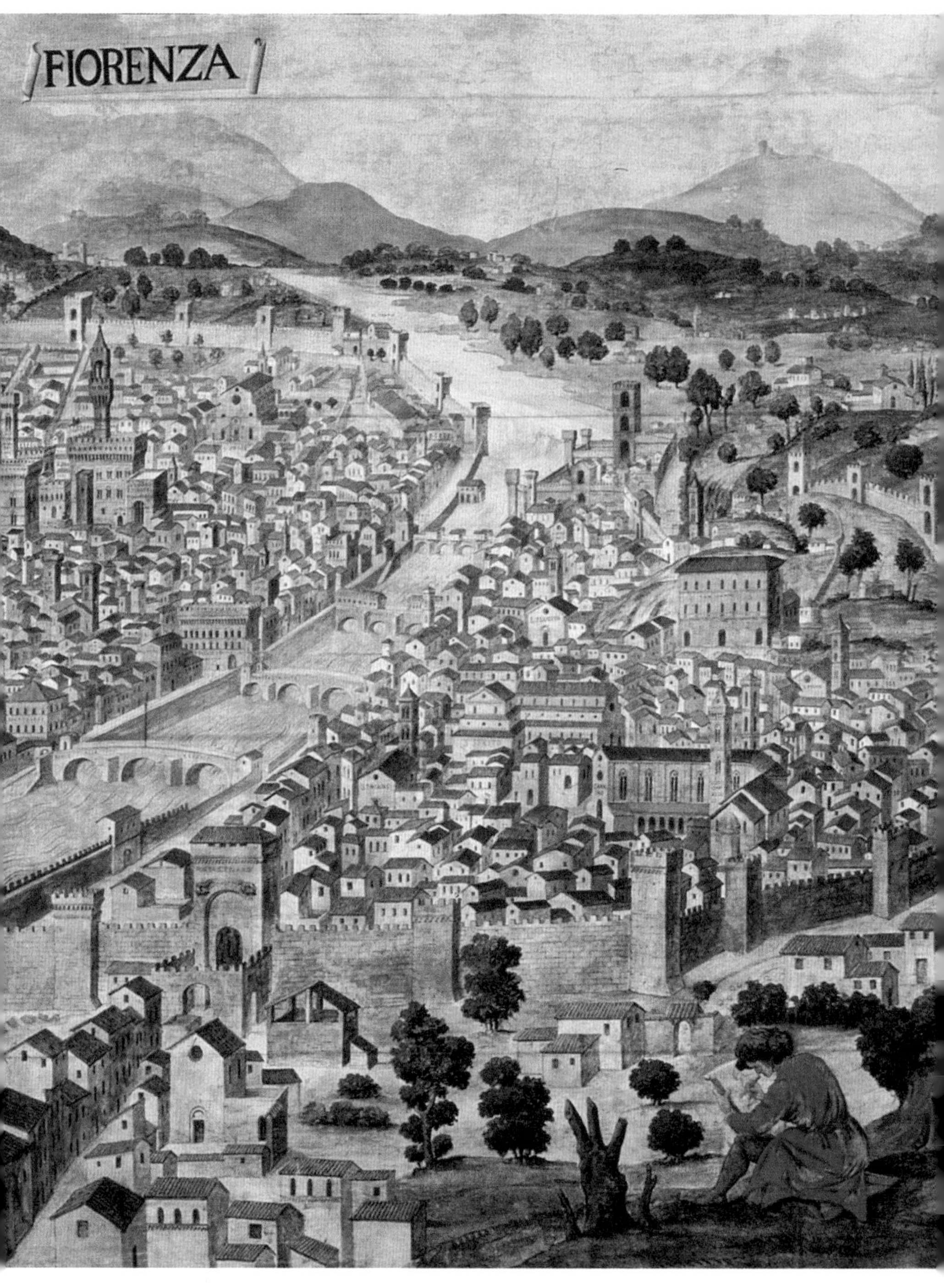
FIORENZA

as a result of large families, irregular employment and taxes. In particular, resentments had grown over the ruthless collection of debts. Up to this point the mass of workers had been excluded from the guilds but now, gathering in the public spaces of the city, notably the area in front of Santa Maria Novella, they demanded their own guild with the right to elect two of the eight priors. They adopted a blacksmith's tongs, suggesting the power of pincers to crush opposition, as a rallying flag. Pouring out into the streets, they forced themselves into the Palazzo dei Priori and proclaimed a new *gonfaloniere*, an artisan called Michele di Lando. In the assessment of one sympathetic to the uprising: 'This was done to give a share of offices to more people, so that everyone would be satisfied, and the citizens united and poor men would have their share because they have always borne the cost, and no one but the rich has ever profited.'[6] Egalitarianism was in the air.

What emerged from the turmoil was not one new workers' guild but three: one for the skilled workers of the woollen cloths, one for those skilled in the clothing trades and one for the unskilled, the Ciompi. The third guild had an estimated membership of 9,000, dramatically larger than the total of 4,000–5,000 members in the original twenty-one guilds. When the nominations were drawn up for the new government, 1,700 of the hitherto unrepresented workers were among the list of 6,000 – far more than had ever been known before – that was put forward for scrutiny.*

The Ciompi now over-reached themselves. The seven major guilds had secured 2,800 of the 6,000 nominations. Mistakenly believing that more of these could be challenged, the Ciompi met at the end of August, once again in the piazza in front of Santa Maria Novella, and demanded a more extensive scrutiny of the names. They proclaimed that they had the authority to do this but when their representatives returned to the Palazzo dei Priori with the demands, the mood had changed. Michele di Lando, in charge of security as *gonfaloniere*, arrested them and then, when the Ciompi rushed towards the piazza in protest, rallied the guilds, now twenty-three in number, against them. Six or so were killed, others wounded and the remainder chased from the square. On 1 September an assembly of the citizenry abolished the Ciompi guild.

The revolt had not been in vain, even if a full democracy had not been achieved. The remaining twenty-three guilds were divided between the original seven major and, now, sixteen minor guilds. It was

* After the scrutiny, where those nominated on the list could be challenged, the priors would be selected by lot.

proclaimed that reforms could not be carried out 'without the full, free, total, and absolute power of the whole Florentine people' meeting in assembly and indeed a more popular government was installed. Over the next four years most of the priors were selected from the skilled artisans: hatmakers, goldsmiths, furriers and glassmakers. As service was only for two months at a time, there was a rapid turnover of priors. Studies show that as many came from minor guilds as the major ones and that there were representatives of 100 families that had not been recorded before. The revolt of the Ciompi has been seen as the closest approximation to a democratic revolution known anywhere during the Renaissance and it shows that even the skilled working class had developed a political identity. However, the dividing line for participation had proved to be between skilled and unskilled. When the crunch came di Lando had abandoned the Ciompi. In the eighteenth century a statue of Michele, the saviour of stability as he was now seen, was placed in a niche in the Loggia del Mercato Nuovo.

As often happens with time, however, the impetus of revolt slackened. By 1382 the elite had regrouped. The figures suggest that out of 1,069 nominations to fill the posts for the priors in 1411, a large majority, 884, were once again from the major guilds. A new ideology based on the fear of another workers' rising became prevalent. Tensions were raised when a new bishop of Florence counselled the *signoria* in 1390, in a message that became public: 'If you want to rule and keep control, keep the *popolo* hungry for bread.'[7]

overleaf The dome of Florence's hallowed baptistery was decorated with sumptuous mosaics in the thirteenth century.

Despite this antagonism, a much broader proportion of the citizenry were still represented among the elected officials. The new government proved to be a stable one underpinned by the continued growth in prosperity. There was a growing demand for luxury goods, which the sophisticated Florentine merchants were able to meet. The skills of many cloth workers were diverted into the making of silk, the city's most successful new industry of the fifteenth century. A mass of commodities, from slaves to spices, were picked up on the trade routes and sold alongside these staples. The shock of the Bardi and Peruzzi bankruptcies led to more efficient methods of managing credit, and the merchant families of Florence remained the most resourceful of all players on the international stage. The narrow streets and the heavy fortress-palaces of Florence give the impression of defensiveness (compare them to the façades of the palaces of Venice visible to all across the canals), so making it difficult for the visitor today to appreciate the extent of the city's international

DNATIONES
POTES

ANGELI

reach and its ruthless exploitation of new markets, whether in Spain and Portugal, Antwerp and Bruges, Rhodes and Jerusalem and – after the fall of Constantinople in 1453 – the triumphant Ottoman empire. A typical Florentine firm may have had twenty-five overseas branches across the Mediterranean and northern Europe.

The century ended successfully when an invasion by the duke of Milan, Gian Galeazzo Visconti, which appeared to be on the brink of victory, collapsed in 1402 with his death from plague. In 1406 Florence finally gained control of Pisa, and its own outlet to the sea. The addition of Livorno and Porto Pisano, bought from the Genoese in 1421, ensured that Florence was now a maritime power. By the early 1400s the Florentines had every right to be proud of their achievements and their new confidence and wealth provided a secure setting for the development of humanism.

One of the most influential studies of the period, *The Crisis of the Early Italian Renaissance* by Hans Baron, first published in 1955, saw the victory of the Florentines against the Milanese in 1402 as the inspiration for a 'civic humanism' that transformed the ethos of the city.[8] As with their responses to Burckhardt, historians of humanism are now more cautious in assuming the sudden appearance of something radically new in 1400. Political debate had been lively in the Italian cities from as early as the twelfth century. Aristotle's influential *Politics* had been translated in 1264 and drawn on by Marsilius of Padua in his *Defensor Pacis*. The famous allegories of *Good and Bad Government*, frescos by Ambrogio Lorenzetti in the Palazzo Pubblico in Siena, date from 1338–9 and again draw on models from Aristotle's *Politics*, who can certainly be seen as an inspiration for 'civic humanism'. Yet there was something in the air of early fifteenth-century Florence that gave it a dynamism that extended beyond the intellectual elite into its public life. Central to this was an adulation of republicanism, even though, as we shall see, the Florentine republic was never as pure as it was proclaimed to be.

Among Baron's favoured humanists was chancellor Coluccio Salutati, already noted for his eloquent letters in defence of his city's freedom. Salutati, an enthusiast for Petrarch (he argued that the humanist was greater than Cicero and Virgil), took the study of the classical world a step further when in 1397 he invited the Greek scholar Manuel Chrysoloras to teach Greek in the city. For the first time in the west for centuries, Aristotle and Plato and other representatives of the great cultural heritage of ancient Greece, including the tragedians Aeschylus, Sophocles and Euripides, began to be read in the original.

And there was more than this. If one was to gain a fuller understanding of the major Latin writers such as Virgil and Horace, the models that they followed had to be absorbed in the original. Although it was to be some decades before mastery of Greek spread through the elite, this was an important initiative and helped broaden the reach of humanism.

One of the first to master the restored works was Leonardo Bruni (1370–1444), another of Baron's favourites. Bruni was from Arezzo, a city which had been acquired by Florence in 1384. Salutati had spotted his talent and recruited him for Florence's chancery. As with so many humanists, Bruni also served in Rome. He was secretary to the papal chancery in Rome under four popes before returning to Florence to become chancellor himself in 1427 until his death in 1444. Bruni was renowned for his eloquence at a time when the discovery of the full text of the Roman orator Quintilian's *The Education of the Orator* (*c.*AD 95) in the monastery of St Gall in 1416 had provided a fine introduction to Roman rhetoric and a model for the training of speakers. Bruni greeted the find with enthusiasm.

Shortly after the failure of Milan to take the city, Bruni composed his *Laudatio Florentiae urbis* (*Panegyric of the City of Florence*).[9] His model came from the great period of Greek rhetoric of the second century AD, the so-called Second Sophistic. By this time the Roman empire was stable and the Greek cities of the eastern Mediterranean lived at peace with one another. The orator Aelius Aristides offered praise to the city of Athens as the defender of Greek freedom against the tyrannical Persians, and Bruni now adopted this for Florence, which had defended its freedom against the tyranny of Milan. Not least, Bruni reasserted the importance of knowing the past as a means of illuminating the present, a key feature of humanism.

The *Panegyric* is blatant propaganda but inspiring nonetheless. Bruni traced Florence's greatness back to its Roman past but its spirit came from the period it was founded, the first century BC when Rome was still a republic. By now the adulation of Rome was pervasive among the educated Florentine elite and so Bruni was able to let himself go, but here stressing the Roman people rather than their imperial masters.

> What nation in the entire world was ever more distinguished, more powerful, more outstanding in every sort of excellence than the Roman people? Their deeds are so illustrious that the greatest feats done by other men seem like child's play when compared to the deeds of the Romans… They governed with the greatest competence for many centuries, so that from a single city comes more examples of virtue than all other nations have been able to produce until *now* [my emphasis]… *Now*, if the glory, nobility, virtue, grandeur, and magnificence of the parents can also make

POSTQVAM LEONARDVS E VITA MIGRAVIT
HISTORIA LVGET · ELOQVENTIA MVTA EST·
FERTVRQVE MVSAS TVM GRAECAS TVM
LATINAS LACRIMAS TENERE NO POTVISSE·

the sons outstanding, no people in the entire world can be as worthy of dignity as are the Florentines, for they are born from such parents who surpass by a long way all mortals in every sort of glory… Nowhere else do you find such internal order, such neatness, and such harmonious co-operation… this very prudent city is harmonized in all its parts, so there results a single great, harmonious constitution whose harmony pleases both the eyes and minds of men.

In addition to the use of Aristides, there are echoes too of a work Bruni is known to have read in detail, the *History of the Peloponnesian War* by the Greek historian Thucydides (*c.*460–400 BC), in which Thucydides records a similar idealizing panegyric by the Athenian statesman Pericles. The *History* was to prove an important model for the humanists. It provided a narrative history of a brutal conflict that its author claimed to be accurate and shorn of myth. This was an approach to history that had become lost with the end of antiquity – the Greek historian Ammianus Marcellinus in the late fourth century is considered its last exponent.

Another Greek work of history that came Bruni's way was Polybius' *Histories*. Polybius (*c.*200–118 BC) was a cultivated Greek aristocrat taken by the Romans as a hostage after their conquest of Greece in the second century BC. The *Histories* cover the period 264–146 BC and include a description of the destruction of Carthage. Polybius became fascinated by the republican political system of Rome and how it had powered Rome's successful rise to empire. This paean to republicanism chimed well with Bruni's own beliefs. In a later work he proclaims that 'the only legitimate constitution of the commonwealth is the popular one, in which liberty is real, in which legal equality is the same for all citizens, in which pursuit of the virtues may flourish without suspicion'.[10] This bore little relation to the tumultuous political life of Florence, not least because the city was a hotbed of aggressive capitalism.

This elegant tomb of Leonardo Bruni (d. 1444) by Bernardo Rossellino celebrates the fine speaker and historian who was also chancellor of the city from 1427 to his death.

Bruni is also known for his *Historiarum Florentini populi* (*A History of the Florentine People*).[11] This major work is often said to be 'the first modern history' and this is justified in so far as the work made a careful use of a variety of sources, bypassing the legendary accounts of early Florentine history that Giovanni Villani had recorded a century earlier. It is resolutely secular in tone – in particular Bruni turned his back on what John Burrow in his survey of historical writing has described as the 'historiographical coup' of the church historians who had portrayed the empire as the providential base for the inevitable expansion of Christianity and shaped their histories accordingly.[12] Now the Roman republic takes precedence. In his first chapter Bruni destroys the legends of Florence's foundations and recasts its history in narrative form, with a succession of battles and set-piece speeches, typical of classical historians such as Thucydides and, for Rome, Livy. Yet this is, of course, a history driven by ideology, the prominence of Florence among other cities and the adulation of republicanism that Polybius had recorded as the catalyst for Rome's greatness. Having laboured at his history for twenty years, Bruni completed the final book, the twelfth, shortly before his death and it was fitting that a copy should be placed on his body at his funeral. The wonderfully elegant Renaissance tomb in Santa Croce, sculpted by Bernardo Rossellino, again shows Bruni with his masterwork lying on his chest. His successor as chancellor composed a fitting epitaph: 'After Leonardo departed this life, history is in mourning and eloquence is dumb and it is said that the Muses, Greek and Latin alike, cannot restrain their tears.'

While working in Rome, Bruni had been happy to tutor other bright students and the one who was to become most famous was Lorenzo Valla, born in the city in 1403. Lorenzo was a difficult man, brilliant in his scholarship but arrogant and polemical.[13] His working life illustrates just how complex was the relationship between the humanists and the church. In his *De voluptate* (*On Pleasure*), he advocated a return to the philosophy of Epicurus, a Greek thinker of the second century BC, who had taught that mental pleasure was the chief aim of life. Valla attempted to marry Epicurianism with Christianity by arguing that God had created a good world that human beings had been given the capacity to enjoy. This conflicted with more austere philosophies, such as Stoicism, that had traditionally underpinned Christian attitudes to pleasure and Valla was pursued by the Inquisition on grounds of heresy; it was only through the protection of the king of Naples that he survived. In 1448 Valla was to enjoy an extraordinary reversal of his fortunes, when the new pope Nicholas V determined to turn Rome into a centre of humanist studies and summoned him to be his secretary, specifically to help with translations from the Greek.

Valla achieved his papal preferment despite the fact that he was the man who had discovered, in the 1440s, that the Donation of Constantine – on which the popes had depended so heavily for the assertion of their power – was a forgery. (It appears that the popes simply ignored the discovery.) Valla showed that words used in the Donation were later accretions, not known at the time of Constantine (and now dated to the mid-eighth century). In this alone he made an important advance in the study of linguistics.[14] Valla's studies showed that Latin had never been static as a language and furthermore how, as a result, literary analysis could be applied to religious texts. He used his knowledge of Greek to look critically at the Vulgate, Jerome's translation of the original New Testament texts, which had been given an unchallengeable authority by the church. As the Renaissance scholar Robert Black has noted: 'To subject the Bible itself to critical textual analysis was a genuine innovation in western history, without precedent either in Antiquity or the Middle Ages.'[15] Another 'humanist achievement' that infuriated theologians was to claim that the so-called 'Apostles' Creed' could not possibly date from the time of the apostles. Again Valla was the first scholar to reject a forged correspondence between the Roman Stoic Seneca and the apostle Paul. He would also be an inspiration for the critical analysis of Catholicism of Desiderius Erasmus (see Chapter 16, p. 392).

In his *Elegantiarum Latinae Linguae* (1435–44), a text that became a humanist bestseller, with sixty editions between 1471 and 1536 alone, Valla followed Petrarch in decrying the lack of learning in the earlier years of the Middle Ages, especially in the way that Latin had been corrupted during this period. The popular *Etymologies* of Isidore of Seville were among his targets. He bitterly attacked the scholasticism of the universities both for its methods of presenting arguments and for its terminology. Valla played some part in breaking down the dominance of Aristotle, reminding his followers that there were other philosophers who deserved respect, that observations reported by Aristotle could be shown, empirically, to be false, and thus providing a stage for the rise of new intellectual perspectives. He expanded the philosophical horizon.

Valla was part of a much wider enthusiasm for humanist education that was now spreading through the princely courts of northern Italy as an alternative to the long years at university.[16] Among those whom Leonardo Bruni had patronized in Florence was a young humanist scholar, Guarino of Verona (*c.*1374–1460), who taught for five years in the city. Guarino was expert in Greek and had even spent some time searching for original manuscripts in the eastern Mediterranean. In 1429 he was recruited by the Este duke of Ferrara to tutor his son, Leonardo. Guarino took the opportunity to open a school in Ferrara and it flourished, attracting the sons of nobility from throughout Italy and even from wider afield in Europe.

Guarino deliberately set out a curriculum that he felt was superior to that offered by the universities. There were three levels. The first level

involved mastering Latin; this was then taken further at the next level when Greek was added and the two languages were used to explore classical history and literature. The third level concentrated on rhetoric and philosophy, including Aristotle and, despite the few texts of his that were known at that time, Plato. There was even a programme for promising students from less elitist backgrounds to attend.*

Meanwhile, in Mantua, at the court of the Gonzaga, another humanist, Vittorino da Feltre (1378–1446), founded a school which was more traditional in its curriculum but which stressed the importance of self-discipline and moral behaviour within a Christian context. It was innovatory in other ways; the duke's daughters were taught alongside his sons, the school was open to all classes and there was a deliberate attempt to break down the barriers between teachers and students. It proved enormously popular and continued to flourish for another twenty years after its founder had died, so spreading ideals of humanism beyond Italy.

The humanists infused an air of optimism to the *studia humanitatis*. There was a powerful endorsement of a reawakening in every sphere of life. Valla in particular argued that painting, sculpture, architecture and other liberal arts had been 'virtually dead', but now 'they were awakened to a new life and flourish among an impressive group of excellent artisans and learned men of letters'. In contrast to scholasticism, the rarified abstraction of whose thinking rarely travelled beyond the cerebral world of the universities, the ideals of humanism infused the world of art.

* In practice, very few of these proved to have the necessary contacts to exploit their education in what remained a hierarchical society.

The *studiolo*, the private study of Federico da Montefeltro (1422–82) at Urbino, displays the range of intellectual, musical and martial activities of a Renaissance prince in its wonderful intarsia panels. The figures above the panels are described in Appendix II, p. 743.

13

The Flowering of the Florentine Renaissance

I used to marvel and at the same time to grieve that so many excellent and superior arts from our most vigorous antique past could now seem lacking and almost wholly lost. We know from remaining works and through references to them that they were once widespread. Painters, sculptors, architects, musicians, geometricians, rhetoricians, seers and similar amazing and noble intellects are very rarely found today and there are few to praise them... Since then I have been brought back to Florence from my long exile and I have come to understand that in many men, but especially in you Filippo and in our great friend Donato the sculptor and others, there is a genius for accomplishing every praiseworthy thing, a genius for which they should not be ranked behind anyone famous in antiquity in these arts.

From the Prologue to *Della pittura*
by Leon Battista Alberti[1]

In the fifteenth century it was once again Florence that provided the catalyst for an outburst of artistic creativity. By the 1420s there was a bustle of activity around the new Duomo (cathedral), the revered baptistery and, a short distance to the south in full view of the cathedral bell tower, the Orsanmichele.[2] The Duomo was almost finished, its octagonal base for the dome gaping open, but a commission to build the dome had been awarded in 1420 to Filippo Brunelleschi (1377–1444), the son of a notary who had trained as a goldsmith but whose confidence as an architect had been boosted by studies of ancient buildings in Rome. Just a year later, in 1421, Brunelleschi marked a moment in the history of technology when he was awarded one of the first known patents, in this case for a barge able to carry marble, granted for three years by the city.*

Brunelleschi had already gained an important commission from the Por Santa Maria, the guild of silk workers and producers, whose industry and wealth was expanding fast. The guilds were effective patrons of charitable activities. The Por Santa Maria had taken responsibility for the orphan children of the city (of whom there were all too many following the Black Death) and was determined to build a suitable *Ospedale* for these *innocenti* ('innocent ones') while making sure that everyone knew of its charitable endeavours. The *Ospedale degli Innocenti* is typical of Florentine architecture in using public space, the

* There is no known English patent before 1565.

Piazza Santa Annunziata, to make a dramatic impact. In the elegant façade Brunelleschi consciously rejected any influence of the Gothic and drew on Romanesque models from Tuscany and earlier classical styles. So the columns are slender and bear rounded semi-circular arches, the arcade is split between them into nine cubes and the spaces, between the columns, for instance, provide a template that is copied in other parts of the design. The *Ospedale degli Innocenti* is usually seen as the first true expression of Renaissance thought in architecture. Yet Brunelleschi's overweening confidence that he would complete the dome of the cathedral was untested. He had taken on the commission from the Lana, the wool guild, by himself and had reacted with fury when they suggested that Lorenzo Ghiberti, a master of metalworking, should work alongside him.

The two had history. Twenty years earlier (1401), the Calimala, the guild responsible for the baptistery, had decided to add a second set of gilded panelled doors to the building and had launched a competition for the commission. Brunelleschi and Ghiberti had been the two finalists and their trial pieces, showing the Sacrifice of Isaac, survive. One can see why Ghiberti won. Brunelleschi tacked on his figures as individual pieces; Ghiberti created a much more coherent and vital design that was also lighter and so less costly to cast. His door, which was made up of scenes from the life of Christ, each set within a Gothic frame, was so successful that he was asked to do another, the famous *Gates of Paradise*, this time depicting scenes from the Old Testament. For this second set of doors, completed between 1425 and 1452, Ghiberti was given free rein. He extended the scenes to the whole panel, exploiting a new way in which artists could accurately represent the world as it exists in reality, the use of linear perspective.[3]

Filippo Brunelleschi's *Ospedale*, commissioned in 1419 for the orphans of Florence, is often seen as the first true Renaissance building and reflects the lightness and harmony of the spirit of the times.

Once again the influence of Alhazen may have been important here. While the classical art of Greece has often been characterized as pure idealism and medieval art as more concerned with symbolic representation, a new realism now penetrates western art after 1420. It is not strictly true to say that there had been no realism before; it can surely be found in the tortured sculpture of the Hellenistic period or the stern portrait busts of republican Romans, but these were three-dimensional. In the two-dimensional wall paintings of architectural scenes from Roman Pompeii there is some attempt to add perspective but it is often clumsy. The use of perspective is then lost. Giotto and his followers from a century earlier had understood the problem and they did their best to provide depth in their paintings, but there was no systematic account of how to create the illusion of a three-dimensional scene on a two-dimensional surface.[4] Brunelleschi appears to have been the first to have found a system of doing this, probably in about 1413.

Brunelleschi has left no records of his procedures and his solutions were only recorded for the first time in the 1480s. What is not in doubt is that his system of defining perspective was seen as a vital innovation and was very soon followed by artists. The humanist polymath Leon Battista Alberti, who had returned to Florence in the 1430s, notes in his *Della pittura*, his treatise on painting: 'He [Brunelleschi] invented arts and sciences of which people had formerly heard nothing and seen nothing, and had no model for them.' Brunelleschi's first biographer, Antonio Manetti, is more explicit. Writing in the 1480s he sees Brunelleschi as having 'propounded and realized what painters today called perspective'.[5] Yet the background to the 'invention' remains obscure and, with the Florentines always ready to recognize one of their own as a genius, any external sources may have been deleted.

Lorenzo Ghiberti's *Gates of Paradise* from the doors of the baptistery in Florence (1425–32) are an early example of the sophisticated use of perspective by a Florentine artist. This scene shows Solomon and the Queen of Sheba.

It is usually assumed that, confronted by the ancient buildings in Rome that he was surveying during his stay there, Brunelleschi had to find a way of recording what he saw accurately. In some way he appears to have come across the work of Alhazen who had, as we have seen, created a mathematical formulation to show how rays from an object might meet and be absorbed by the eye. Back home in Florence, Brunelleschi painted a picture of the baptistery in Florence from just inside the west door of the Duomo. The choice of the baptistery was significant. It was the oldest and most revered building in Florence – many Florentines even thought it Roman in origin – and by selecting it for his painting, Brunelleschi may have been expressing his veneration of the ancients. He made a hole through the back of his painting. He then stood facing the baptistery from the same spot where he had painted it. He next raised the picture he had made of the same building but with the back of the picture in front of him. Beyond this he held a mirror* and looked through the hole, with one eye. Crucially (whether by accident or inspiration from Alhazen), this established a single line of vision where the 'rays' from each part of the baptistery would meet at a central point, the hole in the painting,

* This mirror was apparently from Venice and shows that reflective glass surfaces had now become available.

often termed the 'vanishing point' where the individual rays merge as one. Now he could play with two images, the three-dimensional image of the baptistery as it stood before him and, in the mirror, a two-dimensional image in the reflection of his painting. By ensuring that they matched he had established that he had achieved a geometrically exact representation, the dimensions of any one object co-ordinated with the dimensions of any other.

This use of linear perspective was a revolution in representational art and one can see how Ghiberti exploited it in his *Gates of Paradise*. His buildings do not just frame the painting but can show depth, with the size of figures corresponding to the distance they are from the viewer. So the possibilities of representing a scene, with, say, buildings and figures in the far background, accurately are now realized. By 1435, Alberti had described, in his *Della pittura*, how the artist should approach the issue:

> The painter's duty is to inscribe and paint any given bodies on a surface, with lines and colours, at a fixed distance, and with such a fixed position of the centric ray, that everything which you see in the painting seems exactly like the body in question, and in the same relief.[6]

To illustrate his point he uses the example of painting a picture of a floor with square tiles and showed how the artists could accurately depict the size and shape of the squares as they receded to a distant *punto del centro*, a vanishing point. The rays, again shown geometrically, now converge on a point on the two-dimensional surface.

While Brunelleschi and Ghiberti were hard at work on their commissions, they would have been fascinated by the creations of another great sculptural genius working in the same small area of the city, Donato di Niccolò de Betto Bardi, better known as Donatello (*c*.1386–1466). Donatello, the son of a wool carder, had served Ghiberti as an assistant before accompanying Brunelleschi to Rome to study ancient sculpture. He was soon creating life-size figures for the cathedral and for the Orsanmichele.

Here there was intense activity.[7] It had been decades since it had been agreed that the more prominent guilds should each have their own statues in the tabernacles on the exterior of the buildings, but with many of the city's sculptors diverted to work on the cathedral, the niches remained empty. The city government finally threatened to take away the guilds' right to their niches unless they filled them.

In the second century AD, Greek and Roman cities had been crowded with statues created by private patrons, and this was a chance to revive the tradition. Yet here the subjects were not city worthies but evangelists and saints. Donatello created a St Mark for the Linaiuoli, the linen merchants, and a St Louis of Toulouse for a niche reserved for the ruling Guelph party. He framed it classically with Ionic columns under a pediment. However, his masterpiece (and revered as such in the sixteenth century as superior to the other twelve commissions) is his St George for the Armaiuoli, the guild of armourers and swordsmiths (1420). Here is a youthful and determined figure with a presence that goes well beyond the more static traditions of Gothic. It is Giotto in action. Below it was a lovely bas-relief, of George defeating the dragon. Here Donatello used perspective to show, on one side, the princess George is defending standing modestly in front of a classical building, and, on the other, a cave set well back from the action. By 1425, when creating panels for a baptismal font in Siena, he had mastered the process still further and could use it to show arches and figures under them well behind a banqueting scene (the Feast of Herod) but on a virtually flat surface.

Masaccio's majestic representation of the Trinity in the Church of Santa Maria Novella in Florence (1425–8) shows how perspective has been mastered by one of the city's finest artists.

The appearance of Renaissance humanism and linear perspective in art was not confined to sculpture and architecture. South of the River Arno, in the Church of Santa Maria in Carmine, two painters, Masolino (1383–1440) and his pupil Masaccio (1401–28), were collaborating on a series of frescos showing the life of the apostle Peter.[8] Piero (Peter) Brancacci had founded the chapel in 1367 but it was only now (1426–8) that a descendant was paying for it to be decorated. Masaccio and Masolino would have known Giotto's frescos in the Bardi and Peruzzi chapels in Santa Croce and in the Church of Santa Maria they mastered the skill of creating three-dimensional figures who fill out space within a two-dimensional surface. The effect is intensified by the use of shadow. Buildings provide a backdrop to the scenes from the life of the apostle, but they are contemporary views of Florence while the opulently clad onlookers have the swagger of successful Florentine merchants. Some have seen an unkempt figure, his hands raised in prayer as Peter passes, as Masaccio himself and others might well represent known individuals. The same chapel holds Masaccio's powerful *Expulsion of Adam and Eve from Paradise*, the two shamed figures overcome with desperation at their fate. To show that he was a master of the new perspective, in the same years Masaccio created his majestic *Trinity* for the Church of Santa Maria Novella, in which the crucified Christ is set within a chapel that stretches behind him with God the Father hovering above. The lines which Masaccio drew to delineate the outlines of the perspective can still be seen in the plaster. Tragically, he died at the early age of twenty-seven, probably the victim of plague.

The Polyptych of St Anthony (1467–8) by Piero della Francesca, a geometrician-turned-painter. His brilliant use of perspective, here seen in his *Annunciation* at the very top, astonished his contemporaries.

Perhaps the finest of those artists fascinated by perspective was the Tuscan painter Piero della Francesca (1415–92), described by Giorgio Vasari as 'the greatest geometrician' of his time. Arriving in Florence from his birthplace of Borgo San Sepolcro around 1439, Piero must have been immediately aware of the advances made by Masaccio, Brunelleschi and Alberti, whose *Della pittura* was only just out. Piero contributed his own treatise on perspective, *De prospectiva pingendi* (*On the Perspective of Painting*), and for centuries after his death his reputation as a mathematician overshadowed that of a painter. Among his commissions were the illustrations for an edition of the great mathematician and physicist Archimedes (*c.*287–*c.*212 BC).

Having absorbed the work of the Florentine masters of perspective, Piero left the city to find patrons elsewhere in northern Italy: Arezzo and his birthplace, Borgo San Sepolcro, in Tuscany, Perugia in Umbria

and Urbino in the Marche. One of his most brilliant uses of perspective is to be found in his *Annunciation* placed over the polyptych he created for a convent in Perugia* while his *Flagellation*, which can still be seen in the palace in Urbino where it was painted, has mystified viewers to this day. Here there are two separate scenes, the flagellation of Christ set back in a classical setting, and three men who, strangely, are given far greater prominence.† The picture is a combination of mathematical precision in its use of perspective allied to the mystery of what the two scenes and their relationship to each other are meant to represent. The sensitive use of light adds to its haunting quality and it has become a favourite of many art historians.‡

In all kinds of subtle ways the influence of ancient Rome was entering Florence's public art. Donatello took the style further when he designed a tomb in the baptistery itself for Baldassare Cossa, John XXIII, one of the popes deposed at the Council of Constance (1414–18), when the Great Schism was healed. Cossa was especially honoured for having donated a finger of St John the Baptist, Florence's patron saint, to the city. His tomb, one of the earliest Renaissance tombs in Florence, was beautifully carved and fitted perfectly within the Roman columns of the interior. It was paid for by one Giovanni de' Medici (1360–1429), who had exploited his friendship with Cossa to take on the papal banking. So began a complex relationship between one family and a republic that was sensitive to any form of one-man rule.

The first prominent Medici, Giovanni was a merchant and banker.[9] It was Giovanni's conservative investment policies, mainly of land both in the city and the surrounding countryside, and his shrewd networking with contacts, that led to his steady accumulation of wealth. Through his relationship with Cossa, Rome now provided half the Medici income and Giovanni's loyalty to Cossa after his deposition added to his reputation for trustworthiness. Yet within Florence itself, Giovanni was cautious. He held office as *gonfaloniere* in 1421, and served on other committees, among them the one that awarded the contract for the baptistery doors won by Ghiberti. He put in hand the rebuilding of the family Church of San Lorenzo to a plan by Brunelleschi that resulted in one of the most harmonious interiors of the city, but he was never a great patron of the arts. On major political issues he carefully sided with the lesser guilds, supporting, for instance, the *catasto*, a tax system

* It is now in the Galleria Nationale dell'Umbria in the city.

† There has been endless debate over who they represent, possibly members of the Montefeltro family, dukes of Urbino, but there are many imaginative alternatives.

‡ The art historian and critic Kenneth Clark is often quoted as listing the *Flagellation* as one of his top ten paintings.

that demanded more from the rich, who had to declare all their assets. He died popular and respected, bequeathing to his son Cosimo (1389–1464) a status which could be exploited further, and according to the records of the *catasto* assessments of 1427, the second largest fortune in the city.

Cosimo was already forty when his father died, and, unlike his father, was educated in the new humanism. He read Latin easily even if he could not write it with any competence. He knew the main texts well and commissioned the lovely library in the Dominican convent of San Marco where the humanists deposited Greek and Latin texts. It is usually seen as the first public library since antiquity (1441) and was part of a monastic complex that was carefully calculated to show off the religious orthodoxy of its patron. Cosimo's private library was later to be housed in Michelangelo's magnificent Laurentian Library next to the Basilica of San Lorenzo.[10]

One of Cosimo's first commissions in sculpture, probably in about 1434, was from Donatello: the famous bronze *David* that was to stand inside the courtyard of the new Medici palace.[11] The palace, commissioned from Cosimo's favourite architect, Michelozzo Michelozzi, in 1444, prided itself on its accessibility so the statue was on view to all who entered. Donatello's conception of David as a nude and sensual figure standing on the head of the defeated Goliath was revolutionary. The sculptor appears to have modelled the body on the Roman bronze *Spinario*, the boy taking a thorn from his foot, that he had seen in Rome, but the jaunty cap and boots are those of a contemporary Florentine. Casting bronze was prohibitively expensive and Cosimo must have realized that the startling *David* would arouse suspicion that he was pushing himself into the limelight. He was careful to provide a text at the bottom of the work that stressed that David represented the city's defence of the fatherland against tyranny. The aim was to show that here was a family that was open to the city, with music and food freely laid on whenever there was a public festival. Of course those entering for festivities could not fail to be awed by the palace's grandeur and the quietly stated dominance of the Medici family.[12]

As a politician Cosimo worked carefully behind the scenes. What appeared to be a disaster, his exile at the hands of the conservative Albizi family in 1433, became a triumph when he re-entered the city to general rejoicing the following year. Now he showed himself a relentless networker, sidelining the Albizi and their allies while building up a formidable following of his own. In a fast-changing social scene, in which family businesses regularly rose and fell, the process of spotting and then winning over 'new men' who were on the up required perceptiveness, patience and adroit diplomacy. Cosimo even claimed that one of his Medici forebears had been sympathetic to the Ciompi, thus sustaining the myth that the Medici were on the side of the *popolo minuto*, the 'lesser people'. He would use his allies to restrain or exile enemies and so presented the façade of a settled and well-governed republic to the outside world. Elections continued but most appear to have been manipulated by Medici money.

Cosimo's finest achievement came when he persuaded the delegates for the council of reconciliation of the eastern and western churches to meet in Florence in 1439 (see pp. 331–3). Hardly had the council's business finished than Florence achieved a major victory over the Milanese at Anghiari in 1440, which further boosted Cosimo's position. Many were tempted to compare him with Octavian, later the Roman emperor Augustus, even to the extent of spreading a myth that Florence had been founded by Octavian rather than Julius Caesar. The accolades given to Cosimo – *princeps*, 'first citizen', and, after his death, *pater patriae*, 'father of the fatherland', had, in fact, been used of Augustus 1,400 years earlier.

When Jacob Burckhardt argued in *The Civilization of the Renaissance in Italy* that this period was characterized by the emergence of the autonomous individual, Leon Battista Alberti, already mentioned for his *Della pittura*, was one of his stars. Alberti, born in 1404, was the bastard son of a wealthy father who had been exiled from Florence.[13] His father educated him well, even though, like many of the humanists, he found the study of law at Bologna uninspiring. However, his degree qualified him for a post in the papal Curia. The ban on the family was lifted sometime after 1428 and he was able to settle in Florence as part of the retinue of Pope Eugenius IV, who had been forced to flee Rome. It was here that he became close to Brunelleschi and Donatello. Using Alberti's own assessment of his qualities as a source, Burckhardt presents Alberti as effortlessly brilliant in every sphere of life, athletics, physical strength, music (mastering the art of composition without a teacher), the law, mathematics, aesthetics and the practice of art and architecture.[14] In short this was 'the Renaissance man'. While Florence and Rome remained his primary homes, he was welcomed into many of the courts of northern Italy.

In fact, very little is known about Alberti, the man behind the achievements. Scholars, among them Anthony Grafton in his fine biography, suggest a more conflicted figure, one who had never come to terms with his bastard status. 'The sovereign urban intellectual was at once a hero and a victim, a master of the crowd's applause who was always in search of a cork-lined room,' as Grafton puts it.[15] He took holy orders and appears to have been celibate, although there is nothing to suggest that his commitment to the church was strong. Humanist studies always came first. Mathematics infuse many of his texts and confirm that order and rationality were important to him. Endlessly curious, always ready to praise any activity that satisfied the humanist ambition for *virtu*, he relished the accolades of his admirers. However, achievement did not come as easily to him as Burckhardt implies. There is evidence that he often felt that his image was artificially polished with the result that 'the onlooker thinks that all your accomplishment is the innate gift of nature', as he once put it.[16] One is reminded of one of Alberti's favourite Greek authors, Lucian, another outsider, this time among the sophisticated Greek intellectual elite of the second century AD, who described how one had to learn the correct way of presenting oneself as cultured. Perhaps Alberti's most attractive feature was his willingness to apply his theoretical findings to the practical needs of the craftsmen whose company he enjoyed.

This is where *Della pittura* comes in. Published in 1435, its use of the vernacular made it accessible to those artists without Latin. A Latin version, with technical additions (*De pictura*) followed later. Alberti's studies of perspective had, like those of Roger Bacon, relied heavily on the *Optics* of the Arab scholar Alhazen. He was marrying science and mathematics to aesthetics. In fact, he was one of the first to define the material world in mathematical, especially geometrical, terms, a harbinger of the dominant principle of seventeenth-century science.[17] Alberti went on in *Della pittura* to argue that art should be dedicated to imitating nature but expressing a harmony that would be lost if a single element of the whole was withdrawn. A stress on harmony reflected Greek traditions of the ideal proportions of the human body that went back to the fifth-century BC sculptor Polycleitos. Recreating this was a noble pastime and thus Alberti raised artists to a more elevated plane, far above the status of mere craftsmen that an earlier respected treatise on painting (*c.*1400), by the Tuscan Cennino Cennini, had accorded them.[18] In this he was a forerunner of Giorgio Vasari, who would elevate art and artists to an even greater status in his celebrated *Lives of the Artists* (first edition, 1550).

The problem of how to represent space was one that absorbed Alberti. As has already been seen (pp. 2–6), the *Geographike* of Ptolemy, with its elaborate maps and co-ordinates for some 8,000 locations, had been recreated by scholars in Constantinople and then translated into Latin in the early fifteenth century. Alberti came to know it well and he used its methods for establishing co-ordinates as the basis for creating a plan of Rome. In the 1440s he studied its buildings in detail as Brunelleschi and Donatello had done some years before. Taking lessons from the portolan charts of the Mediterranean sailors and devising a measuring instrument that allowed him to use the Capitoline Hill as a point from which the distance of each building in the city could be gauged (and their distance from each other), he created the first accurate map of any city. His methods were described in his *Panorama of the City of Rome*.

Alberti was now fascinated by the ancient monuments of Rome themselves and examined them minutely.[19] He assumed that the classical architects had a skill and ingenuity that had been forgotten and that their secrets were being lost as the ruins were despoiled or left to decay. The humanist popes were, in fact, rebuilding the city from its own ruins and much was to be destroyed in the next decades. The model for Alberti's *De re aedificatoria* (*On the Art of Building*), eventually published in 1452 and dedicated to the humanist pope Nicholas V, was the first-century BC Roman architect Vitruvius' *De architectura*. Vitruvius provided a systematic manual of procedures for architects in ten volumes, and Alberti echoed him with his own ten volumes, although the buildings he described were mostly from imperial Rome and thus later than Vitruvius. The Pantheon was a special favourite and Alberti lambasted those of his contemporaries who ignored the sophisticated building techniques of their Roman ancestors. Yet he was never slow to advise how an ideal city should be planned. He accepted that a city's layout should reflect the power of its ruler and that the landscape of the ideal city should be envisaged as an organic whole.* His task in *De re aedificatoria* was to establish principles of proportion and harmony in architecture and then apply them to buildings of his own day – notably churches – that had been unknown in classical times. *De re aedificatoria* became the authoritative manual for architecture for the next three hundred years, earning Alberti the title of 'the Florentine Vitruvius'.

Alberti went further, to begin designing buildings himself. In Florence he created a palazzo for his friend Giovanni Rucellai, an immensely wealthy banker. Its elaborate use of columns, from all three

* The harmonious centre of the home town of the humanist Pope Pius II (Enea Silvio Piccolomini, 1405–64), created by him as Pienza, has often been seen as reflecting Alberti's ideals although there is no documentary evidence to link him to its design.

Greek orders, Doric, Ionic and Corinthian, make the façade much less forbidding than the typical palazzo of this period.† Rucellai also commissioned Alberti to design the central door (modelled on his beloved Pantheon) and upper part of the façade of the Dominican Church of Santa Maria Novella. It was an act of genius to connect the upper roof of the nave to the roofs of the side aisles by a scrolled volute that became a popular motif in sixteenth-century façades. The most impressive of Alberti's designs, the building just begun at the time of his death, 1472, was the cavernous Church of Sant'Andrea in Mantua for the ruling Gonzaga family. The city possessed a sacred relic, no less than the blood of Christ gathered from the Crucifixion itself by Longinus, by tradition the Roman soldier who had pierced Christ's side. It was appropriated as their symbol by the ruling family. For Sant'Andrea Alberti drew on the great vaults of late Roman architecture. The church is entered through a monumental triumphal arch and the nave is a vast barrel vault that leads through another soaring arch to the central dome, although this was only completed in the eighteenth century. Again, with side chapels set within the massive walls of the nave, Sant'Andrea provided a model for many later churches. Prominent among its tombs is that of Andrea Mantegna (*c.*1430–1506), the artist who had created stunning frescos of the Gonzaga for their neighbouring palace. The epitaph reflects the raised status of the artist by the early sixteenth century – Mantegna is proclaimed as 'the equal if not superior to Apelles'.‡

* * *

By 1470 another dome, that of the cathedral in Florence, had been triumphantly completed with the placing of a gold ball on its summit. It was a work that had required ingenuity and innovation of a prodigious nature and ranks as one of the greatest architectural achievements in history.[20] It deserves to be placed in context.

The Gothic style pioneered by Abbot Suger at St Denis had provided the most extraordinary architectural creations of medieval Europe.[21] As the French craftsmen had become more confident and accomplished, the height of the naves of their cathedrals soared. So an early example such as Sens reached only 80 feet, while the magnificent cathedral of Chartres, built in its present form in 1193, was half as high again, at

† The Rucellai family still live on the top floor!

‡ According to the *Natural History* of Pliny the Elder, the Greek Apelles (fourth century BC) was the greatest painter of antiquity.

121 feet. The highest vault of all was in the choir at Beauvais: begun in 1230, it reached an extraordinary 157 feet and spanned 51 feet. This was certainly pushing the extremes. The building of this vast and ambitious cathedral was continually interrupted by financial crises, urban unrest and then a catastrophic collapse of part of the choir in 1284. Building went on for another three centuries but the nave was never completed. The choir remains as one of the pinnacles of French Gothic and its height never surpassed by any other Gothic vault.

From the start, the building of the new cathedral in Florence was an ambitious project; two older churches and a mass of houses had to be cleared to make an expanse in the centre of the city where the foundations could be laid out. Progress had been slow, and further delayed when funds were shifted to completing Giotto's elegant *campanile* that rose alongside the new cathedral. Work had only fully resumed as the city recovered in the 1350s from the Black Death. By 1366 the nave was vaulted, by now in Gothic style, and then attention turned to the last phase of the building, the construction of a dome. Here the ambitious Florentines appeared to have over-reached themselves. The largest dome in the world, one that had stood for over 1,000 years, and still stands today, was that of the Pantheon in Rome, built in the AD 120s. The reach of the dome planned for Florence cathedral was already, at nearly 144 feet, wider than that. This was challenging enough but the octagonal base of the planned dome was to be a heady 170 feet above ground, higher even than the vault at Beauvais. This was where building of the dome had to *begin*, with all the stones and bricks raised to that height even before they could be put in place.

By the first years of the fifteenth century the drum on which the dome was to stand had been completed, its walls a solid 14 feet thick so as to carry the weight of the promised dome. The conventional way of building domes, centring a wooden structure on which the masonry was laid, was clearly doomed to fail over such an expanse. Soon rival cities were beginning to ridicule the arrogance of the Florentines. The wealthy Lana guild, which was responsible for the fabric of the cathedral, had somehow to get things moving to avoid total humiliation. Finally, in 1418, with funds in hand, they had announced a competition for an architect who could build the dome.

Brunelleschi was by now in his early forties. Stung by being beaten by Ghiberti for the commission to craft the baptistery doors, he had spent several years in Rome exploring how the Romans had created their vast edifices. The ruins of classical Rome were scattered around a city that was now in a state of deep decay, its population still smaller than that of Florence, and huddled in a bend of the River Tiber, the *abitato*, which often flooded. Brunelleschi would have focused on the Pantheon, the only equivalent dome still standing from ancient times, but throughout the city there were other impressive vaults to study, among them the Basilica of Maxentius in the Forum and the baths of the third-century emperor Caracalla. Brunelleschi must have absorbed the techniques that had left them still standing.

Brunelleschi was back in Florence just before the competition was announced and was soon consulted by the Lana over whether his knowledge of Roman buildings might help them. He then set about constructing, over ninety days, an intricate model of how the finished cathedral might look, but his arrogance was such that he failed to share with the judges the exact way in which the dome was to be built and stay up. He recognized from the start that the traditional methods of centring a dome on a wooden frame would never work; timber of the required length could never be found or constructed. Still, his rejection of centring came as a shock. It was some time before the guild officials swallowed their doubts and awarded him the commission. A separate memorandum outlining the specifications for the building of the dome survives – it presumably originates from Brunelleschi as it contains many of the solutions he devised to raise the first stages of the dome. Then there was the warning that, after 30 *braccia* of height (about 57 feet), when the dome would begin to taper inwards and be at its most vulnerable, the building would be continued 'according to what shall be deemed advisable because in building only practical experience will teach that which is to be followed'. This was certainly leaving things to chance.

Even without centring, it might have been possible to build a dome with a series of circles of brick and stone built one on top of each and tapering towards the centre as they rose. This would be using the principle of an arch for strength, although here the arch would be on a horizontal plane. Unfortunately, the octagonal shape of the drum ruled this out. At each corner the cohesion of the circle would be broken. Brunelleschi did borrow one idea from earlier architects, that of a double shell. If an inner, smaller, and thus lighter shell could form the main dome, then a more elegant one with better weatherproofing could enclose it and the two could be linked together for further support. The gap between them would help make the whole lighter. There were other advantages for the workers. As the double shell rose, they could reach the working area by climbing between the two, in the same way as the dome can still be climbed today. At the top they could position themselves on one shell while working on the other. It proved a life-saver: only one worker, a mason called Nenno di Chello, fell to his death during the construction of the dome.

The problem remained that the thrust outwards would increase as the dome rose and threaten it with an ignominious collapse. One approach, to use buttresses to support the drum as it expanded outwards under the weight of the dome, had been earlier rejected as inelegant – typical of those Gothic barbarians to the north and not worthy of the purer Florentines! Instead, Brunelleschi devised a chain system in which limestone blocks, meticulously cut and measured, were to be clamped together with iron and then laid so that long blocks covered short ones to make a solid whole. At each of the corners of the octagon, where there was a 45-degree change of direction, further iron was used to clamp the ends. There were to be four of the chains, each one to be put in place 35 feet above the other. After each was laid, bricks would be mortared in place, row upon row above it, until a base had been created for the next chain up to lie on. The problem here was that as the brick walls rose, and they had to taper inwards towards the centre of the dome, they risked falling in while the mortar was drying. Brunelleschi solved the problem by placing a brick vertically at intervals along each horizontal course of bricks. Once these had dried another course of bricks could be inserted as if between bookends and held in place until the mortar dried. Brunelleschi also worked at finding a mix of mortar that dried more quickly. As the dome rose he would also fit curved wooden ribs to rise from each of the corners. By using a herring-bone pattern of bricks the stress could be diverted towards the ribs and not downwards to the ground. This was extraordinarily ingenious, yet the project remained an awesome undertaking. Some 37,000 tons of material had to be lifted, including 4 million bricks. Precision would be vital; a small deviation and the dome would not fit together. All this had to be accomplished from a starting point 170 feet above ground.

Brunelleschi's dome for the cathedral of Florence (*right* and *overleaf*) is one of the most extraordinary creations of the Renaissance. It radiates the confidence, imagination and technical brilliance of a single man confronted with what appeared to be an impossible project.

Despite the honing of stoneworking skills throughout Europe during the medieval period, the continent had yet not reached the levels of technological sophistication of the ancient world. The collapse of the Roman empire had been devastating for virtually all forms of technology; almost every skill had been forgotten. One did not need to look far to see how backward medieval Europe still was compared to

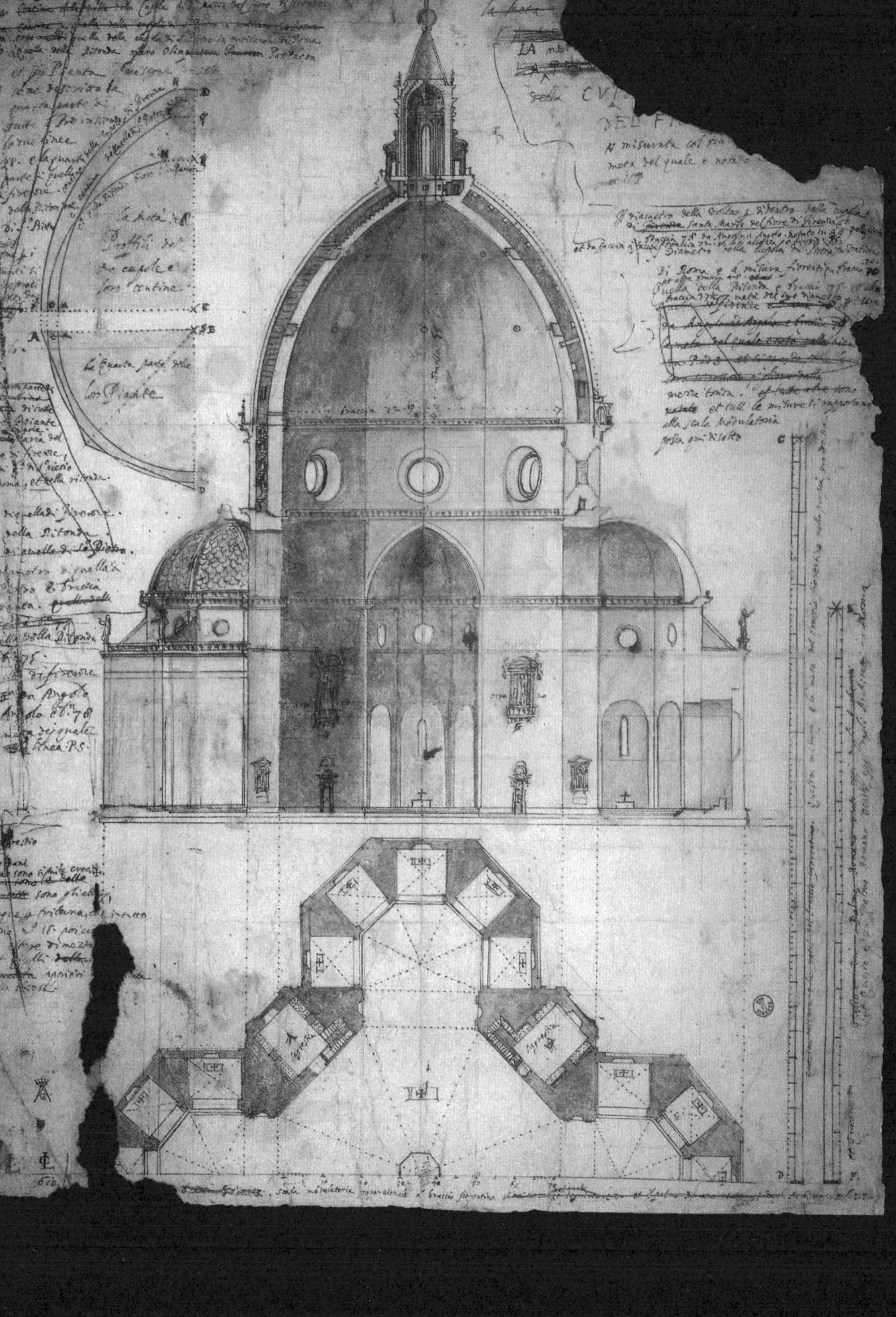

the Roman period. There were few surfaced roads, whereas the Roman empire had been criss-crossed by superbly constructed and enduring ones. There were no aqueducts, let alone any of the magnificence of the best Roman examples such as the first-century AD Pont du Gard. There was no modern equivalent of the Pantheon. It was the supreme exemplar of the use of pozzolana concrete, a process that had taken over 100 years for Roman builders to perfect.* For all the glories of the Gothic cathedrals, it is technically easier to construct a Gothic ribbed vault than a Romanesque barrelled one, and a pointed arch can be used more flexibly than a round one. Advances in building techniques across the high medieval period were relatively few in number. The flying buttress was a pragmatic, if often elegant, solution to the need to support higher, lighter walls, not a technological advance in itself.

Brunelleschi desperately needed whatever craft skills were at hand, but his was also a case where technological innovation was driven by the need to succeed in his project. The first challenge was to devise a mechanism that could lift heavy loads to the right height. Here he had to take the initiative. Lifting devices were already known, but these were hoists that were operated by manpower. Something much more powerful was needed and Brunelleschi decided to use the power of oxen. The oxen would be harnessed to a central shaft that would be embedded in a frame. Its lower end was carved as a helical screw. Higher up the shaft, well above the oxen, were two cogged wheels. Either one could be engaged in a much larger wheel that drove the shaft around which the lifting ropes coiled or unwound as the masonry buckets or limestone blocks were hauled aloft. The helical screw was designed like a clutch; it could be disengaged and the hoist shifted from raising to lowering. This avoided the laborious procedure of unharnessing the oxen and changing their direction.

To actually get this working at all required exceptionally large pieces of wood. One drum was 5 feet across. As the octagon would be open until the final moment of construction, elm was chosen for its ability to resist the elements. Then there was the rope. Here the rope makers of the naval city of Pisa had to be called on. Their order was for a rope 600 feet long, one of the longest and heaviest ever recorded. To make the hoist even more productive it was given lifting shafts of different diameters. A heavy load used the smallest drum, so that one revolution would only raise the block only a short distance to compensate for the greater weight, while the larger drum was able to whisk lighter

* Pozzolana concrete involves mixing volcanic ash with mortar. It could even set hard under water, in a chemical reaction that has only recently been understood.

materials up at speed. What was extraordinary was that the cumbersome machine actually worked and kept on going year after year. After its inauguration in the summer of 1421 it was almost as popular a sight as the rising dome itself. With the ropes continually watered to avoided overheating through friction and a steady production line of blocks of dressed stone arriving under the octagon to be attached to the lifting ropes, fifty loads a day became possible, a turnaround time of ten minutes. Next Brunelleschi devised a separate device, known as the *castello*, that could be perched on the rising walls and swing each block into place as it arrived on the dome.

The dome rose slowly, year by year, on average – it has been calculated – by 1 foot per month. Brunelleschi was meticulous in his supervision; one report claimed that he checked every one of the 4 million bricks. Forests were scoured for tree trunks large enough for the ribs, the ironworkers were taught how to encase their clamps in lead so that they would not rust, the shape of bricks had to be determined so that the complex patterns could be reproduced from templates. The ribs had shelves cut into them so that scaffolding could run between them to allow the bricks to be covered with mortar. For every crisis Brunelleschi found a new solution. The drum was so thick that it proved possible to create a circular vault within the octagonal shape. Horizontal arches were created to link subsidiary ribs to the main ones on the outer shell and so strengthen it still further. By 1434 the right height had been reached for the final chain to be placed at the top of the dome and this was done the following year.

There still remained the covering of the outer shell of the dome, the putting in place of facings of coloured marble on the external ribs and, as a final finishing touch, the construction of a lantern. However, the relieved guild officials felt now was the time to consecrate their cathedral and, on 25 March 1436, Pope Eugenius IV presided at the grand ceremony. Even though the Lana, rather ungratefully, forced Brunelleschi to compete with others for the final design of the lantern, it was his that was ultimately chosen. He designed another form of hoist to reach even higher than his earlier models, to the base where the lantern was to rise. This one was handled by men, but with a brake so that they could rest from their lifting when a load was halfway up. The lantern itself was conceived in an ornate classical style. This time buttresses were allowed but they were classical in form, with flutes and shell niches, and their purpose was to give a suitable unifying focus for the eight external ribs. Eight high-arched windows allowed light to flood the cathedral and later a bronze plate would be added at the base through which the rays of the sun could form a sundial on the floor. Work on the lantern began just a month before Brunelleschi died, aged sixty-nine, in April 1446. Despite his absence the lantern was completed by his friend the architect Michelozzo Michelozzi and eventually topped by a splendid gold ball in the 1460s.

Brunelleschi was certainly a genius. He had shown great confidence in his ability to complete the project and find solutions to each challenge. Mastering the labour force, the machinery and the absolute precision of workmanship needed for success demanded energy and total commitment to the task over twenty-five years. He was the first architect, in the modern sense of the word, as the professional who designs and supervises a building, since antiquity. Part of his genius lay in his intuitive understanding of the stresses within different types of material, where these might prove catastrophic and how they could be diverted. Yet the building of the dome was also a collaborative venture, financed by a confident and determined city that had, after all, set up the ambitious project well before Brunelleschi had come on the scene. It was an extraordinary achievement. In his *Della pittura*, Alberti piles on the adulation of his friend:

> What man, however hard of heart or jealous, would not praise Filippo the architect when he sees here such an enormous construction towering above the stars, vast enough to cover the entire Tuscan population with its shadow… Unless I am wrong, this was a feat of engineering that people did not believe possible these days and probably equally unknown and unimaginable among the ancients.[22]

Coming from a man who was himself a champion of Roman building, this was a rare recognition in this period that the ancients might be surpassed.[23]

Despite massive spending, the fortunes of the Medici family were intact when Cosimo de' Medici died in 1464, and in 1466 they were boosted further through being awarded, by the papacy, the lucrative monopoly on the alum mines in papal territory.* Cosimo's son, Piero il Gottoso (the Gouty), maintained Medici control of Florence against opponents hoping to destroy the family at a time of weakness. Shrewdly building up links with Milan and Naples and marrying his son Lorenzo into Roman aristocracy, Piero consolidated his position and was influential enough to control elections. While his 'gout' appears to have been an acute form of arthritis and he was often bedridden, Piero continued to support scholarship and to add to the Medicis' fine

* Alum was a mineral salt used to fix dyes into cloth.

collection of books. Benozzi Gozzoli's magnificent fresco *The Journey of the Magi*, with the Medici identified with the Magi, in the palace chapel, was his commission. Far from occupying a short interlude between more prominent members of his family, Piero is now being given greater scholarly respect.[24]

When Piero died, in 1469, Lorenzo, by now twenty, was in place to carry on the Medici name and fortunes.[25] In fact, he was immediately approached by a delegation of citizens asking him 'to take charge' of the city. Although still young, Lorenzo was already skilled in the exercise of power. He had visited Milan, Venice and Rome on official business and his wife, Clarice Orsini, came from one of the most ancient families of Rome. He was energetic, intelligent and had a charisma that transcended an ugly face. He was deeply schooled in humanist values and felt at home with intellectuals. One of his circle, the poet Angelo Poliziano (1454–94), was such an erudite classicist that many of his emendations to corrupt Greek manuscripts are still accepted as correct by scholars today. Another intimate, Giovanni Pico della Mirandola (1463–94), was one of the first Christians to master Hebrew in depth and achieved an impressive synthesis of several intellectual traditions in his *900 Theses*. He was heavily influenced by the spirituality of Marsilio Ficino, the translator of Plato, whose achievements will be covered in the next chapter. The links between Lorenzo and Platonism were so strong that many contemporaries regarded Lorenzo as the ideal philosopher-king that Plato had dreamed of.

Lorenzo played his own part in keeping the peace. He intervened to thwart the ambitions of Naples against Florence and supported his father's alliance with Florence's old enemy, Milan, which he was able to use against the papacy, Venice and Naples if they threatened him. Control of the church within Florence's territories was important to Lorenzo. After much wrangling, he persuaded Pope Sixtus IV to appoint his brother-in-law Rinaldo Orsini as the new archbishop of Florence. Orsini remained archbishop for thirty years but hardly ever visited Florence so Lorenzo and his inner circle were able to run the see themselves. It was an arrangement that suited everyone and a further reminder of how independent Florence was from the institutional church.

However, while Lorenzo appeared to be successfully fulfilling the ambiguous role of *princeps* in a city that detested tyranny, not all his fellow citizens were ready to acquiesce in his influence. His youth made him vulnerable and his court of favourites left him isolated from the mass of citizens. Traditionalists resented his marriage to a 'foreign' aristocrat – an alliance with another wealthy Florentine family would have been more acceptable. He was high-handed and abusive in the exercise of power in a way his grandfather Cosimo had never been. He switched around the traditional festivities, even, in 1491, transforming the hallowed celebration of John the Baptist into a Roman triumph as if he was a conquering hero. In fact, he was moving Florence away from its republican oligarchy towards a more aristocratic style of living typical of other courts of Italy.

It was inevitable that resentments would fester. In 1478 Lorenzo was lucky to escape with his life when a plot to assassinate him (the Pazzi Conspiracy) killed his brother Giovanni within the sacred space of the cathedral at the moment of the consecration of the host. However, the backlash was easy to exploit. The crowds rose in support of Lorenzo. The archbishop of Pisa, Francesco Salviati, a cousin of the Pazzi family, who had supported the coup, was ignominiously hanged from the windows of the Palazzo della Signoria (now the Palazzo Vecchio). Lorenzo issued a medal to commemorate his survival and basked in the period of comparative stability that followed. A new Council of Seventy was packed with his supporters. His commissions from Sandro Botticelli, *Primavera* and *The Birth of Venus*, suggest rebirth, a new Golden Age ushered in with the coming of spring and the birth of the goddess of love. Pico della Mirandola gushed, in words more typical of Enlightenment or Romantic thought: 'O great and wonderful happiness of man. It is given to have that which he desires and to be that which he wills.'[26]

Behind the façade, however, things were not so secure. The once lucrative textile industry was now challenged by rival producers in the north of Europe. The Medici fortune was being eroded by economic uncertainty and unwise investments. Lorenzo was not a good businessman, and his manager, Francesco Sassetti, proved hopelessly inadequate. Two important branches of the company, in London and Bruges, had to be closed down and, sensing Lorenzo's weakness, debtors had the temerity to ask for the return of vast loans they had made to him. Resources had to be found elsewhere. As the historian Francesco Guicciardini put it: 'His expenditure on magnificence escalated while his profits dropped… his affairs were in such disorder that on several occasions he was on the verge of bankruptcy and found it necessary to help himself to money belonging to his friends or to public funds', so making another Medici incursion into the republic's affairs.[27]

When Lorenzo died, aged only forty-three, in 1492, his son Piero, still only twenty, no longer had the capital to secure goodwill with largesse as Lorenzo had done. A much weaker character than his predecessors, Piero also alienated the *signoria* through his arrogant behaviour, losing all remaining support when he surrendered some of Florence's possessions to the French king Charles VIII, who had invaded Italy in 1494. An outraged populace drove out the Medici with cries of '*Popolo e Liberta*' and their palace was sacked.* Donatello's *David*, which had been commissioned by Cosimo as a mark of the family's commitment, real or imagined, to republicanism, was repositioned in the Piazza della Signoria. Soon afterwards a Dominican monk, Girolamo Savonarola, gripped this sophisticated city with religious fervour (see Chapter 16, p. 388). After his death, Florentine art turned away from the gentler light-filled world of Botticelli to something more austere, symbolized by the vast nude figure of Michelangelo's *David* (1504) where the classical monumentality of the Roman hero defying his enemies returns to western art. His brooding presence, reflecting the temperament of the statue's maker, dramatically contrasts with Donatello's sensually relaxed *David* from sixty years before. The Florentine civil servant Niccolo Machiavelli's pragmatic and often cynical approach to power politics (pp. 468–73) is a symptom of a new age.

Charles VIII's invasion of Italy, in pursuit of the throne of Naples, marked a turning point. While Charles himself was ridiculed by his contemporaries as uncouth and uncultured, France itself had prospered under his predecessors and had built a strong bureaucracy and effective army that could outplay those of the Italian cities. The French were helped by their light artillery, which was able to break medieval city walls and so move the impact of war to a more destructive level. The peninsula was to be further disrupted when both the Spaniards and the Holy Roman Empire saw the chance of rich pickings in the turmoil that followed. A warrior pope, Julius II (r.1503–13), insisted on leading his own armies and confirmed that the pope was as much a territorial as a spiritual ruler. Rome itself was to be brutally sacked by the Lutheran troops of Emperor Charles V in 1527.

In retrospect the age of Lorenzo was to enter myth as a golden one when civilization had reached a peak. In his *Storia d'Italia*, published posthumously in 1561, the Florentine Francesco Guicciardini (1483–1540) – the finest historian of the sixteenth century[28] – idealizes Lorenzo as the only worthy statesman among the pygmies who would follow him.

---

* One of the unexpected pleasures of visiting the abbey at Monte Cassino is to come across a fine sepulchral monument to Piero, who drowned fleeing a Spanish army in 1503. It had been commissioned by his Medici uncle Giulio (1478–1534), then Pope Clement VII.

Modern historians are more cautious, applauding Lorenzo's patronage of the arts but lamenting that he lacked the measured manipulation of Florence's politics in which his grandfather Cosimo had excelled. For Guicciardini, Charles VIII's invasion brought with it into Italy 'the seeds of innumerable disasters, terrible events and changes in almost everything… subversion of kingdoms, devastation of the countryside, slaughter of cities, cruel murders, but also of new habits, new customs, new and bloody methods of warfare, diseases unknown until that day'.[29] The humiliation of Italy at the hands of foreign powers followed.

Guicciardini's *Storia* runs from 1494 to 1534 and is a detailed account of the troubles Italy faced during this period of turmoil. Guicciardini not only had access to the documents of the day but, like Thucydides in his *History of the Peloponnesian War*, had lived through the events he describes. It competes with the work of Bruni as the first modern history. What is distinctive about the *Storia* is that, despite coming from an ancient Florentine aristocratic family, Guicciardini does not idealize Italy or Florence's past through its roots in Rome's history. He records the tumultuous march of events, episode by episode, in an account that contains no record of inevitable political or social betterment. His account echoes the *Histories* and *Annals* of Tacitus, now available as a penetrating narrative of the corruption of Roman politics under the emperors. The rebirth of the classical past has been forgotten; history, argues Guicciardini, does not repeat itself, and in this sense the *Storia* might be seen as heralding the end of the Renaissance.

But the story of the *Rinascimento* still has some way to run. There were other important cultural developments in Florence in the fifteenth century and one of them was the reappearance of the original works of the philosopher Plato.

Plato Re-enters the Western Mind

Great Cosimo, the father of his country by senatorial decree, at a time when a council was being negotiated among the Greeks and the Latins in Florence under [Pope] Eugenius IV, frequently heard a Greek philosopher by the name of Gemistos Plethon disputing like another Plato on the Platonic theology. From Plethon's fervid lips Cosimo was straightaway so inspired, so ensouled, that from that time forth he conceived deep in his mind a kind of Academy, to give birth to it at the first opportune moment.

Marsilio Ficino, from the preface to his edition of *Plotinus*, 1492[1]

'Few will doubt that had there been no Socrates, no Plato and no Aristotle, there would have been no philosophy for the next two thousand years, nor in all probability then.'[2] The British philosopher John Stuart Mill reflected the nineteenth-century view of the philosophers who had come to dominate the university curriculum. Yet despite, or perhaps because of, the absorption of Platonism within Christian theology the original Plato and his Neoplatonist successors such as Plotinus had almost been lost from the western mind ever since the Christian emperor Justinian had closed down the Academy in Athens in 529, 900 years after Plato had founded it. Of course, Plato's approach to philosophy had not been forgotten and, as we have seen, he had some influence in the university of Oxford (see Chapter 9, p. 218). The memory of the philosopher was discernible in the continuing influence of Augustine, Boethius, Bonaventure and other scholars.[3] Yet as late as 1400 there were almost no translations of Plato's texts in Latin. Among them were the *Timaeus*, which had been exploited in the twelfth century to illustrate the conformity between Plato's view of the creation and the biblical one. Its portrayal of a 'divine craftsman' involved in the creation made it close enough to the Christian version to be acceptable.* It also contained the doctrine of the four elements – air, fire, earth and water – and the need to keep them in balance. The view put forward in the *Timaeus* that the universe (a macrocosm) has a soul of which the human individual is a microcosm was illustrated in the mid-thirteenth-century crypt of the cathedral in the papal city of Anagni near Rome. Other than the *Timaeus*, there were some short extracts of Plato found in Latin in Cicero and Augustine and, in weak medieval translations, the *Phaedo*, the last conversations of Socrates before his death on a charge of impiety in Athens in 399 BC. This was a text that would prove important to Christians as it told of the immortality of the individual soul and provided an exposition of Plato's theory of the Forms or Ideas, arguing for the reality of the immaterial world. The nobility of Socrates as he prepared himself for death also resonated strongly with the humanists. Only two other works of Plato were known, the *Meno* and the *Parmenides*.†

* Plato had argued that a divine craftsman brought into order a pre-existing cosmos; Aristotle, on the other hand, that the universe had existed eternally without any such intervention.

† *Meno* contains a dialogue between Meno and Socrates on the question of virtue. It is best known for a discussion on whether the soul can remember information from an earlier existence (which Plato believes that it can). *Parmenides* is a dialogue between the elderly philosopher of the same name and a younger Socrates over the nature of the Platonic Forms or Ideas.

It was the humanists who were responsible for the rebirth of Plato. Leonardo Bruni, one of the earliest masters of Greek in the west, was a pioneer translator. More than any other humanist, he made the treasures of Greek literature available to his contemporaries. With the growing backlash against Aristotle among the humanists, there was a revival of the tradition that Plato rather than Aristotle was the greatest of the Greek philosophers, not least through the elegance of his language. In the *Phaedo* Plato had elevated the study of philosophy as the true end of life: 'No one may join the company of the gods who has not practised philosophy and is not completely pure when he departs from life, no one but the lover of learning.'[4] This was a view that Catholics could find in the ever-influential Augustine, who acknowledged that Plato was the pagan philosopher who was closest to Christianity. Moreover, it was clear that Plato was committed to finding truth as a moral imperative, something appealing in itself to the humanists. As Petrarch, who had a Greek manuscript of Plato he could not read, put it: 'Plato is praised by greater men, Aristotle by a greater number.'[5] Anyone seriously interested in the classical world or learning for its own sake had to take him into account.

Bruni had already shown his sensitivity towards spiritual texts. His earliest translation from the Greek had been of a letter by the Christian theologian Basil of Caesarea, in which the importance of using selected pagan authors as a foundation for theological work had been extolled.‡ For Plato's works, Bruni began with the *Phaedo* and initiated a revolution in methods of translating. Salutati urged his protégé to turn his back on the word-for-word translations that helped make scholastic Latin so intractable. Instead, the goal was to prioritize the use of the *Phaedo* as a didactic text, a purveyor of moral and religious truths. Bruni took to this approach with enthusiasm:

> In translation the best translator will turn his whole mind, heart, and will to his original author, and in a sense transform him [*sic*], considering how he may express the shape, attitude and stance of his speech and all his lines and colours… he must possess a sound ear, so that his translation does not disturb the fullness and rhythmical qualities of the original.

Nothing could be more meritorious, he said, than to supply a text of Aristotle 'not via the enigmas and nonsense of absurd and false translations but face to face as he wrote it in Greek'.[6] This was not an idle boast. A comparison of Bruni's version with a twelfth-

‡ This was 'The Address to the Youth', made to Basil's nephews.

ALIDVM; V E S T A
HIEMS FRIGI
PLVS ET IN

century word-for-word translation of the *Phaedo* by the Sicilian scholar Aristippus reveals the latter to be hopelessly obscure. In Bruni's work we are witnessing the birth of modern approaches to translation – as well as a major achievement of humanist scholarship. Bruni went on to apply the same skills to Aristotle's *Ethics*, in the preface of which he ridiculed Robert Grosseteste's earlier translation as 'more barbarous than Latin'.

When Bruni moved to Rome he used the arguments of the *Phaedo* to show that Plato believed, unlike Aristotle, in the immortality of the soul, even suggesting to the pope an old tradition, traceable back to the Jewish philosopher Philo in the first century AD, that Plato had inherited his philosophy from the Old Testament prophets. In his next translation, of the *Gorgias*, where Plato shows the inadequacy of rhetoric as a means of finding truth, Bruni claimed that the moral values espoused by Socrates in refuting the orator Gorgias were Christian ones.[7] Yet after he returned to Florence, he became cooler towards Plato. Bruni seems to have been appalled by the authoritarian politics of Plato's *Republic* – and considered the notion that wives and children should be held in common to be particularly distasteful. He found the *Politics* of Aristotle much more sympathetic to an oligarchical system of government and, like Aristotle's *Ethics*, more deeply rooted in everyday life. While he translated the supposed letters of Plato in a presentation edition for Cosimo de' Medici, Bruni appears to have doctored Plato's political philosophy to make it more palatable to the republican ruling elite that he represented as Florence's chancellor.

A fresco in Anagni Cathedral *c.*1250, illustrating the theme of Plato's *Timaeus*. At the centre of the universe, the macrocosm, is a human figure, the microcosm. The surrounding circles represent the ages of man, the seasons and the four humours.

While Bruni, as a practising politician, became increasingly concerned by the otherworldliness and authoritarianism of Plato, a fresh impetus for the study of the philosopher came with the arrival of Greek scholars for an important meeting of the eastern and western churches held under the auspices of Pope Eugenius IV in Florence in 1439.[8] The hope was that there might be some reconciliation of the two churches at a time when the Ottoman Turks were threatening Constantinople. The council had begun in Ferrara but plague had broken out there and a new venue was needed. It was now that Cosimo de' Medici, always on the lookout for ways of boosting his prestige in the city, took the opportunity to bring the council to Florence. He offered to pay transport costs for the Greek delegates. When they arrived in Florence they found that Cosimo had

had himself elected *gonfaloniere* so that he could personally welcome the pope, the eastern emperor and other dignitaries on behalf of the city. The patriarch of Constantinople was already ill when he arrived in Florence, and took no part in discussions. He died in June 1439 and was buried in Santa Maria Novella. This left the emperor, John Palaeologos, in charge of the eastern delegation, an echo of emperors presiding over church councils 1,000 years earlier.

It was a tense occasion; many of the Greeks were haunted by historical memories of the sack of Constantinople by the crusaders in 1204 and the siphoning away of trade by Venice and Genoa in its aftermath. The Byzantine empire had, by this point, lost most of its territory to the advancing Ottoman Turks, who now surrounded and threatened a much-diminished Constantinople. News arrived during the council that an Ottoman fleet was lurking close to the Byzantine capital. Some hoped that the Latins might come to their rescue. In the council sessions, however, the Greeks found themselves under intense pressure from the Latin delegates. After much theological fudging over the crucial question of the *filioque*, Augustine's addition to the definition of the Trinity that had infuriated the Greeks (see p. 74), and an acceptance of the pope as first among the patriarchs as the successor of Peter, a union was declared and celebrated under the now-completed dome of the cathedral in July 1439. By the time the Greek delegation reached home, however, most were having doubts about their submission to the Latins. Some even saw the dramatic fall of Constantinople just a few years later (1453) as God's punishment for their acquiescence. Cosimo, however, had gained enormous prestige and his pre-eminence in Florence was now assured.*

Notable among the Greek experts at the council was the eighty-year-old scholar Gemistos Plethon from the Byzantine city of Mistras, in the Greek Peloponnese, then in its golden age as a centre of Byzantine art and scholarship.† As seen in the opening quotation, Plethon, an enthusiast for Plato, gave lectures on the philosopher during the council. Plethon was a controversial figure among Christians, many believing that his commitment to Plato was so great that he might be in fact a pagan. Some of his contemporary accusers quarried his commentary

* Notwithstanding his expenditure on transporting the Greek delegates, Cosimo managed to work the council to his financial advantage and the Medici profits doubled for the year.

† Mistras was founded in the mid-thirteenth century and soon became an important centre of Byzantine learning that reached its climax between 1348 and 1460 (when it was conquered by the Ottoman Turks). The site is now deserted but its ruins and several of its frescoed churches are intact and interesting to visit.

on Plato's *Laws* to show that he followed Plato in rejecting free will, assuming that the cosmos is eternal, that each human was purely the living form of a soul that pre-existed and survived it, that a supreme God acted through lesser gods. Those who supported him retorted that his commentary on the *Laws* had been deliberately doctored by his enemies to make Plethon appear heretical. What no one doubted was that Plethon was a true scholar, at home as much with the works of the later Platonists such as Plotinus (see Chapter 1, p. 32) and Proclus‡ as with the master himself, and blameless in character. With perhaps a touch of Abelardian arrogance, he saw himself as intellectually superior to those he saw debating theology at the council.

Plethon and his followers had little time for the scholastic theology of the western schools. They preferred a more mystical approach to the divine and rated Plato much more highly in giving access to this than Aristotle who, they felt, was too concerned with material things. This approach initiated a controversy over the relative merits of Aristotle and Plato. Plethon repeated all the original scholastic objections to Aristotle and accused him of denying any divine creator. The Aristotelians hit back and a battle of texts broke out, in which Plethon was challenged by a vituperative pro-Aristotle polemic, the *Comparatio* of George of Trebizond.[9]

The most interesting figure in this debate was Basilios Bessarion, himself born in Trebizond, on the Black Sea, in 1403.[10] An avid student and collector of Greek theological texts, Bessarion was also a consummate diplomat and, despite a fairly humble background, at total ease with the most powerful. He had studied with Plethon in Mistras but the two men were not close (there was an age difference of more than forty years) and it was as archbishop of Nicaea that Bessarion attended the Council of Florence. Here he proved himself a reconciler. He was in favour of union of the eastern and western churches and claimed that the *filioque* could be accommodated with Greek patristic texts. He was the only member of the eastern delegation to actively participate in the Mass of reunion and it was thus hardly surprising that he was welcomed into the Catholic Church, came to live in Italy and was made a cardinal. He became a leading figure in papal politics, and was even – twice – considered as a potential pope. Understandably, Bessarion was deeply affected by the fall of Constantinople and the threatened extinction of Hellenic culture. His palace in Rome became

‡ Proclus (AD 412–85) was an important commentator on the works of Plato. Having studied mathematics and the works of Aristotle in Alexandria, he became dissatisfied with their content and moved to Athens to work at (Plato's) Academy.

a centre of intellectual activity, a Platonic 'Academy' in its own right, where many Italian humanists gathered to discuss Greek philosophy.

Bessarion believed that Plato was altogether a greater philosopher than Aristotle but that they were not necessarily in opposition to each other. It was rather that Plato focused his thoughts on the spiritual in contrast to the materialism of Aristotle. This was the thrust of his *In calumniatorem Platonis* (*Against the Calumniator of Plato*), a response to George of Trebizond's outspoken attack on Plato. Bessarion quoted from many ancient commentaries on Plato, including those of the Neoplatonists of the third century AD, which were not known in the west. Eighty codices of Plato and his followers are recorded in an inventory of Bessarion's library. Thus it was that Bessarion helped ease Plato back into western consciousness, stressing that, while Plato was never a Christian and was often in error, it was as if he had been inspired by God.

It was Bessarion's magnificent collection of Greek manuscripts that restored the achievements of Greek science and literature to the west. From now on it would be the mark of an educated man that he would be aware of this heritage. The great early printer of Greek texts, Aldus Manutius, put it as follows: 'How can he who does not know Greek imitate the Greek authors, who are the most advanced in every field of learning and from whom, as is known, everything that is worthy of praise has passed into the Latin tongue?'[11] Among other initiatives, Bessarion encouraged a new summary of Ptolemy's *Almagest* that contained more recent observations and critical commentary, and which stressed that astronomy was not a closed subject to be taught from a decades-old textbook but a living one.* Bessarion was a patron of Regiomontanus (1436–76), the most sophisticated astronomer of his day, who travelled with him in his household and accumulated mathematical and astronomical texts for Bessarion's large private library.

The rector of the University of Paris, Guillaume Fichet, presents his book on rhetoric (1471) to Cardinal Bessarion. This miniature comes from the presentation copy, itself now in the *Biblioteca Marciana* in Venice.

After the fall of Constantinople in 1453, Bessarion was determined that his library, now with some 750 codices in Greek or Latin, should be preserved and he left it to the Senate of Venice in 1468. However, the gift was not given the care it deserved: a report of 1523 noted that the books were still packed in crates, mouldering in the damp of the city – even though it does seem that interested scholars had access

* It was known that the *Almagest* was considered indigestible by most students and so was hardly read.

to them.* By the early sixteenth century, Aldus Manutius had made Venice the source of the finest printed Greek texts, largely as a result of the accessibility of the originals in the city. Manutius's edition of the dialogues of Plato, dedicated to Pope Leo X, appeared in 1513. In short, Cardinal Bessarion is one of the most attractive figures in the reawakening of the western mind to a cultural heritage that it had forgotten. He died in 1472, having added some of the earliest printed books to his gift.

A much younger enthusiast for Plato was now to take the stage. Marsilio Ficino (1433–99)[12] was born near Florence, the son of a physician who had a good practice and thus intimate contacts with the Florentine elite, including Cosimo himself. Naturally, the young Marsilio was educated in Florence. He was soon drawn to philosophy but two years of studying with a scholastic teacher turned him against Aristotle. He felt that 'the philosopher' provided no moral purpose to learning and that he could not be reconciled with Christianity. This left him philosophically adrift and by the 1450s he had joined a religious confraternity based at the Medici Church of San Lorenzo. Here there was an emphasis on spiritual fellowship and a tendency towards mysticism. In the late 1450s Ficino appears to have had some form of religious crisis. Although the details are obscure, it is known that he had come across the works of Plato and felt them to be both sophisticated and emotionally satisfying. For Ficino and his circle the rediscovery of Plato had a revolutionary effect. It appeared to provide a link back to an earlier pristine knowledge.†

Yet there were many ways in which Plato was in conflict with the teachings of the medieval church. The only way out, Ficino eventually resolved, was to try to find some form of reconciliation between the two traditions. He went back to Augustine to see how the great theologian had found meaning through his study of Plotinus and recognized that the Platonic tradition had been absorbed into Christianity. It was he, Marsilio Ficino, who would revive it. He would do for Plato what Thomas Aquinas had done for Aristotle. Always something of an outsider, Ficino reinvented himself as a spiritual leader who would bring wisdom and profound moral truths to a city that had rejected them through its own impiety. He must have realized that Plato too had been at odds with the Athenian society of his era, resented rule

* Eventually, one of the most impressive library buildings of the sixteenth century, Jacopo Sansovino's Biblioteca Marciana, opposite the Doge's Palace, was built to house Bessarion's bequest.

† The extent to which the early Greek Church Fathers had relied on Plato to give intellectual backbone to their theology was hardly recognized.

by democracy, had been relegated to teaching outside the city and had failed dismally when he had attempted to create a Platonic society in Sicily. Perhaps Marsilio Ficino could do better.

It was in the early 1460s that Cosimo de' Medici, already interested in Platonism through Plethon's lectures, began to offer Ficino his patronage. In September 1462 he provided him with a manuscript containing all the dialogues of Plato in Greek, probably one he had been given by Plethon in 1439. A few months later he gave Ficino a house near one of the Medici country villas and Ficino began to assemble his own Platonic Academy (although it was probably little more than a set of informal gatherings with the young of the local elite families). He had soon presented Cosimo with the translations of ten dialogues. As Cosimo lay dying in the summer of 1464, Ficino was summoned to his deathbed to give spiritual readings. Also at the deathbed was Cosimo's fifteen-year-old grandson, Lorenzo, whom Ficino was tutoring in Greek.

Ficino placed Plato close to the gods. 'His style', he wrote, 'is similar more to a divine oracle than to human eloquence, now thundering deeply, now flowing with the sweetness of nectar, but always enfolding the hidden things of Heaven.'[13] Ficino recreated Plato as a serene unifier, *medicus animorum* ('doctor of souls'), whose benign counsel contrasted with the intractable intricacies of the scholastics. Each of Plato's dialogues, in the eyes of Ficino, was a single lesson within a wider programme of moral instruction, rather than an individual work in its own right. Plato's dialogues, and here Ficino was an innovator, were to be seen as a single corpus, reconcilable with each other. In his *Platonic Theology* (written between 1469 and 1474), Ficino enlisted the support of various texts of Plato to put forward rational arguments for the immortality of the soul. Ficino's ambitious treatise would become the most important Renaissance defence of this critical element of Christian doctrine – in many ways it was his equivalent of the *Summa theologiae* of Thomas Aquinas.

When confronted by the scholastics, Ficino's response was, in the true Platonic tradition, that divine matters, as enunciated by Plato, were necessarily beyond the range of rational discourse and language. Only a scholarly and committed few would achieve any understanding of them and most would have to wait until the afterlife before they would become fully conscious of them. Ficino drew heavily on the mystical works of the Christian philosopher Pseudo-Dionysius, famous for his 'negative theology' (see p. 188). Following Pseudo-Dionysius, Ficino argued that cutting away at the surface of things, just as a

SVSCI PITE O LI CTE RAS
ET LE GES EGIP TII
HERMIS MERCURIUS TRIMEGISTU
CONTEMPORANEUS MOYSI

Hermes Trismegistus, championed by Marsilio Ficino as the source of ancient learning, passes on wisdom texts to the Greeks and Egyptians. From a floor mosaic in Siena Cathedral.

sculptor might reveal a statue by chipping away and discarding stone, would provide an image of the ultimate reality.

Ficino was a brilliant scholar. His translations amazed his fellow humanists with their accuracy and philosophical penetration, and their exalted reputation ensured that they remained respected until the nineteenth century. Ficino was particularly successful in identifying Plato's works as the starting point of a tradition that would culminate, some 600 years later, in the work of Plotinus. Thus he also translated the *Enneads* of Plotinus' student Porphyry, which offer the fullest account of his teacher's ideas. Ficino believed that Plotinus' concept of 'the One' – a supreme and transcendent principle – and the means by which it could be grasped, marked a development of Plato's original thought. More controversially, he assumed that, while Plato was a forerunner of Christianity, he was the successor of much older sources of wisdom, notably those of Hermes Trismegistus and the so-called Hermetic tradition that apparently dated far back in the Egyptian past, to the time of Moses, so possibly representing early revelations of a pre-Christian God. While the mainstream humanists idealized the classical past, Ficino was championing much earlier sources of knowledge through which adherents could begin to grasp the original order of the universe as created by God. (He remained within the humanist tradition, which held that the past was a better place than the present and which therefore needed to be recovered.) In fact, as was realized in the seventeenth century, the Hermetic writings had been written between the first and third centuries AD and had been adopted by a Platonist successor of Plotinus, Iamblichus, in the late third century.* This is where Ficino had discovered them. The esoteric Hermetic writings, with their emphasis on a hidden wisdom originating in Egypt, became enormously popular in the sixteenth century, inspiring natural philosophers with the idea that there was a body of ancient truths waiting to be rediscovered.[14] Ficino did not study Hebrew in depth, but Pico della Mirandola's intensive study of that language was an attempt to master what he believed was humanity's original tongue, and which would therefore uncover a wealth of primal wisdom.

Whatever is said about the authority of Ficino's translations, he took trouble to censor the passages of Plato that Christians found objectionable. Foremost among these were the Greek philosopher's direct references to erotic love between older men and boys. At the beginning of the dialogue *Charmides*, for instance, where Socrates

---

* This was the achievement of the polymath Isaac Casaubon (1559–1614), an expert on deciphering and dating ancient manuscripts.

experiences lust for a young boy, Ficino simply left out the passage.

Both Bessarion and Ficino transformed the references to same-sex relationships into a chaste form of love, noble in its desires; Platonic love, as it became known. Usually between two men, this was seen as an elevated form of relationship and became very much an ideal and a prefiguring of the divine love that would be found in the immaterial world. In short, Ficino revered Socrates as if he were a pagan saint, overlooking his erotic impulses and presenting him as a teacher who goes out in the streets to preach to the young. He saw the 'Socratic method' of questioning as a means of clearing the misconceptions surrounding any philosophic issue so that the mind is left open for the reception of the wisdom of Plato. Ficino's adoption of Socrates' method, through which the teacher withdraws to let the student make his or her own progress towards knowledge, made him an attractive and popular figure among the educated Florentine elite.†

Soon after Ficino's death in 1499, the possibilities of reconciling Aristotle and Plato found favour in the papal court. With the fall of Constantinople and the revival of Greek scholarship, Rome had become the new Athens. In Raphael's *The School of Athens*, a fresco in the *Stanza della Segnatura* (originally the private library of Julius II where he made judicial pronouncements) in the Vatican (1510–11), they are shown side by side in the centre of the fresco, creating a philosophical companionship that has influenced intellectual debate ever since. The figure of Plato, carrying the *Timaeus*, points towards the stars; the figure of Aristotle, with his *Ethics*, towards the ground. On either side of them their followers or predecessors sit or stand in a great vaulted basilica poring over scrolls, globes and drawings. So the geographer and astronomer Ptolemy and the mathematician Euclid are on Aristotle's side, while Pythagoras and Heraclitus, the sixth-century BC philosopher who believed, like Plato, that all is in flux, support Plato.

overleaf Raphael's *School of Athens* (1510–11) in the *Stanza della Segnatura* in the Vatican portrays the reconciliation of the schools of Plato and Athens. Plato carries the *Timaeus* and looks upwards, while Aristotle holds his *Ethics* and points towards the ground.

The concept of reconciliation owed much to one of Ficino's contacts, an Augustinian friar, Egidio da Viterbo, who persuaded Pope Julius II to envisage Greek philosophy as a key element in the spiritual enlightenment of humanity that would culminate in the Christianity of Rome. (In fact, the first fresco Raphael had painted in the Stanza was

† It is said that in a recent inspection of teaching methods, the teachers of philosophy at Oxford University were asked what innovations they had made. They replied that the Socratic dialogue was still good enough.

The Triumph of Theology with theologians also finding reconciliation through debate. On the ceiling a traditional portrayal of Justice, complete with sword and balance, reflects another of Plato's most important Forms.) Egidio drew heavily on a newly discovered work, the third-century AD *Lives of the Philosophers* by Diogenes Laertius, a readable, discursive but unreliable compilation that became one of the most popular texts of the sixteenth century, not least in recovering Hellenistic (330–30 BC) philosophy. Alberti had been one of its first champions. Diogenes had given Plato a whole book to himself and so the rediscovery of the *Lives* embedded the great philosopher deeper in the intellectual fabric of the era.[15]

Yet despite this support, Platonism would always struggle to be heard in the more conservative universities, where Aristotelian scholasticism remained strong. The strength of Platonism was rather in the princely courts of the sixteenth century, where it attracted leading intellectuals. One might see Plato's ideal Republic as a precursor of Thomas More's *Utopia* (see Chapter 20, p. 462). In his highly influential *Il Cortegiano* (*The Book of the Courtier*, published in 1528), a meditation on the attributes of the perfect courtier, the diplomat and writer Baldassare Castiglione uses models drawn from Plato's *Republic*.* Castiglione turns his back on Aristotle's *Politics*, the standard sourcebook on the subject, which he saw as too rooted in the pragmatic problems of ruling. His aim was to provide an idealized vision of the court, to which the courtiers and their prince could aspire. In the fourth, and most Platonist, book of *The Courtier*, Castiglione argues that a prince can only rule wisely if he is a philosopher, while the role of the perfect courtier is to guide him towards this wisdom. Yet the fact that Castiglione also draws on Aristotle's *Ethics* – the book Raphael had depicted in the philosopher's hand – reveals that sixteenth-century philosophy had moved far beyond scholasticism to draw on a wide variety of philosophies, of which Platonism was now seen to be the most spiritual. One might even say that there had been a revival of the atmosphere of the Hellenistic period when the intellectual elite lived easily within a variety of competing philosophies.

Ficino's reputation had been temporarily eclipsed by the fall of the Medici in 1494, but later, during the Counter-Reformation, the Medici, now reincarnated as the grand dukes of Tuscany, would champion him

* Through his Urbino contact with Raphael, some believe that Castiglione was one of the models for the *School of Athens* (where he may be the figure next to Ptolemy, who is holding a globe). It has been noted too that the urbane Castiglione's respect for Raphael is a sign of the rising status of artists in the sixteenth century.

in a revival of Christian Platonism. By now the reputation of Aristotle was in decline in the Italian universities. A chair in Platonic studies was set up in Pisa, while in Ferrara Duke Alfonso II d'Este established one in his own university. The holder of this chair, Francesco Patrizi (Franciscus Patricius), moved to a similar chair in Rome but here, after the Council of Trent had reinforced the dominance of Thomas Aquinas and Aristotelianism, he encountered considerable opposition from conservatives, even to the extent of having one of his works, *Nova de universis philosophia* (*New Philosophy of Universes*), placed on the papal Index of Prohibited Books of 1597.

Plato fared better in northern Europe. Through Ficino's translations, he found supporters in the University of Paris in the 1580s and many of the new German universities lectured on him. The *Timaeus*, the *Phaedo* and the *Republic* continued to be the most popular texts. In Cambridge, the so-called 'Cambridge Platonists'† of the later seventeenth century were theologians who used Plato as a champion of effective reasoning in the search for faith. Like many of their Renaissance predecessors, they used Plato as one of the battering rams against the continuing but diminishing influence of Aristotle.

Now that Plato was well known he would never disappear from philosophical studies, although as the historian of philosophy Paul Oskar Kristeller has noted, by the seventeenth century the intellectual climate was changing: 'The speculative cosmology of the Renaissance was no longer possible within the framework of a natural science based on experiments and mathematical formulas.'[16] It was not until the revival of Greek studies in German and then European universities in the nineteenth century that Plato found a prominent and enduring place in the curriculum.[17]

Florence was not the only city that was a hotbed of cultural innovation in the fifteenth century. North across the Alps, a technological revolution was under way that was to transform the way in which knowledge was presented and spread to those with the literacy and languages to appreciate it. Vast new and productive ways of awakening the western mind were on the horizon.

† A name given to them in the nineteenth century.

The Printing Press: What was Published and Why?

Once it so happened that I was talking with a companion in the pope's garden at the Vatican. In our usual way we were discussing literary matters. As it happens, we agreed that we approved very warmly of the German inventor who has recently made it possible, by making certain imprints of letter, for three men to make more than two hundred copies of an original text in one hundred days, since each pressing yields a page in large format.

Leon Battista Alberti,
De cifra (*On Codes*)[1]

Leon Battista Alberti, the 'Renaissance man', had always been as interested in technical innovation as with the study of ancient texts. Towards the end of his life, sometime after 1465, he was excited to hear of this Italian 'printing press', probably the press at Subiaco near Rome that was working by that date.

By the fifteenth century literacy was rising and demand for reading material growing. The production of handwritten texts had reached new levels of accuracy and sophistication. No longer were readers dependent on the monasteries or university scriveners; texts were also produced by large and efficient secular workshops. When Cosimo de' Medici wanted to build up his library, he commissioned a Florentine bookseller, Vespasiano da Bisticci, to organize the production. Vespasiano, whose shop doubled as a meeting place for Florentine intellectuals, hired fifty-five scribes, each of whom took an average of six months to provide a copy of the quality that Cosimo expected. In less than two years some 200 volumes were ready to be added to Cosimo's library. One of the most famous libraries in Europe was that assembled by Matthias Corvinus, king of Hungary, from the 1480s; Florentine scribes had completed 2,000 volumes for him within seven years. In Paris, Bologna and Oxford the *pecia* system allowed an approved manuscript of a text to be lent out in sections (hence *pecia*, 'a piece') so that it could be copied for students. Translations were also well organized. The popular *Travels of Sir John Mandeville* (1356) survives in manuscripts in ten different languages including Irish and Czech.[2]

So a growing reading public and demand for more manuscripts provided every incentive to speed things up still further, but printing required a cluster of innovations. Luckily, a new material, paper, was at hand that would prove to be an indispensable element in allowing multiple copies of text to be produced at a reasonable cost.[3] Paper was another innovation that had appeared in China, as early as the first century AD, and had made its slow way to the west via the Arab world, the Levant and Islamic Spain, to arrive into Christian Europe in the twelfth century. In China and Korea woodcuts had also developed as an earlier form of printed material and there had been experiments with moveable type, but the sheer number of Chinese characters made printing uneconomical. It remained cheaper to copy out a book than to create the type to print it.* There were also cultural reasons for

* Similarly, printing in Arabic was delayed by the need to create 900 characters to reflect the different combinations of joined-up script.

limiting print production: for many the prestige of a copied text made it more desirable to own than one produced mechanically, just as the printed book is now holding its own against e-books. Still, it is possible that European trade with Asia led to the westward transmission of ideas that would be used by Europeans such as Gutenberg. As with so many apparent innovations in Europe, one must be cautious in assuming that outside influences were not important.

Scholarly humanists, with their disdain for manual work, were of no use here. Papermaking was a skilled process even if the raw material – linen rags and hemp from old sails and ropes – was easy to obtain. In fact, the supply was inexhaustible, certainly enough to provide as much as was needed in the early decades of papermaking. The rags were first broken up, hammered by water-powered mallets and then left damp for the fibres to break down. The resulting pulp was placed in a vat and pure water added – purity was important to maintain the whiteness of the finish – together with animal glue as a binder. The skill was to place a wire frame into a vat of the mixture and draw off a thin film of consistent thickness and appearance. Each sheet was dried out and treated with an agent so that ink applied to it would not disperse. It was then ready for use. If the raw materials had not been fully broken down, the result would be lumpy. It is not surprising that it was in Italy, the home of so much accomplished craftsmanship, that the technique of papermaking first matured and the best surviving examples are smooth and easy to use. The wire frame left its mark, which could be seen when the sheet was held to the light, and each workshop proudly entered its own design on the wire, thus creating a 'watermark'.†

Paper was not cheap in itself, but it was much cheaper than parchment. An inventory from a Florentine stationer of 1476, listing both vellum and paper with their respective prices, reveals that a sheet of vellum was about fourteen times as expensive as an equivalent sheet of paper. Yet a single page of the best quality might cost an artisan's weekly wages and most artists covered both sides with their doodlings and designs. Vellum went on being used for prestige commissions but increasingly paper was chosen for letter-writing and account-keeping and, as will be seen in Chapter 18 (p. 427), by artists and architects for preliminary sketches and drawings. Traders quickly responded.

† The provenance and date of the paper can often be dated from these, and faked editions of rare early books detected. At the Museo della Carta in Amalfi, Italy, an early centre of papermaking, you can create a page yourself using the original method – the author's was a bit ragged!

By the middle of the fifteenth century, mule-loads of stacked paper were making their way over the Alpine passes to the great trade fairs of northern Europe before Italian papermakers themselves travelled north to set up workshops and pass on their skills. By the fifteenth century Germany, France and Switzerland were dotted with mills. England was a laggard in this respect; there is no record of an English paper mill before the 1490s.

Already, in the early fifteenth century, woodcuts had been inked and rubbed through onto paper so that single page illustrations, usually of religious themes, were quite common and could even be joined to others in a primitive book. However, effective and versatile printing required individual letters that could be composed into lines of text, set in a frame, inked and applied to paper many times in sequence. The frame could then be dismantled and the letters reassembled in a new page. Achieving this required a high level of technical expertise and imagination.

The figure who is given the accolade of founder of the European printing press is Johannes Gutenberg. Gutenberg was born between 1397 and 1403 in Mainz on the Rhine.[4] He trained as a gem cutter and probably as a goldsmith, so he was adept at handling metals. He is known to have been designing pilgrim badges in Strasbourg in the 1430s but he was never a businessman, his ambitions being regularly thwarted by his difficulties in raising and repaying capital. How he came to be involved with printing is unknown; scattered references to the process after his return to his home town in 1448 leave much obscure. His earliest production was of the popular grammar book by the Roman writer Donatus, a small volume only using fourteen double-sided pages, of which few copies survive. The first real book, one which was astonishing in its ambition, was his Bible, 1,282 pages printed in 180 copies from 1452, a venture that would take two years to complete in versions that were printed both on paper and – for wealthy clients – on vellum. The first edition sold well to monasteries and clergy around Mainz and fifty copies still survive today. It was expensive; two copies of the luxury edition on vellum would have cost the equivalent of buying a house built in stone. Even the paper edition would have eaten up most of a master craftsman's annual wage. Yet Gutenberg's invention provoked such excitement and wonder that it became an inspiration and model for many early printers. It used the fourth-century Vulgate translation of Jerome, which it helped to consolidate as the authoritative version of the Bible for the Catholic Church. Unfortunately, the financial demands of the project – the type had to be created and the paper amassed before any return could be expected – defeated Gutenberg. He had to surrender his printing shop to two partners: Johann Fust, who provided capital and financial expertise; and Fust's son-in-law Peter Schoeffer, who grasped the technical demands of printing with moveable type and was soon making improvements in typefaces. The immediate result, the Mainz Psalter of 1457, printed only in an edition on vellum and using three colours (so that each page had to be pressed three times in perfect alignment with the earlier pressings) was a triumph.*

Composing a book required extraordinary co-ordination and continuous development of more effective methods of producing type. Gutenberg's Bible had used 300 different letters, if both upper and lower case, punctuation marks and abbreviations are included. There needed to be many copies of each letter. On one page alone the word *filii* was repeated 100 times, so 300 letter 'i's were needed. Each page required 2,600 individual pieces of type in its 42 lines. These figures give some idea of the vast scale of commitment needed to get printing going (and why the Chinese and Islamic scholars with their many more characters had found it unprofitable). They also explain why, in the first instance, printing depended on wealthy monasteries and cathedrals being prepared to pay for religious works, not only Bibles and psalters but calendars of the liturgical year and the works of the Church Fathers, notably Augustine and, from 200 years earlier, Thomas Aquinas. All of these items had been printed in Mainz by 1470.

overleaf The Gutenberg Bible (1452) is a triumphant recognition of the power of printing, not least as it consolidated the Latin Vulgate of Jerome as the authorized text of the Bible.

How was type created? The craftsmen and goldsmiths were among the few with the advanced level of expertise required. They would first create a punch, a rectangular rod into one end of which a letter was carved in reverse. The punch was then driven into a plate of softer metal, the matrix, and this left an impression of the letter. The matrix was then placed inside a mould and the impression was filled with a molten metal which, when cooled, hardened into a single piece of type. This had to stand out in relief on a column perhaps an inch high that could be placed alongside other letters in a compositor's stick to create words. The sticks would be amalgamated to make a forme, a single whole page of text. The surface of each letter had to be perfectly aligned with the others so that the print was uniform in its depth.

The process of making type required the selection of different

* Only ten copies survive, making it rarer than Gutenberg's Bible.

Feruescere faciet q̄si ollā profundum
maris:ponet quasi cū ungenta bulli-
unt. Post eum lucebit semita:estima-
bit abissum quasi senescentem. Non
est super terram potestas que comparetur ei: qui factus est ut nullum ti-
meret. Om̄e sublime videt:ipse est rex
sup universos filios supbie. xlij.

Respondens autem iob dn̄o dixit.
Scio q̄a om̄ia potes:et nulla te
latet cogitacio. Quis est iste qui celat
cōsiliū absq; sciencia? Ideo insipienter
locut⁹ sum:et que ultra modū excede-
rent sciēciā meā. Audi et ego loquar:
interrogabo te et respōde michi. Au-
ditu auris audivi te:nūc aūt oculus
meus videt te. Idcirco ip̄e me rep̄hen-
do:et ago penitenciā in favilla ⁊ cine-
re. Postq̄ aūt locut⁹ est de⁹ verba hec
ad iob: dixit ad eliphaz themanitem.
Iratus est furor meus in te et in duos
amicos tuos: quoniā nō estis locuti
corā me rectū sicut seru⁹ me⁹ iob. Su-
mite ergo vobis septem thauros ⁊ septem arietes: et ite ad servū meū iob:
⁊ offerte olocaustum pro vobis. Iob
aūt seru⁹ me⁹ orabit pro vobis. Faciem ei⁹ suscipiā: ut nō vobis imputet̄
stulticia. Neq; eni locuti estis ad me
recta:sicut seru⁹ me⁹ iob. Abierūt ergo
eliphaz themanites et baldach suites
et sophar naamatites et fecerūt sicut
locutus fuerat dn̄s ad eos:et suscepit
deus faciem iob. Dn̄s q̄q; conversus
est ad penitenciā iob: cū oraret pro a-
micis suis. Et addidit domin⁹ om̄ia
quecūq; fuerāt iob duplicia. Venerūt
aūt ad eū om̄es fratres sui ⁊ universe
sorores sue et cūcti qui noverāt eū pri-
us:⁊ comederūt cū eo panē in domo
eius. Et noverūt sup eū caput:et cōso-
lati sūt eū sup om̄i malo qd̄ intulerat

dn̄s sup eum:et dederūt ei un
ovem unam ⁊ inaurem aure
Dn̄s autē benedixit novissi
magis quā principio ei⁹. Et
ei quatuordecim milia oviū
lia camelorū:et mille iuga b
le asine:et fuerūt ei septē filij ⁊
Et vocavit nomē uni⁹ diē:et
secūde cassiam:⁊ nomē tercie
bij. Nō sunt aūt invente mul
ciose sicut filie iob:in univ̄sa t
ditq; eis pater suus hereditatē
tres eaꝝ. Vixit aūt iob post h
q̄dragita ānis:⁊ vidit filios f
lios filioꝝ suoꝝ usq; ad quar
racionē:⁊ mortu⁹ ē senex et ple
Explicit lib' iob Incipit p
bti Iheronimi presbri i psa

Psalteriū rome d
tus emēdarā:⁊ iux
aginta interpretes
sim·magna tam
correxerā. Quod quia rursu
o paula et eustochiū scriptoꝝ
pravatū·plusq; antiquum er
novā emēdacionē valere:me
ut veluti quodam novali·sci
arvū exerceam·et obliquis su
scentes spinas eradicem:equū
tes·ut qd̄ crebro pullulat creb
cidatur. Unde consueta p̄fa
moneo·tam vos quib; forte
desīdat·quā eos qui exempl
usmodi habere voluerit:ut q
ter emendavi: cū cura et dilig
scribantur. Notet sibi unusqu
iacētem lineā·vel radiācia sig
est obelos·vel asteriscos: et
viderit virgulā p̄cedentem·ab
ad duo pūcta que impressim⁹
septuaginta translatoribus
beri:ubi aūt prespexerit stelle si

cris voluminibꝫ additū noue-
usqꝫ ad duo pūcta-iuxta theo-
s dumtaxat editionē: qui sim-
e sermonis a septuaginta inter-
s nō discordat. Hec ergo et vo-
udioso cuiqꝫ fecisse me sciens-
bigo multos fore-qui vel invi-
supercilio malent contemnere
e predara quam discere: et de
nto magis rivo quam de pu-
fōte potare. Incipit liber
rū vel soli loquentium: 1
Eatus vir qui nō
abijt in cōsilio im-
piorū: et in via pec-
catorum nō stetit:
et in cathedra pesti-
lētie nō sedit. Sed
domini volūtas eius: et in lege
editabit die ac nocte. Et erit
ignū quod plātatum est secus
s aquarū: qđ fructū suū dabit
o. Et foliū eius nō defluet: et
quecūqꝫ faciet prosperabūtur.
sic impij nō sic: sed tanqꝫ pul-
proicit vētus a facie terre. I-
resurgūt impij ī iudicio: neqꝫ
res in cōsilio iustorū. Quoni-
uit dominus viā iustorꝫ: et iter
um peribit. psalmus david. 2
are fremuerūt gētes: et ppli me-
itati sunt inania? Astiterūt
rre et principes cōvenerunt in
dūsus dūm et adūsus cristū ei9.
upam9 vincula eorꝫ: et pciam9
s iugū ipsorꝫ. Qui habitat ī ce-
ebit eos: et dūs subsānabit eos.
t loquet ad eos in ira sua: et in
suo cōturbabit eos. Ego au-
titut9 sum rex ab eo super syon
m sanctū ei9: pdicās preceptū
Dominus dixit ad me filius
meus es tu: ego hodie genui te. Po-
stula a me et dabo tibi gentes heredi-
tatem tuā: et possessionē tuā terminos
terre. Reges eos ī virga ferrea: et tanqꝫ vas figuli cōfringes eos. Et nūc
reges intelligite: erudimini q iudica-
tis terrā. Servite dūo ī timore: et ex-
ultate ei cū tremore. Apprehendite di-
sciplinam: ne quādo irascatur dominus et pereatis de via iusta. Cum ex-
arserit in brevi ira eius: beati omnes
qui confidunt in eo. psalmus david
cum fugeret a facie absolō filij sui. 3
Domine qd multiplicati sunt qui
tribulāt me? multi insurgūt ad-
versum me. Multi dicūt anime mee:
nō est salus ipsi in deo eius. Tu aūt
dūe susceptor me9 es: gloria mea et ex-
altās caput meū. Voce mea ad do-
minū clamavi: et exaudivit me de mō-
te sācto suo. Ego dormivi et soporat9
sum: et exsurrexi quia dūs suscepit me.
Non timebo milia populi circūdan-
tis me: exurge dūe salvū me fac deus
meus. Quoniam tu pcussisti omēs
advūsantes michi sine causa: dentes
peccatorū cōtrivisti. Domini est sal9:
et super populū tuum benedictio tua.
In fine carminibꝫ psalm9 david.
Cum invocarē exaudivit me deus
iusticie mee: ī tribulatione dila-
tasti michi. Miserere mei: et exaudi o-
rationē meā. Filij hominū usqꝫ quo
gravi corde: ut quid diligitis vanita-
tem et queritis mēdacium? Et scitote
quoniā mirificavit dūs sāctum suū:
dūs exaudiet me cū clamavero ad eū.
Irascimini et nolite peccare: qui di-
citis in cordibus vestris in cubilibus
vestris compungimini. Sacrificate
sacrificiū iusticie et sperate in domino:
multi dicunt qs ostendit nobis bona.

metals for each stage. Originally, punches were made of brass or bronze (later it would be steel) and the softer matrixes of lead or copper. The type had to be hard in order to last for many printings; eventually, by trial and error, a composition of specified proportions of lead, tin and antimony achieved the required resilience. At first the styles of typefaces mirrored actual writing, so that books looked as if they had been handwritten. This had the bizarre consequence that some scribes copied manuscripts from printed books. It was some time before clearer and more readable 'Roman' fonts, adopted from the scripts pioneered by the humanists in the fourteenth century, took over from Gothic styles (except in Germany, where Gothic persisted for centuries). By the 1470s type-making had become the business of specialist firms and it is no longer possible for an expert to spot the origin of a book at a specific press by its distinctive font. (Adding the name of the printer to the text was a later development.)

Once a page had been checked, the type would be inked using a soaked horsehair sponge. The consistency of ink was crucial; it needed to be viscous enough to transfer onto the paper but quick to dry on a surface that had been dampened to accept it. One of the achievements of the Mainz printers was to find the right solution early on. Paper and forme would be placed one on top of the other in a frame. Then the frame was placed on a carriage that ran under the actual press, originally of wood but later of metal, which would be screwed down to make the impression. Presses were already in use for crushing grapes and olives and here they were adapted to serve new purposes.

The concept of printing spread fast, not least because of lower prices. In the 1460s the cost of a printed page was roughly one-eighth that of a copied manuscript. The merchant cities of Germany along the Rhine were among the pioneering centres of the printing industry and they were soon followed by other German cities: Bamberg, Nuremberg, Strasbourg, Cologne and Augsburg. Paris had a press by 1470 and was probably the first to print secular texts, although there was powerful resistance to imported books from the efficient university scribes. There is a, possibly apocryphal, report of Johann Fust arriving in Paris with a load of Bibles only to be chased out of town by the resident sellers of manuscripts. By 1480 German printers had migrated to northern Italy to set up presses in the major cities, although printing faltered in Florence, where scribes and their organizers such as da Bisticci still dominated the market. University cities were not foremost in the trade, so in England, London rather than Oxford or Cambridge became the centre of the book trade. It is probable that there were so many manuscript copies of the set books that there was less need for printed versions. While there were sixteen editions of Peter Lombard's *Sentences* before 1500, for instance, the one city where one would expect to find an edition, Paris, did not print any of them. There was a continuing relationship between scribes and printers. Printed books would leave spaces for elaborate capitals or Greek text to be added by hand; manuscripts would leave spaces for printed illustrations.

Many printers remained small scale. The very success of the process meant that, especially in the 1470s, far too many entrepreneurs were drawn into the trade and then found that they had misjudged the market, producing books that were not attractive enough to compete with similar editions or taking a chance with a new text that failed to find a market. One might compare the situation in the late fifteenth century with the explosion of small firms making computers in the 1970s, most of whom failed as the giants drove down costs. The result was that many printers, especially those Germans working in Italy, became migrants, moving their type and presses from town to town in the hope of tapping into a fresh and lucrative new market. Paper was heavy and difficult to move, so it was important for printers to locate their business as close as possible to a paper mill. In many cases, printer and paper mill were run by members of the same extended family. A breakdown of supply would be fatal to the smooth running of a press. A large edition (what modern publishers would call 'a long print run') would result in lower costs per book; but in order to achieve this the printer needed to be based in a prosperous, and hence literate, city with good distribution routes. Printing remained a precarious business. The encyclopaedic *Nuremberg Chronicle* of 1493, masterminded by Anton Koberger, the commercial genius of the printing world, had an edition of 2,500 (1,500 in Latin, and 1,000 in German) and was widely advertised. It became a prestige possession, which helps explain why 1,200 copies survive. Unfortunately for the backers, reprints and new editions so flooded the market that the first edition failed to sell out and the massive outlay was never fully recouped. The more astute printers recognized that they had to alternate larger editions with one-off sheets or pamphlets that would bring in an immediate return.

* * *

The most successful printing city was not a university town at all but one with the resources, the contacts and the outreach to make an immense success of the printing revolution. The supremacy of Venice in the history of printing is still underestimated. There were some 233 printing houses recorded between 1469 and 1500. They had the access to the capital needed to produce large books and exploited the market by sea to Spain and Portugal and over the Alpine passes to Hungary and Poland, lands where the German presses were less successful. A pioneer in the 1470s was the Frenchman Nicolas Jenson (*c.*1420–80), applauded to this day for his elegant Roman font, which became standard. His edition of the works of Julius Caesar (1471), the first in print, marks the transition from imitations of handwriting to a font derived from scripts on Roman monuments. One reason for the Venetian printers' success was their flexibility. This can be seen in the liturgical texts, of which they were the biggest producer of all. They were able to adapt their missals (books containing the texts used in the Catholic Mass throughout the year) to fit the varied rites followed in different parts of Europe. It is estimated that 4,000 different editions had been published in Venice by 1500. However, political difficulties and the freezing of credit brought an economic crisis to the republic at the end of the century and the printers found themselves undercut by lower-quality presses in Germany and the Netherlands.

Aldus Manutius's edition of Pietro Bembo's *De Aetna* is remarkable as an early example of a 'scientific' text and was set in a font (Bembo) that became standard.

An estimated 8 million *incunabula*, the term used for books printed in 1500 or before, were printed in the first fifty years. Religious texts and pamphlets remained dominant, perhaps 45 per cent of the total; in addition to the scriptures, Augustine (his *The City of God* was the most popular) and Gregory the Great, staples from earlier centuries, were to be found alongside the major texts of the twelfth and thirteenth centuries, Aquinas, Bonaventure, the *Sentences* of Peter Lombard, and the saints' lives in *The Golden Legend* of Jacobus de Varagine. So at one level this was a conservative market and it provided both books for the scholar, for the practising cleric (missals and the liturgies), and for the laity. The largest runs of single-sheet pamphlets were receipts confirming that an indulgence had been paid for. The devotional Books of Hours, traditionally produced for the elite, could now be reproduced much more cheaply for a larger clientele. One early bestseller was Thomas à Kempis's *Imitation of Christ*, which was popular for its radical idea that Christ could be imitated even by members of the laity. Another was Boethius' *Consolation of Philosophy*, found in seventy editions before 1500. The popularity of this philosophical text that did not mention Christian belief but did nothing to undermine piety was truly remarkable. The argument that the laity were absorbing religion independently of the church (to be explored further in Chapter 16), is reinforced by the evidence from the presses that shows that there was a real hunger for religious texts.

Overall, some 77 per cent of the *incunabula* were in Latin. Original vernacular texts were also popular: works such as the heavily illustrated *Der Edelstein* (*The Precious Stone*), a book of folk tales in German, Dante and Boccaccio in the original Italian, and Chaucer's *The Canterbury Tales* in London. Here William Caxton, who had run a press in Bruges after learning the trade in Cologne, set up in 1476. Translations from the Latin, including religious texts, were also becoming common. So Varagine's *The Golden Legend* appeared in eighty-eight Latin editions before 1500 but also with eighteen editions in French, five in English, two in German, thirteen in Flemish and six in Italian.

Grammars were early bestsellers as they gave learners access to the more advanced texts in Latin – the original language, of course, of the texts loved by the humanists. Cicero's philosophical tracts, his letters and his speeches were the bestselling of the classics, a total of 316 editions before 1500. The poets Virgil and Ovid were popular and Seneca held his place as a Stoic philosopher. There was a hiatus here.

Quia noueram mores hominum ;tum etiam pertentare te prorsus uolui, q̃ recte ista sentires. Sed omittamus haec iam tandem filĩ; atq; ad eam partem sermonis, ex qua egressi sumus, reuertamur.
B. F. Immo uero pater nec reuertamur: quid enim amplius nobiscum platanis illis? de iis enim loquebamur. Sed (si placet) ad Aetnam potius, de qua sermo haberi coeptus est, properemus.
B. P. Mihi uero pérplacet; ita tamen, ut ne festines: tibi enim ego omnes has pomeridianas horas dico. Sed quoniam me impellente nimium iam extra Aetnae terminos prouecti sumus, non cõmittam, ut te interpellem saepius; nisi quid erit, quod de ea ipsa te rogem. B. F. Sanè mons ipse situ, forma, magnitudine, feritate, incendiis mirus; demum tota sui qualitate ac specie longe conspicuus, et sibi uni par est. Ab aurora mare Ionium bibit; et Catanam sustinet imo in pede: cum sole descendit in insulam, qua Tyrrenum pelagus est; et quae Aeoliæ appellantur: laterorsus, in septentriones uergenti Pelorus obiicitur, et Italiae angustiae sunt: contra reliqua insula súbiacet, tractúsque ii omnes, qui cum Lilyboeo in Africam protenduntur. Ipsa Aetna radices suas ferè in orbem deducit; nisi sícubi orientem, et meridiémuersus promisso cliuo paulisper extenditur: celebs degit; et nullius montis dignata coniugium caste intra suos terminos continetur. circumitur non minus, q̃. c. mil. pass. ascenditur ferè per uiginti, qua breuior uia. Imi colles, ac omnis radicum ambîtus per oppida, et per uicos frequens inhabitatur; Baccho, Pallade, Cerere feraces terrae; armentorum omnis generis supra, q̃ credas, feracissimæ. Hic amoenissima loca circunquaq;: hic fluuii personantes: hic obstrepentes riui:

Printers were craftsmen, not scholars, and they often unknowingly reproduced texts from corrupt manuscripts. It is usually noted that printing helped standardize texts, but it could also standardize errors. It took some time, to a point between 1490 and 1510, before the humanists began demanding that only the most accurate manuscripts should be used. The search for the best manuscripts further stimulated humanist scholarship. Yet here too the status of the major Latin authors was such that translations soon followed. Cicero's letters to his friends were quickly to be found in Italian, French and German editions.

Greek, with its breathings and accents, was difficult to reproduce in type but it found a printing supremo in the humanist scholar Aldus Manutius.[5] Born in Bassiano, south of Rome, in 1449, Manutius studied Greek in Ferrara but found his true home among the bustling printing shops of Venice, where he arrived in 1490. Now he had access to the wonderful collection of Cardinal Bessarion, whom he had met in Rome, the resources of a prosperous and cultured city and, in the skills of Andrea Torresani, a type designer who was expert in creating Greek lettering. He could also draw on Venice's centuries-old trading contacts with the east and, in the 1490s, on the knowledge of Florentine Greek scholars fleeing the repressive regime of Savonarola (see p. 388). Among the meticulous texts that resulted were first editions of many of the great Greek classical writers: the playwrights Aristophanes, Sophocles and Euripides, the historian Thucydides, the philosopher and historian Plutarch (whose *Lives* were highly influential in the century that followed), the aristocratic poet Pindar, the orator Demosthenes and, with his importance restored by Ficino and others, Plato. One of the most celebrated of Manutius's productions was a five-volume edition of Aristotle in Greek that provided a definitive version of the original texts. All this made him the most famous printer of his day, respected by scholars throughout Europe for bringing not only Greek but also Latin texts to a wider scholarly public.

Among Manutius's most influential productions was his first text in Latin, the humanist Pietro Bembo's *De Aetna* (1496), a short account of the author's ascent of Mount Etna in Sicily in which, in a dialogue with his scholarly father, Bernardo, his actual experience of the volcano is contrasted with his father's knowledge of it only through classical texts. It is part of the transition from the authority of those texts to the findings of empirical observation (as will be seen in later chapters on the replacement of Ptolemy's *Geographike* and *Almagest* and Dioscorides' *De Matera Medica*). Its beautifully clear typeface is known to this day as 'Bembo type' and its octavo pages prefigured the modern book. While this page size had been known for some time, Manutius's use of it enabled his works to be easily carried around and so its adoption marks a transition of immense significance for readers to this day.* Yet the superlative quality of his work meant that Manutius was easily undercut by rivals and his press did not earn high profits. An insistence on quality and accuracy was not necessarily the road to financial success; Manutius's press only just survived the collapse of the Venetian trade in the early 1500s.

The flood of new books meant that readers could be overwhelmed. It was often difficult for scholars to know what a book contained and in the 1520s the bastard son of Christopher Columbus, Hernando Colón, collector of one of the largest private libraries of the day, produced a catalogue known as the *Book of Epitomes* summarizing each work. Many could be summed up in just seven or eight lines but now that the works of Plato were translated they had to have thirty pages dedicated to their contents. Much could follow from the *Book of Epitomes*. It was inevitable that the scholar summarizing each book would give some comments on its quality as a text and with an epitome at hand one could group books more easily and perhaps even amalgamate them to make a single authoritative study of a given subject.[6]

In these early years the presses certainly reached a wider reading public, but they did not transform thinking. There was as yet no significant market for new writers and ideas. The vast majority of editions were of established classics and authorities. Even in what might be called science, old favourites were recycled, suggesting that the concept of knowledge being progressive had not yet been grasped. So the encyclopaedic *Speculum Maius* (*The Great Mirror*), a vast summary of knowledge, compiled by the Dominican Vincent of Beauvais in the middle of the thirteenth century, was reproduced in print unchanged. Many other works on natural philosophy that now appeared in print also dated from this century. Avicenna's *Canon Medicinae* (*c.*1025) went through twenty editions before 1500, rivalled only by Albert the Great's Aristotelian treatises on biology. In medicine the authority of Galen

overleaf Regiomontanus's calendar of 1482 was an accurate compilation of astronomical phenomena that included the predictions of eclipses from 1483 to 1530, as illustrated here. The printing of such texts allowed a 'scientific' accuracy to be spread among learned circles.

* A folio, from the Latin *folium*, a leaf, is a book made up with each printed page folded over once to produce two leaves; a quarto book is when the page is folded twice and an octavo book when the original printed page is folded over three times, thus making it a quarter of the size of a folio edition. Depending on the size of the original printed page an octavo page will be roughly eight to ten inches high by five to six inches wide.

1493	1493	149
Eclipsis Lune	Eclipsis Solis	Eclipsis Sol
19 13 58	10 2 38	7 4
Aprilis	Octobris	Martij
Dimidia duratio	Dimidia duratio	Dimidia dura
1 49	1 4	0 4
	Puncta octo	Puncta qua

1494	1494	1497
Eclipsis Lune	Eclipsis Lune	Eclipsis Lu
21 14 38	14 19 45	18 6 3
Martij	Septembris	Januari
Dimidia duratio	Dimidia duratio	Dimidia d
1 46	1 48	1

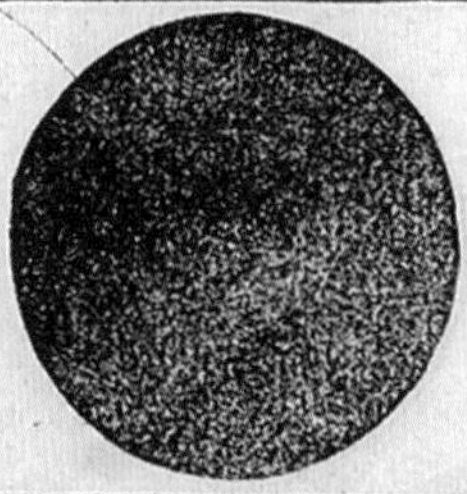

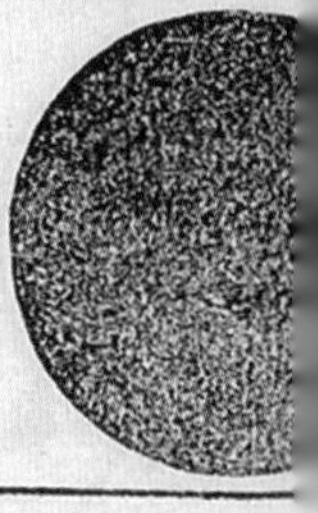

1497	1500	1501
Eclipsis Solis	Eclipsis Lune	Eclipsis Lune
29 3 2	5 14 2	2 17 49
Julij	Nouembris	Maij
Dimidia duratio	Dimidia duratio	Dimidia duratio
0 36	1 37	1 52
Puncta tria	Puncta decem	

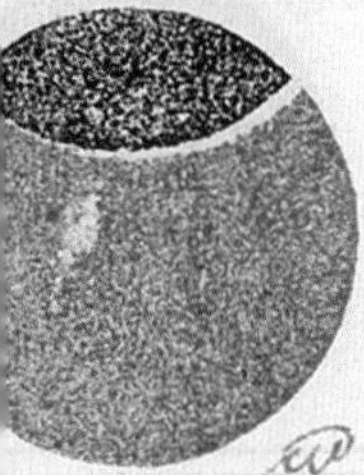

1502	1502	1504
Eclipsis Solis	Eclipsis Lune	Eclipsis Lune
30 19 45	15 12 20	29 13 36
Septembris	Octobris	Februarii
Dimidia duratio	Dimidia duratio	Dimidia duratio
1 7	1 1	1 46
Puncta decem	Puncta tria	

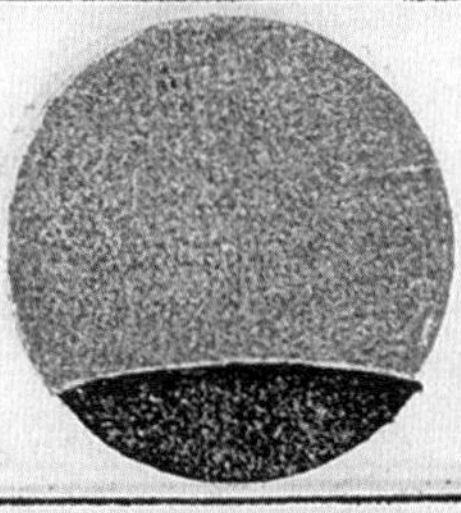

(brought together in a coherent edition for the first time in 1490) and Hippocrates remained secure. We have already seen how the staple university texts endured from decade to decade well into the sixteenth century. Similarly, new important works by mathematicians such as Regiomontanus were first printed many years after they had been written. Regiomontanus's important *Epitome* of Ptolemy's *Almagest* was published in 1496, as many as thirty-four years after it had been completed in 1462. Regiomontanus, however, deserves credit as the publisher of the earliest known printed treatise on astronomy, *Theoricae novae Planetarum* (*New Theories of the Planets*), by his teacher Georg von Peuerbach, in 1472.

Famously, the first edition of Copernicus's *De Revolutionibus*, where the Polish astronomer set out his theory of a heliocentric (sun-centred) universe, published in an edition of 400 copies in 1543, failed to sell out. It was not until 1566 that there was a second edition. However, Owen Gingerich in his *The Book that Nobody Read*[7] does much to redress this by tracking down a wide range of annotated copies of these first two editions to show that the audience who mattered, the astronomers of the day, were aware of it even if they did not grasp the importance of its central thesis. Nonetheless, a dated printed copy of a work established its precedence in a way that a manuscript often failed to do. The publication of *De Revolutionibus* in 1543 confirms Copernicus's priority, over any European competitor, as the first formulator of the heliocentric theory, even if he may have adopted models from Arabic texts (see p. 653).[8]

In short, while the advent of printing was certainly a technological revolution of the greatest importance, it was not necessarily linked to an immediate intellectual revolution. The church was quick to see the problems of allowing printers to operate freely. 'It will be necessary to maintain full control over the printers,' ran a papal bull issued by Pope Alexander VI in 1501, 'so that they may be prevented from bringing into print writings which are antagonistic to the Catholic faith or which are likely to cause trouble to believers.'[9] Yet, millions of books, many of them expensive items, would never have been printed unless there was an existing demand for them. Brilliantly successful for a wider audience was Ludovico Ariosto's *Orlando Furioso* (in its complete form, 1532), a lengthy romantic epic of a knight caught up in the struggles between Charlemagne and the Saracens, and Torquato Tasso's *Gerusalemme Liberata* (1581), another epic, this time set during the First Crusade.

The success of printing is a reminder that by the fifteenth century European trade was well established and there was freedom to travel across the continent in search of profit and learning. Latin still remained the language of scholarship and thus enabled effective communication between the intellectual elites, in what was to become known as the Republic of Letters.* Yet there was also a strong market in vernacular texts, many of them popular works of literature. What remained closed off to the reading public were the scriptures: the church still refused to allow vernacular translations of the Vulgate Bible and it was inevitable that pressure would build up for translations of the scriptures, authorized or not. A conflict between the Catholic Church and a spiritually hungry laity was brewing. The German theologian Martin Luther was to exploit the vacuum brilliantly with outpourings of pamphlets (see p. 525). It was one manifestation of a growing distance between the institutions of the church and the laity, who were increasingly following their own spiritual lives in their local communities. It used to be said that the prominent question for the Roman empire was not 'Why did it fall?' but 'Why did it last so long?' The same might be said of a single Europe-wide Christianity of the Latin west.

overleaf A depiction of two of the artists who illustrated Leonhard Fuchs's *De historia stirpium commentarii insignia* (Basle, 1542). Albertus Meyer draws plants (right), while Heinrich Füllmaurer transfers drawings to a woodblock (left).

* Although this term was only coined in the seventeenth century, the interplay within a community of intellectuals can be traced as far back as the fourteenth century, as it is by the French scholar Marc Fumaroli in his *The Republic of Letters*. See also the chapter 'A Sketch Map of a Lost Continent: The Republic of Letters' in Anthony Grafton, *Worlds Made by Words: Scholarship and Community in the Modern West* (Cambridge, MA, and London: Harvard University Press, 2009) pp. 9–34.

Heinricus Füllmaurer.

PERIS,

Albertus Meyer.

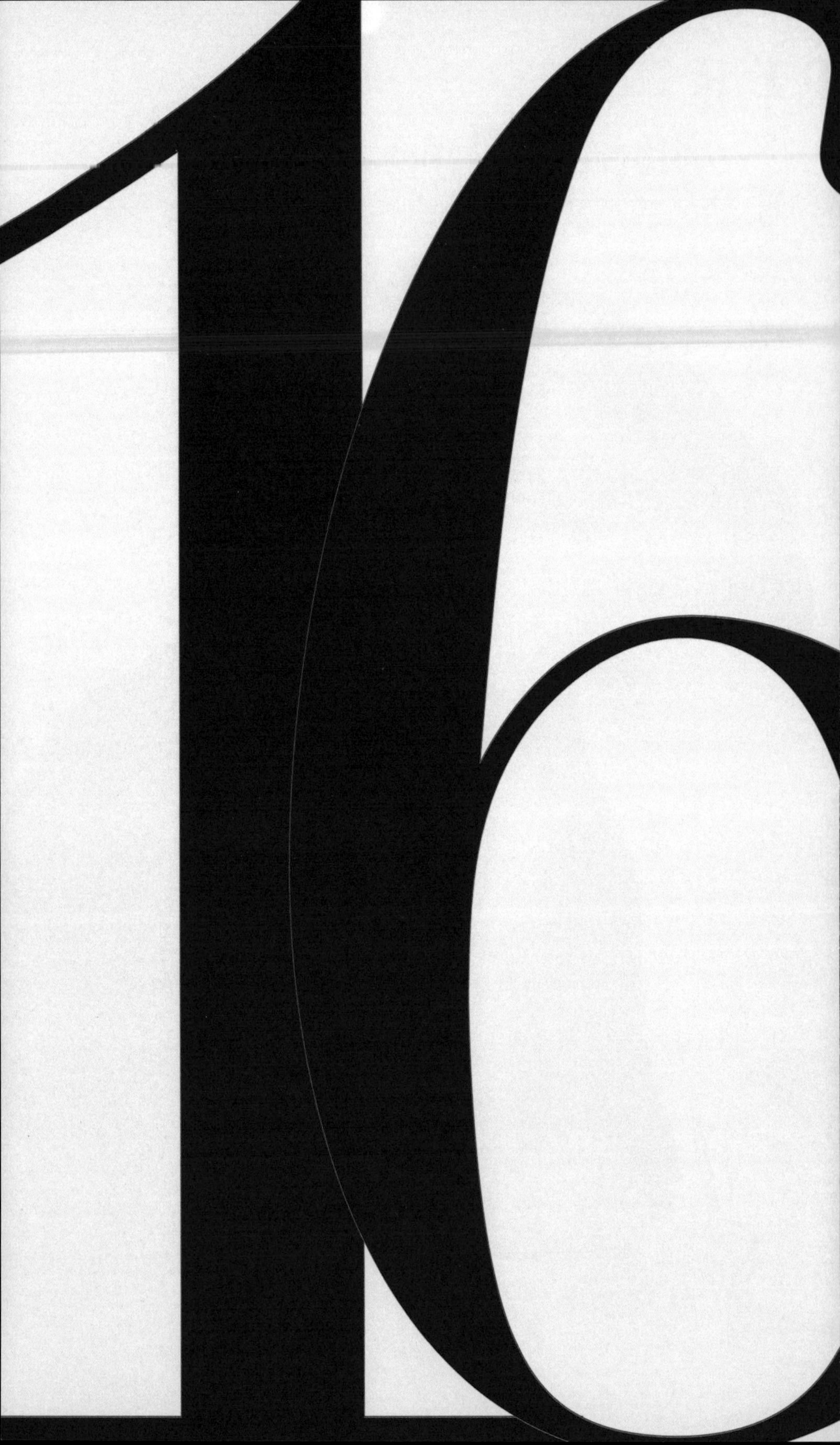

The Loss of Papal Authority and the Rise of the Laity, 1300–1550

Some desirous of fulfilling the law and of serving Our Lord, and often finding certain poor wretches lying in the streets and dying of cold, were moved by compassion for their misery and thought to provide a bed or two in a small house where they could succour these poor; so they began, and as charity grew in them they began to increase the number of beds and so their mercy [*misericordia*] grew and their hospitality, not only towards these poor but also to strangers who found themselves with nowhere to stay.

The motives behind the Roman confraternity Madonna della Pieta della Casa, 1563[1]

Between 1350 and 1600 new ways of being Christian spread throughout Europe and far beyond. They were partly a response to the continuing atrophy of papal prestige and the increasing segregation of the clergy as a caste. Secular rulers were also gaining in authority, developing more efficient ways of raising taxes, using university-trained lawyers to run their bureaucracies and expanding their armies. This shifted the balance of power away from the popes and clergy into the hands of kings and emperors and allowed new movements, both theological and populist, to express themselves. As so often, maps show this shift of power. While the Catalan Atlas of 1375 (see p. 406) placed the names of kingdoms within undefined territories, a map of Europe by Erhard Etzlaup a century later has each state delineated by colour. Arguably, in the history of western thought the rise of secular control of religion, by both Protestant and Catholic rulers and local communities, is as important as the emergence of new Christianities in the form of the so-called Reformation of the sixteenth century. Across the period 1300–1500, greater opportunities had opened up for Europeans to develop their own spiritual aspirations, and the ways in which religious belief could be expressed had diversified significantly. The breadth of religious responses to changing social conditions during these two centuries can certainly be seen as part of the story of 'the reawakening of the western mind'. It was the Reformation that reversed this process by reimposing authoritarian Christianities, notably by reasserting the theology of Augustine. The story will be treated in two phases: first, with an account of the rise of lay initiatives in the fifteenth century; and, second, in a later chapter, with the Reformation (see Chapter 24).[2]

The rule of Innocent III (1198–1216) had seen the zenith of the imperial papacy. By 1300 decline had set in. The most dramatic confrontation of the late thirteenth century between a ruler and a pope came during the papacy of Boniface VIII (1294–1303). Boniface appears to have elbowed aside the fragile Franciscan pope Celestine V and was elected only a day after Celestine's abdication. His legitimacy was therefore questionable and rumours of his lust for sex with both boys and women isolated him further. However, it was his clumsy assertion of his authority that incensed his enemies. He launched a vendetta against the powerful Roman Colonna family, driving them towards the French king Philip IV, who was already in dispute with Boniface over the privileges of the French clergy and his rights to church property and income, and was in the process of crushing the military order of the

Templars. In fact, Philip was exceeding the acknowledged legal powers of a monarch vis-à-vis the church and this marks an important moment in the rise of secular confidence. In retaliation Boniface issued a papal bull, *Unam Sanctam* (*One Holy* (*Church*)), in 1302 that went beyond even the absolutism of Gregory VII, Bernard of Clairvaux and Innocent III to proclaim that failure to acknowledge the authority of the pope both in spiritual and secular matters would result in damnation. The outraged French called for a council to depose Boniface, which was supported by the bishops of Paris, the university clerics, the chapter of Notre Dame, the Dominicans and most of the Franciscans. Back in Italy the emboldened Colonna, with the help of agents from France, stormed Boniface's palace in Anagni and held the pontiff captive for several days. The palace still stands and the room where he was attacked by the nobleman Sciarra Colonna some 700 years ago – in an episode know as the *Schiaffo di Anagni* ('Anagni's slap') – remains unchanged. Whether from natural causes or from the massive humiliation he had suffered, Pope Boniface died shortly afterwards in Rome. Composing his *Divine Comedy* in 1308, the poet Dante, who had been exiled from his native Florence when papal forces had gained control in the city, retaliated by ensuring a place for Boniface in hell.

Any chance of regaining the initiative from the monarchies of Europe was further diminished in the fourteenth century by the long exile of the papacy in Avignon (1309–76).[3] The city of Rome was not a pleasant place to live, especially in the hot summers when disease spread easily. For the popes there were always rival noble factions to deal with as well as a resurgent communal government. Yet the marriage of papal power with the authority of Peter, and his relics in St Peter's, made it almost impossible to conceive of an effective papacy outside Rome. One anonymous Roman cleric had written in the thirteenth century that a pope who lived outside lost half his dignity by doing so, 'as a woman without a husband, so does the city of Rome without a pope seem to be'.

The move to Avignon, by Clement V (r.1305–14), was never meant to be permanent. Clement, who was hoping to mend the breakdown of the traditional relationship between the papacy and the French monarchy, felt that the Provençal city of Avignon, although itself not part of the kingdom of France (it was in the territory of the counts of Provence, then rulers of Sicily), was a better temporary base for doing this. Furthermore, the city's location on the River Rhône would allow effective communications with other Catholic states. Clement's successor, John XXII (r.1316–34) – elected only after two years of infighting among the cardinals – had already served as bishop of Avignon and a move back to Rome never took place. John's episcopal palace was transformed into the grandiose Palais des Papes, a fitting backdrop to the papal monarchy.

The quality of papal administration improved in Avignon as the popes stabilized their finances through asserting greater control of appointments to benefices (or 'provisions', as they were known), allowing rents, endowments and other forms of revenue to be paid to the papal court and then distributed to favoured recipients. However, this also had the effect of undermining local patronage and encouraging a rush of applicants to the court every time a new pope took office (as many as 6,000 after the election of Pope Clement VI in 1342). Now that the appointments were made centrally, outsiders were often appointed by the popes to lucrative bishoprics and then never lived in their new dioceses. These developments had the effect of distancing the church from local politics and so reinforced the image of a wealthy institution that operated independently

Between 1309 and 1376 seven successive popes resided in Avignon, in southern France, rather than Rome, leading to a marked increase in French influence on the papacy.

of the mass of its subjects. One long-term result of the short reigns of individual popes was to encourage the sale of posts whose salaries then had to be financed by later pontiffs. By the mid-1520s 30 per cent of papal income was spent on bureaucracy, by 1560 it was 50 per cent.[4] As the humanist Petrarch, who worked in the papal administration, wrote:

> Here reign the successors of the poor fishermen of Galilee; they have strangely forgotten their origin. I am astounded, as I recall their predecessors, to see these men loaded with gold and clad in purple, boasting of the spoils of princes and nations; to see luxurious palaces and heights crowned with fortifications, instead of a boat turned downward for shelter.[5]

It says something about the priorities of papal government that the Palais des Papes alone absorbed 18 per cent of the income of Pope Benedict XII (r.1334–42). For the English and Germans this impression of isolation was intensified by the close relationships of the popes with French culture. The Avignon popes were all French, as were 112 of the 134 cardinals they created, and they were ridiculed by many as

subservient to a more powerful French monarchy. So withdrawn were the popes that there was only a single church council (the Council of Vienne, 1311–12) held in these years and that was firmly under the control of Clement V.

It was the Italians (the Florentine Petrarch among them) who were most offended by the Avignon exile. The Romans had become used to the wealth of the church sustaining the city, and the absence of the popes allowed aristocratic rivalries to fester. In 1346 a popular uprising led by the charismatic Cola di Rienzo took months to exhaust itself. Outside Rome there was widespread unrest in the amalgam of territories that made up the papal states. John XXII was so determined to suppress it that he spent two-thirds of his income on mercenary troops and the buying off of rival contestants. Following a crushing defeat of the papal armies at Ferrara in 1333, Bologna was temporarily lost to the papacy. Important political works such as the *Defensor Pacis* of Marsilius of Padua (1324) challenged papal authority more coherently than ever before (see pp. 250–3). In 1375, as has been seen, Florence, once the most loyal of the papal allies, declared war on the popes.

Respect for the papacy was further destroyed by the schism that followed Pope Gregory XI's (r.1370–8) decision to return to Rome in 1377 after his conscience had been aroused by importunate pleading from Catherine, a mystic from Siena, who took it upon herself to intervene in politics.*[6] Gregory died soon afterwards but the cardinals, determined to discard French popes in favour of an Italian who would stay in Rome, elected Urban VI (r.1378–89), the former bishop of Bari in southern Italy. He proved to be highly disturbed, vigorously asserting his authority in fits of rage and imprisoning and even torturing the cardinals who offended him. Several of them fled and elected a rival 'antipope', another Frenchman, Robert of Geneva, a former archbishop of Cambrai, as Clement VII (r.1378–94), to restore papal rule in Avignon.

While the popes who remained in Rome are considered to be the legitimate line from Peter, it hardly appeared so at the time as western Christendom split in its allegiances. The French naturally sided with Clement; England, Germany, central Europe and Italy with Urban. For thirty-nine years rival popes excommunicated each other, causing such frustration that an important movement, conciliarism, emerged in the vacuum. Championed by the theologians of the University of Paris (and four church councils held in Paris), conciliarism promulgated the

* Catherine of Siena (1347–80) has since become one of the most venerated saints of medieval Europe.

belief that the church as a whole, as represented in a council, might even depose an errant pope, or even two simultaneously and then elect a single successor. The politics needed to achieve this were tortuous and it was not until 1417 that a council meeting at Constance finally elected a single pope, Martin V (r.1417–31). Martin, a Colonna, from the family that had ousted Boniface, took up residence in his family's palace in Rome in 1420.

The Christian emperors had effectively used councils as a way of controlling the church, notably the Council of Nicaea in 325, the Council of Constantinople in 381 and the Council of Chalcedon in 451, all of which took place under the auspices of the emperor. In the west, a pope could similarly take charge as Innocent III had done at the Fourth Lateran Council in 1215 when he set out a clear agenda to be achieved under his formidable supervision. Now the conciliarists were taking the initiative, determined to create councils as permanent features of church administration even to the extent of being able to depose a pope.

The leading advocate of conciliarism was the chancellor of the University of Paris, Jean Gerson. Gerson had become so frustrated by the infighting between followers of Aquinas, Scotus and Ockham that he had threatened to resign as chancellor of the university in 1400. He recognized that the intricate debates of the scholastics had taken theology way beyond the understanding of the ordinary faithful. Gerson preferred a more emotional approach in which the love of God was allowed to suffuse the mind. The knowledge that mattered was that which touched the heart and stimulated charitable thoughts and, for Gerson, only Bonaventure among the scholastic theologians came close to this. It was the traditional theologians, Gregory the Great, Eusebius (for history) and Augustine, Gerson argued, that should be restored as compulsory reading.[7]

Gerson saw papal absolutism as a medieval deviation from an earlier, more mystical, church that had been led by a dedicated clergy. He could draw on canon law in support of his belief that power could be transferred to others within the church. Gratian, the authority on such matters (see Chapter 4, pp. 91–2), had accepted that there were circumstances in which a pope might be deposed: 'If the pope, neglectful of his own and his brethren's salvation, is proved useless and remiss in his duties and moreover drags innumerable people down with him horde-like away from the good, he will suffer many afflictions in the slavery of hell for all eternity.'[8] Deposition, Gratian went on, was possible if 'he deviates from the faith'. Dante had, of course, portrayed those popes he believed deserved to be in Hell but the practical steps to achieve deposition had never been formulated.

There was never a consistent ideology of conciliarism. From Marsilius at one extreme (who believed that the Christian community as a whole must rule) to councils summoned by the pope and their decrees subject to his approval at the other,* there was a host of possible ways of defining the relationship. It was hard to agree how the members of a council might be selected and how, in the power struggles between rival papal claimants, there might be clear principles for deposing a pope and choosing his successor. Moreover, secular rulers, now more confidently in charge of their kingdoms, would be very sensitive to any revival of church power, whether from popes or councils.

In fact, the popes still held the stronger hand. While the Council of Constance had achieved the restoration of a single pope, Martin V, it failed in its objective, put forward in a decree, *Frequens* ('repeated' or 'frequent'), of making council meetings a permanent feature of church government. Such a 'democratic' vision would only have succeeded if a pope had been ready to renounce his traditional authority and work creatively with a council for future reform, but no pope was prepared to do this. A council that met at Basle between 1431 and 1439 was outmanoeuvred by Pope Eugenius IV (r.1431–47). Eugenius convoked a rival council, which eventually met in Florence – over which he would preside – and negotiated a union between the eastern and western churches, thereby temporarily enhancing papal prestige (see Chapter 14, pp. 331–3). This was such an effective move that some members of the council in Basle even moved over to its rival in Florence. A more confident papacy now took the initiative. The papal bull *Execrabilis*,† issued by Pope Pius II in 1460, declared any appeal above the pope to a council as 'erroneous and abominable'. A century later the Counter-Reformation Council of Trent (1545–63) would meekly offer its canons to the pope for his approval. Conciliarism had failed. The burning of John Hus by the Council of Constance, an execution that Jean Gerson backed, showed that councils were as likely to be as conservatively authoritarian as any pope. (See pp. 386–7 for the burning of Hus.)

After 1420 the popes were busy creating a Renaissance city in the core of ancient Rome, a city still riven with factional infighting and malarial swamps. It was a costly business, culminating in the rebuilding of a vast new St Peter's but sadly destroying many fine ancient buildings such as the remaining façade of the magnificent early third-century

---

* As was to be the case with the Council of Trent (see pp. 546–9).

† Execrable in the sense that it is execrable for a pope to appeal to a council.

Septizodium.‡ While there were many features of a typical Renaissance court, that of the popes was, officially at least, an assembly of a celibate male elite with a pretended supervision of the morals of Europe.§ Many of the cardinals and their retinues set up subsidiary courts from which intrigues over any forthcoming succession were orchestrated, simply confirming the isolation of the clerical hierarchy from the rest of Europe. Between 1417 and 1600 twenty-three of the twenty-six popes would be Italians. Attempts to reform, as in the brief reign of Adrian VI (1522–3) when the bloated bureaucracy and the ambitious building programmes were cut back, offended the artists and wealthy families who had come to depend on papal largesse. The long-running conflict between maintaining the wealth of the church and restoring its spiritual ethos continued.

Increasingly centred on its temporal concerns in Italy, the papacy was becoming irrelevant to the spiritual needs of its flock. The greatest crisis of the century was the conquest of Constantinople by the Ottoman Turks in 1453. Pope Pius II did attempt to call a crusade to rescue his fellow Christians in the east, but its only supporter was Vlad III ('the Impaler'), prince of Wallachia, and the project was abandoned. Yet the continuing expansion of the Ottomans, across Greece and the Balkans and even in raids on Italy,¶ haunted the Christian imagination and added another dimension to religious and political life. The popes were hardly likely to compromise their own authority when Christianity itself appeared to be so threatened from the east.

Church councils were never open to the laity, and yet by the fifteenth century it was among the laity that the healthiest expressions of religious fervour and practical Christianity were to be found. It is easy to decry bishops who never visited their dioceses, but this had the advantage of allowing communities to develop their own forms of religious identity. Whatever Jacob Burckhardt said about the Renaissance as the birth of the individual (see p. 277), this did not extend to religion, where collegiality developed new forms.

If one takes the prosperous trading city of Ragusa, now better known as Dubrovnik, on the coast of what is now Croatia, all visitors remarked on the piety of its citizens.[9] There were forty-seven churches, the Franciscans being the most popular order. There was a town

‡ This was a three-storey fountain built by the emperor Septimius Severus (r. AD 193–211).

§ Many scholars have traced the rise of the courtesan in sixteenth-century Europe to the sexual loneliness of prelates in Rome.

¶ Otranto in Puglia, southern Italy, was taken briefly in 1480 and the skulls of those massacred are still honoured (and displayed in a side chapel) in the city's cathedral.

orphanage and bequests made for the poor, lepers, widows and the ransoming of captives. Italian visitors noted how much more generous the Ragusans were in alms-giving than the typical Italian. The citizens honoured their patron saint, St Blaise, a fourth-century Armenian bishop, known as a healer of sore throats, whose cult was boosted when the lessening in severity of the Black Death was credited to his intervention. The church dedicated to him was in the political, not the religious, centre of the city (just as St Mark's Basilica was in Venice). The canons of the cathedral were in effect the leading members of the city's clergy as the archbishop was appointed by the popes and seldom resident. The canons were drawn from the local aristocracy and had acquired the right to appoint bishops in Ragusa's territories. Foreigners were not allowed to join the city's preaching orders and the city ran its own inquisition. It was not surprising that a visitation from Rome in 1560 lambasted the appointed archbishop, from Calabria in southern Italy, for allowing the city to go its own way.

Ragusa provides a good example of a community where Catholic liturgies and practices were still followed, but largely independently of any direct control by the church hierarchy. In central Europe, Nuremberg, Augsburg, Constance and Zurich were among cities that ran their own religious affairs and in the countryside many princes had similar influence. In Wittenberg, it was the (Catholic!) Elector Frederick who protected Luther from the revenge of the church. In Italy, Venice insisted on appointing its bishops from among members of its own nobility and so sustained its independence for centuries to come. As has been seen in Ragusa, many cities focused their religious devotions on a communal saint; St Mark in the case of Venice, of course. In Florence the feast day of John the Baptist, the city's patron saint, on 24 June, was the high point of the year. The processions finished not at the city's cathedral but at its baptistery, which was venerated as an ancient symbol of the city's past. In Lucca, it was the city that organized the procession and celebration of the *Volto Santo*, the face of Christ that had miraculously appeared on a wooden cross. Religion and a strengthened civic identity went hand in hand. A powerful expression of this was the *Misericordia*, the image, often carried in civic processions, of the Virgin Mary protecting the city faithful under her cloak. In an extraordinary display of divine disharmony, she shelters them from an angry God who is depicted above her.[10] In Siena the riotous Palio, the no-holds-barred horserace

A banner of the confraternity of San Francesco in Perugia, in which the Virgin Mary protects the citizens and city of Perugia from plague. Note the angry Christ figure who rains down plague in the form of arrows.

F.V.R°
·1464·

around the city's central Campo, was and still is held in the honour of the Virgin and the winning rider is still 'crowned' in the cathedral.

It is clear, therefore, that a faltering church did not mean that religious life itself was any less vibrant. In the words of one distinguished scholar of church history: 'Many of the most popular activities of late medieval religion depended on *doing* something, on participation, activity, movement, essentially on experiencing an event fraught with sacral power, more than on learning or understanding a message. Everyone loved a parade.'[11] The Dominican and Franciscan orders permeated the cities through their passionate preaching. They moved religious life away from the enclosed orders and a remote papacy into the streets, where vast crowds were drawn into what became popular theatre. There were power struggles here, between the city authorities who hoped to use preachers for political purposes, and the preachers themselves, who saw their chance to denounce the corruption of rulers. The most successful preacher of the early fifteenth century was the Franciscan Bernardino of Siena (1380–1444), who was able to speak extemporaneously in colloquial Italian for four or five hours to massed audiences as he moved from city to city.[12] Anti-Semitism, condemnation of sodomites and the denunciation of 'vanities' coloured his rhetoric as he exploited his listeners' fears of the Last Judgement. Naturally, the popes were worried by this apparent threat to their authority and Bernardino, summoned to Rome in 1427, narrowly survived being condemned for heresy. In Florence the sermons of the Dominican Remigio de' Girolami (1235–1319) emphasized the achievements of the city to be seen in its wealth, skills and, in his words, 'a civilized way of life'. Aware of his highly educated audience, he extolled Cicero as the exemplar of patriotic citizenship. All the more shameful, therefore, he fulminated, that the city was riven with factional conflict and its wealth dissipated when it could be used for the good of the community. The Franciscans of the city railed against the corruption of the papacy and were prominent supporters of the war of 1375.[13]

There was also vigorous lay participation through the confraternities that became a prominent feature of life not only in Ragusa but throughout Europe in the fifteenth century. They offered a more sober and ritualized approach to religious expression. The most intensely pious of the confraternities arose from the movement known as *Devotio Moderna*.[14] The movement originated in the late fourteenth century in the Netherlands, a highly urbanized part of Europe, where growing resentment over the wealth of the church and the lack of any firm commitment to spiritual renewal led to the laity forming their own communities, of both men and women, that adopted monastic rituals and personal prayer. These eventually became formalized as the Brethren of the Common Life with houses that spread beyond the Netherlands. The movement was, in fact, rooted in the belief that the laity were as capable of achieving sanctity as the clergy. While there was no formal taking of vows or isolation from the local community, life within the houses demanded obedience, chastity and poverty. The brethren engaged in intense study of early texts, especially those of monasticism and asceticism, which were copied out to create a library for each house. The most famous, and influential, product of the movement was *The Imitation of Christ* by Thomas à Kempis (composed sometime between 1418 and 1425). Even suggesting that a mere human being, mired in original sin, as Augustine had described it, and not even a member of the clergy, could imitate Christ was unprecedented. Yet despite its ambivalence towards the institutions and apparent corruptions of the church, the movement remained resolutely Catholic and resisted the lure of the reformers.

The confraternities provided a more mature form of religion than one in which the laity lived in subjection to the church hierarchy. It was the diversity and flexibility of the confraternities that was remarkable. There were often specific requirements for membership, promises to observe correct behaviour and sexual continence. Some confraternities, especially in northern Europe, welcomed both sexes. The founding statute of one Italian confraternity specifically states that the souls of men and women are equal in the eyes of God and hence it was open to all. In Bergamo the confraternity of Misericordia Maggiore was restricted to women and had almost 2,000 members. As the emphasis within confraternities was on repentance and continence, such confraternities provided a home for former prostitutes.[15]

overleaf The *Scuola di San Giovanni Evangelista* carries its relic of the True Cross in the celebration of the feast day of St Mark in 1496. The *scuole* carried out important charitable functions and helped sustain the political stability of the Venetian republic.

The confraternities were especially strong in Venice, where they were known as *scuole*. The five major confraternities, the *scuole grandi*, sucked in as members those wealthier citizens who lacked the noble status that allowed them to participate in the city councils that were reserved to the patriciate. Most came from the manufacturing classes, the makers of textiles and clothing, the builders and sailors of boats, members of the luxury trades, such as books and jewellery, and builders. By the mid-sixteenth century their total membership was some 5–6,000 and their meeting halls were sumptuous expressions of their presence. The

grandest, the *scuola* of San Rocco, has magnificent chambers painted by Tintoretto. The *scuole grandi* ran most of the city's welfare services, even giving out pensions for naval veterans; their success in doing this did much to account for the political stability of the city. On major feast days they were welcomed to participate alongside the doge, nobility and other civic dignitaries in the processions that filled the Piazza San Marco. Yet, while the *scuole* were ostensibly 'Catholic' institutions, their members attending Mass and taking the sacraments, Venice was notoriously the most anti-clerical city in Europe. The Council of Ten, which was responsible for security in the city, even forbade them to have direct links with the church. This highlights the importance of confraternities as an often sophisticated expression of religious beliefs and ideology outside the direct control of the church but compliant with its rituals.

The *scuole grandi* flourished in Venice alongside many smaller and less opulent ones. Many of these had originated as guilds of specialist artisans who put themselves under the protection of a particular monastery or patron saint and then developed a confraternity for their own poor and sick. Expatriate communities would form a *scuola*, as in the case of San Giorgio degli Schiavoni, for the Dalmatian community, with the exquisite paintings by Vittore Carpaccio in their beautiful meeting hall. The blind had their own, the *Scuola degli Orbi*, as did the lame, the *Scuola dei Zotti*. The members of the *Scuola di San Fantin* would accompany criminals to their executions. Other *scuole* had specific devotions as the focus, such as the Eucharist or a favoured saint. In 1521 some 120 *scuole piccole* were on parade with their banners at a doge's funeral. One sign of the spread of confraternities through the laity of the fifteenth century was the use of the vernacular rather than Latin to set out their statutes.

While most scholarship has focused on the confraternities of the cities of northern Italy, they were widespread throughout Europe and responsible for the same variety of functions as those in Italy. By the nature of their membership they had access to sophisticated administrative skills, probably exercised more effectively than the poorly educated lower clergy could manage. This seems to have been grasped by testators who, in the period after the Black Death, left their money to confraternities at the expense of the older religious houses. In Cortona, in Tuscany, for instance, the city elite contributed four times as much to their local hospital, the Santa Maria della Misericordia, as they did to the local bishop, and five times as much as they left to the cathedral chapter. After a magnificent hospital had been built in the centre of the city, the surplus revenue was distributed as food and clothing to the poor.[16] Cortona was now ruled from Florence and Florence was again at the vanguard of the charitable confraternity movement. While there are forty-three confraternities recorded in Florence in 1348, by 1400 there were sixty-eight. In the same year there was a total of 180 confraternities scattered through Florence's territories. The chronicler Villani counted thirty hospitals and hospices in the city with 1,000 beds for the poor and infirm. The confraternity running the Orsanmichele accumulated vast wealth from the pious, especially after the Black Death of 1348, and became in effect the city's most important distributor of poor relief – even the city government gave it an annual grant.* One group of confraternities, the *laudesi* companies, specialized in hymn-singing and between them gave hundreds of Florentines the rudiments of a musical education.[17]

The mendicant orders, the Dominicans and Franciscans, provided important support to the confraternities of Florence. While there were undoubted tensions between the various religious communities, most confraternities proved able to co-exist alongside the religious orders and the cathedrals and parish churches. The Guild of Our Lady at Boston in Lincolnshire, which grew rich on the sales of indulgences, was able to construct a side chapel in one of England's finest parish churches, known with its dominating spire as 'the Boston Stump'.[18] The relationship worked both ways. As Martin Heale has shown in his study *The Abbots and Priors of Late Medieval and Reformation England*,[19] these high-ranking clerics were adopting grander lifestyles and more prominent roles in secular life as well, especially in the decades just before the Reformation. So Cardinal Wolsey in England and Cardinal Ximenes de Cisneros in Spain are early sixteenth-century examples of senior clerics becoming leading figures in royal administrations.

Other developments, such as the retreat of individuals into private devotions, were not threatening to the church. The Books of Hours – anthologies of psalms built around other sacred texts, litanies and the Office of the Dead – were the most sumptuous illuminated manuscripts found in aristocratic households. By the later fifteenth century cheaper editions had spread even among artisans and shopkeepers and especially among women, so disseminating new devotional texts among the laity.[20] It was perfectly possible in hindsight that Europe might simply have evolved in a quasi-Catholic religious network, with the papacy becoming increasingly irrelevant outside Rome and its possessions in Italy.

---

* One of its main sources of income was the sale of candles to pilgrims visiting its miracle-working image of the Virgin.

Yet, however much the confraternities fulfilled local needs, the corruption of the church remained and it was inevitable that direct challenges would be made to its authority.[21] These might spring from anywhere. In England in the 1370s an Oxford lecturer, John Wyclif (or Wycliffe), already distinguished for his work in logic, turned to biblical studies and elaborated a distinctive theology that was to become ever more polemical and radical with time. Wyclif began with attacking the wealth of the church; possession of land by the church should only be temporary and dependent on the righteous living of the occupier. Many clergy, he felt, fell far short of this. Wyclif's approach was hardly controversial when there was already substantial anti-clerical feeling in the English royal court and in parliament. When the pope, Gregory XI, condemned Wyclif in 1377 and ordered the university to arrest him, the university refused. Stung by the condemnation and horrified by the Great Schism of the following year, Wyclif now launched a devastating and comprehensive attack on the church, despite the risk of his extremism losing him many of his early supporters.

By now Wyclif had lectured extensively on the scriptures and claimed that there were hidden truths in them that even a layman could grasp. The scriptures, he argued, together with commentaries on them by such authorities as Augustine, provided the model by which the contemporary church should be judged. The gospels made clear, for instance, that the church had been founded by Christ and Christ remained its head. Nowhere was there any support for a clerical hierarchy or an institutional church, let alone a pope. While Wyclif never mentions Marsilius of Padua by name, it is likely that he drew on *Defensor Pacis* as he uses many of the same supporting texts. Although Wyclif argued, following Augustine's *City of God*, that there was a heavenly church of the elect, it could not be known who was a member and so no member of the clergy could claim to have valid authority, in the giving of sacraments, for instance. Another major target was monasticism, not only for the apparent corruptions Wyclif saw around him but for the way in which it isolated monks from the community of the church. Moreover, in what proved his most provocative argument, Wyclif rejected the doctrine of transubstantiation, claiming that the bread and water might acquire the presence of Christ at the consecration but could not lose their original substance. Material reality could not be destroyed (a view Wyclif may have adopted from the Stoics). Those remaining in the clergy should divest themselves of all wealth and concentrate on following the example of Christ. Similarly, the laity could follow this example and, in the vacuum that would follow the loss of the clergy, religion should be brought under the supervision of the state. Wyclif now faced increasing opposition both within the university and from his aristocratic supporters and he prudently left Oxford. By the time he had been formally condemned by the archbishop of Canterbury, he had already suffered a stroke and he was left to live out his days, dying in 1384.

Wyclif, like Marsilius, had provided theological backing for the view that Christianity should be absorbed into the secular state. In this sense he was part of the wider movement in which the laity could follow a committed religious life within the community. However, Wyclif had gone far beyond the followers of the *Devotio Moderna*, who had never rejected the church. Yet he had no control over the movement that emerged after his death, known conventionally as Lollardy, a dismissive term meaning 'mumbling'. Lollardy began among followers of Wyclif in Oxford and spread from there. However, the Lollards occupied an ambivalent position in society, attracting some sympathy from the literate classes. This made the movement one in which texts, including a Bible translated from the Latin Vulgate, were prominent. The chosen texts were read and reread (as can be seen from the tattered copies, including those of some 300 Bibles that survive) but, as time passed, without the fervour of Wyclif there was little new theology. While the Lollards followed Wyclif in rejecting transubstantiation, the authority of the pope and the power of the priesthood in the giving of sacraments, it was hard to see how they could develop into a cohesive community. It was relatively easy for the English crown to ally itself with the church in hunting down a movement that appeared to be both socially and theologically subversive. Vernacular Bibles were banned in 1407. The Lollards were targeted by general laws against heresies that were eventually consolidated in the *Constitutions* of the archbishop of Canterbury, Thomas Arundel, in 1409. At Oxford a Committee of Twelve drew up a list of 267 defined heresies and ordered the burning of Wyclif's works. By 1412 all members of the university had to make an oath that they would uphold orthodoxy, a sign of the growing conservatism of the university. In 1414 a Lollard revolt led by Sir John Oldcastle was easily crushed (and Oldcastle burned), reinforcing the alliance of church and state against the movement. Yet Lollardy survived underground until the Reformation; Lollards were still being sought out and ordered to recant in the first decades of the sixteenth century. A debate continues as to whether Lollardy was an effective forerunner of the Reformation or a stagnant group who were bypassed by more lively spiritual movements. The Lollards certainly did not have the impetus or powerful support needed to make an effective break with Rome.

Wyclif's most successful 'convert' was a Czech, Jan Hus.[22] While England and Bohemia appeared distant from each other, there was a connection. In 1382 the English king Richard II had married Anne, the daughter of Charles IV, the Holy Roman Emperor who was then also king of Bohemia and who had rebuilt Prague in some splendour, making it one of the great capitals of Europe. Czech students were attending Oxford and bringing theological tracts, including those of Wyclif, back with them.

Hus was dean of the faculty of philosophy at the new Prague university and later, 1412, its rector. Energetic and deeply committed to his cause, he was set on church reform, and Wyclif's works provided the inspiration for his own programme. Hus followed Wyclif in desiring a purer church, centred on direct devotion to Christ and free of the corruptions of wealth and lax morality. The clergy should not be respected unless their lifestyles followed biblical teachings, while women would be given a place as reformers and preachers. The movement spurned relics as an obstacle to direct expressions of faith and indulgences were rejected as a false way of achieving salvation. Yet Hus was never a slave to Wyclif. His views on transubstantiation remained orthodox. It became a symbol of his movement, in fact, that the Eucharist could be taken in both kinds, bread and water now consecrated as the body and blood of Christ. The chalice became the Hussite emblem.

Hus hoped that the king of Bohemia and the ruling council would take responsibility for spiritual life but this assumed that they would be prepared to make a break with the church. Battle lines were being drawn between traditionalist Catholics and followers of Hus, who could draw both on the hunger for reform and an incipient Czech nationalism. The University of Prague was dominated by German theologians who had formally condemned Wyclif's works in 1403. Now the Czechs took over the university, forcing out 1,000 German masters and students. Yet the Catholic authorities stood firm and the king protected the church. This was hardly surprising when one of the papal concessions to the kingdom had been the right of the king to collect money from indulgences, and Hus was demanding they be abolished.

By now, during the Great Schism, there were three popes competing for authority and, one of them, John XXIII (r.1410–15), now regarded as an antipope, excommunicated Hus. Hus refused to quieten down, effectively using a base in the Bethlehem Chapel in the Old Town to press home his message through impassioned preaching. He appealed to the church council that was now meeting at Constance and he was offered free passage there by the emperor. When he arrived he found the conservatives arraigned against him. Trapped by the assembled clerics in defending himself against accusations of views he claimed he had never held, he was sentenced to death and burned.

The burning caused an outburst of fury in Prague, the Czech nobility taking the initiative in what was developing into a nationalist and independent church. As with many reforming movements, it became split between those who wished to effect moderate reforms under the auspices of King Sigismund (r.1419–37) whom they hoped to persuade to support them, and a group of radicals, the Taborites,* who were determined to destroy the church hierarchy and its properties and found a community of Christian purists. When German crusaders, backed by Pope Martin V – and, after some initial hesitation, Emperor Sigismund – entered Bohemia to extirpate what was now a popular movement, the reformers sustained a fragile unity.

In his study of religious warfare, Norman Housley discusses the powerful forces that intensified the Hussite wars. The urge to reform the church was, of course, the most prominent but it was strengthened by the sense, especially among the Taborites, that they were the elect of God. They could ally this to a growing sense of Czech identity (most of the Hussites within the kingdom of Bohemia being ethnic Czechs). Christianity and nationalism were to be important bedfellows after the Reformation. In this the Hussite wars were precursors of new expressions of Christianity that threatened any idea of a universal church.

There would be a long period of struggle, from the martyrdom of Hus in 1415 to an eventual compact agreed at Jihlava in 1436, before a Hussite church was in place across much of Bohemia. As many of the leading Hussites were landed nobles, political stability mattered to them and they were ready to compromise and work with the kings of Bohemia to achieve it. Hence the emerging Hussite church was moderate in tone. It clung to the Czech language as its means of expression and retained communion in both kinds. The Taborites were eventually recognized as a self-governing community. The Catholics survived and were tolerated within Bohemia but much of the church's wealth was lost. The very first use of the term 'Roman Catholic' defined these remaining Catholic communities in a kingdom that had moved beyond papal control. It was an important moment in the process by which independent nationalist churches emerged.

* They were named after the town they founded in southern Bohemia, inspired by the biblical Mount Tabor.

They could also emerge within a Catholic context. Ferdinand of Aragon and Isabella of Castile had married in 1474 but kept the jurisdictions of their kingdoms, which between them covered most of Spain outside Portugal, separate.[23] In 1492 their combined forces conquered the Nasrid emirate of Granada, the last Muslim redoubt in the peninsula. Following the frustrations of the crusades, this *Reconquista* was greeted throughout Christian Europe as a triumph. Yet by now *los reyes catolicos*, 'the Catholic monarchs', had become contaminated by the rigours of the reconquest of the Spanish peninsula. Their independence from any papal restraint ensured they could embark on a ferocious programme of conversion and expulsion of both the Muslims now under their control and the Jews. Isabella had already persecuted the Jews in Castile in the 1480s and now they were to be forced to convert or leave Spain. Nicholas Terpstra, in his *Religious Refugees in the Early Modern World*,[24] argues that her decree marks the true beginning of the Reformation, insofar as it was the first of many mass displacements of religious dissenters. Even those who converted were the subject of continuing suspicion that they were not fully committed to their new faith. Proving the purity of one's blood became a mark of the true Catholic. In 1500 the monarchs' chief inquisitor, Cardinal Cisneros, launched a campaign of forced baptisms on the Muslims of Granada.[25] In a former mosque, 806 were baptized within two days. This went beyond anything the popes condoned, but the popes were happy to acquiesce in the extinction of these rival civilizations, and so too with the later imposition of Catholicism on the new American colonies. The Spanish Inquisition was able to operate under its own rules. While the mystical intensity and harshness of Spanish Catholicism owed much to the *Reconquista*, this was a reminder that secular rulers did not support religious tolerance. Their policy towards non-Christians also provided an unhappy precedent for the treatment of the Indians within the Spanish empire of the New World (see Chapter 22). The concept of religious toleration remained unborn.

* * *

In 1494, as described in Chapter 13, Charles VIII of France had invaded Italy and brought immense disruption with his undisciplined troops. In Florence there was a feeling of intense humiliation when Charles forced an alliance on the city that he had occupied after the expulsion of Lorenzo's son, Piero de' Medici. It was in this political vacuum that Savonarola, a Dominican monk from Ferrara, based in the Medici monastery of San Marco, found himself.[26] Savonarola was deeply learned in the best Dominican tradition and he had even won the favour of Lorenzo de' Medici, who had protected him at San Marco. His sermons of the early 1490s had condemned the Christianity of Florence as superficial but this was standard polemic for the times. However, with Piero expelled, Savonarola was opportunistic in exploiting the resentments over Medici 'tyranny' that had always simmered below the surface of an ebullient city. By December 1494, his charismatic preaching had already made him the most influential figure in Florence and many were anxious that he was stirring up uncontrollable forces. This was something much more dangerous than the sermons of the itinerant Bernardino of Siena.

By 1495 a new government had emerged in Florence with an unwieldy Grand Council of 3,000 citizens that included many artisans. The very first meeting had over 1,700 attendees and, while a typical attendance was between 800 and 1,000, there was nothing like this raucous assembly anywhere else in Europe. It was, as a contemporary commentator, Piero di Marco Parenti, noted, genuinely *populare*.[27] Transformed by the religious ideology of Savonarola, this Florentine Council might be seen as a precursor of the Christian city that John Calvin would found in Geneva in the 1550s. The preacher linked political reform to moral regeneration in a prophetic message that a purified city would earn the special favour of God: 'The revived republic became a moral cause, a central chapter of sacred history and of the Almighty's plan for his

The hanging and burning of Girolamo Savonarola in Florence's Piazza della Signoria, as depicted by a sixteenth-century Italian artist.

people.'[28] So the uniqueness and superiority of Florence was harnessed in a new cause. 'God, for justice also, will increase the city's empire, as he did that of the Romans… since there is good government in the city, it will abound with riches and there will be work for everyone and the poor will earn a living.'[29] It was as if the renunciation of wealth would suddenly bring honour and prosperity back to the community after its humiliation by the French.

The fantasies lasted for three years. Vigilantes roamed the streets, obsessed with finding evidence of sodomy. A campaign was launched against Jews and money-lenders. 'Vanities' were brought into the city squares to be burned. Among them were fine editions of Petrarch and Virgil and sensual statues by Donatello and other masters. Yet despite the mounting hysteria, there were always those who resisted the *frateschi*, as the supporters of Savonarola became known. Many of his attempts to change the laws of the city were blocked or watered down. Only one 'sodomite' was ever executed – the vigilantes who went in search of them were in fact taunted by rival gangs. A few Jews were expelled but the laws against them would eventually be rescinded.

Gradually, the conservatives regrouped. The Borgia pope, Alexander VI (r.1492–1503), may have deserved the denunciations hurled at him by Savonarola but he had the power to order the friar to stop preaching and threaten the city with an interdict that would have closed down religious life and crippled Florence's banking activities. Savonarola defied the pope and was excommunicated in 1497. What proved decisive was the failure of Savonarola's programme to bear any fruit. Gradually, the middle classes of the city abandoned him. Youth gangs, the *compagnacci*, began to heckle his sermons. Challenged to show that he had the favour of God, Savonarola failed. His enemies rounded on him. Tortured and forced to confess that he had always known his prophecies to be false, Savonarola was formally declared a heretic on 23 May 1498. He was hanged and his body burned in the Piazza dei Signoria the same day. Yet his brief reign had shown that a community, while remaining Catholic, could find an ardent republican identity. The Protestant alternative, Calvinism, was to sustain itself more successfully.

The fifteenth century ended in a tumult of religious fervour. It did not help that these were years of poor harvests. A children's pilgrimage to the shrine of Wilsnack* in 1475 seems to have been impelled as much by hunger as by piety. As the year 1500 approached, biblical passages were manipulated to suggest that the turn of the century – in this case representing the halfway point of the second millennium – would usher in the Apocalypse. There was talk of the arrival of 'Spiritual Men' who would herald the coming of a supreme religious leader, perhaps a pope, who would restore the love of God. Apparitions of the Virgin Mary warned that poor harvests or plague were punishment for the wickedness of humanity. Pilgrims flocked to the sites where she had appeared. Rural folk naturally attributed the vagaries of the agricultural year to divine or satanic intervention, and this uncertainty was a cause of profound unrest. There was a surge of belief in witches and demons. In his *A Short Work on Witches (*1505), the Tübingen theologian Martin Plantsch highlighted particular shrines that would provide protection against the forces of evil. But by arguing that God himself had the power to act through devils, Plantsch obscured the distinction between those events that were the work of God and those that were the work of the devil. Campaigns involving the burning of supposed witches were to continue into the sixteenth and seventeenth centuries.

In contrast to this volatility, the popes, the Borgia Alexander VI and Julius II (1503–13), *il papa terribile* (*terribile* in the Italian sense of 'awesome'), did nothing to enhance the prestige of the papacy among the laity. Alexander was notorious for fathering a string of children and elevating his relations to high office, while Julius marked a further step in the secularization of the papacy by leading his own forces into the chaos that had engulfed Italy after the French invasion of 1494. Yet the popes were also playing an important role in invigorating cultural life. The great artists of the day, Bramante, Raphael and Michelangelo, who was commissioned to paint the Sistine Chapel by Julius, were drawn to Rome by papal largesse. The ambitious project of a splendid tomb for Julius that Michelangelo undertook, but never completed, showed two of the most powerful men of the period aiming for supremacy one over the other. Who would be most remembered by the extravagant monument if it had ever been completed: Julius or Michelangelo?

What did follow was one of the great moments in the history of western art. 'Never before or since have two masterpieces of this order been created concurrently in such close proximity,' wrote the

* Wilsnack, in northern Germany, was a shrine which housed consecrated communion wafers which had been found intact with blood on them after their church had been consumed by fire. As they had been consecrated, this was believed by pilgrims to be the actual blood of Christ.

art historians Hugh Honour and John Fleming of Raphael's *Stanza della Segnatura* and Michelangelo's Sistine Chapel.[30] In his plan for the Sistine Chapel, Michelangelo once again tried to outdo Julius by producing a much more ambitious design than anyone had thought a sculptor was capable of and then executed it triumphantly, not least in its blatant adulation of male nudity. (This, and his poems, has led to endless scholarly, and not so scholarly, speculation about Michelangelo's sexuality.[31]) Honour and Fleming echo Giorgio Vasari who, in his celebrated *Lives of the Artists* (first edition, 1550), placed Michelangelo (and Leonardo da Vinci) as among the first painters to surpass the ancients. Vasari not only raised the status of individual artists – he had championed Giotto and Brunelleschi – but he also established art as one of the key features of western civilization to the extent that artists are at the forefront of studies of the Italian Renaissance to this day.[32]

Raphael's portrayal of the Greek philosophers, *The School of Athens*, in the Vatican, explored earlier, shows how deeply embedded humanism had become within Catholic circles. Humanist scholarship had been critical of the church but many humanists also served in the papal bureaucracy, so widespread were the opportunities it offered as it expanded in the fourteenth and fifteenth centuries. The overwhelming economic power of the church, with all the privileges that it brought for those lucky enough to find a position, further hampered any reform despite many calls, especially from the mendicant orders, for a return to the poverty of the early church. The humanists were careful to avoid any open conflict with the church over its teachings but criticism of blatant abuses was acceptable across a wide spectrum of society. The question was whether they could go further and themselves act as a catalyst for reform. The extraordinary achievements and impact of the Dutch scholar Desiderius Erasmus suggested that they might.

* * *

In many ways Erasmus marks a culmination of the intellectual currents that we explored in the chapters on humanism: a distrust of scholasticism, a profound knowledge of both Latin, and by now, Greek, classics, and frustration with the corruptions of the church hierarchy and the superstitions of the masses.[33]

Where Erasmus was exceptional was in his championing of the integration of ancient learning with Christianity, in his application of scholarship to the biblical texts in their original Greek (as against the Vulgate of St Jerome) and in wielding a merciless pen that used the printing presses to spread his message. He was also optimistic about his fellow humans, perhaps to the point of naivety, but in vivid contrast to those who stuck with Augustine's pessimistic view of human nature.

Erasmus was probably born in 1466, in the Burgundian Netherlands, the illegitimate son of parents who both died of the plague when he was still young. Forced to enter an Augustinian order, such were his skills in Latin that he was freed to work as a secretary to a bishop and having acquitted himself well was able to progress to further study. He hated the exclusion demanded by a monastery and managed to achieve papal dispensations from living in one for the rest of his life. Studious but sociable at the universities of Paris and Padua, he travelled throughout Italy and eventually arrived in England for the first time in 1499, where he became close to the humanists John Colet and Thomas More and spent time in Oxford and Cambridge. He taught at Queens' College, Cambridge, between 1510 and 1515. Returning to northern Europe by 1516, he never had a settled home but was sustained by a web of devoted contacts that he maintained through incessant letter-writing. Erasmus was an assured self-publicist, brilliantly overcoming his tainted social background and gaining a Europe-wide audience. His *Adagia*, a collection of Greek and Latin proverbs and sayings, perfect as an introductory text for the classics, was to be found in almost every schoolroom and was expanded from edition to edition.* It was typical that one of his classical mentors was Lucian, a Greek scholar and satirist of the second century AD, like Erasmus an outsider and versatile intellectual who was able to use his wit to ridicule Greek religious life of his day. Among the classical dramatists, the down-to-earth plays of Euripides were Erasmus's favourites.

Irritated by the way that Aristotle had become entangled in scholasticism, Erasmus was also a champion of Plato, whom he felt was the philosopher who was most closely attuned to Christianity and who shared the moral commitment that he believed all humanists should make. The erudite John Colet was an important influence in this respect. 'When I listen to Colet, it seems to me that I am listening to Plato himself' was Erasmus's generous tribute.[34] This was a feature of a movement among Erasmus's coterie of English humanists that denigrated Roman texts in comparison to those of the Greeks. As one follower of Erasmus, the Tudor diplomat Richard Pace, put it: 'Philosophy among the Romans was so feeble that nothing could seem more stupid to learned ears than to compare Roman philosophers to

* There were commentaries attached to the entries, which some scholars see as the foundation of the essay.

the Greeks.'[35] In Oxford in the 1520s a culture war broke out between those supporting Rome or Greece.

Faith, for Erasmus, would always consist of a reordering of the mind towards the divine, independently of all the relics and finery of the medieval church. 'The flesh profits nothing, it is the spirit that gives life' (John 6:63) was a favourite verse. He was led back to one of the Platonist Church Fathers, the Greek Origen of Alexandria (*c.*185–254), who had taught, in contrast to Augustine, that human beings could freely aim for salvation through their own efforts. Origen had argued that eternal punishment in hell was unworthy of a loving God and, if he had been born in a later age, would have ridiculed Augustine's doctrine of original sin, not least because Augustine was unable to read the Greek theological debates in which Origen was steeped. Sadly, Erasmus's championship of Origen was never brought into mainstream debate and the Protestant reformers would prove conservative in their continuing attachment to Augustine.

Having been inspired by John Colet to acquire expertise in Greek, Erasmus realized that there was an urgent need for an authoritative version of the Greek scriptures, the New Testament. The work that resulted, the *Novum Instrumentum Omne* (*The New Testament Revised and Improved,* 1516), later revised as the *Novum Testamentum* (1519), was his masterwork. The western church had ignored the original Greek texts of the gospels, Paul and the Church Fathers ever since Augustine had shown that he did not have the learning to read them. Erasmus translated the Greek into Latin, preserving the original alongside his translation, and in so doing he exposed the inadequacies of Jerome's Vulgate translation. This had startling results. Western theology had been based on Jerome's text, but all too often Jerome had shaped his translation to fit with the church doctrine of his day. The classic case came in Matthew 3:2 where, in the Greek original, John the Baptist had demanded of his audience that they 'repent'. Jerome had translated the Greek word *metanoeite* as *paenitentiam agite* ('do penance'), and this had been used as support for the sacrament of penance. Erasmus replaced Jerome's translation with the Latin *resipicite*, 'repent'.* Could such a sacrament now be justified and did the original Greek texts even support the concept of such a ritual? In another example, Luke 2:51 – 'And he went down with them, and came to Nazareth, and was subject unto them: but his mother kept all these

Hans Holbein's celebrated painting of Erasmus (*c.*1523) captures not only the character of the sitter but the atmosphere of cultivated humanism which he represents.

* The King James Bible followed Erasmus by translating *metanoeite* as 'repent'.

ΠΟΝΟΙ

sayings in her heart' – suggested that the young Jesus had shown his obedience to his parents after they had found him preaching in the Temple. It had been assumed that he had remained in obedience to his mother Mary and that therefore intercessions to Christ could be made through her. This had then been elaborated by medieval theologians to include intercessions through the saints. Erasmus showed that this was an erroneous interpretation of Luke and by doing so 'threatened one of the great principles of medieval western piety – that God could and should be approached through his courtiers the saints'.[36] Again Erasmus, although accepting the orthodox position that Mary remained a virgin even after the birth of Jesus, had to accept that there was no scriptural backing from the original text. The Greek word used by Matthew, *parthenos*, a virgin (1:22), had been a mistranslation from a Hebrew prophecy of Isaiah, which had talked only of 'a young woman'. Subtly, Erasmus had exposed the crucial question that all theologians must tackle: where does authority lie, in the scriptures themselves or in tradition that may have evolved independently of, and even in conflict with, the original texts? Meanwhile, Erasmus's Greek version of the New Testament provided the basis for vernacular translations of the Bible, notably those of Luther (1522) and the acclaimed King James English version (1611).

Erasmus was frustrated by the way the clergy had cut themselves off from the laity, especially through their claim that only the theologically trained could interpret scripture. In a letter of 1519, he noted how the term 'heretic' had been expanded from its original use – of denoting one who dissented from the gospels or agreed articles of faith – to anyone who 'disagrees with some newfangled reasoning thought up yesterday by some sophister in the schools'. In his *In Praise of Folly* (1511), perhaps the most popular of his works, using the figure of Folly to playfully reveal the superstitions and corruption of the church, Erasmus attacked the confusion caused by these schools: 'These subtle refinements of subtleties are made still more subtle by all the varied lies of a scholastic argument, so that you could extricate yourself more rapidly from a labyrinth than from the tortuous obscurities of Realists, Nominalists, Thomists, Albertists, Ockhamists and Scotists.'[37]

While lamenting that even speaking Greek, the language of the gospels and the letters of Paul, was seen as suspicious, Erasmus argued that it was in the works of the Greek Fathers that purity and beauty of language were to be found: 'The great [Greek] Christian writers of the past were able to treat even the most arid subjects with a beautiful prose.' He explored the writings of the theologians who had been lost to the western tradition, including another Platonist, Clement of Alexandria, and the father of eastern monasticism, Basil the Great.

The vision that Erasmus had for Christians was as a community who absorbed the scriptures as part of their daily working life, thereby achieving what he called *consensus fidelium*, the collective wisdom of the Christian congregation. This was the theme of his *Enchiridion Militis Christiani* (*Handbook of the Christian Knight*) which followed the tradition of the *Devotio Moderna* in championing a faith centred on Christ. The Christian did not require any intermediary between himself and his maker; nor was there any need to become lost in mysticism. Recognizing that the authority of the papacy was irretrievably damaged (a text, *Julius exclusus e coelis*, attributed to Erasmus suggested that Pope Julius II would be shut out of heaven when he arrived there), he argued instead, on Platonic principles, that society should be run by peace-loving and idealistic princes. But such rulers were nowhere to be found in the strife-ridden Europe of the sixteenth century. The high hopes Erasmus had of the young Emperor Charles V were to be dashed in 1527, during the Habsburg–Valois wars, when mutinous troops from Charles's army, many of them Lutheran, ransacked and pillaged the city of Rome.

Nor were the laity likely to make a commitment to their religious lives as Erasmus would have liked, especially as he believed that they were easily led astray by the mass of shrines clamouring for their attention. In one of his most engaging texts, *Pilgrimage for Religion's Sake* (1526), Erasmus narrates a visit made by one Ogygius to the shrine dedicated to the Virgin Mary at Walsingham in eastern England, followed by one to Canterbury, where the martyr Thomas Becket lay buried. Ogygius, describing his pilgrimage after his return, ridicules the pilgrims for being manipulated into parting with their money and for being so easily convinced that the saints' relics on display originated in early Palestine. Walsingham boasted a replica of the house of the Virgin Mary in Nazareth, which according to legend had been revealed in a vision to the shrine's founder, a noblewoman named Richeldis de Faverches. Ogygius was also shown a phial of Mary's breast milk together with the thighbone of St Peter.

Erasmus and the humanists of his generation still dreamed of an ideal Roman church, the restoration of dignity to a degenerate Catholicism. Imaginative and open-minded though he was, Erasmus could not conceive of an institution that was starting afresh. There was a psychological chasm between Erasmus and the reformers. Typically for a humanist, Erasmus was disciplined and resistant to upheaval.

He understood that the meaning of texts was often obscure and that therefore disputes over scriptural meanings would be inevitable. To insist on one interpretation and to persecute those who disagreed was unacceptable – a point that would be elaborated by seventeenth-century philosophers such as John Locke. Erasmus dreaded the confusion that a complete breakdown of traditional authority would bring. Moreover, the reformers presented human beings as perpetually anxious, caught in the turmoil of their original sin. Calvin, in particular, intensified the existential terrors of human life by insisting that his followers had to be on constant guard against the commission of sin. Erasmus was, in the traditions of ancient philosophy, more concerned with finding intellectual satisfaction and emotional peace. In his later years, he came across the second-century BC pagan philosopher Epicurus, who had regarded the achievement of *ataxia*, a tranquil mind free of worries, as the aim of life. Erasmus took the daring step of linking Christ to Epicurus, as Lorenzo Valla had done before him (see p. 294). Erasmus believed that Christians had a right to be happy and had the means in their free minds to achieve this. Luther and the Protestants argued that, on the contrary, as inheritors of original sin Christians could not afford to be at ease.

As Luther's revolution unfolded, Erasmus was horrified and his last years before his death in 1536 were unhappy ones. While there was no chance of his leaving the church, he was attacked by Catholics for having instigated a Reformation that went well beyond anything he had envisaged. The church even went so far as to place his books on the *Index Librorum Prohibitorum* (*Index of Prohibited Books*). Even today, one encounters traditional Catholics who argue that Erasmus 'caused' the Reformation. Erasmus had indeed created his own fame through his relentless propagandizing, but he had never called for the overthrow of the church, only its unworthy servants and distorted theology. While his uncluttered erudition and the brilliance of his attacks on superstition and corruption made him stand out as the key scholarly personality of his times, Erasmus's intellectual broad-mindedness, together with the eclecticism and penetration of his knowledge, made him unsuited to any leadership role. Unlike Luther and Calvin, he was seldom dogmatic; in the best traditions of humanist scholarship, he had the confidence to leave his ideas open to debate.

Another development was the focusing of veneration in new directions. In her book *Christian Materiality* the scholar Caroline Walker Bynum has explored the emotional fascination with material objects, notably relics and images of the suffering of Christ, in the late medieval period. They added new dimensions to Christianity, in particular the belief that the miracle-working activity of a potent relic was a symbol of the triumph of life over death, good over evil.[38] This was one more feature of a Christianity that was becoming less centralized.

* * *

Traditional histories of the Reformation often treat the emergence of Luther in 1517 as a shock event or a sudden reaction to the corruption of the church. Yet Luther was hardly unique in complaining of the corruption of the Catholic Church. Calls for reform of a wealthy and bloated church had been made for centuries without much success. As will be seen, it may have been no more than chance that it was Luther who set off the collapse of papal authority. One reason why the Reformation spread so quickly is that he and Calvin were able to exploit the lack of popular support for Catholic authority. This does not mean that religious belief in itself was in decline before the Reformation; as this chapter has shown, there was intense religious activity within local communities. 'The Reformation', writes Peter Marshall, 'was neither a detached and unheralded post-medieval arrival, nor simply a reaction against the religious culture of the Middle Ages. It was itself a flowering of late medieval developments, seeded and germinated in the political, cultural and religious soil of the decades around 1500.'[39] Much of this activity was concerned with the efficient administration of the welfare of the sick and the poor, the carrying out of Christian duties, as the quotation that opens this chapter suggests.

The narrative of the Reformation will be continued in Chapter 23. The important question is whether Lutheranism and Calvinism stifled certain healthy and decentralizing developments in Christianity that had been successful largely because they reflected – and responded to – local needs. Meanwhile, it is time to consider the extraordinary widening of the European consciousness brought about by the voyages of discovery – undertakings born of a growing curiosity about the world and of a desire for increased trading opportunities, which were all part of the gradual awakening of the western mind.

Defining Global Space: The Mapping of the New World

A general delineation of the various lands and islands, including some of which the ancients make no mention, discovered lately between 1497 and 1504 in four voyages over the seas, two commanded by Fernando of Castile, and two by Manuel of Portugal, most serene monarchs, with Amerigo Vespucci as one of the navigators and officers of the fleet, and especially a delineation of many places hitherto unknown. All this we have carefully drawn on the map, to furnish true and precise geographical knowledge.

The legend on the Waldseemüller World Map, 1507[1]

In the preface, I described the enormous impact that the discovery of Ptolemy's *Geographike* had on the mapping of the Earth's surface. If the *Geographike* was to prosper it had to dislodge two earlier types of map, the *mappae mundi* and the portolan charts, both of which were very different in conception from Ptolemy's map.

The function of *mappae mundi* was to help the faithful to understand the world as God had created it based on the teachings of the Bible and ancient traditions.[2] Naturally, the cities of Rome and Jerusalem are highlighted, but Asia is always placed at the top as the original home of Christianity (so making east rather than north the 'top' of the map). Within Asia, Paradise is represented as if it was on earth, with the four rivers, Euphrates, Tigris, Pishoon and Gihon, running outwards from it. Jerusalem appears just below. Land predominates, with the Mediterranean and the Black Sea little more than a large L-shaped lake between Asia, Europe and Africa. Because Aristotle (and later Ptolemy) had argued that the world must be symmetrical in form, consisting of four pieces of land, a separate region is often added in the south, and thus on the right of the *mappa mundi*, cut off from Africa by a stretch of water. In order to balance the other three continents this southern region was believed to be equal in size to them. In Ptolemy's time, this southern continent was only a hypothesis, and Ptolemy does not include it on his map. Al-Idrisi, in the twelfth century, had shown Africa as one enormous land mass extending beyond his boundaries. Typically, a *mappa mundi* is presented as a circle with sea around the edges, so enclosing the three continents of the assumed world, or four if Aristotle was followed. Some of the *mappae* drew on Aristotle's division of the globe into five *klimata*, or zones, with one torrid zone across the centre, a temperate zone either side of this and a frigid zone at the poles (the original Greek is the root of the English word 'climate').*

A *mappa mundi* would have been of little practical assistance to those departing on pilgrimage or crusade to Jerusalem. Their best bet would have been to head for the port of Venice, which possessed both the ships and the maps needed to make a journey to the eastern Mediterranean. By the thirteenth century, having helped bring about the collapse of the Byzantine empire in the Fourth Crusade of 1204 (see

* The best surviving example of a *mappa mundi* is the large parchment dating from the early fourteenth century that is now on display in Hereford Cathedral in the west of England. It is so crammed with images, including a Last Judgement and references to the crusades that had just ended in failure, that it is virtually unrecognizable as a map of the known world.

Chapter 4, p. 100), Venice had grabbed access to the empire's best ports and made itself a wealthy maritime power. According to one estimate, as many as 10,000 Venetian merchants were active in Constantinople in the thirteenth century. These traders, together with their rivals in other north Italian port cities such as Genoa and Pisa, began plotting charts that showed the ports and safe anchorages around the coast of the Mediterranean and the Black Sea. In the west, the Genoans charted the Straits of Gibraltar and the Atlantic coast of Spain. These nautical maps are known as portolan charts.[3]

The portolan charts were based on compass settings. The cartographer would take a set landmark and sail to another known mark, recording the compass bearing between the two. He would also estimate the distance separating the two places. Then he would place a compass 'rose' with thirty-two points on the parchment to mark the starting point. He would use the relevant point on the 'rose' and the estimated distance to the next landmark to draw a straight line to it, the rhumb line (possibly from the Portuguese word *rumbo*, meaning 'a direction'). Gradually, new landmarks would be introduced along the shoreline and their names written in. Eventually, the whole mapped coastline would be bristling with the names of ports and other features. Armed with the portolan chart, the sea captain could then follow his compass from one landmark to another. Medieval mapmakers were aware of magnetic declination, which created an angle of between 7 and 11 degrees from north to west on a compass.† Allowance was made for this in the portolan charts. The drawback of the portolan charts was that, as the sailor was following a straight compass line on what was in reality a curved surface, they were accurate only over short distances. This hardly mattered in the Mediterranean, where landfalls were close together, but things became trickier on the Atlantic coast of Africa. Some islands were several hundred miles distant from the African shoreline, and deviations were inevitable. A rhumb line on the flat surface of a map would, if followed on sea and land, eventually deposit the traveller at the poles.

overleaf Portolan charts used compass settings to map the locations of ports and other features of the Mediterranean and Atlantic coastlines. This example, showing the Mediterranean and the Western part of the Black Sea, dates from the first half of the seventeenth century.

In the fourteenth century the portolan charts became very sophisticated as sailors continuously revised them on the basis of their sailing experiences. These advances in maritime knowledge allowed

† Because magnetic north and geographical north do not coincide, there is an angular deviation of a compass needle from true north.

EVROPA
AMERICA
AFRICA

ASIA

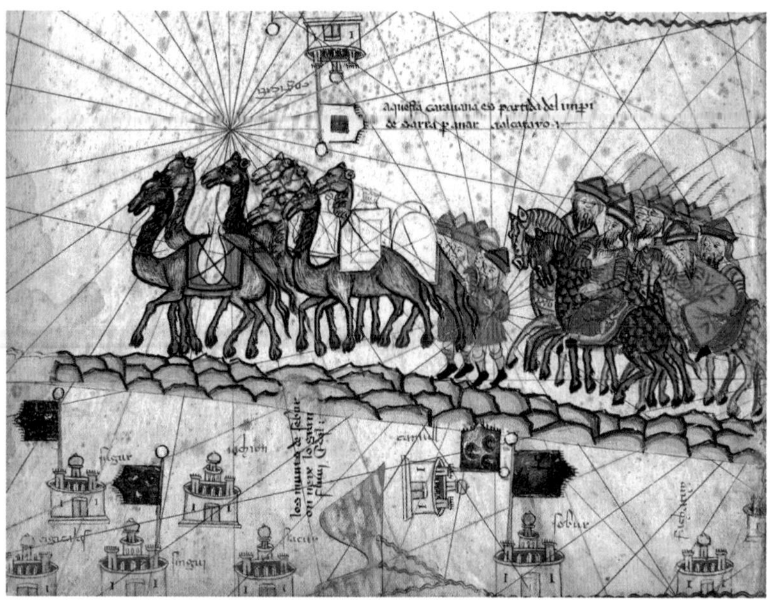

The travels of Marco Polo, legendary or otherwise, gripped the medieval imagination. The extraordinary *Catalan Atlas* of 1375 depicts his progress in the east.

the sumptuous *Catalan Atlas*, made in 1375 for the future king of France, Charles VI (and still in the Bibliothèque nationale in Paris), to represent such far-flung locations as the Canary Islands (off the Atlantic coast of what is now Morocco) and the British Isles (clearly recognizable as such) in the west, together with the entirety of continental Europe, and, in the east, large parts of Asia as far as China.[4] The Mediterranean and Black Sea were by now accurately plotted, but, although the *Atlas* was able to draw on the bestselling travels of Marco Polo, published in the late thirteenth century, for its representation of China, much of that land remained obscure. The Indian Ocean, well known to Roman traders, was now, after the Arab invasions and papal restrictions on trade with Muslims, beyond the reach of the European mariners so mapmakers had to rely on Arab sources.

Ptolemy's instructions for composing maps in his *Geographike Hyphegesis*, rediscovered in 1295 by Maximus Planudes (see p. 2), would provide an essential framework within which to accurately map the world beyond the Mediterranean. In 1477 the very first printed edition of any atlas, Ptolemy's *Geographike* with maps included, was rushed out in Bologna to beat a rival project under way in Rome. Printed in black and white, and embellished with some imaginative waves on the seas and winds blowing from the maps' edges, the printed *Geographike* was part of a revolution that would transform people's knowledge of the world's geography. The rush to be first in print led to numerous typographical errors and other infelicities, but – as the opportunities opened up by printing were more fully grasped – further progress in the printing of maps and atlases would soon be made. In 1468 a German cartographer, Nicolaus Germanus, had created a richly coloured map of Ptolemy's *Geographike*. This incorporated a map of Scandinavia – probably the work of a Danish geographer named Claudius Clavus – which the Frenchman Guillaume Fillastre had included in an earlier codex of Ptolemy's work. When Nicolaus's map was printed in 1482, its wide distribution allowed Europe's full extent to become known to a large audience for the first time. It was also the earliest map to be coloured in by artists after the printing had been completed. Typically, they defined the contrast between sea and land by rendering the former in blue. Soon magnificently coloured maps were being published. They were based on woodcuts that relied heavily on the skills of the carvers to give exact delineations of the land masses. The invention of printing now allowed text to be added to the maps.

In 1450 perhaps 15 per cent of the world's shorelines was known to Europe's sailors. Much of this was still poorly mapped, and knowledge of it was based on travellers' tales that were not always reliable. Essentially, the scope of mid-fifteenth-century geographical knowledge was little more than it had been at the height of the Roman empire. In 1450 very few Europeans had ever seen a map. By the start of the seventeenth century, however, millions of them had been printed and few Europeans would not have recognized what a map represented. There can be few more dramatic cases of the reawakening – and for the most part the awakening for the first time – of the western mind.

overleaf Henricus Martellus's world map of 1489 was the first to show the southern tip of Africa, following the rounding of the Cape by Bartholemeu Dias in early 1488. As depicted here, Africa in fact extends too far south.

Other sources were forthcoming. In 1439 western knowledge of the geography of the classical world had been enhanced considerably by the arrival in Florence – in the baggage of the Byzantine scholar Plethon, who was attending the ecclesiastical council in that city – of a significant work of scholarship of the first century AD. The *Geographia* of the Greek polymath Strabo (64/63 BC–*c.*AD 24) offered a wide-ranging survey of the known world, covering the whole of Europe and large tracts of western Asia and reflecting on how different environments influence the peoples who live in them. Plethon's Greek text was translated into

Mare glaciale
OCEANVS
mare gotticum
LIVONIA
norvegia
OCCIDETAL
mare germanie
OCEANVS
TARTARIA
pontus euxinus
hircanum f. caspium
MARE
MEDITERRANEVM
AFRICA
insule portugalensium
rio de gambia
rio grande
1489
SINVS PERSICVS
mare arabicum
ARABIA
Mare rubrum
MONTES LUNE

Hec est vera forma moderna
Affrice secundum descriptionem
Portugalensium inter mare
Mediterraneum et oceanum
meridionalem

Ad hunc usque montem qui vocatur niger
pervenit classis serenissimi regis portugalie cuius
classis prefectus erat diegus canus qui in memo
riam rei erexit columpnam marmoream cum
crucis insigne et ultra processit usque ad
Serram Pardam que distat ab monte nigro
mille miliaria et hic moritur

ALIS
tartaria per totum
SINVS GANGETIC
CEANVS
NDICVS
ERIDIONAL

Latin in 1458 and soon became a standard addition to Ptolemy.

In the fifteenth century the Portuguese unexpectedly emerged as the most successful traders and navigators in Europe. By finding new routes to the east, via Africa, they would help to fill in some of the blank spaces on the Ptolemaic maps.[5] Historically, Portugal was a vulnerable state with relatively few resources and a small population. Its larger neighbour Castile was a persistent threat to its independence and it had no tradition of international trading. Its nobility was powerful and its kings correspondingly weak. However, under Portugal's second royal dynasty, the house of Aviz – established towards the end of the fourteenth century – Portugal became a significant European and global power. The Aviz proved to have clear objectives, and its monarchs reigned for long enough to be able to effect them. There were only five monarchs of the dynasty between 1385 and 1521 (as against sixteen popes) and they were committed to commercial expansion, not least to give them the wealth to challenge the nobility. Prince Henry (1394–1460), the third son of King Joao I (1385–1433) and his English wife Philippa, is often seen as the catalyst for Portuguese expansion. Henry, known to the English as 'the Navigator', participated in the capture of the first Portuguese overseas possession, Ceuta, on the coast of north Africa, in 1415. From Ceuta, Henry went on to explore the north-west coast of Africa. Soon he was building up his resources – and more would flow in from his appointment in 1420 as Grand Master of the Military Order of Christ, a successor to the Knights Templar in Portugal. Intelligent, well educated and an explorer by temperament, Henry's thirst for expansion combined a mission for conversion of Muslims with an appetite for gold and readiness to capture slaves. The numbers of these were few, but the precedent established the brutal exploitation of human resources as a corollary of European imperialism. Henry and the kings of Portugal who followed his father gradually won control over the Azores and Madeira and the maps of these islands became ever more accurate. The Canary Islands came under Castilian control by the end of the fifteenth century.

A powerful incentive was the desire to know what lay beyond Cape Bojador, a headland on the Atlantic coast of what is now Western Sahara, whose shifting winds and currents had wrecked many land-hugging ships. Cape Bojador was a formidable obstacle, seen as the dividing line between the inhabited world and a mysterious southern world beyond. Henry's mariners passed the Cape for the first time in 1434, using the navigational technique that would come to be known as the *volta do mar* ('turn of the sea'), which involved sailing further out to sea in order to catch more favourable winds. Gradually, Portuguese voyages ventured further down the coast of western Africa, establishing trading posts and bringing back gold and slaves. The coast was soon plotted as far south as Sierra Leone and Guinea where it turned eastwards. Exploration continued during the reign of King Joao II (r.1477–95).

Ptolemy had assumed that Africa was one enormous land mass and that there was therefore little point in travelling south in search of a route to India. Other ancient sources, including Strabo – who became increasingly popular as an 'authority' in the sixteenth century – and Pliny the Elder in his *Natural History*, disagreed. Reports reached Lisbon that a crossing of the southern end of Africa had been made from the east. Joao tried to establish the truth of these rumours by sending men overland across Africa in the hope of reaching the Indian Ocean. Portuguese adventurers disguised as Arab merchants attempted to make their way across land from Alexandria in Egypt to the Red Sea. Their journeys confirmed the richness of the Indian spice trade and encouraged Joao II to launch a new series of voyages down the west African coast. It was Bartholemeu Dias, a noble of the royal household, who had been trading in Guinea in the 1470s, who finally rounded Africa's southern Cape – the 'Cape of Storms' for Dias, optimistically renamed the 'Cape of Good Hope' by Joao – in early 1488. Dias's voyage revealed that the coastline ran eastwards and then northwards. There was now a potential sea route from Europe to the Far East.

The news spread fast. Only a year later, 1489, a world map by the German Henricus Martellus would show the tip of southern Africa and clear water around it leading directly into the Indian Ocean, even though Martellus extended the Cape 10 degrees too far south. While he relied on Ptolemy for the bulk of his geographical information, Martellus's map was proof that new discoveries were rendering some of Ptolemy's claims obsolete. Empirical knowledge was trumping the authority of antiquity, even if the world maps were now a combination of a creative relationship between old and new.

In 1492 a citizen of Nuremberg, Martin Behaim, who knew of Henricus Martellus's map, and thus of the southern tip of Africa, and who himself had sailed along the coast of Africa, created the earliest known globe, the *Erdapfel* ('the earth apple'), which is still on display in the Germanisches Nationalmuseum in Nuremberg.* Behaim

* In his introduction to his map, al-Idrisi mentioned that Roger II ordered the making of a silver sphere which he, al-Idrisi, would use as the basis for his description of the world.

followed Ptolemy in overestimating the breadth of the three known continents, thus making the Atlantic much smaller than it really is, placing legendary islands in its midst and giving the false impression that Japan, known then as Cipango, and from there India, could be reached easily from the west. This representation of the world would fire the imagination of an exuberant and obsessive sailor from Genoa, Christopher Columbus, who was pestering Queen Isabella of Castile to finance an expedition to find out if the Indies could be reached by sailing west.

By now the Portuguese voyages in the Atlantic had stimulated changes in shipbuilding. Galleys, which could use oarsmen and sails in combination, had been part of Mediterranean life for centuries. However, in hot climates it was not feasible to keep large numbers of oarsmen supplied with the water they required on long sea voyages; furthermore, rough seas were clearly dangerous to a ship with openings for oars close to the waterline. In the Atlantic a more robust boat, able to use its sails effectively to take advantage of shifting winds and with a small draught so that it would not run aground in uncharted waters, was vital. One type of medieval ship, the cog, a sturdy boat with a large hold, which had been widely used since the twelfth century, could ride the seas but its square sail made it manoeuvrable only with a following wind. The caravel, developed by the Portuguese during the fifteenth century from Atlantic coast fishing boats, was slimmer and easier to steer and its large lateen sail was able to exploit shifting winds. Yet the lateen sail needed a large crew to handle it and this meant less space for cargo. Its long boom, extending in front of the mast, also made the ship's bow vulnerable to being driven under the waves. This led to the reappearance of square sails, which allowed a forecastle to raise the bow well above the waves. Eventually, the carrack emerged – a large cargo ship with square sails that were rigged to make them more flexible to shifting winds. The stability of the carrack, which enabled cannons to be mounted on the decks, gave it an immense advantage over its competitors, especially Arab traders in the eastern seas. Yet the very size of the carrack made it vulnerable in high winds. Thousands of these ships would be lost, many of them driven onto a lee shore, in the centuries to come. When a carrack managed to return home safely from the Atlantic, however, there were fabulous fortunes to be made from the contents of its commodious hull.

In 1492 Christopher Columbus finally persuaded Ferdinand of Aragon and Isabella of Castile to finance a small expedition across the Atlantic.[6] He had failed to convince Joao II in Portugal but it may well have been the success of Bartholomeu Dias in opening up an alternative route to India, one which would be under the control of the Portuguese, that impelled the Spanish monarchs to fit Columbus out with a carrack, the *Santa Maria*, and two caravels, with a total crew of eighty-seven men. Columbus believed, or had manipulated travellers' tales and Ptolemaic maps to make his patrons believe, that the crossing was very much shorter than it was. In fact, having left Spain in early August 1492, it was mid-October before Columbus reached the Bahamas archipelago. Their exact landfall in the Bahamas is unknown, but Columbus continued his voyage, landing on Hispaniola and Cuba.

Those expeditions that returned home with new discoveries to report quickly became famous. While still at sea on his way home Columbus had written letters to Ferdinand and Isabella and Luis de Santangel, an Aragonese official who had given support to the expedition. Columbus arrived back in Spain in March 1493 and by April his letter to Santagel had been printed and news of 'the islands of India beyond [i.e. to the east of] the Ganges recently discovered', which had been claimed for the Spanish crown, spread across Europe. The letter emphasized how suitable were the resources of the islands for exploitation and how ready its people for conversion. The parameters of Spanish rule in the Americas were already being defined.

Columbus's discoveries revived the traditional hostility between Spain and Portugal, and for a few months in 1493 war seemed imminent. Their rulers realized, however, that a vicious war over trade routes would be counterproductive. Spain had the support of Pope Alexander VI, who was a native of Aragon. The Portuguese knew the loss of their African possessions would be disastrous. The ensuing treaty, of Tordesillas, signed in June 1494, by drawing a line of demarcation 370 'leagues' west of the Cape Verde Islands (a nautical league is 3.452 miles), protected all the Portuguese-owned islands and trading posts along the African coast. This treaty was endorsed by Pope Julius II in 1506. What was not known at the time of the signing of the treaty in 1494 was that the eastern part of what would later be Brazil jutted out across the line and so could legitimately be claimed by Portugal when Pedro Álvares Cabral landed on the coast in April 1500. Cabral was searching for a way to the Indies that would avoid the Arab merchants who thronged the route around Africa from the west. He claimed the territory for the Portuguese crown, but made no attempt to settle the coastline that he had landed on. After exploring the Brazilian coast, Cabral headed back east across the Atlantic.

There had, in fact, been some hesitation in exploiting the discovery of Dias. It was not until 1497 and a new king, Manuel I, that the impetuous and ruthless Portuguese mariner, Vasco da Gama (*c.*1460s–1524), embarked on a hazardous voyage that took him round the Cape, up the eastern coast of Africa and then across to India, as far as the spice trading centre at Calicut (in the modern Indian state of Kerala).[7] Da Gama sailed on two further expeditions to India, dying of malaria in Cochin in 1524 during his third voyage. Despite his achievement, the journey from Portugal to India and back – the longest sea voyage known at that time – was too perilous for immediate trading exploitation. The route had entered western consciousness, nonetheless. In 1519 a sumptuous atlas of Portuguese possessions was presented as a gift to Manuel I.*[8] It shows the coast of Kerala bristling with names just as on a traditional portolan map, the Indian Ocean crowded with shipping and the Indian subcontinent filled with beautifully drawn animals – including elephants – trees and cities (see pp. 452–3). 'Library' atlases such as this were prestige objects.

What was left unresolved between Spain and Portugal was where the demarcation line of the Treaty of Tordesillas would run if it described a full circle around the globe. It was hard enough to plot it in the Atlantic, let alone where it would run on the other side of the world. In 1519 Charles V, the Habsburg emperor and – as Charles I – the new king of Spain, was persuaded by the Portuguese mariner Ferdinand Magellan (1480–1521), who had fallen out with the king of Portugal, to allow him to sail westwards in a search for the Spice Islands. While the eastern coastline of both North and South America were by now beginning to be accurately plotted – John Cabot, a citizen of Venice, had explored the coast of Newfoundland in a series of English-funded expeditions in the 1490s – it was still not clear whether a way through could be found further to the west. (The search, in the north, for the north-west passage, was to consume lives for centuries.) Magellan was convinced that there was a way through to the south and he was proved right. In late 1520 he sailed through what are now the Straits of Magellan at the tip of South America into an ocean that he found 'pacific' and then onwards, over a vaster stretch of sea than he had ever imagined, to the Philippines (named as such later, after Charles V's son, Philip II of Spain) where he was killed in a skirmish with natives. After Magellan's death, Juan Sebastián Elcano took command of his carrack, the *Victoria*, which was the sole surviving ship to limp home

* It is known as the Atlas Miller, from the name of its donor to the Bibliothèque nationale in Paris in 1897.

to Spain in 1522 to complete the world's first circumnavigation. There was a subsequent agreement, in 1529, that a new line should be drawn that left the Philippines Spanish and the Moluccas, the Spice Islands, subject to Portugal.

The constant flow of new discoveries kept cartographers busy. The Waldseemüller map of 1507 was the achievement of a German monk, Martin Waldseemüller, working in Lorraine, then part of the Holy Roman Empire, whose duke, René, had patronized a group of printers and mapmakers.[9] They had published the travel diaries of the Florentine explorer Amerigo Vespucci, whose colourful accounts of the 'wild inhabitants' of what is today Brazil had become very popular, especially in Germany (see p. 499). The term *Mundus Novus* ('the New World') was publicized in 1503 in a pamphlet in Latin allegedly by Vespucci.† This suggested, correctly, that these lands were not India but something apart. Waldseemüller and his colleagues compiled the *Cosmographiae Introductio* (*An Introduction to Cosmography*) which set out 'certain necessary principles of geometry and astronomy', together with a map showing the four voyages that Vespucci had written about. The authors then announced that, as Vespucci had discovered so much of the 'fourth continent', it was only right to name it Amerigo in his honour. The name has stuck. In the map that contains the name for the first time on the shorelines of what is South America, Ptolemy with a quadrant faces Vespucci with a pair of compasses, the wisdom of the ancient world meeting the discoveries of the new. Contemporary sources suggest that 1,000 copies of the map were printed, but so far only one has ever been found, this by a German Jesuit, Joseph Fischer, in a castle in south-west Germany in 1901. In 2003 the United States Library of Congress paid the castle's aristocratic owner $10 million for this single printed page, the first time on a map that part of 'America' had been shown as separate from Asia.

The quadrant and the compasses are indicative of a more scientific approach to 'cosmography', as the study of the Earth and the stars and their relationship to each other was termed. The new discoveries gave the cosmographers an elevated status; they were responsible for creating a uniform perspective of the universe. Many attempted to elaborate this with a chronology of the Earth's history. Time needed to be measured, not only on the mundane level of a clock ticking with some accuracy, but to describe the full extent of God's creation and the possible timing of the end of the world with its expected Last Judgement. Both

† In an earlier authentic letter by Vespucci the term was in Italian.

Portugal and Spain set up administrative departments that gathered maps, received accounts of voyages and sent out expeditions to make new measurements. The 1529 world map by the Portuguese-born Diego Ribero, head cosmographer of the Spanish *Casa de Contratación de las Indias* ('House of trade of the Indies') in Seville, was the most accurate known to that date. There is no mention now of Amerigo but Vespucci's title *Mundus Novus* is adopted for Spanish America. The map has illustrations of scientific instruments, quadrants and mariners' astrolabes, as well as the tables of scales for measuring latitudes.

The most popular handbook for measurement, however, did not come from Spain or Portugal but from Landshut (now in Bavaria) where a German mathematician, Petrus Apianus, had published his *Cosmographicus liber* (*Book on Cosmography*) in 1524. Apianus was obsessed with the precise measurement of borders, those between land and sea, plains and mountains, rivers and land. To identify their exact positions it was necessary to establish the markers between lines of longitude (meridians) and latitude as well as the divisions between climatic zones. There was the added problem of how to represent a sphere accurately on a two-dimensional surface. Apianus was one of the first to illustrate the land and seas as being part of one Aristotelian sphere, not two (water above earth), as Sacrobosco and earlier astronomers had believed (see p. 176). This was the inevitable result of the discovery of the New World, which rendered obsolete the belief that water gathered to a greater height outside the known land mass.[10] Apianus's work marked another step in the representation of the world in mathematical terms and technology followed suit. The *Cosmographicus* illustrated all the scientific instruments of his day that were used to measure the angles of stars, sun and moon. These included armillary spheres, originally conceived in Hellenistic times, which had now developed into beautifully crafted models of the Earth with the stars orbiting around it (a view of the universe that was soon to be challenged by Copernicus's discovery of the solar system).

One of Apianus's proposals was to use the relationship between the moon and the stars to plot the position of ships at sea using the tables of a nautical almanac. The problem remained the difficulty of taking precise measurements on board a moving ship. It was also grasped that longitude could not be measured without an accurate timepiece showing the time of departure from the home port, which could then be set against the time of midday taken from the sun at its greatest height. Each hour of difference would mark 15 degrees of longitude, but it would be 200 years before the English clockmaker

John Harrison made a marine chronometer that was both sufficiently accurate and was not disturbed by the motion of the sea. Failing to know exactly where you were remained a hazard.

Gerard Mercator (1512–94) will always be remembered for his famous projection of the world's surface that overcame the deviations of the rhumb line.[11] However, Mercator achieved very much more than this. He never travelled very far from his birthplace in what is now Belgium and is not known to have ever stepped aboard an ocean-going ship. He had a good humanist education (he adopted the name 'Mercator' – 'merchant' – as a Latinized version of his birth name) and learned to write an elegant italic script that was to become a celebrated feature of his maps. But he was brought up in a Europe that was now polarized between Catholic and Protestant. While cartographers in the early part of the century had been able to draw maps without interference by the church, now the way that the world was represented was scrutinized for any bias towards one denomination rather than another. Lutherans expected maps to highlight the glories of God's creation, the Holy Land and the travels of the apostle Paul. Moreover, the proof of God's existence could be found in examining the wonders of the natural world. 'In accordance with God's will we may trace His footprints in this world by studying the sciences,' wrote Luther's friend Philip Melanchthon.[12] This emotional response to the creation was expressed in a map in which the world is shown as heart-shaped (or cordiform). Lutherans regarded the cordiform projection 'as a devotional act of looking into one's heart or conscience, for signs of grace'.[13] Maps of this kind were soon interpreted by Catholics as symbolic of heretical dissent.

Mercator, a Catholic by birth, was fascinated by theology and apparently sympathetic to Lutheranism. One of his early world maps was indeed cordiform, but he never repeated this shape and the search for scientific accuracy became his lodestar. Yet in 1544, after a round-up of 'heretics' by the Catholic authorities in Louvain, he was imprisoned for six months. The exact charge is not known but there were references to 'inauspicious letters' that have not survived.[14] Other evidence suggests that Mercator preferred to follow an individual path of piety and was not sympathetic to the more flamboyant forms of Catholicism. In 1552 he migrated to a more tolerant city, Duisburg in the duchy of Cleves, where he lived with his family until his death some forty years later.

Mercator's own description of himself illustrates his many skills: 'Geographer, cosmographer, manufacturer of scientific instruments, engraver and publisher.'* One of his achievements was to perfect the technique of engraving on copper, rather than wood. Even though woodcutting had become highly professional and wood was much cheaper than copper, a copper plate could take more intricate detail and also print off large numbers of copies without becoming worn or cracked. It was an easier surface on which to inscribe the flowing Renaissance scripts that had now replaced older Gothic forms. Mercator was also an accomplished networker, finding experts in mathematics, engraving and making instruments to help him develop his own models. One of his most fruitful contacts was the English astrologer and scientist John Dee (1527–1608), who was obsessed, as Mercator was, with solving the theoretical problems associated with navigation, notably the problems with the deviations in rhumb lines. Using an impressive globe he had created in 1541, Mercator could illustrate how, if one followed a rhumb line on a curved surface, one would spiral round the globe to the pole. The problem of how to help long-distance sailors to avoid spiralling towards inevitable shipwreck was to worry him for decades.

By 1554, Mercator had already begun to make important corrections to Ptolemy's calculations. A vast map of Europe published that year showed the extent of the continent to be 9 degrees less than Ptolemy had calculated. Ten years later he produced a map of the British Isles. These maps sold well and the patronage of the local duke gave Mercator the security to indulge in further ambitious projects. Like many of his contemporaries, Mercator could not envisage a map as fixed at a single moment of time but saw it as having a past behind it and a future ahead of it. This led to his compiling the *Chronologia*, a sweeping chronology of world history. Drawing on Hebrew, Greek, Egyptian and Roman sources, he created columns of information attached to each civilization so that one could run a finger across the columns in order to discover what was happening in different parts of the ancient world on the same date. When there were apparent conflicts between the different sources, he used Hebrew dates as the most authoritative. Theology always remained central to Mercator's work; he composed a map of the Holy Land and even attempted to harmonize the four gospels as a single narrative. Yet when he included Luther and other events of the Reformation in his *Chronologia* it was placed on the papal Index of Prohibited Books, making it off limits for Catholic readers.

* By this time a distinction was beginning to be made between 'cosmographers', who studied the universe as a whole, and 'geographers', who studied only the surface of the Earth.

The *Chronologia* was published as an independent text in 1569. Later that year, Mercator brought together the fruits of decades of research and calculation in the form of an enormous world map, over 2 metres across, made up of eighteen separate printed sheets. One of Mercator's contacts, Abraham Ortelius, who was based in Antwerp, was about to publish one of the most beautiful books of the Renaissance (*Theatrum Orbis Terrarum*, or *The Theatre of the World*), a wonderfully accurate atlas of the known world, fully up to date, and containing seventy maps accompanied by commentaries. Mercator's 1569 world map, however, looked very different.† Rather than using an oval, circular or heart-shaped frame, it was set in a rectangle, and the lands towards the poles were vastly extended, apparently denying all the findings of recent exploration. In an accompanying text (in his beautiful script), Mercator made his point clear. It was one thing to look down on the world from above, as traditional cosmographers aimed to do; it was quite another to produce a map on which sailors could follow compass bearings and end up where they wanted to be, rather than being launched into a spiral.[15]

Mercator had noted that on a globe the meridians – the lines of longitude stretching up towards the pole – would converge as they neared it and meet together at the top. He calculated (a mathematical representation of his findings was only produced after his death) that at, say, 60 degrees north, the distance between two converging meridians would be half what it was at the equator. Then recognizing that 'on account of their curvature and convergence to each other, they [the meridians] are not suitable for navigation' he hit on the concept of doubling the distance between them on his map at 60 degrees, making the meridians in effect lines that were parallel to each other (and stretching into infinity). This, of course, meant that the area of the world that they were covering also doubled, leading to the distortions on the map. (It would prove, of course, virtually impossible to draw any land mass above 70 degrees, as the land around the poles would stretch across the whole map.) However, if a mariner now plotted a straight line connecting the two locations between which he wished to travel, it would lead him from one to the other without any deviance. The adjustment was so brilliant that, despite a slow start – partly due to Mercator's failure

overleaf This world map, *Theatrum Orbis Terrarum*, by Abraham Ortelius (1570) is considered one of the most beautiful of the late sixteenth century. While there are inaccuracies in the depictions of the Americas, the coastlines of both east and west have been explored.

† Ortelius's archive has survived. It shows that he corresponded with hundreds of informants and drew on eighty-seven different maps in order to compile his own.

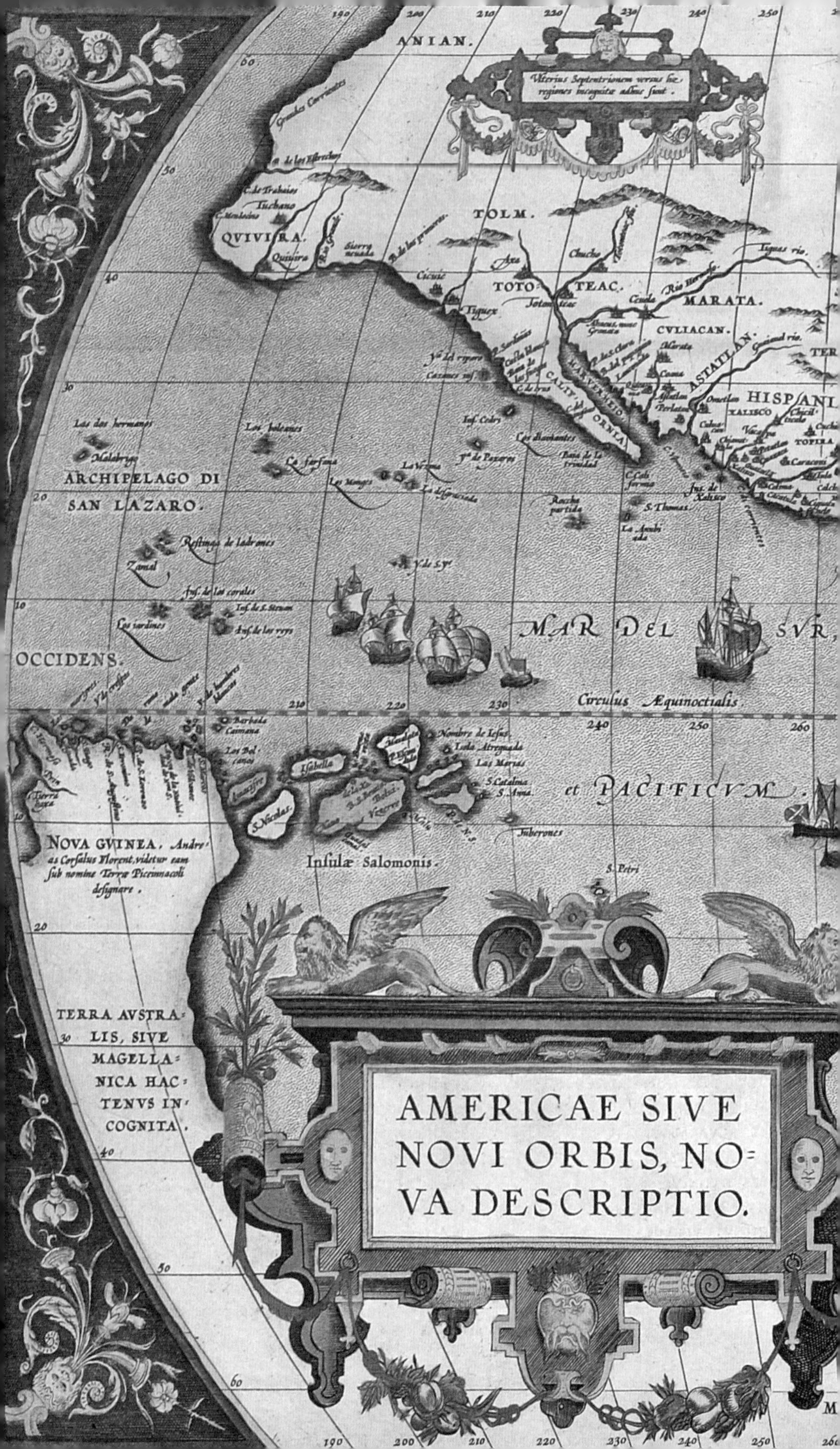
ANIAN.
Vlterius Septentrionem versus hæ regiones incognitæ adhuc sunt.
TOLM.
QVIVIRA.
TOTO
TEAC.
MARATA.
CVLIACAN.
ASTATLAN.
HISPANI
CALIFORNIA
MAR VERMEIO
ARCHIPELAGO DI SAN LAZARO.
OCCIDENS.
MAR DEL SVR,
Circulus Æquinoctialis
et PACIFICVM.
Insulæ Salomonis.
NOVA GVINEA. Andreas Corsalus Florent, videtur eam sub nomine Terræ Piccinnacoli designare.
TERRA AVSTRALIS, SIVE MAGELLANICA HACTENVS INCOGNITA.
AMERICAE SIVE NOVI ORBIS, NOVA DESCRIPTIO.

ESTOTILANT
SAGVENAI
NOVA
CANADA
TERRA CORTEREALIS
CHILAGA
FRANCIA
NORVMBEGA
MOCOSA
AVACAL
APALCHEN
WINGANDEKOA
LA FLORIDA
CVBA
IVCATAN
HISPANIOLA
La bermuda
Sept cites
Santana
Las Açores
Ansulæ de C. Verde
S. Brandani
Caribana
Tisnada
Paguana
PERV
Picora
Amazones
BRESILIA à Lusitanis A°. 1504. inuenta.
ORIENS
PARANA
ACVTIA
CHARCAS
CHILI
Mepenes
Ningatas
Rio de la Plata
PATAGONES, vel REGIO GIGANTVM
FRETVM MAGELLANICVM
TERRA DEL FVEGO
Golfo de S. Sebastiano
Cum Priuilegio decennali
Ab. Ortelius delineab.
et excudeb. 1587.

to advertise his achievement – the Mercator projection has been used to this day even though its distortions are geographically ridiculous. Greenland becomes the same size as South America while in reality it is only one-eighth of the size of that continent. From the nineteenth century English Ordnance mappers and British Admiralty chart makers found the Mercator projection invaluable and it has even been used by the NASA space agency to map the solar system.

Before his death in 1594, Mercator produced two more sets of maps. In one (1578) he ignored all the inaccuracies and misconceptions of Ptolemy's *Geographike* and reproduced them as the master had decreed. By now this was little more than a tribute to a genius whose achievement had been surpassed. While Ptolemy had believed in an Earth-centred universe, his *Almagest* was also being made redundant by Copernicus's theory that the sun was the centre of the solar system. Just before he died, Mercator produced a very accurate series of maps which ignored his projection of 1569. When they were published in 1595, they were the first compilation of maps to bear the title 'atlas' on their front page. Mercator's coinage honoured the mythological Atlas, the Titan who supported the heavens and, according to one version of Greek myth, was king of Mauretania and the first astronomer.

Mercator's achievements were only part of an outpouring of collections of knowledge that appeared during the sixteenth century. In 1544 Sebastian Münster, a professor of Hebrew at the university of Heidelberg, produced his *Cosmographia*, a vast encyclopaedia of the known world. An extended edition appeared in 1550. Besides its maps, it contained 1,200 pages, including 1,000 woodblock images, of historical events and individuals, flora and fauna, peoples and city plans. It was written in German rather than Latin and so found a literate audience from the start. By 1628 thirty-five editions had been printed, including translations into English, Czech, French and Italian.

Thus did the European discovery of the New World play a major part in the reawakening of the western mind. Adam Smith, the apostle of free trade, writing in 1776, was in no doubt about this: 'The discovery of America, and that of a passage to the East Indies by the Cape of Good Hope, are the two greatest and most important events recorded in the history of mankind.' And, he added, 'the full extent of their consequences [is] still unseen'.[16]

The 'discoveries' of the age of exploration provide an excellent example of how ancient knowledge invigorated both intellectual inquiry and more practical avenues of investigation, but was rapidly surpassed as more 'scientific' ways of approaching the natural world became established. As the explorer of far northern America, Jacques Cartier, put it in 1545: 'The simple sailors of today have learned the opposite of the opinion of the philosophers by true experience.'[17] Cartier's words seem to capture a triumph of empirical evidence over ancient theory, marking a key moment in the history of science. But at the same time as the voyages of da Gama, Magellan and Cabot were extending human knowledge of the world's far-flung oceans and continents, other, similarly curious individuals were attempting to enhance the accuracy with which artists rendered objects rather closer to home. It is to their efforts that we will now turn.

How Europe Learned to See Again: Leonardo and Vesalius

Do you not see that the eye embraces the beauty of the world. The eye is the commander of astronomy; it makes cosmography; it guides and rectifies all the human arts; it conducts man to the various regions of the world; it is the prince of mathematics; its sciences are most certain; it has measured the height and size of the stars; it has disclosed the elements and their distribution; it has made its predictions of future events by means of the course of the stars; it has generated architecture, perspective and divine painting… And it triumphs over nature, in that the constituent parts of nature are finite, but the works that the eye commands of hands are infinite.

Attributed to Leonardo da Vinci,
Trattato della Pittura[1]

If science, in the sense of understanding the natural world, was to resume the progress that it had made in the ancient Mediterranean, accurate ways of observing it needed to be found. A good starting point for tracing the progress of what was to prove a lengthy journey towards achieving this end is the life of the Italian humanist and antiquarian Cyriacus of Ancona (1391–*c*.1453). Cyriacus has been called 'the father of archaeology'.[2] He was inspired to take an interest in antiquities when, on seeing the Latin inscription on the emperor Trajan's arch in his native city crumbling away, he decided to copy it. Cyriacus went on to learn Latin and Greek and travelled extensively in the eastern Mediterranean, financed by his trading of antiquities, carpets and slaves. In contrast to Petrarch, who loved ancient texts, Cyriacus was fascinated by surviving monuments. He talked of reviving 'those glorious things that were alive to those living in antiquity but had become buried and defunct… to bring them from the dark tomb to light, to live once more'.[3] Even as he travelled, he noticed that old buildings were being lost, columns falling over, walls disintegrating, and he copied down as many inscriptions as he could find. His findings remain an important source for classical archaeologists to this day.

In 1436 Cyriacus arrived in Athens, by then a backwater of the Byzantine empire and soon to be absorbed by the expanding Ottoman empire. Here he carried out work that has been of immense worth to posterity. His drawing of the second-century AD monument to the Commegene king Philopappos on the Mouseion Hill recorded reliefs that are now lost. He then turned to the Parthenon, the great fifth-century BC temple high up on the Acropolis, the most glorious creation of the classical city, which was now a church.

Cyriacus's is the earliest drawing of the Parthenon that has survived. The temple was to suffer dreadful damage when it was blown up by a Venetian shell in 1687, so drawings of it in its undamaged state are especially valuable. Alas, Cyriacus was conditioned by his times and it might be said that he drew what he expected to see. The figure of Athena was drawn in a fifteenth-century dress rather than in a classical *chiton* and many of the figures on the western pediment appear as *putti*. He even managed to get the angle of the pediment wrong.

So here observation is not accurate. Later, in about 1510, the architect Giuliano da Sangallo copied Cyriacus's drawing and added some classical columns on his own initiative that made the Parthenon look as if it were a Roman temple. This fed a completely distorted view of the Parthenon into western Europe. Although the name of Pheidias, the mastermind behind the sculptures of the Parthenon, was well known, no accurate depiction of his work could be seen in western Europe until the drawings of the Frenchman Jacques Carrey in the seventeenth century, a few years before the Parthenon was blown up. Some 'scholars' even believed that the much more complete temple of Hephaestus which looks over the Agora might be the Parthenon itself.

As well as continual practice, drawing requires a commitment to trying to depict what is actually seen. It takes discipline. Until the need for this level of accuracy was recognized, scientific progress would be slow. One major constraint was the lack of a relatively cheap medium on which drawings could be done. With the spread of paper, sketching became much easier. Only a small number of these examples survive from the fourteenth century but many, including whole sketchbooks, from the fifteenth.[4] Few were finished works of art and most of them must have been discarded or recycled. The unsociable and introspective Michelangelo (1475–1564) is known to have burned most of his drawings, in order that – he is reputed to have said – no one would 'see the way he toiled and stimulated his creativity'. Private collections of drawings only became the vogue around 1550; Giorgio Vasari, the author of the influential *Lives of the Artists*, was one of the first collectors.

Most of these early survivors, therefore, are preliminary drawings, but they are still of great interest to scholars exploring the development of commissions or seeking out some record of paintings that have disappeared. As the art historian Hugo Chapman notes: 'The revolutionary developments in Italian Renaissance art were rehearsed and took place on paper, and the practice of drawing was vital to producing the enquiring, analytical, observational and creative reflexes of the artists whose works define the period.'[5] The accurate rendering of the structure of objects required a mind which grasped that the depiction of the body of a human or an animal would be enhanced by an understanding of its inner form. The contrast must be made between accurate observation for accuracy's sake and what artists refer to as *disegno*, a word used to describe the conceiving of an object in the mind and then working out how to portray it on paper. Essentially, this involved a process of experimentation, which was doubly important in that the Renaissance stimulated interest in the depiction of a variety of subjects for which no ancient models existed. Michelangelo is usually seen as the finest exponent of *disegno*, although his contemporary Raphael equals him in his exuberance.[6] In his *Lives of the Artists*, Vasari praised Michelangelo and Raphael as the first painters to surpass those of antiquity.

One can hardly deny Michelangelo a place in the history of observation when one looks closely at his *Pietà* (1498–9) in St Peter's Basilica in Rome. However, his sculpture is always distorted by his desire to convey emotion rather than accuracy. In the *Pietà*, Mary, holding the body of her thirty-three-year-old son among her voluminous skirts, is depicted as no more than a teenage girl. This is what gives the sculpture its pathos. His *David* is not well proportioned – the head and the hands are exaggerated – but his primary aim was to show the resolution and power of Florence, whose city authorities had commissioned the work from the twenty-six-year-old Michelangelo in 1501. In his many tortuous representations of the nude, Michelangelo broke all the accepted conventions of classical harmony. Among them the *Dying Slave*, intended for the tomb of Pope Julius II but still unfinished after forty years, is a brilliant illustration of his internal frustrations. While his so-called 'gift drawings', made in the 1530s for a young Roman nobleman, Tommaso Cavalieri, to whom Michelangelo was deeply attached, are brilliant, they are *disegni*, compositions primarily designed for emotional impact rather than to demonstrate accuracy of representation.

opposite and overleaf
The extraordinary sophistication and accuracy of Leonardo's anatomical drawings are evident in these studies of *c.*1510.

The supreme genius of 'scientific' observational art was Michelangelo's older contemporary and rival, Leonardo da Vinci. Leonardo was born in 1452, the illegitimate son of a Florentine notary, and was bought up by his mother, probably Caterina Lippi, an orphaned fifteen-year-old, in the small hill town of Vinci in Tuscany.[7] He moved into nearby Florence to begin an apprenticeship in the workshop of the painter Andrea Verrocchio. Leonardo had had no more than the basic education of the day in numeracy and literacy and does not seem to have mastered much Latin; throughout his life, he preferred to read vernacular Italian. Perhaps one reason why he became so interested in the human body is that medical texts were by now often translated into Italian and so he would have been able to understand them. We know that he carried sketchbooks around with him, jotting down aides-memoires of whatever caught his attention. One text describes him as virtually buried by the reams of paper around him in his studio. 'No one', in the words of the Leonardo scholar Martin Kemp, 'covered the surface of pages with such an impetuous cascade of observations, visualized thoughts, brainstormed alternatives, theories, polemics and debates, covering virtually every branch of knowledge about the visible world known in his time.'[8] In his surviving drawings one can often see

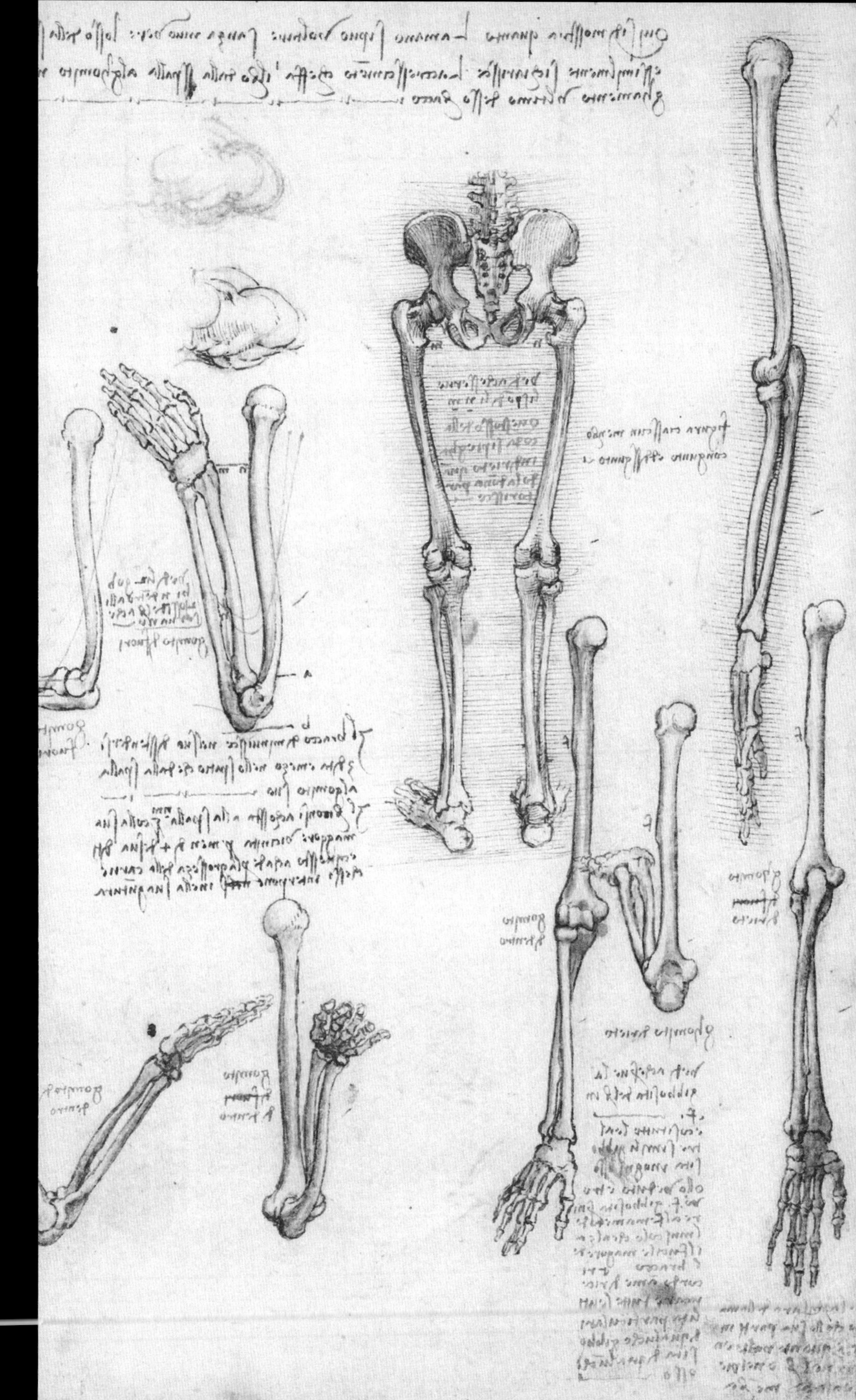

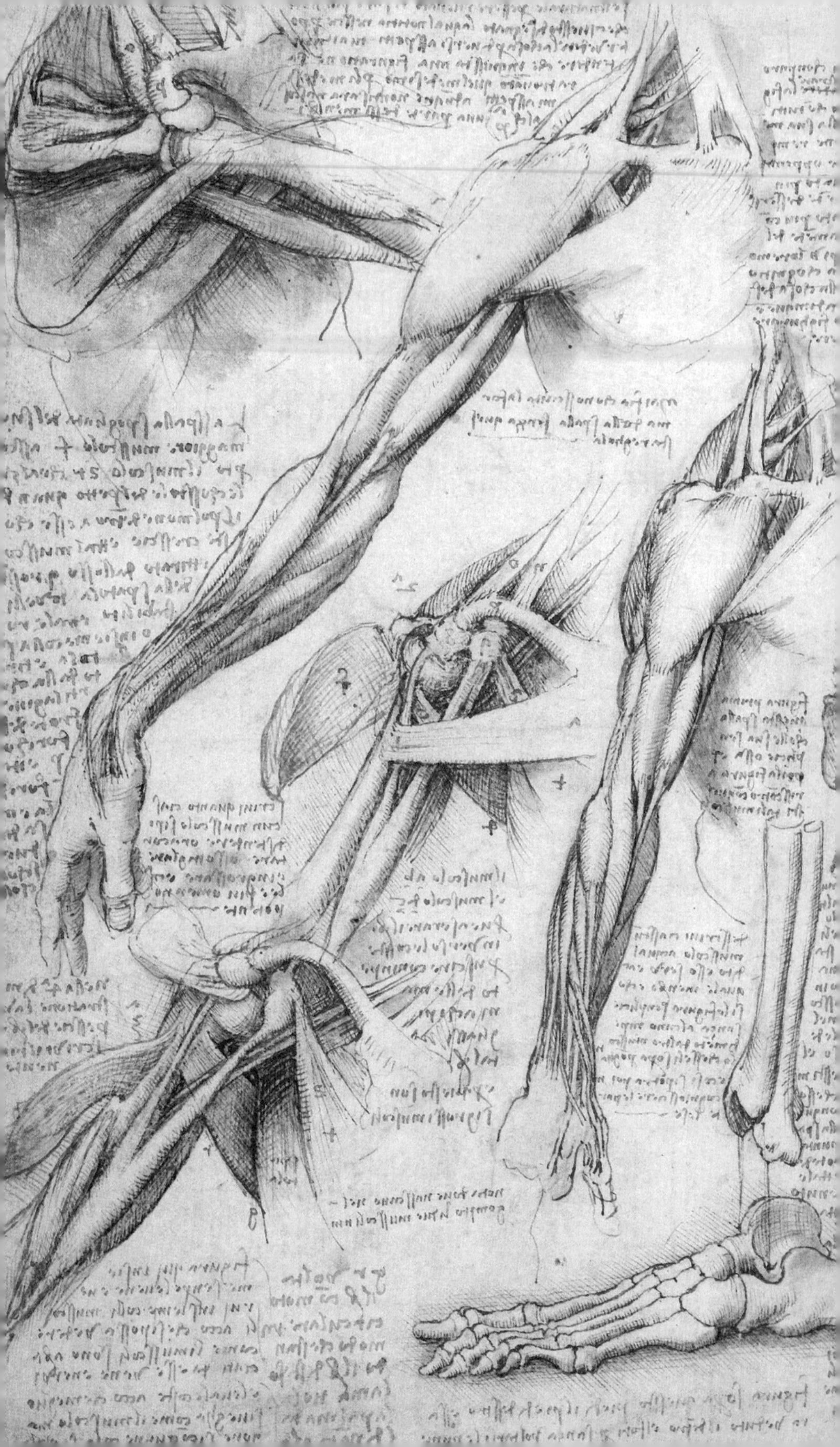

how his mind works as he covers a page (from right to left) with the elaboration of ideas as they enter his mind, one drawing often infusing or influencing the next.

By the 1480s, in his early thirties, Leonardo had moved north from Florence to the opulent and scholarly court of the Sforzas at Milan. He was well trained, fully confident of his abilities and he must have felt that the city would give him more scope for his talents. There is another possible reason for his move. As we saw in Chapter 14, intellectual life in late fifteenth-century Florence was heavily influenced by Neoplatonism and so encouraged introspective thought, the search for truths that could only be grasped through meditation on eternal realities. This went against Leonardo's own instincts and it seems that a more Aristotelian approach, reaching outwards to the material world, was prominent in Milan. It was certainly attractive to him. A surviving fragment from the 1480s confirms the markedly Aristotelian cast of Leonardo's thinking: 'All science will be vain and full of errors which is not born of experience, mother of all certainty. True sciences are those which experience has caused to enter through the senses, thus silencing the tongues of the litigants.'[9] He also wrote in his notebooks, again in contrast to those in thrall to the works of antiquity: 'A painter who imitates the work of other artists instead of Nature herself, becomes Nature's grandchild when he could have been her son.'[10] Yet mere observation of 'Nature' is not enough; there must be thoughtful consideration of the underlying structures of living things. When Leonardo highlights the difference between those who paint as if they are simply producing a mirror image of an object and those who aim to capture its essence, his outlook seems to be moving closer to Platonism. As Ernst Gombrich, the great Austrian art historian, noted, Leonardo is the 'most important witness' for those 'convinced that the correct representation of nature rests on intellectual understanding as much as on good eyesight'.[11]

In the 1480s Leonardo produced his first anatomical drawings. He was still conditioned by outside influences, notably the belief that a human body was a harmonious whole. Inspired by the ideas of Vitruvius on proportion from the Roman architect's text *De architectura*,* he drew his famous 'Vitruvian man', probably about 1487. It remains one of the defining images of Renaissance humanism, a perfect male body stretching out to fill both a circle and square simultaneously. Of course, Leonardo recognized that this was an ideal body, perhaps seldom encountered in real life, so it can hardly be called a 'scientific'

* It had been discovered in a manuscript in 1414 and printed for the first time in 1486.

illustration, but after the degradation of the human form in so much medieval art, it was an important statement.

In 1489 Leonardo described in a text, *On the Human Body*, how he would create a set of drawings that would show the progress of an embryo through conception to birth and then to the first year of life. He would then concentrate on the fully grown human body. The questions he asked are 'scientific' ones. 'Which tendon causes the motion of the eye, so that the motion of one eye moves the other?' Never before had the human body been so rigorously examined. And Leonardo's genius had endowed him with the artistic skills to match his intense curiosity. Among the fruits of this anatomical inquisitiveness was Leonardo's studies of the human skull. These appear at first sight to be accurate drawings, but they too are created within an ideology that draws on ancient texts, in this case Aristotle and Galen, the outstanding physician of the second century AD. It is clear from his accompanying notes that Leonardo was as much concerned with understanding the metaphysics of the human soul, its location within the skull, as in creating an accurate picture of the skull itself. 'If man's construction should appear to you to be of marvellous artifice, remember that it is nothing compared to the soul which inhabits such architecture, and, truly, be what it may, it is a divine thing.'[12] This is typical of his intense desire to understand the issues he confronted in their most comprehensive form. As the distinguished Leonardo scholar Martin Kemp has put it: 'No artist or scientist has ever possessed a stronger sense of man in motion as a sentient, responsive and expressive being.'[13]

Yet inevitably, Leonardo was constrained by his sources and these appear to have conditioned his depictions of the human body. He drew on classical and medieval notions of the nervous system and shaped his studies of the spinal cord to represent them. Of course, he faced enormous challenges with dissection, as his corpses decomposed quickly in the warm climate. The dissected eye is notoriously difficult to draw as it 'rapidly collapses into a gelatinous heap'.[14] It is evident that Leonardo allowed himself to be influenced by earlier conceptions of optics to make up for the inadequacy of his specimens. So while we can say that Leonardo showed a 'scientific' approach to the human body, as yet he had not made any groundbreaking progress in the representation of one. It is not even certain, this early, that he was involved in dissection himself.

Even so, he was an inveterate observer of the natural world. It seems that there was no area of life that Leonardo did not penetrate and transform with his imagination. So quite apart from his achievements as a painter – his mural of *The Last Supper*, in the convent of Santa Maria della Grazie, Milan, even in its decayed form, provides an extraordinary example of how Brunelleschi's rules of perspective, and the academic development of them by scholars such as Alberti, can be exploited – there are endless studies of movement in Leonardo's work, swirls of water (a particular obsession), engineering gadgets, fortifications, ambitious plans to build a canal to make the River Arno navigable to the sea, and a famous map of the town of Imola, near Bologna. The Imola map, designed for Cesare Borgia, shows how Leonardo was able to adapt surveying techniques to produce pinpoint accuracy without depriving the town plan of an aesthetic life of its own.

Back in Florence by 1500, after the expulsion of his Milanese patron, Ludovico Sforza, from his court, Leonardo was restless and unsettled but no less productive. He was now devouring texts – his library contained 116 named items plus another 50 unclassified works. He had developed an interest in mathematics and possessed Euclid's *Elements*, the most common primer for mathematical proofs, as well as works of Archimedes. As was the case with Galileo after him, Leonardo appears to have regarded Archimedes as the greatest mathematical figure of the ancient world, and he explored Archimedean principles obsessively through his geometrical drawings. Like many other artists (notably Piero della Francesca; see p. 306), he appreciated the certainty that mathematical logic could bring.[15]

overleaf Like most 'scientists' of his time, Leonardo was fascinated by light. In these diagrams and accompanying notes he shows the way that light rays are transmitted from mirrors.

Leonardo's preoccupation with the human body led to a burst of creativity around the year 1508, when he famously dissected a man aged over 100. Here he took an anatomically more sophisticated approach; his uncovering of the veins of the old man, withered and narrowed in comparison to those of a two-year-old child, led him to explore how blood and air were transported around the body. His own studies of fluids, many of them natural water flows, further informed these investigations. Over the course of some twenty years, therefore, Leonardo had moved towards observations that broke free from ancient precedent. In his studies of the female body, now in the Royal Collection of drawings at Windsor, he attempted to depict the respiratory, vascular and urino-genital tracts together as a whole. While not wholly accurate, this ambitious juxtaposition of organs showed that he was now aware of just how complex the structure of the human body is.

In 1510 Leonardo set out on a final quest to depict the inner workings of the body. The only way he could do it was to show the

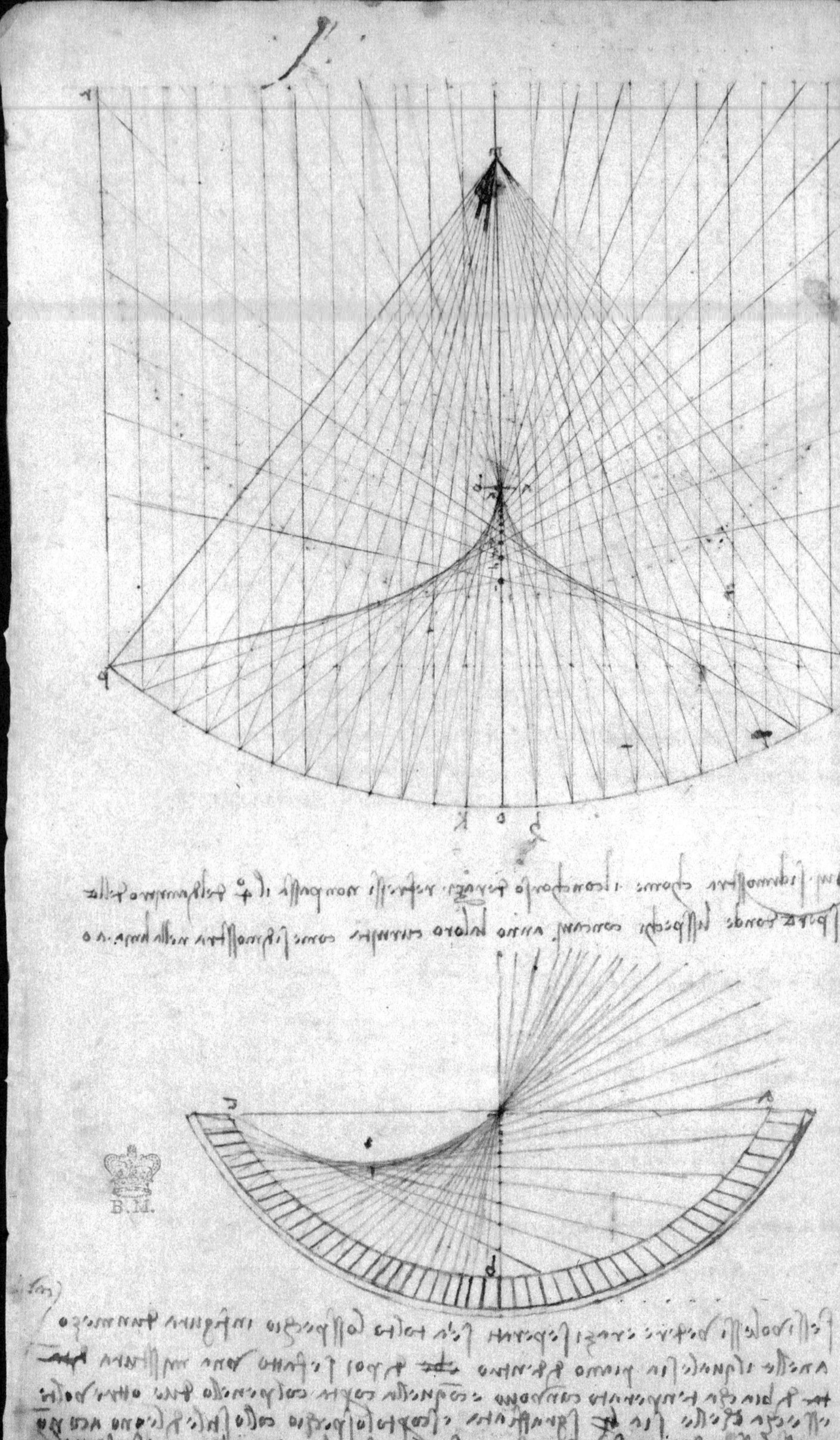
B.M.

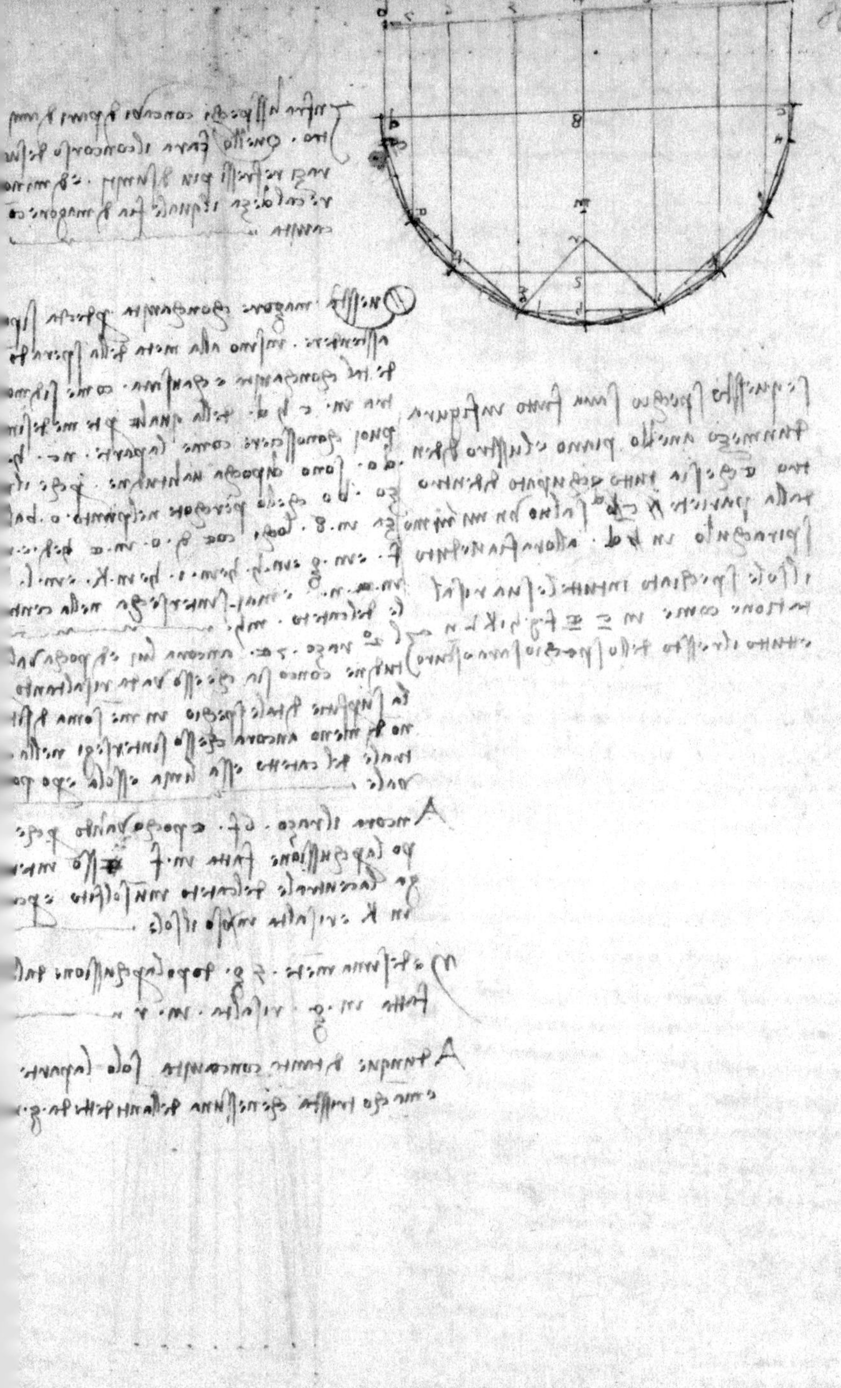

flesh, muscles and bones of each limb stage by stage as it was dissected. His aim now was clarity, so the different elements of the limb are first shown separately and then as they are when they are reassembled. This was an innovative approach and has been enormously influential in technical drawing. Leonardo exulted in what he had achieved in an age when anatomical texts lacked illustrations. He knew that his drawings encompassed knowledge that a written text would never be able to provide. He had become a true empiricist, rejecting in the process the external 'causes' of the organs, which the classical sources had defined for him, in favour of what he could actually see. As he put it: 'Nature begins with the cause and ends with the experience: we must follow the opposite course, that is beginning with the experience and from this investigate the reason.'[16]

Leonardo concluded his researches in 1514 with a magnificent series of studies of the heart of an ox. His determination to define cause and effect, to portray how the valves actually worked, led him to insist that it was essential to achieve the precision of a mathematician. Everything had to fit together as a working instrument. His greatest anatomical achievement was his accurate portrayal of the functions of the three-cusp valve at the base of the pulmonary artery. His depiction is so exact that modern research has confirmed his insights and his design is similar to the artificial valves used by surgeons today.

Despite his being acknowledged as a genius, Leonardo did not publish his drawings during his lifetime. After his death in France in 1519, where he was living at the invitation of King François I, they were gradually dispersed across various different collections and many of them were lost. A more public display of anatomy, and one that was capable of contributing to scientific advance, would have to await the emergence of Andreas Vesalius.[17] Vesalius was born into a family of physicians in the Habsburg Netherlands in 1487, and he studied at the University of Paris, where the works of Galen were still considered authoritative. The rediscovery of Galen's *De anatomicis administrationibus* (*On Anatomical Procedures*), a Latin translation of which appeared in 1531, provided a more logical method of approaching dissection but most of Galen's anatomical research had been carried out on animals, especially Barbary apes, rather than on human bodies, which had been difficult for him to obtain. It was only when Vesalius moved to the most advanced medical school in Europe, at Padua, where he became professor of anatomy and surgery in 1537, that he had the chance to dissect bodies in front of students.

Even though Galen had clearly made serious errors in his observations, some physicians continued to declare that he was always right even when the bodily organs exposed before them showed him to be wrong. Faced with overwhelming evidence of Galen's errors, some argued that the human body must have changed over the intervening 1,400 years – or that his texts had been wrongly copied! It was Vesalius who broke the stranglehold of such thinking on the western mind by declaring that what he could actually *see* as he dissected a body proved that Galen had been wrong – not least because he had based his conclusions on the dissection of animals.

Andreas Vesalius, as depicted in his *De humani corporis fabrica* of 1543. Vesalius's masterwork represented a quantum leap in the accurate portrayal of the human body, revealed here in his reconstruction of the human skeleton (*overleaf*).

Vesalius first presented his findings in a series of six *Tabulae anatomicae* (*Anatomical Pictures*) published in Venice in 1538. These are fascinating in that Vesalius still reproduced many of the original findings of Galen that we now know to be inaccurate, but alongside them are his own drawings that represent organs, among them the liver, as they truly are. The culmination of Vesalius's work was his *De humani corporis fabrica* (*On the Fabric of the Human Body*) of 1543. By now, with the bodies of a number of executed criminals to work from, he had the confidence to discard Galen and the other medieval texts that anatomists had relied on. He spotted, for instance, that the sternum has three, not seven, segments. He corrected Galen's conception of the liver and, in perhaps the most important breakthrough of all, questioned the permeability of the septum in the heart. Galen had assumed that blood somehow passed through tissue. By 1559 Realdo Colombo (*c.*1515–59) was noting the importance of the pumping heartbeat, thus laying the ground for later anatomists such as William Harvey (1578–1657) to discover the circulation of the blood. Vesalius also made progress in bringing consistency to the confusing mishmash of nomenclature that had

HVMANI COR- PORIS OSSIVM
TERIS QVAS SV- STINENT PART.
LIBERORVM, SVAQVE SEDE POSITORVM
latere delineatio.

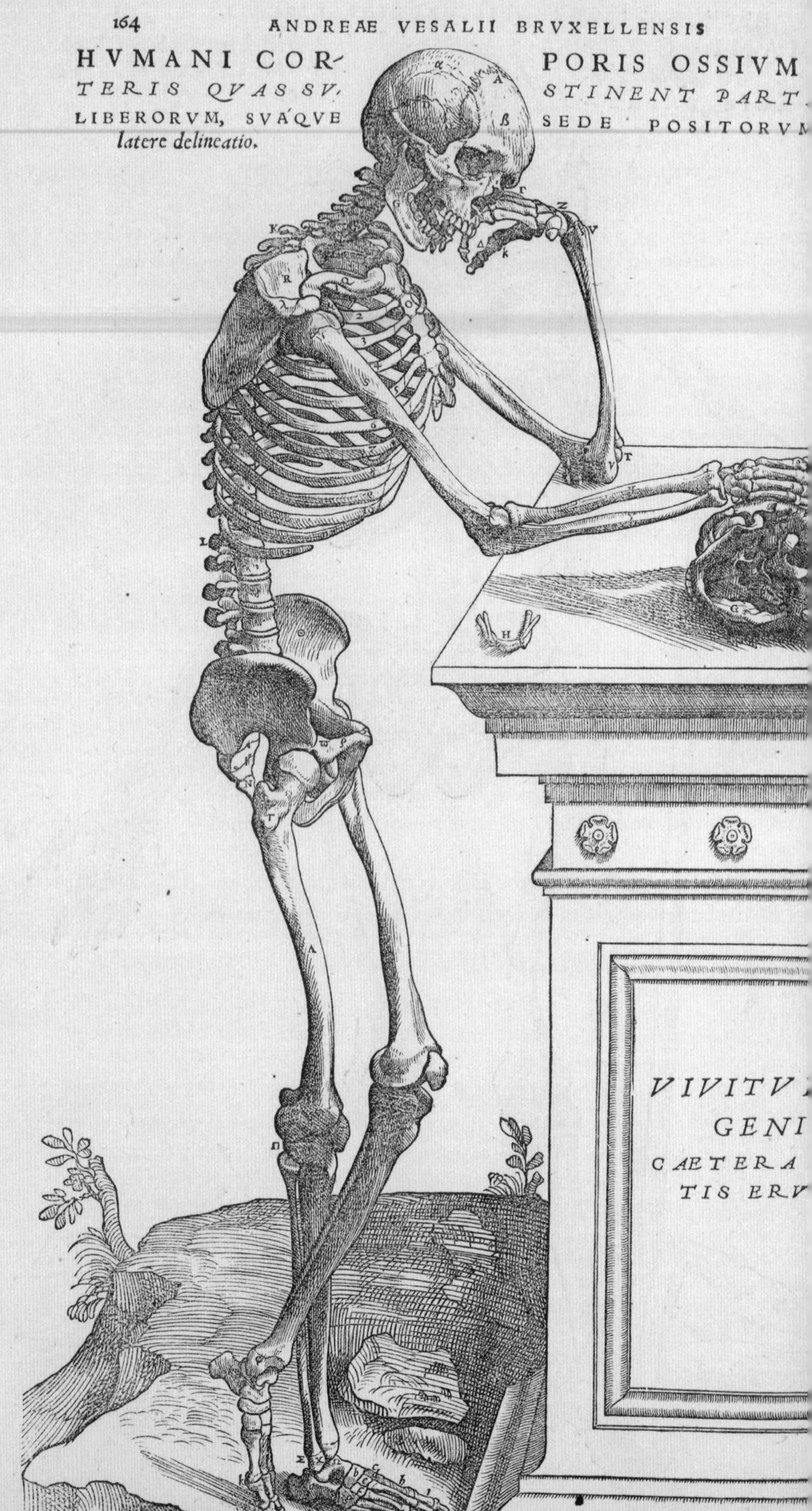

resulted from different linguistic traditions, Greek, Latin, Hebrew and Arabic. This was essential if a scientific community that worked from the same perspective and same language, Latin, was to be created.

De humani was not simply a set of illustrations. It included detailed instructions for dissection and so was, in effect, a teaching manual. As such it was rather formal in that it adopted the order of dissection outlined by Galen in his *De anatomicis*, moving from the skeleton to the various organs and vascular system with the brain as the final organ to be dissected. In practice only the most determined dissectors would have been able to follow this order, since without any method of preservation the internal organs would have decayed by the time the anatomist reached them and the stench would have been unbearable. In his work of 1538, Vesalius had provided his own drawings but in *De humani* he relied on a professional artist, Jan Stephan van Calcar, also from the Netherlands, working under his supervision. Van Calcar's extraordinarily accomplished illustrations – which were both accurate and imaginative – were another pointer to the future. The development of accurate woodcuts, which had already been seen in the drawings of plants by the German artist Hans Weiditz (see p. 442), marks another important step forward in the history of science.

Images cut on woodcuts were inked, then pressed against paper and rubbed on the reverse to transfer the image. The earliest examples, in the fifteenth century, were often crude drawings of common themes, such as the Virgin Mary. The new emphasis on using illustrations as a teaching tool demanded greater technical expertise. Books with a mass of woodcut illustrations became prohibitively expensive, well beyond the means of most students, but they shifted scholarship towards accepting the superiority of observation and investigation. Virtually every anatomist who followed Vesalius adopted the primacy of the eye over theory or ancient authority.

It has to be recognized, however, that the study and practice of medicine remained highly conservative. Galen would continue to be seen as the ultimate authority for decades to come. The English historian Hugh Trevor-Roper wrote a fascinating study of Théodore de Mayerne (1573–1655), one of the most famous physicians of seventeenth-century Europe. In it he explores how one of the most committed and famous physicians of his day moved within a medical world still hedged about by superstition but containing glimmers of scientific understanding.[18] At this time, despite the empirical advances made by Vesalius and others, accurate observation had not yet been used to provide much benefit to the sick.

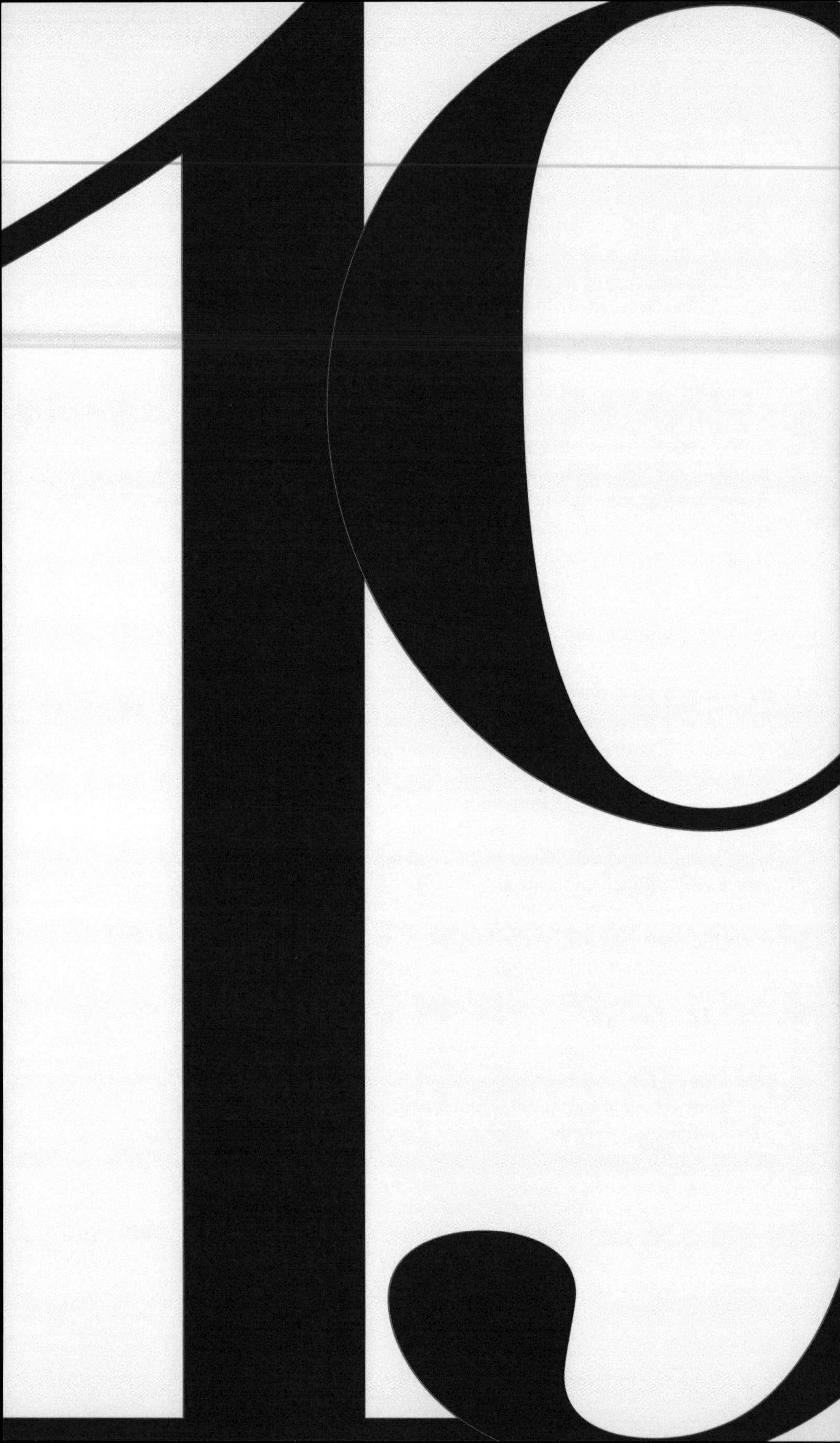

Exploring the Natural World in the Sixteenth Century

This plant emerges in the spring about the same time that Aron [a star] first appears. It is not very common, and its usual place is in very dark and moist woods. It is a plant with one or two leaves, similar to those of the Meyenblumen. The leaves acquire stems like that of garlic; at the end of April they bear little white flowers, which are also like those of Meyenblumen. But they are not hollow, like the Meyenblumen, but star-shaped, and the petals are separated one from another. The roots of this flower are white and longish, like a small garden garlic plant that is not more than a month old.

From Hieronymus Bock,
Kreuterbuch, Strasbourg, 1577

Among Leonardo da Vinci's books, from a list of 1504, were a large herbal and the Bolognese Pietro Crescenzio's *Libro della agricultura*, the Italian version of a standard (Latin) text on the subject. From his surviving drawings scholars have suggested that Leonardo considered writing a treatise on the structure of plants with illustrations that would have been as accomplished as his anatomical drawings. It was never completed and instead it was the Nuremberg-born Albrecht Dürer (1471–1528) who set the standards for the naturalistic depictions of plants and animals. Shortly after Dürer's death one of his pupils, Hans Weiditz (1495–*c*.1537), produced the *Herbarum vivae icones* (*Living Portraits of Plants*) in three parts between 1530 and 1536. It was illustrated with 260 superb woodcuts.

The text for the *Herbarum* was based on a famous work of antiquity, the *De Materia Medica* of Dioscorides. Dioscorides was a natural scientist of the first century AD who came from Anazarbus in Cilicia (present-day south-eastern Turkey). He is a good example of the driving force of curiosity that enabled the Greeks to lay so many of the foundations of modern science. Fascinated by the medicinal properties of plants and animals, he had imposed on himself what he termed 'a military discipline' and travelled far and wide in search of specimens. We know he was in Greece, Crete and Egypt and reached Petra, the capital of the Nabataeans, who traded eastwards across the Arabian deserts. Eventually, he was able to list some 700 plants, describing their natural habitats insofar as he was able to locate them. In the five books of his works that survive he grouped his subjects into categories: whole animals, parts of animals, minerals and then plants, which were further subdivided into roots, fruits, trees and herbs. He also wrote about their medicinal properties that he observed closely, distinguishing groups of drugs according to the effect they had on the human body. This is practical science with no mention of any supernatural intervention in the curing of sickness.

Albrecht Dürer was a pioneer in the representation of plant life. His *The Great Piece of Turf* (1503) is a masterpiece.

The *De Materia Medica* had been treasured by the Arabs and was well known in the Middle Ages, in Latin versions of the original Greek; and, as with most ancient texts, it was considered authoritative. An edition translated and annotated by the Sienese physician Andrea Mattioli was the sixteenth-century's bestselling natural history book. Mattioli resolutely defended it against critics who tempered their admiration with criticism of its errors as these gradually became apparent. Even

as late as 1598, Dioscorides was the textbook used in classes at the University of Leiden in the Dutch Republic.

Another text that had been popular in the Middle Ages was Pliny the Elder's *Natural History*, dating from the first century AD. Pliny's curiosity was such that during the devastating eruption of Vesuvius in AD 79 he attempted to cross the Bay of Naples in order to obtain a closer view, but died from suffocation on the shore.[1] His *Natural History*, a massive compilation of material about the natural world, had been copied and recopied, but the surviving manuscripts had been reproduced without any critical editing and the work contained numerous passages that were difficult to understand. Since Pliny was believed to have been an important and accurate authority, something clearly had to be done to fashion and make available a coherent text of the *Natural History*. It seemed to be a matter of attempting to recover the original from the mass of corruptions that had crept in through careless copying. Scholars got to work and when the humanist Ermolao Barbaro published his *Castigationes plinianae* in 1493, he claimed to be providing an original text stripped of no fewer than 5,000 later errors. Whenever Pliny's meaning remained unclear, Barbaro dug into an earlier text, usually one by Aristotle, Theophrastus (Aristotle's successor as head of the Lyceum) or Dioscorides, on the assumption that Pliny had copied from them, and then simply filled in the gaps. Barbaro believed that Pliny must be trusted.

So in the late fifteenth century, the authority of classical texts on matters relating to the natural world was still accepted uncritically.[2] Yet change was in the air. In 1492 the humanist Niccolò Leoniceno published his own study of Pliny, *De Plinii et aliorum medicorum in medicina erroribus*. Leoniceno taught moral philosophy and practical medicine at the university of Ferrara. He had already attracted attention for his criticism of Arabic medical texts and one of his correspondents from Florence, another humanist, Angelo Poliziano, wrote in support of the view that Pliny was to be trusted and that his 'errors' were corruptions of his original text. Would Leoniceno advise him on this? 'I will rejoice if a Latin author is not in the same straits as the barbarians' was his hope.[3]

He could hardly have expected the riposte he received in Leoniceno's work. The wording of his title, 'on the medical errors of Pliny and others', already contained a warning. Leoniceno's first blow was to reveal a grievous error in Book 2 of Pliny's work, the claim that the moon is larger than the Earth. This error alone did lasting damage to Pliny's reputation as an authority on the natural world. Having made his point, Leoniceno warmed to his theme. He showed that Pliny had muddled the names of plants, so that in one case two plants with similar Greek names were assumed to be the same one. Then there were the plants that were the same, but which had different names in Greek and Latin, and which Pliny had listed as two different plants. Leoniceno exposed Pliny to be an armchair scholar who had simply relied on texts that he had not the linguistic competence to decipher; he had never bothered to check for himself from actual specimens. The *Natural History* was deeply flawed.

Leoniceno's work had set a new tone. The ancient authorities were not sacred. Earlier writings on plants clearly did not constitute the last word on them – and nor indeed did writings on other aspects of the natural world. It was at this time (1496) that the famous Manutius edition of Pietro Bembo's *De Aetna*, in which the author showed that ancient descriptions of Etna did not correspond with what he saw for himself, was published. In Rome there is an extraordinary record of a new approach to the depiction of fruits and vegetables. They were painted in festoons in the loggia of the Villa Farnesina on the banks of the Tiber. The rooms of this sumptuous 'rural' retreat (it was in the centre of Rome but protected by large gardens) of the fabulously rich banker Agostini Chigi were decorated by Raphael and his followers. The loggia depicted the love affair of Cupid and Psyche and involved a good deal of nudity – in keeping with the myth and the ambience of a private space.[4] It is only recently that a full study of the festoons, in this case the work of Raphael's follower, Giovanni da Udine, has been undertaken by a team led by the botanist Giulia Caneva.[5] The frescos were begun in 1518 and depict some 160 different flowers and fruits. There can be no better example of the fascination with plant life that was beginning to grip the cultivated minds of the period. Remarkably, the frescos feature many plants from the New World, including maize, but the colours are so bright and the details so accurate that it has been argued that the artists must have used specimens from the greenhouses and flowerbeds of Chigi's now-lost gardens.

The study of plants as objects in themselves, irrespective of any medicinal use they might have, developed slowly from the 1530s. Physicians who simply repeated the mantras of existing herbals, without carrying out their own experiments to see if a drug worked, came under increasing criticism. More intensive study of Dioscorides, and earlier ancient writers on natural history, such as Aristotle and Theophrastus, began to take place. Their originality was respected, as was their attention to detail and observation, but they too were soon

Psyche and Cupid dominate the richly festooned ceiling of the Loggia di Psiche in the Villa Farnesina, in Rome. Executed by Giovanni da Udine, an assistant of Raphael's, the frescos contain more than 160 varieties of plants and fruit.

found to be full of errors, often because they had relied on second-hand reports. The new naturalists now saw themselves as heirs to a great tradition that they were reviving in a more sophisticated form after a decline of study of natural history in the Middle Ages. They would carry out their own observations and refuse to be cowed by the ancient texts.

They were helped by the arrival of the first 'scientific' gardens. The Villa di Castello, on the outskirts of Florence, has one of the most delightful gardens of Renaissance Italy. Still largely neglected by the hordes of visitors spending their time in queues waiting outside the museums and galleries of the city, it is perhaps the finest example of a Renaissance garden. The villa itself was bought by the Medici family in 1476 and some of Sandro Botticelli's most famous paintings, including *The Birth of Venus* and the *Primavera*, once hung here. This is a fitting place to begin to explore one of the most productive fields of observation of the sixteenth century, that of plant life or botany.

It was Cosimo I, duke of Florence – and, from 1570, the first duke of Tuscany – who began the planning of the garden in the 1530s. His architect was Niccolò Tribolo, often known as 'the father of the Italian garden', whose primary concern was to create a showcase of Medici beneficence through the elaborate use of water. The Villa di Castello contains some of the first elaborate fountains and grottoes that would become features of most formal gardens by the end of the century.

For botanists, the interest of the garden lies in its magnificent collection of citrus trees, still set out every summer in large terracotta tubs. There are about 1,000 of them and they contain over 100 examples of citrus, some of which are over 300 years old and now unique, descendants of the original specimens. There are few collections in the world to rival them and they are a vivid testimony of how the new spirit of Renaissance and humanist thought expressed itself in a preoccupation with the natural world of plants. The Renaissance garden combined different functions, presenting an aesthetically pleasing display as well as a living catalogue of plant varieties. This 'academic' focus was to be emphasized by the establishing of the first university botanical gardens, in Padua, Pisa and Florence, in the 1540s. As scholars returned home from their education in Italy, similar gardens would be created further afield, in northern Europe.

This shift towards a more academic study of natural phenomena can be seen in the thoughts of one of the greatest naturalists of the sixteenth century, the Swiss Conrad Gessner (1516–65). Gessner is best remembered now for his wonderfully comprehensive *Historia Animalium*, an erudite and beautifully illustrated study of the animal kingdom, published in five volumes in the 1550s.[6] Although it was placed on the Index of Prohibited Books in 1559 on account of Gessner's Lutheranism, it was to become the bible of zoology for the next 200 years. Gessner saw himself as the centre of a community of scholars. As he wrote in the preface to the first volume of *Historia Animalium*: 'One wish: that anyone wishing to contact me write sincerely and modestly, and that they write neither to increase their own glory nor to reprehend me, but to promote the *respublica literaria* [*Republic of Letters*].'[7] Luckily, for posterity Gessner jotted down the details of those informants he actually met and made them enter their names in his notebooks. Those that survive record 217 such autographs. Gessner and his fellow naturalists communicated in Ciceronian Latin, now the lingua franca of humanist studies. Anyone who trained to be a physician or apothecary learned Latin as a matter of course but so did any educated gentleman (and a few aristocratic ladies, such as the future Elizabeth I of England) and so it was possible for discussion to take place across class barriers and national boundaries. Socially speaking, Gessner seems to have been as much at ease with scholars as he was with the herdsmen he lived alongside when he was researching in the mountains.

Despite his later fame as 'the father of zoology', Gessner was best known in the 1540s for his work in botany. But he was no armchair scholar – he revelled in scrambling up the mountains of his native country. The records of his expeditions show an important contrast with Petrarch; while Petrarch was so overwhelmed with spiritual feelings that he hardly relates to the natural world, Gessner found spirituality in the experience of being in nature itself. He describes the joy he experienced in drinking water from a gushing spring. Gessner undoubtedly set off into the mountains with a scientific purpose – to find new plants – but his relationship with them was a sensuous as well as an intellectual one. He always tells us what a newly discovered plant smells like. It is the combination of 'the harmonious pleasure of all the senses' with the 'contemplation and admiration of so many works of the Great Artificer' that brings him true delight.

This outburst of what almost appears to be proto-Romantic feeling, with God becoming the divine creator of nature rather that the stern judge of the medieval world, might well have resulted in sloppy observations. However, Gessner's greatness as a scholar rests on his passionate commitment to accuracy of representation and description. He depicted what he saw without sentimentality. He drew his own illustrations, portraying the plant as a whole, of course, with separate details such as the flowers or seedpods added in enlarged ancillary drawings. He also included a text to elaborate on each part of the plant.

One of the creatures European explorers encountered for the first time in the New World was the turkey, a splendid depiction of which appeared in Conrad Gessner's *Historia Animalium*, published in the 1550s.

Gessner's plant drawings were large and formal, intended to be studied only in libraries, although it was possible, at vast expense, to order a hand-coloured copy. These were not items that walkers could take with them on rambles in the mountains to identify the flora they encountered there. The works of Carolus Clusius (1526–1609), on the other hand, were small enough to be packed away in a knapsack or a pouch on a saddle. Clusius was born Charles de l'Écluse at Arras in Flanders and studied botany at the University of Montpellier, where it was part of the curriculum of the famous medical school there.[8] Clusius is important because he broke with the tradition of trying to match plants to ancient descriptions and he did this by

deliberately searching out plants that the ancients had never described. In the 1560s he travelled in Spain and Portugal, discovering 200 plants that had never before been recorded. In 1573 Clusius was appointed director of the imperial medical garden by the Holy Roman Emperor Maximilian II in Vienna. Establishing the garden was to remain his focus for the next sixteen years. Like Gessner, however, he preferred to be in the mountains. He took every opportunity he could to escape the stifling ritual of the Habsburg court and breathe the clean air of the Austrian Alps, where he is credited with yet more botanical discoveries. He was also fascinated by the way similar plants associated with each other in the wild and he would visit the same spot each year to see how they had spread. Gradually, he became aware of how the same plant would flower at different times in different locations according to its height or the mildness of the air. Clusius was also a significant figure in the history of gardening. He was one of the first to see the colour of

Vitis Idæa rubra, in
saxis montis pilati.
Sali minoris species, ibid.
VIII
7
VII
VI
5
6
G
Rhododaphnen alpina Aldroanā
nominat. quod si Ledon alpinū
169 a

flowers as an important distinctive feature of a species, but he also loved colour for its own sake and acted as a go-between for the sale of exotic species. In the 1590s Clusius moved to Leiden in the United Provinces, where he cultivated tulips in the city's botanical garden, thereby laying the first foundations of the Dutch tulip industry. His richly descriptive writings can be regarded as forerunners of the work of such later nature writers as Izaak Walton, Gilbert White and Charles Darwin.

By now gardens were being used for experimentation as much as for enjoyment and one can talk of a way of writing about and depicting the natural world that is rooted in observation and which has broken with the ancient authors altogether. This approach required illustrations that were drawn from real-life specimens. In this respect, Hans Weiditz's woodcuts from the 1530s, which achieved remarkable levels of realism in their execution, were – like Giotto's frescos – immediately recognized as setting a new standard. The texts that accompanied such illustrations also grew in sophistication and quality. By the 1570s plants were being described in relation to other plants. When the writer of the words quoted at the start of this chapter compares the species he is describing with the arrival of the star 'Aron' and the plant 'Meyenblumen', he does so on the assumption that his readers know exactly what these are. In essence a new scientific discipline had been born.

This was only a beginning. With the discovery of the New World, vast numbers of new plants previously unknown to Europeans were found and recorded, even if few had yet been accurately described.[9] In 1577 a natural history of the West Indies by the Spaniard Nicolás Monardes appeared in an English translation under the title *Joyfull Newes out of the New Founde Worldes, wherein is declared the Rare and Singuler Vertues of Diverse and Sundrie Hearbes, Trees, Oyles, Plants and Stones...* Monardes's work marked an extraordinary broadening of European knowledge. A typical herbal of the 1530s depicted 800 plants. The landmark publication *Pinax theatri botani* (*Illustrated Exposition of Plants*), published by the Swiss botanist Gaspard Bauhin (1560–1624) in 1594, described some 6,000 species.[10] Bauhin promises on the *Pinax*'s title page to list plants 'methodically according to their genera and species'.[11] He had grasped that plants might be classified in groups, in which a number of species comprised a genus common to all of them. Here can be seen the

The images in Conrad Gessner's *Historia Plantarum* (compiled between 1555 and 1565) typified a new scientific approach to the observation of plant life.

overleaf The Atlas Miller, a Portuguese atlas of 1519, showcased the richness of the fauna and flora of Portugal's new-found territories in Asia and South America. India and its elephants form the centrepiece of this section of the atlas.

DESSERTO
PAROPANISAD
SVSIANA
EVFRATES
PERSIA
SOPI
RIO
ARABIA DESERTA
MARE PERSICV
PSIDIS
GEDROSIA
CARMANIA
MECHA
CIRCVL9
MARTI MOTES
ADEM REGIO
ARAB
IA
FELI
X
ORMANVS
MELA MONS
MARE INDIC
COCOTORA
SINVS
ARABICVS
OPIA
ELEPHAS MO
IR
CVL
V

BEGALA REGIO
XENTUS MONTES
GANGES FL.
GAGEA REGIO
ARDONIS MOS
SINUS GANGETICUS
RETIGOM
INDIA
BAZACATA ISULA
PEALEGUS INDICUS
GATABEDA
TEMALA
PEGU REG
ISULE NICOBAR
CEILAM ISULA
FINIS COMORIA
MANIOLE ISULE
Hic lapis gignitur herculeus obque hec nauigia qie clauos ferreos habent retinentur harum incolae anthropophagi unt.
EQUI NO C CI AL I
chaull
dabull
danda
os ylheos queymados
vilhas degoa
calecut
panane
coulam

Parte ſegun da delas coſas que ſe traen

do de aquellas partes .De que tẽ
go en tendido que no menos vti
lidad y prouecho vendra q̃ del
paſſado:porque ſe verã enel co/
ſas nueuas,y ſecretos que põdrã
admiracion,nunca haſta oy vi/
ſtos ni ſabidos. Y pues las coſas
de que enel tratamos, y los Rey
nos y partes de a do vienen,ſon
de vueſtra Mageſtad ,y el que
la s eſcriue es vaſallo de vueſtra
Mageſtad,ſuplico avueſtraMa
geſtad , lo reciba y ampare y a/
ya la mereed que las obras dedi
cadas a vueſtra Mageſtadrece
bir ſuelen.

Vaſſallo de vr̃a Mageſtad.

El Doctor Monardes.

EL TABACO. 3

A3

beginnings of the system of binomial nomenclature that Carl Linnaeus* would later develop in more scientifically rigorous fashion. By modern standards Bauhin's classification was somewhat hit and miss. Some of the genera he identified were accepted by Linnaeus in the eighteenth century and are still used today, but he failed to define any underlying principles through which new discoveries could be classified.

Another aspect of this growth in curiosity about the natural world was the presentation of physical specimens to the public. In Bologna, the naturalist Ulisse Aldrovandi (sometimes known as Aldrovandus; 1522–1605) and his colleague Antonio Giganti (1535–97), were amassing important collections. Both drew heavily on ethnographical material

* Carl Linnaeus (1701–78) was 'the father of modern taxonomy'. His *Species Plantarum* (1753) with its 7,200 plants laid down the nomenclature for plants that still reigns today.

from the New World, and Giganti in particular exploited his relationship with leading members of the church to acquire numerous objects from the Americas. He was especially interested in documents and inscriptions in non-European languages, those of India and China in the east, and those of the native American Indians in the west. Aldrovandi was more attracted to the natural world: animals, plants, fossils and rocks. His annotated collection contained 18,000 specimens, including fifteen volumes of 7,000 dried plants. By the time of his death in 1605 he had published four volumes of birds and insects. He left his collection to the senate of Bologna, who housed it in a 'theatre of nature', perhaps the first museum devoted to natural history. Aldrovandi's students compiled a further nine volumes describing his collection. Their contents ranged from trees, fish and serpents to minerals, molluscs and crustaceans.

In short, the sixteenth century had witnessed the birth of 'scientific' natural history. Throughout this period, the use of plants for medical purposes remained predominant; Conrad Gessner, Carolus Cluvius and Gaspard Bauhin had all studied medicine and it provided an important incentive for their researches. By the end of the century, however, it was clear that a fascination with plants in themselves had taken over. Botanical curiosity had increased enormously the stock of plants known to European collectors. And this spirit of inquisitiveness was enriching other areas of human inquiry. Not to be outdone, the writers of the period were also creating new approaches to political thought.

The 1569 edition of Nicolás Monardes's natural history of the West Indies was the first publication to depict the tobacco plant, which the author saw as a cure-all for many ailments.

Imagining Princely Politics, from *Utopia* to the Machiavellian Ruler

If a king should fall under such contempt or envy that he could not keep his subjects in their duty but by oppression and ill usage, and by rendering them poor and miserable, it were certainly better for him to quit his kingdom than to retain it by such methods as make him, while he keeps the name of authority, lose the majesty due to it.

Thomas More, *Utopia* [1]

Being unarmed makes you despised which is one of those indignities that a prince must studiously avoid… It does not stand to reason that someone who is armed will willingly obey someone unarmed or that someone unarmed will be safe amongst those who serve him who are armed.

Niccolò Machiavelli, *The Prince* [2]

In his panegyric applauding Florentine republicanism (see Chapter 12, p. 291), delivered in 1403 or 1404, Leonardo Bruni characterized the city as the inheritor of the values and ideals of the Roman republic. He was aiming his rhetoric at Florence's traditional enemies, notably Milan, which had come under the rule of princes, the Visconti. One of Bruni's most powerful arguments was that liberty flourishes if it is protected by law. Bruni cites Florence's republican constitution, according to which each of the nine priors who made up the city's governing *signoria* could hold office for two months only, as a bulwark against tyranny. He goes on to argue that, as a result, the law reigns supreme:

> All classes of men can be brought to trial; laws are made prudently for the common good, and they are fashioned to help the citizens. There is no place on earth where there is greater justice open equally to everyone. Nowhere else does freedom grow so vigorously, and nowhere else are rich and poor alike treated with such equality.[3]

This was a hopelessly optimistic view of the efficacy of a constitution which could not prevent successive generations of the Medici family from dominating Florentine politics for much of the fifteenth century. Yet Bruni's words reflected one view of republicanism that had matured in Florence and Venice. Its roots lay in the Roman authors such as Cicero, who had argued in his *De officiis* that liberty is that value 'for which a high-minded man should stake everything'. The panegyric also drew on the Roman historian Tacitus (AD 56–120), who had noted in his *Annals* and *Histories* how the emperors had corrupted republican politics. In the sixteenth century the Venetian cardinal and diplomat Gasparo Contarini would present a magisterial – but similarly glorifying and idealized – portrait of the institutions of republican government of his native city: council, senate and doge. *De Magistratibus et republica Venetorum* (*On the Officials and the Republic of Venice*) (1536) would become an inspirational text, not only for Venetians but for those, such as Thomas Jefferson, founding father of the United States, who believed that a 'mixed' republic was the highest form of government.

Yet the princes had their champions, who argued that they could better provide security for their states, both in defending them against outsiders and in protecting the rights and property of their citizens. Again there were Roman precedents, in that Roman law placed a strong emphasis on the rights of property owners. In his *Speculum principis* (*A*

Mirror for Princes) of 1373, Petrarch had gone even further in his account of princely virtue. Drawing on the example of the emperor Augustus in restoring Rome after the civil wars, he argued that a prince should be generous in his patronage, and that he should also uphold justice and seek the glory of his state. As a result of his work Petrarch attracted the support of a number of emerging Italian rulers and was welcomed into their courts. In the century that followed, numerous other advocates of princely rule contrasted the need for order with the turmoil allegedly brought about by republicanism. In his 1471 *De principe* (*Concerning the Prince*), addressed to Federico Gonzaga of Mantua, Bartolomeo Sacchi laments the inevitable and damaging effects of personal ambition; when they are allowed a role in government, individuals will compete with each other to the detriment of the community. Only a virtuous prince, one who puts the stability and wellbeing of the city before all else, can achieve glory for his state. Increasingly the courts were where patronage was to be found and careers advanced. From the early fifteenth century the *studiae humanitas*, a curriculum that focused on Greek as well as Latin and the study of classical texts of history and philosophy in addition to rhetoric, catered for the noble elite in cities such as Ferrara under the Estes and Mantua under the Gonzaga. Students were attracted from all over Europe (see pp. 295–7).[4]

The world of the princes is brilliantly explored in *Il Cortegiano* (*The Book of the Courtier*, 1528) by Baldassare Castiglione (1478–1529). Castiglione served as a courtier and soldier in Milan, Mantua, Rome (he died in Spain while on a papal mission there) and, most famously, at the elegant court of Guidobaldo da Montefeltro, duke of Urbino, where *The Book of the Courtier* is set. Castiglione is depicted in a striking portrait by Raphael, now in the Louvre (and Castiglione may have been one of the models for Raphael's *School of Athens*, see pp. 342–3). Castiglione would have been acquainted with the exquisite *studiolo*, or private study, of Federico da Montefeltro in the ducal palace, which ranks among the finest artistic expressions of classical humanism. Castiglione insists that in a court the humanist ideal of *virtu* can be cultivated by both the prince and his courtiers. Like his contemporary Machiavelli, he knew only too well the horrors of the French invasion and its consequences, but he insists that a harmonious court can restore civilized living to a war-torn peninsula. Italian has a good word for it: *sprezzatura*, the ability to create great things without apparent effort. (Castiglione can be seen as the embodiment of *sprezzatura*: he laboured over *The Book of the Courtier* for sixteen years but boasted that he had run it off in *pochi giorni*, 'just a few days'.)

The Book of the Courtier is presented as a series of conversations involving nineteen real individuals, including a son of Lorenzo the Magnificent, the intellectual future cardinal Pietro Bembo and four ladies of the court. This approach allows the participants to show off their eloquence but also to explore opposing views. There is, for instance, a spirited debate over whether women can show *virtu* and, if so, are feminine expressions of this similar to masculine ones. The men display some willingness to accept women as active participants at court, but the meagre contribution of the two women present during this dialogue, which takes place in the drawing room of the duchess of Urbino – the duchess herself and her sister-in-law Emilia Pia – tends to reinforce the idea that their role should be a largely decorative one, in support of the men. But fifteenth-century Italian courtly culture in fact offered some fine examples of active female *virtu*: the lives of Isabella d'Este (1474–1539), brought up in the intellectually brilliant court of Ferrara, and now marquise of Mantua, who corresponded with Castiglione and Pietro Bembo, and Ginevra Sforza (1440–1507), wife of Giovanni II Bentivoglio of Bologna (r.1463–1506), show that a woman could flourish in a supportive court and contribute to its functioning.

Castiglione's ideal courtier is of noble background, schooled in Greek and Latin texts, with grace and verbal agility. He also fights well but can turn to music when at home. The beautiful inlaid marquetry of the *intarsia* wooden panels in the *studiolo* in Urbino depict armour and weapons alongside musical instruments. The courtier's role is to win the approval of his prince so that he can support and advise him on the road to *virtu*: 'He will know in every situation how to smoothly make his prince see how much honour and utility he and his supporters can gain from justice, generosity, magnanimity, gentleness and the other *virtu* which are required of a good prince.' *The Book of the Courtier* was an instant bestseller, one of the most widely printed books of the sixteenth century, and it provided a model for the ideal 'gentleman' that lasted centuries. But it also perpetuated the myth that those who concentrated on making money were somehow not worthy of respect, an attitude that persisted in some European societies well into the twentieth century.

Raphael was a close friend of the diplomat and humanist Baldassare Castiglione, author of *The Courtier*. This striking portrait (1514–15) of Castiglione is considered one of his masterpieces.

Among the major virtues of a Christian prince, as seen by Erasmus, was the ability to maintain peace and security. Erasmus had noted two major weaknesses of the Roman state: its love of war and its pursuit of wealth. Both he considered corrupting. He went further by following

Plato in believing that goods should be held in common. The aim of government was to achieve *eudaimonia*, the flourishing of individuals, and this would only follow when equality was enforced. These ideals were also followed in one of the more important works of political philosophy of the period, the humanist Thomas More's *Utopia*.[5]

Utopia responds to the new discoveries of the Americas, not least in being presented as the apocryphal travel journal of a sailor who had accompanied Amerigo Vespucci in the early sixteenth century. (These discoveries and their impact have chapters to themselves; see Chapters 17 and 22.) More (1478–1535) is a hard figure to place. He was a deeply erudite man, and a friend, together with his colleague John Colet, of the liberal humanist Erasmus. More and Colet were part of the first generation of English scholars to become proficient in classical Greek. Yet he was also a hardline Catholic, happy to condemn heretics to the fire. Having risen to the high office of Lord Chancellor in the fraught atmosphere of the court of Henry VIII, he was executed when he refused to accept Henry's Act of Supremacy of 1534, which established an English church free of papal control.

Thomas Hobby's English translation (1561) of Baldassore Castiglione's *The Courtier* became the essential handbook for the Elizabethan gentleman.

It is equally hard to place *Utopia*, written when More was starting out in public life on a delegation to the Netherlands (1516). The title, meaning 'nowhere' (based on the Greek *ou*, 'not', and *topos*, 'place'), alerts us to the possibility that More is describing a society that he knows cannot exist, yet he presents it as a riposte to the abuses and corruption of contemporary England (as related to him by the sailor Raphael Hythloday, whom he meets in Antwerp). Hythloday (the Greek derivation of the name suggests 'purveyor of nonsense'), who, unexpectedly, has an extensive knowledge of Greek philosophy, follows Plato in seeing all evil originating in the possession of private property. A few always accumulate more than their fair share of the wealth of the community, leaving the majority in poverty. This was relevant to the situation in early sixteenth-century England, where sheep farming was driving the peasants off the land. A remarkable feature of Book 1 ('The Communication of Raphael Hythloday, Concerning the Best State of a Commonwealth') is its argument, described by one scholar as one of 'startling originality',[6] that evil-doing, in this case theft, might be the result of deprivation. It raises the question of whether God can justifiably condemn those who are driven into sin by society. There is also a discussion here of philosophy as an abstract subject of debate which More suggests is inadequate for the actual experience of

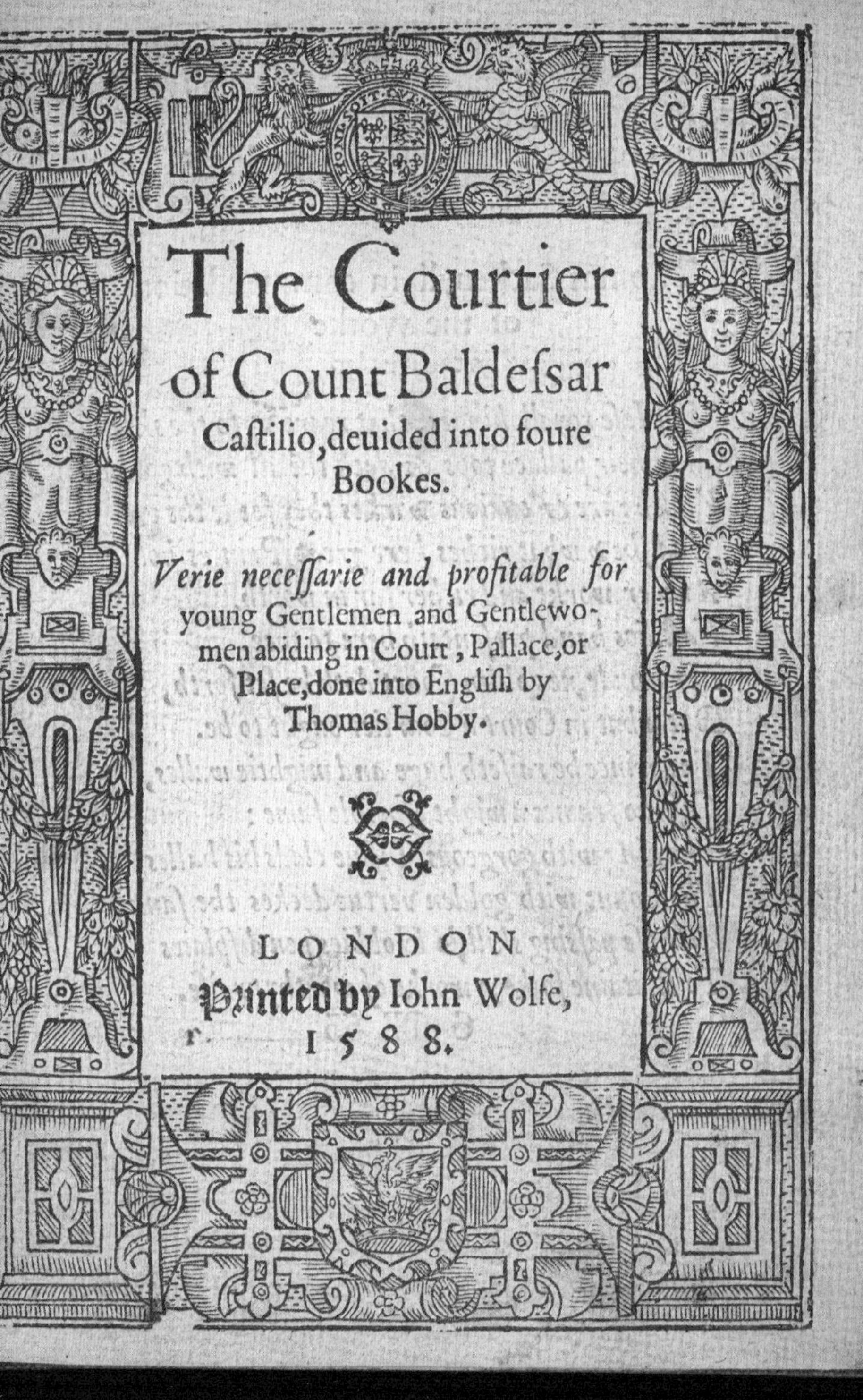

The Courtier of Count Baldessar Castilio, deuided into foure Bookes.

Verie necessarie and profitable for young Gentlemen and Gentlewomen abiding in Court, Pallace, or Place, done into English by Thomas Hobby.

LONDON
Printed by Iohn Wolfe,
1588.

Amaurotũ vrbs.
Fons Anydri.
Ostium anydri
Hythlodaeus.

living in a court, where you must use 'a crafty wile' to achieve good. As in many other Renaissance contexts, rhetoric is recommended as a tool for survival.

It is probable that More wrote the second book of *Utopia* first, when he had the freedom to think more freely, and the first book later, as he contemplated entering the king's service. In fact, many editions of *Utopia* omit the first book altogether. However, the link between the two is provided by More's wish for Hythloday to tell him about Utopia. In Book 2 ('Discourse on Utopia') Hythloday describes the 'Utopian' island state the sailor has come across on his travels. It has been brought into being by a king, Utopus, who took it over by force and who then moved a primitive society to a higher state of being without recognizing private property. No one is allowed to own their own homes, and in fact they change their houses by lot every ten years. Utopus is, in short, a philosopher-king on the model of Plato. Government is conducted through the election of magistrates, the Syphogrants, by groups of thirty households who then elect further magistrates to form the prince's council. There are opportunities for the whole island to meet together in a senate.

Freed from the desire to acquire possessions and protect them, the citizens have an excess of energy, which they channel into producing the wealth of the community. So abundant is their energy that they only need to work for six hours a day, although many willingly labour for longer. Many of these hours are devoted to agricultural work, periods of which are compulsory. Simple crafts are especially valued. Women work alongside men. More notes the time wasted by the idle in Europe, especially the clergy. In Utopia, there will be such a surplus of resources that everyone will be able to help themselves from the foodstuffs and materials that have been stored. Once two years' worth of supplies have been accumulated, the rest can be exported. Abundance is assumed: Utopia is an island where the climate is benign and there are plentiful supplies of water. 'I never saw anything more fruitful nor better trimmed in any place', says Hythloday as he describes the well-stocked gardens. Even the coastline seems designed to help the flow of commerce. A woodcut map of Utopia was included in a 1518 edition of the work published in Basle and 'it is likely that this was the first work of fiction to contain a map of a non-existent place'.[7]

A woodcut by Ambrosius Holbein which appeared in a revised Latin edition of Thomas More's *Utopia* printed in Basle in 1518. It depicts the traveller Hythloday describing Utopia to More himself.

With so much free time and fertile land, all the citizens are expected to master a craft and cultivate the mind. An elite of scholars provide lectures and standards are high – the Utopians 'have made the same discoveries as the Greeks, in music, logic, arithmetic and geography'. Despite these intellectual achievements the emphasis in the curriculum is on moral uprightness, with contributions from both the austere self-discipline of Stoicism and from Epicureanism,* in which the individual finds peace of mind through contemplation and good fellowship. While there is no emphasis on asceticism, spiritual values are important (as Plato had taught). Suicide is forbidden but euthanasia is permitted. The Utopian way of life is set within a religious framework; reason orientates its users towards the notion of a single supreme God, but diversity of opinion is accepted. There is nothing of original sin here. 'The soul is immortal and by the bountiful goodness of God ordained to felicity', a view that Augustine would have found shocking. As a result of the acquiescence of the citizens of this happy community, laws are few and magistrates are benign. Yet a closer reading of the text suggests that this is still an authoritarian society. Punishment is inflicted through making wrongdoers temporary slaves who will carry out menial jobs. Travel outside the community is restricted and luxuries are despised. It is iron rather than silver and gold that is the most precious commodity for this hard-working society. Hythloday talks of some visiting ambassadors who appear in all the finery of smart diplomatic dress and simply invite ridicule. Utopia is undoubtedly an austere society: daily life follows a pattern of communal eating in barns, listening to lectures and being in bed by 8 p.m.

More makes it clear enough that he does not believe Utopia could exist. At one point he puts forward Aristotle's argument in favour of private property, that it encourages the owners to keep good order and take responsibility for the wellbeing of society (this argument would later be used to justify the restricting of voting rights to property owners). Yet it is remarkable that a man so wedded to Catholic orthodoxy could even envisage a society in which human beings are so well developed in body and mind and free of the guilt of original sin. This is a long way from Augustine's fallen mankind. The philosopher Anthony Kenny, in a biographical essay on More, notes that 'wherever we turn in Utopia, it seems that we find something that is contradicted in More's life'.[8] Kenny notes in particular the conflict between More's own stern

* The philosopher Epicurus (341–270 BC) believed that this life was the only one we had and that its purpose was to find pleasure, not so much sensual, but psychological, from peace of mind and companionship. Diogenes Laertius had dedicated a whole book to him together with many of his writings.

religious Catholicism and the religious tolerance he describes in *Utopia*. Again, how could he serve in a luxurious and licentious court subject to the whims of an increasingly irritable monarch while extolling the democracy of Utopia? The one theme of Utopia that *is* consistent with the values according to which More lived his own life is his attack on the linking of the exercise of *virtu* with status, fine clothes and aristocratic superiority. And the best means of destroying this, *Utopia* suggests, is to ban all private property. More is clearly ambivalent on this matter. It may be that implicit in Utopia's proscription of luxury and private riches is a condemnation of an entrenched nobility who flaunted their wealth and education as if that alone was enough to demand respect.

These contradictions have generated intense scholarly debate over More's intentions in writing the work: 'In no other literary work is the question of authorial intention at once more pressing and more unanswerable,' writes Susan Bruce, in her introduction to the World Classics edition of *Utopia*.[9] Some have argued that More was genuinely concerned with the poverty and corruption of England and, as a young man whose convictions were still evolving, was trying to imagine how society might be better run. It might even be that More had composed a satire on idealism, expecting the reader to realize that he is setting out the impossible. As a committed humanist, steeped in classical texts, More would also have known of the ideal of the 'Golden Age', in which societies lived in a state of prosperity, stability and mutual harmony that had been forever lost, and which was a familiar topic in such texts. In introducing Hythloday as a sailor who has journeyed to the west, More may also have been influenced by what he had heard of native societies in the Americas. Or it may simply be that, at the time when More was writing – when he was based in Flanders during long-drawn-out trade negotiations with the Holy Roman Emperor – he may have had the leisure to let his mind run riot.

Whatever More's motives, over the centuries since it was published *Utopia* has gripped the imagination. It is the only one of More's works that has lasted. At its core is the belief that a state can be reorganized for the common good, providing not only a fairer society but one which releases positive energies and a commitment to harmonious living. More's name is even to be found, improbably, on an obelisk in Moscow honouring the forerunners of communism. Sadly, the twentieth century showed, in the collectivization plans of Stalin in Soviet Russia and Mao Zedong in China, for instance, that abolishing private property is not enough to encourage the population to work joyfully in an ordered way. The result has been chaos, breakdown in cultivation and eventually famine. Individual self-interest has been impossible to subdue.

Utopia's imagined society and its prescriptions did not provide a model which the states of early sixteenth-century Europe could realistically follow. The French invasion of Italy in 1494 spawned a mood of sober reflectiveness, which would lead to important discussions on the nature of authority and the effective use of power in a world where violence was an everyday occurrence. Of the voices prominent in these debates the name that resonates down the ages is that of Niccolò Machiavelli (1469–1527). Assessing Machiavelli's views is challenging. Writing to his close friend the historian Francesco Guicciardini in 1521, some years after his most controversial work, *The Prince* (1513–14), had been written, he confessed that 'for a long time I have not said what I believed, nor do I ever believe what I say. And if sometimes I do happen to tell the truth, I hide it among so many lies that it is hard to find.'[10] *The Prince* had been conceived within the turmoil of Florentine republican politics, in which Machiavelli had played a leading part until he had been tortured and thrown out of the city in 1512 when the Medici returned from exile.

Niccolò Machiavelli as depicted in a posthumous portrait by Santi di Tito (1536–1603) in the Palazzo Vecchio in Florence.

Machiavelli was a typical humanist of his time; he especially valued the cultural and military heritage of ancient Rome. In a famous letter to his friend Francesco Vittori in December 1513, the year after he had been released from prison, he would tell of how, on returning from a day in the fields, he would change clothes and steep himself in the Roman classics. The early days of Rome, when republican values were prominent in building the state, were his favourite period.[11] Yet Machiavelli was no armchair theorist. He had been brought up in the 'reign' of Lorenzo the Magnificent, witnessed the French invasion and had lived through the Savonarola years. Following the fall of Savonarola in 1498 he was given a senior position in the government as second chancellor, responsible for foreign affairs and later the conduct of war. For fourteen years he travelled widely, helping to sort out the numerous disputes that threatened Florence's interests. In 1500 he was in France to negotiate with the new French king, Louis XII, who had claimed the right to rule in Milan, Florence's old enemy. He travelled with the *papa terribile*, Julius II, and met with Emperor Maximilian I. He supervised the tortuous campaigns to retake Pisa, during which Machiavelli learned that a citizen army raised from within the state was vastly more effective

than the mercenaries Florence had previously employed. This was a view derived from his studies of the Roman republic and its citizen legions. When his advice was heeded and Pisa finally fell in 1509, he could take credit for the success. In short, this was a confident and able man who had matured within the maelstrom of European politics. However, after the dissolution of the Florentine republic by the Medici in 1512, the forty-three-year-old Machiavelli was brutally discarded. A year later, he would be tortured, then briefly imprisoned for conspiracy. On his release, he retired to his Tuscan estate.

This is the context in which *The Prince* was written. *The Prince* was dedicated to the newly returned Medici as if, despite his treatment, Machiavelli was prepared to re-enter political service under their rule. It ends with an exhortation for them to use their *virtu* and good fortune (see below) to confront the barbarians who have taken over Italy. Yet there is no evidence that they ever read it.

The Prince was never published during Machiavelli's lifetime and its first appearance was as a conversation piece to be distributed among his coterie of humanist friends. It is also written in the vernacular Tuscan, by now an elegant language, and one which those who had mastered Latin to perfection felt able to use. *The Prince* uses Latin for its chapter headings and is laced with Latin quotations. This is Machiavelli showing off his erudition to earn respect among his small group of readers.[12]

The Prince is usually seen as a cynical justification for the unrestrained use of power by a prince determined to dominate his subjects. It is undeniable that Machiavelli rejects the idealized views of the benign, compassionate ruler who respects justice and prudence as cardinal virtues. This unsentimental attitude of course reflects the brutal realities of a violent age, but *The Prince* is also rooted in Machiavelli's experience of the corruptions and instabilities of political life. He had achieved a political objective through the citizen army he organized to subjugate Pisa and it was understandable that he would expect 'his' prince to arm himself. So there is an emphasis (in chapters 12–14) on the justified use of military force. Machiavelli's confidence can also be seen in the forceful way in which he presents his case, something that adds immensely to the power of the narrative.

In essence *The Prince* is a far more sophisticated analysis of power than it is often given credit for. The problem lies rather in its lack of coherence. The work examines the various ways in which a ruler might achieve and maintain supremacy. For instance, Machiavelli contrasts the state which has already known hereditary rule, where a new ruler may easily fit himself in, with one which has hitherto been a republic and is therefore resistant to one-man rule. It is Machiavelli's advice to the prince, here *il principe nuovo* (a prince who has recently come to rule), on how to deal with the latter that constitutes the most infamous part of his text.

Like most humanists, Machiavelli sees the achievement of *virtu* as intrinsic to a successful society. *Virtu* was what led Rome to greatness. Quentin Skinner, in his celebrated *The Foundations of Modern Political Thought* (1978), notes that for Machiavelli 'the *virtu* of the ruler is treated as an astonishingly creative force, the key to "maintaining his state" and enabling him to fight off his enemies'.[13] This would involve calculating the means through which one could survive, especially when one's status was threatened. Machiavelli knew only too well from his own experience how quickly *fortuna*, whether good or bad, could turn against one. He highlighted the case of Cesare Borgia, son of the notorious Pope Alexander VI, who had been attempting to carve out a kingdom for himself in central Italy. Cesare's plans collapsed after his father's death in 1503 when Alexander's rival Giuliano della Rovere was elected as Pope Julius II. Machiavelli suggests that *virtu* consisted in planning for this kind of reversal and being ruthless in doing so. Even deliberate lying and deception is justified and the prince can 'act in defiance of good faith, of charity, of kindness and religion'. Steeped as he was in ancient texts, Machiavelli used as one of his examples Agathocles, the late fourth-century BC tyrant of Syracuse. While decrying his cruelty, Machiavelli praises Agathocles for his skill and courage in overcoming hardships in his drive for power.

The jaded Machiavelli was critical of his more philosophical contemporaries who underestimated the need for coercion. He must have had in mind Piero de' Medici and his abject surrender to Charles VIII of France in 1494. He subverted the traditional humanist argument that a prince should be loved rather than feared. Indeed, Machiavelli's argument tended towards the opposite; that the use of fear could be justified as a means to an end. And it is here that his use of *virtu* becomes much more ambiguous and embraces amorality. Where the people themselves lack *virtu*, Machiavelli argues, a prince might well have to use *virtu*, in the amoral sense of the word, in the short term, to stabilize society and turn it towards *virtu* in a more positive sense. One can see why this manipulation of expression has earned Machiavelli such a bad reputation. He seems to have moved beyond any stable interpretation of good or evil. One might find an echo here of the Greek historian Thucydides' portrayal of the civil war in Corcyra (modern Corfu), where Thucydides notes how recklessness came to be called 'courage' and aggression was recast as 'manliness'. Moreover, in *The Prince* Machiavelli often assumes that 'the people' are happy to be made dependent on their ruler, even to the extent of allowing themselves to be suppressed. Quentin Skinner has suggested that underlying *The Prince* is Machiavelli's belief that acting harshly in the short term will avoid greater cruelty and disorder in the long term. Machiavelli also notes how acting decisively earns respect, whereas acting irresolutely, as Piero de' Medici had done in the face of the invading French, simply invites contempt.[14]

So was this the authentic Machiavelli? The Machiavelli scholar Erica Benner talks of *The Prince*'s 'impression of different voices, the maddening ambiguities'.[15] In his *Discourses on Livy* (Livy being the famous historian of republican Rome), which evolved from his conversations with friends in the same years that he was writing *The Prince*, Machiavelli shows a much more positive attitude in his discussion of republics. He was able to find an ideal in the Roman republic from which he had already drawn his model for a citizen army (for the subjugation of Pisa) 'so that young spirits who happen to read what I write will flee from present examples and imitate those of the ancients',[16] but he goes further in stressing the virtues of a mixed government in which different classes are represented. He stresses all the advantages of popular involvement and even when he admits that a strong man may be needed to take control during times of social or political breakdown, he muses on whether such a person exists. The violent application of power might even make things worse. He notes too that 'good' men are reluctant to resort to evil. There is another report that he believed that gross inequalities in a society would invariably lead to unrest, contrasting Germany with Italy.[17] So in the *Discourses* one finds Machiavelli adopting a much more nuanced approach to power, here set within the republican tradition in which he had served.

Of course, few readers would have bothered to explore the ambiguities and hesitations in Machiavelli's work. He was soon criticized for raising the will of the ruler above any spiritual concerns. At best he appears to see his rulers using religion as a means of manipulating power, a justified stance, perhaps, but one which could hardly be defended in public. There were those Florentines who feared that the Medicis to whom the text was dedicated might actually take it as a tyrannical model for princely behaviour. After its first printing in 1532 (seven years after Machiavelli's death), *The Prince* quickly became seen as a work that broke through established traditions of humanist writing and injected a disturbing realism into political thought. Virtually every commentator was soon reacting to it, for or against its apparently bleak message. As early as 1538 the English cardinal Reginald Pole denounced Thomas Cromwell and his master Henry VIII as inspired by the 'Satanic' Machiavelli. In 1559 the first papal Index of Prohibited Books included every one of Machiavelli's works, despite the plea of his grandson that offending passages could be cut out. They remained on the Index until 1890. (Ironically, *The Book of the Courtier* was also placed on the Index for giving too great an emphasis to Fortuna at the expense of recognizing God's power to intervene.) This did not stop both authors from being widely read by both Catholics and Protestants. England was particularly receptive: Shakespeare's analysis of the power of rulers in his plays owes much to Machiavelli. The character Machievil in Christopher Marlowe's *The Jew of Malta* (1589) pronounces that 'Might first made kings, and laws were then most sure when, like the Draco's,* they were writ in blood.' In his *The Politics of Opera: A History from Monteverdi to Mozart*,[18] Mitchell Cohen credits to Machiavelli the prominence of tyrannical princes in early opera. He highlights, for instance, Monteverdi's *L'incoronazione di Poppea* (*The Coronation of Poppaea*, 1643), which showcases two unscrupulous 'Machiavellian' characters, Emperor Nero and his mistress Poppaea. Despite the efforts of Machiavelli scholars such as Erica Benner to portray a softer, more reflective, Machiavelli, the condemnatory term 'Machiavellian' seems to be here to stay.

Castiglione, More and Machiavelli were all steeped in ancient texts, but this was a restless age. James Hankins, a leading scholar in the history of Renaissance thought, notes how the sixteenth century showed 'a profound dissatisfaction with the existing resources of European intellectual life and a determination to appropriate the wisdom and knowledge of other cultures and religions'.[19] This can be seen both in the recovery of new classical texts but also in a readiness to learn about other civilizations. The European discovery of the New World would be the most dramatic example of this (see Chapters 17 and 22), but intellectual life was also enriched by the rediscovery of the ancient world, and, concomitantly, of the embracing of new ways of looking at it. These are the subject of our next chapter.

* Draco was an Athenian legislator of the seventh century BC, known for the harshness of his laws.

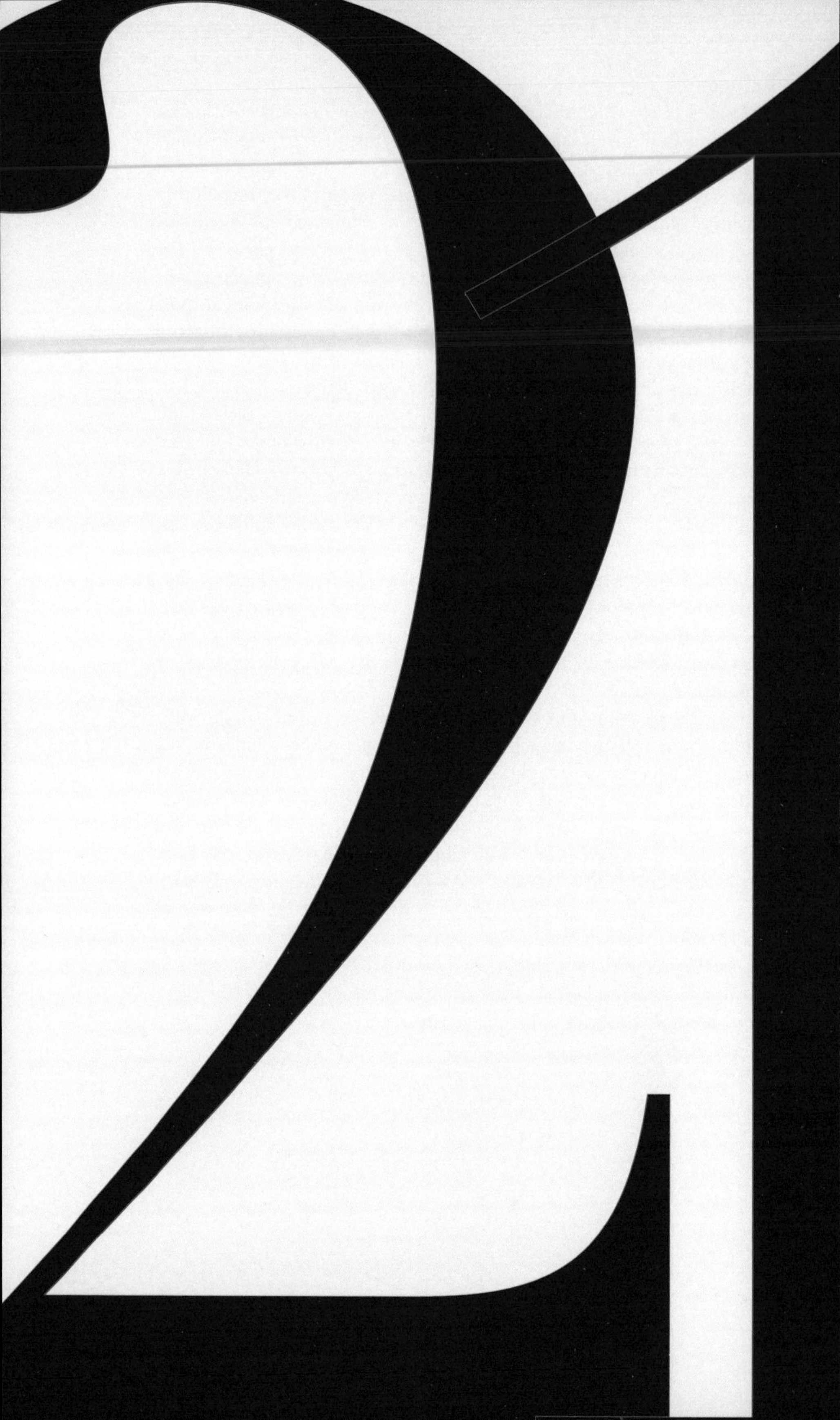

Broadening Horizons: From the Laocoön to the Academies

The first time I was in Rome when I was very young, the pope was told about the discovery of some very beautiful statues in a vineyard near Santa Maria Maggiore. The pope ordered one of his officers to run and tell Giuliano da Sangallo to go and see them. He set off immediately. Since Michelangelo Buonarroti was always to be found at our house, my father wanted him to come along too. I joined up with my father and off we went. I climbed down to where the statues were when immediately my father said 'That is the Laocoön, which Pliny mentions.' Then they dug the hole wider so that they could pull the statue out. As soon as it was visible everyone started to draw, all the while discoursing on ancient things, chatting as well about the ones in Florence.

Francesco da Sangallo, son of the architect Giuliano, both of whom were present at this discovery[1]

It was inevitable that if scholarship was to be creative in the sixteenth century it would be curious about other civilizations. In 1492, Columbus had made the sensational discovery of other societies whose existence had been completely unknown. How they were portrayed and understood will be the subject of the next chapter. This chapter will explore the rediscovery of ancient cultures that played such an important part in broadening the western mind in the fifteenth and, predominantly, sixteenth centuries.[2]

The story of the rediscovery starts in Rome.[3] Already in the 1490s there had been great excitement when a domed room from Roman times had been broken into on the Esquiline Hill and found to be part of Nero's opulent *Domus Aurea*, 'the Golden House' (*c.*AD 65). Its frescos were still intact and Raphael and Michelangelo were among those who were lowered down on ropes to study them. The room's *grotteschi* designs, full of fantastical human and animal figures, were to reappear, first in decorations in the Vatican and then throughout northern Italy.

A few years later there was an even more dramatic find, the Laocoön. Laocoön was a Trojan priest who had warned the city of the dangers of the Trojan Horse but two snakes had come across the sea to strangle him and his two sons. The scene had been vividly portrayed by the poet Virgil in his epic the *Aeneid* and a statue of the three figures entangled in the snakes had been described in Pliny's *Natural History* with named sculptors from Rhodes. As noted in the opening quotation, just such a statue was discovered in a private garden on the Esquiline Hill in 1506. It was assumed to be the one described by Pliny and its anguished depiction of the tragedy was an immediate sensation. On hearing the news of its discovery Michelangelo hurried to see it being dug out and he too gave it the seal of approval. The tortured figures of the priest and his sons may have inspired Michelangelo's (unfinished) sculptures of slaves now in the Accademia in Florence.[4]

The discovery of *Laocoön and his Sons* in Rome in 1506 was a powerful moment in the revival of enthusiasm for the classical past. The ancient statue was soon acquired by Pope Julius II for his gallery in the Belvedere in the Vatican.

The Laocoön was bought by Pope Julius II, who had a perfect place to display it. The Belvedere garden had been built further up the Vatican Hill behind the papal palace and then incorporated into the palace by the architect Donato Bramante, who was redesigning St Peter's for the pope. Bramante was already famous for his exquisite Tempietto on the Janiculum Hill (1502). Modelled on nearby Roman buildings, the small

circular domed building was recognized as a masterpiece that confirmed the high status of Greco-Roman architecture that Alberti had extolled. A dome placed above columns became an essential feature of many later churches and ceremonial buildings.*

The Belvedere garden was planted with orange trees and had fountains that were graced with antique statues, suitably of personifications of the Nile and Tiber. Julius was as enthused with the idea of incorporating classical sculptures into the Christian patrimony as he had been over the Greek philosophers of Raphael described earlier. He let it be known that he was 'eager to acquire all the most wonderful and beautiful antiquities in order to place them in his garden'.[5] The Laocoön was set up here beside another of Julius's acquisitions, an Apollo, known as the 'Apollo Belvedere', and these two became the star attractions. By 1543 the niches of the garden had been filled with other statues, the last of them to be put in place being a sensual Antinous, the youthful beloved of the emperor Hadrian, which became one of the most popular in the collection. What was revolutionary about the Belvedere was that it became a public gallery in which the presence of the statues was itself a guarantee of their supreme quality. 'The whole concept of displaying art in this way – this very notion of art in itself – was as new as it was unique, and it is hardly surprising that the impact was overwhelming.'[6] For the next 300 years the Belvedere statues set the standard of excellence and it became mandatory for any artist to begin their training by copying either the statues themselves or plaster casts of the originals. When Louis XIV was commissioning statues for the gardens of his palace at Versailles, many of them, including the Apollo Belvedere and the Laocoön, were copies from the Belvedere.[7]

Of course, there had been major collectors and collections before Pope Julius displayed his collection of Roman sculpture in the *Cortile del Belvedere.* In the fifteenth century Cosimo and Piero de' Medici filled their family palace with a treasure trove of antiquities, gems, paintings, and *objets d'art.* Lorenzo de' Medici added to the collection after he had acquired a large array of gems, coins and small bronzes from an earlier papal collection. Pope Sixtus IV (r.1471–84) had donated wonderful ancient bronzes to be displayed on the Capitoline Hill in Rome. Copies of these were diffused among *cognoscenti* in the shape of bronze statuettes, one of the most attractive expressions of Renaissance art. By the sixteenth century collecting ancient sculptures had become all the rage. In 1538 the Farnese Pope Paul III (r.1534–49) transferred

* Among these are St Paul's Cathedral, London, the Pantheon in Paris and the Capitol in Washington.

one of the most imposing statues of all, the equestrian statue of Marcus Aurelius, which had been preserved because it was believed to be of the Christian emperor Constantine, from the Lateran Palace to the centre of the *piazza* that Michelangelo was designing on the Capitoline Hill. It was to become an inspiration for those sculptors commissioned to portray dukes and monarchs on horseback. By 1543 Paul had set about making his own collection of antiquities. The Farnese family owned the extensive ruins of the Baths of Caracalla, which had been decorated with sculptures in the third century AD, and they began digging there. Among the first finds was the Farnese Bull, the largest group of figures known from antiquity, and the massive Farnese Hercules. The Farnese Bull was found in fragments but the pope ordered it to be reconstituted so that this pagan statue would 'certainly be the most beautiful thing in Christendom'.[8] By the time of his death, Paul had the most prestigious private collection in Rome, some 300 statues, equal to that of the Vatican. Unlike many of these collections, it was preserved intact and was taken to Naples by a Farnese descendant in the eighteenth century, where it is still on display in the Archaeological Museum.

There was still at this time little understanding of how to distinguish between Greek and Roman sculpture. Many sculptures believed to be Greek were in fact Roman copies of the originals. Even so, they, and the accompanying works of contemporary artists, caught the imagination of artists and scholars alike. In the words of the art historian Ingrid Rowland, Raphael's *School of Athens*, with its array of philosophers, 'helped to create a widespread passion for the careful study of Greek in Italy'.[9] This vogue for classicism caught another mood, a fascination with the philosophies themselves that was becoming pervasive in intellectual circles. The eighty-two Greek philosophers in the *Lives* of Diogenes Laertius may have been presented in a disorganized and uncritical format (one view is that Diogenes died before he could bring his work into order) but the mass of anecdotes, the eccentricity of his subjects and their obsession with finding the best way of living, endeared them to his Renaissance readers. Could their teachings be reconciled with Christianity as Raphael had done in the frescos in his *Stanza della Segnatura*?[10]

* * *

With the many attacks on the sterility of scholastic Aristotelianism by the humanists, it comes perhaps as a surprise that, in the sheer quantity of editions of his works and commentaries on them, Aristotle is by far the most influential philosopher of the sixteenth century.[11] New texts of his were arriving from the east and even the best-known ones were invigorated by humanist translators such as Leonardo Bruni and his sixteenth-century successors. Disputes over how best to translate him simply added to the number and variety of Latin editions. The Counter-Reformation further embedded the traditional Aristotelian content of the Catholic universities' curriculum. So the revival of the Hellenistic philosophers needs to be placed in context of the continuing dominance of 'the Philosopher'.

Yet while one can hardly see the sixteenth century as an age of innovative philosophy, there was a widespread belief that the study of the philosophy of the ancients was a balm for the soul. One philosophy that gained new support was Stoicism. While Stoicism had always attracted some Christians for its insistence on resolution in the face of fate and suffering, as a pagan philosophy it was regarded with some suspicion. During the Renaissance, attitudes to its best-known proponent, the Roman statesman and philosopher Seneca (4 BC–

AD 65), were ambivalent. The belief that he had corresponded with the apostle Paul had been rejected by Lorenzo Valla (see p. 295) and this left him exposed for his paganism and above all his decision to commit suicide during the reign of the emperor Nero. As more texts were discovered, and the intricacies of Stoic debate appreciated, some were critical of a philosophy that was full of 'overly subtle arguments, cavils and sophistries'.[12] Many found it difficult to accept the emotional distance from the calamities of everyday life that the Stoics preached. It was the French philosopher Michel de Montaigne (1533–92) who, while respecting aspects of Stoicism, regretted that 'to the Stoics pity is a vicious passion: they want us to succor the afflicted, but not to unbend and sympathize with them'.[13] The Stoic insistence that an individual must take responsibility for their own happiness undermined any role for God.

The most sophisticated scholar of Stoicism, the Fleming Justus Lipsius (1547–1606), proved as important in the revival of Stoicism as Ficino had been for Platonism. Lipsius was writing at a time of religious strife and was no stranger to suffering. His house was sacked twice during the religious wars of the era and he wavered between Catholicism and Lutheranism. In his *De Constantia* (*On Constancy in Times of Public Calamity*, 1584), he provided a guide to how Stoicism could be revived as a living philosophy that allowed the individual to deal with public evils. It was futile, Lipsius argued, to try to escape the real world by moving around; rather, it was important to train the mind to resist external events. (Today one would see him as a champion of mindfulness!) While *De Constantia* remains his most influential work, Lipsius's *Manuductionis ad Stoicam Philosophiam*, a guide to Stoic philosophy (1604), was a vast compilation of the works of all the known Stoic philosophers and of those Christian writers whose commentaries on them had consolidated the relationship between Stoicism and Christianity. Lipsius managed to portray Stoicism in terms of an active, rather than passive, ethical system and so stress an overlap with Christianity.[14] For the next fifty years Stoicism provided a backbone to Christian ethics; European artists even applauded the suicide of Seneca. In a famous portrayal (1615) Peter Paul Rubens fits him into the iconography of Christian martyrdom.

Lorenzo Lotto's portrait of the Renaissance scholar Andrea Odoni (1527) shows him surrounded by antiquities. Yet his hand is also pressed against a Christian cross hanging round his neck, illustrating the harmony between the two traditions.

The most important revival of Greek philosophy in the sixteenth century was the tradition of Scepticism, the questioning of what could be known, if anything at all, for certain. This was not a feature of medieval thought (although some scholars have seen Scepticism in the works of William of Ockham). It was only in the fifteenth century that manuscripts of the works of the second-century BC Sextus Empiricus highlighted Pyrrho of Elis, a philosopher of the fourth century BC who also appeared in Diogenes Laertes' *Lives of the Philosophers*. Pyrrho had argued that all belief should be suspended as there was no effective way of achieving truth. At first this hardly resonated. The breakthrough came with the recognition, by Gianfrancesco Pico della Mirandola (1469–1533), nephew of the Florentine philosopher Giovanni Pico della Mirandola, that Pyrrhonism could be used against itself – in the sense that, if the pagans *knew* that they knew nothing, the 'truths' of Christianity achieved through divine revelation were more easily defended. Uncertain of everything, we need to be humble, aware that there is little we can provide ourselves that will help us attain an understanding of God. By the middle of the sixteenth century, once new editions of Sextus Empiricus had been published, Scepticism had again become a battering ram against the scholastics; but many humanists, including the essayist Montaigne, saw it rather as means of escaping from tortuous arguments. If our senses deceive us and reason often leads to different conclusions from the same premises, then we have an excuse not to get involved. One can live peacefully within society.

There were two other figures from the classical world whose prominence in the sixteenth century carried great influence. The first was Titus Lucretius Carus (98–*c.*55 BC), author of *De rerum natura* (*On the Nature of Things*), a sophisticated portrayal of Epicureanism. *De rerum* has been described as 'one of the rarest of literary accomplishments, a successful didactic poem on a scientific subject'.* For Lucretius, as with Epicurus, there is no place for religion; the world is purely material, made up of atoms which are always rearranging themselves, swerving backwards and forwards to make contact with each other. There is no afterlife, so the fear of judgement after death is unnecessary. Lucretius praises the power of reason to bring the fruits of civilization, among which he includes seamanship, agriculture, law, poetry, painting and sculpture. None of this suggests the sheer exuberance of the poem, its delight in the natural world and the joys of friendship.

The one surviving manuscript of *De rerum* had been discovered in a German monastery in 1417 but at first its anti-religious tone made it of little interest other than as a text to be emended. Machiavelli certainly knew it – his annotated edition survives and scholars have found some

* This was the view of the nineteenth-century Scottish botanist Alexander Dalzell.

traces of its ideas in his writings. However, it was not until 1580 that Lucretius was fully championed, this time by Montaigne in his *Essays*. Montaigne tells how he found himself 'enthralled by some of Lucretius' finest passages' and places him among his other Roman favourites, Virgil, Catullus and Horace.[15] By the next century, Lucretius' influence had become pervasive among scientists.[16]

The second major figure was Plutarch (*c.*AD 45–120), one of the most interesting Greek historians and philosophers of the first century AD. Not so long ago when I was crossing central Greece, we stopped off at his home town, Chaeronea in Boeotia, to pay homage at a memorial to him. Plutarch came from a landed family, mixed easily with both Roman and Greek intellectuals, and, as a priest at Delphi, was deeply interested in spiritual affairs. He gives a vivid picture of intellectual life in his times through his *Table Talk*, a series of discussions of subjects that range from the topical to the abstruse, from 'What God is worshipped by the Jews?' to 'Why women do not eat the middle part of lettuce'. Plutarch was a Platonist, a believer that the material world is unstable and chaotic compared to the true unchanging one beyond. In his *Moralia*, a collection of his essays on ethics, he argues his point, adding a great deal of material about his opponents, the Stoics and Epicureans, that is not recorded elsewhere. Plutarch's originality broadened out the debate and so his works were of great interest to Renaissance philosophers. Yet his *Parallel Lives*, in which Plutarch compared celebrated Romans with selected Greek equivalents, has probably been his most influential work, not only for the details of now lost sources but because of his interest in the moral characters of his subjects. His accounts, which include descriptions of the deaths of Cicero and Mark Antony and the arrival of Cleopatra in her barge to meet her lover-to-be, are intensely atmospheric.

The sixteenth-century mind was too curious to neglect other ancient traditions. There was a growing interest in Hebrew, partly for scholarly reasons in an age where study of the scriptures had become important.[17] It was assumed that Hebrew had been the language of the Garden of Eden and that the Virgin Mary might respond better to prayers if addressed in the language.[18] The German scholar Johannes Reuchlin published a Hebrew grammar and dictionary in 1506 but when he opposed an imperial edict of 1510 designed to destroy Jewish books throughout the empire he was ridiculed and branded a heretic. Erasmus was more cautious, endorsing the study of Hebrew but balancing this with attacks on the Jews. Yet the importance of Hebrew for the study of the Old Testament led to the founding of the *Collegium Trilingue* at Louvain in Belgium in 1517, where Latin, Greek and Hebrew were taught together on the curriculum. Henry VIII instituted professorships of Hebrew at both Oxford and Cambridge in the 1540s. By now, the first polyglot Bible (known as the Complutensian Bible, after the Latin name of the town where it was composed) had been published in Spain. The Old Testament was presented in three columns, the Latin Vulgate of Jerome in the centre with Greek and Hebrew texts running either side of it. The whole was accompanied by a Hebrew and Greek dictionary but there was no attempt to reconcile the different texts with each other. In fact, the Latin Vulgate, a translation of the earlier texts, was considered so authoritative that a Latin verse added to the Vulgate by Jerome to make a point about the Trinity and removed by Erasmus as spurious was recreated in Greek in this Bible as if it had been in the original Greek all along! Traditionalists still assumed that the Vulgate had somehow (through divine intervention?) transcended the original languages of the scriptures, a view later endorsed by the Council of Trent.[19]

Yet while the Catholic Church endorsed this Bible, allowing copies to be printed in 1522, the weight of anti-Judaism still militated against effective scholarship. And things would get worse in both Protestant and Catholic communities. The anti-Semitic pamphlets of Luther were the most vitriolic of the onslaughts but by the 1550s the Catholic Church had also launched a massive campaign against the Talmud, the principal text of Rabbinic Judaism. Copies were burned in Rome and other Italian cities and it was placed on the papal Index of Prohibited Books. Under Gregory VIII (r.1575–85) it was again forbidden to own or even read a copy and Jews were increasingly confined to ghettos.* In the papal index of 1596 even copies of the Talmud that had been purged of 'calumnies against Christianity' were banned.

Despite the invective of Luther, it was the Protestant reformers who kept the study of Hebrew alive. In tolerant Amsterdam, where the debilitating conflict against Spain† had challenged traditional prejudices, Calvinists and Jews worked together in the early 1600s on an agreed Hebrew version of the Old Testament, while Sephardic Jews in the city began shaping their own works so that they were acceptable to Christians. The Ashkenazi chronicler David Gans of Prague rewrote the history of Judaism in such a way as to minimize Christian violence.

* The term comes from the Jewish quarter in Venice, the original word relating to a nearby iron foundry, or *ghèto*. The Jews were confined here from 1516.

† The Eighty Years' War (1568–1648), in which the seven largely Protestant provinces of the Netherlands – who seceded from the original seventeen Habsburg provinces in 1581 – fought against the rule of the Catholic Spanish Habsburgs.

Other Jews believed that providing translations of Hebrew sources for a wider public would help defuse anti-Judaism.

Toleration of Jews was little more than a pragmatic response. Prejudice and active hostility was only slightly mitigated by the opportunist exploitation of Jews as money-lenders and trade negotiators, exemplified in Shakespeare's acute portrayal of the character of Shylock in *The Merchant of Venice* (written between 1596 and 1599). In the capital cities of Prague, Berlin and Vienna, Jews were given privileged status in return for their expertise in raising large sums of cash or army provisions at short notice. The Habsburg emperor Rudolf II (r.1579–1612) actually attracted a growing population of Jews to Prague after they had shown their usefulness as marketers of agricultural surplus.

The opening of the western mind to Judaism followed a slow and faltering course. While Oliver Cromwell had allowed Jews to resettle as a community in England and practise their religion in 1656, just eight years earlier tens of thousands of Jews had been killed during the Chmielnicki rebellion in Polish Lithuania, the home of the largest European population of Jews (an estimated 300,000 in the mid-seventeenth century). This was especially tragic since in the sixteenth century this region had been one of the most tolerant in Europe. By the end of the century a revived Catholicism had intensified anti-Semitic prejudice in Poland. Overall, Jews remained marginalized, their ancient traditions – more ancient than those of Christianity – insulating them from conversion into the mainstream.

Christians were more ready to accept Egypt as a provider of ancient wisdoms. Marsilio Ficino's rediscovery of the Hermetic works was influential in positing Egypt as the most ancient source of knowledge. Some Renaissance writers regarded Hermes Trismegistus, whom they believed to have been a contemporary of Moses, as prefiguring Christianity. The first printed edition of *Hieroglyphica*, a Greek translation – probably of the fifth century AD – of a purported original Egyptian text on the subject was published in 1505. While parts of the text may be based on genuine knowledge of Egyptian hieroglyphics, it is fragmentary at best. Nonetheless, the text soon became popular among humanists. Throughout the sixteenth century traditions of magic and esoteric learning permeated intellectual life. In her book *Giordano Bruno and the Hermetic Tradition* (1964) Frances Yates linked the hermetic tradition to Giordano Bruno and argued that his adherence to its 'magic' was the true cause of his burning by the church in Rome in 1600. It was not until the scholar Isaac Casaubon (1559–1614) dated the corpus on stylistic grounds to the third century AD, many centuries later than had been believed, that the enthusiasm for hermeticism was quietened and by the eighteenth century it was obsolescent.

Gradually, it was appreciated that Egypt was only one of a number of civilizations of the ancient world that had been neglected, despite the extended description given it in Herodotus' *Histories*.* In his *De emendatione temporum* (*On Improving the Chronology of Time*, 1583, and revised throughout his remaining life) the French scholar Joseph Scaliger (1540–1609) insisted that ancient history should be expanded beyond Greece and Rome to include Egypt, Persia and Phoenicia. Scaliger was also fascinated by the origins of languages and began the serious study of how they had evolved. He scandalized the traditionalists by showing that the Jews had been able to read Greek, in the Septuagint

* Herodotus devoted Book 2 of his *Histories* to the geography, history and culture of Egypt, to which he may have paid a brief visit. He was clearly bewildered by Egyptian civilization and his account is not considered reliable.

translations of the Hebrew scriptures, and so were worthy of respect for their learning. Scaliger was lucky to receive the patronage of Leiden University, which, unlike other universities of the time, allowed its lecturers to carry out research into ancient history. His most dangerous discovery, so far as conventional Christian thinking was concerned, was the list of Egyptian dynasties compiled by Manetho, an Egyptian priest of the third century BC, which took Egyptian history further back than the generally accepted date for the Creation. The traditional chronology of Christian history was gradually being dismantled. While *De emendatione temporum* was not fully appreciated at first, it was a major step forward in setting the classical tradition in the much wider context of contemporaneous civilizations.

In 1586, Domenico Fontana re-erected an ancient Egyptian obelisk in St Peter's Square. This engraving of the period depicts Fontana's prodigious feat of transportation and engineering.

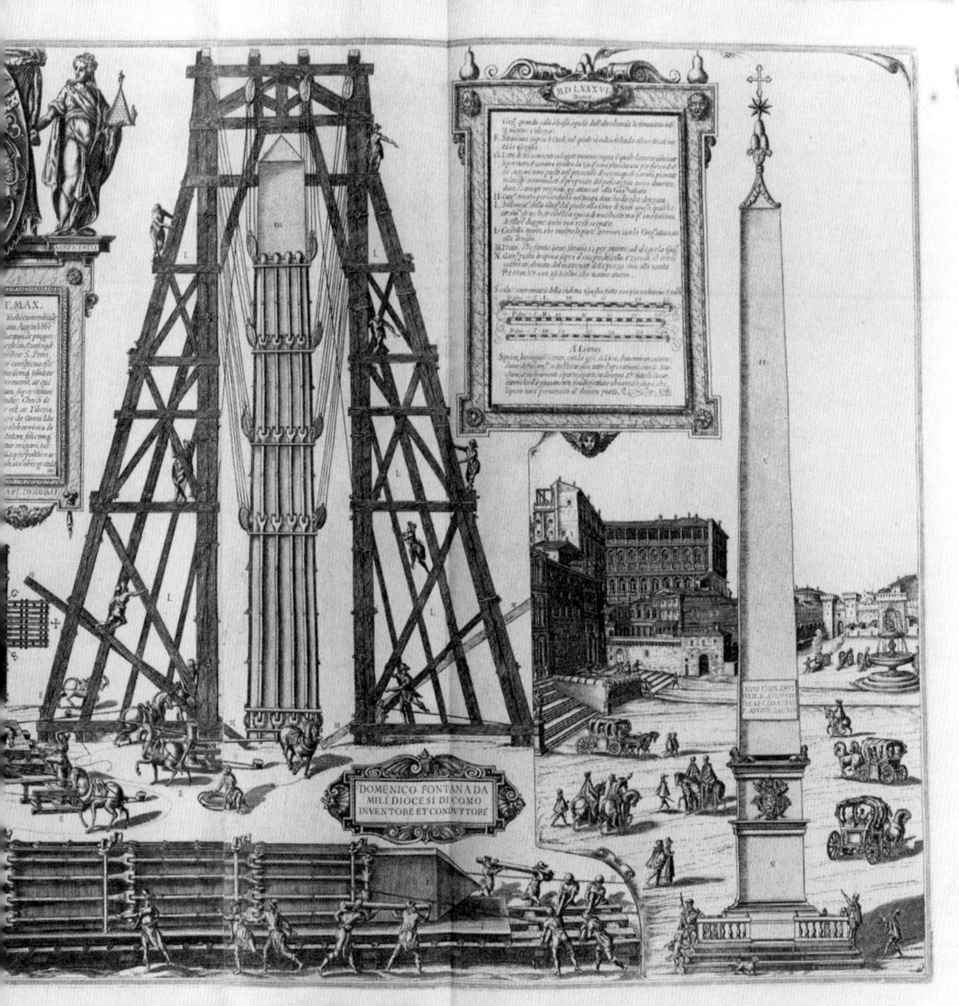

By now there had been contact with Egypt itself.[20] The Ottomans had conquered Egypt in 1517 and soon afterwards the country became open to European traders. The French were given special protection by the sultans. Not surprisingly the visitors were astonished by the pyramids. Medieval legends had described them as the granaries of Joseph, but this idea was soon discounted by sixteenth-century observers. The first eyewitness descriptions date from the 1540s. In the 1590s Prosper Alpinus, a Venetian, became the first to attempt to make accurate measurements of the pyramids. By 1610 it was accepted that the pyramids were tombs of kings and John Greaves, professor of astronomy at Oxford, correctly allocated them to named pharaohs in 1646. By then the German Jesuit Athanasius Kircher (1602–80), often known as 'the Father of Egyptology', claimed to have deciphered hieroglyphics. In fact, he got no further than establishing a link between Coptic and hieroglyphic scripts and his decipherment was little more than fanciful, not least in his attempt to relate hieroglyphs to Chinese characters. It was not until much later, the 1820s, that the French scholar Jean-François Champollion used the three texts of the Rosetta Stone to provide a reliable decipherment.

The pyramids of Giza, as imagined by Athanasius Kircher (1602–80), German Jesuit scholar and so-called 'father of Egyptology', in his *Sphinx Mystagoga* of 1676.

Perhaps the most dramatic moment in the rediscovery of Egyptian antiquity was the triumphant re-erection of obelisks in Rome by the irrepressible Pope Sixtus V (r.1585–90). Augustus, the conqueror of Egypt in 31–30 BC, had brought back two obelisks, probably to celebrate his absorption of pharaonic power. One was erected on the *spina*, the central barrier of the Circus Maximus, the largest racing circuit of the city, the other formed the needle for a large sundial. Others followed over the next 400 years.* By the fifteenth century most of them had collapsed or been buried, but Sixtus was determined to re-erect four of them at focal points in the city.

The most ambitious project was to move the so-called Vatican obelisk, originally placed by Emperor Caligula on the circus on the Vatican Hill where by tradition early Christians, including St Peter, had been martyred. Here was a further chance to link Christianity with Egyptian antiquity. The obelisk was still standing in the sixteenth century and the plan in 1586 was to move it 275 yards in front of the new St Peter's to give honour to its venerable status. It was a colossal project. The obelisk was 83 feet high and weighed 331 tons and the

* Thirty-four are recorded in ancient sources, but many of these have never been found.

De
CŒMITERIIS,
ſive
ADYTIS ÆGYPTIORUM
Veterum.
A
C
C
D
E
C. Decker, in. et fe.

TRVM HOC

aim was to place it on a heightened base. The task was taken on by Domenico Fontana, a young architect who created an elaborate system of wooden towers to encase the obelisk before lowering it within the framework, transporting it on rollers and then re-erecting it. It needed meticulous planning and once completed the relocation was seen as one of the engineering miracles of its day. It was easier to re-erect three of the other obelisks as they were already broken. One of those brought back by Augustus for the Circus Maximus is now in the Piazza del Popolo, and two others were re-erected in front of two great churches of Rome, St John Lateran and Santa Maria Maggiore.*

While this dramatic transfer was taking place, a less publicized but perhaps more influential building project was taking place in Vicenza, in the north-east of Italy. This was a permanent theatre, one of the first known to have been built since antiquity, and the earliest of these Renaissance theatres to be preserved intact. Its original scenery, including streets stretching back from the stage, has survived in its original state. Although its architect, Andrea Palladio (1508–80), died soon after construction began, his close colleague Vincenzo Scamozzi finished it to his design and the first production, appropriately enough of a Greek tragedy, *Oedipus Rex*, by the playwright Sophocles, took place on 3 March 1585. So began a rich tradition of theatres and opera houses that would add a new dimension to cultural life.

previous pages The Teatro Olimpico in Vicenza, designed by Andrea Palladio, opened with a performance of Sophocles' *Oedipus Rex* in 1585. The original scenery remains in place.

The theatre's patrons were the *Accademia Olimpica*, a group of local intellectuals who had dedicated themselves since their foundation in 1555 to cultural activities of every kind – literary, philosophical, historical, scientific; anything, as they put it, that could foster the artistic, cultural or progressive life of Vicenza. The *Accademia*'s membership embraced individuals from varied backgrounds, including Andrea Palladio, the man who had designed the theatre according to ancient Roman models. Palladio had begun life as a stonecutter but through sheer persistence had become the most influential architect of north-eastern Italy.[21] His genius lay in adapting classical models to build houses for the cultural elite of his day. Many of his villas and palaces survive. His fame spread beyond his native region with his *Quattro Libri dell'architectura* (*Four Books on Architecture*, 1570), which set out his principles together with elevations and plans. That

* One might talk of sixteenth-century technological 'miracles', but the obelisks had been successfully erected by the Egyptians, taken down by the Romans, brought by sea to Rome and then re-erected there – all the while remaining intact!

a man of such humble birth could be accepted within this intellectual community tells us much about the nature of the new phenomenon of the *Accademia* or academy.[22]

Humanism had always encouraged informal groups of scholars who enjoyed each other's company and sharing ideas. Marsilio Ficino and Cardinal Bessarion had hosted such gatherings; Machiavelli would read extracts from his *Discourses* to his coterie. In the second half of the sixteenth century these gatherings became more formal. They would draw up foundation documents explaining their cultural ambitions, the procedures for electing officers, and setting out the criteria for membership and the rules that members were expected to follow. While only 30 academies are recorded in 1530, by 1600 there were 400 of them in Italy and by 1700 there were 1,000. No self-respecting city would be without one. Most academy members came from a male intellectual elite, but since the academies were independent entities, the focus could be on sociability and discussion rather than pandering to the formalities of court life. This more tolerant atmosphere meant that artists and even artisans who had skills could be admitted. This is how Palladio came to be a member of the Vicenza academy. He had much to offer. He would design palaces and villas for many of his fellow members, and he had an in-depth knowledge of classical architecture.

For all their organizational formality, the gatherings of the sixteenth-century academies appear to have been conducted with a certain light-heartedness, as if knowledge did not have to be taken too seriously. (The term *sprezzatura*, in the sense of showing off without effort, seems especially appropriate here.) Their members largely came from the leisured classes and such men could show off to their fellows the breadth of their reading and the range of their interests without having to apply their intellects to more serious business. The academies offered an arena where urbane and cultured individuals could unwind and find entertainment in like-minded company. Their rise has been linked to the growing sterility and austere rituals of court life. The names of the academies reflect this mood of refined good humour. So in Bologna one found the *Gelati* ('the frozen ones'), in Naples the *Ardenti* ('the impassioned ones'), in Genoa the *Addormentati* ('the sleeping ones') and in Siena the *Intronati* ('the dazed ones'). The *Intronati* complained that they had been so 'dazed' by the confusion of life around them that they had decided to withdraw from it to study literature – they became well known for their comedies – and woo women, even if these were only the educated daughters from the local aristocracy.

Gradually, however, a more serious tone entered the proceedings of the academies. One can spot it in Florence in the activities of a group who called themselves the *Brigata dei Crusconi* ('the Brigade of the Discarded Chaff') who had set themselves up as a loose grouping of poets and writers after they had found the more formal city academies too pompous. Chaff, the husks left after corn had been threshed, was useless and so were their discussions – which, they prided themselves, never came to any conclusions. One of the *Brigata*'s members, Leonardo Salviati, who joined in 1582, was passionate about vernacular Italian as spoken in his native Tuscany.* He persuaded his fellows to look back to their Florentine literary heroes, Dante and Boccaccio, and observe how they used the Italian language. From this starting point, the *Brigata* decided in 1583 to create a dictionary which would place Tuscan as the true form of Italian, superior to all the other dialects of Italy. In the same year they renamed themselves the *Accademia della Crusca*. Their motto was a line from Petrarch, *il più bel fior ne coglie* ('the most beautiful flower is chosen'). This was now a serious intellectual enterprise. They were no longer the chaff. Rather, the chaff had been the linguistic infelicities and corruptions they had winnowed out, leaving the pure Italian behind. The first of many editions of their dictionary came out in 1612 and those writers whose Italian had been learned through dialects adopted its authoritative pronouncements just as earlier humanists had used Cicero as a model for Latin. The *Accademia della Crusca* continues to this day as a guardian of the Italian language and inspired the foundation of a similar Academy in France in 1635. Its members meet today in the Medici Villa di Castello, next to the gardens of citrus fruit described in Chapter 19.

The citrus garden of the Villa di Castello, near Florence, country house of Cosimo I de' Medici, Grand Duke of Tuscany.

The new dedication to serious intellectual activity can be seen in the *Accademia dei Lincei* founded in Rome in 1603 by Federico Cesi, an aristocrat who was predominantly interested in mathematics and the study of the natural world.[23] The *Lincei* were 'lynxes' and the name suggests the sharp eyesight needed for close observation of natural organisms. The Lynxes' stated aims reflect the tone of such academies: 'Knowledge and wisdom of things to be obtained not only through living together with honesty and piety, but with the further goal of communicating them peacefully to men without causing any harm.' Galileo was made a member in 1611 and he treasured this enough to add '*Linceo*' to his signature.

* In the spirit of the group Salviati was nicknamed Infarinato ('one who is coated with flour').

The *Lincei* were responsible for some of the finest studies of natural history, the first to benefit from microscopes after Galileo had presented one to the Academy in 1624, well before the work of Robert Hooke (described in Chapter 30, pp. 686–7). Unfortunately, the declaration that Copernicanism was a heresy split the Academy and it closed in 1630 on Cesi's death. Many of the *Accademia*'s beautifully illustrated 'painted books', the *libri dipinti*, were bought by the great collector of drawings Cassiano dal Pozzo (1588–1657) for his celebrated 'Paper Museum' and survive today. The *Lincei* was seen as the forerunner of other academies dedicated to science, notably the Royal Society of London, founded in 1660, which will be described in Chapter 30 (see pp. 684–5).

Encountering the Peoples of the 'Newe Founde Worldes', 1492–1610

When we saw so many cities and villages built in the water and other great towns on dry land and that straight and narrow causeway going towards Mexico, we were amazed and said that it was like the enchantments they tell of in the legend of Amadis, on account of the great towers and buildings rising from the water, and all built of masonry. And some of our soldiers even asked whether the things we saw were not a dream. It is not to be wondered at that I here write it down in this manner, for there is so much to think over that I do not know how to describe it, seeing things as we did that had never been heard of or seen before, not even dreamed about.

Bernal Díaz, *The Conquest of New Spain*, 1568[1]

One of the most successful mapmakers of the early seventeenth century was the Dutchman Willem Janszoon Blaeu, who had settled in Amsterdam, by then a leading centre for cartography, in 1599.[2] An adept mathematician, astronomer and expert on navigation, Blaeu's maps were soon in high demand, not least from the Dutch East India Company, which became his customer in 1603. In 1607 he produced a world map that portrayed a personification of the continent Europa on a throne.* The text that follows describes the continent as 'the supreme ruler, with the world at her feet, most powerful on land and sea through war and enterprise, she owns a wealth of all goods'. The trading links shown include Mexico and Peru, India, Africa and Russia as well as the Far East, where the Dutch were making major inroads into Portuguese commerce and breaking up the trading links between the different Asian communities. Among the fruits of that trade were gold, silver, skins, sugar cane, furs, silk, balsam and ivory. A later Blaeu map would describe Europe as dominating through 'its virtue and knowledge of the divine will which is more powerful than all the treasures and riches of the world'. These words sum up the results of the first century of European engagement with the New World. They suggest that a superiority based on war and opportunism, trade and religion, is already secure. How had this happened?

Europe had long benefited from commodities and technologies originating in India and China, including silk, spices, weaving looms and paper. During the medieval period, stories had proliferated about the peoples of the east. Their ancient civilizations – several of them more advanced and opulent than Europe – had been described in the works of Sir John Mandeville and Marco Polo.[3] The purpose of Columbus's Atlantic voyages had been to find a western sea route to these 'East Indies', and to profit from its lucrative spice trade.

The shock of European discovery of the peoples of the western Atlantic set in place a revolution in the way human societies were conceived. Each new voyage brought fresh perspectives and a re-evaluation of what had actually been discovered. The ease with which the Spanish were able to penetrate the interior of the central American mainland, where they encountered many millions of indigenous inhabitants (an estimated 11 million in the Aztec empire alone), made the discoveries even more intoxicating.[4]

Columbus remained convinced that the lands he had discovered

* The original map was lost during the Second World War but records of it survive.

were part of the Asian land mass. The earliest commentator to appreciate that the lands of the New World were not part of China or India had been Amerigo Vespucci (1454–1512) after whom America was named (see p. 415).[5] While Vespucci appears to have travelled four times to the New World, it is still unclear what he actually discovered and how far his accounts are first hand or accurate. Every observer interpreted Indian customs through their own preconceptions and Vespucci appears to have read other travellers' tales and reconciled them with his own biases. His vivid, journalistic style allowed his accounts of a supposedly uncultured and barbaric people to become embedded in the European mind. 'We found no evidence that these people followed any law,' he wrote. 'They cannot be called Moors or Jews and they are worse than Gentiles because we did not see them making any sacrifices, nor even did they say prayers.'[6] His description of the Indians' apparent lack of shame at their own nakedness and their alleged offering of their wives and daughters to visitors helped to create a picture of sexual depravity. Vespucci went on to accuse one group of Indians of cannibalism – the kind of canard that was to sure to grip his readers' imaginations. It was undoubtedly the case that Indians taken prisoner by neighbouring tribespeople were occasionally eaten by their captors, but, as the essayist Michel de Montaigne observed, a European society that burned heretics and committed terrible atrocities in its wars was hardly setting a high moral standard.

Some writers offered more measured descriptions of Indian society than Vespucci's. An early letter (1500) to King Manuel of Portugal by Pero Vaz de Caminha, who had accompanied Cabral on his landings in what is now Brazil, showed that as Caminha learned more about the way of life of the Tupi Indians, the more respect he had for them.[7] His letter reads like the evolving diary of a man who wants to observe and to understand; in his earliest reports Caminha sees the Tupi as barbarous, living in the open as if they were incapable of establishing settled communities, but then he visits a village and recognizes a more ordered way of living. Although he is prurient about the nakedness of their women, he does not follow Vespucci in seeing this as a sign of sexual depravity, but rather as evidence of their living in a state of innocence. They represent no threat to the Portuguese and Caminha concludes by arguing that the Tupi were so amenable that it would be easy to convert them to Christianity. This letter remained unpublished until the nineteenth century, however, and it was Vespucci's more sensationalist accounts that influenced the outlook of European readers.

Papal support for the division of the New World between Spain and Portugal implied that these nations were entrusted with the task of converting the Indians. There was lively debate over how this might be done. Spanish history offered unhappy precedents, notably the conquest of Granada in 1492 and the mass conversion of the Jews in Spain, which suggested forcible conversion was justified. The immediate debate focused on the existing religious status of the Indians. Had they already heard the word of God? Might they have been converted at some remote earlier time, perhaps by the apostle Thomas, whom tradition already linked to the conversion of India in the first century AD? According to one account, Thomas had paused in his westward journey to visit the country now known as Brazil. This raised the possibility that the Indians of South America *had* heard the word of God but had rejected it – which would have left them in mortal sin and destined for hell. Some speculated that the Indians were a lost tribe of Israel, but closer inspection revealed that they did not practise circumcision.

Perhaps, on the other hand, the Indians had never been Christian and so could be placed in the same category as pagans who had lived before Christ. They could hardly expect to go to heaven but perhaps there was a midway place such as Limbo, decreed by Pope Innocent III as the destination of unbaptized infants who had died. Those who had read their Dante would have known Limbo to be the home of those who live 'without hope but with desire' at the edge of hell. None of this lessened the need to convert or reconvert the Indians to Catholicism. When Charles V became king of Spain in 1516, and thus ruler of the Spanish possessions in the Americas, he declared this to be his priority.[8]

Other preconceptions about the status of the Indians, relative to Europeans, fuelled the debate. In his *Politics*, now well known in educated circles, Aristotle had graded human beings according to their ability to reason.[9] Some races were classed as natural slaves with strong bodies and weak minds, incapable of reasoning or making moral choices, and so ideal for labour whether they had been legally made slaves or not. In his *Physics*, Aristotle had proposed that as the universe was naturally hierarchical and harmonious, and so it was fitting that 'lower' races be fitted into that harmony by being made subject to the 'higher' ones.[10] It could be argued that, like animals, the Indians would prefer the security of domestication rather than persist in living in depravity.

None of this led to a satisfactory placing of the Indian communities. An alternative approach could be made through the concept of natural law. As we saw earlier, Aquinas believed that certain eternal

Human sacrifice was a feature of religious festivals in the Aztec calendar, as shown here in the mid-sixteenth-century *Codex Magliabechiano*.

principles and moral values that were common to all humanity could be appreciated through the use of reason by Christians, Muslims, Jews and pagans alike. They included the concept of God, a rejection of incest and adultery, the institution of marriage and a sense of justice. The Indians could be studied for the degree to which they had proved their ability to use reason through the way they ran their societies. As had already been seen in the approaches of Vespucci and Caminha, Europeans found it impossible to view the Indians without bias, a problem that was exacerbated by the difficulty of gaining access to their communities. There was no model against which they could be judged, a point that was recognized by some more percipient observers. Gonzales Fernández de Oviedo was an active participant in Spain's colonization of the Caribbean and lived and worked for a number of years in Santo Domingo, on Hispaniola. His *Historia general y natural de las Indias*, the first part of which was published in Seville in 1535, grappled with the problem of accurately describing a society that had few points of contact with his European readers. He could do little more than validate his assessment by saying that he had had personal experience of what he had seen.[11]

Since the newly discovered territories were soon found to be rich in silver, gold and other desirable materials, it was inevitable that the Spanish would seek to dominate and exploit them. In practical terms the argument concerning the status of the native inhabitants of the Americas was settled by the Doctrine of Submission, which was established in Spanish colonies by 1513.[12] King Ferdinand of Spain relied heavily on a report by a lawyer, Palacios Rubios, who had made a careful survey of Indian life but had concluded that behind a peaceful façade Indians lacked the capacity to reason: 'They are so inept and foolish that they do not know how to rule themselves.' If they had had this attribute, then surely God would have revealed himself to them. Rubios went on to outline what he considered to be the proper hierarchies of society and argued that no 'civilized' society could survive if it did not use lesser races to carry out menial tasks. The Spanish colonial authorities in the New World needed to put in place a process by which this could be legally enforced. With Ferdinand's support, Rubios drew up a document entitled *El Requerimento* (*The Requirement*), which was to be formally read out to Indian communities even though they would not have been able to understand its contents. *El Requerimento* described Ferdinand as a 'subduer of the barbarous nations' and proclaimed his right to rule as given to him by the pope. Those communities who accepted this would be allowed to live in freedom and would not even be required to convert to Christianity, although the document insisted that missionaries be given free rein to move among them. *El Requerimento* also offered other undefined privileges. Should the native Americans refuse to submit to the demands of their new overlords, *El Requerimento* warned them that 'with the help of God, we shall powerfully enter your country, and shall make war against you in all ways and manners that we can and shall subject you to the yoke and obedience of the Church… we shall take your wives and children and shall make slaves of them'. This was not so much a proposal as a decree which in effect offered the Indians no choice but to submit to Spanish rule. It was justified in the eyes of those who imposed it by biblical and other sources, including classical histories, where a powerful state had imposed its will on a poor, subject people on pain of war. The crusades and the *Reconquista* offered recent precedents. There were many Spanish who protested, including those Dominicans who followed Aquinas in arguing that peaceful peoples could not be subjugated, but the pressures to impose control on the Indians were too great for their voices to be heard. *El Requerimento* set the pattern that was to be followed through the rest of the conquest of the Americas. Alongside *El Requerimento*, the *encomienda* system was established, by which named individuals were given absolute rights over labour allocated to them in perpetuity. This was in effect a form of slavery in that the *encomenderos* were able to move their allotted labour around and break up communities in doing so. The rationale was that conversion could only take place if Indians were removed from their traditional pagan societies.

El Requerimento promised free status to those who acquiesced to its demands. But the debate over whether Indians could be legally made slaves or not – rooted in arguments outlined in Aristotle's *Politics* – still raged. The church could offer little help. In the late fourth century Gregory of Nyssa, perhaps the most brilliant of the so-called Cappadocian Fathers, had denounced the institution of slavery. He argued in his *Fourth Homily on Ecclesiastes* that God would not have created two species of humanity, one slave, one free, and if man is indeed made 'in God's image', then he cannot be a slave. His voice was a lone one – Augustine, in fact, had seen slavery as part of God's punishment for sin* and trade in slaves had continued in Europe in the first millennium (see p. 132). Nevertheless, within Europe the practice of enslaving fellow Europeans had died out by 1500, with the church forbidding the slavery of Christians by Christians. The discovery of Africa and the New World allowed slavery to flourish again. There was biblical backing for it in the form of the curse by Noah of his son Ham (who was believed to be the ancestors of all Africans) which had been used in the Middle Ages to justify serfdom and now, in the new context of the sixteenth century, to support slavery. The serfs and slaves were descendants of Ham in that 'all his posteritie after him should be so blacke and loathsome' as one English source put it.† Roman law had also legitimized the enslaving of those captured in war, whose lives had been saved when they might otherwise have been killed by the victors. But now race entered the picture. The racial characteristics of the black

---

* Augustine argued in his *Questiones in Heptateuchum* that slavery was the result of sin. While not insisting that slaves be freed, he did argue that they should be well treated.

† This was an English sailor, George Best, who included his views in an account of his travels, published in 1577. It is widely quoted in studies of sixteenth-century slavery.

Africans who had come within the compass of Portuguese exploration had made them easy to segregate. Many of these black slaves had already been taken captive during conflicts between local peoples, and then passed on to Europeans via local African elites.[13]

Slavery was given papal sanction by Pope Nicholas V, who had granted the right of enforcing perpetual slavery on Africans to the Portuguese king Alfonso V in 1455. In 1518 Emperor Charles V licensed the import of African slaves into the Spanish colonies, so perpetuating one of the most brutal exploitations of human beings of modern history, one that was to set patterns of racial control and subjection for centuries to come. Slave trading remained a Catholic enterprise until the early seventeenth century but thereafter it was also conducted by Protestant trading communities.

The debate over Indian slavery was transformed by the inexorable spread of Spanish control. The Spanish had encountered sophisticated and well-established empires that proved easy to conquer. Traditionally, this ease of conquest has been attributed to superior European fire-power. While the Spanish cavalry proved formidable, recent research has revealed that the Spanish were able to exploit alliances and recruit bodies of native mercenaries – far larger in number than the Spanish troops – to isolate their opponents. The Aztecs, in what is now Mexico, had been defeated by Hernán Cortés between 1519 and 1521, after their numbers had been diminished by the spread of smallpox. The Inca were overcome by Francisco Pizarro in 1533, again after smallpox had spread among them and the Spanish had recruited support among the peoples the Inca dominated. While Amerigo Vespucci had suggested that those Indians he had encountered had no religion (a misconception that was to be corrected over the next century), the Inca and Aztecs had in fact built magnificent temples, where priests performed elaborate ceremonies. Moreover, they had kings, a nobility and a merchant class that was engaged in trading with nearby communities. Their buildings and artefacts showed that they had developed craft skills. Unlike the Indian societies of the Caribbean coastline, the Aztecs and Inca had built large cities. If there was one feature that spoke of civilization, it was city life, a view that had been embedded in European thought since the time of the Greeks. So they could hardly be fitted into Aristotle's category of natural slaves.

Faced with this new evidence, the most respected Spanish theologian of the day, the Dominican Francisco de Vitoria, explored the issue in a lecture *On the Indies*, written in 1539.[14] Vitoria was deeply affected by Thomas Aquinas's belief in a natural law and he attempted to interpret it in relation to the unexpected discoveries of the New World. He was profoundly concerned by the alacrity with which Spanish control had been justified. While the pope might have jurisdiction over fellow Christians, did he have the right to extend this to pagans? The answer was, to Vitoria, clearly 'no', and he used Aristotle in his argument as much as he did Aquinas's concept of natural law. Nowhere, Vitoria argued, had Aristotle accepted that 'slave-like' peoples should actually be enslaved. While the Spaniards had the right to be in the Americas they had a duty to treat the Indians with respect. After all, the Aztec and Inca empires had made it quite clear, through their recognition of family relationships and organization of life of their cities, that they understood the concept of natural law. In carrying out human sacrifices and idolatrous practices, on the other hand, they had not. So they might be said to occupy a kind of halfway house on the way towards full civilization. Here Vitoria went back to Aristotle. 'The Philosopher' had argued that women and children lacked the use of reason. Yet male children would one day achieve the capacity to do so. So perhaps the Indians could be equated to boys. While they would not learn reasoning through growing up, it might yet be instilled in them through education. While Vitoria is often seen as a pioneer in recognizing that the Indian populations had rights and should be treated with respect, his accompanying belief that the Spaniards had the right to be in the Americas was hopelessly naive if he expected the Indians to be left undisturbed. The growing dependence of the Spanish empire on the resources of the Americas killed any chance of that.

Vitoria accepted the right of the Spaniards to convert the Indians. But trying to expound Christian theology was a major challenge, especially across the linguistic divide. Even Europeans found it hard to explain or to grasp the nature of the Trinity or the function of the Holy Spirit. When Indians were told that the Eucharist, the central sacrament of the Christian church, involved ingesting the body and blood of Christ, it must have left them confused over the wickedness imputed to them for their own practice of eating their captives. The missionaries foundered in the confusion and there were reports of Indians claiming that the Christian God may have been comprehensible to Christians but meant nothing to them. Attempts were made to convey Christianity through picture books but it was gradually accepted that only by teaching the Indians Spanish first could there be any hope of meaningful conversion. This, of course, implied that Christianity was specific to one cultural tradition and not necessarily transferable elsewhere, but such an idea could hardly be entertained in the sixteenth century. Only in the changed climate of the eighteenth-century Enlightenment would philosophers be able to make this point. The impact of Catholic evangelism was also limited by the fact that relatively few of the vast numbers of Indians were actually converted. In many cases local elites simply had to be left in place under Spanish suzerainty and little more could be asked of them than that they provide local taxation. These communities were beyond the reach of the *encomiendo* movement.

Despite these various initiatives and practical constraints on their effectiveness, the debates continued. The argument that the Indians were 'natural slaves' was expounded in the *Democrates Secundus* (*A Second Democritus: on the just causes of war with Indians*), a violently racist book by Juan Ginés de Sepúlveda, written in 1544.[15] Sepúlveda, who had never visited the Americas himself, described the Indians as subhuman, 'given over to every sort of intemperance and wicked indulgence'. He made great play of their failure to have developed writing so that they could not have any understanding of their past or an evolved system of written law. They had offended natural law through their idolatry and human sacrifice and they deserved to be subjugated.

Spanish rights over the Indians were further justified by Sepúlveda on the grounds that they had indeed been conquered and so were abject subjects of their new masters. The emotional rhetoric of Sepúlveda's work outraged the theologians whose approach had been much more measured and sober. To Sepúlveda's fury, Vitoria used his influence to have his book banned. Sepúlveda then vented his frustration on the man who had made the most sophisticated defence of the Indians against their conquerors. This was Bartolomé de Las Casas.[16]

Las Casas had arrived in the Spanish Indies for the first time in 1502. At first he was a conventional colonist, even importing slaves from Africa and participating in the system of *encomienda*. Increasingly aware of the abuses of the practice and after experiencing a massacre of the native Cubans by Spanish sailors in 1512, he underwent a profound conversion (the key biblical verse was Ecclesiasticus 34:21–2) and became a Dominican friar in 1522. He then devoted his life to the observation and support of the Indians. Famously he declared that 'just as we regard the peoples of the Indies as barbarians, they also judge us to be barbarians because they do not understand us', a point made by the Greek historian Herodotus writing about the different cultures that surrounded the Greek city-states 2,000 years earlier.[17] In 1537 Las Casas persuaded Pope Paul III to issue an encyclical, *Sublimis Deus* (*The Sublime God*), which outlawed the enslavement of Indians on the grounds that they were rational human beings who could not be deprived of their rights. His next campaign was to abolish *encomienda* but, despite gaining the agreement of Emperor Charles V, now king of Spain, to relax the system by transferring the rights to control Spanish labour to the crown (in the so-called New Laws of 1542), he met with fierce resistance from the *encomenderos*, especially in Peru.[18] Las Casas's position as a bishop in Mexico was made untenable after he confronted the *encomenderos* with a refusal to offer them absolution and the threat of excommunication. In 1547 he was forced to return to Spain, where his opponents attempted to condemn him for treason against the state.

The Cuban chief Hatuey is burned at the stake by Spanish soldiers for resisting the imposition of Christianity. Bartolomé de Las Casas exposed the atrocities committed by the Spanish colonists in his *The Destruction of the Indies*, published in 1552.

Despite the opposition of both the crown and the church to the *encomienda* system Charles simply did not have the power to enforce his will on his remote subjects. The tiny minority of Spanish settlers who lived within the Indian communities had made themselves acutely vulnerable and they pressurized Charles constantly to support them. But he never had enough accurate information to be able to evaluate their demands. Charles was also bound by the need to keep the vast resources of the Americas flowing into his coffers to support the costs of maintaining his European empire.[19]

Las Casas's accusers naturally called on Sepúlveda for support and the two men met for a celebrated public debate at Valladolid in 1550.[20] Sepúlveda reiterated his arguments: that the Indians were pagans who merited punishment, and who had to be pacified in order to convert them to Christianity, and that living as they did, without any order, they deserved to be disciplined by their Spanish masters. Las Casas countered by arguing that the Bible nowhere condoned the conquests of pagans simply because they were such, and that, far from living in sin and disorder, Indian society showed signs of being ordered and civilized. The only way that they could be converted, therefore, was through peaceful means. He went on to argue that sacrifices of the Indians carried out by the Spanish in honour of their own goddess, whom he entitled Greed (!), far outweighed the sacrifices the Indians had made to their gods in the previous hundred years. While the judges of the debate offered no conclusive decision, both sides claimed victory. Las Casas hammered home his argument in his *A Short Account of the Destruction of the Indies*, published in Seville in 1552, which is seen as offering the first detailed description of the brutality of Spanish colonialism. Las Casas championed those who resisted Spanish rule, notably the Cuban chief Hatuey, who had been burned at the stake in 1512 for resisting the imposition of Christianity. In Las Casas's opinion, the Spanish regarded the Indians as they did the Moors – as pagans deserving of a *Reconquista*.* However, while it could be argued that 'the Moors' had conquered Spain and the Spanish were therefore justified in trying to reclaim it, in the case of the Americas it was the Spanish themselves who were the unprovoked conquerors. *The Destruction of the Indies* was, of course, seen as a direct attack on his own people and Las Casas was vilified by Spanish historians well into the twentieth century. Protestants used the book as evidence of the wickedness and brutality of Spanish Catholicism.†

In his last years, Las Casas elaborated his case in his *Apology*. As a Dominican he was used to developing intricate theological arguments through which he minimized the nature of Indian idolatry and even

* One viceroy of Mexico, Antonio de Mendoza, who had been involved in the reconquest of Granada in 1492, justified using similar brutality on the American Indians. See Parker, *Emperor*, p. 359.

† *The Destruction* was translated into English by John Phillips in 1656 and then recast as a play, *The Cruelty of the Spaniards in Peru*, by Sir William Davenant, which was given a rare performance licence by Oliver Cromwell in 1658.

managed to declare that their paganism was superior to that of the Greeks and Romans, whose societies he analysed in detail. The *Apology* is especially interesting for placing the Indians within their native environment and stressing that this would influence the way that their society had developed – and would continue to develop towards greater complexity. Las Casas dwelt a great deal on Inca and Aztec cities, the Indians' skill in craftsmanship and their readiness to learn from Europeans. In one of his most imaginative arguments, Las Casas claimed that offering sacrifice was a sign of the acceptance of a supreme deity and that the more precious the sacrifice, the greater the veneration of God. And what could be more precious than a human being? The Indians, he contended, had now reached the moment when they were ready for the highest state of civilization, Christianity. 'All these Indian peoples are, without taking them away from their natural state, well disposed and well proportioned to receive noble souls.' As the Indians were, unlike the Europeans, relatively uncorrupted, he suggested that their lives as Christians would quite possibly be superior to that of their conquerors.

Las Casas has been accused of exaggerating the atrocities of Spanish rule. He claimed that the Spanish had killed 4 million men, women and children 'by sword and lance and by burning alive', although recent research suggests such massive depopulations were largely due to disease. But this should not diminish the significance of Las Casas's thinking. His was the first serious attempt, in a Christian context, to endow pagans with rights, and it has earned him the accolade as being one of the founders of the concept of human rights. However, he stopped well short of a doctrine of equal rights for all. Las Casas remained a Christian, confident of the superiority of his faith. He never argued that the religious mission of the Spanish should be aborted. He acknowledged, for instance, the right of the church to punish those who convert to Christianity and then revert. As long as Christians continued to regard non-Christians as somehow less worthy of respect, any arguments they put forward for the rights of those non-Christians would lack genuine moral force. There was a paradox here. The more advocates such as Las Casas argued that the Indians had reason, the more difficult it was for theologians to understand why this 'reasoning' did not lead them to Catholic truth.

overleaf Aztec herbs, including remedies for swollen eyes, sleeplessness and earache, as illustrated in the Aztec herbal known as the *Codex Badianus*. Shown here is a Latin edition (1627) of the Spanish original, compiled in Mexico *c.*1550.

Even though the *Apology* was never published in a printed edition during Las Casas's lifetime, it was known and read. Its arguments

Tetzmitl. Tequixquiçacatl. Azcapan yxhua-tlazcolpalitli: Hi... ch...

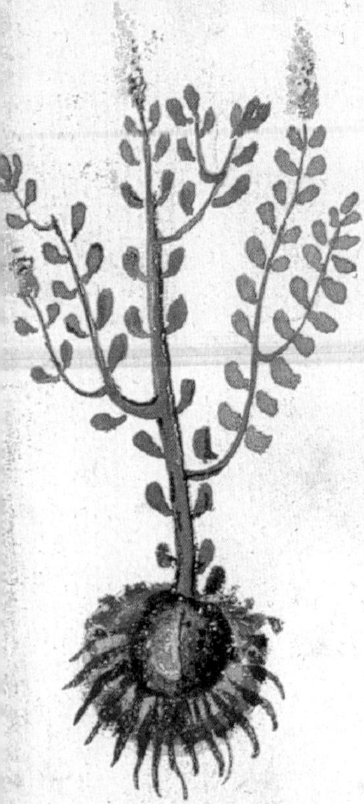

Oculi tumescentes

Frutices Tetzmitl et Tequixquiçacatl et lapillus qui in hirundinis uentriculo albus siue pumiceus inuenitur trita in sanguine eiusdem auiculę oculos turgescentes, et faciem calore flagrantem prohibent, comprimuntque.

Som

Somnum intermissu
çolpalitli, quę iuxta
cihuitl cum hirundin
herbulę Huihuitzyocc
expresso corpus ungi

Somnole

Somnolentias fugab
nas proijeceris et fu
auribus suffimenti
facto ut eis conten
leporem euulsis, et
piuras sine aqua c
eius cinerem in a

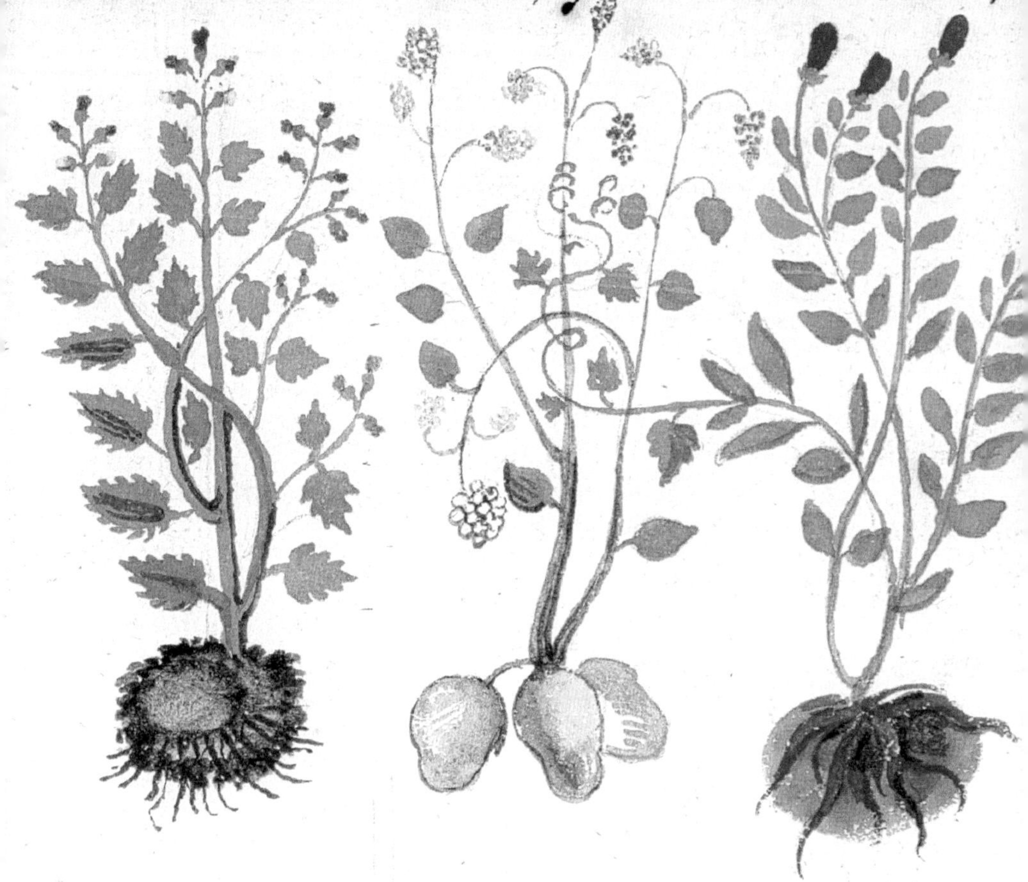

Cochiztzihuitl. Maçayelli. Xoxouhiqui p

el intermissio.

et conciliant herba tlah
eam nascitur, et Cochiz
frondesq illita, tritę uero
ex frondibus liquore

o.

nos capillos super pru-
dorem olfeceris, et tuis
m afflauerit. Hoc
oua testa uel olla
uisceribus illius super
carbonis. Ubi combustum=
[illegible]

Caput tertium de aurium p
de surditate, uel clausul

Putrescentibus auribus radix maç
tę xoxouhiqui pahtli semen, ali
quilin folia cum salis mica in aq
instillata comedant plurimum
riculis duas arbusculas. frondes trite
Arbusculę uocantur tolona et Tlap
pretiosi tetlahuitl, tlahcalhuatz
xoxouhqui chalchiuitl cum arbori
quarę frondibus tritis in calfacta
bi, instillatique conclusas aures ad

reappear in other contemporary studies. During their revolt against the Habsburgs in the 1570s, the Dutch seized with alacrity on the *Apology*'s descriptions of Spanish atrocities. In his seminal *The Fall of Natural Man: The American Indian and the Origins of Comparative Ethnology* (1982), Anthony Pagden sees the *Apology* as 'an expansive piece of comparative ethnology, the first, so far as I am aware, to be written in a European language'.[21]

By 1560 the Spanish royal censors had clamped down on any discussion of the Indian question; it was too unsettling a subject. In 1590, however, José de Acosta published the *Historia natural y moral de las Indias*, a sophisticated study of the Indian way of life that avoids polemics and attempts to provide an objective and coherent portrayal.[22] Acosta was born in Spain in 1540 and entered the Jesuit order when still a boy. He travelled to Peru as part of the Jesuit missionary expansion, arriving in 1570, and later became a professor of theology in Lima. He probably witnessed the symbolic beheading of the 'Last Inca', Túpac Amaru, claimant to the Inca throne, in the public square at Cuzco in September 1572. The Spanish governor Francisco de Toledo lined up 100,000 Amerindians to witness Túpac Amaru acknowledge the Christian God before his execution. The episode left Acosta with no illusions about the reality of Spanish domination. While he was never as condemnatory of Spanish atrocities as Las Casas had been, he was still determined to explore the Indian way of life. Despite ill health, he made three major journeys into the interior of Peru and another in Mexico on his way back to Spain in 1587. Having crossed the Cordillera of the Andes, he wrote the first known account of altitude sickness. Acosta also exploded Aristotle's contention that life near the equator would be impossible because of the tropical heat. Altitude, winds and the Pacific Ocean all acted to cool the climate. Once again the ancient sources were being challenged by experience. Acosta wrote up his *Historia* on his return.

Acosta realized that the missions to convert the Indians had been hampered by their failure to understand the nature of their society and their languages. Far too often generalized comments about the 'Indians' were made without any appreciation that there were many different Indian cultures, a diversity as great as the many different species of plants. Acosta felt that he had gone further than other observers in his accumulation of knowledge from his travels in Peru and Mexico. He divided his cultures into three groups, in descending order of sophistication, according to the degree to which individual societies and peoples lived in cities, accepted the rule of law and had a system for changing or electing their rulers. Acosta's is the first known classification that tries to create a global ethnology encompassing Europe, the Americas and Asia. His most advanced group would include the Chinese. Most of the Indian communities were in Acosta's second group; they lived in communities with some concept of government and family life but had no sophisticated system of social organization. The third group was what we would now call hunter-gatherers. They had no stable family structures, made do with rudimentary food such as rats and lizards, and were essentially nomads. Acosta believed that this had been the original form of society but that most Indian communities had moved beyond it into the second group. Just as the forms of social organization varied from group to group, so did their ideas of religion and the sophistication of their language.

Insofar as there was a natural progression from one group to the one above it, a point would be reached when the Indians would be ready to be brought into the highest group of all, the Christians. This would be the natural end of the evolutionary process. A tradition that went back to Aristotle held that the ability to reason was the highest state of being. Theologians such as Aquinas, who took on this line of thinking, believed that this faculty would lead to a recognition of a single God. And an early Christian belief could be resurrected, namely that God had created the Roman empire specifically to provide a cradle for the spread of Christianity. Acosta argued that the Spanish empire was decreed by God to fulfil the same function.*

overleaf Amerigo Vespucci of the Old World wakes up a native American of the New in an engraving of *c.*1615, 'An Allegory of America'. The imagined landscape includes native flora and fauna and what appears to be a cannibals' feast.

The *Historia* was consciously groundbreaking in that it included both a narrative description of the history of the Indians and an analysis of their society. Yet Acosta relied heavily on ancient authors. In fact, an early French translator related the text to the Greek historian Herodotus for its narrative and to Pliny's *Natural History* for its analysis; Acosta himself paid tribute to Theophrastus' work on botany and also to Aristotle.† He had, typically for a Jesuit, been schooled in Aquinas's scholastic Aristotelianism but he also wished to emphasize Aristotle's collection of empirical observations of the natural world. Naturally, he had to accept that even with acute observation many aspects of Indian life were hard to evaluate. For Acosta

* British readers will be familiar with the first lines of the patriotic song 'Rule, Britannia!' (1740), which characterizes the rise of a later imperial power as divinely ordained: 'When Britain first, at Heaven's command / Arose from out the azure main...'

† The Greek polymath Theophrastus (*c.*371–*c.*287 BC) was Aristotle's successor at the Lyceum and was known as 'the father of botany' for his works on plants.

Ioan. Stradanus inuent.
Theodor. Galle sculp.
Phls Galle excud.

there was the problem of what he called 'a forest of languages', in which tribes living close to each other were divided by mutually unintelligible languages. Indeed, a major part of Acosta's work consists of exploring the nature of language and how it had evolved in so many different forms. Were there universal concepts that underlay all languages or had each developed its own unique structure?

The further Acosta delved into the nature of Indian societies, the more he recognized how deeply embedded local cultures were. The earliest observers had been too simplistic in their assumption that Indians could be treated as *tabulae rasae*, blank slates onto which European civilization could be inscribed. Acosta condemned those who had destroyed the written records of the Aztecs, making it harder to understand their culture. He argued that native customs that did not conflict with Christianity should be maintained, so that the fabric of Indian society could be preserved. Christian theology should be presented to the Indians in such a way that it meshed with their existing beliefs. In practice, this meant that local deities could be amalgamated syncretically with Christian saints and other holy men and women – just as in the Mediterranean the Virgin Mary had taken on many of the attributes of the goddesses of the Greeks and Romans. The plethora of saints that made up such a large part of European Catholicism could be adapted to absorb Indian cults. In 1531 an apparition of a woman with Mexican features, in what is now the northern part of Mexico city, was believed to be that of the Virgin Mary and venerated as the Virgin of Guadalupe among the converted Aztecs. The image remains a massive pilgrimage draw to this day.[23]

A watercolour (1585) by the English settler John White, showing a Secotan Indian village in North Carolina. White's illustration is a positive representation of an Indian community, portraying the good order of their village life.

Acosta also discussed the origins of the Indian communities, distant as they seemed to be from any other human society. He subscribed to the traditional belief that humans and all animal species had been created in the six days described in the biblical book of Genesis, and that, after the Flood, the world had been repopulated by those saved by Noah, who were dispersed from the ark's final resting place on Mount Ararat. But Acosta rejected the notion that the Indians had somehow crossed the Atlantic at an early moment in history, on the grounds that a migration of so many millions of people across the sea would have been impossible. He posited that there must be a land route in the north from Asia through which the Indians had entered the Americas. Twenty-first-century scholarly orthodoxy suggests that Acosta's hypothesis is correct, and that human

Their greene corne.

Corne newly sprong.

Their sitting at meate

The place of solemne prayer

rm the Tombe of their Herounds standeth.

SECOTON.

beings migrated from Asia to North America across the Bering Strait when sea levels were lower during the period 45,000–12,000 BC. And Acosta could build further on his theory by suggesting that the American Indians and the Chinese had certain physical similarities to each other. Since migration involved nomadism, the less advanced state of the Indians could be explained by the fact that they had spent so many years on the move. Only when they had settled could they begin to evolve towards the higher level of society enjoyed by the Chinese and then the Christians. Acosta wisely made no attempt to date the migration, but he assumed that it had been a continuing process: the more nomadic the society, the more recent the migration.

The *Historia* was sensationally successful. It was published in Spain in 1590 and by 1604 there were Latin, German, French and English editions. It remained the most authoritative account of the American Indian communities until the late eighteenth century.

It is hard to over-emphasize the importance of the events described in this chapter for the future not only of European but of global history. At the most basic level it is the story of the suppression of peoples who were unable to stand up to the firepower of their conquerors and

the subsequent exploitation of their resources. They were locked into a condition of subservience in which many of them remain to this day – despite the formal abolition of slavery. Christianity reinforced its predominantly European identity as the highest form of religious life. European warfare was exported into the New World as open and accessible places with resources became easy to occupy but hard to defend.

Europeans were forced to think about what it meant to be a human being and how far one society was justified in exploiting another. They faced the challenge of relating European 'values' to the very different communities of the New World. If a single voyage, that of Columbus to the west, or Vasco da Gama's to the east, could revolutionize knowledge about the world to such a degree, then the status and authority of Europeans and their intellectual achievements were surely vulnerable. One of the earliest chroniclers of the New World, Peter Martyr d'Anghiera (1457–1526), who compiled reports for King Ferdinand of Aragon, had grasped that for the first time Europeans were able to progress beyond the knowledge of the classical texts. Writing in 1620, the English philosopher Francis Bacon argued that 'it would be disgraceful, in a time when the regions of the material globe, that is, of the earth, the sea and the stars, have been opened far and wide for us to see, if the limits of our intellectual world were restricted to the narrow discoveries of the ancients'.[24] So far as philosophy and science were concerned, the authority of the ancients was confronted by the mass of new flora and fauna and geographical information that became available. This was the setting within which the findings of the microscope and the telescope could be accepted and the notion of unending progress in the unfolding of knowledge become dominant. As Louis Le Roy, the French humanist and a professor of Greek, put it in 1575:

The mission of San Xavier del Bac, south of Tuscon, Arizona, in the southwestern United States. One of the finest examples of Spanish mission architecture, San Xavier del Bac was originally founded in 1682 by the Jesuit missionary Eusebio Francisco Kino.

> How many secrets of nature have been first knowen and found out in this age. I say, new lands, new seas, new formes of men, manners, lawes and customes; new diseases, and new remedies, new waies of the heaven, and of the Ocean, never before found out... That which is now hidden, with time will come to light; and our successors will wonder that we were ignorant of them.[25]

Acceptance that the accumulation of knowledge is progressive is a crucial part of the 'reawakening of the western mind'.

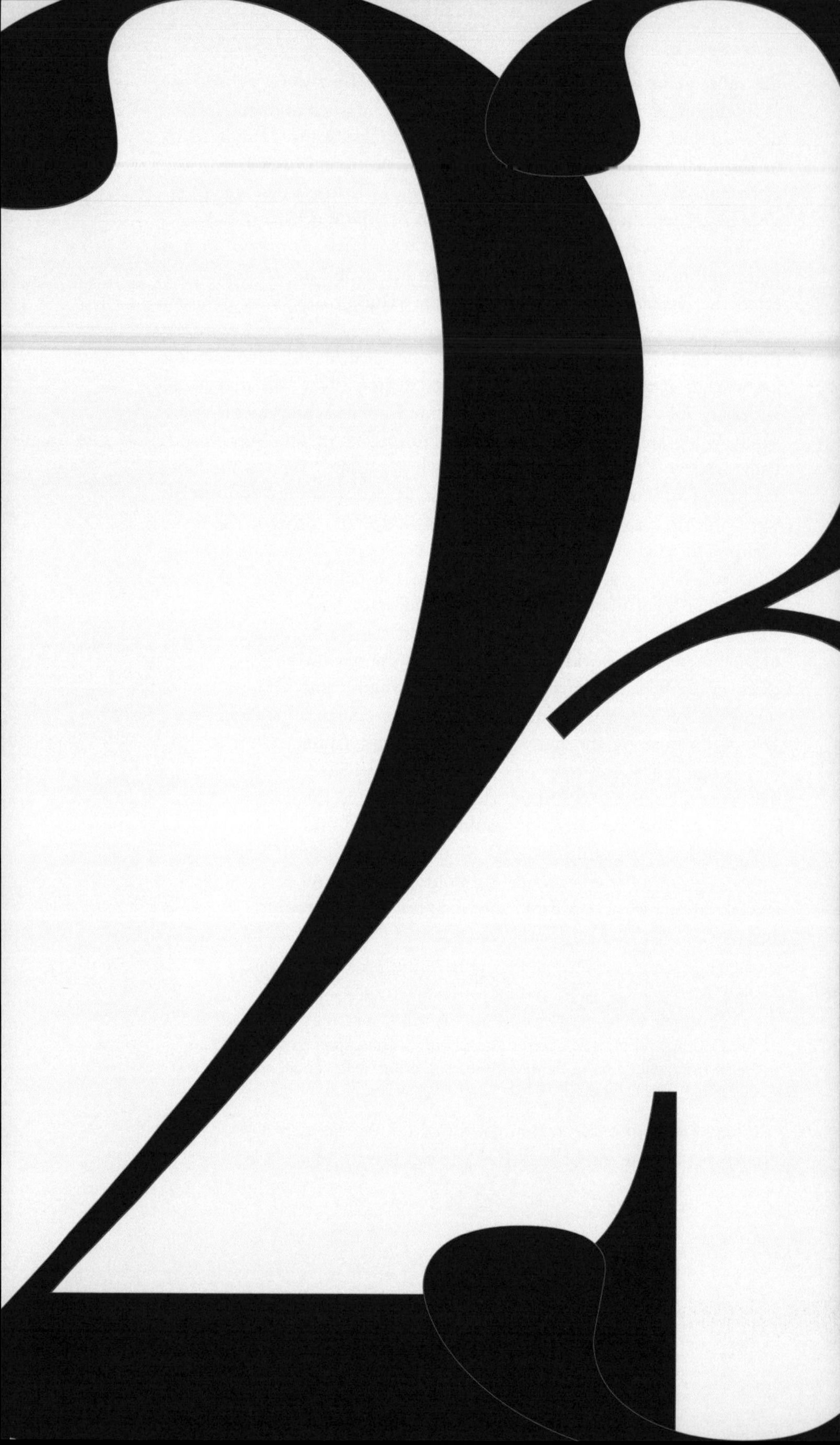

The Reformation and the Reassertion of Christian Authority?

The true fear of God and charity are fallen and grown cold. Although opinions are almost as numerous as men, nevertheless there is hardly any sect that does not condemn all others and desire to reign alone… if you are orthodox in one city or region, you are held for a heretic in the next… Hence arise banishments, chains, imprisonments, stakes and gallows and this miserable rage to visit daily penalties on those who differ from the mighty about things hitherto unknown, for so many centuries disputed, and not yet cleared up… Satan could not devise anything more repugnant to the nature and will of Christ.

Sebastian Castellio, *Concerning Heretics and Whether They Should Be Persecuted*, 1554[1]

The previous chapters have shown the vitality of the medieval and Renaissance mind set against the backdrop of global discovery. As seen in Chapter 16, there had been considerable progress in the way that laity took responsibility for their own religious beliefs and carried out charitable activities effectively through the confraternities. It was an uneven process. As papal rule atrophied, it was as likely that an unscrupulous preacher such as Savonarola or a dictatorial monarch like those in Spain would exploit the vacuum. What followed was not the further disintegration of Christian authority, as might have been expected, but its reassertion in new forms; the aptly named Reformation, which saw the crushing of local expressions of spirituality, not least in the widespread destruction of shrines, their art and their treasured relics. The Catholic Church was to make a spirited response, a renewal of its original doctrinal message, the so-called Counter-Reformation. In short, the development of European thought between 1550 and 1700 takes place against a backdrop of fragmented and mutually intolerant Christianities. Traditional accounts that the Reformation led in itself to intellectual and social progress are hard to sustain. In many ways the integration of religion with secular nationalism restricted rather than fostered freedom of thought. The following two chapters provide the background to these important developments in the evolution of Christianity.[2]

The Reformation saw the first war of pamphlets. Martin Luther was the most effective propagandist of the period, but this hard-hitting Catholic woodcut, dating from *c.*1520, shows the Protestant reformer communing with Lucifer.

While the conciliarists, humanists, Lollards and Hussites had all talked of a church without a pope, the man who actually began the campaign that successfully removed him from much of northern Europe never set out to destroy the church. Martin Luther was born in 1483 into a relatively prosperous family from the mining district of Saxony. The story of how this young but tormented theologian found himself committed to a vituperative confrontation with the Catholic Church has often been told and need not be repeated in full here. His legacy was remarkable and, as the Reformation could not have been carried through without his determination and stubbornness, his – hardly attractive – personality has been ruthlessly analysed.[3]

Luther began by challenging the popular but exploitative practice of selling indulgences for the rescue of souls in Purgatory. In 1476 Pope Sixtus IV had issued a papal bull claiming the right of the pope alone to grant indulgences and receive the revenue. The fabulously wealthy

Luthers vnd Lutzbers

eintrechtige vereinigung/so in xxij
eygenschafften sindt allenthalben gleychförmig verfüget/
Durch M. Pet. Syluium der Christenheyt zu seliger warnung trewlich
beschriben/vnd mit Götlicher schrifft vnwidersprechlich ergrün-
det/wie es am letzten blat ist volkomlicher berürt.

entrepreneur Jacob Fugger of Augsburg, in one of his most lucrative deals, took a cut of the money raised via the sale of indulgences in Germany. This money was then forwarded to Rome and diverted by the pope, now Leo X (r.1513–21) of the Medici family, to fund the rebuilding of St Peter's. Luther's Ninety-Five Theses denouncing the practice were no more than an invitation for debate, the document by tradition nailed to the church door of the castle at Wittenberg in October 1517. This moment was later mythologized as the beginning of the Reformation.[4] The debate widened to encompass a bitter onslaught on the papacy and the Curia. The responses from distant Rome were erratic and ham-fisted. Pope Leo's bull *Exsurge domine* (*Rise up, O Lord*) gave no proper theological response to Luther's Theses (as the scholarly Erasmus was quick to point out) and simply inflamed Luther further. He reacted ever more provocatively to each counter-attack on him. His public burning of the papal bull excommunicating him in 1520 and a celebrated debate with the young Emperor Charles V in 1521 at the Diet of Worms were perhaps the true beginning of the Reformation.[5] Now past the point of no return, with widespread support in many of the small German states, Luther, always a man of intense emotions, took on a messianic role, pouring out an avalanche of tracts as he attempted to create a new Christian confession. As Andrew Pettegree has shown in his study, *Brand Luther*,[6] his exploitation of printing was particularly effective. The flow of short and powerful tracts with striking title pages created a momentum of their own that drew ever-larger

Religious statues are committed to the flames, Zurich, 1524. Protestants abhorred the mass of relics in churches and the Reformation witnessed widespread destruction of even authentic relics.

audiences. Many of Luther's fellow clergy were emboldened by his stand to express their own frustrations with the church. The Catholic Church could never match his propaganda and what remained of papal authority in the German states crumbled.

Luther's home territory of Saxony, which had long escaped the reach of Rome, supported the excommunicated and outlawed priest. Critically, the patron of the university at Wittenberg, the Elector Frederick 'the Wise', offered him his protection, thereby enabling Luther to avoid the fate that Jan Hus had suffered in the previous century.* Luther lived out the rest of his turbulent life in safety at Wittenberg. What was now needed was a theology that went beyond the conventional demands for reform to formulate a complete break with papal authority. Here again Luther played a crucial role. He put forward the scriptures as the foundation of his theology: *sola scriptura*, 'scripture alone', is needed. This was truly revolutionary as the Bible had been hitherto inaccessible to those who could not read Jerome's Latin Vulgate. Luther argued that since the church had betrayed the teachings that the scriptures proclaimed, it was essential that they were restored to primacy. His stance also fuelled an attack on the university curriculum. Peter Lombard's *Sentences* should be replaced by the Bible, and Aristotle was to be condemned. 'It grieves me to the quick that this damned, conceited, rascally heathen has deluded and made so many fools of so many of the best Christians with his misleading writings.'[7] It followed that there must be a vernacular text of the scriptures and Luther set about providing one. His German translation of the Bible (from Erasmus's Greek text) was perhaps 'his most lasting achievement',[8] not least for the enduring and influential quality of its prose, although as Lyndal Roper has pointed out Luther 'built his own theological understandings into his translations', especially when dealing with matters of 'faith'.†[9]

The concept of *sola scriptura* was essentially an unstable one in that it would lead to interminable wrangling over the meanings of biblical passages. Luther claimed that one should look for the message of Christ's salvation through a literal reading of the texts, yet he gave priority to some texts, in particular Paul's Epistle to the Romans, above others, such as the Book of Revelation. He also accepted that the books of the Old Testament, notably Isaiah, should be interpreted as prophecies of

---

* Frederick remained a Catholic, at least until his deathbed. He did not have much personal contact with Luther but felt that it was his duty as his ruler to offer him protection.

† Luther's translation of the New Testament was published in 1522, the complete Bible in 1534.

the coming of Christ. But where did this leave individuals who were reading the Bible for the first time? Here Luther was ambivalent. While insisting that the message of the scriptures was straightforward, in time he, and the other reformers, had to accept that trained interpreters were needed to keep doctrinal coherence.[10]

One of the paradoxes of Lutheranism is that despite placing scripture first, Luther relied heavily on Augustine's theory of original sin, which had left the human race 'totally depraved' and dependent on the undeserved grace of God, granted through Christ, for salvation. By promising that souls could be released from Purgatory and suggesting that individuals might work for their salvation, the church was cheating them of the truth. It was only through having faith, 'a living, bold trust in God's grace', that one made oneself open to the possibility of salvation. This was justification through *sola fide*, 'faith alone', the cornerstone of Lutheranism. Good works, 'righteousness', would follow *from* faith, not lead towards it or earn it. The French reformer John Calvin, who agreed with Luther on this, would express this incisively: 'Justified by faith is he who, excluded from the righteousness of [good] works, grasps the righteousness of Christ through faith and, clothed in it, appears in God's sight not as a sinner but as a righteous man.'[11]

In so far as one was totally dependent on the grace of God, free will was a fiction 'with no reality because it is in no man's power to plan any good or evil'.[12] Luther went on to claim that he was, in fact, happy not to have been given free will as he would have been incapable of making choices for himself. He 'was a man who retained a healthy mistrust of Reason, "the whore"'.[13] Yet if there is no freedom of will, and the adoption of 'faith' was the essential requirement of Christian belief, then why bother to participate in and contribute to society at all? In practical terms, surely there had to be some kind of reward for the individual who worked for the good of the community, whether that person was saved or not. Luther himself went so far as to argue that doing good works was in fact sinful, in that the individual's real motive was to receive praise. This interpretation of human motivation stood in stark contrast to the Renaissance (and classical) ideal of the socially engaged and creative individual.

Erasmus was aroused to counter-attack. In the ensuing debate, the humanist challenged Luther on his own ground by citing many scriptural exhortations to do good. Human beings, Erasmus riposted, were hardly lumps of clay but thinking and willing beings. They could surely play some part in their own salvation. The fiery monk and the thoughtful and intellectually detached scholar were as far apart in temperament as in theology and there was never a chance of a resolution to the debate. When Erasmus died in 1536, without making confession, Luther insisted that he would have gone straight to hell.[14]

Concomitant with the denial of free will was that ancient philosophical conundrum of predestination, that God knew from eternity whom he would and would not save. Whatever an individual believed his condition might be in the eyes of God, it was already foreordained. It followed that God knew who would be born but not saved. This left the intractable theological problem of whether there was such a thing as divine mercy. Luther, like many others before him, was perplexed by the issue and clearly wished to refrain from declaring God to be the author of evil. In the predestination debate he chose to emphasize the possibility of salvation rather than the likelihood of condemnation. Later, Calvin was to be more ruthless in insisting that God did in fact know who would be condemned to hell and, as a result of the Fall, one could hardly expect otherwise.[15]

As with reformers such as Wyclif before him, Luther was adamant that the distinction between clergy and laity should be dissolved. The clergy were deprived of their traditional and elevated status and confined to a role as teachers, preachers and administrators of the sacraments. They would now be able to marry – Luther himself married a former nun – and communion for the laity would no longer be restricted to the bread but, as with the Hussites, include the wine. Luther rejected the doctrine of transubstantiation.* He taught instead that Christ would be a real presence at the Eucharist rather than transforming the bread and wine or being present there only in a symbolic sense, the position taken by most of Luther's Protestant rivals.† The doctrine of the Real Presence became an obsession with Luther, albeit one which he failed to justify to his opponents. His return to the scriptures as the ultimate authority led to his questioning of the seven sacraments that were central to Catholic practice. The only other sacrament for which he could find scriptural support was baptism, the offering of an infant to the grace of God. He condemned monasticism on the grounds that an individual could not achieve purity in isolation from the community. These fundamentals formed the Augsburg Confession of 1530, still the primary document of Lutheran theology.

Another critical aspect of Luther's thinking was his vision of the

* According to this doctrine, the elements of the Eucharist, when they were consecrated, were wholly converted into the body and blood of Christ.

† The word 'Protestant' comes from those German political leaders who 'protested' against attempts to ban Lutheranism.

relationship between the Lutheran confession and civil society. In his popular address *To the Christian Nobility of the German Nation* of 1520 he called on the princes to become 'emergency bishops' to replace the Anti Christ, the pope. This was now a Christian community that was evolving under the supervision of the existing rulers (on whom the clergy now depended for payment). What would emerge was a conservative and authoritarian church. In Wittenberg and elsewhere, there were those who wished to embrace a more radical programme of reform. Luther managed to curb these developments in Wittenberg, but further afield millenarian preachers such as Thomas Müntzer attracted support from both the urban poor and disaffected peasants. Luther's attacks on the church hierarchy had awakened in them the hope that he might back them in an all-out assault on the nobility. But when the Peasants' War erupted in Thuringia, Franconia and Swabia in 1524–5, he called for its brutal repression. Luther was savage in his criticism of those with whom he disagreed. Thomas Aquinas was condemned for his compromises with the pagan Aristotle and his 'unchristian, profane, meaningless babblings'. And Luther was vindictive against his enemies, including those who made alternative confessions of Protestantism. He reserved special venom for Jews. Luther's virulent 1543 pamphlet on *The Jews and their Lies* was openly used by preachers as a justification for anti-Semitism in Nazi Germany.

The success of Luther's church depended on rulers deciding to be Lutheran. After a bitter conflict between Lutheran principalities and the emperor, a religious settlement within the empire was thrashed out in the Peace of Augsburg in 1555, nine years after Luther's death. The peace allowed individual rulers to decide the religious allegiance of their subjects, with the choice restricted to Lutheranism or Roman Catholicism. So Christianity became, for the first time in its history, territorial, different confessions being allocated to different territories (thus aligning the chosen Christianity with nationalism). What Luther never resolved – extraordinarily for a man who had challenged the authority and the office of the pope – was how Lutherans would deal with an unsatisfactory ruler. To their credit many Lutheran rulers took on the role that Luther had allotted them. When monasteries were dissolved, they distributed their wealth for the public good in schools and hospitals.* In so doing they were continuing a tradition established by the confraternities in the previous century. Despite large regions

* While Luther saw monasticism as an unjustified (and unscriptural) diversion of spirituality away from the needs of the world, some monastic communities adopted Lutheranism and continued in existence.

of Germany, notably Bavaria, remaining Catholic, by the eighteenth century Lutheranism and German nationhood (in this case Prussian nationhood) were firmly intertwined. Frederick the Great of Prussia called Luther 'the liberator of the Fatherland' while the German philosopher Johann Gottfried Herder (1744–1803) described Luther as the man who gave a nation asleep 'under the yoke of foreign words and customs... its authentic speech'.[16] So Luther entered into German nationalist mythology, one further step in the fragmentation of the Christian religion.

By its very nature and its embedding within the civil hierarchy of the German states, Lutheranism had respectability but lacked dynamism. Luther had never laid down any principles for the survival of his movement.[17] Lutheranism was adopted by the rulers of Denmark, Norway and Sweden but otherwise spread very little outside its original home territory except when it was later carried overseas by German settlers. Luther's inability to brook any opposition risked creating a static religion (as had happened with the follower of Wyclif). After his death, however, the fervid nature of the Reformation made it inevitable that impassioned debates would break out. There was an inherent tension between those who wished to commemorate and respect Luther with volumes of his writings and a plethora of accompanying images and those, such as Philipp Melanchthon, who fought to create a church that could live fully in society. The consolidation of Lutheranism was helped by the continuation of traditional practices, in the use of vestments, images and above all music,† with the sublimity of Bach to come.

Philipp Melanchthon (1497–1560), great-nephew of the Hebraic scholar Johannes Reuchlin, was steeped in humanism and a brilliant Greek scholar in his own right (his adopted name meant 'Black Earth' in Greek). He met Luther when he was appointed a lecturer in Greek at Wittenberg at the age of twenty, just as the Reformation was starting. He played a vital role in clarifying doctrine, especially for the Augsburg Confession of 1530, the primary confession of faith of the Lutheran church. Melanchthon was by nature conciliatory and gradually moved away from the vindictiveness of Luther's own theology, allowing some place for free will and stressing the evidence that good works were a sign of the transmission of God's grace. He even maintained good

† Luther was a fine hymn-writer, one of his best-known hymns being 'Ein feste Burg ist unser Gott' ('A Mighty Fortress is our God'). The German baroque composer J. S. Bach would later include numerous Lutheran hymns (or chorales) in his cantatas and oratorios.

relationships with Erasmus. Melanchthon was especially important as an educationalist, not only plotting out a curriculum for schools but playing an important part in founding and reforming German universities. He certainly helped Lutheranism to fit more harmoniously into German society but he was also revered by the English Protestant reformers who were offended by the crudeness of Luther's polemics. It is to Melanchthon, above all, that Lutheranism owes its survival.

Luther's intransigence was inherited by a new wave of Protestants who did not think it radical enough. The leading figure of Reformed Protestantism, as the new movement has become known, was John Calvin. Calvin was born in northern France in 1509.[18] As he grew up and studied in Paris, the first waves of Protestantism were beginning to sweep through France and Calvin was forced to flee to Switzerland where reformers were already in control. Committed to the cause, he wrote his celebrated *Institutes of the Christian Religion* (1536 in Latin; 1541 in French), a preparation for those studying the Bible that provided a much more coherent expression of the new theology than Luther had ever attempted. The fact that Calvin never had any formal training in theology may have worked to the book's advantage, in that he had a brilliantly concise and logical writing style in both Latin and French. The first edition had an immediate impact where a more conventional theological tome might have failed. The *Institutes* demanded an absolute dedication to God and went further than Luther in condemning any ruler who did not proclaim God's glory and build a Christian state. Although Calvin had had a humanist education, he rejected 'the whole body of philosophers' who had 'adulterated pure religion'. Laws were to be based on biblical precedent. The *Institutes* prompted a wave of intense study of the scriptures, which led in turn to the chapters of the scriptures being split up into distinct verses for the first time, for easy reference.

Like Luther, Calvin was saturated in Augustine. One meticulous scholar has counted 1,708 quotations from Augustine in Calvin's works. So he believed in the total depravity of human beings as a result of original sin and their absolute dependence on God's grace for salvation. As Augustine had argued, the damage even extended to the capacity to reason. 'Sound reason in man was seriously injured by sin', as Calvin put it, leaving the human race as diminished beings.[19] The corruption of the Catholic Church and the evils of society were the direct result of human sinfulness and now purity had to be restored. There was to be a rejection not only of the pope and all his panoply of power but of any material objects that might stand between the Christian and his or her maker. His condemnation of images, altars, crucifixes and relics as idolatrous led to a sweeping-out of such objects from churches that was often violent. Calvin himself wrote a damning *Treatise on Relics* (1543) which, incidentally, provides an excellent survey of what pilgrims might have found as they travelled across pre-Reformation Europe. Even those relics whose authenticity was secure had to be gathered up and destroyed. The challenge to materialism had an important impact on the doctrine of the Eucharist. Calvin believed that Christ himself could not be present at the sacrament other than in a spiritual sense. Of course, this meant a powerful rejection not only of transubstantiation but also of Luther's doctrine of the Real Presence. The ensuing controversy further poisoned relations between Calvinists and Lutherans.

While Luther had prevaricated on how the elect might be recognized, Calvin gave a new dynamism to the concept of predestination. He stated in the *Institutes* that God had already chosen those whom he would save and take with him to heaven. Those people he had not chosen for salvation would go to hell: 'All are not created on equal terms, but some are preordained to eternal life, others to eternal damnation; and, accordingly, as each has been created for one or other of these ends, we say that he has been predestined to life or to death.'[20] While this might imply that human beings were helpless and there was nothing they could do to save themselves, the followers of Calvin soon believed that they were indeed the elect. Calvin preached that they should show this by their enthusiasm for creating God's kingdom on earth. As a result there was an earnestness and commitment to Calvinism that would carry it far beyond its original 'capital' in Geneva where Calvin eventually made his permanent home as an exile from France in 1541.[21]

Geneva had asserted its independence from the dukes of Savoy in 1535 after much of the Savoy territory had been overrun by the French. The Lutherans had gained the support of the city's popular assemblies in the 1530s and the city had become a centre for exiles fleeing from regions that had stayed Catholic. Many of the refugees brought skills with them and, once established, Calvin built up his influence in Geneva by exploiting their specialities, predominantly in printing and the law, so as to become the dominant figure in the city. Not a single minister was drawn from the city's native population between the 1540s and 1594. Under Calvin's rule, Geneva became a theocratic city and, to the fury of the Catholic censors, the centre of the Protestant printing trade.

The compactness of Geneva led to an exportable model of a Christian society. The clergy were placed alongside the civil magistrates as fellow administrators with roles specified for those selecting the clergy, those teaching the gospel as Calvin interpreted it and those overseeing the morals of the community. Far from Protestantism providing liberation from a supposed Catholic tyranny, the faithful were now disciplined, their private lives supervised, even to the extent of suffering execution for heresy as defined by Calvin. Calvin was particularly harsh on those who followed approved rituals of worship without signs of any inner commitment and extended his disapproval to his fellow Protestants in France – known as Huguenots – who had compromised with the dominant faith by continuing to attend Catholic services. By ordering them to live openly as Protestants, Calvin set up a confrontation between Huguenots and Catholics. Later in the century France was to be racked by religious wars, one of many low points of which was the infamous slaughter of Huguenots by Catholics in the St Bartholomew's Day Massacre of 1572 (see illustration pp. 568–9).* The French Wars of Religion only came to an end when the Huguenot king, Henry IV, proved flexible enough to convert to Catholicism and grant toleration for the Huguenots in the Edict of Nantes of 1598. This initiative was an important moment in strengthening a Catholic French monarchy as the arbiter of the national religion, something that a later king, Louis XIV, would exploit (see pp. 592–3).

Calvinism's expansionist energy took his movement to Scotland, where the fiery preacher and theologian John Knox introduced reformed principles, and, via refugees from Germany, to many parts of the Netherlands where it gave backbone to the gruelling revolt of the Dutch against Spanish rule. In central and eastern Europe Calvinists were adept at creating communities in any political or geographical niche that would allow them in. Calvinist ideas travelled to England, inspiring the austere Puritan movement that would prove a thorn in the side of the established church. Calvinists were also prominent in the European settlement of North America, where they made religion a powerful and often frightening force. With the sacrament of confession now eliminated, the fear of God was transmitted through sermons and the prurient supervision of sexual behaviour.

In contrast to the mix of principalities, bishoprics and free cities of Germany, England had developed a stable centralized monarchy under the Tudors. If one is searching for the most effective secular monarch of his age, Henry VII (r.1485–1509) fits the bill even if his spartan rule

* In celebration of this massacre, the artist Giorgio Vasari was commissioned by Pope Gregory XIII to record the scene in the Sala Regia in the Vatican. The painting still exists.

aroused much resentment.[22] His son Henry VIII (r.1509–47) initiated the English Reformation after the pope refused to annul his marriage to his first wife, Catherine of Aragon. He assumed the role of Supreme Head of the Church through the Act of Supremacy of 1534. (Henry's chief minister, Thomas Cromwell, had arranged for Marsilius of Padua's fourteenth-century tract *Defensor Pacis* – which challenged the church's right to exercise legal or political power (see pp. 250–2) – to be translated into English so that its arguments could provide support for the implementation of royal supremacy.) Henry worked his way through five more marriages but remained theologically conservative. More radical theologians, many of them already imbued with European Protestantism, achieved power only in the brief reign of his young son Edward VI (r.1547–53). A Catholic reaction under Edward's half-sister Mary Tudor (r.1553–8), who married the intense Philip II, king of Catholic Spain, saw the burnings of Protestants. If Mary had lived longer, England might have remained a Catholic country. The return to Catholicism was reversed as Mary's shrewd half-sister, Elizabeth (r.1558–1603), sensed that a judicious Protestant settlement might be enforced; her Act of Settlement and the moderate Thirty-Nine Articles, finalized in 1571, founded what would eventually become an English church in a form still recognizable today. Its reliance on three sources of theology, the scriptures, tradition and reason, allowed it to become a broad church that would embed itself within the mainstream of English rural life.

It would be wrong to underestimate the upheaval in English society caused by the Reformation. In his meticulous study of the English Reformation, *Heretics and Believers*, Peter Marshall describes it as 'a volcanic eruption of change, whose seismic impact remains fundamental to an informed understanding of almost all the country's subsequent social and political developments'.[23] Anglicanism, the name adopted only much later for the English church, was essentially an elitist movement supported by a highly educated core of reformers such as Thomas Cranmer and Hugh Latimer,† many of whom had close links with their continental colleagues such as Melanchthon. They worked with Henry VIII's ministers, notably his henchman Thomas Cromwell, to effect the overthrow of the papacy and create an independent church. The great defenders of the rituals, images and feast days of traditional religion were – as the studies of Eamon Duffy have shown – the laity. The tragedy of the English Reformation (as

† Both were burned during the reign of Mary. The site of their 'martyrdom' is still commemorated by a memorial in Oxford.

in much of the rest of Protestant Europe) lay in the destruction of local Christianities that had grown up around shrines and the patterns of the agricultural year.[24] However, there could be no return to papal rule. By 1547 much of the panoply of saints, images and relics had been burned or desecrated and the monasteries left to decay once their wealth had been transferred to the royal treasury by Thomas Cromwell. Clergy would be allowed to marry and services would be conducted in the vernacular. The liturgical and sacred texts – the Prayer Book, Psalms and the Authorized King James Version of the Bible – that were to be the vehicles for Anglican worship would provide some of the finest of all expressions of English prose. The new church cleaved to the traditional Christian doctrines of the Trinity, the nature of Christ and original sin. It retained a church hierarchy of archbishops, bishops and clergy. The latter were chosen overwhelmingly from the middle or even upper classes and fitted in well with leaders of the conservative rural society around them.* The great cathedrals of medieval England, with their peaceful closes, remained intact. Elizabeth encouraged their choirs, ensuring a rich legacy of Anglican church music and a tradition of choral singing that remains vibrant to this day.

Elizabeth's finest quality was her ability to retain authority without 'opening windows in men's souls'.† Her careful manoeuvring allowed Catholics to operate underground (as 'recusants') unless they supported priests who had been sent from abroad to foment opposition to her rule. Such men were assumed to be in league with the Catholic Philip II of Spain who launched his Armada against Elizabeth in 1588, and dealt with brutally as traitors. The Elizabethan church and national identity were being consolidated. By 1901 the scholar-bishop Mandell Creighton was crediting the English Reformation with making 'the national spirit of England become more resolute, adventurous and practical' leading to 'greater honesty, greater straightforwardness, greater love of justice and a more exalted standard of national morality'.[25] Puritans, inspired by the teachings of John Calvin, remained a constant irritation. In Scotland, John Knox preached a much purer church without hierarchy and decoration and with less compromise with the upper reaches of English society. As will be explored in Chapter 27, these ideas were to be central to the politics of the seventeenth century.

---

* By the eighteenth century it was difficult to become a bishop in England without an aristocratic patron to support you. See Robert Ingram, *Reformation without End: Religion, Politics and the Past in Post-revolutionary England* (Manchester: Manchester University Press, 2018).

† These words have often been attributed to Elizabeth, but while they reflect her attitude, their origin is unknown.

It was inevitable that European Protestantism would splinter further as the problems in finding stable foundations for theology were exposed. Yet in many ways, Protestant Christianity remained conservative, not least in arguing that it was returning to the ideals of the early church that had been corrupted by papal government. Even Calvin claimed that he was not inventing a new theology but returning to the old. The Trinity was still accepted as the only legitimate way of giving Christ and the Holy Spirit equal dignity and substance with the Father. No one thought of discarding the Old Testament as the superseded scriptures of the Jews (as had been proposed by some in the early church) or challenging the canon of the Bible as it had been finalized in the fourth century. The theology of the church councils was accepted to include that of Chalcedon in 451, the council that had decreed the indivisibility of the human and divine natures of Christ. After that, it was argued, absolutism had asserted itself both in Constantinople and Rome and so destroyed the harmony of the ancient church. Augustine remained in place as the most authoritative of the western theologians and the doctrine of original sin, the loss of dignity and the perpetuation of helplessness of a depraved and undeserving humanity, remained unchallenged. Eternal punishment in hell awaited most. God's continuing outrage against the sin of Adam left little room for mercy.

Yet the differences between the confessions were real enough to create barriers between them that were vigorously defended. 'Although opinions are almost as numerous as men, nevertheless there is hardly any sect that does not condemn all others and desire to reign alone', was, as seen in the opening quotation to this chapter, the bleak assessment of Sebastian Castellio, whose call for tolerance between the warring French churches went unheeded.[26] 'The Reformation', states Diarmaid MacCulloch in his authoritative history of the religious upheavals, 'might indeed be viewed simply as two centuries of warfare'.[27] These wars, in France, in the Netherlands over eighty years, in central Europe (the Thirty Years War, 1618–48) and the civil wars in the British Isles, stood out for their atrocities. Concurrent with these conflicts was a steady wave of persecutions. To the horror of more tolerant Christians Calvin acquiesced, with much conservative support, in the burning of the Spanish theologian and humanist Michael Servetus in Geneva in 1553 when Servetus argued that there was no scriptural support for the Trinity. (He was fleeing a previous condemnation when he was arrested as he passed through Geneva.) When one popular sect, the Anabaptists, proclaimed that baptism should be seen as an adult commitment to Christian living, based on a mature understanding of scripture, they

MICHAEL SERVETUS HIS
DE ARAGONIA
Fritsch Sculpsit Hamburgi.

were violently persecuted. They responded to the challenge by quoting the scriptural passages that taught that persecution was only to be expected and stood firm. There were more Anabaptist martyrs than those of any other confession.*

It was the burning of Servetus that outraged Sebastian Castellio. Castellio (1515–63) was born into poverty in the duchy of Savoy, but his intellectual brilliance was soon recognized and led to study in the rich humanistic environment of Lyons, where he studied at a municipal college. He then converted to Protestantism and came to Geneva to work alongside Calvin, but the two soon fell out. Castellio was scandalized by what he saw as the lack of personal commitment by Christians living in the city. For him charity and tolerance of religious differences were more important than doctrine. If Christians could allow people who were leading dissolute lifestyles to live among them, they could surely tolerate those who interpreted the scriptures differently.

Castellio eventually moved to Basle, where he became a professor at the university. His tract of 1554, *Concerning Heretics and Whether They Should Be Persecuted*, published the year after Servetus's death, detailed the Christian thinkers who had argued for tolerance, showing how many of them, including Luther and Calvin, had abandoned their stance as soon they had achieved authority for themselves. Castellio argued that the concept of heresy was itself a fluid one, often no more than disagreement over minor doctrinal issues. Intellectual freedom was important, not least because it allowed disagreements to be aired in debate. To the fury of Calvin, he showed how many biblical passages are obscure, and open to a variety of interpretations (Erasmus had made the same point in relation to Luther). Anticipating the seventeenth-century English philosopher John Locke, Castellio argued that it was no business of magistrates to judge heresies unless there was a breakdown of peace. Using coercion was never a way of changing beliefs.

The Spanish theologian Michael Servetus portrayed in an eighteenth-century engraving. Servetus, who argued that there was no scriptural support for the Trinity, was arrested on the orders of Jean Calvin in Geneva and burnt at the stake for heresy in October 1553.

There followed a bitter war of words between Castellio and Calvin, whose *Defence of the Orthodox Faith of the Trinity Against the Prodigious Mistakes of Servetus* (1554) argued that everyone guilty of 'grave errors' in religion – clearly denoting those who did not follow Calvin – deserved

* One result of insisting on infant, rather than adult, baptism was that most children were conditioned into the faith they were born into and never experienced alternative expressions of Christianity.

to die. In response, in a new tract that was only published after his death, Castellio cleverly quoted biblical passages to support his views for a pluralism within which different religious views can exist in harmony. In his later writings, he followed Erasmus in championing free will against Calvin's predestination. Castellio's last years were marred by the outbreak of religious warfare in France. While he was still read into the seventeenth century, his voice was lost in the turmoil. For the historian Perez Zagorin, who champions him, 'his significance depends less on his influence than on the character of his thought and his intellectual and moral firmness as a great pioneer in the struggle for toleration'.[28] Largely forgotten when compared to the champions of toleration we will meet in later chapters, Castellio deserves to be remembered here.

The religious rigour of Geneva was certainly not replicated everywhere. The emphasis on religious conflicts in western Europe in the sixteenth century blinds us to the compromises that the rulers of eastern Europe – in Poland, Transylvania and what is now Romania – made to keep peace among the plethora of confessions that arose in the sixteenth century. The Declaration of Torda (1568) in Transylvania, for instance, acknowledged the right of clergy to preach according to their own understanding of their faith on the grounds that this faith was a direct gift to an individual from God. Here, as in moves towards toleration after the Thirty Years War in the following century, it was as much the futility of conflict that influenced the development as any idealism.[29]

The title page of the Great Bible of 1539, the first authorized edition of the Bible in English, translated by Miles Coverdale. Henry VIII is depicted as Supreme Head of the Church. He is surrounded by clerics and courtiers while the crowds below applaud him with cries of *Vivat Rex*.

There is a persistent myth, reinforced by the celebrations of the 500th anniversary of Luther's hammering the Ninety-Five Theses on the church door at Wittenberg, that the Reformation was a moment of liberation from superstition and the corruption of the Catholic Church and a turning point in the history of the Western World. This view must be treated with caution.[30] The Reformation had certainly showed how impossible it was to find a coherent doctrine of Christian belief and thus offered an immense challenge to traditional theology. But rather than accepting that this might lead to the mutual tolerance that Castellio had argued for, the vast majority of believers were trapped into the confession of their birthplace and were condemned if they tried to escape from it. As has already been seen in the case of Servetus and Castellio, toleration grew outside the churches rather than from within it. Later chapters will provide more examples of the slow chipping away by philosophers

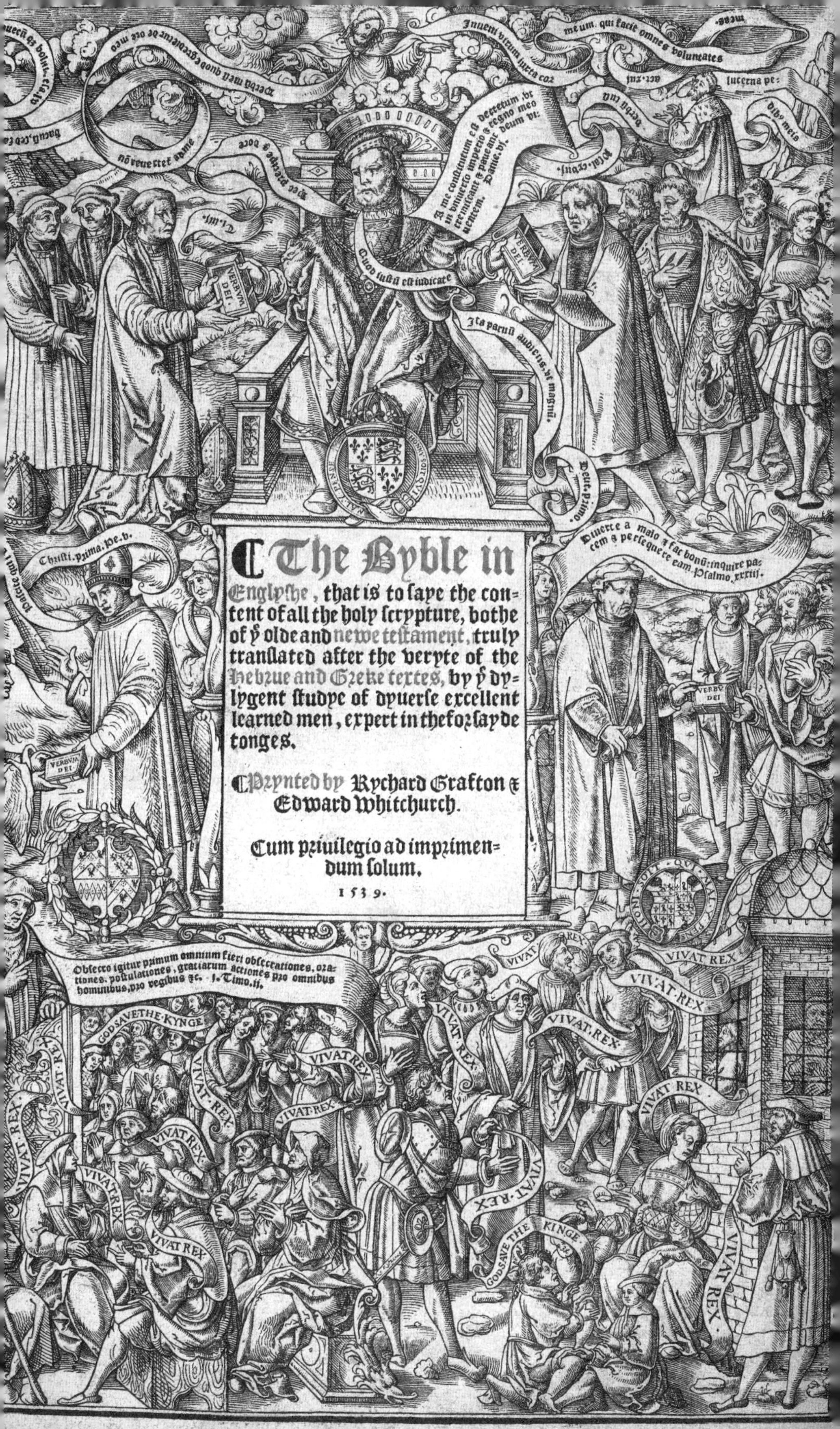
The Byble in Englyshe, that is to saye the content of all the holy scrypture, bothe of ye olde and newe testament, truly translated after the veryte of the Hebrue and Greke textes, by ye dylygent studye of dyuerse excellent learned men, expert in the forsayde tonges.
Prynted by Rychard Grafton & Edward Whitchurch.
Cum priuilegio ad imprimendum solum.
1539.
Inueni virum iuxta cor meum, qui faciet omnes voluntates meas. Act. xiij.
Lucerna pedibus meis verbum tuum
A me constitutum est decretum, vt in vniuerso imperio & regno meo tremiscant & paueant deum viuentem. Danie. vi.
Haec praecipe & doce. Ti. iiij.
Quod iustum est iudicate
Ita paruum audietis vt magnum. Deut. primo.
VERBUM DEI
Diuerte a malo & fac bonum: inquire pacem & persequere eam. Psalmo. xxxiij.
Obsecro igitur primum omnium fieri obsecrationes, orationes, postulationes, gratiarum actiones pro omnibus hominibus, pro regibus &c. i. Timo. ij.
VIVAT REX
GOD SAVE THE KYNGE

of the resolutely defended structures of Christian authoritarianism.

Overall, the Augustinian pessimism reinforced by the Reformation ensured that Protestantism could seldom, in itself, be a vehicle for progressive thought. The clergy, or their assemblies, proved relentlessly conservative in the face of social change. Biblical precedents, most of them from the Old Testament, could be found to justify slavery (see p. 503) and the use of violence in achieving God's will. Augustine's theory of the just war remained powerful. The Calvinist emphasis on individual effort meant that the 'undeserving poor' would not be given help; in this the Protestants were often less generous than the Catholic confraternities.* There was what can only be described as an obsession with the control of sexual behaviour. The sociologist Max Weber's famous hypothesis that the work ethic of the Calvinists was a major factor in the development of modern capitalism is now questioned by historians. Free enterprise had already flourished in the Roman empire and one can hardly argue that the ruthlessly acquisitive Catholic merchants of northern Italy were not capitalists within the markets to which they had access. Despite the outpouring of Protestant prints and engravings in which the sober and hard-working Christian is contrasted with the idle and dissolute pagan, it may have been more of a change of context, the opening of new global markets for those able to exploit them from the Atlantic seaboard, that drove economic advance in Protestant countries after 1600.

Tintern Abbey: The Crossing and Chancel, looking towards the East Window, watercolour painting by J. M. W. Turner, 1794. The 'bare, ruined choirs' of the dissolved monasteries haunted the English landscape.

Neither Luther nor Calvin had shown any interest in the study of the natural world, but it is sometimes claimed that Protestantism challenged the supernatural superstitions of the Catholics and so introduced a more 'scientific' age. Before 1600 the Lutherans condemned Copernicus's sun-centred universe much more quickly and forcefully than the Catholic Church. It is true that access to God through the saints and the Virgin Mary was no longer permissible but this was replaced by the continuous intrusion of God into one's inner conscience. In the world at large, portents, even illness, were seen as acts of God.† Worst of all, it was believed that individuals could be possessed by the devil. Augustine had talked of contracts between the

* 'In a US poll 46 per cent of Christians said that a lack of effort is generally to blame for a person's poverty, compared with 29 per cent of all non-Christians.' *Washington Post*, 3 August 2017.

† During the HIV/AIDS crisis of the 1980s, in which large numbers of gay men were afflicted, some Christian evangelicals expressed the belief that the disease was God's punishment for homosexuality.

devil and those submitting to him, and this was another of his ideas that was adopted by the Protestants of the period. The trauma of the resulting witch-hunts – possibly as many as 100,000 'witches' were put to death in Europe between 1500 and 1750 – challenges the argument that Protestantism could be seen to have transcended superstition. Its credo was that human beings deserved to see themselves as abject and unworthy sinners subject to the scriptures. In fact, far from opening up a new age of reason, the Protestant reformers were distrustful of reason as a means of finding truth. It was Luther who called reason 'the Whore'. As Augustine and Calvin argued, the capacity to reason, with which Adam and Eve had been originally endowed, was forever diminished by their sin. This admission of the incapacity of the human mind had important implications for intellectual life, as did the insistence by most of the reformers that there was no such thing as free will.

Yet there were strands of Protestant thought that could be seen as an impetus to scientific progress. Philipp Melanchthon believed that the wonder of God's creation made it worthy of further study and there were others who followed him in the seventeenth century. It has even been argued, by Peter Harrison in his *The Fall of Man and the Foundations of Science*,[31] that the belief that the reasoning power of human beings was damaged by original sin fostered a more intense and precise approach to experimental science. What is difficult to sort out is how far Christianity was a force that in itself encouraged an exploration of the natural world and how far deeper psychological traits, the 'natural curiosity' that had been seen as a universal trait by Aristotle, were the catalyst for the rebirth of science. Certainly, as the career of Isaac Newton showed, one could carry out science and mathematics at the higher level without losing a fascination with, and acceptance of, the scriptures.[32] This is a question that will deserve further discussion in the concluding chapters. The argument is complicated in that in the seventeenth century no 'scientist' could afford to publicly divorce his findings from the framework of a Christian view of the world. Newton was never able to openly express his own view, based on years of study, that there was no scriptural support for the Trinity.

In short, the view that the Reformation was a triumph of light over darkness and set Europe on the path to modernity is far too simplistic. Too much energy was dispersed in the maintenance of authority and conservative social structures and in conflict with rival denominations. What had changed most significantly is that national governments were now in charge of religious affairs, with the result that in conflicts to come, notably the Thirty Years War, nationalism and religion became entangled and often reinforced each other. With the decline of papal authority this was as true in Catholic countries, such as France and Spain, as it was in the new Protestant states. This added an unpleasant dimension to European politics. By the early twentieth century, and the outbreak of the great European war of 1914–18, each nation was able to call on the Christian God for support.

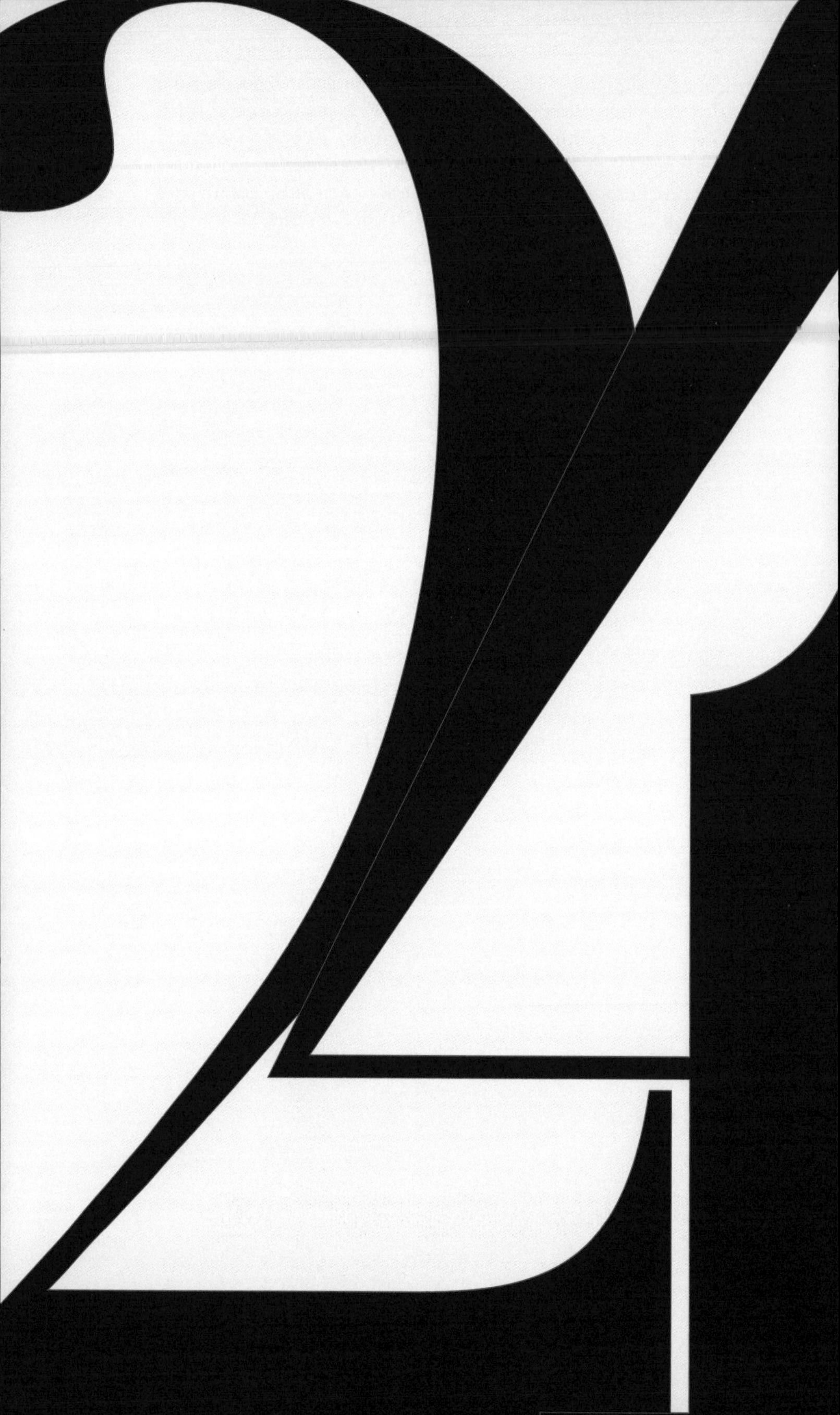
24

The World of Catholic Renewal

The holy synod enjoins on all bishops that they especially instruct the faithful diligently touching the intercession and invocation of saints; the honour paid to relics; and the lawful use of images: teaching them that the saints, who reign together with Christ, offer up their own prayers to God for men; that it is good and useful suppliantly to invoke them, and to resort to their prayers, aid, and help, for obtaining benefits from God…

Decree on 'Veneration and on Relics of Saints and Sacred Images', Session XXV of the Council of Trent, 1563

While Protestantism became tied to specific territories, the Catholic Church was able to reassert itself globally as the handmaid to Spanish and Portuguese colonization. Traditionally, this recovery has been called the Counter-Reformation, a term first used in the eighteenth century. However, this gives the impression that the consolidation of traditional Catholicism was solely a response to the Protestant Reformation. It can in fact, also be seen as a wider process of reform that had earlier roots. The strategy of founding new orders to galvanize reform, for instance, was already under way by the time of the Reformation. The earliest of the new orders, the Theatines, was inaugurated by Pope Clement VII in 1524 and another, the Capuchins, by the same pope in 1529 when it was still unclear that Lutheranism would prevail in Germany. In 1537 there was a remarkably hard-hitting report from within the hierarchy itself, the *Consilium de emendanda Ecclesia* (*Recommendations for the Correction of the Church*) written by Cardinal Gaspara Contarini (already cited as the champion of Venetian republicanism) at the request of the Farnese Pope Paul III (r.1534–49). It lambasted the worldly nature of the papacy and the dependency of its bloated bureaucracy on heavy taxation.

The opening session of the Council of Trent by Nicolò Dorigati (1711).

A broader perspective on sixteenth-century Catholicism is reflected in the title of the scholar R. Po-Chia Hsia's *The World of Catholic Renewal, 1540–1770*, one which I have appropriated for the title of this chapter.[1] This 'renewal' encompassed the reassertion of papal supremacy, the restating of traditional Catholic teaching, and pastoral reform through the ecclesiastical council held at Trentino (Trent). Alongside this more new orders were created, of which the Jesuits were the most dynamic, but which also included a number of women's orders, such as the teaching Ursulines.

Trentino was an Austrian imperial state in the north of Italy, under the authority of a prince-bishop. The council met there over three sessions between 1545 and 1563. By the time the Council of Trent opened, Protestantism was well established and the hopes of some that the council might form a forum for reconciliation were disappointed.[2] Instead, the council first concentrated on clarifying those Catholic doctrines that had been thrown into doubt by the Protestants, notably the problem of justification, the relieving by Christ of the burden of sin.[3] Luther believed that this could be achieved only through a declaration of faith.

XIV
I
III
II
VIII
XV
IX
IX
IV
VI
V
VII
X
XI
XI
XIII
D. O. M.
DIVISQVE DEI GENITRICI, IOANNI, VIGILIO, MAXENTIÆ, ADA
SISINIO, MARTYRIO, ALEXANDRO, MAGORIA

The council fathers wanted to emphasize more active participation by Catholics in the process. So, while following Augustine's belief that undeserving human beings were utterly dependent on God's grace for salvation, the bishops accepted, after exhaustive debate, that the faithful had the free will to 'convert themselves to their own justification, by freely assenting to and cooperating with that said grace'. This was a much more proactive response to Augustine's pessimism than the one the Protestants had preached (and Luther's claim that faith alone was necessary). However, the council decreed that no one, despite their efforts and good works, could be sure of being among those predestined for salvation and individuals also had the freedom to reject God's offer. This decree on justification is seen as an intellectual high point of the council's deliberations, but wrangling over the issue would continue for another 150 years.

As far as doctrine was concerned, the council reinforced the authority of the theology of Thomas Aquinas (or Thomism, as it became known). One result of this was that Aristotelian scholasticism would become a mark of an orthodox Catholic education and, ominously as it turned out, this included Aristotle's cosmology. The seven sacraments were recognized as having scriptural backing, and the miracle of transubstantiation reaffirmed for the Eucharist. The council accepted that the scriptures, as translated from the originals in the Vulgate, were the basis for Christian doctrine, but emphasized that tradition was also important: the church upheld the *magisterium*, the teachings that were said to have originated with the apostles and been passed down from generation to generation. In a direct riposte to Luther, the council decreed that no one was allowed to offer personal interpretations of the scriptures contrary to the teachings of the church. The practice of interceding with Christ through the Virgin Mary and the saints was confirmed and the council acknowledged the importance of arousing religious emotions through the arts. The practice of acquiring indulgences – and, implicitly, the continued existence of Purgatory – was reaffirmed, although abuses, somewhat vaguely defined, of the former were forbidden.

No ruling pope attended any of the sessions (although several delegates later became popes), and the council made no official statement on papal authority, but Pope Pius IV put the final *imprimatur*, a declaration that they should be printed, on the agreed decrees. Unlike the councils of Constance and Basle, the Council of Trent did not define a continuing role for itself. It was assumed by the bishops that the pope held ultimate authority as divinely appointed by God and the later sixteenth-century popes themselves made this clear by their actions. With Dominican support, Pope Paul III had already set up a more effective Roman Inquisition in 1542. A Tridentine* Profession of Faith, issued in 1565 by Pius IV after the council, included a promise of obedience to the popes that was now required of the clergy. The power of the popes to declare who had attained sainthood was strengthened still further at the expense of local initiatives. There was no decree requiring the reform of the papal Curia and, in fact, the cardinals would adopt even more opulent lifestyles in the seventeenth century, the great age of Roman palace building. The Roman aristocracy would become increasingly dependent on the immense patronage of each new pope.[4]

It was also accepted without question that it was the popes who issued the Indexes of Prohibited Books.[5] The first papal Index of Prohibited Books compiled under the supervision of Pope Paul IV in 1559 was as draconian as would be expected from one of the most austere of popes: the works of some 500 authors were banned completely, and the Index also included over 100 individual books and some 300 anonymous works. In addition, forty-five translated Bibles were prohibited alongside the works of sixty-one publishers, mainly from Germany and Switzerland, where John Calvin's Geneva was a major source of Protestant texts.

The severity of the Index triggered protests even from within the church, but once the process had begun it grew inexorably. An updated Index of 1596 comprised more than 2,000 items. They included a bewildering array of titles and authors of subjects from theology to philosophy, extensive areas of Italian literature, even including all or parts of selected works of Dante, Petrarch, Castiglione and all vernacular translations of the Bible. The ban on the latter was to be enforced with especial vigour. Bishops could no longer give permission for theologians to study these translations. Censorship grew steadily; the Index of 1707 contained as many as 11,000 entries.

The easiest way of dealing with the accumulating piles of confiscated books was, of course, to burn them. There was good scriptural backing for the practice. Acts 19:19 told how, in Ephesus in the presence of the apostle Paul, 'many of those who had formerly practised magic collected their books and burnt them publicly'. Pope Gregory the Great (r.590–604) had apparently endorsed the process by burning a pagan library from the Palatine Hill in Rome and St Dominic had

---

* 'Tridentine' is the descriptive term applied to the doctrines emanating from the Council of Trent.

also strongly recommended it as a way of dealing with heretical works. With the coming of the Reformation the practice gathered pace. Naturally enough, the works of Martin Luther were to be burned. (Luther planned to retaliate by burning the works of the Catholic theologians Duns Scotus and Thomas Aquinas, but he was thwarted when no scholars in Wittenberg would agree to surrender their valued copies.) The energetic cardinal Michele Ghislieri, later Pope Pius V, boasted that he had burned between 10,000 and 12,000 books on one day, 18 March 1559, in Rome. Years later, in 1620, the inquisitor in Genoa, Elisio Masini, berated his fellow inquisitors for their laxity. He looked back fondly to his earlier book-burning days when he had sent 5,000 or 6,000 volumes up in smoke, thereby purging Genoa 'of the Aretinos, the Machiavellis, the Bodins, the Boccaccios and of a thousand other filthy authors, of vernacular Bibles, of historical compendiums and of innumerable other totally prohibited books'.[6] His haul showed the extent of the inquisitors' reach. Aretino and Boccaccio represented Italian literature, Niccolò Machiavelli and (the French thinker) Jean Bodin political philosophy. The ban on vernacular Bibles was particularly destructive of learning as humanist scholars such as Antonio Brucioli had mastered the Greek and Hebrew sources and their translations into Italian were authoritative.

The church's attitude to works of 'science' was inconsistent, largely because the discipline itself was not clearly defined. The *Historia Animalium*, a major work by the Swiss Conrad Gessner (1516–65), which was to become the 'bible' of zoology for 200 years, was placed on the 1559 Index on the grounds of Gessner's Protestantism, while works on natural history by Catholic authors remained unscathed. The Jesuits, whose order will be explored below, contributed enormously to the flood of knowledge of flora and fauna and ethnography that swept back into Europe from Asia and the Americas. There was nothing threatening to theology from knowing more about the properties of plants. When a work of science challenged biblical texts, on the other hand, the scriptures took precedence and this sealed the fate of Copernicus, the German astronomer Johannes Kepler and Galileo (see pp. 653–8), whose works on heliocentrism remained on the Index from 1616 until the nineteenth century. Overall, the damage to cultural life, especially to the rich tradition of Italian literature, by the Index was immense.

Yet the council also made provision for the reform of the church. Each bishop now had to reside in his diocese, and was, to have no more than one diocese. (Oddly enough, this was the subject of much

contention in that it challenged the traditional right of the papacy to grant a bishop the privilege of non-residence.) A bishop was obliged to visit each of the churches under his jurisdiction once a year. Each diocese would have a seminary for the training of priests.* The segregation of a celibate clergy was to continue. One important move was to extend the control of the church over marriages, many of which had previously been clandestine. Marriages now had to be made public, and recognized as a sacrament in a ceremony conducted by the parish priest.

Three members of the Jesuit mission to China are shown bringing 'science' to two of their converts, Xu Guangqi and his granddaughter. The figure at top left is Father Matteo Ricci, who in 1601 became the first European to enter Beijing's Forbidden City.

At their best these decrees were highly effective in ensuring action. When Cardinal Carlo Borromeo arrived in Milan in 1565 he was the first archbishop to take up residence in the city for eighty years (a

* While, with the decline in vocations, they are now empty shells, one can still find these forbidding buildings in many Italian cities.

reminder of how lax the ecclesiastical supervision of even a large city had become).[7] When plague broke out in Milan in 1576 many leaders fled, but Borromeo stayed, a move that helped restore confidence among the poor. (One of the reasons why Sebastian Castellio condemned the Calvinists of Geneva was because, he claimed, they did not help the afflicted during a plague in the city.[8]) As the decadent clergy, monks and nuns of his archdiocese soon found out, this was a man who was uncompromising in his fight to reform the church. Borromeo battled to improve the education of the clergy, cleaned out dissolute monasteries (he found that the monks were often 'lazy, ignorant and debauched') and dealt with witches, heretics and Protestants to the extent of burning them if necessary. He laid down detailed instructions on how churches were to be built and decorated. Even the correct design for the *latrinas* got a mention. Borromeo was obsessive about the importance of regular confession and the confessionals still found lining the walls of many a Catholic church were made to his design. His role in the plague became a symbol of his saintliness* as the magnificent baroque Karlskirche in Vienna, constructed in thanksgiving for the end of a plague in the city, bears witness.

Alongside the energetic spiritual and administrative efforts of men like Borromeo, the age of Catholic renewal saw the founding of new missionary orders, of which the Jesuits were the most prominent.[9] The Jesuits marked a break with the contemplative life of established orders such as the Benedictines. The founder of the Jesuits, Ignatius of Loyola, was a Basque nobleman with a military background. Driven by personal religious crises from Spain to the Holy Land and then to France, his commanding presence and ascetic practices drew a small coterie of admirers to share his commitment to preaching among the poor. Pope Paul III identified how his gifts might be used to found a new order dedicated to reliving the lives of the apostles, although the Jesuits never had the same emphasis on poverty that other orders demanded. Crucially, the Jesuits, founded in 1540, were to be subject directly to the pope and Ignatius, and his successors as general superior. Free from allegiance to any particular monastic house, the order possessed considerable flexibility. Individuals could be moved wherever they were needed. The missionary successes achieved by the Jesuits in India, Japan and China in the later sixteenth century were remarkable not only for their conversions but for the vigour with which they collected information about the peoples among whom they worked. Later, they would also be a powerful force in Spanish America.

* Borromeo was canonized in 1610 by Pope Paul V.

In comparison to other orders, the Jesuit ministry was defined in broad terms as missionary work among the poor and in prisons and hospitals, or working as arbiters of moral issues, but above all they were formidable educationalists. In the seventeenth century 'the Jesuit colleges remained the largest and most coherent educational system in the world',[10] with 444 colleges and 100 seminaries by 1626. They disciplined their pupils into a sophisticated understanding of the complexities of Catholic theology – based on the works of Aquinas – and became the teachers of first choice for the Catholic elites. The Jesuit *Collegio Romano* in Rome, established by Loyola in 1551, schooled eight future popes. In Vienna, where some 70 per cent of nobles became Protestants, they spearheaded the restoration of Catholicism. By the seventeenth century the Jesuits were prepared to supplement their austere curriculum with mathematics, science and history. The Flemish Jesuit Johan Boland (1596–1669) launched the *Acta Sanctorum*, a vast compilation of documents relating to the saints that would take centuries to complete. But the Jesuits' very success and their closeness to the popes aroused resentment from the bishops and older orders. They were actually suppressed by the pope in 1773, only to return in the early nineteenth century. Despite their many activities they did not, however, staff the Inquisition.

It is within Rome that one sees the fruits of the Catholic renewal and the contradictions at its heart. The simply furnished rooms occupied by Ignatius of Loyola when he was superior general of his order can be visited from the Piazza del Gesù in the centre of the ancient city. While he was here his *Spiritual Exercises*, a series of meditations and prayers, were printed for the first time, in 1548, with the support of Pope Paul III. Traditionally followed in solitude over thirty days, the *Exercises* were one of the most effective ways in which the Jesuits communicated with the faithful, as mentors for those participating in the rigorous 'exercises' that would bring them personally closer to God. Yet the humble rooms lie between two of the most ostentatious churches in Rome. The first, the Gesù, was the sumptuous church of Ignatius's order. Built between 1568 and 1578, the effect as one enters is overwhelming. Heavily decorated with gilded pilasters and a marvellous vaulted ceiling, it is also the site of the tomb of Ignatius that is swathed in marble, lapis lazuli and bronze. There are statues on either side of the imposing edifice, suitably of *Religion Triumphing Over Heresy* and *Barbarians Adoring the Faith*. Opposite the tomb is another, that of Ignatius's companion Francis Xavier, who had died while evangelizing in Goa. His arm is preserved here in an opulent reliquary, confirming

INFERNORVM + DONAVIT ILLI NOMEN
IHS
NOMINE IESV SACRVM

the decree of the Council of Trent that relics were a valid means of accessing the saints and through them God.

Ignatius was canonized in 1622 and it was decided to build a new church, Sant'Ignazio, in his honour, one which could also serve the staff and students of the *Collegio Romano*. It is every way as magnificent as the Gesù, decorated with the rarest of marbles and an extraordinary painted ceiling that uses *trompe l'oeil* to draw the eye up towards the heavens. Its creator, Andrea Pozzo, was a member of the order and this is his masterpiece, with every niche and corner of the vault exploited to create the illusions of a limitless space. The prevailing theme that emerges from the mass of images here is the missionary work of the Jesuits and the triumph of St Ignatius. Elsewhere in Rome there is similar opulence. Pope Sixtus V (r.1585–90), a swineherd in his youth, began designing the extraordinary Capella Sistina in Santa Maria Maggiore as the site for his tomb as soon as he came into office. Not to be outdone, the Borghese Pope Paul V had an equally luxurious chapel built opposite, using the leading artists and sculptors of his day. It had been Paul V who had completed the enormous new St Peter's in 1605 and it was his name, rather than a biblical verse, that graced the façade. Fifty years later St Peter's would be fronted by the superb colonnade designed by the master of baroque architecture, Lorenzo Bernini.[11]

The magnificent ceiling of the Church of the Gesù, in Rome, opulent mother church of the Society of Jesus.

Yet however sumptuous the backdrop to papal power, the popes had now lost much of their influence within Europe. In a confrontation between Pope Paul V and Venice in 1606 over the extent of papal prerogatives in the city, the local clergy, led by the theologian and ardently republican statesman Paolo Sarpi, took the side of Venice. Among the clergy only the Jesuits supported the pope, and they were summarily expelled from the city. To his dismay, Paul V found that he did not even have the backing of the French and Spanish monarchs and he had to make a humiliating diplomatic climbdown. This is often seen as a further turning point in the loss of papal authority, the moment the popes could no longer use the threat of excommunication or impose an interdict on a secular state.

A pope and his supporting Curia could use his influence through the Index of Prohibited Books and the Inquisition to maintain control over the minds of the faithful, but even this power was limited. In Spain, for example, no papal bull could be promulgated without royal approval, the Spanish Inquisition was independent of the papal equivalent and the kings controlled senior ecclesiastical appointments.

Likewise, France and most other Catholic states would not let the papal inquisitors in but instead used their bishops, sometimes very effectively, to uphold Catholic teaching and morals on behalf of the state. Even in Italy, bishops resented the intrusions of the Inquisition into their dioceses. In fact, there was powerful popular resentment to the Inquisition. Only in the papal states could the popes be said to exercise their restored spiritual authority in untrammelled fashion, but even here there were challenges to their authority. After the death of Pope Paul IV in 1559 a Roman mob sacked the offices of the Inquisition and destroyed its archives. Papal power was further hampered by the steady decline of the Italian economy as wealth in trade shifted to the Atlantic seaboard. By the middle of the seventeenth century, the continuing shortfall in papal revenues, the consolidation of a religious settlement at the Treaty of Westphalia (1648) and the rise of absolutism in states such as France left the popes even more isolated.

The challenge faced by the Italian Inquisition, run as it was by cardinals in Rome, was to provide a coherent and stable definition of what might be heresy in a world where new ideas were proliferating. There were too many shades of opinion and personal rivalries among the inquisitors that would affect the outcome of any trial. Galileo became the scientist who caused most confusion and frustration for the church – his 'trial' will be described later (see p. 664). An earlier *cause célèbre* was the burning of Giordano Bruno in Rome in 1600.[12]

Bruno was a Dominican monk, born close to Naples in 1548 and educated there. He was an impetuous character, brilliant and imaginative but also combative and his life was one of continual conflict. Whether teaching or writing in Germany, Oxford or Paris, he infuriated those he encountered by, in the words of one critic, his 'vain and chimerical imagining of novelties'.[13] Among the provocative titles he gave himself was one as 'the tamer of presumptuous and stubborn ignorance'.[14] George Abbot, later an archbishop of Canterbury (1611–33), who heard Bruno expound Copernicus in Oxford, noted that rather than the Earth moving and the universe standing still 'it was his owne head which rather did run round and his braines did not stand still'.[15]

Yet, as his support for Copernicus showed, Bruno had important ideas, although his varied reading and overactive imagination make it hard to make much sense of them. He was strongly influenced by the Islamic philosopher Averroes in his view that theology should be totally independent of scientific exploration and he went beyond the heliocentrism of Copernicus in arguing that there must be many solar systems, even with the possibilities of alien life on them. At a time when Aristotelian scholasticism still had powerful backing within the church, Bruno made penetrating criticisms of Aristotle's physics, preferring to see the world as made up entirely of atoms that joined with each other to form objects. This had been the view of the Roman philosopher Lucretius, of the first century BC, whose 'scientific' poem, *De rerum natura*, was becoming more influential as the sixteenth century progressed (see p. 482). Not surprisingly for someone who made such trouble for himself by his incessant questioning, Bruno argued for toleration between religions.

Bruno would have been better left alone, but fortune was not with him. Thinking he might be safe in the more tolerant atmosphere of Venice, he was, in fact, extradited from there by the Roman Inquisition in 1593. Many years of tortuous argument with the inquisitors followed as he claimed that, as a philosopher, he was not interested in theology and that even if he were, nothing he believed conflicted with Catholic teaching. Ordered to retract his ideas, which in the trial centred on theology rather than Copernicanism, he refused and was burned as a heretic in the Campo de' Fiori in Rome in February 1600. Bruno remains a secular hero and it was fitting that one of the first acts of the government of the newly unified Italy, when it absorbed Rome into its national territory in 1870, was to set up a statue to him on the site of his burning. The pope, now confined to the Vatican, retaliated by spending the day prostrate before a statue of St Peter.[16]

How far can one place Reformation and Counter-Reformation Christianity as the core of 'western civilization'? There are difficulties in making the case. By 1600 Christianity had fragmented and different variants were now competing with one another. The question 'What is the nature of a Christian society?' becomes difficult to answer if one surveys the possibilities on offer – from Calvinism to Catholicism, and from the austerity of committed practice in bare chapels to the passive enjoyment of the opulence and emotional impact of Catholic architecture and ritual. Christianity's success has, of course, partly depended on the many ways it can be expressed or experienced, but this makes it challenging to generalize about the contribution of Christianity to society. Its impact has been so varied. Bizarrely, that most isolated of Christian intellectuals, Augustine, whose impact never travelled beyond western Christendom and its missions, was common to all. So too was authority. Conversion involved signing up to a set of non-negotiable doctrines that varied from one confession to another. Infant baptism ensured that most believers grew up with little understanding of competing confessions. What religion you belonged to and how you practised it became central to everyday life.

One inevitable response to Christian authoritarianism was for there to be more secrecy, notably in the practice of forbidden forms of worship, from the priest holes of English country houses to the hidden meetings of radicals in the backstreets of cities. Some minority religious groups, such as the Jews of Spain or the Huguenots of France, were forced to flee their homeland or were expelled. The Renaissance scholar Nicholas Terpstra argues that 'the Reformation stands out as the first period in European and possibly global history when the religious refugee became a mass phenomenon... Never before had so many people of so many different faiths – hundreds of thousands certainly and perhaps millions – been forcibly relocated by the demands of religious purity.'[17] It is impossible to understand the religious life of the United States without acknowledging the pressures that led Puritan settlers to establish their communities in New England.

As yet, freedom to openly express one's own religious beliefs – or lack of them – remained virtually impossible. But it was also impossible for the Christian churches actually to control individual minds. A few more philosophical thinkers realized the absurdity of believing that one form of Christianity was superior to another, but it took time for their ideas to become accepted. As Jonathan Israel has argued in the second volume of his major study of the Enlightenment, there was little possibility of tolerance emerging from within the Christian communities: 'Resistance to any kind of theoretically grounded toleration remained everywhere extremely tenacious and to the extent it was broken down was reduced only by a dogged combination of practical pressures and philosophical argument.'[18] And yet there were many ways in which individuals could explore their creativity with marginal reference to the Christianity into which they were born. Two of the most celebrated are the subject of the next chapter.

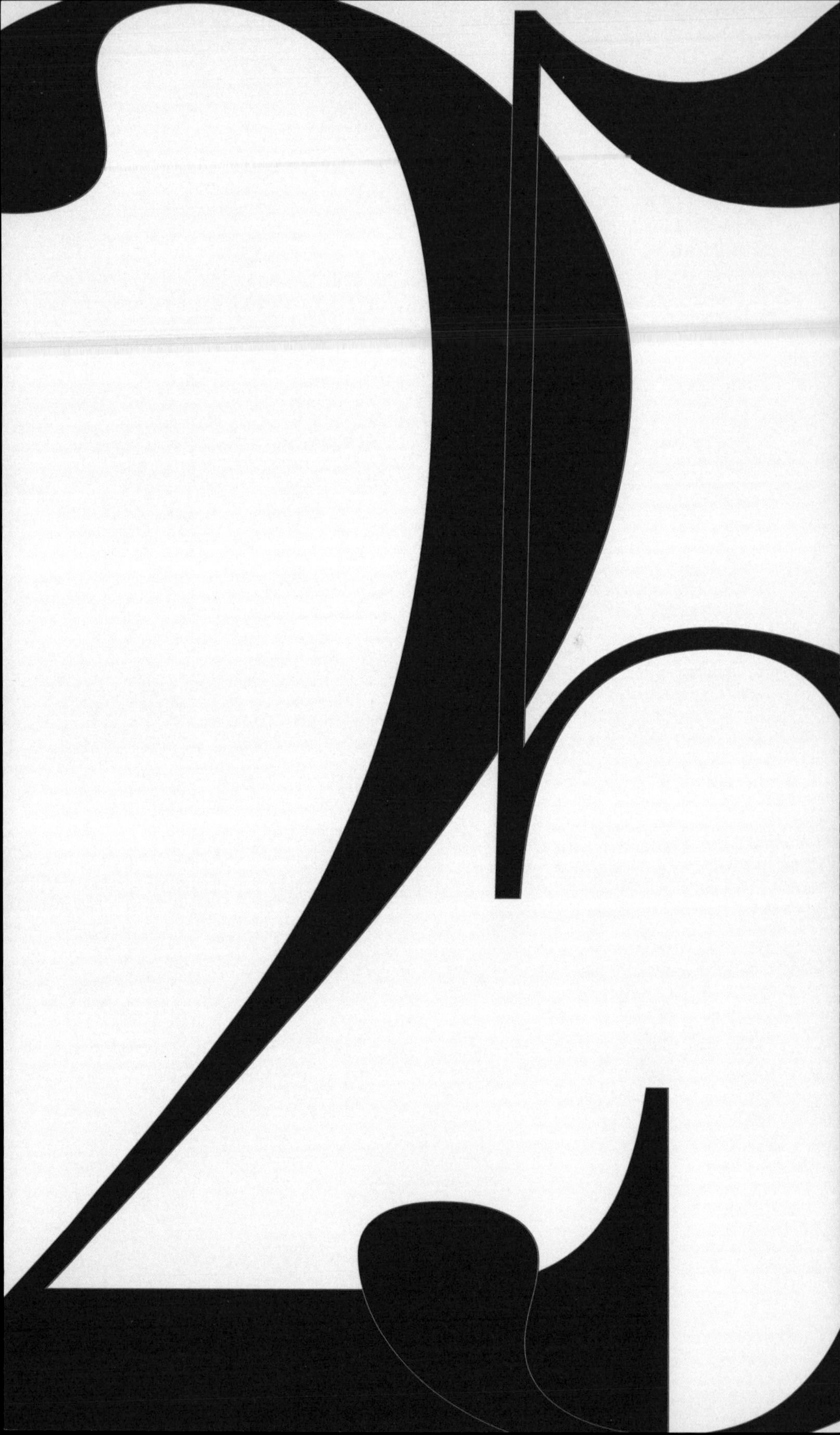

Montaigne and Hamlet: Peace or Turmoil in the Solitary Soul?

Let us leave aside that infinite confusion of opinions which we can see among the philosophers themselves… It really is the truest of presuppositions that men – I mean the most learned, the best-endowed and the cleverest of men – never agree about anything, not even that the sky is above our heads. Those who doubt everything doubt that too… Many's the time I have taken an opinion contrary to my own and (as I am fond of doing) tried defending it for the fun of the exercise: then, once my mind has really applied itself to that other side, I get so firmly attached to it that I forget why I held the first opinion and give it up.

Michel de Montaigne, from his essay 'An Apology for Raymond Sebond'

There is nothing either good or bad but thinking makes it so.

Hamlet, *Hamlet*, Act 2, Scene 2

The leading intellectuals of the sixteenth century were, of course, infused with classical learning and none more so than Michel de Montaigne (1533–92).[1] 'Plutarch leads us, while Seneca drives us' was how the famous essayist described his mentors. Montaigne was born into a minor noble family in Bordeaux. The family had worked its way up through gathering estates, made up largely of vineyards, and entering public service as mayors and magistrates. Montaigne's father was no scholar himself but was so obsessed with educating his son that he devised a strict pedagogical programme for him which from an early age required him to speak only Latin – even the servants had to learn some in order to communicate. The boy grew up somewhat isolated but feeling he was someone special, and he was anxious to find a role that took him beyond the confines of his conventional background. He began a career in law and local politics, but in his late thirties he was profoundly shaken by a sequence of tragic and unsettling events. In 1563 he was devastated by the death of his close friend, the poet Étienne de La Boétie; two years later he married, but lost his first-born child in infancy (only one of his six children would grow to adulthood). He also had an accident while riding which might have killed him. Then, in 1568, his father died, leaving him to manage the family estates.

The southern tower of the Château de Montaigne, family home of the Renaissance thinker Michel de Montaigne. It was here that Montaigne housed his library and wrote his celebrated *Essays*.

The combined shock of these events made him sensitive to the minutiae of everyday existence. He decided to withdraw from public life and meditate on life as it affected him, working in the isolation of a tower in his château in the Dordogne. 'Let us cut loose from all the ties that bind us to others; let us win from ourselves the power to live really alone and to live that way at our ease.'[2] He had, of course, absorbed the immense resources offered by the classical tradition. A thousand books were accommodated in his tower and he could draw on these for the meditations that became immortalized as the *Essays*. Outside Montaigne's civilized world of quiet contemplation, France – the state where the immediate legacy of the Reformation was at its most devastating – was split by the religious warfare described in later chapters.

In one standard edition, the Penguin Classics, edited and brilliantly translated by the Renaissance scholar M. A. Screech, the *Essays* run to over 1,250 pages. It is hard to open the volume at random without being drawn into Montaigne's musings on whatever subject he is exploring.

As he puts it in one essay, 'On Affectionate Relationships': 'In truth what are these things I scribble, other than grotesques and monstrous bodies, made of various parts, without any certain figure or any other than accidental order, coherence or proportion?' Montaigne admits that these are not formal essays; they are often not well structured and one may follow on from the other in what would later be called 'a stream of consciousness'. The English novelist Virginia Woolf noted how the third, and final, book of essays reached no conclusion but was simply suspended at Montaigne's death.[3] This is perhaps too dismissive; Montaigne's last essay, 'On Experience', does appear to offer a summing-up at a time when his health was deteriorating. But it is fair to say the *Essays* contrast with the self-disciplined writings of the earlier Renaissance humanists. However, they are absorbing for their insights and use of classical examples and this is one reason why their early readers enthused over them when the first edition was published in 1580.

One can understand why Plutarch is Montaigne's favourite author. There are at least 400 references to Plutarch, described as 'my very own Plutarch, so perfect, so outstanding a judge of human actions' and 'a philosopher who teaches us what purity is'.[4] Despite their distance from each other in time, they came from very similar backgrounds, supported by country estates, a solid grounding in the classics, and a life in public service – although in later life Montaigne avoided the latter as much as he could. They have the same exploratory and undogmatic approach to philosophical issues and in his *Parallel Lives* Plutarch provided a mass of examples with which Montaigne could illustrate the *Essays*. Unable to read the original Greek, he came across the *Lives* through the elegant French translation (1559–65) of Bishop Jacques Amyot. It is said that the quality of the translation inspired Montaigne to write the *Essays* in French, not Latin, as might have been expected.* In his essay 'On Books' he praises Plutarch for writing lives that 'linger more over motives than events, over what comes from inside more than what happens outside'.

Montaigne's *Essays* were inspired by his study of classical writers such as Plutrarch and Lucretius. Shown here is Montaigne's own copy of the latter's *De rerum natura.*

This emphasis on the inner life is supported by Montaigne's eclectic espousal of Stoicism and Epicureanism. These philosophies suit his detached tone. He is determined to moderate his emotions and open himself to the rhythms of the natural world. Here he followed the standard Stoic belief that the universe followed a sequence of rise

* Amyot's translation was in turn translated into English by Thomas North (1579), from where it fed into Shakespeare's plays.

TITI LVCRETII CARI DE RERVM NATVRA LIBRI SEX.

A DIONYSIO LAMBINO Monstroliensi litterarum Græcarum in vrbe Lutetia doctore Regio, locis innumerabilibus ex auctoritate quinque codicum manu scriptorum emendati, atque in antiquum ac natiuum statum ferè restituti, & præterea breuibus, & perquàm vtilibus commentariis illustrati.

PARISIIS,
Et Lugduni habentur.

In Gulielmi Rouillij,
Et Philippi G. Rouillij Nep.
ædibus, via Iacobæa sub Concordia.

CVM PRIVILEGIO REGIS.

and fall with new life sprouting from the old. There is no place for a cataclysmic and final Last Judgement. It is wrong to try to subvert or challenge this inevitable process of birth, death and rebirth. This is one of the themes of his meditative essay 'On Experience': 'Our life is composed, like the harmony of the world, of discords, as well as of different tones, sweet and harsh, sharp and flat, soft and loud.' We must live with these discords. Montaigne followed, via Lucretius' *De rerum natura*, the philosopher Epicurus (341–270 BC), who embraced withdrawal from public life and an active concentration on the pleasures of the mind. The traditional Greek argument against Epicureanism was that the philosophy played down the importance of active involvement in political life, and Montaigne was often to be condemned by later readers for his apparent indifference to the suffering around him. His response would be that involvement was as likely to cause harm as good.

Aware of the religious tensions sweeping his country after the Reformation, Montaigne remained a loyal but hardly zealous Catholic. His acceptance of Stoicism was underpinned by his correspondence with Justus Lipsius, who had reconciled the two philosophies (see p. 481).[5] Yet the teachings of the church or the life of Christ hardly feature at all in his writings. The Greek philosopher Socrates is far more prominent. More committed Catholics would have shown some concern over their fate in the afterlife, but Montaigne talked as if death was merely an entry into darkness. And he diverges from traditional Catholic theology in the opening lines of his essay 'On Cruelty', where he talks of the 'tendencies towards Good that are born in us', a riposte to Augustine's concept of original sin. One gets the feeling that Montaigne frees his mind by simply accepting the revelations of God as a matter of faith – a doctrine known as fideism – which lets him off the hook so that he can concentrate on the philosophies that actually engage him: Stoicism, Epicureanism and Scepticism. There are virtually no references in the *Essays* to Luther or Calvin even though they had initiated the turmoil that was sweeping the France of his day. Montaigne's fideistic stance worked in that he was accepted as a loyal Catholic by many of his contemporaries and he was even received by Pope Gregory XIII on a visit to Rome in 1580. However, in the more austere climate of the seventeenth century his commitment to Catholic orthodoxy was seen to be half-hearted and by the end of the century the *Essays* were even placed on the papal Index.

One of Montaigne's views that came to offend the church was his sympathy towards animals. This came not merely from an abhorrence of cruelty to either man or beast but from an awareness that they have qualities we ignore. He notes how animals and insects can co-operate, have sophisticated instincts and possess attributes – for instance, an acute sense of smell – which in humans are less developed. In his 'Apology for Raymond Sebond',* his longest essay and the fullest expression of his views on animals, Montaigne described the prayer-like gestures made by elephants after they have washed themselves and wondered if they had 'some participation of religion'. To the modern reader, and to many in Montaigne's day, this seemed a natural reaction but his religious detractors saw these sympathies as breaking down the absolute barrier that God had created between man and animals, even to the extent of degrading humans. In theological terms, this was unforgivable and the *Essays* remained on the Index for nearly 200 years.

Raymond Sebond was a fifteenth-century Catalonian theologian whose *Theologia naturalis* (*Natural Theology*) had been published in 1484. Montaigne translated it from Latin into French for his father. Sebond had argued that it was possible to prove the existence of God through reason and the experience of nature. Montaigne starts off by supporting Sebond but the major theme of the essay is why scepticism is justified. This is one of the best expositions of the claim that there can be no certainty about anything, other than, as Montaigne concludes, the revelations of God. He draws heavily on Sextus Empiricus' analysis of Pyrrhonism (see pp. 481–2).

The central theme of the 'Apology', and one that Montaigne enjoyed exploring, was that one can look at almost everything from different perspectives. To return to animal life, Montaigne made the point that the world as seen by himself was not the same as the world seen by his beloved cat. 'When I play with my cat who knows whether I do not make her more sport than she makes with me?' He was profoundly affected by his meetings with the Tupinamba Indians who had been brought back to Europe from Brazil on a French ship.[6] In his essay 'On the Cannibals', where he discusses the meetings, he notes how it is only ignorance that condemns them for their lifestyle. In fact, he wishes they had been discovered sooner as earlier generations might have appreciated their way of life more than the present, less tolerant, one. Montaigne waxes lyrical about their free and untroubled life, thus helping to create the image of the 'noble savage' that was to become prominent among eighteenth-

overleaf Tensions between French Catholic groups and Protestant Huguenots overflowed in August 1572 in the massacre of St Bartholomew's Day. In the left rear of François Dubois' painting, Catherine de Medici – traditionally regarded as the instigator of the massacre – inspects a pile of Huguenot bodies.

* 'Apology' here means 'defence'.

century philosophers. While Montaigne accepted that the Indians had rituals that included cannibalism, he sets this alongside the barbarities practised by Europeans, such as the burning alive of heretics: 'We may well call these people barbarians, in respect to the rules of reason, but not in respect to ourselves, who surpass them in every kind of barbarity.' Montaigne was particularly shocked by the mass killing of Protestants by fanatical Catholics in Paris in the St Bartholomew's Day Massacre of 1572. In his 'Apology', he deplored the failure of the Spanish not to improve the peoples and land they had discovered by 'adding the Greek and Roman virtues to those originally in that region'. Instead, the intruders had embarked on an orgy of destruction.

Montaigne's scepticism was underpinned by more profound questionings. One of the few New Testament texts he uses in the *Essays* is the apostle Paul's attack on 'the wisdom of the wise', from First Corinthians (3:19). It is pretentious, he argues, to think that human beings are 'wise'. If one examines the debates of the ancient philosophers they never come to coherent conclusions. Logic appears to offer an unassailable way of achieving truth but in practice logicians disagree. Montaigne follows the early Greek philosophers such as Heraclitus and Plato, who talk of the fallibility of the senses. There is a telling passage in the 'Apology' in which he asks his readers to:

> Take a philosopher, put him in a cage made from thin wires set wide apart; hang him from one of the towers of Notre Dame de Paris. It is evident to his reason that he cannot fall; yet when he looks down from that height he is bound to be terrified and beside himself.

Is the act of reasoning itself distorted by the emotions? Montaigne asks. How can one find a standard by which to judge the accuracy of what is perceived? Then there is scientific knowledge. Montaigne notes the two conceptions of the solar system: the traditional Earth-centred view, or the one in which the sun is placed in the centre, as postulated by Copernicus in 1543. Not only are these incompatible, says Montaigne, but in 100 years' time they might both be superseded by new discoveries.

Montaigne was read by every literary figure of the seventeenth century. His *Essays* became part of a conventional education and his relativism permeated European thought through to the Enlightenment. In his influential *The History of Scepticism*, Richard Popkin sees Montaigne's analysis of scepticism in the 'Apology' as 'one of the crucial forces in the formation of modern thought'. Popkin argues that it highlights three crucial philosophical issues of the times: the theological, thrown up by the Reformation; the humanist, arising from the mass of ancient authors in conflict with each other; and the scientific. 'By extending the implicit sceptical tendencies of the Reformation crisis, the humanistic crisis, and the scientific crisis into a total *crise pyrrhonienne*, Montaigne's genial *Apology* became the *coup de grâce* to an entire intellectual world.'[7] In the next century Descartes would become obsessed with the problem left by Montaigne: how one could find a starting point for any form of certainty.

Montaigne is an excellent example of how a sensitive and original mind can use but also transcend classical sources. While nominally a Catholic, he stays well clear of the religious tensions of his age, even to the extent of being criticized for doing so. He does not stick rigidly to any single philosophy, although his favourites all come from the schools of the Hellenistic period (330 BC–AD 30). He takes us into new territory by using the example of other cultures as a riposte to the condescension and rigidity of European society.

* * *

Montaigne's sceptical approach might be said to have been further developed in one of the great plays of the late sixteenth century, Shakespeare's *Hamlet*, probably written in its earliest form in 1599 or 1600.

By then William Shakespeare (1564–1616) had emerged from his early career as an actor in the rival groups that jostled for attention in late Elizabethan England to become an accomplished playwright. His whereabouts between 1585 and 1592 are uncharted. These 'lost years' have always given rise to much scholarly speculation as to exactly how this brilliant and innovative mind evolved. He must have soaked himself in his sources, both classical and contemporary, perhaps even travelling abroad, and developing a fascination with the psychological impulses of his subjects. In his *How Classics Made Shakespeare*, the Shakespeare scholar Jonathan Bate finds the poet Ovid to be the most pervasive influence in Shakespeare's plays.[8] But he also discovers traces of Horace, Cicero, Tacitus and Seneca, about whom Shakespeare, like many of his contemporaries, was ambivalent. Shakespeare was extraordinary in the way that he was able to use a huge variety of sources – including classical drama and poetry, as well as historical chronicles, folk tales and legends – but, rather than being dominated by them, transformed them into something totally original.

Shakespeare's acting career had been rooted in the revenge tragedies influenced by the plays of Seneca, which had been known in English since the 1560s. Famous examples include Christopher Marlowe's *The Jew of Malta* (1589) and Thomas Kyd's *The Spanish Tragedy* (1580s). One of Shakespeare's earliest plays, *Titus Andronicus* (written between 1588 and 1593), is in this genre but his inventive mind was already encompassing comedy, as in *The Taming of the Shrew* of the early 1590s. His famous history plays – *Richard II*, the two parts of *Henry VI* and *Richard III* – followed later in the 1590s. This is a confident and wide-ranging mind. Yet by 1599 the Elizabethan skies were darkening. The earl of Essex had returned to England after a humiliating campaign that had failed to subdue Ireland. The queen was ailing and after forty years of comparative stability the succession was insecure. *Hamlet* mirrors the anxieties of the age.

Hamlet, which one scholar has described as 'the first great story in Europe of a man growing up',[9] has haunted theatregoers since its earliest performances. This can be seen from the language alone. There are around 600 words in the play that Shakespeare had never used before and two-thirds of these he would never use again. It is also, at 3,900 lines, his longest play, as if he were making some form of statement rather than providing something that could be acted within the usual time limits of Elizabethan theatre. A Cambridge academic, the late Eric Griffiths, suggested that this leaves us speculating what kind of play this actually is. He suggests that one reason for *Hamlet*'s popularity is that the audience is kept guessing as to how its complex characters will develop. Griffiths went on to note how the play 'abounds in hints of unrecounted lives'.[10] The playwright Tom Stoppard picked up on these 'hints' in his tragicomedy *Rosencrantz and Guildenstern are Dead*, first performed in 1966, where he explored the exploits of two of the minor characters in *Hamlet.*

The title page of an early edition of *Hamlet*, the so-called Second Quarto, published in 1604/5. *Hamlet* was one of Shakespeare's most popular plays during his lifetime and remains one of the most performed of all his works.

For his sources Shakespeare drew on a lost revenge play that was playing on the London stage in the 1580s and 1590s and which included the ghost scene that begins his *Hamlet.* The storyline goes back much further than this lost play, to a saga of a Danish revenge seeker, Amleth, first recorded in the twelfth century. Amleth's uncle kills his father and then marries his mother. Amleth then acts as if he is mad in order to plot to avenge his father, but in this saga he kills his uncle and survives to become king. The lost play that Shakespeare knew (*Ur-Hamlet*, as it is known to scholars) seems to have not only included the ghost but also to have developed the theme of the feigned madness of Hamlet

THE

The Tragicall Hiſtorie of HAMLET, *Prince of Denmarke.*

By William Shakeſpeare.

Newly imprinted and enlarged to almoſt as much againe as it was, according to the true and perfect Coppie.

AT LONDON,
Printed by I. R. for N. L. and are to be ſold at his ſhoppe vnder Saint Dunſtons Church in Fleetſtreet. 1604.

and his death. The famous 'play within the play', in Act 3, Scene 2, may also have originated here.

The story begins on the battlements of Elsinore, the castle in which Hamlet had been brought up by his father, also called Hamlet, and his mother Gertrude. The older Hamlet, now dead, was a traditional prince, so resolute in action that he has killed a rival, Fortinbras, king of Norway, in battle. He now appears as a ghost to tell of his murder by his own brother, Claudius, who has made himself king. His son, pushed aside by his uncle's usurpation of the Danish crown, is very different from his father. Deprived of his entitlement to the kingdom, he has to formulate some response in a court fraught with tension as his uncle, aided by his own mother, asserts his illegitimate authority. Yet after what must have been many years studying at university (Luther's Wittenberg!), he lacks resolution. The psychological uncertainty of the eponymous hero is what gives *Hamlet* its enduring fascination and human resonance. As one Shakespeare scholar notes: 'What manifests the writer's original genius from the beginning is his unique sense of what makes experience fully human, shareable yet monolithic in its elements.'[11]

Shakespeare may have believed that the storyline would have been well known to his audience and that he could therefore refocus the original play so as to concentrate on the psychological drama that highlights Hamlet's irresolution over the way to deal with the usurpation. This irresolution – captured in the striking image of the 'native hue of resolution... sicklied over with the pale cast of thought' – is presented in a series of famous soliloquies. 'To be or not to be, that is the question,' Hamlet asks, gripped by the dilemma of whether to remain alive in a flawed world or to kill himself and so encounter 'what dreams may come when we have shuffled off this mortal coil'. The afterlife resonates through the play. 'O... that the Everlasting had not fixed his canon 'gainst self-slaughter', laments Hamlet, as if that that were the only reason not to carry out his thoughts of suicide to fruition. When Hamlet has the opportunity to kill Claudius while the latter is at prayer, he holds back with the excuse that by doing so he would send Claudius in a purified state to heaven rather than to hell.

By hovering between action and inaction, Hamlet defies the image of the traditional 'Machiavellian' prince who has no compunction about dealing brutally with those who have offended him. As the Shakespeare scholar Margreta de Grazia has noted, the question 'Why does Hamlet delay?' is 'the Mona Lisa of literature', argued over for 200 years.[12] It was truly revolutionary of Shakespeare to present a prince who is so beset by doubts, and he does it in such a sophisticated way that anyone who plays the role of Hamlet is faced by a plethora of interpretive possibilities. While it might have been impossible for Hamlet, still in mourning for his father, not to have been deeply disturbed by his uncle's brutal coup, and to have felt disgust for his mother's apparently lustful feelings for Claudius (which is hinted at in one text of the play as the cause of the murder), he still has the resourcefulness to provide some 'method in his madness', as one famous line records. In the words of the Shakespeare scholar James Shapiro: 'The sense of inwardness is something that no dramatist had yet achieved'.[13]

Yet scholars have noted that the emphasis on the introspection and indecision of Hamlet that most moves an audience today only first appears in commentaries of the eighteenth century. Eric Griffiths stresses that Hamlet is only alone on the stage for 200 of the play's 3,900 lines and suggests that we are perhaps wrong to see him as an anguished outsider from the volatile community of the court. He is after all shrewd enough to manipulate the action, especially by arranging the staging of the 'play within the play', which depicts – before an audience that includes his uncle and Gertrude – a Player King murdering his royal rival by pouring poison in his ear. Was Hamlet driven by some deeper impulse? The scholar Barbara Everett puts forward the idea that the principal catalyst for Hamlet's actions is the loss of his entitlement to the throne of Denmark. Everett notes that Shakespeare lost his only son, the eleven-year-old Hamnet, in 1596, just at the same time as his own father had, after several setbacks, been awarded a coat of arms as a gentleman. The chance to pass on this new status to a son had been snatched from him and it may have been this trauma that caused him to create a character who had endured a similar loss (and who had a similar name).

Hamlet returns from England, having evaded a plot by his uncle to kill him, and is confronted by the gravediggers hollowing out a grave for a – to him as yet unknown – corpse. As the diggers uncover the bones and skulls of other burials, Hamlet is forced to come to terms with death; the names that come up are classical heroes, Alexander the Great and Julius Caesar, who have been great men in their times but reduced to earth once they have died. The discovery of the skull of Yorick, the court jester who had been like a father to the child Hamlet, brings the reality of death still closer.

Then the corpse arrives. It is Ophelia, the girl that Hamlet might have married but whom he tormented by his indecision. Her death by drowning leaves her as possibly unworthy of a Christian burial; the solution chosen here is to bury her in sacred ground but without the normal rituals of committal. When Ophelia's brother Laertes embraces her corpse in the grave, Hamlet jumps in to confront him, a rare moment of passion, as if his lack of resolution is finally overcome by the power of emotion. It is hard to disentangle Hamlet's motives – there is no hint that he may have felt himself responsible for Ophelia's death, but in the following climactic scene where he and most of the characters will die, he seems to have accepted the power of providence, the 'divinity that shapes our ends rough-hew them how we will'. This is a resolution of sorts but leaves open the dilemma that pervades the play, whether free will exists or not.

As meditations on death and its aftermath form such a large part of *Hamlet*, scholars have wondered whether the playwright had read the essays of Montaigne.[14] Hamlet and Montaigne both bring death into the foreground, not as something to be put aside but to keep constantly in mind as inevitable. There is also, as the Stoic philosopher Seneca had shown with his own suicide in Nero's Rome, the option of taking one's own life. Yet the first English edition of Montaigne's *Essays*, that of John Florio, a man of Anglo-Italian parentage, came out in 1603, three years later than the play. There is circumstantial evidence that Shakespeare would already have known Florio, as the go-to man for those who wanted to know more about Italy, by the time he was writing *Hamlet*. So it is possible that he absorbed some of Montaigne's ideas at this point. He certainly knew Florio later and passages from *The Tempest* (*c*.1610), for instance, reflect material directly taken from the Italian's translation of the *Essays*.[15]

Even if Shakespeare did not know directly of Montaigne, examples of the essay, a new literary genre, had started to appear for the first time in English before Florio's translation of Montaigne was published. Francis Bacon's *Essays* of 1597 are the earliest known and these definitely *do* draw on Montaigne. The advent of the essay, which was a means through which the writer could communicate his personal thoughts directly to the reader, may have exerted an influence on Shakespeare. While in *Hamlet* Shakespeare made an astonishing conceptual leap in creating the soliloquies, the essay may have been the catalyst for the confidence and sophistication with which he did so.

A great work of art often becomes so through ambiguity, and this may explain the enduring appeal of *Hamlet* across the centuries. Whether Shakespeare knew of Montaigne's essays or not, the two men would have concurred in seeing the world as one fraught with confusion, both in the turmoil of the times and in the challenges that the individual faced in seeking for certainty.

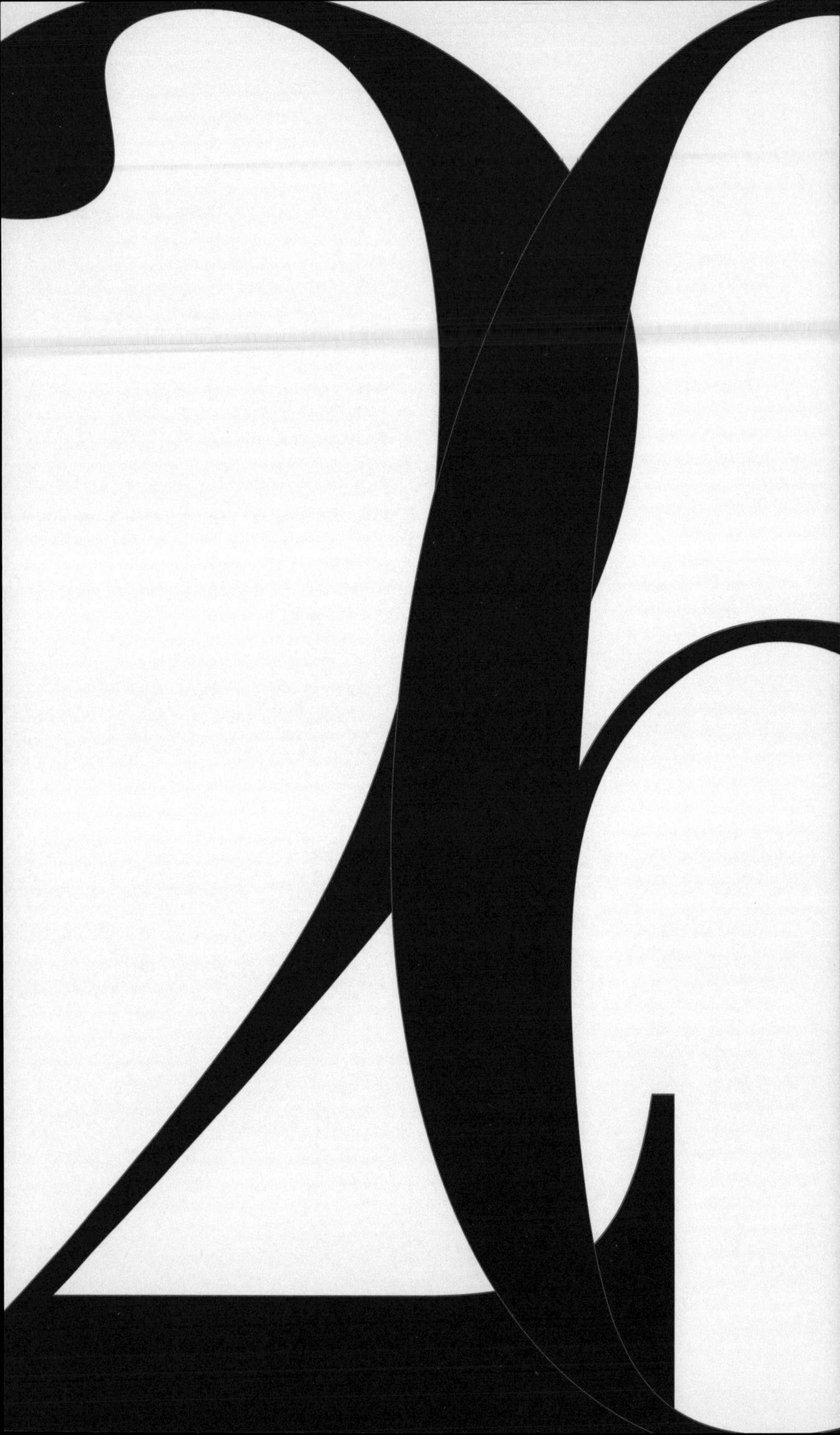

Absolutist France versus the Dutch Republic: A Study of Political Contrasts

God Almighty has a quarrel lately with all mankind, and given the reins to the ill spirit to compass the whole earth; for within these twelve years and strangest revolutions and horridest things have happened, not only in Europe but all the world over, that have befallen mankind, I dare boldly say, since Adam fell, in so short a revolution in time.

Welsh preacher James Howell, 1645[1]

The words of the seventeenth-century Welsh preacher James Howell, spoken in an era of bitter religious conflict, characterize accurately the events of the first half of a troubled European century. The reformers had highlighted the persistent anger of God at the sin of Adam. Now that Christendom was divided into doctrinally irreconcilable camps, each claiming a monopoly of understanding of the nature of man's relationship with God, it could well be believed that the wars that swept Europe in the first half of the seventeenth century were the direct result of divine displeasure. In seventeenth-century Europe religion played an ever-increasing role in politics, either through guiding the consciences of politicians and monarchs or through being meshed into the authority of the state. The papacy no longer possessed the power to enforce religious belief. Confessional orthodoxy, whether Catholic or Protestant, could only be imposed by political institutions, via the laws they passed. As the French lawyer Étienne Pasquier (1529–1615) put it:

> The general foundation [of a state] is principally dependent on the establishment of religion, because the fear and reverence of religion keeps all subjects within bounds more effectively than even the presence of the prince. Therefore the magistrate must above all other things prevent the mutation of religion or the existence of diverse religions in the same state.[2]

For most rulers, religion became a means of imposing authority on their realms.

This leaves a challenge for the historian in distinguishing between the roles played by nationalism and religion in the conflicts of the seventeenth century. Struggles between the European states depended as much on the manipulation of religious identity as on the effective use of military resources by determined and charismatic leaders. Traditionally, scholars used to point to the end of the Thirty Years War in 1648 as the moment when secular politics became more important than religious politics, but this view has gradually been eroded as the continuing prominence of religion – from the late seventeenth century and forward into the eighteenth – has been recognized. Louis XIV of France, the most powerful European monarch, gave notice that this would be the case when, in 1685, he revoked the Edict of Nantes, which had protected the rights of Huguenots, causing a flood of refugees across Protestant Europe. Any hope that the coming century would necessarily lead to more religiously tolerant governments receded.

Against such a backdrop, it is hard to discern signs of a Europe breaking free of confessional dogmatism and monarchical autocracy to embrace the tolerance of free speech and religion that the philosopher Voltaire would champion in the following century. Indeed, as we will see presently, Louis XIV was able to manipulate classical precedents to maintain an absolutist monarchy, the adulation of classical sources opening up the possibility of reviving models of Roman imperial authority. Royal absolutism did not flourish everywhere, however. In England, the 'Glorious Revolution' of 1688, which brought to the throne the Dutch Stadtholder, William of Orange, and his wife Mary as joint monarchs, is usually seen as setting Great Britain – as it became after the union with Scotland in 1707 – on the road to full parliamentary democracy. Even here, however, despite England's earlier readmission of the Jews and legislation (in 1708) allowing for the naturalization of tens of thousands of French Protestant exiles, religious bigotry remained stubbornly alive and well: the Restoration religious settlement – while nothing like as punitive as Louis's Revocation of the Edict of Nantes – imposed constricting civil disabilities on both Roman Catholics and nonconformists.

It is impossible to give a coherent account of the horrific Thirty Years War (1618–48) within the limited space available here and I will not attempt to do so.[3] The war saw a shifting set of alliances that brought devastation to much of mainland Europe. The three states that emerged as important players after the Treaty of Westphalia had brought the conflicts to an end in 1648 were Catholic France, soon to be under the control of Louis XIV (born in 1638) after the regency of his mother ended in 1651, the Catholic Habsburg empire, which had expanded beyond Austria and Hungary northwards into Bohemia, and Lutheran Sweden, which was the leading power in the Baltic until defeated by the Russian tsar Peter the Great early in the following century. The Protestant Prussians had also begun their long rise to power that would eventually lead to the unification of Germany as an empire in 1871, but much of Germany, still split into small principalities, had been laid waste by the impact of war. The Calvinist Dutch Republic also finally brought its conflict with Catholic Spain to an end and was able to embark on a 'Golden Age' during which it prospered as a trading nation far beyond what its size might have predicted. The Spanish were already in a period of decline following their spectacular exploitation of South America in the sixteenth century but they retained a strong position in the Spanish Netherlands and in parts of Italy, including the former duchy of Milan and the south. Franche-Comté, inherited by the Spanish branch of the Habsburgs, helped provide a corridor between the north and south. England was entering the seventh year of a debilitating series of civil wars that would witness the execution of its monarch, Charles I, in 1649. For eleven years it was a republican Commonwealth, until Charles I's son, Charles II, was restored as monarch in 1660.

War between France and Spain continued beyond the Treaty of Westphalia. Spain was desperate for a settlement and had something to offer in the form of the infanta, Maria Theresa, daughter of the Spanish king, Philip IV. Cardinal Mazarin, chief minister to the young French king, had concerns about Louis's health and was intent on a speedy marriage and heirs. The ensuing Treaty of the Pyrenees of 1659 won the infanta for France but recognized the weakness of Spain and ensured an expansion of French territory to the south and into parts of the Spanish Netherlands, its most vulnerable border as far as France was concerned.

France was now the most powerful state in Europe, with a large population, relatively robust economy and an army to match. Success was consolidated by Louis. On starting his personal rule in 1661, at the age of twenty-two, following the death of Mazarin, this resolute young monarch brought a stability and dynamism to his kingdom after periods of civil war. He cut a formidable and decisive figure, with the charisma and guile that his rival European monarchs lacked. His controller-general of finances, Jean-Baptiste Colbert, fostered new commercial and industrial enterprises and the combination made France a redoubtable opponent, well placed to strengthen still further its international position. Throughout the 1660s the methodical Colbert expanded his roles to include virtually every area of the administration except the conduct of war.[4] Among his responsibilities, and one he took to with great gusto, was the supervision of the nation's cultural life.

Louis XIV of France drew heavily on classical precedents to promote his rule. In this allegorical painting by Joseph Werner, dating from the 1660s, he is represented as Apollo, the god of reason, driving the Chariot of the Sun.

It was, in effect, through the arts, literature and scholarship that Louis imposed himself, publicizing his every achievement to proclaim a unity of *roi* (king), *loi* (law) and *foi* (faith).* He had a brilliant array of talents to support him: Racine, Molière and Corneille in the theatre, Jean-Baptiste Lully and Marc-Antoine Charpentier in music, Le Brun in painting, Le Vau in architecture (whose works included the vast new palace at Versailles) and Le Nôtre in formal garden design,

* It was said that his chief, and probably most accomplished, mistress, Madame de Montespan, would, during their most intimate moments, address him simply as 'France'.

again at Versailles. The ancient world acted as a powerful inspiration. The playwrights in particular provided new interpretations of the tragedies of ancient Greece. Colbert instituted an impressive set of new *Académies* covering painting, sculpture, music and the other arts. One of these, the *Académie de France à Rome*, had the important role of strengthening the cultural links between France and the classical city.* The *Académie des Sciences* mirrored the Royal Society set up in England in 1660 (p. 684–5). The *Académie des Inscriptions* sorted out epigrams and suitable mythological scenes for the portrayal of the king. Members of an *Académie* were expected to provide active support for the king, who further guaranteed their loyalty by granting them pensions.

In short, this was a monarchy centred on the personality and ambitions of Louis, *le Roi-Soleil* ('the Sun King'), as he became known after he adopted the sun as his symbol. It had been drummed into him as a boy that 'royalty is almost all action' and he played the part to the full, holding council meetings almost every day of the week throughout his reign.[5] While his rule was certainly absolutist, in that his ministers were always subservient to him and he retained the power to effect his foreign and domestic policy with an enormous, if expensive, army to back him, Louis was also pragmatic. He was no Napoleon or Frederick the Great. (Summing up Louis's strengthening of his northern frontiers to the Rhine, his most recent biographer, Philip Mansel, notes that Louis 'understood geography better than Napoleon, who believed that France extended to the Elbe and the Tiber'.)[6] As the brilliant court preacher Jacques-Bénigne Bossuet (1627–1704) continually reminded the king, he might have been divinely appointed to rule France but he still had to respect the teachings of the church. Under Louis, expansion was directed towards strengthening France's borders rather than conquest of territory for its own sake. Stress was placed on diplomatic relationships through which France would patronize its neighbours and flaunt its supremacy over them.

Louis XIV was an adept propagandist. Here he shows off his intellectual interests by visiting the *Académie des Sciences*, 1671.

In retrospect Spain can be seen to be in serious decline, even if this was not apparent at the time. Louis might have married into Spanish royalty, but Spain was still regarded as France's major enemy. The Austrian Habsburgs, the other power that had gained from the peace of 1648, were too busy absorbing new territory in central Europe

* It is still to be found in the imposing Villa Medici at the top of the Spanish Steps in the city.

and fighting off the Turks* to be a threat to France. So the isolation of Spain was the primary focus of Louis's foreign policy. This meant creating diplomatic relations with the English under their restored monarch Charles II and maintaining the so-called League of the Rhine, an alliance of fifty German states with France under the terms of which the Germans promised not to allow foreign powers, the Habsburgs or Swedes, to pass through their territories. The Spanish were now isolated in north-western Europe in their remaining possessions in the southern Netherlands and Franche-Comté. The new king, Charles II, the half-brother of Maria Theresa, succeeded in 1665 when he was only three but he was already seriously disabled and would never be able to rule for himself. Spain was therefore left even more vulnerable. A further humiliation came when Portugal (and its African and Latin American empire), which had been annexed by Philip II of Spain in 1581, became independent with France's support in 1668.

Louis successfully 'fabricated' an image for himself that relied heavily on classical models.[7] In June 1662, at a flamboyant celebration of the birth of his son, the dauphin, the previous year, Louis appeared dressed as a Roman emperor. His reign shows once again how powerfully the Roman inheritance could be manipulated in the service of politics, although here, in contrast to republican Florence, it was one-man rule that was to be celebrated. Augustus, the title given to Julius Caesar's great-nephew Octavian by a grateful senate in 27 BC after he had brought the civil wars of the Roman republic to an end, provided one of the models. Augustus had defeated his rivals – brutally, in fact – but then presented himself as the man who had brought peace and glory to the state. He was particularly successful in linking his name to the cult of Rome in temples throughout the empire and he also initiated the triumphal arch as a symbol of victory.† While Augustus behaved as if the Roman senate still held responsibility for the running of affairs, he skilfully built up his authority by respecting traditional Roman religious cults, by using poets such as Virgil to praise the empire and by launching a campaign in which his deeds, the *Res Gestae* ('the matters accomplished'), were promulgated through the empire together with imposing statues of himself as *princeps civitatis* ('first citizen').

The exploits of Augustus were well known to the classicists of the seventeenth century. There were obvious differences between the first

* The Ottomans twice laid siege to Vienna itself in the sixteenth and seventeenth centuries, in 1528 and 1683.

† The earliest example of a triumphal arch is at Aosta in north-eastern Italy and dates to 25 BC.

Roman emperor and his Bourbon imitator. Louis was the legitimate king of France and did not have to fight his way to power as Octavian had done. His absolutism was there for the taking; it did not have to be slowly consolidated over a long reign and he used his power to crush any pretensions the *parlements* – these were essentially law courts, albeit with a strong sense of their political importance – may have had. Yet Louis could, like Augustus, exploit the desire for peace after the civil wars that had divided France, act as a patron of buildings, art and literature, and publicize his victories through triumphal arches and statues. He could present himself as a pious upholder of traditional religion, in this case Catholicism, and a restorer of the ancient laws of France in the same way that Augustus claimed that he was respecting the values of republican Rome.

It was Colbert who crafted the presentation of Louis when he took the reins of power in 1661. The court painter Charles Le Brun composed a majestic ceiling painting for the new palace at Versailles with the theme: 'The king takes over the conduct of his dominions and gives himself up entirely to business.' Louis holds a rudder to show he is now in charge of the ship of state. A personification of Discord is subdued by another representing France while other personifications, Minerva (the Roman Athena), as a symbol of wisdom, Victory and Fame, cluster around a monarch who is crowned by the Graces. In accompanying medals, the king is shown as having restored order and made himself accessible to his people and so echoing what had been the expected virtues of a Roman emperor.

In 1665 the opportunity arose to show the king off as a conquering hero, an essential element of the public image of any successful seventeenth-century monarch. On the death of Philip IV of Spain in that year Louis decided, through his wife, the half-sister of the new king, to press a claim to further territory in the Spanish Netherlands.‡ The ensuing war had a moderately successful outcome for France: at the Peace of Aix-la-Chapelle of 1668, Louis was able to strengthen his border with the acquisition of the city of Lille. The peace was celebrated by an extravagant outburst of adulation in which Louis was now celebrated as the successor to an even greater conqueror than Augustus, the Macedonian Alexander the Great. Paintings by Le Brun, together with ballets and plays, pressed home the aggrandizing comparison with the great conquerors of antiquity, its propagandist message further reinforced with Roman iconography. One of the first triumphal arches

‡ His case was helped by the fact that the Spanish had never paid her dowry.

Les VICTOIRES Remporté par les VENITIENS
La prise de la Ville de Napoli de Romanie
La prise du Château d'Argos et l'Armée des Turcs taillé en pieces.
La Reduction de la Ville de Napoli de Malvasie, par le General Cornaro.
Conquestes dans la Dalmatie.
Dans l'Epire.
L'AUDIENCE donné aux Ambassadeurs Extraordinaires du ROY de S
ALMANACH POVR L'ANNEE M DC LXXXVII

to be built in Europe since the time of the Romans was erected in Paris.* Among a number of expansions made to the palace at Versailles was a grand new staircase, the Stair of the Ambassadors, commissioned as worthy of the monarch 'when he returns from his glorious conquests'.

Yet, as so often, one war led to another. Louis's intrusions had aroused the anger of the Dutch Republic, which had recruited England and Sweden as allies in a Triple Alliance that forced him to make peace. In 1672 Louis bought off the English with promises of sharing the Dutch commercial empire and attacked the Dutch in retaliation for their opposition to him, though it was also said that he wished to show off his virility to the now-favoured Madame de Montespan. At first the war was enormously successful; city after city was taken and the Dutch were in disarray. It was only the flooding of the lowlands and popular outrage over Louis's vindictive terms of surrender that saved them from utter defeat. The atrocities committed by French troops on the civilian population created an image of the cruelty of Louis that diminished his reputation as prints of the conflict spread through Europe.[8] Yet French court propagandists now redoubled the adulation of their monarch. The high point came when Louis and his troops reached the Rhine, traditionally the boundary of the Roman empire, and crossed it without needing to build a bridge, as Julius Caesar had done. Paintings depict Louis on horseback in front of the river, while his troops swim across en masse.[9] Some show a river god, cowering before the king; others bring in Hercules, always a symbol of strength, and Minerva, to represent his wisdom. A new element enters the propaganda; the monarch who surpasses the ancients. One bust of Louis carried the inscription *Augusto augustior* ('more august than Augustus'). The court propagandists proclaimed that his acts were 'never equalled in the past and impossible to repeat in the future'. Colbert shrewdly urged Louis to construct more 'public monuments which will carry the glory and grandeur of Your Majesty further than those of ancient Rome did their builders'.[10] Among the triumphal arches erected in Paris, that at the Porte Saint-Martin contained a relief of Louis receiving homage from his defeated foes just as earlier Roman emperors such as Trajan had portrayed themselves.† As well as portraying the crossing of the Rhine,

Louis XIV gives an audience to the Ambassadors Extraordinary of the King of Siam, in an engraving dated 1687. By now the reach of the European powers extended to the Far East.

* It was not the first. A triumphal arch celebrating Emperor Charles V, dating to 1548, still stands at the northern entrance to the city of Lecce in southern Italy.

† Trajan's column in Rome depicts scenes from Trajan's conquest of Dacia (modern Romania) in the early first century AD.

the arch at Porte Saint-Denis was festooned with images of Roman armour and trophies over the inscription *Ludovico Magno* (cf. *Carolus Magnus*, Charlemagne). Some 1,200 years after the fall of the empire, the influence of Rome remained strong.

Despite such encomia, under William III, a resolute and resourceful new Stadtholder,* the Dutch situation gradually improved after the disasters of 1672, and Louis's armies began to withdraw. In the Peace of Nijmegen of 1678 the French restored commercial concessions as well as territory to the Dutch, while themselves making gains in the Spanish Netherlands.† Despite these concessions, William remained obsessed with taking revenge on France, an attitude that underpinned his long-term strategy to isolate it.‡ Spain was the main loser, bullied into surrendering Franche-Comté and so giving France a more secure north-eastern border. In the light of these modest gains, the propagandists now had to make do with stressing Louis's moderation. In fact, the discrepancy between the images of Louis as conquering hero and the expensive reality of his debilitating wars was to become more glaring after the 1680s.[11] After the deaths of Colbert, mastermind of the propaganda campaign, and the painter Le Brun (in 1683 and 1690 respectively), new modes of presentation were devised for the Sun King – one of the most successful of which was to display him on horseback. Among classical models, the second-century AD statue of the emperor Marcus Aurelius, which Michelangelo had repositioned on the Campidoglio in Rome in 1538, was a rare surviving equestrian statue of a pre-Christian emperor. In a 'statue campaign' of 1685–7, statues portraying Louis XIV astride his horse were distributed around the provinces. The most colossal was that created by the court sculptor, François Girardon, for the Place Louis-le-Grand in Paris.§ Inaugurated with great ceremony in 1699, it echoed the statue of Marcus Aurelius by showing the monarch in Roman dress.¶

While his image was being disseminated across the provinces, Louis was embarking on the vast building programme for which he is most famous, the palace at Versailles. There was no doubting, as the shrewd

---

* The Stadtholder was the presiding magistrate in a Dutch province; William had been appointed Stadtholder of all seven provinces in 1672 (see p. 596).

† Marc-Antoine Charpentier wrote a Te Deum to celebrate the 'victory', the prelude of which lives on, implausibly, as the theme music of the Eurovision Song Contest.

‡ Later, Louis would attempt to restore relations with William by offering him one of his illegitimate daughters in marriage. A withering reply came back: 'In my family we marry the daughters of great kings, not their bastards.'

§ Now the Place Vendôme.

¶ It was destroyed during the French Revolution and now exists only in the form of a maquette.

Colbert recognized, that this project was for the personal glory of Louis. Yet it was also a deliberate attempt to assert his authority against the troublesome aristocracy whose squabbles had caused the Frondes,** the civil wars that took place early in his reign between 1648 and 1653. Paris, the largest city in Europe, was 'a cauldron of combustible institutions, at once the support and the rival of the monarchy'.[12] In the 1640s, the powerful *parlement* of Paris had raised some of the same complaints as the English parliament, in particular over arbitrary imprisonment and taxation. Despite the frictions that led to rebellion in the Frondes, there was never the same deep breakdown in relations between monarch and parliament as took place across the English Channel ('They were separated, not divorced', as Mansel puts it).[13] A system of royal patronage that was dependent on nobles asserting their status through attendance on the king at Versailles had the advantage for the monarch of weakening the link between the aristocracy, Paris and the provinces. At court Louis knew how to manipulate his majesty, either by dazzling his courtiers through the flamboyance of his bejewelled robes or by granting favoured individuals absurd privileges such as the honour of carrying the candle lighting his way to the royal bedchamber. ('As the king boasted in his memoirs, one of the most visible effects of his power was to give "an infinite value" to something which in itself was nothing.'[14])

The result was often the impoverishment of those who wished to compete for favours. Versailles, in short, was a key component of Louis's absolutism: aristocratic status was preserved here, but only on the king's terms. This was no Escorial, the gloomy monastery north of Madrid that Philip II of Spain had made his royal residence a century before. While Versailles possessed a chapel, it was subordinate to the royal apartments. The state rooms were named after pagan deities: Mars, Venus, Diana, Mercury, Jupiter and Saturn, possibly echoing the similar rooms in the Palazzo Pitti in Florence.[15] The countries defeated by Louis were displayed in the *Salon de la Guerre*, reached via the ostentatious Stair of the Ambassadors. The fabulous Hall of Mirrors, deliberately created to be the grandest room in Europe, looked out onto gardens where nature had been tamed by the landscape architect André Le Nôtre. On the façade of the palace facing Paris were eighty-four marble busts of Roman emperors backed by the French royal crowns and fleurs-de-lys. 'You will see there [at the palace] ancient and modern Rome', exclaimed one observer.[16] While the workforce at the palace itself numbered 36,000 at its peak, a further 30,000 were employed

** The name comes from a French word for a type of sling used to throw stones.

to build a canal to provide supplies for the *bassins* and fountains that stretched to the horizon. Even their endeavours resulted in no more than a few hours of water displays at a time.[17] Attitudes to the daily life of the court varied. The diaries of the duc de Saint-Simon, whose fascinating if inaccurate descriptions of court life still intrigue, described it as 'the saddest most unrewarding place in the world'.[18] He was one of a number of writers who ridiculed the court favourites, whose absurd posturings and endless jostling for precedence was played out against a background of profligacy, card playing, masques and sexual intrigue. Despite Saint-Simon's jaded observation, it seems unlikely that anyone at Versailles, whether waspish observer or enthusiastic participant in the revels, could have been bored.

However much Louis depended on the classical past, the inspiration for his religious policy could only come from Christian models – and a seventeenth-century French king was spoiled for precedents from which to choose. The Merovingian Clovis had been the first of the rulers of France to embrace Catholicism (AD 496). At his coronation in 1654 at the age of fifteen, Louis had been anointed with oil said to have been delivered directly by the Holy Ghost for Clovis's baptism. Charlemagne was another obvious model, as was Louis IX (1214–70), who had been canonized for playing an active role in the Seventh and Eighth Crusades. All three former kings figured prominently in the propaganda used to consolidate Louis XIV as the upholder of traditional Catholicism. In the chapel of the Invalides, a vast building to house invalided or aged soldiers, completed in 1679 on the left bank of the Seine in Paris, frescos of Clovis, Charlemagne and St Louis were placed alongside those of Louis.

The most far-reaching of Louis's moves to assert his Catholicism was the Revocation of the Edict of Nantes (in the Edict of Fontainebleau of 1685).[19] Most French Protestants, known as Huguenots, followed the Reformed Church of Jean Calvin. The Edict of Nantes (promulgated by Henry IV in 1598) had guaranteed some freedoms of worship for them, but from the start of his reign Louis had fostered discrimination, closing down Reformed churches when he could and harassing their congregations. He claimed in 1685 that most Huguenots had converted to Catholicism and that the edict was no longer needed. In fact, there were probably some 2 million Huguenots still active, some 10 per cent of the French population. The revocation was ruthless in its banning of services, schools and rites of baptism. Those who refused to accept the Catholic 'Last Sacrament' of Extreme Unction could be dragged off to the galleys if they recovered. Even though the new edict banned emigration, an estimated 250,000 Huguenots went into exile, to England, the Dutch Republic, Sweden and Prussia and some overseas to the Americas. A highly skilled community, they took their talents with them to enrich the economies of their new homes, damaging the French economy and further damning the image of France – and of Catholicism more widely – among Europe's Protestants. The clergy, notably the Jesuits, praised Louis for his destruction of heresy. He was applauded by Bossuet, the formidable bishop of Meaux, as 'a new Theodosius', a reference to the first Roman emperor to have persecuted pagans (r.379–95). Despite such approbation, the revocation was an impetuous move, and one that hardly enhanced Louis's reputation for benevolence. The renewed persecution of Protestants in France that followed the edict acted as a spur to philosophers such as John Locke and Pierre Bayle to elaborate principles of religious toleration. The revocation ushered in a downturn both of Louis's reputation and of his political and diplomatic fortunes. The wars he prosecuted after 1688 – the year he crossed the Rhine for a second time in pursuit of territorial claims against the Holy Roman Empire – were met by determined alliances from both Catholic and Protestant Europe. From the beginning of this 'Nine Years War' until the end of his reign in 1715, the former bright radiance of the Sun King was greatly diminished.

* * *

Earlier in his reign, religion had also played a significant part in Louis's war against the Dutch between 1672 and 1678. While Louis presented the war as a punishment on the United Provinces for their opposition to his invasion of the neighbouring Spanish Netherlands, there was little doubt that ideological differences were central to the conflict. Here was a republic of merchants (who after 1660 were outperforming those of France) and Calvinists who represented everything the Catholic absolutist Louis most abhorred. The Republic of the Seven United Netherlands,* with its population of 2 million souls, appeared to be small fry compared to France's 20 million inhabitants, but they had distinguished themselves during a seventeenth-century Golden Age, when their commercial enterprise,

overleaf In 1651 the States General of the United Provinces met in The Hague to discuss constitutional reform following the death of the Stadtholder William II. Bartholomeus van Bassen's splendid painting shows the Hall of Knights of the Binnenhof decorated for the occasion with flags representing the Dutch states and their struggles against the Spanish.

* This was the country's official name (in Dutch, *Republiek der Zeven Verenigde Nederlanden*) from 1581 to 1795.

RVÆ CRESCVNT

sophisticated urban lifestyles and reputation as the most tolerant society in Europe gained them many admirers. Some observers highlighted the air of good order and cleanliness in their cities, others the efficiency of their hospitals and orphanages, others again the Dutch achievements in art, philosophy and science. As one English ambassador, Sir William Temple, who had brokered the Triple Alliance against France, enthused in his *Observations* of 1673, the republic 'created a general liberty and ease, not only in point of conscience, but all others that serve to the commodiousness and quiet of life, every man following his own way, minding his own business, and little enquiring into other men's'.[20]

How had this small but vibrant 'Dutch Republic' emerged, 'infinitely transcending all the ancient republics of Greece', as William Aglionby, a Fellow of the Royal Society, put it?[21] Just as ancient Athens had been stimulated by its successful defence against the Persian invasions and medieval Florence by the defeat of its rivals, so Dutch resistance to Spanish rule, starting in earnest in 1572, embedded a powerful sense of national identity. Yet this was a federal republic. There were seven provinces, of which Holland, with its capital Amsterdam, was by far the most cohesive and powerful in the late sixteenth century. Each province had an assembly, the States. These would meet together in a States General that gradually absorbed more powers – over foreign policy, decisions of peace and war, the regulation of shipping, church affairs, a national budget and the promotion of colonial expansion – as the republic evolved. Outside these powers, the provinces controlled their own lives. Under Article 13 of the founding treaty, the provinces chose their own religion. Each province had a leading official, the Stadtholder, who held command of the armies and oversaw the administration of justice. He was responsible for resolving disputes in the States. The original leader of the Dutch revolt against Spain had been William of Orange (William the Silent) and his prestige ensured that with time members of the Orange-Nassau noble dynasty accumulated a number of the provincial Stadtholder posts,* so becoming unofficial leaders of the nation and traditionally living in appropriate style.

As with Florence in an earlier century, certain ideological myths gave backbone to Dutch patriotism. The humanists looked back to the Batavians, mythologized as a hardy, frugal people who had stood up to the Romans but later fought alongside them as free allies. The Batavians were credited with being innately tolerant and nurturing a love of debate. These virtues, it was claimed, had been preserved through the centuries to inspire their descendants in their own fight against another

* It was possible to hold several Stadtholder posts at the same time.

expansionist enemy. This mythology co-existed with the influence of the theology of Calvinism, institutionalized in the Dutch Reformed Church. Up to 50 per cent of the Dutch population, including the vast majority of the elite, were Calvinists. They saw themselves and their nation as God's chosen people fighting against Catholic tyranny. Naturally, this belief was reinforced by their experience of fighting against both Spain and France, the leading Catholic states of Europe. Las Casas's denunciation of the atrocities of the Spanish (see p. 507) was soon translated into Dutch. The first known European national anthem, the 'Wilhelmus von Nassouwe', linked William the Silent to David in another manipulation of that Old Testament king as a symbol of resistance to tyranny. The migrations of Protestants from the Spanish-ruled southern Netherlands were compared to the Israelite Exodus from Egypt. This combination of noble past and Christian present was neatly expressed in a prayer that ended in a history of the nation, the *Nederlantsche Gedenck-Clank* ('Netherlands Anthem of Commemoration'). 'O Lord… you have wrought all manner of wondrous things and despite the covetousness of our enemy, have made the golden liberty and olden laws of the Netherlands renowned throughout the world: proof of the covenant made with your believers…'[22]

This republican government was underpinned by commercial success. Its roots lay in the 1590s when there was a massive influx of migrants from the southern Netherlands, perhaps as many as 150,000, following the outbreak of war with Spain. The cities of the United Provinces grew fast and, as a result of the Reformation, a wealth of disused monastery buildings available to house new enterprises. Expansion was underpinned by the reclamation of land, some 200,000 acres between 1590 and 1640. It could be said that the fight against the sea was as important as the fight against the Spaniards in establishing a national identity. When a dyke burst, a drummer would call out the community, men and women alike, to rebuild the breach. The reclaimed land was fertile and could feed the growing population. Large imports of grain allowed Dutch farmers to specialize in other more lucrative crops, such as hops and flax. The turmoil in Germany during the Thirty Years War led to desperate demands for food that the Dutch could supply. Yet the migrations from the south would not have been so beneficial to the republic if there had not been an enormous expansion in overseas activity. The most significant shift was from the traditional Dutch trade, notably in the Baltic, of bulk goods, grain, timber, salt and fish, to the so-called 'rich trades' – fine cloths, silks, copper, processed sugar and tobacco – based on the East Indies, Spanish

America and eastern Mediterranean routes, which brought wealth back into the republic. By 1670 the Dutch merchant fleet was larger than that of France, England, Spain and Portugal combined.[23] The Dutch East India Company, founded in 1602, spread its tentacles throughout the world from southern Europe, the eastern Mediterranean, New York (originally New Amsterdam) to southern America and notably to the Far East where the spice trade, prised ruthlessly from the Portuguese, brought in profits twice that of the outlay. Dutch shipbuilding undercut its rivals and Amsterdam became the world's most successful money market, notable above all else for providing insurance. The ensuing affluence in its turn supported luxury specialist trades, diamonds, fine furniture and ceramics (Delftware), tapestries and wood marquetry. There were fluctuations, trade slumps and interruptions caused by war, but this was a prosperous state supported by a mass of skilled artisans. It was not until the first half of the eighteenth century that Dutch commercial dominance was challenged by Britain and France.

This immense wealth fed back into a society where prestige rested with the merchant classes rather than with the landed nobility. Intermarriage between the two classes was easily accepted. So this became a predominantly bourgeois society where the well-run home was a microcosm of a well-run state. No one pretends that Dutch women were given equal status in public life, but they played dominant roles in controlling households, as the artists of the age have shown well. Free of the extravagance of the Counter-Reformation, Dutch art focused on secular scenes, portraits (Rembrandt, with his extraordinary psychological insight, was, of course, the star figure

BIBLIOTHECÆ LUGDUNO-BATAVÆ CUM PULPITIS ET ARCIS VERA IXNOGRAPHIA

The library of the University of Leiden in 1610. Jan van 't Woudt's drawing reveals the order and seriousness of the Dutch Republic, not least as a place of learning.

here), landscapes or the quiet domestic interiors that Johannes Vermeer and Pieter de Hooch (both active in Delft) have made so famous. Science and philosophy also flourished within a tolerant and innovative society that provided a haven for dissidents. One of Rembrandt's most famous paintings, *The Anatomy Lesson* (1632), marries the arts and science with its psychological insights into the minds of the participants.

There is no more vivid way of showing the differing natures of France and the Dutch Republic than to compare their most costly building projects of the seventeenth century. While Louis was flaunting his absolutism at Versailles, the town of Amsterdam, the richest in the Dutch economy, was constructing a majestic town hall, which became the largest administrative building of its time. The brainchild of the architect Jacob van Campen (1596–1657), who had absorbed a restrained Palladian classicism from early studies in Italy, it was unprecedented in its impact as a symbol of republicanism. Begun in the year of peace, 1648, and inaugurated with great fanfare in 1655, it had its own 'Hall of Mirrors', a vast central hall whose barrel-vaulted ceiling was over twice the height of its French competitor. The decoration in painting and sculpture that followed its inauguration placed more emphasis on the noble Batavians than on the Bible. The town hall was also designed to reflect and glorify the republic's global dominance in seafaring. From the windows beneath its cupola, viewers could observe merchant vessels and their lucrative cargos returning to harbour. Appropriated by Louis Bonaparte when he was made king of Holland by his brother Napoleon in 1806, it has remained a royal palace. The palaces of the Orange family were modest in comparison.

Outsiders agreed that the Dutch Republic was more accepting of religious diversity than other states. But this may have been due less to a public commitment to an ideal than to a necessary tolerance of communities within a state that owed its prosperity to a population of diverse confessional allegiances and which prided itself as open to the world.[24] The Calvinists had provided the backbone of the fight for independence and through the Dutch Reformed Church had attempted to impose Calvinist uniformity on a population that not only contained a significant Catholic minority but also Lutherans, other Protestant sects and Jews. Yet there were important splits within the church, notably over the commitment to predestination, which Calvin had made a core principle of his theology (see p. 531). A breakaway group, the Remonstrants, founded by Jacob Arminius (1560–1609), revived the traditional objection that, if the salvation of an individual was already predetermined, the possibility of free will

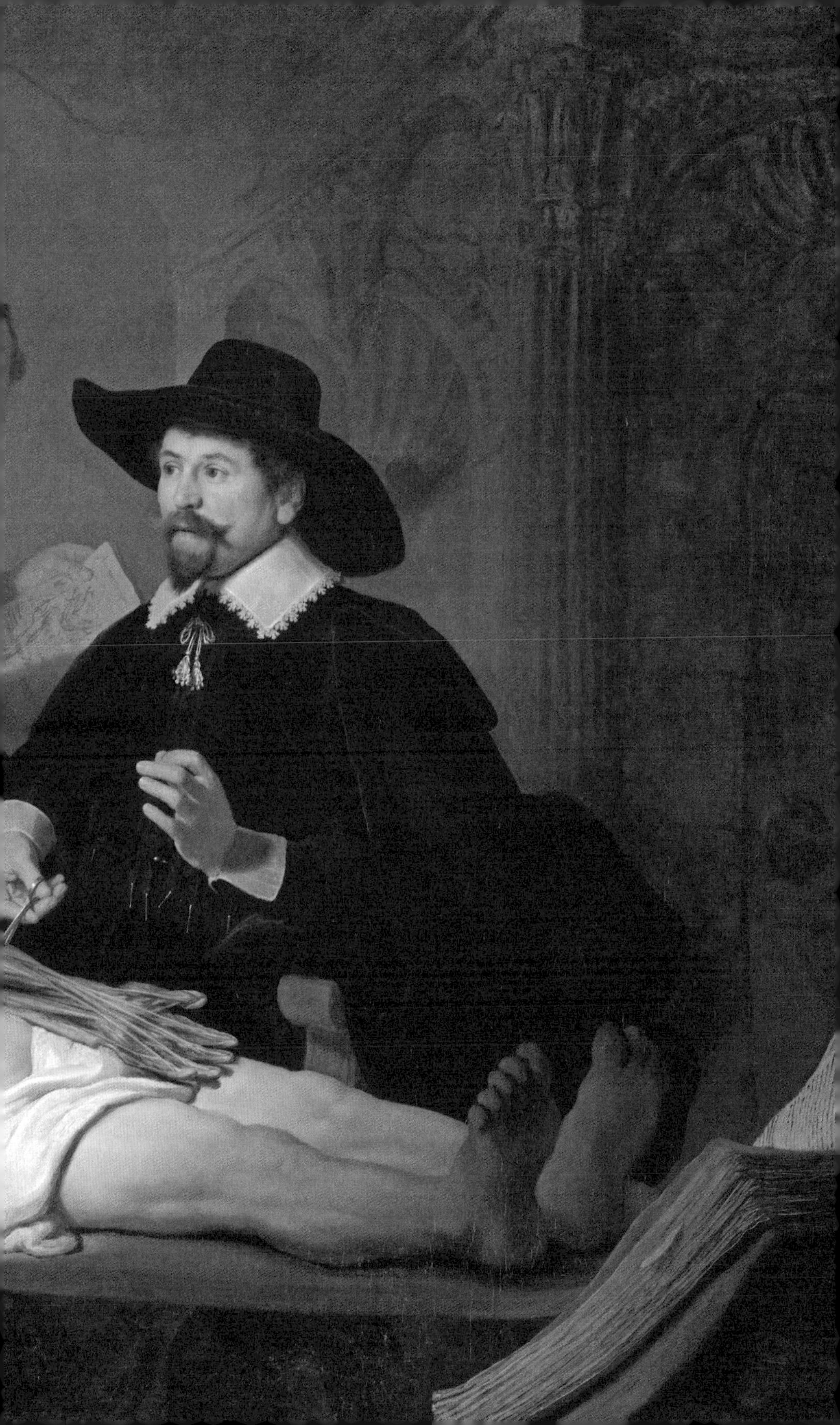

was denied. Arminius identified biblical texts that supported him. Yet the early Remonstrants were not in favour of religious toleration as such. Their aim was for greater toleration *within* Calvinism so that their congregations could be contained within the wider church. As long as the core tenets of Calvinism were accepted, they argued, there could be friendly debate over remaining differences. The Remonstrants also demanded that religious matters be judged by magistrates rather than the clergy, since they alone could preserve the civic peace that was the ultimate end of a stable society.

The most radical, and theologically the most profound, supporter of Arminius was Simon Episcopius (1583–1643). After a period as a professor of theology at the university of Leiden, Episcopius had been exiled for his beliefs in 1619 and only returned to the republic in 1626 when hostility to Arminianism had abated.* Following his return Episcopius became the prominent exponent of Arminianism, notably in his *Free Worship of God* (1627) and his *Apology for the Remonstrant's Confession* of 1629. He argued that as the scriptures could be interpreted in a variety of ways, theological debate should be respected and was in fact healthy. Persecution of alternative views undermined the stability and wellbeing of the nation by creating disaffected minorities. The only religious opinion that was beyond toleration was outright blasphemy. Having experienced intolerance himself, Episcopius's abiding concern was that religious belief should be free of coercion by either state or church. He was even prepared to tolerate Catholics as long as they made an oath of allegiance to the state.

previous pages Rembrandt's *The Anatomy Lesson of Dr Nicholaes Tulp* (1632). The painting is remarkable for the accuracy of detail in its depiction of muscles and tendons, and for the intense level of interest of the assembled observers.

Episcopius's hopes for toleration of religious pluralism and dissent proved to be too optimistic. The Reformed Church – still benefiting from official support and state finance – remained immoveable. Even so, Episcopius and his followers had their impact. In the words of Perez Zagorin, 'through their criticisms and subsequent influence, they helped to weaken the theological ascendancy of Calvinism and to promote the development of religious and, indirectly, also of intellectual freedom in parts of Protestant Europe'.[25] John Locke had the works of Episcopius on his shelves.

Ultimately, a pragmatic approach to the toleration of religious minorities was to prevail. Officially, Catholicism continued to be

* The distinguished jurist Hugo Grotius was among those imprisoned and forced into exile at this time (see also p. 632).

banned, but in practice areas with large Catholic populations were left alone and their congregations grew. By the 1630s persecution of the Remonstrants had subsided, even if they remained forbidden to build their own churches. Lutherans and other Protestant sects also survived, as did a small community of Jews. During the French invasion of 1672 these Dutch Jews were noted for their patriotism, which helped to deflect traditional anti-Semitism. Yet the dominance of the Reformed Church remained. It was free to denounce its rivals while the latter were not free to respond. No other denomination thrived, other than – in a limited way – the Catholics. As a de facto toleration spread, the Remonstrants lost their impetus (although a small Remonstrant community still exists today). In the conclusion to his magisterial survey of Dutch religion during this period, Jonathan Israel talks of an 'ambivalent semi-tolerance... a partial tolerance seething with tension', something that outsiders did not always recognize in their idealization of the Republic.[26] It was enough, however, for radical thinkers such as René Descartes, John Locke, Pierre Bayle and, as an internal exile, Baruch Spinoza to shelter there. (Philosophical approaches to religious toleration will be covered in Chapter 31.)

In 1685 the idea that the Stadtholder William III would within three years be ruling another kingdom, one that was much larger than his own, seemed remote. The death of the English king, Charles II, in that year was followed by the succession to the throne of Charles's brother as James II. William was married to James's eldest daughter Mary and if he did not have a son she would succeed him. However, it was unlikely that Mary's husband, a Dutch Calvinist, would be welcomed in England, especially after decades of hostility between the two nations over their commercial ambitions. An invasion in Mary's cause seemed strategically impossible; after all, there had been no successful invasion of England from the continent since 1066, and there did not seem any faction in England ready to welcome William. Within the provinces and above all in Holland, which gloried in its republican traditions, William would never have been able to find support for what appeared to be a personal and costly war against a powerful neighbour to win its throne. Yet by 1688 circumstances were to lead to him launching a brilliantly organized expedition across the North Sea that was to result in a so-called 'Glorious Revolution', a watershed in the constitutional history of England.

7

Britain's Revolutionary Century

All men have stood for freedom… and those of the richer sort of you that see it are ashamed and afraid to own it, because it comes clothed in a clownish garment… Freedom is the man who will turn the world upside down, therefore no wonder he hath enemies… True freedom lies in the community in spirit and community in the earthly treasury, and this is Christ, the true manchild spread abroad in the creation, restoring all things to himself.

Gerrard Winstanley, *A Watch-Word to the City of London*, 1649[1]

The term 'Glorious Revolution' to describe the events of 1688–9, when James II was replaced as king of England by Mary II and her husband William of Orange as joint monarchs, was much favoured by those 'Whig' historians – men such as Thomas Babington Macaulay (1800–59) – who saw Britain's history as following an inevitable progress towards a constitutional monarchy, enlightenment, liberalism and parliamentary democracy. But the word 'revolution' has also been applied – especially by Marxist historians – to the events of the period of the English Civil War and Commonwealth earlier in the same century (1642–60). Before analysing the consequences of what happened in 1688, it is worth exploring the outburst of radical thought that took place as a result of breakdown of relations between King Charles I and Parliament after his accession in 1625.[2]

There has been vigorous debate among historians as to the causes of the English Civil War, but central was the king's claim to rule by divine right and through his prerogative powers, and Parliament's assertion of its own rights. The king's inflexibility and narrowness of political vision exacerbated the tensions between them. As the antagonism between king and Parliament grew in the 1620s, the parliamentarians revived ancient traditions of liberties.[3] While at this stage, and certainly as late as 1648, the vast majority wished to preserve the monarchy, they drew on sources as varied as precedents from classical Rome, the republican examples of northern Italy, notably Venice* and Florence, and homegrown proclamations going as far back as Magna Carta and the authoritative works of the thirteenth-century lawyer Henry de Bracton.† In his *De legibus et consuetudinibus Angliae* (*On the Laws and Customs of England*) completed in the 1250s (see p. 156), Bracton, following Justinian's *Digest*, had emphasized the contrast between the free man and the slave. Bracton broadened the Roman definition of slave to include all those bound to the will of others, through, for instance, feudal dues.[4] These were the sources that invigorated the parliamentary debate when, in the Five Knights Case of 1627, Charles claimed the right to impose billeted troops and forced loans on his subjects and imprison them when they refused to comply. Parliament's Petition of Rights of 1628, an important milestone in English constitutional history,

* Gasparo Contarini's famous defence of the republic of Venice (see Chapter 6, p. 135) had appeared in English in 1599.

† It was not until the eighteenth century that William Blackstone's *Commentaries on the Laws of England* (1766) supplanted Bracton.

reasserted the ancient liberties of 'free men', notably the right not to be imprisoned without good reason, not to be forced into paying loans to the crown or have troops billeted on them. The king dismissed the petition, claiming that his prerogative overruled the claimed liberties and attempted to rule without Parliament.‡ He was forced to relent and recall Parliament in 1640 when he ran out of money. The battle lines were by now drawn. As one parliamentarian, Lord Digby, concluded, his intransigence meant that 'our Liberties, the very spirit and essence of our weal, which should differ us from slaves, and speak to us as Englishmen, are torn away'.[5] The parliamentary pamphleteer Henry Parker offered a more sophisticated analysis in his *Observations* of 1642, where he argued that the sovereign power rested not with the king but with both houses of Parliament. In a later tract, *Ius Populi* (*The Rights of the People*, 1644), Parker contended that 'Parliament is nothing else, but the very people itself artificially congregated or reduced by an orderly election and representation', into a body 'proportionable' to the 'rude bulk of the universality'.[6]

These incompatible theories of government, stubbornly asserted by both sides, made civil war inevitable. By 1645 the king's forces had been defeated by the New Model Army raised by the parliamentarians and skilfully marshalled by generals such as Oliver Cromwell. Charles escaped in disguise from his last 'capital', Oxford, in April 1646, and refused to enter into negotiations, leaving his opponents in a political vacuum. It is in contexts such as these that new and often radical ideas are born.

The Parliament that had been elected in 1640 was still sitting (and would continue in a truncated form until 1653, so earning itself the name 'the Long Parliament'), but its members had been bypassed by events. Most would have been happy with a constitutional compromise that retained many of the powers of the sovereign and the essentials of the Elizabethan religious settlement but confirmed specified liberties for the monarch's subjects. Others, more determined and more vocal, wished to eliminate bishops and establish a church on the Presbyterian Scottish model. Opponents of episcopacy also claimed that bishops, by virtue of their appointment by the monarch as head of the church, were subservient to him and thus inimical to the rights of 'the People'. Yet here there was a further split between those who wanted one uniform church administered, and its doctrine enforced, by the state

‡ Traditionally, Whig historians called this period the 'Eleven Years' Tyranny'. In his study *The Personal Rule of Charles I*, the historian Kevin Sharpe introduced the more neutral term 'personal rule'.

and those who wished each congregation to run its own affairs. The latter naturally stood for liberty of conscience.

At this moment the New Model Army, proud of its achievements but frustrated by the failure to find a settlement (as well as angry with delays in its pay), came close to mutiny when attempts by Parliament to discipline the soldiers and impress them for a campaign in Ireland backfired. The regiments began to elect 'agitators' who demanded respect for their victories and a reform of Parliament, the dissolution of the Long Parliament and new elections on a broader franchise. It was an important moment in the history of political thought, comparable to the revolt of the Ciompi in Florence in 1378, when a group normally considered to be outside any traditional arena of politics was forced by circumstances to formulate radical proposals.

The most vociferous debates of the 'agitators', who had formed themselves in a 'Council of the Army', took place in October 1647 at Putney, then a village on the southern banks of the Thames. Today a visit to the built-up site makes it hard to envisage the drama of the times but, happily, written reports of the speeches were made (and rediscovered in the nineteenth century). The soldiers were joined by a body of radicals – dubbed 'Levellers' by their opponents – who brought their own manifesto, the *Agreement of the People*, which called for the abolition of the monarchy and a Parliament with supreme authority elected by manhood suffrage based on property ownership which would respect religious freedom (no one was yet prepared to extend the suffrage to women or toleration to Catholics). Like the Ciompi, the Levellers drew support from tradesmen and craftsmen. Their most influential leader, the volatile John Lilburne, was an ardent pamphleteer, who had already served several prison terms for his activities.*

The trial of the Earl of Strafford, in an engraving by Wenceslaus Hollar. The parliament of 1641 assembled to impeach the king's minister for 'high misdemeanours' during his time as Lord Deputy of Ireland already had a sophisticated grasp of its threatened liberties. Strafford would eventually be attainted and executed in May 1641.

The debates that followed were intense but uncoordinated. A division opened between those who, in the famous statement of Colonel Thomas Rainsborough, believed that 'the poorest he in England hath a life to live as the greatest he', and most of the officers, who supported a property qualification for the electorate. As Rainsborough put it, even the poorest should have the right to give their consent to the government that ruled them

* 'Leveller' was originally a term of abuse and Lilburne himself resented being called one. It has since lost its opprobrium and is used more positively of those fighting for radical change.

and they should not be bound by its laws if they had not done so. His was an eloquent plea for an effective social contract between people and government that, in various forms, was already being advocated by the philosophers (see Chapter 28, pp. 634–47).

The rising power of the army frightened those in Parliament who were still hoping for a moderate settlement and those in the country who longed for a return to stability after the four years of high taxation and disruption that had followed from civil war. Charles clumsily tried to exploit the confusion, hoping to gain Scottish support for his survival in return for a promise to establish Presbyterianism as the national church (and abolish bishops). However, a Scottish invasion in support of Charles was brutally repulsed by the army under its commander, the increasingly influential Oliver Cromwell. A series of royalist uprisings across England was quelled in the summer of 1648. The army now saw itself as destined by its victories to be the real power in the land, the true representatives of the people, and for the first time its radicals began building up a revised *Agreement of the People* which would ask for the trial of the king, the dissolution of a Parliament

regarded as corrupt and self-seeking, and manhood suffrage (this time for all adult males except servants, beggars and Royalists) through which to elect a new one. They forced a purge of the more moderate members of Parliament but it was the continued intransigence of the king that led inexorably to his trial by the republican minority now at the centre of power. Accepting that he would never regain his status in any political settlement, Charles began to see himself as a martyr. Yet he had no hope of sympathy. According to the charge laid against him, Charles had 'traitorously and maliciously levied war against the present Parliament, and the people therein represented'. The indictment declared him 'guilty of all the treasons, murders, rapines, burnings, spoils, desolations, damages and mischiefs to this nation, acted and committed in the said wars'. Inevitably found guilty, the king was executed outside his own palace in Whitehall on 30 January 1649.

The execution was greeted with shock throughout Britain and Europe. Republicanism could draw on honourable precedents in Greece and Rome that provided examples of 'tyrants' who had been executed, but the aura of monarchy was still immensely powerful across the continent. There were reprisals against English shipping and a mass of pamphlets exploited the shock of the event. Ten days after Charles's execution, *Eikon Basilikei* (*Icon* or *Portrait of the King*), a propagandist Royalist text purporting to be written by Charles himself and portraying him as a martyr, was published in England. *Eikon Basilikei* would run through many increasingly elaborate editions. Its frontispiece showed Charles communicating directly with heaven. Biblical support for monarchy came largely from the Old Testament Books of Kings or, in the New Testament, from the apostle Paul's call to respect authority in his *Letter to the Romans*. Yet biblical precedent could be found for just about every political system, and it was used just as powerfully by radicals, who released their own flood of pamphlets during this period. A common device of such tracts was to evoke an image of human society in its earliest, simplest forms: Adam and Eve after their expulsion from Eden or Noah and his family after the Flood. How had these primitive societies turned into hierarchies divided between a rich few and an impoverished majority if not through the seizure of goods and the exploitation of the poor? In his *Declaration from the Poor Oppressed People of England* (1649), the radical Gerrard Winstanley (1609–76) claimed that it was only through the sword and murders that a few seized the common land of the people and passed it down to their children. Such a state would continue 'till your bloody and thieving power be rooted out of the land'.[7]

The lively debates took place within a maelstrom of religious enthusiasm. As Winstanley's *Watch-Word*, quoted at the beginning of this chapter, suggests, Christ could also be transformed into a radical. Radicalism was always present in the gospels, of course, but it had been lost in the authoritarian and conservative Christianities of the previous centuries. Now it could be recovered. Millenarian groups such as the Fifth Monarchists saw the execution of the king as a harbinger of the imminent coming of Christ. Even those who did not go so far welcomed the chance to create a perfect society based on the teachings of the gospels. All the old debates, over predestination and free will, the nature of baptism, the interpretation of the scriptures, resurfaced. This was the moment when new Christian movements, which have endured to this day, among them the Baptists and Quakers, became established in England. Inevitably, each of these churches wanted to be tolerated by the state. But was toleration to be extended to this plethora of rival sects? Was any interpretation of the gospels to be permitted? This was to be a major issue within British politics for the next 200 years, over which period there would be a gradual acceptance of alternatives to the state religion of Anglicanism. The vigorous debates that took place in England in the 1640s, and the emergence of new, 'nonconformist' Christian denominations – dissenting from the established Church of England – can be seen as part of a broadening of the western mind.

The radical polemics of the period extended beyond religion to include attacks on the privileges of lawyers and the universities. A myth was born, according to which Anglo-Saxon freedoms had been suppressed by a 'Norman yoke' after 1066. Winstanley, the myth's most prominent advocate, argued for a return to communal living, even though his followers, the aptly named Diggers, failed miserably when they set up an agricultural commune. The republican poet John Milton (1608–74) offered his own take on the turmoil: 'More just it is that a less number compel a greater to retain their liberty, than a greater number compel a less to be their slaves.'[8] His statement remains a worthy subject for debate.

Milton's is the voice that resonates most from this era of English history. Following seven, largely disappointing, years at Cambridge, his mastery of the classical languages and immersion in biblical texts led him to become preoccupied with the nature of tyrannical rule. The fate of Galileo, whom he met while travelling in Italy, especially haunted him. In the 1630s he began to find his intellectual niche. By the time of the execution of Charles I in 1649, he had become a doughty and accomplished writer of poetry and prose in the cause of liberty. He

ΜΟΝΩ
ΤΩ ΘΕΩ
ΔΟΞΑ
I will never faile thee, nor forsake thee
Bee still and know that I am GOD
Ararat
Per flatus per fluctus
Remora
Scylla
Caribdis
Floreant Protector
et Parliamentum Angliæ &c
Pro Deo lege et grege
Constantia Fortitudo
Lex Corona Columna
Salus Populi Suprema Lex
Magna Charta
Honos pro Bonis
Salvalit Insula Legibus Munita
Ex Charta Charitas
Fame
Tollo Perlego Protego
Anglia
Scotia
Hibernia
Vis unita fortior
Mons Sion
Error
Babilon
Uror dum alij non uruntur
The Embleme of ENGLANDS Distractions As also of her attained, and further expected Freedome, & Happines Per H. M. 1655.
Anglia ne mentas, sistas innota Triumphans
Pacis Oliva tibi vere Olivarus erit
They shall beat their Speares into Pruneing hooks
And their Swords into Plowshears

argued passionately for freedom of speech in his *Areopagitica* of 1644, and also championed the right of couples to divorce.

Milton's support for the king's execution earned him a place in the civil service of the Protectorate from 1649, as Secretary for Foreign Tongues. Among his next works was a devastating critique of *Eikon Basilikei* and its supposed author. But tragedy was soon to strike: Milton was completely blind by 1652, and endured the deaths of his first wife and infant son in that same year. His enemies interpreted these afflictions as the just response of an enraged deity, but Milton replied that adversity simply drove his mind inwards, enabling him to concentrate more intensely. In 1660, to his despair, came the Restoration of Charles II. Milton was lucky to avoid the retribution of a restored monarchy; his works were publicly burnt and he was briefly imprisoned.

Milton had rejected the hierarchy of the Anglican church along with monarchy. He was, however, deeply committed to asserting the providence of God. Whatever the evil in the world, the goodness of God, as represented on earth by the love of Christ, would shine through, but individuals must find their own way through the scriptures. He was an impassioned apostle of religious tolerance. The question for Milton as a poet was how to craft his beliefs in suitably dramatic form. He chose to revive the classical precedent of the epic: God was to be the hero, and Adam and Eve the victims of Satan whose terrifying capacity to corrupt would be overcome in a celestial struggle with God. *Paradise Lost* (1667), which had – quite possibly – been taking shape in his mind for decades, erupted from deep in his unconscious with enormous power, 11,500 lines by the second edition of 1674. A major role is given to Satan, expelled from heaven but determined to exact revenge on God. So it is the cajoling Satan who tempts Adam and Eve and arranges the 'Fall of Man'. In some ways he is the hero of the epic but it is providence, in the shape of the eventual redemption of humankind by Christ, that will win through.

The Embleme of England's Distractions, 1658, portrays Oliver Cromwell as triumphant Lord Protector, having defeated his enemies and upheld the laws and freedoms of England by divine providence.

Milton's intellect and erudition were unmatched in his own time; he embodies an English radicalism – intellectual, religious and political – that has proved enduring even when the impact of the Biblical creation has become diminished. He deserves his place here.

Yet the immediate issue was whether a stable republican government could emerge in a country that remained profoundly conservative and longed for peace. The eleven years that followed the execution of

Charles in 1649 saw a succession of failed attempts to find a settlement that would balance republicanism with an efficient executive. The Rump Parliament (as it became known as its membership dwindled) continued to sit and sustained the republic, but it was challenged on every side, with continued royalist opposition from Ireland and Scotland – which proclaimed Charles's son as the lawful monarch, Charles II – economic crises and a war with the Dutch Republic over trade. While paying lip service to the need for radical reform, most members of Parliament were hardly revolutionaries and vacillated over creating an effective new constitution. The ever-vociferous John Lilburne was on hand to denounce the Rump's failure to act – and thus, in his eyes, to perpetuate tyranny – in his pamphlet *England's New Chains Discovered* (1649). Lilburne was tried for high treason and briefly imprisoned, at which his wife Elizabeth Lilburne organized a petition demanding not only her husband's release but also equal rights for women, which attracted 10,000 signatures.[9]

On 20 April 1653, in a dramatic and decisive move, Oliver Cromwell entered the chamber, backed by musketeers, denounced the members and dismissed them. As commander of the army, still with its political ambitions intact, the years of drift had made his role as a go-between impossible and ultimately he sided with the army.

As with Julius Caesar at the time of the disintegration of the Roman republic, and as would be the case with Napoleon following the collapse of the French Directory in 1799, political breakdown had given Cromwell (1599–1658) the opportunity to rise to power through military victory. Where he differed from these two was in the time he took to do so. He was well into his forties before his command of the New Model Army brought him renown and he was already fifty when a brutal campaign in Ireland in 1649, still remembered today for its atrocities, and the ensuing destruction of Scottish armies, at Dunbar in September 1650 and then at Worcester a year later, gave him an undefined but unassailable position in the emerging republic.

While Cromwell's letters and speeches survive, it has proved challenging for historians to assess his motives as he struggled to find a political role. He was not afraid to show off his victories. After the battle of Worcester, he paraded 4,000 of his Scottish prisoners through the streets of London. It is telling that one of the few works of art from the king's collection that was not sold off was Andrea Mantegna's magnificent tableaux of the *Triumph of Caesar* (painted 1484–92), housed in Hampton Court Palace where they remain to this day. John Milton referred to these successes as 'Rome in the making'. Yet

Cromwell also insisted on being painted 'warts and all', a vivid contrast to the glorified portrayals of Charles I by court artists such as the Dutchman Anthony Van Dyck. He could be described, to quote his own words, as 'an honest man that knows what he fights for and loves what he knows'. His 'honesty' was deeply rooted in his religious beliefs, which committed him to creating some form of 'Godly' society. His opponents claimed that this was merely a cover for his lust for power, and with the return of the monarchy in 1660 his reputation would be damaged beyond repair. A more balanced view would be that Cromwell *did* have a vision for society where greed and the abuses of politicians were eliminated but that his efforts to achieve it were frustrated by his being forced to share power with an elected Parliament that was more focused on stability than reform.

After an abortive attempt to create a new Parliament of nominated members between July and December 1653 (the so-called Barebones Parliament), a new republican constitution was drafted by John Lambert, a leading member of Cromwell's advisory Council of State. The Instrument of Government provided for a single-chamber assembly (the House of Lords had been abolished by the Rump Parliament), elected every three years and sitting for at least five months every year. Election was largely by county but restricted to men holding £200 worth of property. Parliament had the right to elect a Lord Protector, who in the event could be none other than Cromwell, supported by an advisory council which had the power to issue ordinances when Parliament was not sitting. The most interesting provision was for a moderate toleration of religious differences. While Catholicism was banned and so too the return of bishops (and thus traditional high church Anglicanism), other sects were tolerated so long as they did not threaten the peace. (One achievement of the Protectorate was to welcome back Jews. They had been expelled in the Middle Ages but from 1656 they were allowed to settle in England and practise their religion.) Within this framework, local gentry continued to be permitted to nominate clergy, although a Commission of Triers and Ejectors was empowered to dismiss ministers considered to be unsuitable. Anglicans were able to continue to worship unmolested within their country houses. As time went on, however, attitudes to radical Christian sects hardened and laws forbidding 'blasphemy', a flexible term, which, in effect, allowed savage treatment of recalcitrant dissenters, reappeared. The year 1656 witnessed a national crackdown on Quakers, who were increasingly seen as a disruptive force for their refusal to pay tithes and rejection of conventional social behaviour.

It was the contradictions of the new regime that made it unworkable. The government largely avoided corruption and was administratively competent in matters such as the Poor Laws. Its foreign policy was successful in standing up to the Dutch, running an enlarged navy and encouraging trade. Yet there was never any way that there could be a compromise between country gentry electing Parliaments from a conservative franchise, the army that still clung to its privileged status as the bringer of victory, and Cromwell set on the reformation of the moral behaviour of the nation. Members of Parliament of whom the Protector disapproved were excluded when they arrived in London. A ham-fisted attempt to impose reformation at local level through the rule of ten major-generals was deeply resented. The restoration of an Upper Chamber and an offer to Cromwell to make him a hereditary king – which he refused – suggested a drift back to a quasi-monarchical constitution. Following Cromwell's death in September 1658, he was succeeded by his son Richard, who was to rule for less than a year. The Protectorate collapsed in May 1659, opening the way for Charles I's son, Charles II, to return to the throne in 1660. England has remained a monarchy to this day.

* * *

Historians have disagreed over the nature of the impact of these twenty years of turbulent politics. The Marxist Christopher Hill, one of the most sophisticated analysts of the intellectual life of the period in the 1960s, argued in his *The World Turned Upside Down* that this was a time of profound change, 'a period of glorious flux and intellectual excitement... when [between 1645 and 1653] there was a great overturning, questioning, revaluing, of everything in England'.[10] *The World Turned Upside Down* was an enormously influential book that resonated with readers of the early 1970s (although it has been criticized for seeing a unity among the radicals that may never have existed). Perez Zagorin, a historian of the popular revolts of this period, described the years 1640 to 1660 as 'the first great manifestation of the modern revolutionary temper'.[11] The contemporary writer John Rees champions the Levellers as 'pioneers of revolutionary political organisation... who bequeathed us a dramatic ideological heritage of democratic ideas'.[12] While Hill relied heavily on published sources (the mass of pamphlets) the Stanford professor David Como, in his *Radical Parliamentarians and the English Civil War*,[13] has explored grassroots opinion especially in the thriving streets of London where the fear of retaliation by Charles loomed large as early as 1642. Como posits a much more deep-rooted and early genesis of radical ideas.

In short it can be argued that, just as the French Revolution – which similarly ended in a restoration of a conservative monarchy, following the reign of Napoleon – utterly changed perceptions of political possibilities, so the shock of war, the execution of a monarch and the unleashing of a plethora of radical alternatives challenged conventional thinking. Yet, as Christopher Hill laments in the concluding chapter of *The World Turned Upside Down*, the return of the monarchy and the restoration of a traditional Anglican hierarchy in 1660 saw a stifling of the political and religious clamour of the previous years. (In fact, Hill dates their suppression as early as 1656.) There was certainly no religious tolerance with the return of the monarchy. The Corporation and Test Acts (1661 and 1673 respectively) required those seeking to join town corporations or the civil service or to hold public office to be practising members of the Anglican church, so excluding Catholics and dissenting Protestants, who were now known as nonconformists. Clergy had to accept ordination through a bishop and some 2,000 dissenting clergy were banned from the church in the so-called Great Ejection of 1662.

Despite constraints such as these, in the wake of the events of 1649–60 there was more popular involvement in public affairs. During the Interregnum, royalist gentry had often been excluded from their traditional roles and this had opened the way for activists from the towns to become involved in local government. They became mayors or aldermen, leaders of the militia or justices of the peace. Once involved they seem to have remained active after the Restoration. An act by the Rump Parliament (passed in November 1650) required all legal proceedings to be in English rather than Latin or French and there is some evidence, hard though it is to quantify, that the period saw an increase in public understanding of legal issues. The Justices of the Peace, a vital lynchpin for everyday justice, were recruited more widely. It was the novelist Tobias Smollett who wrote (albeit a century later) of a Mr Gobble, a low-born journeyman hosier who 'had picked up some law terms, by conversing with hackney writers and attorney's clerks of the lowest order',[14] enabling him to become a Justice. In the major cities coffee houses became new centres of debate. Coffee was cheap and classes could mix together – 'a boatman and a Lord smoke at the same table', as one French visitor observed. 'The emergence of the coffeehouse [from the 1650s], perhaps more than any other institution, both transformed and marked the transformation of English national culture.'[15] The world of the Renaissance, in which controversy was confined to an educated social elite communicating with each other in Latin, was passing. This was graphically shown in the Exclusion Crisis of 1679–81 when a new political grouping, the Whigs, organized popular support in an ultimately unsuccessful attempt to exclude Charles II's Catholic brother James from the throne. (Their opponents, the Tories, retaliated in support of the succession and these two loose groupings would remain the most prominent actors in British political life for the next 180 years.)

In an important study, *The Invention of Improvement: Information and Material Progress in Seventeenth-Century England*,[16] the historian Paul Slack argues that there was a commitment to and belief in a steady rate of 'improvement' during this period. He characterizes it as pragmatic, promoting skills that ranged across the economy, from working the land more effectively to engaging in industry and commerce. A key figure here was William Petty (1623–87), who initiated what he called 'political arithmetic', the application of statistics to the calculation of the wealth of the country with the implication that growth could be measured. While Giovanni Villani, in fourteenth-century Florence, had attempted to create an accurate portrayal of his society through tabulating an array of numbers, from the production of bolts of cloth to participation in education, Petty marks a step forward in that he integrated the possibility of material progress within his economic calculations. Wealth, Petty stressed, was not an end in itself but a means of enjoying the finer things of life and of satisfying intellectual curiosity. He provided a model through his own activities. The son of a cloth merchant, Petty was a founder member of the Royal Society, had held professorships of medicine and music and even served as a Member of Parliament. His confidence that society was improving is borne out by estimates that incomes rose by 50 per cent between 1650 and 1700.

William and Mary defeating tyranny, in a painting (1707–26) by James Thornhill that adorns the ceiling of the Painted Hall of the Royal Naval College, Greenwich. The crushed figure cowering below William is his arch-enemy, Louis XIV of France.

So how does the 'Glorious Revolution' of 1688 fit into this culture of 'improvement'? James II had succeeded his brother in February 1685, at the age of fifty-one, determined to create a more efficient centralized government on the model of his contemporary, Louis XIV. However, the emerging absolutism risked riding roughshod over a population that, as has been argued above, was now more politically aware. Central to James's purpose was the restoration of Catholicism. He believed that once legislative discrimination had been removed, the Catholic Church would revive naturally. This ambition led James to urge Parliament to

repeal the Test and Corporation Acts and support Catholic leaders in Ireland – a risky and unpopular strategy. Opposition from both the Anglican establishment and the nonconformist communities, whom he attempted to win over with promises of toleration and patronage, was profound. The Revocation of the Edict of Nantes in October 1685 and the subsequent arrival of many Huguenot refugees in England made it politically impossible. Attitudes hardened further when the birth of a male heir to the throne in June 1688, another James, meant that a Catholic monarchy might be perpetuated.

None of this made a revolution or even an abdication inevitable. James had a large standing army and there were deep-rooted fears of plunging the country back into civil war. The impetus now came from William of Orange who began to see the advantages of intervening directly in English politics. William had, of course, a link to England through his wife, whose right to succession had been lost by the birth of the baby James, but his predominant motive, based on the experience of the invasion of 1672, was fear of French expansion. He grasped the importance of breaking the ties James had with Louis XIV and bringing England into a coalition against his formidable enemy. It was especially important for William to neutralize the British navy which, were it to join to the French, would have isolated and outgunned the Dutch. The flood of Huguenot refugees arriving in the Netherlands after 1685 further shifted Dutch opinion against France and helped eliminate domestic opposition to William's projected adventure.

However, even after secret meetings that had promised William support from the English opposition, in practical terms the invasion seemed over-ambitious and fraught with risks in its planning and execution. William may in fact have intended no more than to force his father-in-law into accepting that he would have to compromise with Parliament. In public he would admit only to travelling to England to investigate civil and religious liberties. Yet what would happen if James resisted and so plunged the country into a civil war in which he could rally support against an intruder? In the event luck and good planning worked together. The French had been diverted by a campaign in the Palatine. Favourable winds kept the English fleet in port but swept the Dutch across the Channel, enabling William and his forces to land unopposed at Torbay in the south-west of England. 'Measured as an organizational achievement, the Dutch invasion of Britain in November 1688, marks the high point of the Republic's effectiveness as a European great power… it was arguably one of the most impressive feats of organization any early modern regime has ever achieved' is the assessment of Jonathan Israel in his magisterial *The Dutch Republic*.[17] Most important of all, James's army deserted, giving William free passage to enter London. William, reluctant to create another Stuart martyr-king, allowed James to escape to France, where he sought refuge with his ally Louis XIV.

With the throne now vacant, the only way of maintaining political stability was through William and Mary's accession. William insisted that he should be given full rights as a monarch to reign alongside his wife. In the event, Mary proved a quiet supporter of her husband, more interested in reshaping the royal palaces and supervising charitable activities than in politics. She died five years later, still only thirty-two. With no alternatives the different factions in English found reasons to explain their acquiescence: the Tories saying that there was a vacuum that had to be filled, and the Whigs claiming that a contract between crown and people had been broken by James's absolutist behaviour.

A similar ambiguity pervaded the Declaration, later Bill, of Rights that purported to set out the principles under which William and Mary would rule. Crucially, the declaration did not attempt to place new restrictions on royal power. It was 'not for making new laws but declaring old', and provided an opportunity to settle the many grievances that had arisen under the early Stuarts when Parliament had asserted its presumed rights. The declaration preserved the rights of the monarch to select his own ministers and to declare peace and war, allowing William to turn the foreign policy of Britain against France. He was to be given an agreed sum for his expenditure and he could not raise more without the consent of Parliament. No standing army could be maintained in peacetime without the consent of Parliament and the monarch could not dispense with laws as he or she willed. Yet his power to influence events in Parliament through patronage remained, even if William did not use it effectively during his reign. Other rights, such as free elections to Parliament, freedom of speech within Parliament, and an end to cruel and excessive punishment, were more vaguely drawn. Key clauses defined the succession, first to Anne, sister of Queen Mary, while no future monarch could be a Catholic or married to one. This implied parliamentary control of the right of succession and thus a constitutional monarchy. The declaration was read to William and Mary during the ceremony in which they accepted the offer of the crown, but they did not give it their formal assent. Once promulgated as a Bill of Rights in August 1689 it would come to be seen as one of the most important documents of a constitution that remains to this day largely unwritten.

Yet this was far from a 'Glorious Revolution'. A so-called Act of Toleration in the same year (1689) in effect confined full participation in public life to Anglicans with only a grudging acceptance of worship by nonconformists, who had to have their premises licensed and services open to inspection. Its aim was to offer a sop to the nonconformists in the hope of keeping them on side against Catholicism. In Ireland the Catholic leaders encouraged by James were brutally crushed in a conquest personally led by William and John Churchill, later duke of Marlborough, his most accomplished general. The decisive Battle of the Boyne (1690) resonates among Catholic and Protestant communities to this day. In Scotland the Jacobite cause (from *Jacobus*, the Latin form of James) remained strong and much of the Highlands proved ungovernable. It was only under William's successor, Anne, the daughter of James II and sister of Mary, that the Act of Union of 1707 created a single nation, Great Britain.

So how far was this a revolutionary settlement that marked a turning point in the history of Britain? This would be the view put forward by one of England's greatest historians, Thomas Babington Macaulay, in the nineteenth century, and it would become, for many, part of the traditional narrative of British history.[18] The 'Whig theory of history' saw history unfolding as a narrative of inevitable progress as the country had moved away from divine kingship to a more secular state where Parliament remained supreme. It was gradualism that was important to Macaulay, in contrast to the violent upheaval of the French Revolution, when an intransigent and incompetent monarch was overthrown in a political convulsion that culminated in a Reign of Terror. For Macaulay, 1688 was the crucial turning point of English history and he began his *History* in 1685 (and ended it with the death of William in 1702). Was he right to highlight this moment?

In his *1688, The First Modern Revolution*, Steve Pincus challenges the conventional view, held even by the Whigs, that this was essentially a conservative settlement in that it disturbed relatively little in English life. (Christopher Hill went so far as to describe it as 'a restoration to power of the traditional ruling class'.)[19] Pincus explores a much deeper level of popular discontent with what he calls the modernizing policies of James.[20] He claims that 1688 was primarily a reaction against James's determination to move decisively in creating a more absolutist regime on the model of Louis XIV. However, for Pincus such discontent had deeper roots, 'set in motion in the wide-ranging crisis of the 1620s',[21] with which this chapter began. Pincus thus extends the revolutionary period and sees a fundamental shift in the path taken by England in comparison to that taken on the continent. He calls 1688 the 'First Modern Revolution'.

Nothing can undermine the extraordinary nature of the political change that took place in 1688, the peaceful succession – albeit only so in England – of one unpopular monarch by a married couple, one of them a Dutch Calvinist, who were readily accepted by the gentry and nobility. Yet one can doubt that the 'Glorious Revolution' transformed English society as radically as Pincus claims. Popular participation in parliamentary politics can hardly be said to have increased. The electorate was confined to adult males with property (electoral rights varied from one borough to another), just 4.3 per cent of the population. There was to be no expansion of this until the Great Reform Act of 1832. Parliament was dominated by the aristocracy, with the peers who sat by hereditary right in the House of Lords controlling many of the seats of the House of Commons. As Pincus notes, there was virtually no increase in the percentage of merchants sitting as members of the Commons.[22] However, by the provisions of an act of 1694, elections were to be held every three years and Parliament had to meet annually. This led to a more energetic assembly as the Tories, those conservative royalists who had originally supported the right of James II to succeed his brother and who clung to the idea of a strong monarchy, confronted the Whigs, who championed the supremacy of Parliament and greater tolerance for nonconformists. While William attempted to balance his ministries, politics during his reign and that of his successor, Anne, remained volatile until the Whigs achieved an ascendancy following the accession of George I in 1714.

The revolution of 1688 was sustained by other factors. One reason for the shift of focus from monarchy to Parliament was the heavy demands of finance for wars with France, which required continuous parliamentary approval. The relatively untroubled trajectory of this change in political dynamic was greatly assisted by the growing wealth and industrial success of the country. Another crucial factor was the readiness of the monarchs, first Anne and then, with the failure of the Stuart dynasty, the Hanoverian Georges, to accept their circumscribed role. Here England was lucky. An intransigent monarch might have destroyed the fruits of the 'Glorious Revolution'. The exercise of a royal veto by Anne when she withheld royal assent from the Scottish Militia Bill in 1708 was the last ever by an English monarch. Essentially, this was a conservative settlement that provided a stable framework within which Parliament could grasp the initiative. While the 'revolution' of 1688 cannot be said to have been designed to set Great Britain on the path of parliamentary government, it provided the means by which an evolving commercial and industrial nation could achieve this. No other state in Europe took this path, and here Pincus's argument has validity. The Dutch Republic went into decline after 1700. The death of William III in 1702 saw a reaction against the traditional powers of the Stadtholder and a breakdown in order in many provinces as conservatives and republicans jostled for power. The War of the Spanish Succession was the last European war in which the Dutch Republic took part as a major power. Its commercial supremacy was eroded as its competitors caught up.[23]

Where Macaulay overstated his case was in assuming that this progress was inevitable as a direct result of 1688. The nineteenth century might be seen as an age of progress, but it brought also the horrors of urban poverty arising from industrialization, the injustices of laissez-faire liberal economics and the nightmare of the Irish famine. The Whig theory of history was roundly criticized by Herbert Butterfield in *The Whig Interpretation of History* (1931). In his 1992 biography of another Whig historian, G. M. Trevelyan (Macaulay's great-nephew), the historian David Cannadine assailed the concept: 'Whig history was, in short, an extremely biased view of the past: eager to hand out moral judgements, and distorted by teleology, anachronism and present-mindedness.'[24] Whig historians downplayed the subjugation of Ireland even though the Protestant Ascendancy that dominated the country from seventeenth to the early twentieth century was to leave an enduring legacy of resentment and prejudice. This should not overshadow the fact that the British Parliament was able to make significant improvements to British society in the nineteenth century, widen the electorate (though still denying the votes to women until 1918), and remove the restrictions on Catholics and nonconformists. Qualified approval of the *English* revolutions of the seventeenth century, for successfully challenging absolutism and allowing alternative ideologies to be expressed, seems justified. The Catholic Irish, subjected to the brutal reassertion of Protestant supremacy, would not have agreed.

Envisaging an Ideal Society in the Seventeenth Century

Men being, as has been said, by nature all free, equal, and independent, no one can be put out of this estate and subjected to the political power of another without his own consent, which is done by agreeing with other men, to join and unite into a community for their comfortable, safe, and peaceable living, one amongst another, in a secure enjoyment of their properties, and a greater security against any that are not of it. This any number of men may do, because it injures not the freedom of the rest; they are left, as they were, in the liberty of the state of Nature. When any number of men have so consented to make one community or government, they are thereby presently incorporated, and make one body politic, wherein the majority have a right to act and conclude the rest.

John Locke, *Second Treatise on Government* (1689)[1]

It would have been impossible for the dramatic political events covered in the previous chapters not to have had an impact on political thought. The seventeenth century was a time of intense debate over the nature of sovereignty, rights of participation in government and the underlying laws that might act as a template for an ideal society. New questions arose. At what point had one a right, even a duty, to resist a ruler? Was God the ultimate source of authority and did this mean unquestioned obedience was owed to his dictates (whatever they were considered to be)? Or could secular philosophy help define the rules of political conduct? Before the Reformation, there was arguably general agreement over the nature of the law required by a (Catholic) God, but would a Lutheran, Calvinist or Anglican God have different concerns? If you were a Catholic subject to a Protestant ruler, or vice versa, where did your obligations lie? It is not hard to see why philosophers explored many new perspectives, not only on political relationships within states – between rulers and ruled – but also, in a world of nations competing for commercial advantage, on those between different states.

One does not expect to find a monument to a seventeenth-century Oxford professor of law in a small town in the Italian Marche, but I spotted one when lunching with my family in the main square of San Ginesio some years ago. San Ginesio was the birthplace of the jurist Alberico Gentili (1552–1608), seen by many as one of the founders of international law.[2] Gentili had learned his law at Perugia and was deeply influenced by Roman law and the conservative interpretation of it by the celebrated fourteenth-century jurist Bartolus da Sassoferrato. He always preferred ancient sources because of 'that degree of prestige which we assert they have, and which age so easily adds to all things'.[3] He stressed Roman law's distinction as a tradition from canon law and strongly rejected the influence of religion over legal principles. Having abandoned his Catholic heritage, Gentili was harassed by the Inquisition and fled from Italy in 1579. After some wanderings he arrived at Oxford and impressed the university so much with his learning that he was appointed Regius Professor of Civil Law in 1587, a post he held until his death. In Oxford he was there at the same time as his fellow Italian Giordano Bruno. Whether because of his association with Bruno or because of his falling-out with the Catholic Church, all Gentili's works were placed on the papal Index of Prohibited Books in 1603.[4]

In 1584, after the unmasking of the Catholic Throckmorton Plot against Queen Elizabeth, Gentili was called on to advise the government on the treatment of the Spanish ambassador, who had been implicated in the conspiracy. Gentili argued that the ambassador should be expelled for his involvement, rather than being tried in the English courts as popular opinion demanded. This set an important precedent for the conventions of diplomacy. The body of an ambassador should be inviolable.

During his time in Oxford, Gentili would produce a number of influential works on international law. His ability to argue his own case, independently of other pressures, brought him increasing respect. Away from his Italian background, he absorbed new influences, especially from the French political theorist Jean Bodin (1530–96), who endorsed a more flexible and pragmatic use of Roman law than Bartolus had done. In his *Les six livres de la République* (*The Six Books of the Republic*, 1576), Bodin argued for the absolute sovereignty of each state and the need for any community to have a strong government in which the power of enforcing law is embedded. This fitted well with what Gentili saw around him, the emergence of nation states that were now competing with each other globally. He recognized that there had to be some basis for evolving the rules governing their relationships, but in a famous saying – *silete theologi in munere alieno* – ' Silence, theologian, in matters that do not concern you' – he insisted that theology must be kept out of it. Where Gentili and his followers differed from the theologians, such as Thomas Aquinas, was in assuming that natural law was not necessarily to be interpreted as having been founded by God. This was an important moment in the secularization of law and it distinguished Gentili from the Dominican Francisco de Vitoria (see p. 504), who had placed his arguments for the defence of rights within the theological perspective of Aquinas. In contrast, for Gentili, a legal system needed to be based, pragmatically, on the actual practice of civilized nations. Religion was a private matter between individuals and their God.

What was important for Gentili was to find a way in which traditional natural law, 'the set of principles that are true for all peoples at all times' and which regulate the desire to live in a peaceful and rational social order, could be incorporated into the law of nations. As we have seen, the concept of natural law goes back to ancient times, and to ideas of the Stoics, for example. In his *De re publica*, a dialogue on Roman politics, Cicero echoed Stoic thought when he wrote that 'true law is right reason in agreement with nature. It is valid for all nations and all times. Human legislation cannot repeal it. We know it by looking within ourselves.' Gentili relied heavily on the Law Code of Justinian, which had formed the basis of his education in Perugia and which he believed to contain the values of natural law. He put his case strongly:

> Are not the following principles from the books of Justinian applicable to sovereigns: to live honorably, not to wrong another, to give every man his due; to protect one's children; to defend oneself against injury; to recognize kinship with all people; and to maintain commercial relations, along with other similar and cognate matters which make up almost the whole of the books? These belong to the law of nations and to the laws of war.[5]

Gentili's approach was therefore to marry the sovereign rights of nations, of whatever religious persuasion, with the principles of Roman law as he saw them. While he accepted that there were evil rulers, bent on the destruction of others, he believed that, if taken as the foundation of ethical living, natural law would result in harmonious living not only within states but between states. He was an advocate of trading relationships as a means of helping maintain friendships. Gentili stressed the importance of diplomacy as a means of avoiding conflict: 'Those who avoid... arbitration and resort at once to force may understand that they are setting their faces against justice, humanity and good precedent.'[6]

War was justified at times, but there were ways in which it could be waged, in accordance with justice. Gentili elaborated his views in his *De jure belli libri tres* (*Three Books on the Law of War*, 1588–9), written in England during the turmoil caused by the Spanish Armada. The *De jure* is heavily dependent on examples from Roman republican and imperial politics. While critical of many aspects of Roman policy, Gentili exalted Roman law as providing the basis for civilized living. The first book deals with the right to go to war, the second with the actual conduct of war ('just as you ought to observe justice in beginning a war, so you should wage it and carry it on justly'), and the third on how to bring conflicts to an end and restore peace. Where Gentili was distinctive was in his argument that a pre-emptive attack could be justified if it served the legitimate cause of self-defence. At the time he naturally had Spanish aggression in mind, but he formulated his argument in general terms: 'that one man may not have supreme power and that all Europe may not submit to the domination of a single man'.[7] This was an important statement in that it introduced the concept of a balance of power.* Gentili tempered his approach by stressing the need for

---

* The term was first used in a European treaty in 1713, but the principle, so far as the European states were concerned, had been established by Gentili and others in the seventeenth century.

proportionality. There should be no attacks on women and children, lands should not be ravaged nor public buildings destroyed. The use of torture is forbidden. Prisoners of war should be treated humanely. The war should be conducted in such a way as not to leave resentments that would impede the restoration of peace. It seems fitting that a plaque recording the thanks of British fugitives sheltered by the people of the Marche during the Second World War is attached to Gentili's statue in San Ginesio.

Gentili's dismissal of religion as an important factor in politics meant that he transcended the bitter disputes of his age. (He is another case of an individual whose own experience of religious harassment fuelled a desire for toleration.) It followed that differences between states in religion were not in themselves a justification for war unless they posed a threat to another country. Gentili therefore renounced the view – held by many of his contemporaries – that a war against the Ottoman empire would be justified if its primary aim was to convert the Ottomans to Christianity. Yet, as Noel Malcolm has shown in his book *Useful Enemies*,[8] Gentili was ready to include the Ottoman empire – in the late sixteenth century seemingly still set on further expansion into Europe – as deserving of a pre-emptive strike. He never supported one form of government over another; what concerned him above all was the unjustified use of power by rulers.

I was pleased to find the monument to Gentili and am happy to argue here for his importance as a counterblast to Machiavellian politics. For Gentili it was justice and humanity that mattered, values that would be entirely absent from the Thirty Years War, which broke out just a decade after his death and would be fought with unremitting brutality. However, his work was soon overshadowed by the Dutchman Hugo Grotius (1583–1645), who drew heavily on Gentili for his own elaboration of international law. It was only in the nineteenth century that Gentili's works and importance was rediscovered.

Grotius amazed everyone by his brilliance from childhood: he was already studying at university at the age of eleven; he published his first book, on Martianus Capella's seven liberal arts, at sixteen; and was Pensioner (governor) of Rotterdam by the age of thirty.[9] Called upon to help solve commercial disputes with England, he became an advocate of the freedom of the seas, notably in his *Mare Liberum* ('The Freedom of the Seas') of 1609. While the right to private property could be defended by taking possession of a tract of land or an object, the sea could not be isolated in this way and so appeared to be the property of no one. The concept of the sea as belonging to no one was perhaps self-serving in that it was used to justify the Dutch breaking up the various trade monopolies of the Far East. The English challenged the idea, claiming that the seas around Britain, extending to 3 nautical miles, the distance that could be defended by a cannon based on shore, were part of their own empire. It was some time before treaties settled the principle of territorial waters within which a coastal state had jurisdiction, but Grotius's idea, that the seas should be open to all in both peace and war, was adopted as a key element of US President Woodrow Wilson's Fourteen Points in 1918.

Grotius was horrified by the religious conflicts of his day and believed that if only Christians could agree on certain fundamental tenets, then peace and toleration might be possible. He argued for the toleration of Jews in Holland, on the grounds that they had a mature sense of the divine. However, his views were considered too radical and in 1619, at a time of conflict between the civil and religious authorities over Arminianism (see p. 599) in the Dutch Republic, he was tried and imprisoned. He escaped from his cell, concealed in a trunk supposedly containing books, and made for Paris, where he could at last get down to work on his most important text, *De iure belli ac pacis* (*On the Law of War and Peace*), published in 1625. This massive work won him immediate fame and Sweden, now a major power, recruited him as its ambassador to France, a post he held for ten years. As the Thirty Years War raged around him, he never abandoned his passionate belief that Christians could be reconciled.

Philosophically, Grotius made an important contribution to the concept of natural law. While he was prepared to accept that natural law might show the will of God, he claimed (controversially for many of his contemporaries) that its precepts would hold true even if God did not exist. Natural law is so intrinsic to human existence that even God cannot change it. 'Just as even God cannot cause that two times two should not equal four, so he cannot cause that which is intrinsically evil be not evil.'*[10] As a result Grotius has been seen by some as marking a new beginning in moral philosophy, 'the secularization of virtue'.[11] He narrowed the precepts of natural law down to two: the right of self-preservation and the right to live socially with others. It was clear to Grotius that these two precepts need to be carefully balanced: the right of self-preservation must be limited so that it does not conflict with social relationships. In other words you could act 'in pursuit of innocent profit' but not in such a way as to injure others. But the individual had no obligation to help others to make their own

* There is an echo here of the Latin Averroists (see p. 199).

'innocent profit'. Grotius believed that his precepts were as important in regulating relationships between states as between individuals and it is as one of the fathers of international law that he is best remembered.

When defining the basis on which such a law could be justified, Grotius accepted that *ius gentium*, customary law, had validity. It would concern such things as the law of treaties and relationships between states through the exchange of ambassadors. These could be changed by agreement. Yet something more profound was needed and it was here that Grotius's interpretation of natural law became important. He translated the right to self-preservation into the right of a state to defend itself. Similarly, a state had the right to recover its property just as an individual might do. Grotius went further by developing the concept that a state had a right to uphold natural law and so punish those who offended against it. This was deeply problematic. Grotius acknowledged that the exercise of this right could easily descend into anarchy, so he reserved the right to punish to sovereigns, not to private individuals. Even so, it was all too easy to use this as a justification for European states' occupying the lands of non-Europeans and punishing their inhabitants, in the interests of bringing Christian 'civilization' to 'savages'. One of the major debates between scholars is how far Grotius was fundamentally a Dutch nationalist whose ideas were always underpinned by the self-interests of his country. When Grotius praised the fruits of commerce, for instance, he was clearly outlining principles that would allow the burgeoning trade of his country to flourish.[12]

When it came to the actual conduct of foreign policy, Grotius stayed true to his belief that conciliation and moderation were essential. Ultimately, as a Christian he believed that God's law required humane treatment of others. He appealed to a higher moral sense.† He suggested that the impact of war should always be limited to the end desired, that victory did not justify imperialist occupation and that every effort should be made to restore peaceful relationships once 'punishment' had been carried out. So women, children and old men should not be killed, clergy and 'men of letters' should not be injured and prisoners of war treated well. Land should not be devastated and sacred objects should be left untouched. The value of the property of an enemy that could be seized might be no more than the damage that the enemy had done.

A more critical analysis of Grotius's writings has left scholars divided over his real contribution to a coherent theory of international law.[13]

† It is not clear why this 'moral sense' was distinct from the precepts established from natural law.

Yet while Grotius was influential even in his day and certainly among the Enlightenment thinkers of the eighteenth century, he was especially inspiring for the peace movements of the later nineteenth century. At the Hague Peace Conference of 1899, the US delegate Andrew Dickson White championed Grotius as 'the real founder of the modern science of international law'. He is recognized as having introduced a moral imperative to the relationships between states, and while his originality may have been overestimated (Gentili, as we have seen, was arguing for a more ethical approach to the waging of war some years decades before Grotius), the breadth of his concerns and his overall humanity of his philosophy is undeniably impressive.*

Grotius was also concerned about the extent to which the individual could surrender rights or liberties to a government. In principle he accepted that rights could be transferable, even to the extent that there could be a total surrender of rights. But Grotius was less clear when it came to the circumstances in which rights could be reclaimed or a ruler resisted. The idea of a contract between the individual and the state was a key feature of seventeenth-century political thought. And, as we have seen, disagreements about the proper limits of royal authority fuelled the breakdown in relations between monarch and Parliament that led to the English revolution. Social contract theory found one of its most influential proponents in the person of the English philosopher Thomas Hobbes.

The frontispiece of Thomas Hobbes's *Leviathan* shows the supreme ruler constituted from his subjects, with human (left) and divine (right) authority competing equally for recognition.

Born in Wiltshire in the year of the Armada, 1588, Hobbes claimed he absorbed the tensions of that year from his mother.[14] He was also doubtless influenced by the wayward life of his clergyman father, who fades into oblivion after violent conflicts with his fellow clergy. Whatever the influences of his childhood, Hobbes comes across as a frustrated individual, always ready to engage in interminable debates with those he perceived as his opponents. At Oxford he found the Aristotelian curriculum sterile. His condemnation of scholasticism, not least its imprecise use of language, was profound and lasting and embedded in him a deep suspicion of religion. Luckily, Hobbes enjoyed a lifelong attachment to the Cavendish family, later dukes of Devonshire; this gave him the opportunity to travel (as tutor to the young Cavendishes) but also a relatively secure base from which to work and to survey the political scene from close up. One of his earliest publications

* Elihu Lauterpacht, my supervisor when I was studying international law at Cambridge in the late 1960s, was a great fan of Grotius, as was his father, the celebrated jurist Hersch Lauterpacht, who plays an important part in Philippe Sands's recent memoir *East West Street* (2016).

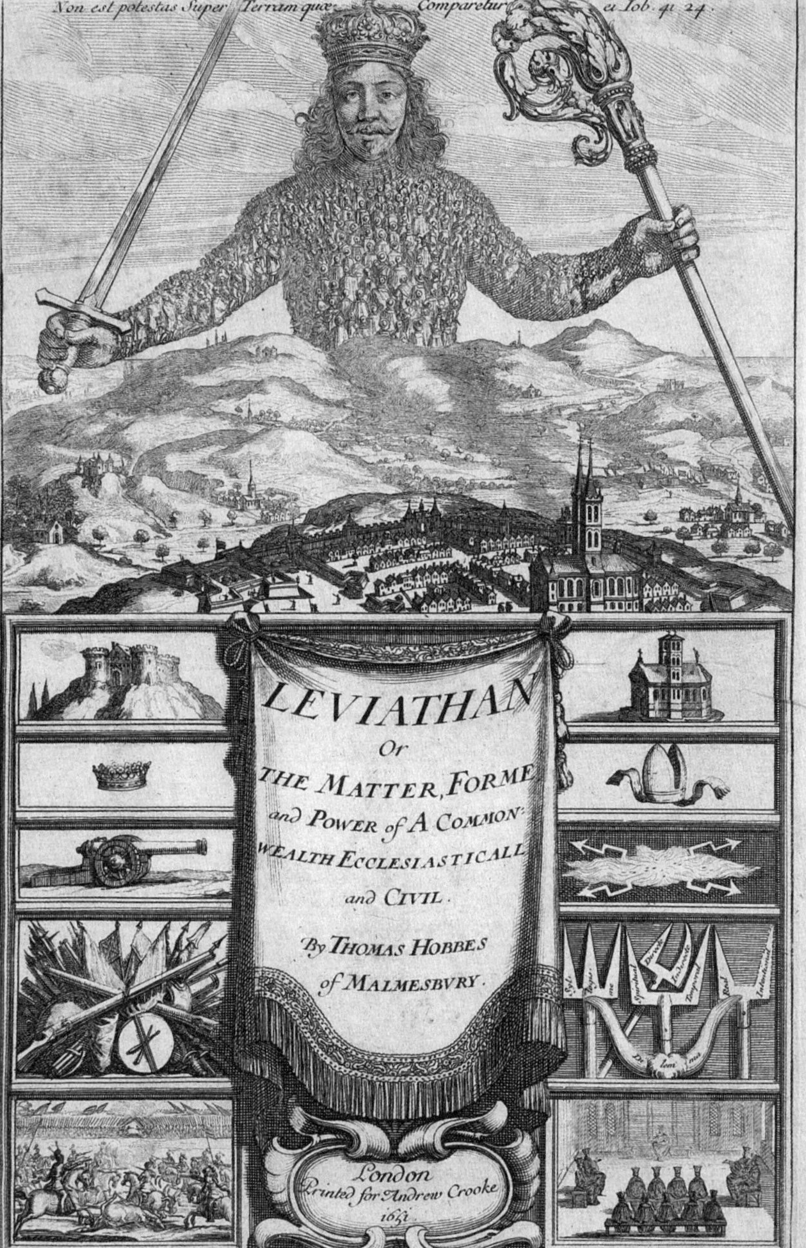
Non est potestas Super Terram quæ Comparetur ei Iob. 41 24.
LEVIATHAN
Or
THE MATTER, FORME and POWER of A COMMON-WEALTH ECCLESIASTICALL and CIVIL.
By THOMAS HOBBES of MALMESBURY.
London
Printed for Andrew Crooke
1651.

(1629) was a translation of Thucydides' *History of the Peloponnesian War* – the very first from Greek to English. Thucydides' account of civil war in Corcyra (modern Corfu) is a brilliant analysis of how easily a society can degenerate into breakdown, each faction justifying its atrocities. Perhaps another of Thucydides' celebrated set-pieces from the *History* (and a classic case-study in cold realpolitik) – his dramatization of the negotiations between the Athenians and the rulers of Melos, which is followed by their brutal subjection of the island when the stubborn Melians refuse their terms – either created or confirmed Hobbes's cynical approach to human nature.

Disillusioned as he was by established religion, Hobbes began to look for more defensible foundations for human knowledge. He found inspiration in Euclid's approach to mathematical knowledge from first principles, which confirmed for Hobbes the critical importance of geometry as the foundation of scientific thought. Hobbes was also clearly influenced by Francis Bacon's empiricism (see Chapter 30). In the 1630s Hobbes became engrossed by the latest scientific ideas, especially optics. For several years he lived in Paris, engaging in abrasive confrontations with his fellow intellectuals, notably Descartes, with whom he strongly disagreed on dualism. (For Descartes's dualism, see pp. 706–7.) He also met Galileo and is known to have been impressed by William Harvey's discovery of the circulation of the blood. So this was a man of wide scholarly interests, but our principal concern is with his political thinking, notably as expressed in his work *Leviathan*. Published in 1651, in the early years of the English republic, when Hobbes was already well into his sixties, *Leviathan*'s title refers to a biblical sea monster – here seen as a symbol of the sovereign state.

Hobbes was a materialist. He was heavily influenced by Lucretius, to the extent that a preface to a 1686 edition of *De rerum natura* noted that 'admirers of Mr Hobbes may easily discern that his politics are but Lucretius enlarged'. Lucretius' descriptions of a primitive society from which civilization emerged accorded with Hobbes's own views. While remaining a believer, he distrusted the 'dreams' of Christianity and its ministers.[15] (He once likened theologians to clumsy countrymen arriving at court and becoming embarrassingly entangled in their hats and cloaks.) Nor did he accept the view of philosophers such as Plato and Aristotle that some are naturally inferior or subordinate to others. For Hobbes, all human beings are equal[16] and there are no natural hierarchies; his world has little room for heroes or natural leaders. This was not so much based on any high-sounding principle of egalitarianism as on the recognition that all are equally vulnerable.[17]

The most polemical part of *Leviathan* is a savage and bitingly ironic attack on the universities for their collaboration with the church and for perverting knowledge through their adulation of Aristotle. Hobbes had always resented the fact that he could not study geometry at Oxford. He would later argue that skills such as navigation, knowledge of 'the face of the earth' and the ability to trade were essential.

Hobbes lived through the era of the Thirty Years War and the English Civil War – whose brutalities must have seemed consistent with the portrayal of humanity at war that he had encountered in Thucydides. It is perhaps understandable therefore that *Leviathan*'s most famous passage describes human life in its primitive state as 'solitary, poor, nasty, brutish and short'. Some have seen *Leviathan* partly as a philosophical meditation on current European affairs. Hobbes followed this pessimistic description of life with the premise that humans living without law, in a state of nature, for instance, would have every reason not to trust each other, since there was no effective restraint on one person killing another or stealing their goods. He acknowledged the individual's right to self-preservation, but what was to prevent this being enforced by the killing of those who threatened it? 'The wickedness of bad men also compels good men to have recourse, for their own protection, to the virtues of war, which are violence and fraud.'[18] All are made equally vulnerable by the evil behaviour of the few. In this Hobbes was specifically repudiating theories such as those of the parliamentary pamphleteer Henry Parker (see p. 607) that 'the people' were in some way a united or even benevolent community.

The natural response to all this might be to crawl into a cave and hope for the best, but Hobbes provided a solution. He did not believe that moral values could be established through reason – this was incompatible with his pessimistic view of human nature – thus the only solution was a political one. He argued that the horrors – and likelihood – of social breakdown were such that at some point humans had agreed to surrender their apparent liberty to a ruling power who would have absolute sovereignty over them. As Richard Tuck has averred: 'This must count as Hobbes's most distinctive contribution to political theory.'[19] (While Hobbes tended towards a single ruler such as a monarch, he did accept that there could be other forms of ultimate authority.) The end result was similar to the status conferred by the divine right of kings in that the ruler had absolute power and was responsible only to a higher authority for its exercise. This even allowed him to tutor the young Charles II. However, Hobbes was providing a *secular* justification for the same power, involving a total surrender of rights to the sovereign in the hope that he would exercise his power wisely. Yet insofar as there was a social contract, it was between those who chose to surrender their power, not between the people and the sovereign, who remained unrestrained. The unity of the people was only achieved when they surrendered their individual existences to the sovereign. But how was the transition between warring individuals and a mutual agreement to accept the rule of a sovereign ever to be negotiated? At the end of *Leviathan*, Hobbes appears to have accepted that such an agreement was rarely achieved.[20] Hobbes recognized that nations would often go to war with each other as a result of the failure of leadership.[21]

However, Hobbes was proposing some kind of ideal – of a society in which all would be equal under the sovereign and would work together productively. This was the state or commonwealth – the Leviathan itself – an entity independent of both ruler and ruled. The organizing principle of this state for this society, the 'higher authority' as he put it, would be the laws of nature. Rather than adopting an idealized view of these laws as being self-evident or even established through custom, Hobbes took the pragmatic view that they are those laws that enable human beings to live as they wish without the fear of exploitation by others. His starting point was the premise that every creature seeks to preserve its existence and that this should be enforced collectively by the ruler – who was also interested in his *own* self-preservation. It followed that values such as justice and mercy had some place in society, and that equity should be sought through the fair distribution of goods. As the Hobbes scholar Catherine Wilson has argued in an essay on *Leviathan*: '[Hobbes's] Laws are the ground rules of a well-ordered and productive society that is remarkably egalitarian in its distribution rules, impartial and corruption-free in its dispensation of justice, and kind and mannerly with respect to personal relations.'[22] This ideal, often overlooked in summaries of Hobbes's thought, suggests – optimistically – that the simple imposition of absolute rule by a sovereign will exert a positive influence on his subjects, who would otherwise be killing each other.

There remained the issue of how far the sovereign could exercise his power over and above the need to preserve the lives of his subjects. Hobbes did not suggest that individuals had rights beyond that of the preservation of their lives. As he states in *Leviathan* in relation to freedom of speech: 'It is annexed to the Sovereignty to be judge of what opinions and doctrines are averse and what conducing to peace.'[23] This aspect of Hobbes's thinking has understandably attracted criticism, but he may well have been influenced – in taking such an authoritarian stance – by the mass of radical, especially religious, pamphlets in circulation at the time he was writing *Leviathan*. More than most of his contemporaries he was deeply suspicious of religious dogmatism and he must have hoped that his sovereign would enforce a civic religion that would keep the peace.

Having surrendered rights to the monarch in the hope of self-preservation, the individual was justified in resisting the monarch if their right of self-preservation were violated (if they were about to be killed, for instance). Hobbes argued, however, that there was no justification for forming an alliance with others to resist the sovereign. Hobbes had a profound belief in the sanctity of contracts and he was convinced that such an alliance would lead, inevitably, to civil war. The only option in such a situation was to attempt to replace one sovereign by another and the two would then fight it out in the civil war that ensued. This, of course, was what was happening just as he was writing *Leviathan*.

Hobbes's philosophy contained a contradiction that was to prove its weakness. He must have known that history was full of examples of tyrannical rulers and that his ideal society was unlikely to be created by a single ruler with absolute power. There were surely distinctions to be made between the Stuart monarchy and Cromwell, yet according to Hobbes's philosophy each had the right to rule absolutely. He believed the execution of Charles was unjustified but since he believed sovereignty to be the natural state of things, the emergence of a new sovereign was no surprise. It was simply a case of one – unrelated – ruler replacing another. The right of royal inheritance through birth meant nothing to Hobbes. And nor did he hold with the notion of an inviolable constitution (of the sort that would underpin the 1689 Declaration of Rights). Hobbes has thus been criticized for his failure to explain the philosophical argument for political obligation on the part of the subject. Why should we surrender what freedoms we have to a dictatorial sovereign who might well abuse them? Are there not alternative ways of managing power structures so as to defend liberties and ensure peaceful transitions of power? In the religion-obsessed seventeenth century, it was Hobbes's attack on the clergy and his ambivalence over the role of God that most affronted his readers. When a House of Commons committee tried to ban *Leviathan* in 1666, they did so on account of its 'atheism, blasphemy and profaneness'. In the event Hobbes was protected from prosecution for heresy by his former pupil King Charles II. But from then until his death in 1679 he faced a domestic ban on publishing any work describing human behaviour.

Hobbes is similar to Machiavelli in that he tends to be known for a single idea – that of the authoritarian ruler as the only means of keeping order in a volatile age. As one critic, the Swiss Protestant Jean Barbeyrac, put it in the following century, according to Hobbes 'the will of the sovereign alone constitutes, not only what we call just and unjust, but even religion, and that no divine revelation can bind the conscience, till the authority or rather caprice of his Leviathan has given it the force of law'.[24] The great Scottish philosopher David Hume complained that 'Hobbes's politics are fitted only to promote tyranny, and his ethics to encourage licentiousness'.[25] As with Machiavelli, a more nuanced assessment is possible. While no one doubts that Hobbes was an abrasive man, he did show some insight into the difficulties of governing and did maintain an ideal: that the firm order imposed by a sovereign in the name of preservation of the individual existences of his subjects was for the public good. Hobbes must be seen within the context of the age in which he lived, when he was faced with the brutal reality of the social breakdown and atrocities of war, in which religion played a significant part. Against such a backdrop, he was naturally eager to create a sound theoretical basis for political authority.

A contemporary thinker who did not agree with Hobbes on the natural brutality of human beings was Samuel von Pufendorf (1632–94). His name is little recognized today but this German philosopher was enormously influential in his own time and for 100 years afterwards, especially among the philosophers of the Enlightenment and the Founding Fathers of the United States. Born in Lutheran Saxony, Pufendorf began his studies as a theologian but, like many outstanding minds of this generation he soon ranged more widely, over philosophy, jurisprudence and history. He wrote a controversial critique of the political structure of the Habsburg empire and, later in his life, a history of contemporary Sweden in thirty-three volumes. Yet his focus on natural law was so pronounced that the very first chair in this subject was created for him at Heidelberg, where he taught between 1661 and 1668. After his position in Germany was made untenable (he often found himself at the centre of controversies), he spent twenty years teaching the same subject at Lund in Sweden, where he was respected and protected. He expounded his mature political philosophy in *De jure naturae et gentium libri octo* (*Of the Law of Nature and Nations*), 1672, and, in a resumé of this, in his *De officio hominis et civis* (*On the Duty of Man and Citizen*) of 1673.

Pufendorf drew heavily on Grotius, whom he admired as a pioneer, and also Hobbes, who was still alive (he died only in 1679). Pufendorf differed fundamentally from Hobbes, however, in believing that human beings are naturally sociable. It followed that 'the fundamental natural law is that every man ought to do as much as he can to cultivate and preserve sociability'.[26] This 'fundamental law' originated with God, who had created man as a sociable creature, but the precepts of natural law could also be grasped through reason. Following Grotius, Pufendorf assumed that these precepts would be self-evident even if God did not exist. In fact, he prided himself that his theories held good independently of theology but were based on a 'scientific' approach that was also receptive to the experience of the societies around him. Here too was an echo of Hobbes.

Pufendorf agreed with Hobbes that there were no natural hierarchies. Any differences in status originated in agreements to that effect between individuals. Thus the ideal political system would respect the rights of all to live equally and in harmony with each other. Human beings had a duty of care to others. But this harmony would not happen naturally, however much individuals might desire it to do so. In relationships between individuals, 'something good must also be conferred on the other, at least if the minds of men are to be conjoined by a still closer bond'.[27] Individuals were thus given a moral purpose. A ruling power was required, to maintain peace and with the right to impose sanctions when it was threatened. This was 'the state', very much as Hobbes had imagined it, as an entity independent of ruler and ruled.

Pufendorf did not follow Aristotle in believing that his states emerged naturally, but rather envisaged state formation occurring in two stages. First, a process of agreement that a government was needed had to take place, followed by the granting of authority to a ruling body. Pufendorf again differed from Hobbes in not insisting on an absolute sovereign. He refused to believe that sovereign and people were different entities, one exercising absolute authority over the other. They were, in fact, united in a single state. A monarchy, an aristocracy or even a democracy were legitimate ways of ruling a state and the scope of a state's powers could be limited by the people. Pufendorf was proposing a social contract. Once in power a state was primarily responsible for enforcing natural law, to the extent that it was obliged to maintain the innate sociability of its subjects, but was otherwise free to formulate its own laws. Once the rights of individuals had been freely surrendered, the primary obligation was to obey. Pufendorf felt that resistance would lead to chaos. He recognized only a limited right of resistance, in circumstances where the original agreement made on the formation of a state was breached by the ruling authority.

Pufendorf extended the idea of natural law to nation states and so made important advances in areas such as the just war, where he develops the ideas of Grotius (and Gentili). In chapter 2 of *De officio hominis et civis*, Pufendorf insists that disputes between nations should primarily be settled through arbitration, but that war is justified for self-preservation, defence against invasion or to collect reparations for an injury. Even when justified, the conduct of war must be restrained: 'Humanity commands that, so far as the clash of arms permits, we do not inflict more mischief upon the enemy than defence, or the vindication of our right, and security for the future, require.'[28] Here he was close to Grotius.

Pufendorf wrote with great clarity and followed through his arguments in detail. Intellectually, they were profound and they fitted well with the needs of the times, offering a more benign view of human nature and a less rigid way of understanding the relationship between human beings and the form of power they chose to rule over them. According to Quentin Skinner, Pufendorf is the first philosopher to conceive of the 'civil state' as one entity with a single will. His writings had the right degree of polemic and controversy to be noticed and so his works were widely translated. One English philosopher who warmed to them, to the extent of recommending them to English readers as introductory texts, was John Locke. Locke never met Pufendorf but read him closely: 'readers knowledgeable in Pufendorf can find many tracks of the German thinker all through Locke's writings on politics' is one scholarly assessment.[29] So Pufendorf's importance deserves to be recognized.

Locke was born near Bristol, in England's West Country, in 1632. After a traditional education in the classics at Westminster School (he is said to have been upset by the groans of the nearby crowd when Charles I was beheaded), he went up to Oxford, where he was no more impressed with the scholastic curriculum than Hobbes had been. In words reminiscent of Petrarch and Erasmus, he only 'learned Gibberish' and found the dons 'cover their ignorance with a curious and inexplicable web of perplexed words'.[30] (Two of the finest minds of the eighteenth century, Adam Smith and Edward Gibbon, were to find Oxford sunk even deeper in lethargy.) Attracted to more practical matters, he focused first on medicine while he carried out administrative duties within the university. His interest in science led to contacts with Robert Boyle and Robert Hooke (see pp. 681–88). But at this stage there was nothing to suggest that Locke harboured any radical ideas – in fact, he welcomed the return of royal authority in 1660.

It was a chance meeting in 1667 with Anthony Ashley Cooper, a member of the king's council, that changed his life. Ashley Cooper was to rise high, as first earl of Shaftesbury, and then Lord Chancellor, in Charles II's administration, and Locke moved to London with him as an amanuensis compiling papers on economics while also continuing his studies with the leading doctors of his day. Ashley Cooper, who was later to be a prominent member of the Whig faction, shook up Locke's opinions. His change in attitude can be seen in his *Letter Concerning Toleration* (1689) (see also p. 716) which revealed a much more generous approach to dissenters than his earlier (unpublished) pamphlets. Ashley Cooper lasted only a year as Lord Chancellor (1672–3) before the king dismissed him, but this released Locke from his administrative duties and he was able to spend three years in France. His mind was now turning to deeper issues of philosophy. He immersed himself in the works of Descartes, who, although he had been dead for over twenty years, was still enormously influential. It was also at this time that Pufendorf was publishing his most distinguished works. Returning to England in 1679, Locke found England in the midst of the Exclusion Crisis, the attempt by the Whigs to exclude James from the throne on account of his Catholicism. Shaftesbury led the Whig party but was forced to leave England when accused of treason after the attempt failed and the Tories retaliated. Locke was caught up in the debacle and himself left for exile in Holland in September 1683. He only returned to England in 1689 in the wake of the 'Glorious Revolution'.

A fuller account of Locke's philosophy will be provided in Chapter 31. Here, in a chapter dealing with natural law and social contracts, I concentrate on his *Two Treatises of Government*. While these were published, anonymously, in 1689, and include references to the revolution of 1688, most of their text was probably written under the influence of Shaftesbury between 1679 and 1683. This was the time when Shaftesbury was actively involved in trying to exclude James from the throne and so Locke was naturally interested in finding a philosophical justification for this act of disobedience. The immediate target of the *Treatises*, particularly the first, was, inevitably, the divine right of kings. An influential work in support of the doctrine, *Patriarcha*, had been published in 1680. Its author, Robert Filmer (1588–1653), was long dead. He had probably composed his work before 1642, at a time when anti-royalist sentiment was growing, and during the Exclusion Crisis it seemed relevant for monarchists to print it. Filmer's rationale was heavily based on Old Testament precedents. He claimed that Adam as a father had absolute power over his family and this had been passed down to be taken up by Noah and his family after the Flood and then on through the generations. By analogy a king had absolute power over his subjects, who had no right to dispute his authority.

The first of Locke's *Treatises* aimed to refute Filmer. It was not difficult to do so. The fundamental problem that Locke exposes again and again is that even if Adam did have absolute power this cannot provide an argument for the absolute power of any monarch. Moreover, there is no biblical evidence that God granted Adam absolute authority, let alone dominion over the whole world. Similarly, there is no evidence that God intended Adam, diminished as he was by his sin, to pass on what power he had to his descendants, and, even if he had, there is no way of knowing who these heirs might be. Locke ends with the example of the Hebrews, God's chosen people, who had only experienced monarchical government for a third of their history. This in itself makes it obvious that monarchy is not a God-ordained system of government. Despite the strength of his arguments, Locke's *First Treatise* did not succeed in destroying Filmer's reputation and *Patriarcha* continued to have enormous influence well into the eighteenth century.

The *First Treatise* allows Locke to introduce his most important thesis, one which he would elaborate further in the *Second*. Far from human beings being born helpless slaves and continuing in that servile state throughout their lives, as Filmer argued, they were free and equal in their original 'state of nature' and created as such by God. (Locke was happy to accept that the law of nature was divinely founded, existed eternally, and could be recognized through reasoning, 'being unwritten and so nowhere to be found but in the minds of men'.[31]) He imagined the first human communities as ones in which there were enough resources for all and in which each individual* had the right 'to order their actions, and dispose of their possessions and persons as they think fit'. Locke recognized the importance of private property, which he argued was originally accumulated through labour, and the right to pass it on through inheritance. He supported the right of women to own their own property. Natural law required, however, that we do not take so much as to deprive others of resources and that we do not waste what we have. The autonomy of individuals and their right to preserve 'property' – which comprises not only our possessions but also our status – against intrusion, provides the essential core of Locke's political

The title page of the first edition of John Locke's *Two Treatises of Government* (1690).

* As with Hobbes, there has been much scholarly discussion over Locke's attitude to women. While regarding them theoretically as equal to men, many of his writings imply that they will be in subservient roles.

TWO TREATISES OF Government:

In the former,

The false Principles and Foundation

OF

Sir *ROBERT FILMER*,

And his FOLLOWERS,

ARE

Detected and Overthrown.

The latter is an

ESSAY

CONCERNING

The True Original, Extent, and End

OF

Civil-Government.

The Second Edition Corrected.

LONDON, Printed for *Awnsham* and *John Churchill* at the *Black Swan* in *Pater-noster-Row*, 1694.

philosophy. By staking out his ground so resolutely, he left no room for theories that claimed that there were natural hierarchies allowing slavery (as in Aristotle) or kingship. Like Pufendorf, Locke held that we are social creatures and that societies will flourish when there is mutual respect between individuals.

Clearly, there was much imaginative idealism in Locke's account of the 'state of nature' and he came under pressure to show that such societies existed. He tried hard to find examples from across the world, as his large library of travel books attested. Locke believed that, as societies developed, the difficulties of living within a 'state of nature' – 'inconveniences' as Locke termed them – in which each individual had the right to his or her own preservation and autonomy but not to offend that of others, would inevitably lead to a common agreement that there should be an overriding government. Locke, finalizing his text in the England of 1688, assumed that this would be made up of a legislative assembly backed by an executive that would implement laws. Following Pufendorf, he envisaged a sequence of stages: the people agree to form a political entity, then decide what form the government is to take and finally carry out the act of delegation to the legislature. Consent was essential in each case. Locke found it hard to find any historical examples of this transfer actually taking place and he had to fall back on the argument that a stable society was in itself evidence of this (tacit) consent. Locke's critics have raised the question of the validity of such consent, especially if there are no alternatives for the people to give their express consent to.

As the subjects had freely surrendered their rights to this assembly, it had acquired no more authority than to preserve those rights and legislate to that end. As Locke puts it in the *Second Treatise*:

> The rules that [legislators] make for other men's actions must, as well as their own and other men's actions, be conformable to the law of Nature – i.e., to the will of God, of which that is a declaration – and the fundamental law of nature being the preservation of mankind, no human sanction can be good or valid against it.[32]

The assembly could not acquire rights other than those that individuals had to give. It followed that the assembly could not act arbitrarily but only through 'promulgated laws and authorised judges'. The impartiality of government was crucial. Since the authority of the assembly derives directly from the people, the assembly does not have the power to transfer law-making powers to any other body. This left unresolved the coercive power of the assembly. While a right of self-defence clearly existed in the 'state of nature', did the assembly have the power to punish offenders? In order to maintain his logic Locke had to create an original right – this being the right to punish others so as to uphold the law of nature, which could be transferred to the government.

Fundamental to Locke's theory of natural rights was the right to reclaim the rights surrendered to the assembly if they, or the executive that actually implemented the laws, abused their powers. Locke's primary purpose when he was finalizing the *Treatises* before publication in 1689 may have been to legitimize a specific case, namely the transfer of power from James II to William of Orange. He invokes the right of resistance in circumstances where 'the Governour makes not the Law [of nature], but his Will, the Rule; and his Commands and Actions are not directed to the preservation of the properties of the Peoples, but the satisfaction of his own Ambition, Revenge, Covetousness or any other irregular Passion'. [33]

Partly as a result of their anonymity (Locke only revealed his authorship in his will), the *Two Treatises* had little immediate effect. It would take some time for the notion of inalienable rights that can be surrendered to government for the good of all but reclaimed through resistance if there was abuse to enter the mainstream of political philosophy. But in the long term the influence of Locke has been overwhelming. The ideas that 'natural' rights of man accrue to each individual simply as a result of their birth, the insistence that government must be instituted by popular consent and that this consent can be withdrawn, the requirement that the arbitrary use of power is illegitimate and that government must act for the community as a whole with total impartiality have become essential features of the western democratic tradition. Locke also argued for religious toleration, on the grounds that trying to bring about the salvation of the individual was not an appropriate aim of government and that, in any case, no government could enforce religious conviction. (This theme will be explored further in Chapter 31.) There remained many questions to answer regarding the nature and extent of individual and governmental rights. Does the right of self-preservation give freedom to bear arms? To what extent is a government entitled to raise taxes if this infringes the right to private property? Can lines be effectively drawn between unrestrained capitalism and the use of goods for the good of the community? At what point does violent revolution become justified? Locke framed the context in which these issues could be discussed, and this is his lasting legacy as a political philosopher.

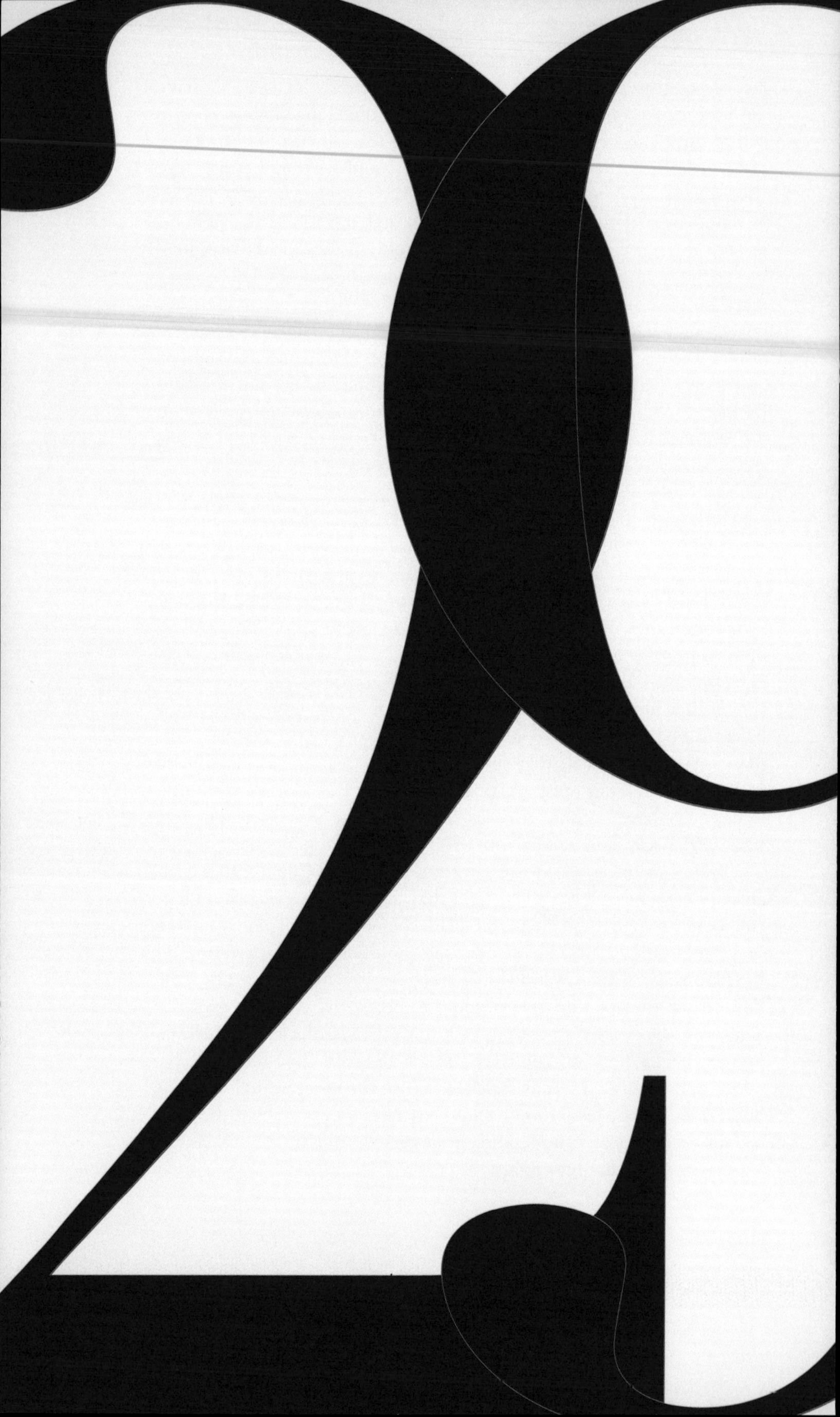

From Natural Philosophy into Science: The Astronomers

Some years ago, as Your Serene Highness well knows, I discovered in the heavens many things that had not been seen before our own age. The novelty of these things, as well as some consequences which followed from them in contradiction to the physical notions commonly held among academic philosophers, stirred up against me no small number of professors as if I had placed these things in the sky with my own hands in order to upset nature and overturn the science… They hurled various charges and published numerous writings filled with vain arguments, and they made the grave mistake of sprinkling these with passages taken from places in the Bible which they had failed to understand properly, and which were ill-suited to their purposes.

Galileo Galilei, Letter to the Grand Duchess Christina of Florence, 1615[1]

The sixteenth and seventeenth centuries witnessed a dramatic growth of interest in the natural world, sparked off not least by the European discovery of the Americas. For the first time since antiquity there was an enthusiastic commitment to what it was possible to know empirically about the world around us. The search to understand the sources of knowledge intensified, made easier by new instruments such as the telescope and microscope, which allowed more accurate observations. Mathematics was to play an important role in contributing models for the universe that was now seen as acting under uniform laws, as would be brilliantly defined by Isaac Newton. The elements of Aristotle, earth, fire, air and water, were replaced by an understanding that material might be made up of small particles of different chemical 'elements'. Scientists – or 'natural philosophers' as they were then known – were eager to find ways of proving their theories and thereby to provide the foundations for the development of new ones. Experimentation thus became the rage. Of course, it is only in hindsight that one can see which experiments bore fruit in the sense of providing accurate representations of reality and which led nowhere. This would make the development of scientific knowledge a cumulative process, a crucial development in the history of European thought and one that has proved enduring.

What unites the figures to be discussed in this chapter is a deep-rooted desire to understand the nature of the universe. The roots of this desire are hard to define, since they varied from individual to individual, but all of these astronomers, physicists and mathematicians of the era of the Scientific Revolution were united by their commitment to observing and calculating. As we shall see, some were committed Christians and some were not. Religion in its varied forms does not appear to have been a powerful force in encouraging or hampering the progress of science (see the end of Chapter 30 for further discussion of this issue).

Telling the story of the transformation of natural philosophy into what might be seen as science involves many complex issues, not least because so many natural events appeared inexplicable unless it was assumed that they were controlled by forces beyond human observation. Were there sources of ancient wisdom – the works of Hermes Trismegistus championed by Marsilio Ficino, for instance – that might hold the secrets of knowledge? An influential work on magnetism by the Englishman William Gilbert (1544–1603), *De Magnete*

(1600), raised the question of how one object, the lodestone, could influence another without any physical connection. Gilbert compared the action of the lodestone with the effect that certain substances, if ingested, can have on the human body – such as the laxative influence of rhubarb – and with the relationship between the phases of the moon and the tides. Was God acting in some way through objects or were there invisible forces underlying the natural world which were present in certain substances? Gilbert made his own suggestion: 'We consider that the whole universe is animated, and that all the globes, all the stars, and also the noble earth, have been governed, since the beginning by their own appointed souls and have motives of self-preservation.'[2]

In contrast to Gilbert's 'animated' universe, Descartes put forward the notion of the universe as a machine, in which every particle was in contact with each other (see p. 668). Others, such as the astronomer Johannes Kepler (see below, p. 660), attempted to classify natural phenomena in relation to their creation by God. The alchemists remained influential – if esoteric – investigators of the physical world and were valued for their skills in working with metals, in particular. Meanwhile, the findings of those who used empirical methods often contradicted classical sources, raising concerns about the authority of each. Studies of the classification systems of the private libraries that were now a feature of cultural life for the elite reveal that it was only slowly that the study of nature and the universe sorted itself out into recognizable disciplines. Rather than attempting to define a coherent sequence of events, traditionally termed the 'Scientific Revolution' and taking place somewhere in the seventeenth century, some scholars prefer to identify – to quote the historian of science Steven Shapin – 'a diverse array of cultural practices aimed at understanding, explaining, and controlling the natural world, each with different characteristics and each experiencing different modes of change'.[3] The relatively coherent term 'science', 'the disciplined enquiry into the phenomena and order of the natural world', that we know today struggled to be born from many different philosophical and empirical sources.

Many histories of 'modern' science begin in 1543 with Copernicus's hypothesis that the Earth and the other planets move around the sun. He had his predecessors. Aristarchus of Samos (*c.*310–*c.*230 BC) had posited a sun-centred system and Copernicus knew of this. However, the sophisticated, Earth-centred description of the cosmos by the Greek geographer and astronomer Ptolemy had held sway since the second century AD. In the *Almagest* (see Chapter 7) Ptolemy used this geocentric model of the known universe to explain the movements of the six known planets (Mercury, Venus, Earth, Mars, Jupiter and Saturn), in addition to the sun and the moon. Ptolemy insisted that all planetary movements were in perfect circles. Once this and the central position of the Earth had been accepted, Ptolemy had had to construct elaborate models to explain the recorded observations of the planets. In the geometrically based Ptolemaic universe, the planets move clockwise in a small circle, the epicycle, which at the same time moves clockwise around a larger circle, the deferent. This model had in fact been used by Greek astronomers for centuries, but the problem for Ptolemy was that it did not entirely square with available observational data relating to the speed of planetary orbits. In order to reconcile these planetary movements with his hypothesis of uniform circular motion, Ptolemy developed the mathematical concept of the equant, a point close to but outside the Earth, from which point a planet would always appear to be moving at a uniform speed. This did actually account for the many astronomical observations.

Understandably, very few medieval astronomers had managed to grasp the breadth of Ptolemy's work in its Latin translations. The accepted explanation of planetary movement was the Aristotelian cosmos, in which the planets moved in concentric spheres. Several centuries earlier than Ptolemy, and with less observational data to go on, Aristotle had argued that the passage of the planets was perfect and unchanging. Once put in motion by the Supreme Mover, they simply went on moving, each planet travelling entirely within its own sphere. The Earth was thus surrounded by concentric spheres, one for each planet, beyond which, in the Christian interpretation of the system, was heaven itself. While Aristotle had talked of the aether above the fire, air and water that surrounded the Earth, there had been much speculation what the substance of each celestial sphere actually was. One suggestion was that it consisted of a form of invisible crystal, within which the planet travelled. What was agreed was that no planet or other star could break out of its sphere. The universe was in itself finite, with the fixed stars in a sphere of their own, not that far beyond the planets. (The Aristotelian system is shown in the sky above Dante on pp. 238–9.)

However complicated, Ptolemy's system claimed superiority over the simpler Aristotelian system because it was based on a mass of observations, some adopted from Babylonian sources; Ptolemy had listed 1,022 stars in 48 constellations. Gradually, however, its problems had become apparent. In the *Epitome*, or abridgement, of the *Almagest*, completed by the German astronomer Johannes Müller, known as Regiomontanus, in 1462 (although not printed until 1496), Regiomontanus had noted that, following Ptolemy's logic, the moon should have appeared much larger as it neared the Earth in the course of its orbit. He began speculating as to whether Ptolemy's geometrical models actually worked. The study of astronomy had been stagnant for many centuries, the university texts inadequate and there had been more concentration on astrology, notably the prediction of the course of diseases based on star charts for an individual. The German astronomer Johannes Kepler would later remark that astrology was like a foolish but well-off daughter without whose help astronomy proper would starve. Even in the papal court, star charts were still being drawn up in the seventeenth century (and an auspicious date picked for the laying the cornerstone of the new St Peter's in Rome).

Copernicus (1473–1543) became interested in astronomy while at the University of Cracow in his native Poland, although his doctorate, from the university of Ferrara in Italy, was in canon law.* While in Italy, he also studied the humanities in Bologna and medicine in Padua, but he was already committed to understanding the motion of the planets and, rather than being worried by the size of the moon, he seems to have been frustrated by the lack of coherence in Ptolemy's system. It appeared to him to have been built up piece by piece rather than having a harmonious simplicity. To put it bluntly, it was inelegant, and Copernicus, who had absorbed Platonism, found this unacceptable.

In 1503 Copernicus returned home to Poland. Here, despite a busy life as a cleric, he continued his investigations into astronomy and postulated for the first time that a system based on the sun as the centre of the planets provided a more elegant representation of Ptolemy's observations. There is some doubt as to the originality of Copernicus's criticisms of the latter. Research into the work of Islamic astronomers has shown that they were aware of the problems with the *Almagest*, notably that of the equant, which appeared simply to have been added to 'save the phenomena', in other words providing an artificial solution to explain what could be observed. The most celebrated Islamic scholar of his age, Nasir al-Din al-Tusi (1201–74), made a more fundamental challenge to Ptolemy in positing an alternative system of rotating spheres, which he claimed also matched Ptolemy's observations. These were based on viewings from the observatory he constructed at Maragheh, in modern Iran, in 1269. Remarkably, Copernicus appears to have based his criticisms of Ptolemy on similar data, and there is lively discussion among scholars as to whether Copernicus, rather than

* A plaque by the cathedral commemorates his studies there.

being a pioneer, 'can be looked on as, if not the last, surely the most noted follower of the Maragheh School'. Copernicus did not know Arabic but it is quite possible that he used a go-between who had access to the texts of the Maragheh school and transferred them to him.[4]

Wherever Copernicus obtained his hypothesis, from the Arab world or as a result of his own genius, there were few new observations in it. What he put forward was essentially a mathematical solution; because it placed the sun at the centre of the planetary system, it matched Ptolemy's observations (which Copernicus accepted as reliable) but had the added benefit of explaining the order of the planets and their relative distance from the sun, something Ptolemy's system had failed to do. Noting the speed of each planet, Copernicus could see that those planets that moved more slowly must be those furthest from the sun. The Earth could find its appropriate place in the order of the planets between Venus and Mars. Other anomalies in the Ptolemaic system, periods when a planet seemed to be going backwards, for instance, could be explained in terms of their observation from the Earth, now postulated as a moving rather than stationary platform. By now it was fully accepted that the Earth was a single sphere, rather than Aristotle's four terrestrial spheres of earth, air, fire and water, so that the argument that a rotating Earth would slide under the water was no longer relevant. Essentially, Copernicus was part of the trend towards searching for mathematical understandings that reflected reality rather than the views that had become incorporated into Christian theology. The question now was whether new observations would confirm his hypothesis.

The Persian scientist and astronomer Nasir al-Din al-Tusi (1201–74) at work with his colleagues in the observatory of Maragheh. He may have initiated objections to Ptolemy that were later adopted by Copernicus.

A sun-centred universe was abhorrent to those who believed the Old Testament story of God stopping the sun during a battle (Joshua 10:12–13). If the sun was immobile in the centre of the universe it could not be stopped as it would not be moving in the first place. Copernicus's *De Revolutionibus* (*On the Revolutions of the Heavenly Spheres*), which set out his calculations in full, was published in 1543, just as its author was dying. Its immediate impact was limited. A Lutheran minister by the name of Andreas Osiander, who had taken responsibility for seeing the work through the press, had realized the implications of Copernicus's theory for those who knew their Bible. As a precaution he had provided an unsigned introduction that claimed that this was no more than a hypothesis from which more efficient mathematical models of the universe might be made. The sheer quantity of mathematical calculations provided by Copernicus also helped obscure the importance of the work, even though the early copies do seem to have been read.[5] Yet Osiander was proved right. *De Revolutionibus* was soon condemned by the Lutherans, both by Luther himself and by Philipp Melanchthon. The Catholic Church took longer to respond. One reason for its muted response was the relatively low status of astronomy and the sheer difficulty of persuading people to believe that the Earth was rotating on its axis as Copernicus demanded. There was simply no evidence for this rush of movement. One study claims that only ten thinkers are known to have accepted the physical truth of Copernicus's theory before 1600.[6]

Four key astronomers engaged seriously with Copernicus's solution and embraced the questions that it left unresolved. It says something for the breadth of European learning that one was a Dane (Tycho Brahe), another German (Johannes Kepler), the third Italian (Galileo Galilei) and the fourth French (René Descartes) and that Latin still acted as a language of scholarly communication between them. The development of science in the seventeenth century was a Europe-wide enterprise.

Tycho Brahe (1546–1601) was lucky to be born into wealth. At the age of thirteen, enthused by an accurately predicted eclipse of the sun, he began to make observations of the stars by night, which he continued alongside his daytime studies in law. In 1563 his first published observations showed that the tables put forward by Copernicus were as much as two days out. Brahe now became obsessed with accuracy, eventually becoming the most proficient astronomical observer of his age. Here he proved a worthy follower of the German cartographer Petrus Apianus (whose *Cosmographia* he is known to have read). A breakthrough came in 1572 when Brahe observed a new star beyond the moon. His *De nova stella* of 1573, if not immediately appreciated, was revolutionary, as Aristotle had always argued that the universe beyond the moon was eternally immutable and the discovery of any new star impossible. In the late 1570s the Danish king, Frederick II, financed the building of an observatory for Brahe on the island of Hven. While the Arabic astronomers had enjoyed state-financed observatories, such as that at Maragheh, in the thirteenth century, this was a European first and raised the status of astronomy considerably. The Uraniborg, as Brahe called his magnificent establishment, gathered a community of artisans and intellectuals who worked together to perfect his instruments. He could now achieve a reassessment of the position of the stars; the 777

The title page of Nicolaus Copernicus's *De Revolutionibus Orbium Coelestium*, in which the Polish astronomer outlined his heliocentric theory, backed up with an impressive array of mathematical calculations.

NICOLAI COPERNICI TORINENSIS DE REVOLUTIONIbus orbium cœlestium, Libri VI.

IN QVIBVS STELLARVM ET FIXARVM ET ERRATICARVM MOTVS, EX VETEribus atq; recentibus obseruationibus, restituit hic autor. Præterea tabulas expeditas luculentasq; addidit, ex quibus eosdem motus ad quoduis tempus Mathematum studiosus facillime calculare poterit.

ITEM, DE LIBRIS REVOLVTIONVM NICOLAI Copernici Narratio prima, per M. Georgium Ioachimum Rheticum ad D. Ioan. Schonerum scripta.

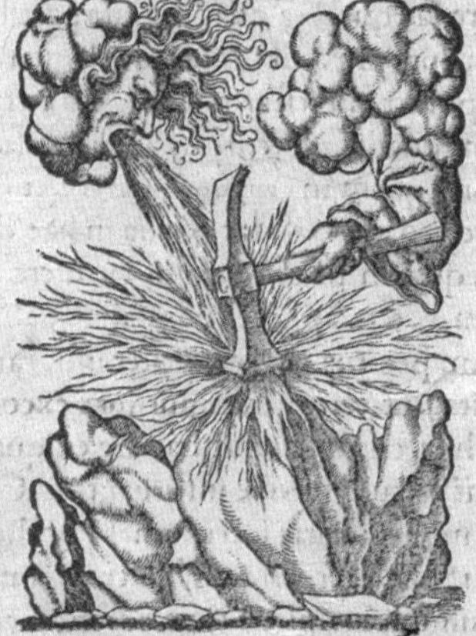

Cum Gratia & Priuilegio Cæs. Maiest.

BASILEAE, EX OFFICINA HENRICPETRINA.

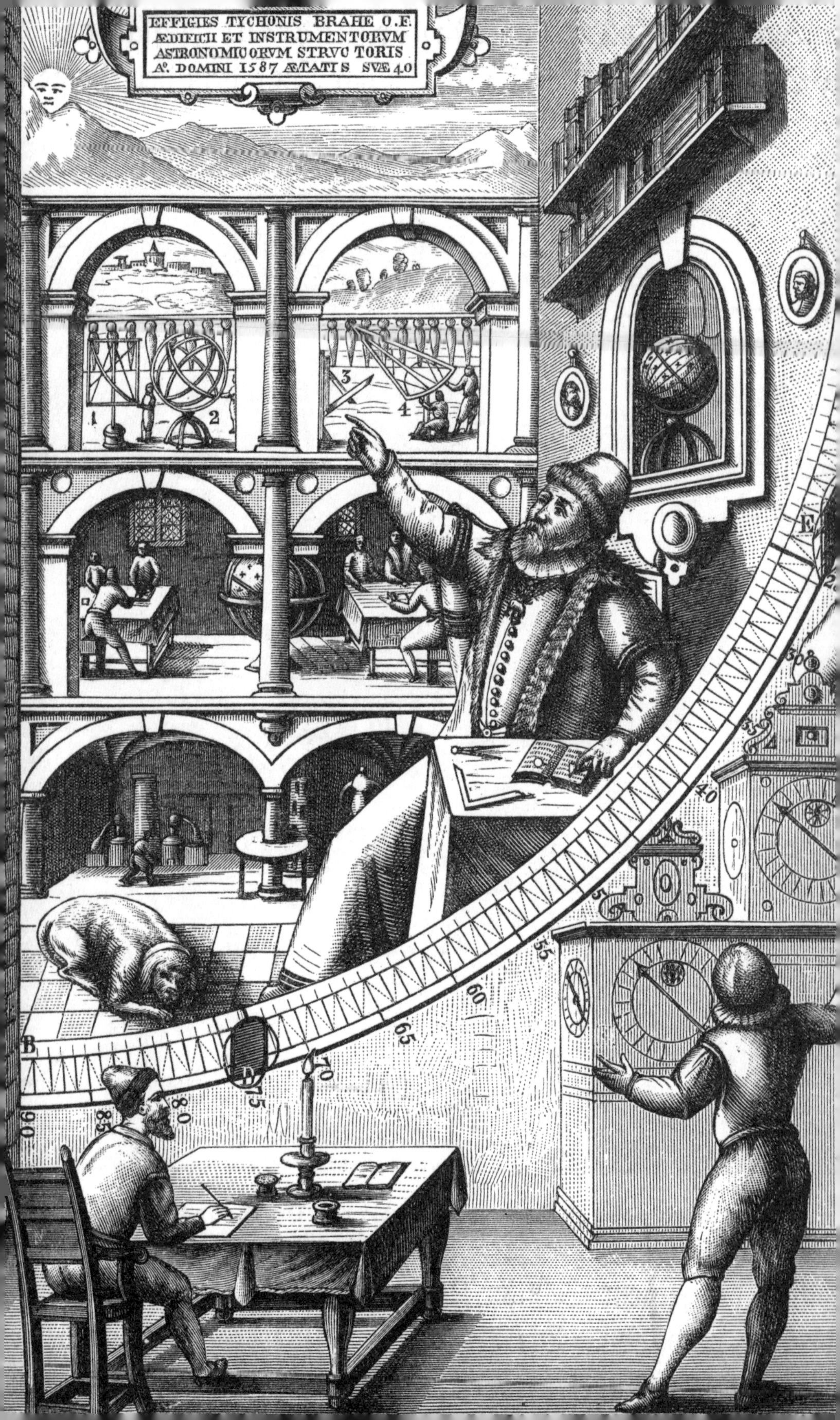
EFFIGIES TYCHONIS BRAHE O.F.
ÆDIFICII ET INSTRUMENTORVM
ASTRONOMICORVM STRVCTORIS
A°. DOMINI 1587 ÆTATIS SVÆ 40

stars whose positions he plotted superseded the earlier catalogue made by Ptolemy. It was not only in astronomy that Brahe was influential; he had shown the importance of accuracy of measurement and this was to be extended to other areas of science, as astronomical instruments, clocks and other measuring devices improved.[7]

In another breakthrough, published as a finding in 1588, Brahe described a comet that he had observed travelling beyond the far side of the moon. Up to now it had been assumed that comets were atmospheric phenomena occurring close to the Earth, but Brahe now proved that the comet travelled through what Aristotle had claimed were closed spheres. This was an important advance, suggesting that stars might follow independent itineraries. It was another blow to the notion of a fixed and unchanging universe and led to a crisis in Aristotelian philosophy that was almost as devastating as Copernicanism. As a sign of just how well established printing was by now, Brahe's comet was discussed in no fewer than 180 different publications. Interestingly, Brahe was unconvinced by Copernicus's radical solution. He insisted that the Earth was still the centre of the universe with the sun and moon circling around it. At first placing only Venus and Mercury in orbit around the sun, as in the *Aratea* (see p. 60), he later placed Mars, Jupiter and Saturn there also. Still mindful of the authority of the scriptures, which described the Earth as being at rest, and confronted by the problem that the Earth did not seem to rotate, Brahe was essentially caught halfway between Ptolemy and Copernicus. But using only the naked eye, his findings had presented a challenge to both Aristotle's and Ptolemy's systems.

Uraniborg, Tycho Brahe's observatory on the Danish island of Hven, in an engraving from Brahe's book *Astronomiae instauratae mechanica* (1598), was the first custom-built observatory in Europe.

Funding for Uraniborg faded with the death of Frederick and in 1599 Brahe moved to Prague to become imperial astronomer to Rudolf II. Here he recruited a young assistant, Johannes Kepler (1571–1630), who came from a poor background but had been awarded a scholarship at the University of Tübingen and become a teacher of mathematics. Kepler had read, and was convinced by, Copernicus's hypothesis but this did not deter Brahe from recognizing his abilities and employing him. After Brahe's death in 1601, Kepler succeeded him as imperial astronomer and inherited his meticulous observations of the planet Mars. He then made a crucial discovery: Brahe's observations did not tally with a circular movement of the planets. They fitted only if Mars, and by extension all planets, actually moved in an ellipse rather than a circle round the sun. The sun was not at the central point of the ellipse but slightly apart from it (at a point known as the focus). Kepler explained this by positing some form of magnetism or light from the sun that alternatively attracted or repulsed the encircling planet. (He knew of William Gilbert's work on magnetism.) He put forward his first 'law', that a planetary orbit is an ellipse with the sun at one focus. His 'second law' concerned the speed of orbit of a planet, which would vary according to its closeness to the sun: faster if close, slower if further away. But Kepler progressed yet further. Copernicus had already spotted that the further a planet was away from the sun, the longer it took to complete a circuit. Kepler discovered the arithmetical rule that made this so. So if one took a period of time for any planet, say a year, squared it and then cubed the average distance from the sun for that year, the ratio between the two would always be the same whichever planet one was dealing with.* This was Kepler's Third Law. The concept of a scientific law, that a phenomenon is observed so consistently that it is assumed it will always occur under the same circumstances, is an important development. It enables the scientist to predict with confidence.

Kepler's final work, *The Epitome of Copernican Astronomy* (1618–21), reflected his (Protestant) belief that God was the great mathematician who had arranged the heavens so that they followed regular movements. He produced elaborate arguments to support the apparent fact that God had produced six planets, no more and no fewer. (Of course, the seventh and eighth planets, Uranus and Neptune, were not known at this time.) This was, he concluded, the only way God, conceived by Kepler to be a geometer, could have put the universe together. Yet his own work on the movements of the planets was more that of a physicist and in the *Epitome* he set them out in detail with fuller explanations of his 'laws'. The question was whether his own hypotheses, based on Brahe's observations, could provide a more accurate representation of the solar system. Kepler had drawn up new tables in 1627 and after his death fresh observations of the relationship between planets turned out almost exactly as he had predicted. His tables were in fact thirty times more accurate than those that Copernicus had provided. Progress was being made.

Kepler's older contemporary, Galileo Galilei (1564–1642), took Copernicus's theory further. Galileo had been born in Pisa to a musical family, but his early studies were in medicine at the university there.[8] However, mathematics, especially ways in which the discipline related to the works of Aristotle, became his passion and his reputation grew;

* The same holds for an artificial satellite circling the Earth.

he became a professor of mathematics, first at Pisa (1589–92), and then at Padua (1592–1610). Galileo became increasingly critical of Aristotle, who was still strongly defended within conservative university circles. One, possibly legendary, experiment involved dropping balls of different weights from the Leaning Tower of Pisa to show that Aristotle's claim that they would travel at different speeds was false. Among ancient scientists Galileo reserved his admiration for the mathematician Archimedes rather than Aristotle. He did much to revive the issues that Archimedes had researched (devoting a paper, written in 1612, to a discussion of how different bodies float in water).

It was while Galileo was at Padua that he heard of the first rudimentary attempts to place lenses within a tube in such a way as to bring distant objects closer. He taught himself how to grind lenses so as to create a 'telescope' that magnified by as much as twenty times. Now he could begin to see the planets and stars far better than the naked eye had ever managed. He discovered that the moon, like the Earth, had a rough surface, and that four 'moons' could be seen circling Jupiter. A panoply of new stars came within his vision. These findings challenged Aristotle's notions of planetary spheres each with its own single planet and a fixed and unchanging number of stars. They also showed that a planet could attract and sustain a smaller 'moon', which meant that whether the sun or Earth was the centre of the universe, neither was the only centre of motion. The breadth of these discoveries led Galileo to ask whether the universe might be infinite, a view that had been among the speculations of the polymath Giordano Bruno (see p. 556). It was clear that Aristotle's theory that the celestial and terrestrial regions were materially distinct was becoming redundant. Galileo was an astute publicist and he wrote up his findings in his treatise *Siderius Nuncius* (*The Starry Messenger*) which he dedicated to the duke of Tuscany, Cosimo II de' Medici. He shrewdly named the Jupiter moons 'the Medicean Stars'. This calculated fawning reaped its reward; Galileo was appointed mathematician and philosopher to Cosimo's court, returning to his native Tuscany from Venetian territory in 1610. He was to be based there for the rest of his life.

Galileo had become convinced that Copernicus was right, perhaps as early as 1596. Further observations with the telescope showed that Venus presented progressive 'phases' of lighting, from a crescent through to its full face, which could only be explained if it was orbiting the sun. This was the first time that Ptolemy's observations had been successfully challenged. Up to now they had been considered compatible with both Copernicus's and Brahe's hypotheses. It was another important breakthrough: the authority of the standard textbook by John of Sacrobosco, so influential in the universities for centuries, (see p. 174), was collapsing swiftly. Of course, Galileo was aware that his findings offended the scriptures. In his 'Letter to the Grand Duchess Christina' (the mother of Cosimo), written in 1615 and quoted in part at the beginning of this chapter, he suggested that scripture could not stand up to 'sensory experience and natural demonstration' and that perhaps certain passages of scripture needed to be reinterpreted so as to fit with what actually could be seen. While the holy office, the Inquisition, might not have worried too much about some abstruse and hypothetical theories concerning the universe that few could understand, once Galileo was seen to have deliberately challenged scripture, and hence the Council of Trent's canons on the fusion of Aristotelianism and Catholic orthodoxy, he became vulnerable. News of the letter soon reached Rome. Galileo travelled to the city to defend himself, probably making his position worse by his arrogance and propensity to argue. The interest of the Inquisition was aroused. In February 1616 the Copernican system was declared heretical and Copernicus's *De Revolutionibus* and Kepler's *Epitome* were placed on the Index of Prohibited Books. Galileo, still in Rome, was summoned to be warned that he was not 'to hold, teach or defend' the Copernican system. There remains some confusion over what exactly he was forbidden to do.

Hindered from expressing his true thoughts, Galileo embarked on a new work that would set out his approach to the scientific method. *Il Saggiatore* (*The Assayer*, in the sense of one who weighs up the quality of a metal), which appeared in Italian in 1623, was essentially a spirited polemic directed at his enemies, with Galileo presented as the persecuted genius. Tycho Brahe and Kepler were among those he criticized, Brahe for his arrangement of the planets. John Heilbron, an authority on Galileo, describes how *Il Saggiatore* 'amused Galileo's friends, multiplied his enemies, and [as he had used the vernacular] brought him new readers who could appreciate the brilliance of the style and the asides that have made excerpts from it chestnuts in the history of science'.[9] In its most famous passage, *Il Saggiatore* confirms the new status of mathematics in the study of the universe:

> Philosophy is written in this grand book, the universe, which stands continually open to our gaze. But the book cannot be understood unless one first learns to comprehend the language and read the letters in which it is composed. It is written in the language of mathematics, and its characters are triangles, circles, and other geometric figures without which it is humanly impossible to understand a single word of it.[10]

Thus did the mathematical rigour that underpinned the advances made by Leon Battista Alberti and others in perspective, and the achievements of the cartographers in presenting more accurate images of the surface of the Earth, now reach the centre of the cosmographic stage. In this they were returning to Plato, who had taught that the path of reasoning started with geometry, Archimedes and, as ever, the *Elements* of Euclid. Here were the ancient sources reasserting themselves, a tribute to their quality and insights.

While some hints of Copernicanism can be found in *Il Saggiatore*, no trouble ensued, and in the same year Galileo was encouraged by the election of a new pope, the genial and erudite Maffeo Barbarini, who took office as Urban VIII. Barbarini was a patron of the arts and of his family. No less than 25 per cent of the papal income was absorbed by his brothers and nephews in the twenty years of his reign. The majestic Palazzo Barbarini, a joint architectural project of Bernini and Borromini, survives in Rome. Galileo, always the opportunist, dedicated *Il Saggiatore* to Urban, who enjoyed its barbs – not least those aimed at the Jesuits, whom he despised. Galileo returned to Rome and had no fewer than six audiences with Urban, who clearly warmed to him. It helped the relationship that Urban, like Galileo, was a Tuscan. He was given to understand that he could continue to write so long as he avoided opening the Copernican question again and did not deliberately provoke his enemies.

Galileo, however, was too confident and unguarded to acquiesce. The work that followed, the *Dialogue Concerning the Two Chief World Systems*, as it came to be known, was essentially a discussion comparing the Copernican system with the traditional ideas of Ptolemy and Aristotle. There are three characters: Salviati, who argues for Copernicus, and could therefore be said to represent Galileo's position; Simplicio, who presents the conventional views of those who continued to support Ptolemy and Aristotle; and Sagredo, who is intended to be neutral but who is shown to be convinced by the arguments of Salviati as the work progresses. Galileo would have been safe if he had merely put forward the alternative positions without any obvious bias, but the very name Simplicio left little doubt as to Galileo's view of those who espoused traditional views, and the character portrayed by Galileo certainly lived up to his name. Galileo managed nonetheless to acquire an *imprimatur** for his work and there was no immediate controversy on its first printing in Florence in 1632, dedicated to Ferdinand, son of Grand Duke Cosimo.

* An imprimatur ('let it be printed') is the licence issued by the Catholic Church to confirm that a work does not offend Catholic teaching.

It was when copies arrived in Rome and Urban, normally so responsive to Galileo, recognized that he might be seen as Simplicio that the clouds began to gather. Galileo, most unwisely, had incorporated conversations he had held with Urban into Simplicio's narrative. When Urban was made aware of the injunction of 1616, it became clear that there were simply too many people, notable among them the Jesuits, whom Galileo had offended and the pope placed the matter in the hands of the Inquisition. In 1633 Galileo was ordered to come to Rome to be interrogated. Now nearly seventy, he was browbeaten until at last he gave in and admitted that the church had been right to follow Aristotle. On 22 June 1633 Galileo was declared to have committed the offence of 'being under suspicion of heresy' and forced 'to abjure, curse and detest the abovementioned errors and heresies [that the sun is the centre of the world and motionless], and, in general, each and every other error, heresy and sect contrary to the Holy Church'.* He was to be confined to his house in Tuscany for the remaining eight years of his life and all his works on Copernicus banned. Among those who were shocked into concealing their own support for Copernicus was another prominent intellectual of the day who was preaching a mechanistic model of the universe, René Descartes.

The title page of *Selenographia*, a study of the moon (1647) by the Danzig astronomer Johannes Hevelius, shows Alhazen (left) opposite Galileo (holding a telescope).

The condemnation of Galileo by the Inquisition has become symbolic of the confrontation of religion and science in the seventeenth century. But such a view simplifies what was a complex individual case. The geocentric view of the universe was a specific issue which the church, immersed as it was in the authority of scripture and the tradition of Aristotelian scholasticism, felt bound to defend. The church would always be vulnerable to new knowledge that could be demonstrated to be empirically unchallengeable. In the 1630s the idea that the extent of human knowledge could advance cumulatively was still in its infancy and in any case the church was too embedded in its traditional ideology to adapt. In the world of the Counter-Reformation no scientist or thinker who was pushing at the boundaries of (Tridentine) orthodoxy could afford not to have a stratagem for coping with the inevitable reaction of a conservative church and the investigations of its Inquisition. Galileo can hardly have been unaware of the punishments meted out to heretical thinkers such as Giordano Bruno, yet he persisted in presenting Copernicanism – a theory that

* Scholars have noted that Copernicanism had not previously been condemned as a heresy, only as 'contrary to the scriptures'.

Contemplatio
Attollite in sublime oculos vestros, et videte quis creaverit ista. Esai. 40
IOHANNIS HEVELII,
SELENOGRAPHIA:
sive,
LVNÆ DESCRIPTIO;
tam macularum,
quàm motuum diversorum,
aliarumq omnium vicissitudinum,
phasiumq Lunarium,
telescopii ope,
deprehensarum,
delineatione accuratâ,
atq locupleti,
rerum Coelestium,
auctario exornata:
prodiit,
GEDANI.
Anno à Christo nato, 1647.
Autoris sumtibus,
Typis Hünefeldianis.
ALHASEN
RATIONE.
GALILÆUS.
SENSU.
Adolf Boÿ delineav.
J. Falck Polonus sculps.

had hitherto ruffled relatively few orthodox feathers – in a deeply provocative way. This was imprudent, to say the least, especially since it was never clear which new ideas might arouse suspicion of heresy. In areas where new research did not conflict with established teachings, on the other hand, the church did not intervene. The Jesuits, for instance, carried out important new work in natural history and mathematics without official censure.

As long as he did not express what were now heretical views, Galileo's writing career was not yet over. His *Dialogue of the Two New Sciences* (1638) went back to another important area of his research, mechanics.[11] Once again Salviati, Sagredo and Simplicio are the central characters. Their discussion takes place in the docks in Venice where there are beams, suction pumps and ropes to experiment with. The *Dialogue* is structured around four days of discussion, each of which centres on a different area of the two 'new sciences' (the latter being respectively the strength of materials and the motion of objects). The three men, who represent Galileo at different stages of his life, debate various questions to which Galileo wishes to find answers. They compare the resistance to tension of different materials, depending on where pressure is placed, and the points at which they fracture. Salviati, who seems to represent Galileo's latest thinking, dwells on the 'strength of hollow solids... which are employed... for the purpose of greatly increasing

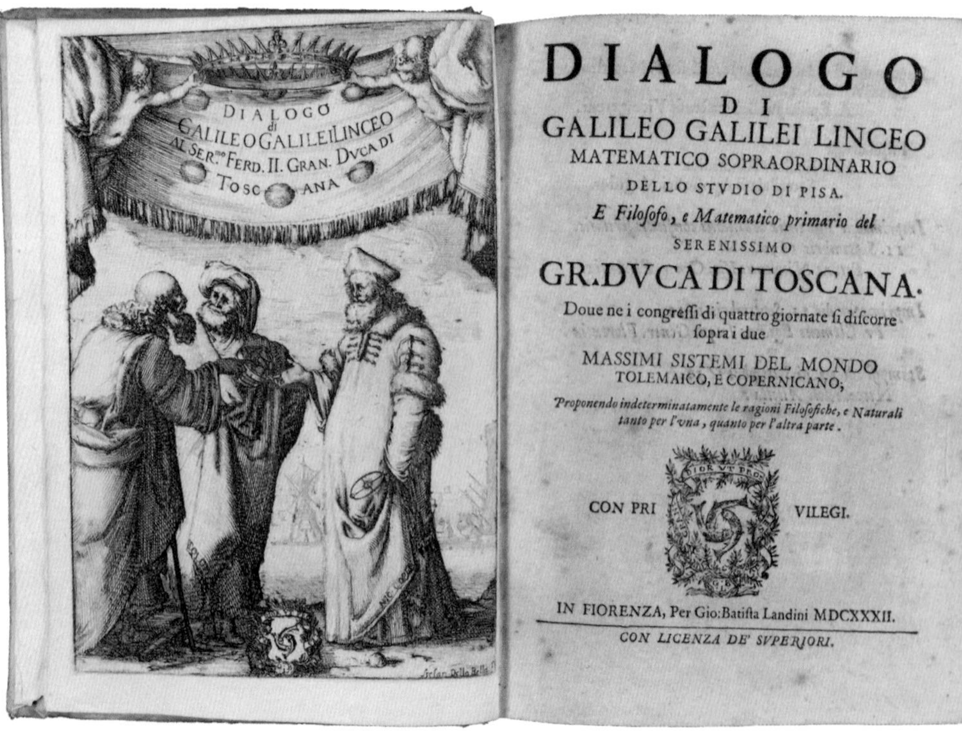

DIALOGO
DI GALILEO GALILEI LINCEO
AL SER.mo FERD. II. GRAN. DVCA DI
TOSCANA

DIALOGO
DI
GALILEO GALILEI LINCEO
MATEMATICO SOPRAORDINARIO
DELLO STVDIO DI PISA.
E Filosofo, e Matematico primario del
SERENISSIMO
GR. DVCA DI TOSCANA.
Doue ne i congressi di quattro giornate si discorre
sopra i due
MASSIMI SISTEMI DEL MONDO
TOLEMAICO, E COPERNICANO;
Proponendo indeterminatamente le ragioni Filosofiche, e Naturali
tanto per l'vna, quanto per l'altra parte.

CON PRI VILEGI.

IN FIORENZA, Per Gio: Batista Landini MDCXXXII.
CON LICENZA DE' SVPERIORI.

Galileo's *Dialogue Concerning the Two Chief World Systems*, first printed in 1632, was primarily an exploration of Copernicus's system against Aristotelian and Ptolemaic alternatives. Linking the figure of the traditionalist Simplicio to the views of Pope Urban VIII guaranteed trouble at the Vatican.

strength without adding to weight; examples of these are seen in the bones of birds and in many kinds of reeds which are light and highly resistant both to bending and breaking'. In experiments involving the dropping of weights Galileo (using Salviati to express his views) had shown that weights fall at the same velocity however heavy they were, but he also had to recognize that there was some resistance from the air (which explained why a feather would float downwards). On the third day, Salviati goes on to consider how velocity increases with the time elapsed after an object has been dropped and how gravity affects a metal ball rolling down a slope. What matters for the velocity of the ball, he discovers, is the height from which the descent begins, not the steepness of the slope. (Lurking behind these observations of the movement of bodies is a problem that Copernicus – and Nicolas Oresme before him – had identified: how the Earth could rotate on its axis without any apparent disturbance to the material objects upon it.) Galileo was able to show that all movement required an external force to break up the stationary relationship between objects that existed despite the rotation. Exploring the problem of impetus, one in which he may have been influenced by the medieval philosophers (although the evidence is elusive), he explained how the twin forces of air resistance and gravity brought a moving object down to the ground. If these forces had not been present it would have continued forever.

The Dialogue of the Two New Sciences also describes experiments using pendulums, in which their speed of movement is measured in relation to their length. Provided the pendulum was heavy enough to overcome any resistance from the air, its speed could be calculated. Galileo had long been fascinated by pendulums and by 1637 he had recognized that the period of swing of a pendulum is approximately the same for different sized swings. This discovery opened the way for the invention of the pendulum clock by the Dutchman Christiaan Huygens (1629–95) in 1656. Huygens's long-term intention was to use his work on the pendulum as the basis for the invention of a viable marine chronometer, but in trials at sea his models were rendered useless by the rocking of the ship in bad weather. Nevertheless, the accuracy of timekeeping on land was improved from a variance of fifteen minutes a day to just fifteen seconds.

In the *Dialogue*, Galileo had demonstrated something of critical importance for the future of science and technology: practical experiments spawned fundamental laws that could take the science of mechanics in directions that made possible the invention of new devices – such as the clock. As Sagredo puts it in the *Dialogue*: 'When these demonstrations have passed into the hands of others of a speculative turn of mind, they will become the path to many others, still more marvellous.'[12] Thus was possibility of a scientific revolution recognized, and the authority of ancient authors further diminished.

The manuscript of the *Dialogue* would be first printed not in Venice or Paris, but in the Protestant Dutch Republic, in the university city of Leiden. Galileo's condemnation by the Inquisition had made him a hero-martyr among Protestants. In his declining years he received visits from the radical English poet John Milton and the philosopher Thomas Hobbes, and his genius was universally recognized. He had shown the vital importance of experimentation and had played a crucial part in establishing a mechanical philosophy that explained the relationship between objects as if they were part of a machine, one part acting in conjunction with another. This was a dramatic rejection of the Aristotelian view that objects had forces within themselves (see p. 229). It went hand in hand with a return to the Atomists, the philosophers such as Democritus (*c.*460–370 BC), Epicurus (341–270 BC) and Lucretius, who had seen the world as made up of indivisible atoms.

René Descartes (1596–1650) is known primarily as a philosopher and will be explored as such in Chapter 31. He is also an important figure in the development of mechanical philosophy even if his views were soon shown to be untenable. The foundation of his approach was that if one started with simple principles or axioms, one could reason from there, just as Euclid had done for mathematics in his *Elements*. Descartes started with the axiom that there was no such thing as a void (a view that had been inherited from Aristotle). This proposition was in fact invalid, as voids do exist, but it was fundamental to Descartes's conception of a universe made up of particles that filled every space. Nothing could move unless through direct contact with another particle. In this Descartes rejected the idea of the existence of invisible forces that caused objects to be attracted or repelled by others. Rather than there being one enormous undifferentiated space, the particles accumulated in vortices, a circulation of flow such as in a whirlpool. Larger particles form denser objects such as planets and these swim around in their own vortex, bumping up against the swirl of smaller particles and thus retaining their motion. Some lesser planets were swept into the vortices of larger ones, as happens with moons orbiting planets or planets moving around the sun. Once God had set the universe in motion, he conserved that motion from one moment to the next. This thinking was all highly speculative but it proved influential. Descartes appeared to have married physics with mechanics and so had implanted the idea that the world was a machine whose every element was in some way in contact with the others. He even suggested that animals were no more than machines, so rejecting Aristotle's idea that they had souls of some sort. (How human beings fitted into this apparently godless universe will be discussed on pp. 702–8.) Not surprisingly, Descartes's materialist philosophy aroused Catholic outrage and his works were placed on the Index in 1663. His science of the vortices would later be demolished by Robert Hooke and Isaac Newton.

If the universe was now seen as a perfectly operating machine, the concept of God as its creator and engineer had to be recalibrated. This in turn encouraged new methods of exploring that machine on the assumption that it worked smoothly. The question remained as to whether there were forces *within* the material world, a view rejected in Descartes's mechanical philosophy. The French priest and philosopher Pierre Gassendi (1592–1655), for instance, attempted a marriage between Epicurus' atomism and Christianity by supposing that atoms held within them some vital force, placed there by God. 'Through the force which is continually received from the Author from the beginning, they [atoms] give motion to all things.'[13] Gassendi suggested that atoms might 'disentangle themselves, free themselves, leap away, knock against other atoms, turn them away, move away from them, and similarly [they have] the capacity to take hold of each other, to attach themselves to each other, to join together, to bind each other fast.'[14] It was, of course, impossible to assess this empirically as atoms could not yet be seen. Gassendi had to argue from reason and classical sources other than Epicurus that certain atoms must have some natural impulse that allowed them to move or initiate new life from seeds. So, he argued, God *could* act creatively within what was essentially a mechanistic universe.

From the vantage point of the twenty-first century, these all seem important developments that underlie the emergence of modern science. For the seventeenth-century observer, however, they were often disturbing in the way they challenged conventional ways of thinking. As the French mathematician Blaise Pascal (1623–62) put it:

> When I consider the short duration of my life, swallowed up in the eternity before and after, the little space which I fill, and even can see, engulfed in the infinite immensity of spaces of which I am ignorant, and which knows me not, I am frightened... The eternal silence of these infinite spaces frightens me.[15]

Was There an English Scientific Revolution?

To throw some light on the question, whether the cooling of a body results from the entry of some kind of special atoms of cold, just as it is believed that it is heated by atoms of fire, we had two equal glass flasks made, with their necks drawn out extremely fine. These were sealed with the flame and we placed one in ice and the other in hot water, where we let them stand for some time. Then, breaking the neck of each under water, we observed that a superabundance of matter had penetrated the hot one, blowing vigorously out of the flask… it seemed to some of us that the same thing should have occurred when the cold one was opened, should the cooling of the air in it have proceeded in the same way… But it turned out quite the other way.

Saggi of the Accademia del Cimento, 1667, published as *Essayes of Natural Experiments*, 1684[1]

In the frontispiece to Thomas Sprat's *History of the Royal Society* (1667), two figures are shown beside a bust of Charles II, the monarch who gave the society his patronage. One is the society's first president, Viscount Brouncker; the other is Francis Bacon, who had died forty years earlier. His books are among those displayed in the image alongside those of Copernicus and William Harvey (1578–1657), the first man to describe the circulation of the blood. Measuring instruments hang from the walls and columns. It is a fitting illustration of a new scientific age.

Francis Bacon (1561–1626) was an intellectual hero for this new group of scholars, who had formed what was the first English learned society totally dedicated to science.* The second son of a second marriage whose father died young, he had to make his own way. While it helped that Bacon's father had been Lord Keeper of the Seal and his uncle Lord Burghley, the great councillor of Elizabeth, Bacon's intellect ensured him a successful early career in the law, and he also became a Member of Parliament at the age of just twenty. However, his plain speaking offended Queen Elizabeth and he languished until her successor James I recognized his talents and promoted him. Bacon finally reached the top of the legal hierarchy as Lord Chancellor in 1618. Membership of the House of Lords followed, as Baron Verulam in 1618 and Viscount St Albans in 1621. He was at the centre of political and legal affairs, enormously industrious and with the ability to see to the heart of an issue and express it clearly in his voluminous writings. His *Essays* covered an astonishing array of subjects, and were beautifully expressed in Bacon's cultivated prose. There are still some who persist in believing that Bacon also crammed the writing of Shakespeare's plays into this busy life. In 1621, however, his career ended in public disgrace. He had accepted gifts of money from two men whose case was before his court; this was within the parameters of the customs of the age, and not decisive proof of corruption on Bacon's part, but in the febrile atmosphere of Jacobean politics, his enemies pounced. His fall was complete: he was thrown out of Parliament, landed with an enormous fine (later waived) and banned from court. But his exclusion from public life allowed him to devote the remaining years of his life – from

The frontispiece to Thomas Sprat's *History of the Royal Society* (1667). Formed by followers of Francis Bacon (shown on the right) to promote discussion of the physical sciences, the Society received its charter from Charles II in 1662.

* The Accademia dei Lincei (founded in Rome in 1603) and the Accademia del Cimento (founded in Florence in 1657) can claim European precedence.

NVLLIVS IN VERBA
CAROLVS II. SOCIETATIS REGALIS AVTHOR & PATRONVS
SOCIETATIS PRÆSES
Ld. Brouncker
K. Cha. 2d.
ARTIVM INSTAVRATOR
Ld. Bacon

Sr. Francis. Bacon, Lord
Keeper and afterwards
Lord Chancellor of
England, 1617

1621 until his death in 1626 – to his passion, the philosophy of science.

Bacon was never an active scientist. He seems to have had little detailed knowledge of the great works of his contemporaries, Gilbert on magnets, Copernicus on the solar system and Galileo. In an age when knowledge was increasingly being expressed in mathematical terms, his mathematics was weak. What he achieved was a synthesis of earlier work on experimentation, notably the work of the English astronomer and practitioner of occult studies Dr John Dee (1527–1608), who had shown how mathematics could be applied to practical skills including surveying and navigation, and continental philosophers such as the Calabrian Bernardino Telesio (1509–88) who wanted to break out of the straitjacket of traditional Aristotelianism and rediscover the Greek philosopher's empiricism, which had been submerged by scholasticism.

In his first major work on science, *The Advancement of Learning* (1605), Bacon rejected the narrowness of Aristotelian scholarship on the grounds that it would never be able to generate new knowledge. It was too heavily based on deductive logic: that is, it started with first principles and worked from there. Euclid had followed this method in his *Elements* but, however valid the reasoning, one could never progress beyond was contained in the original principles. Bacon put it succinctly: 'The sciences we now have are no more than elegant arrangements of things previously discovered, not methods of discovery or pointers to new results.'[2] He went on to provide an appropriate analogy. A spider makes a web from material within its own stomach; that material may now appear in the form of a web, but there is nothing in the web that was not there before. The original material has simply been rearranged. Bees, on the other hand, go out and about collecting pollen from plants and flowers and then return to their hives to create something new – nutritional honey. This is the model for Baconian science. Bacon favoured the view of nature of the Greek Atomists Democritus and Epicurus over Aristotle's. This left him to speculate – like other natural philosophers of the period – whether particles might be endowed with some form of internal spirit that animated living things.

The polymath Francis Bacon (1561–1626), championed an empirical approach to scientific discovery, which was taken up some three decades after his death by the Royal Society.

Fundamental to the Baconian method was the systematic collection of material. In the world around him he saw new discoveries and inventions: the New World took pride of place, of course, but there were also technological innovations such as the printing press and – from an earlier period – gunpowder. None of these had come about through working from first principles; they were brought into being in the practical world, by hands-on artisans and explorers. What was actually discovered was often the result of chance. If Columbus had never hit landfall in the western Atlantic, America might have remained unknown to Europeans for much longer. For Bacon, 'the true and legitimate goal of the sciences is to endow human life with new discoveries and resources', and, in order to attain this goal, an effective methodology was essential.

Bacon worked at his philosophy of science over decades. His last major project, *The Great Instauration* (*The Great Renewal*, reflecting the belief that humanity could recover the knowledge lost at the Fall), remained unfinished. Bacon planned it as six books, echoing the six days of Creation. His ideas have consistency over time. The first book of *The Great Instauration* – Partitions of the Sciences – (1620), for instance, was an enlarged edition of his *The Advancement of Learning* of 1605. The second book, the *Novum Organon* (*Novum*, 'new', as opposed to the 'old' *Organon* of Aristotle), contains the most detailed elaboration of his scientific method. Central to his work, and perhaps Bacon's most lasting achievement, was the idea of continuous progress in knowledge, leading to as yet unrealized possibilities of a better world over which the enlightened knower (and, Bacon believed, the state) would exercise power. This was a decisive break with the immutable nature of the universe as conceived by Aristotle. Having rejected scholasticism, Bacon also moved beyond the humanist preoccupation with historical and literary texts: 'They [the humanists] hunt more after words than matter.' It was natural philosophy that should take precedence. There had been two earlier revolutions in learning, the first among the Greeks, the second during the era of the Roman empire, and now the third: 'the renewal' of his own time. This optimistic view – of the potential of increased human knowledge to facilitate progress in the social, scientific and technological spheres – would greatly enhance Bacon's later popularity.

Francis Bacon's *Novum Organum* was read widely across Europe. The frontispiece of the 1645 edition displays the tag line *Multi pertransibunt et augebitur scientia* ('Many will travel and knowledge will increase').

Yet Bacon was acutely aware of the difficulties in seeking new knowledge. He noted that some had a psychological need to show off their learning, while others could become bogged down in the minutiae of their subject. In the *Novum Organon*, Bacon elaborates on what he calls the 'idols', the hindrances that come between the mind and reality. The senses, he says, are always unreliable: we can be led astray by information that conforms with what we already believe and we can

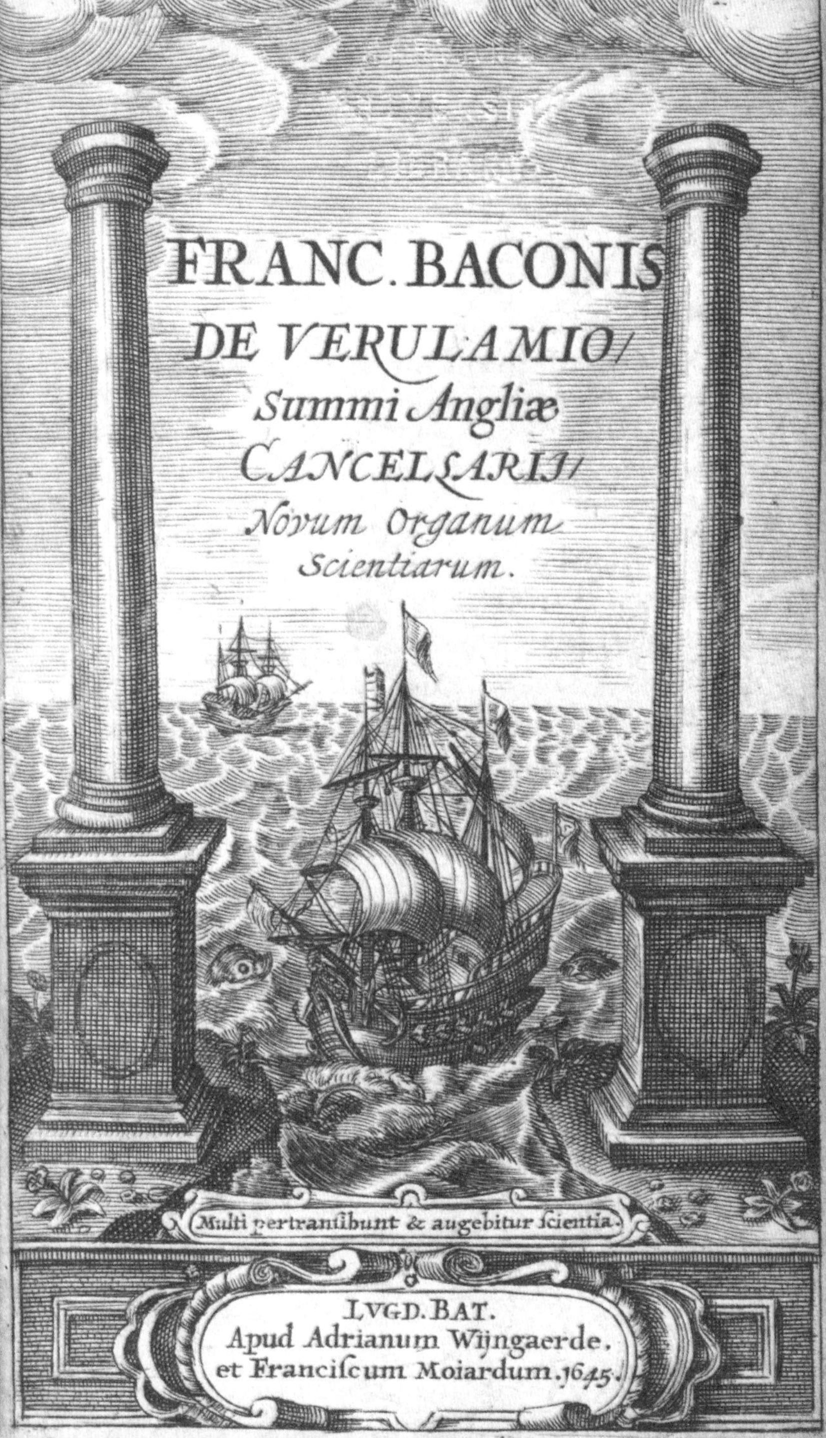
FRANC. BACONIS
DE VERULAMIO,
Summi Angliæ
CANCELLARII,
Novum Organum
Scientiarum.
Multi pertransibunt & augebitur scientia.
LVGD. BAT.
Apud Adrianum Wijngaerde.
et Franciscum Moiardum. 1645.

easily be swayed by the opinions of the marketplace. It is important to separate scientific knowledge from theological belief, which is based on textual authority rather than material evidence. Ultimately, however, there was a place for God in Bacon's system: certain knowledge could be found in 'the true signatures and marks set upon the works of [divine] creation as they are found in nature… all knowledge appeareth to be a plant of God's own planting'. The trick was to mend 'the cracked mirror' of the mind so as to distinguish what God had actually created from what were vain imaginings.

Bacon's chief aim, in outlining his method of inductive reasoning, was the eradication of sloppy thinking. He berates those who try to draw a circle without using a compass or a straight line without a ruler. To take an example that is not drawn from Bacon himself but follows his typical method of reasoning: we see some white swans in front of us and, on this basis, claim that all swans must be white. This, for Bacon, would not be good enough. We must broaden the body of evidence on which we are going to base our judgement; in other words, by trying to see as many swans as we can. It may be that in doing so we track down a single black swan, thereby undermining the validity of our original claim. Once sufficient material has been gathered to form the basis of a reasonable hypothesis, the hypothesis itself has to be tested. For Bacon, it was as important to find evidence to refute it as it was to find evidence to confirm it. This was one of Bacon's most important contributions to scientific method.* His approach is close to that of the fact-finding community Tycho Brahe established in the Uraniborg, but it lacks the imaginative leaps of a Copernicus or Galileo. Bacon also never considered the possibility of using mathematics to create a model that could then be tested. The material that he gathered tended to come from the natural sciences – physics, chemistry and biology.

One drawback of the Baconian method was that while it took only one contrary instance to destroy a hypothesis, it was not clear how *many* swans one had to see before one could say for certain that 'all swans are white'. One could spend one's whole life recording vast numbers of white swans – whose incidence appeared to make the whiteness of *all* swans a racing certainty – but never come across a species of black swans because they dwelt only in a far-off country, such as Australia, in this case. Surely there has to be a moment at which one judges it reasonable to suppose that a particular conclusion is valid. Isaac Newton was to sum up the issue pragmatically in his *Opticks*:

---

* Bacon can be seen as a forerunner of the philosopher Karl Popper (1902–94), who elaborated much the same approach.

> Although the arguing from Experience and Observation by Induction be no Demonstration of General Conclusions; yet it is the best way of arguing which the Nature of Things admits of, and may be looked upon as so much the stronger by how much the Induction is more general. And if no Exception occur from Phenomena, the Conclusion may be pronounced generally.[3]

According to the *Brief Lives* of John Aubrey, Bacon died a death appropriate to a man who rejoiced in the empirical testing of a hypothesis: he caught cold after stuffing a chicken with snow, in an attempt to discover whether snow would preserve meat. He left a utopian novel, *New Atlantis*, which was published the following year (1627). A crew of Europeans adrift in the Pacific finally come across an island – Bensalem, in the language of its inhabitants. Like Thomas More's Utopia, it is a benign and fruitful place 'free of all pollution and foulness', but its most important community is one of scientific researchers organized in Salomon's (Solomon's) House. The governor tells the narrator that their aim is to acquire 'knowledge of causes' and 'the secret motions of things' (a reminder of the seventeenth century's preoccupation with forces that could not be observed). Salomon's House has many of the characteristics of a sophisticated modern scientific research facility. Its teams of trained scientists collect data and conduct experiments. In the words of the 'Father of Salomon's House':

> We have twelve that sail into foreign countries… who bring us the books, and abstracts, and patterns of experiments of all other parts… We have three that collect the experiments which are in all books… We have three that draw… experiments… into titles and tables, to give the better light for the drawing of observations and axioms out of them… We have three that bend themselves, looking into the experiments of their fellows, and cast about how to draw out of them things of use and practice for man's life.[4]

Two vital aspects of Bacon's work can be seen here: the building up of new knowledge through collaboration, and the central place given to the design and application of experiments. Here he made common cause with Galileo.

In the immediate aftermath of his death, Bacon was little read, but thirty years later he would be regarded as a hero, the instigator of a new intellectual era.[5] The diarist John Evelyn (1620–1706) wrote that Bacon was 'celebrated as far as knowledge has any empire… the learned rise up at his very name'. In the Netherlands there were forty-five printings of his works by 1700. The famous *Encyclopédie* conceived by Denis Diderot (twenty-eight volumes appeared between 1751 and 1772, with

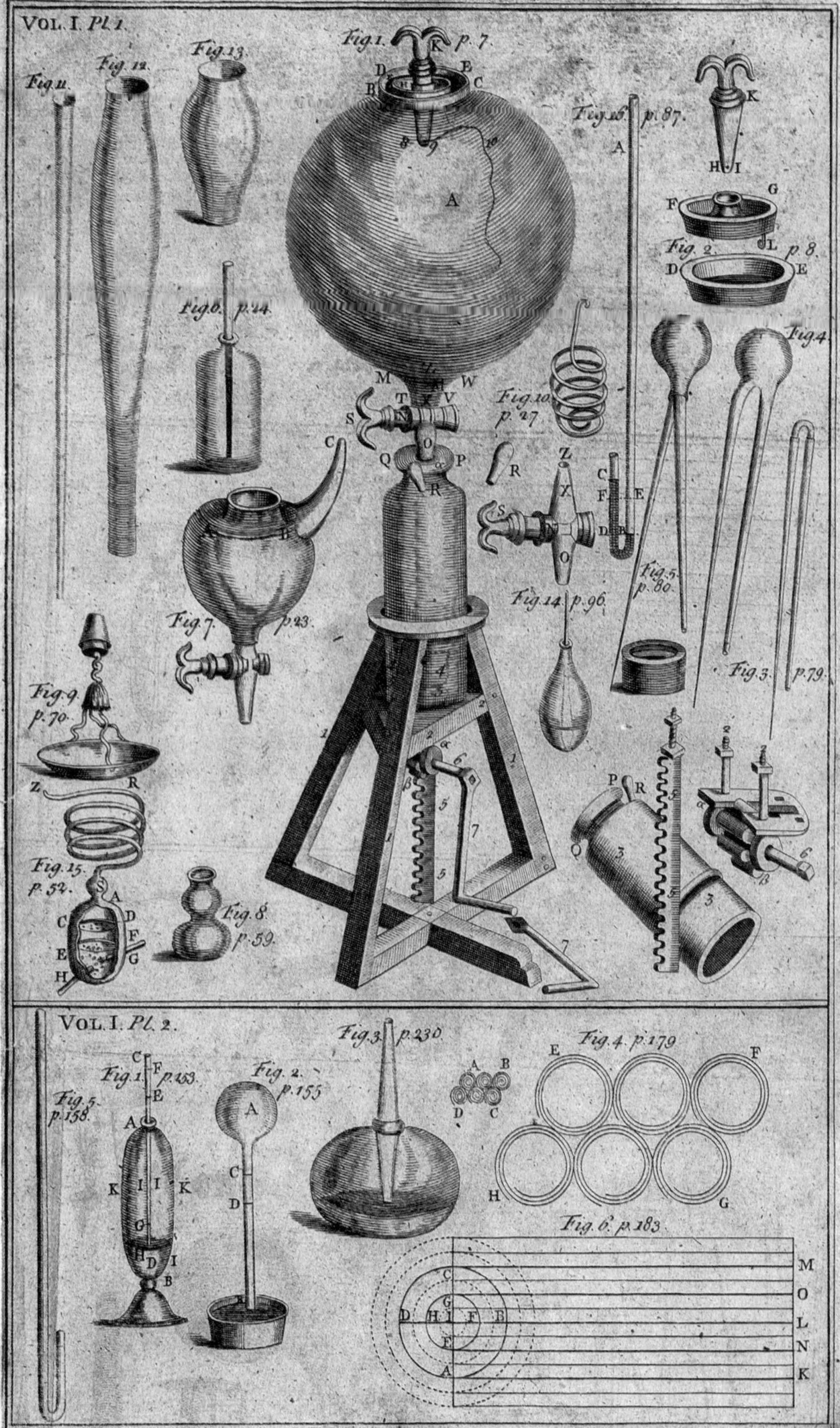

Vol. I. Pl. 1.
Fig. 1. p. 7
Fig. 2. p. 8
Fig. 3. p. 79
Fig. 4
Fig. 5 p. 80
Fig. 6. p. 24
Fig. 7. p. 23
Fig. 8. p. 59
Fig. 9. p. 70.
Fig. 10. p. 27
Fig. 11.
Fig. 12.
Fig. 13.
Fig. 14. p. 96.
Fig. 15. p. 52.
Fig. 16. p. 87.
Vol. I. Pl. 2.
Fig. 1. p. 153.
Fig. 2. p. 155
Fig. 3. p. 230
Fig. 4. p. 179
Fig. 5. p. 158.
Fig. 6. p. 183
J. Mynde f.

Diderot the prime contributor) was permeated with Baconism. As with any imaginative thinker, different readers took different insights from his work but he proved inspirational to all those who wished to join together to find new knowledge that could be used for the benefit of humanity. The Puritans warmed to him as they felt that greater knowledge of the natural world might allow them to refashion it according to the will of God (see p. 693).

The scientist who followed most immediately in Bacon's footsteps was Robert Boyle (1627–91).[6] Boyle was the fourteenth child of an Irish adventurer, Richard Boyle, who had risen through fair means and foul – including well placed bribes – to become earl of Cork in the reign of James I. In the 1640s, just as the English Civil War was about to break out, Robert was sent by his father to travel across Europe. It was said that his passion for science was aroused when he visited Florence and learned of the achievements of Galileo, whose works he read avidly. Eventually, he was able to set himself up with his own laboratory in Oxford and begin experimenting. He was well aware of Galileo's own practical experiments with weights but he was also inspired by Bacon's approach to collecting evidence through observation, although Boyle would always stress that he had made his own way free of mentors.

Robert Boyle's air pump, depicted in the 1662 edition of his *New Experiments Physico-Mechanicall.*

The experiment for which Boyle is best known involved pouring mercury into a closed J-shaped tube and watching how the air pocket at the end of the tube contracted under the pressure of the mercury. In a beautifully simple experiment he demonstrated that doubling the pressure of the mercury would halve the volume of the air. Thus did Boyle's Law – which states that the volume occupied by a gas is inversely proportional to the pressure placed on it – come into being. Boyle published his law in 1662, in the second edition of his *New Experiments Physico-Mechanicall, Touching the Spring of the Air and Its Effects*. Boyle conducted a number of other experiments with pressure, using an air pump made for him by his assistant Robert Hooke (see p. 687). They discovered that the lower the air pressure, the lower the temperature at which water would boil, and that a pump from which air was extracted would contract inwards. While Boyle did not discover oxygen himself, many of his experiments suggested that there was something in air that sustained life and kept flames alight. Another discovery of Boyle's was that sound required air in order to be transmitted. Boyle was, however, not the first scientist to work with an air pump or to experiment with mercury in a tube. The German inventor Otto von Guericke pioneered the air pump in the 1650s, while the Tuscan Evangelista Torricelli, a friend and student of Galileo, carried out experiments with mercury in a vacuum tube that would lead to his inventing the barometer in 1643, well before Boyle.

Although it was not at first appreciated, Boyle was at the forefront of attempts to understand the way in which substances were composed, what came to be known as 'chymistry', as opposed to physics, which dealt with substances in motion. His work *The Sceptical Chymist* (1661) argued for the separation of chemistry from alchemy (which relied heavily on occult knowledge rather than experiments). Boyle attacked Aristotle's theory of causes by which each substance was analysed in terms of its matter, form, efficient cause and final cause.* He was part of the movement that would replace these 'causes' by laws that explained how a universe that was essentially mechanistic worked. In his *Corpuscular Philosophy* (1666), he argued that all materials work only through 'the motion, size, figure and contrivance of their own parts [corpuscles]'. Everything would eventually be reduced, not to earth, water, fire and air as Aristotle had argued, or salt, sulphur and mercury as Paracelsus, the scourge of Galenic medicine, had claimed, but to 'corpuscles' (as Boyle called atoms). He suggested that there might be some 'primitive and simple or perfectly unmingled bodies', in other words what we now call elements, although these would not be defined as such until the nineteenth century.

Evangelista Torricelli demonstrates the experiments that led to the invention of the barometer, 1643.

While alchemy had received a bad press for its search to find gold from a remixing of metals and the use of a 'philosopher's stone', Boyle still believed that transmutation was possible, although he showed that gold was so dense that lighter metals would never be able to create it. Transmutation was not as speculative as it seemed. Anyone casting a metal object would have known that the addition of tin to copper lowered its melting and solidifying points dramatically and created a much more tensile material, bronze. By analysing the ways in which substances might be composed, either through compound mixtures where the individual components lost their identity in the mix, or in mixtures where each component retained its separate identity, Boyle's work has led to him being called 'the father of chemistry'. Alchemy, with its reliance on

* Thus a statue might be made of bronze (its 'matter'); its 'form' conceived by the sculptor who then created it ('the efficient cause'); 'the final cause' was the finished statue itself.

Iconismus X. pag. 185.

ancient Hermetic texts and secret processes, was effectively dead by the early eighteenth century.*

Boyle was a prolific writer, able to express himself clearly and so attract a wide audience. He was also a devout Anglican. As well as many scientific works his output included theological treatises in which he explored the relationship between religion and the new sciences, of which he was a pioneering practitioner. He was a founding member of the Royal Society of London for Improving Natural Knowledge, which held its inaugural meeting in 1660 and was given royal

* The impenetrable nature of the Hermetic texts is preserved in the phrase 'hermetically sealed'.

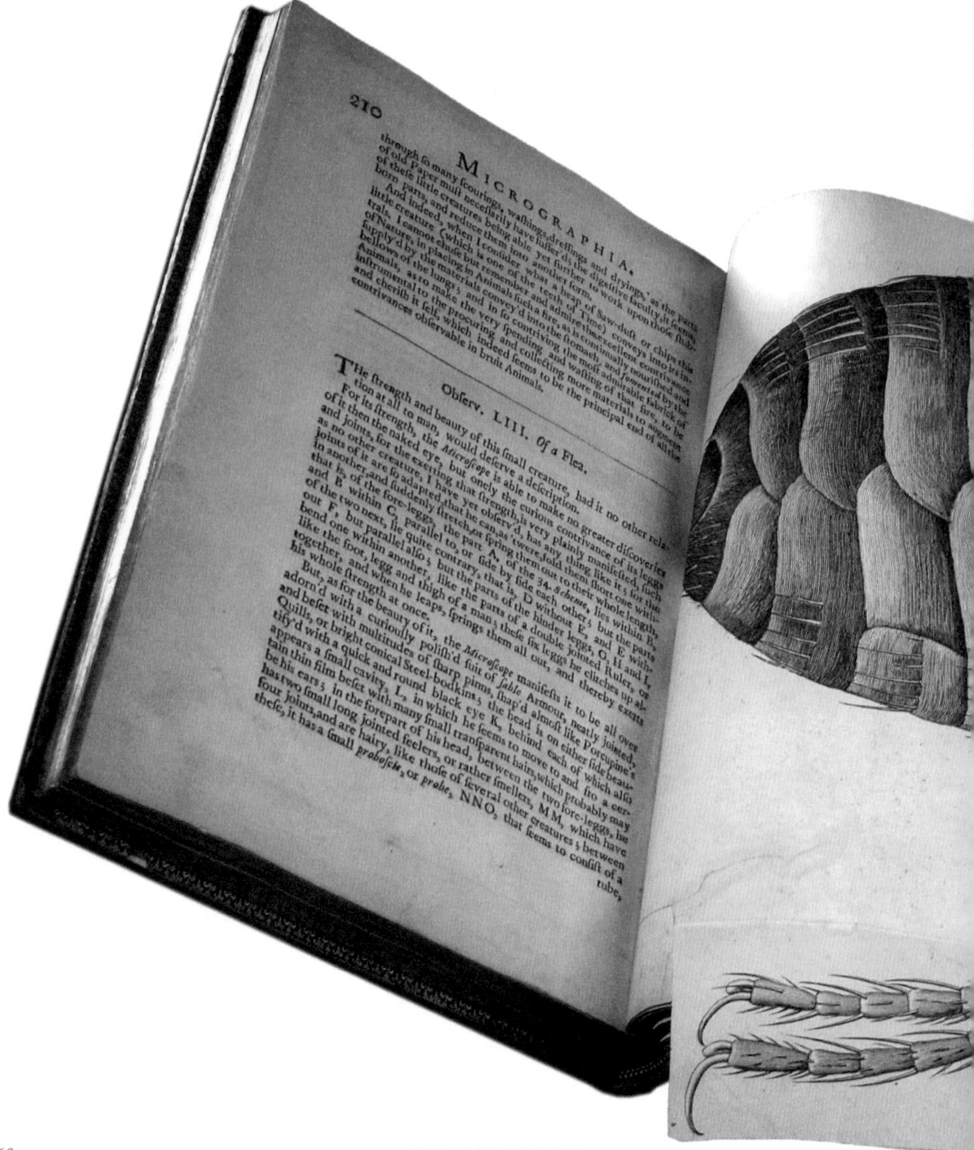

210

MICROGRAPHIA.

through so many scourings, washings, dressings and dryings, as the parts of old Paper must necessarily have suffer'd; the digestive faculty, it seems, of these little creatures being able yet further to work upon those stubborn parts, and reduce them into another form.

And indeed, when I consider what a heap of Saw-dust or chips this little creature (which is one of the teeth of Time) conveys into its intrals, I cannot chuse but remember and admire the excellent contrivance of Nature, in placing in Animals such a fire, as is continually nourished and supply'd by the materials convey'd into the stomach, and *fomented* by the bellows of the lungs; and in so contriving the most admirable fabrick of Animals, as to make the very spending and wasting of that fire, to be instrumental to the procuring and collecting more materials to augment and cherish it self, which indeed seems to be the principal end of all the contrivances observable in bruit Animals.

Observ. LIII. *Of a Flea.*

THe strength and beauty of this small creature, had it no other relation at all to man, would deserve a description.

For its strength, the *Microscope* is able to make no greater discoveries of it then the naked eye, but onely the curious contrivance of its leggs and joints, for the exerting that strength, is very plainly manifested, such as no other creature, I have yet observ'd, has any thing like it; for the joints of it are so adapted, that he can, as 'twere, fold them short one within another, and suddenly stretch, or spring them out to their whole length, that is, of the fore-leggs, the part A, of the 34. *Scheme*, lies within B, and B within C, parallel to, or side by side each other; but the parts of the two next, lie quite contrary, that is, D without E, and E without F, but parallel also; but the parts of the hinder leggs, G, H and I, bend one within another, like the parts of a double jointed Ruler, or like the foot, legg and thigh of a man; these six leggs he clitches up altogether, and when he leaps, springs them all out, and thereby exerts his whole strength at once.

But, as for the beauty of it, the *Microscope* manifests it to be all over adorn'd with a curiously polish'd suit of *sable* Armour, neatly jointed, and beset with multitudes of sharp pinns, shap'd almost like Porcupine's Quills, or bright conical Steel-bodkins; the head is on either side beautify'd with a quick and round black eye K, behind each of which also appears a small cavity, L, in which he seems to move to and fro a certain thin film beset with many small transparent hairs, which probably may be his ears; in the forepart of his head, between the two fore-leggs, he has two small long jointed feelers, or rather smellers, MM, which have four joints, and are hairy, like those of several other creatures; between these, it has a small *proboscis*, or *probe*, NNO, that seems to consist of a tube, patronage for the first time in 1662.[7] The Royal Society was financed by its own members, who actively recruited those whom it considered eminent in its fields of interest, as it still does today. In contrast to the established universities, it banned religious and political discussion and dogmatism of any kind and this is why Baconian science proved so attractive to it. The members had to provide experimental results rather than theories. In his *Invention of Science* David Wootton traces the first use of the term 'hypothesis', in its present sense as an idea that needs confirmation or rejection, to the early years of the society.[8] Fellows such as Boyle, who was courteous and modest in the extreme about his abilities, helped create an air of civilized discourse. In his *History*, Thomas Sprat told of the 'satisfaction of breathing a freer air,

Robert Hooke's *Micrographia* (1665), with its fine illustrations, opened up a new world to its many readers. The diarist Samuel Pepys was among those who were spellbound.

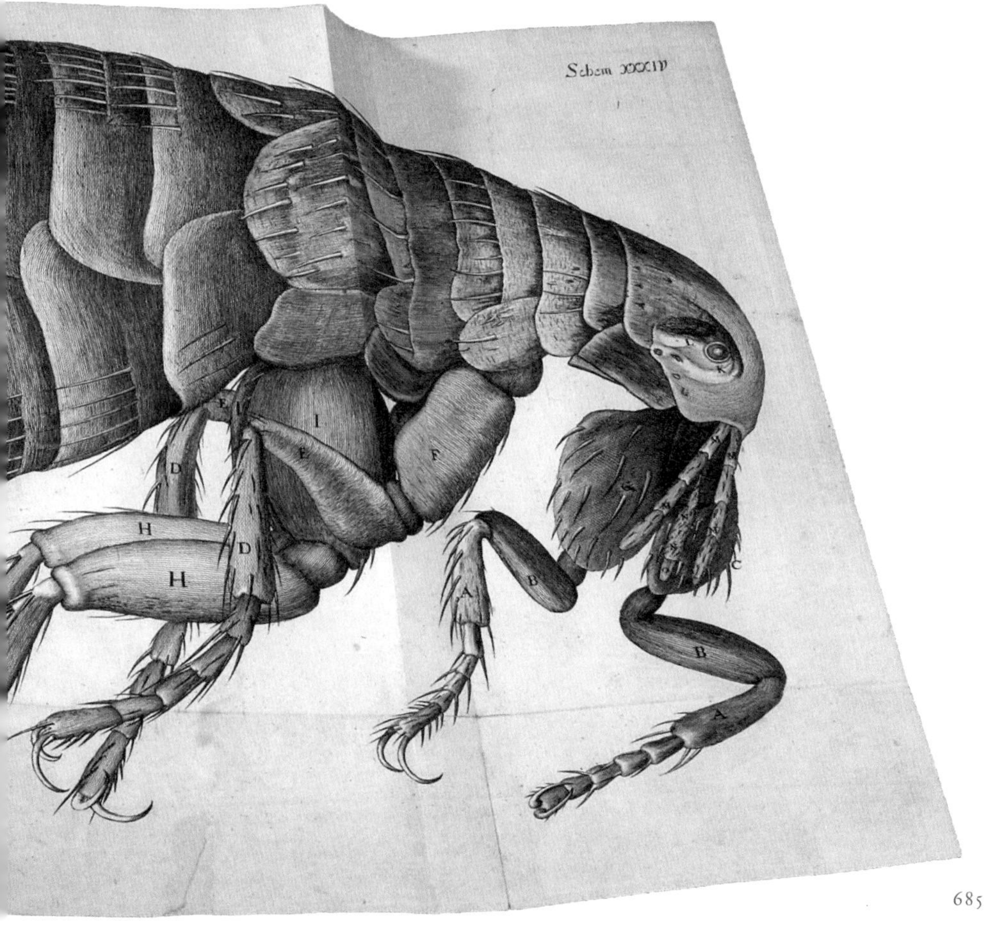

and of conversation in quiet one with another, without being ingage'd in the passions and madness of that dismal age'. By 1666 Louis XIV (at the suggestion of his minister of finances Jean-Baptiste Colbert) had followed the example of Charles II and founded the *Académie Royale des Sciences* in Paris where Christiaan Huygens (see p. 667) became the leading figure. While its members were limited in number and graded in a hierarchy, its aims were very similar to those of the Royal Society: to work collectively to improve the welfare of the nation through the promulgation of scientific knowledge. Jesuits were banned from membership in order to keep the *Académie* free of religious influence.

The Royal Society needed administrators, a secretary and a curator of experiments to oversee and report on any experiments that were carried out. Robert Boyle put forward his assistant Robert Hooke (1635–1703), the son of an Isle of Wight clergyman, as the curator. Hooke had been lucky to survive childhood illness and was described by a contemporary as 'somewhat crooked' but he was well enough to live a life of formidable scientific activity.[9] Even as a child he was fascinated by practical experiments and making things, even a chronometer, for himself. It was while he was at Christ Church, Oxford (as a choral

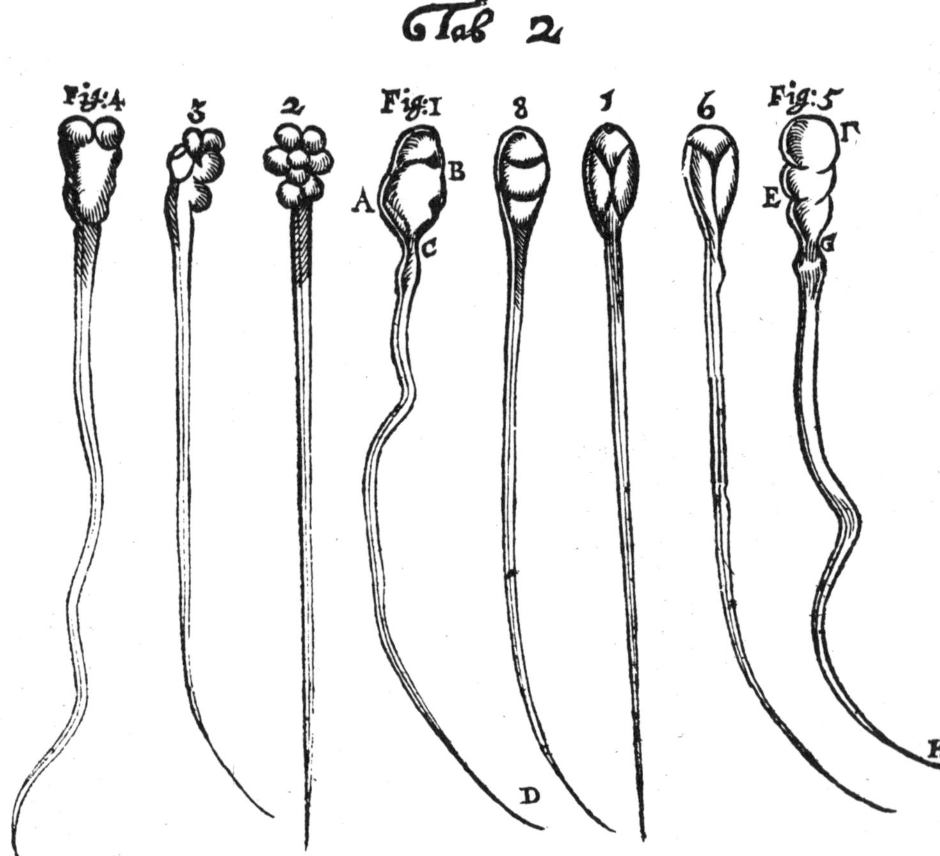

scholar), that he came into contact with the scientists of his day, including Boyle. He was formally elected a Fellow of the Royal Society in 1663. In 1665 he became professor of geometry at Gresham College in London, a post he held for the rest of his life. One of his best-known 'laws' describes how a stretched spring has a force of resistance in proportion to the extent to which it is stretched. He was always touchy about his achievements, not least because of his relatively humble background, which left him feeling socially isolated among the grandees who made up the fellowship.

Hooke's most influential work, his *Micrographia* (1665), brilliantly illustrated the findings of a microscope. Once the idea of the lens being used as a magnifier had been grasped, smaller objects could be seen in a way that had never been imagined. One pioneer, the Dutch Antonie van Leeuwenhoek (1632–1723), had even glimpsed spermatozoa for the first time, thus showing that males produced living organisms, or 'animalcules' as Leeuwenhoek called them, although the mysteries of conception and generation would remain unexplained for a while longer. *Micrographia*, with its precisely descriptive sub-title *Some Physiological Descriptions of Minute Bodies Made by Magnifying Glasses. With Observations and Inquiries Thereupon*, was beautifully produced and was found utterly absorbing by its readers. The diarist Samuel Pepys remarked in his diary entry of 21 January 1665: 'Before I went to bed I sat up till two o'clock in my chamber reading of Mr. Hooke's Microscopicall Observations, the most ingenious book that ever I read in my life.' Close-ups of sections of cork were described by Hooke as 'cells' (after those in a monastery), a name that stuck when the basic unit of all living organisms was identified in the nineteenth century. Hooke was prepared to offer his own interpretations of what he saw under the microscope: thus he suggested that fossils had once been living organisms, that the sea might once have covered the land, and that light was refracted through very thin layers of material such as the wing of an insect. Imaginative speculation such as this inspired others to make their own scientific investigations.

Drawings of the sperm of rabbits and dogs sent to the Royal Society by the Dutch scientist Antonie Van Leeuwenhoek. Van Leeuwenhoek's letters to the Society were published in 1678.

In the 1670s Hooke turned his attention to the motion of the planets. He rejected the Cartesian whirlpool, Descartes's conception of the material universe (see p. 668), in favour of positing a force that kept objects anchored to the surface of planets but also attracted other planets in some way. This force resulted in their moving in perpetual circles or ellipses when otherwise their motion would be in a straight line. By now well established and respected, Hooke was furious to find that a younger Cambridge intellectual, by the name of Isaac Newton (1642–1727), who had become the second Lucasian Professor of Mathematics in 1669, was challenging him on the refraction of light. In his *Micrographia,* Hooke had noted that rainbow colours appeared at the edge of transmitted white light but had not pursued his investigations further. He had also compared the spread of light to the movement of waves in water. In 1672 Newton presented a paper on optics to the Royal Society, in which he argued that light was made up of particles. He described how he had used a sophisticated method of prisms set up to transmit light over a longer distance. Newton demonstrated that white light could be separated into the seven distinct colours of the light spectrum, and that these colours could then be transmitted through another prism to become white light again. He had used his knowledge to develop a telescope that eliminated the way diffuse colours could obscure the edges of a telescope's vision. Newton was elected a Fellow of the Royal Society in 1672, nine years after Hooke.

Hooke disagreed with Newton's particle theory, and made his doubts about it all too clear, thereby sparking an acrimonious rivalry that would disturb the calm discussions that the Royal Society liked to think was its hallmark. Hooke eventually recognized that Newton had taken the study of optics further than he had, while Newton wrote uncharitably that he had gone further because he stood 'on the shoulders of Giants', a phrase that some have interpreted as a deliberate humiliation of the diminutive Hooke. Another bone of contention between the two men was planetary motion. In 1679 Hooke wrote to Newton describing his belief that gravity is dependent on an inverse-square law, which relationship might also govern the movement of the planets. Newton developed this idea further but without, in Hooke's opinion, crediting the latter sufficiently for his insights. He removed all mention of Hooke from the third volume of his *Principia Mathematica* (1686) and did not publish his major work on optics until 1704, a year after Hooke's death.

Newton's childhood, in Lincolnshire, was a solitary one, but he had a good education and started his career as a student at Trinity College, Cambridge, in 1661 under the patronage of a Fellow named Humphrey Babington.[10] It seems to have been a bleak beginning, partly because Newton was a preoccupied loner, obsessively guarding his ideas from his contemporaries. By 1663 he was starting to go his own way intellectually, adding his own reading of Descartes, Copernicus, Kepler and Galileo to the university's Aristotelian curriculum. By the second half of the

1660s, when he was still in his twenties, he was enormously productive: he discovered the generalized binomial theorem in 1665, the year he took his degree. It was not only mathematics and physics that absorbed him; he dabbled in alchemy and then spent years showing that the Trinity was a false doctrine that elevated the status of Jesus beyond any scriptural evidence. His Unitarian views would have disqualified him from public life if he had not kept them to himself.[11]

So far as his physics was concerned, apart from his work on optics, Newton became obsessed with the problem of gravity, although the truth of the story of his being inspired by an apple falling from a tree will never be known. What Newton realized, or absorbed from reading his contemporaries, is that the force of gravity decreases the further one is from the Earth. Crucially, the decrease could be defined precisely. One might assume that, if the force of gravity at sea level was x, doubling the distance from the centre of the Earth up into the sky would halve x, so one over two or half of the sea-level force. Instead, it fell as one over the *square* of the doubled distance, so not a half but a quarter. If one extended the height above the Earth one further unit of distance so as to make two units from sea level and three units of distance from the centre of the Earth, the force of gravity would be one over three squared, so a ninth of the original gravity at sea level. This is the so-called inverse-square law, which explains why there is weightlessness in space, since the force of gravity has been reduced to almost nothing. Yet the very same force caused a stone to fall to earth, finally destroying Aristotle's claim that the physics of the terrestrial and celestial world were distinct. Another force, the centrifugal force caused by the rotation of the Earth (or the sun or other planet), forced objects outwards. At sea level this would not matter as the force of gravity was many times the centrifugal force of the Earth's rotation, allowing objects to fall towards the Earth and stay where they fell. As one moved further from the Earth, however, there would be a moment when the weakened force of gravity would equal the centrifugal force, and an object held in this place would be caught in a perpetual circle or ellipse. Newton now faced the challenge of showing this mathematically. Thus it was that he developed calculus, the procedure by which, if one starts at a fixed point, one can calculate movements that vary as time passes, as with the position of a planet. He established that an elliptical orbit, as first observed by Kepler, was the only mathematically possible way for a planet to circle the sun.

The universe that Newton conceived could not have been more different from that of Descartes. Instead of a crammed universe with the vortices jostling up against each other, Newton painted a picture of a largely empty universe containing isolated planets. Each of these planets possessed forces that attracted one to the other. In Newton's universe, comets moved in towards the sun and then away from it in orbits whose periodicity could be predicted. The astronomer Edmond Halley (1656–1742), a contemporary of Newton, showed from earlier records – the latest being 1682 – that one such comet would reappear at seventy-five-year intervals, and that its next return would be in 1758. 'Halley's comet' did indeed return in that year, but Halley himself did not live to see the reappearance of the celestial body that would henceforth bear his name. Once the principle of mutual attraction was recognized, a large number of other phenomena became explicable. Forces from the moon (and the sun) pulled on sea water, causing the tides. One of the great observational achievements of the ancient world, the precession of the equinoxes of Hipparchus (working *c.*160–*c.*125 BC), which caused the Earth to wobble on its axis, could be explained by the pull of the moon and the sun on the Earth.

Newton brought his theories together in his great *Philosophiae Naturalis Principia Mathematica* of 1687, a work so mathematically dense that at first its author's achievement was not fully appreciated.* But it can now be seen as representing one of the great intellectual breakthroughs of world history, in the sense that it gave a full explanation of the workings of the universe in a way that could be verified mathematically. As John Gribbin, a contemporary historian of science, has put it, Newton:

The title page of the first edition of Isaac Newton's *Principia*, which relates gravity to the movement of the planets. Newton's magnum opus is seen by many as marking the coming of age of modern science.

> laid the foundations for the whole of physics, not only spelling out the implications of his inverse law of gravity and the three laws of motion, which describe the behaviour of everything in the Universe, but making it clear that the laws of physics are indeed *universal* laws that affect everything... The publication of the *Principia* marked the moment when science came of age as an intellectual discipline, putting aside most of the follies of its youth and settling down into grown-up investigation of the world.[12]

There were still uncertainties over where the forces of attraction originated. Newton could not tell, for instance, whether the closeness of one planet to another was caused by one planet having a greater force of attraction than the other, or by a force from a third planet pushing

* It was reported that 'the students at Cambridge said there goes the man who has writt a book that neither he nor anyone else understands'. Quoted in Guicciardini, *Newton*, p. 151.

PHILOSOPHIÆ NATURALIS PRINCIPIA MATHEMATICA.

Autore *JS. NEWTON*, *Trin. Coll. Cantab. Soc.* Matheseos Professore *Lucasiano*, & Societatis Regalis Sodali.

IMPRIMATUR.
S. PEPYS, *Reg. Soc.* PRÆSES.
Julii 5. 1686.

LONDINI,
Jussu *Societatis Regiæ* ac Typis *Josephi Streater*. Prostant Venales apud *Sam. Smith* ad insignia Principis *Walliæ* in Cœmiterio D. *Pauli*, aliosq; nonnullos Bibliopolas. *Anno* MDCLXXXVII.

one of the first two towards the other. The lack of an explanation for the ultimate origins of the forces of attraction was a point hammered to exhaustion by the great German mathematician-philosopher Gottfried Wilhelm Leibniz (1646–1716) (see p. 717). Leibniz had already been involved in a feud with Newton over who had been the first to discover calculus. The laurels for this achievement were Newton's, in fact, but he had not published his findings whereas Leibniz, having discovered calculus independently, and with a better system of notations, was the first in print. Now the two men argued over the role of God in moving the universe. Newton argued that he might well be needed to intervene to sort out irregularities, Leibniz that once started by a perfect God the universe would need no further intervention. As he put it in a letter criticizing the Newtonians: 'According to their [Newton and his followers] doctrine, God Almighty wants to wind up his watch from time to time: otherwise it would cease to move. He had not, it seems, sufficient foresight to make it a perpetual motion.'[13]

Despite their disagreements both Newton and Leibniz accepted the reality of God. Newton, who was president of the Royal Society from 1703 until his death in 1727, provided for 'an intelligent and powerful Being… eternal, infinite, absolutely perfect' in the second edition of *Principia* (1713). Yet the dispute shows how far the advance of science was forcing new conceptions of the deity.

* * *

The extent to which Christianity facilitated the birth of modern science has been the subject of vigorous debate. No serious response can be provided without deconstructing the terms of the original proposition to ask, on the one hand, 'Which Christianity?', and, on the other, 'Which of the myriad activities that might be described as science in the seventeenth century?' The relationship between two such disparate forces can hardly be neatly encapsulated in crude terms of cause and effect. The idea that there were coherent entities ('religion' and 'science') in conflict with each other was a construct of the nineteenth century. It is not a useful way of approaching the diversity of intellectual life in the seventeenth century. Yet some form of assessment must be made.

It goes without saying that Christianity's main interest lay in securing the salvation of the faithful, not in understanding the natural world. No biblical exhortation requires the study of nature, although Augustine had argued that such study should take place in order to foster a better understanding of the scriptures. Yet, whatever the denomination of the scientific enquirer, the concept of God had to fit in somewhere. Atheism was impossible in the climate of the seventeenth century so scientists were forced to define the Almighty in a way that fitted with findings that were increasingly focused on empirical research and experimentation. One response was Deism, the belief that God was some kind of ultimate power whose contact with the material world was minimal. This gave scientists a free hand to discover the workings of the world, but they risked reproach from orthodox Christians for masking their atheism. 'At this day Atheism is slyly called Deism by those that are indeed Atheists: they would disguise it by a false name and thereby hide the heinousness of it', as one English pamphleteer fulminated in 1695.[14]

Any relationship between religion and science was made more complicated by the way in which Christianity had become embedded in specific political and religious structures of authority, which make the direct influence of religion harder to discern. Were books banned because they contained science or for other, often political, reasons? In the name of the Catholic Church, the Inquisition and the Index of Prohibited Books condemned an extraordinary range of books and people, many of which were scientific but the vast majority of which were not. Which forms of scientific enquiry were banned and which allowed into the schools and universities became arbitrary. The *Essays* of Montaigne were banned on the grounds of his recognition that animals had feelings; other scientific works simply because their authors were Lutherans. In the Protestant world, any expression of atheism or lack of religious orthodoxy was more likely to be condemned than any work of science. Newton would have been driven from Cambridge University and banned from public office if his views on the Trinity had become known.

In 1938 the American sociologist Robert Merton published his *Science, Technology and Society in Seventeenth-Century England*.[15] He posited, somewhat cautiously, a link between English Puritanism and the rise of science. His thesis has more recently been explored by Joel Mokyr in his *Culture of Growth: The Origins of the Modern Economy* (2016).[16] Mokyr acknowledges that many Puritans were focused on the Bible and metaphysical issues rather than on science. He notes too that in other contexts, that of the Lutheran Pietists in Germany, for instance, Puritanism appears to have retarded rather than encouraged both scientific and economic progress. Francis Bacon himself was no Puritan, but Mokyr believes Bacon's methods may have spurred the English Puritans towards an ethic of hard work, and to making close observations of natural phenomenon, in the belief that greater understanding of the natural world would heighten their awareness of the glory of God: 'In their stress on empirics, admiration for mechanical knowledge, faith in experimental discoveries and devotion to education, they did a lot to raise the prestige of science.'[17] While Mokyr accepts that by the eighteenth century religion was losing its power as a force for scientific and technological progress, in the seventeenth-century context he gives qualified support for a link – via Bacon – between Puritanism and the promotion of an ideology that economic and technological progress was concomitant with God's will. This did not mean, however, that it took precedence. The first three years of the curriculum at Harvard University (founded 1636) were devoted to Hebrew, Greek and Latin with the aim of fully understanding the scriptures. Most of Harvard's early alumni become ministers and their training was the university's academic priority.*

In defence of the contribution of religion to scientific inquiry one could also invoke the words of the Reformation theologian Philipp Melanchthon: 'In accordance with God's will we may trace His footprints in this world by studying the sciences.' This is not far from Francis Bacon's view a century later – that to closely investigate the world is to try to discern the fundamentals of divine creation. A book by the English parson-naturalist John Ray (1627–1705), *The Wisdom of God Manifested in the Works of the Creation*, first published in 1691, quickly went through eleven editions. Of course, the 'footprints' might equally be those of the Islamic or Jewish god, as both those religions have also produced many great scientists. It is hard, therefore, to argue that Christianity, rather than its monotheistic relations, provided a particular impetus for scientific discovery. At the time of the Scientific Revolution of the seventeenth century, wider cultural influences were in play, just as they had been for the Arab scientists of the early medieval period and for the Greeks in the classical world. The achievements of the Greeks in understanding and measuring the natural world and in creating academic disciplines devoted to its investigation were prodigious in scope, and show that there was no necessary correlation between Christianity and 'scientific' curiosity. For Europeans it seems clear that the discovery of the Americas and its peoples was a decisive causative factor for the emergence of a belief that knowledge, whether

* The nine men who passed the first examination in 1642 were able to progress to a fourth year that included logic, natural and moral philosophy, arithmetic, geometry and astronomy. For the transfer of learning to New England, see Rée, *Witcraft*, pp. 63–8.

derived from theological or classical sources, was not set in stone.†

While it is instructive to identify those early scientists who were prompted by their Christian faith to study the natural world, there were also those whose enthusiasm sprang from sheer curiosity. As Aristotle had acknowledged, 'man is naturally curious', and it is important not to underestimate this impulse. In this chapter we have looked at a number of outstanding minds who were attracted to study the natural world for a variety of reasons, many of them beyond psychological or historical recovery. The evidence that Christianity was the common motivating force is elusive. The intellectual and emotional impact of the discovery of the New World or simple wonder at the night sky appears to have been as much a catalyst for scientific progress as anything provided by religion. 'Wondering' at the majesty of the natural world does not necessarily lead to belief in God.

It is certainly true that there were many cases where Christian authorities did not ban specific advances in science, and many clergymen who accepted the new developments, but it does not follow that Christianity was the prime mover for the likes of Huygens, Hooke, Newton and Leibniz, though the case might well be made for Robert Boyle. There was never, as I have argued throughout this book, a coherent or monolithic Christianity that conditioned the way humans thought, even in the medieval period. At the very least any serious study of the matter has to distinguish between those Christian confessions that were more sympathetic to science (the seventeenth-century English Puritans?) and those that were not. Superstitions remained. In North America the appearance of Halley's Comet in 1682 was still regarded as a portent of divine punishment rather than as an astronomical phenomenon (see the views of Pierre Bayle on this, p. 722). The continuing conflict between creationists and evolutionists reminds us that there are significant groups of Christians, a majority in some societies, who still reject the findings of science. Ultimately, empiricism and experimentation, not Christianity, were to provide scientific truths that would help change lives for the better and provide the impetus for continued research. Science *works* in that by understanding the world as it exists in reality, we are able to manipulate it effectively – for good or ill.

In face of such achievements, theologians have had to play catch-up, continuously revising conceptions of the divine in order to keep up with scientific progress. Bede's 3,952 years between the Creation and the coming of Christ were expanded to between 20 and 400 million

† This is the main theme of David Wootton's *The Invention of Science* (notably Chapter 3, 'Inventing Discovery', and Chapter 4, 'Planet Earth').

years by Lord Kelvin in 1862.* The Augustinian view that the two original human beings, Adam and Eve, had been created perfect but that they and their descendants were eternally diminished by their sin of disobedience has been replaced by one in which imperfect human species emerged through evolution to a more advanced form, a complete transformation of the theological view of human development. In this sense science has exerted as much influence on defining theology as theology has exerted on science. As long as theologians remain intellectually flexible they can avoid conflicts between the expanding horizons of science and their own beliefs.

In his *The Invention of Science*, David Wootton quotes a young clergyman, William Wotton, a Fellow of the Royal Society, who summarized what had been achieved by the end of the seventeenth century in his *Reflections on Ancient and Modern Learning* (1694).[18] 'Matter and motion' had replaced 'occult qualities and idiosyncrasies', there was a much more critical attitude to authorities such as Aristotle, mathematics was seen as 'absolutely necessary to the comprehending of the Oeconomy of Nature, in all her works' and older hypotheses had been disproved by experiment and observation. Some understanding of the workings of the natural world had been achieved, not least through telescopes, microscopes, pendulums and barometers, and a more effective use of mathematics. In his conclusion Wootton also notes how the language of science had changed, as terms such as 'hypothesis', 'scientific law' and 'fact' now conditioned the way the issues were conceived.

Yet conservative forces remained strong. What we can now define as important breakthroughs, those representations of reality on which one could build a more profound understanding of the material world, were not necessarily seen as such at the time. It would take a long time before steam was seen as a more effective source of power than the traditional wind and water that had long been harnessed to machinery.[19] Niccolò Guicciardini, in the introduction to his biography of Newton, shows how his legacy was fragmented by a variety of opponents and enthusiasts following the publication of *Principia Mathematica*.[20] To talk of the achievements discussed in the last two chapters as a 'revolution' may be premature and conceived only in hindsight. As yet science had not been consciously used as a means of improving the human condition, to the extent of exercising power over the natural world, and I would prefer to postpone use of the word 'revolution' until that point is reached. For that was the moment of real breakthrough.

* Today the age of the universe is set at nearly 14 billion years, with the Earth emerging 4.5 billion years ago.

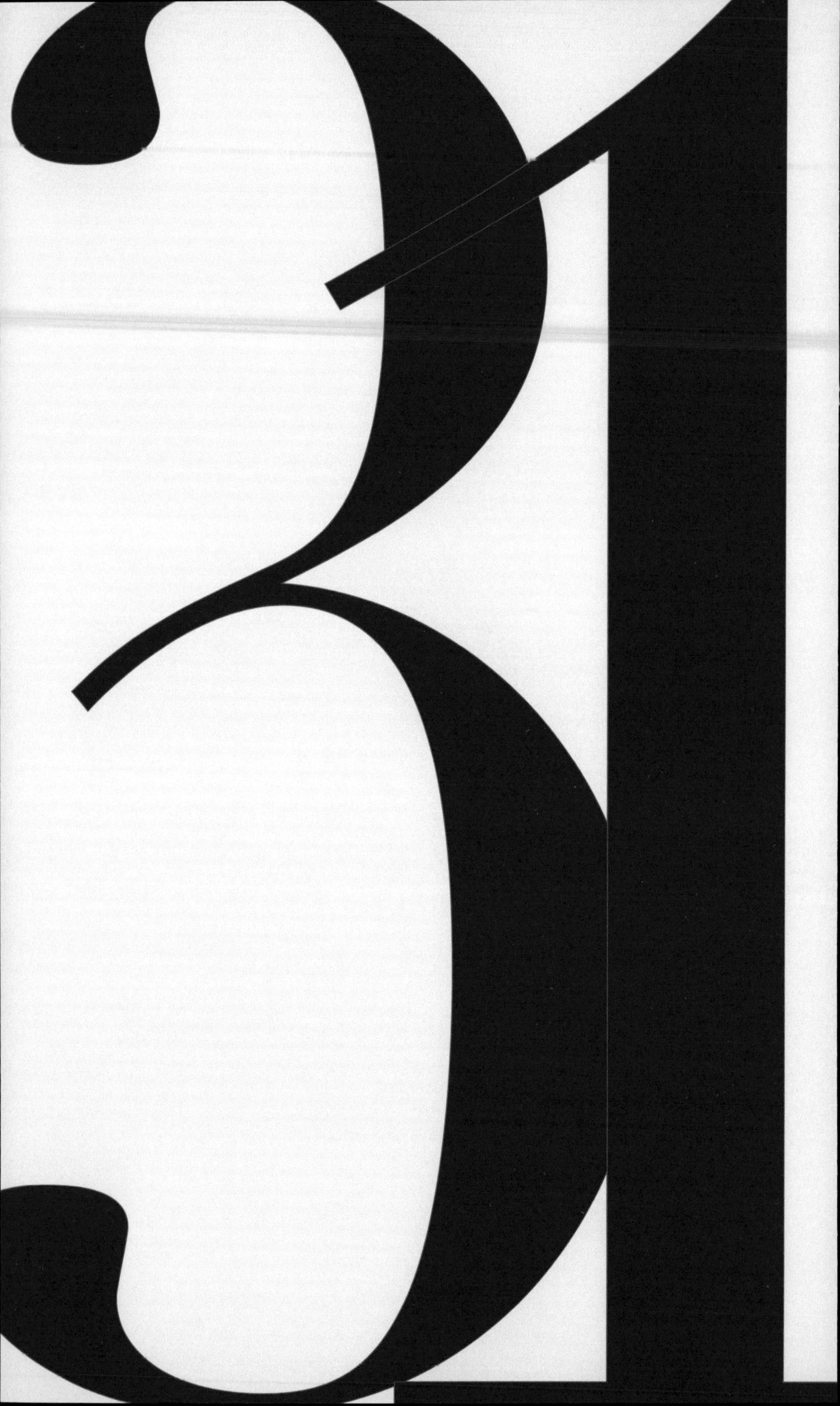

Did the Seventeenth Century see the Making of the Modern Mind?

Reason is a guide that leads one astray; and philosophy can be compared to some powders that are so corrosive that, after they have eaten away the infected flesh of a wound, they then devour the living flesh, rot the bones, and penetrate to the very marrow. Philosophy at first refutes errors. But if it is not stopped at this point, it goes on to attack truths. And when it is left on its own, it goes so far that it no longer knows where it is and can find no stopping place.

Pierre Bayle, from his *Dictionnaire*[1]

Perhaps the most substantial and stimulating book describing the intellectual life of this period is Jonathan Israel's *Radical Enlightenment: Philosophy and the Making of Modernity 1650–1750*.[2] Israel demands that we look beyond the England of Locke and Newton and the French Encyclopedists as sources for the Enlightenment to recognize that this was an intellectual 'drama played out from the depths of Spain to Russia and from Scandinavia to Sicily'.[3] Furthermore, he argues that: 'No major cultural transformation in Europe, since the fall of the Roman Empire, displayed anything comparable to the impressive cohesion of European intellectual culture in the late seventeenth and early eighteenth century.'[4] Israel's most consistent argument, in this and subsequent volumes, notably *Enlightenment Contested: Philosophy, Modernity and the Emancipation of Man, 1670–1752*,[5] is that there was a 'radical Enlightenment' based on a rational materialism inaugurated by the Dutch philosopher Baruch Spinoza and a more moderate Enlightenment pioneered by such figures as John Locke. The difference between the two Enlightenments depended largely on the extent to which God was retained as the ultimate authority and source of knowledge. Israel laments that in the eighteenth century the moderates eventually triumphed over the radicals.

René Descartes in a portrait after Frans Hals. The Dutch painter made a quick portrait of Descartes for a friend of the philosopher in 1648. Most representations of the enigmatic Frenchman are copies of Hals's original, but they nonetheless provide us with an iconic portrayal of the man regarded as 'the father of modern philosophy'.

This was an age that buzzed with intellectual vigour, as journals, newspapers, salons and coffee shops all contributed to the ferment of ideas. Debates of great intensity rocked society. It was the moment in western thought when 'alarming rifts and fissures'[6] began to fragment traditional structures of, mainly religious, authority. In 1935, in a pioneering book, the Belgian historian of thought Paul Hazard (1878–1944) highlighted the conflict between philosophy and theology with the publication of *La Crise de la conscience européenne* (English translation, *The Crisis of the European Mind, 1680–1715*).[7] From around the 1630s, after centuries in which 'philosophy' was no more than a handmaid to theology, 'philosophers became a new breed, formidably different from the subservient, abstract theoreticians of former times'.[8] A survey of these philosophers provides a fitting conclusion to this account of the 'reawakening of the western mind', even if, for reasons of space, I must restrict myself to five of the most important thinkers: René Descartes, John Locke, Gottfried Leibniz, Pierre

Bayle and Baruch Spinoza. The first three still argued within a Christian framework; the last two were prepared to think more radically.[9]

'Once in a lifetime we must demolish everything completely and start again right from the foundations.' This is certainly what René Descartes attempted to do. He was born in a small French town, between Tours and Poitiers, in 1596. His mother died when he was fourteen months old and he had limited contact with his father, who remarried. He was brought up by well-to-do relations and followed a traditional education in classics, mathematics and philosophy at the hands of the Jesuits, by then the leading Catholic educators, at the respected college of La Flèche in the Loire Valley. During these years Descartes received a solid grounding in the philosophies of the ancient world and the orthodox Catholic responses to them. He studied law at Poitiers for a brief period but otherwise had no further contact with any university. He became deeply distrustful of conventional methods of education and would later develop an ambition to replace the entire structure of Aristotelian scholasticism. He would not succeed in this, but he articulated his alternative philosophy with such clarity that it became a focus of debate that has lasted to this day, to the extent that he is known as 'the father of modern philosophy'.

As an individual Descartes remains an enigma. He was never well – he preferred to stay in bed, where he claimed to do his thinking, until late in the morning. Yet he first appears in 1617 as a nobly born mercenary soldier in the army of a Dutch Stadtholder, and the Dutch Republic was to be his home for much of his life, a practising Catholic in a Calvinist state. He claimed that the more tolerant intellectual climate of the United Provinces was a favourable one in which to work, but he also wandered in Germany and Italy and returned to his native France for a couple of years. Even in Holland he moved around frequently, suggesting an unsettled and solitary disposition. In his *Discourse on the Method* (1637), he describes himself 'as a spectator rather than an actor in all the comedies of life'. He never married, but he is known to have fathered a daughter by his housekeeper, though she lived for only five years. He was notoriously prickly about criticism.

A chance meeting in the garrison town of Breda in November 1618 with a Dutchman named Isaac Beeckman, an accomplished mathematician, seems to have been crucial in giving purpose to Descartes's life. The search for certainty began to dominate his imagination and mathematics provided the precision and logic that he craved. His *La Géometrie*, published in 1637 as an essay attached to his best-known work, the *Discours de la Méthode* (*Discourse on the Method*), united algebra and geometry into a single subject, analytic geometry, an achievement which alone would have made him influential. From the 1620s he was reading more widely in science and philosophy, examining issues in the fields of optics including rainbows (confirming the findings of Roger Bacon from the mid-thirteenth century) and refraction through water. He even dissected animals and, as his *Discours de la Méthode* shows, he was aware of Harvey's discovery of the circulation of the blood only a few years after it was published. This activity may seem haphazard, but Descartes's biographer Adrien Baillet describes an episode that took place on the night of St Martin's Day, 1619:

> On the Tenth of *November* 1619, laying himself down *Brim-full of Enthusiasm*, and wholly possess'd with the thought *of having found that day the Foundations of the wonderful Science*, he had three dreams one presently after another; yet so extraordinary, as to make him fancy that they were sent him from above; he supposed he discerned through their shadows the tracks of the Path which God had chalked out for him, to perform his Will in his choice of life; and inquiry after truth, which was the occasion of all his disquiet.[10]

This sequence of dreams gave Descartes his purpose: no less than to start with the basic foundations of philosophy and move from there to a system that would encompass all knowledge. Yet one early attempt at this ambitious synthesis, *The World* (written between 1629 and 1633), which included a heliocentric universe, was withdrawn when he heard of Galileo's condemnation in Rome. Descartes always had an uneasy relationship with the church and in this case he drew back from the threat of excommunication.

In 1637 Descartes published a selection of scientific papers, but it is the accompanying text, the *Discours de la Méthode,* that has lasted. He wrote it in French, not the expected Latin, and its steady pace and coherent argument make his ideas easy to follow. He begins by rejecting his conventional education, accepting that it had some value but did not provide him with truths with which he could be satisfied. He next argues that a mind working alone is far more likely to achieve an intelligible system of philosophical laws than a community of scholars. By Part 2 of the *Discours* he is setting out four criteria which he would always abide by in his philosophy. These seem almost banal to us today, but it is important to list them nonetheless. The first was to accept as true only that which he could securely know as such. The second was to divide up the inherent difficulties of any issue with which he was confronted into as many parts as possible. The third was to start with the simplest of objects and then work from there towards objects of greater complexity. Finally, it was important to cover every aspect of an issue to make sure that nothing was omitted.

By Part 4 of the *Discours*, 'Of God and the Soul', however, Descartes has reached the idea that has made him famous. He starts (and here the influence of Montaigne's 'Apology for Raymond Sebond' – see p. 567 – seems likely) by showing that rational thought in itself leads nowhere and, above all, that the senses are unreliable. One can never be absolutely sure whether one is awake or dreaming. The only thing one can be certain of is that one *is* thinking and the act of thinking means that one must exist. *Cogito ergo sum*, 'I think, therefore I am'. This would not get us very far on the way to a fuller philosophical system, however, if Descartes had not gone on to create an argument for the existence of God. He starts with an idea – that there is a perfect being, someone more perfect than he, Descartes – but claims that that idea can only be held if that perfect being has planted it in our minds in the first place. So the very act of having the thought of a perfect being strongly suggests that a being of perfection must exist. 'God's existence is inferred directly from the fact that necessary existence is contained in the clear and distinct idea of a supremely perfect being', as the *Stanford Encyclopedia of Philosophy* neatly puts it.[11] Descartes uses a geometrical analogy. One can imagine a triangle, but implicit in the idea of that triangle is that its angles add up to 180 degrees. Just as one cannot imagine a triangle without accepting that by its nature it will have 180 degrees, so too one cannot imagine a perfect God without acknowledging that he must exist. Descartes's argument could be compared with the much earlier ontological argument of Anselm (see p. 112) but it could be – and was – criticized as offering no more than an intuition that God existed.

René Descartes's *Meditations* of 1641 provide the fullest exposition of his philosophy and argue for the complete separation of mind and body. The thinking mind is the basis of all knowledge.

Descartes offered the fullest expression of this argument in his *Meditations on First Philosophy*, published in 1641. This time he wrote in Latin; a French translation only came in 1647. There are six 'meditations', of which the first two, where Descartes reiterates the philosophical problems of finding certainty, are the most influential. For Descartes the primary source of knowledge was the human mind as illuminated by God, who, he argued, could not possibly deceive. This did not absolve the philosopher from using reason as far as it could take him. The quality of the knowledge depended on the cognitive attributes of the knower. Yet the mind was immaterial, even to the extent that it would survive the death of the body. 'This "I" by which I

RENATI DES-CARTES, MEDITATIONES DE PRIMA PHILOSOPHIA, IN QVA DEI EXISTENTIA ET ANIMÆ IMMORTALITAS DEMONSTRATVR.

PARISIIS,
Apud MICHAELEM SOLY, viâ Iacobeâ, ſub ſigno Phœnicis.

M. DC. XLI.

Cum Priuilegio, & Approbatione Doctorum.

am what I am is entirely distinct from the body and could exist without it.'[12] It is possible that, in saying this, Descartes was ensuring that he would be seen as an orthodox Catholic who accepted the survival of the mind/soul, but the notion of a complete split between mind and a material body, or dualism as it became known, became a key feature of his philosophy. The mind, in short, was 'the ghost in the machine'.* Descartes never completely resolved the problem of how the 'ghost' and the 'machine' were actually connected to one another. While he accepted that God could act on the mind through the senses, he continued to be distrustful of what the senses could actually tell us. He would only accept mathematical properties – matter, shape and motion (in the sense of relationships between objects always being in flux) – as describing material things. Perceptions of light, colour and sounds were too volatile to provide any certain knowledge. (There are shades of Plato here, although Descartes liked to claim that he was being original.) Outside the human mind, all material things existed and operated as mechanical objects with everything linked to each other, as in the vortices of the universe, which we explored in Chapter 29. Unlike many of his contemporaries, Descartes did not explore the ultimate purposes of God or explain what role the soul had within the material universe.

Descartes sent the *Meditations* to a close friend of his in Paris, a Franciscan friar named Marin Mersenne, a polymathic arch-networker among seventeenth-century intellectuals. Mersenne was another old boy of La Flèche, interested in new scientific developments and an innovative mathematician, but he is most remembered for his dissemination of new ideas, including those of Galileo, which met a much warmer reception in France than they did in Rome. Mersenne had previously disseminated Descartes's *Discourse* among Parisian intellectuals. When he distributed the *Meditations* he went further, asking readers to state any objections they might have to the work and then printing them, along with Descartes's own lengthy replies, which often failed to satisfy his opponents. Thomas Hobbes was among those from whom Mersenne solicited comments on the *Meditations*.

In the last seven years of his life (1643–50), Descartes enjoyed a fruitful correspondence with Princess Elisabeth, the daughter of the Palatine Elector Frederick. Elisabeth had a knack of pinpointing the difficulties in Descartes's philosophy. On his division between the immaterial mind and the material body she remarked: 'It appears to

* This was how it was described by the Oxford philosopher Gilbert Ryle in his critique of Cartesian dualism, *The Concept of Mind* (1949).

me that an immaterial thing can't possibly touch anything else. So I ask you for a definition of the soul that homes in on its nature more thoroughly than does the one you give in your *Meditations*.' It is widely believed that Descartes was unable to provide a precise answer, and certainly not one that satisfied Princess Elisabeth's acute mind. In a little book that he wrote for her, *The Passions of the Soul* (1649), Descartes acknowledged that her 'mental powers were so extraordinary that she can easily understand matters that seem very difficult to our learned doctors'.

Perhaps Descartes was flattering the princess's intellectual prowess in claiming that Elisabeth was receptive to his philosophy. He always felt that he, and he alone, was on the edge of discovering a system that would explain everything simply by stating what the mind, as provided by God, could discover through its own reasoning. In *The Principles of Philosophy*, originally written in 1644 for Elisabeth, he set out the principles by which a mechanistic universe actually worked. He described a tree of philosophy whose roots lie in metaphysics, whose trunk lies in physics and whose branches encompass all the other sciences, including medicine and mechanics, the true fruits of knowledge. Descartes believed in a philosophically unified body of knowledge that could, he hoped, replace Aristotelian scholasticism as the university curriculum. In a context of mounting intellectual frustration at the narrowness of university curricula, this facet of Cartesian thinking helps explain the philosopher's widespread popularity by 1650.

When he completed *The Passions of the Soul* Descartes dedicated the treatise not to Elisabeth but to a much less doughty philosophical contact, Queen Christina of Sweden. Descartes made his way reluctantly to Sweden to teach her but her life was so full and disciplined that she could only schedule their classes at 5 a.m. Whether owing to the cold of the Scandinavian winter, the weakness of his physical constitution or the shock of getting out of bed so early, Descartes died from pneumonia in February 1650.

By insisting on a new start for philosophy, Descartes had thrown down a gauntlet; reaction was inevitable. It was hard from now on for any writer or student of philosophy to avoid him. Many were dismissive. Voltaire remarked, with his characteristic lapidary wit, that Descartes was 'born to discover the errors of antiquity and at the same time to substitute his own'.[13] Others claimed that he was repeating arguments of old and was not as radically innovative as he claimed to be. Descartes was sensitive about this, responding with invective when Beeckman later insisted that he had provided Descartes with new ideas.

For Catholic conservatives, his attack on Aristotelian scholasticism, deeply embedded as it was in the universities, was enough to condemn him. In the old debate over the existence of free will, which had been revived in France by the Jansenists* – who supported Augustine on the depravity of humankind – Descartes was accused of sympathizing with Augustine's opponent, the heretical Pelagius. Others argued that Descartes's mechanical concept of material constituted a denial of the doctrine of transubstantiation. The Jesuits were instrumental in Descartes's works being placed on the Index of Prohibited Books of 1663, while some Protestants found that Descartes's rational concept of God denied the more mystical side of religion. In 1642 Gisbert Voetius, rector of the Calvinist university of Utrecht, persuaded the university senate to issue a condemnation of Descartes and to impose a ban on the teaching of his philosophy. This marked the beginning of a particularly vicious feud between the two men.

Despite the religious authorities lining up against him, Descartes's views remained popular in France and the Netherlands. They spread widely among the *salons* and in those universities where they could be taught. His central idea – how much the mind could know and what did it mean to be a knower – was particularly influential. So too was the concept, which can be traced back beyond Descartes to the Stoics, that the physics of the universe and those of the Earth are unified (something that was to be confirmed and elaborated by Isaac Newton, who would destroy Descartes's own theory of vortices in the process). Above all, by challenging the foundations of traditional philosophical thought and raising questions (albeit ones, such as the mind–body problem, that many philosophers did not feel he solved satisfactorily) Descartes had made himself indispensable.

Descartes's insistence that knowledge-making was concentrated in the mind and that the senses were inherently unreliable, threatened the entire notion of learning through observation. This explains why the Bacon-obsessed British philosophers were not as attracted to Descartes as were many on the continent. While Newton demolished Descartes's science of the vortices, it was John Locke who, having read deeply in the works of Descartes when he was in Paris, provided an alternative philosophy that gave primacy to the senses. The conflict between the two approaches was to invigorate philosophical debate in the centuries to come.

* Jansenism was a French theological movement of the seventeenth and eighteenth centuries, based on the writings of the Dutch Catholic bishop Cornelius Jansen (1585–1638) and characterized by moral rigour and asceticism.

The key work here is Locke's enormously influential *An Essay Concerning Human Understanding*, probably conceived as early as 1671 but not published until 1690. It appeared in four revised editions and had been translated into French and Latin by the time of Locke's death in 1704.[14] The breadth and quality of Locke's work was immediately recognized, not least in the many intellectual journals of the day through which ideas travelled fast across Europe. The finest accolade to be given to a philosophical work is for future generations to draw different insights from its major themes. Despite attracting much hostility on its first publication, the tenor of the *Essay* sat comfortably within the intellectual and philosophical concerns of the emerging age of Enlightenment and so became an essential text for philosophers, as it has been ever since.

Godfrey Kneller's portrait of Locke as an older man (1704) suggests a fraught, otherworldly figure caught up in his own thoughts. Yet those who approached Locke with some trepidation 'were perfectly amazed to find him nothing but affability, good humour, humanity, pleasantness'.[15] As we saw in Chapter 28, Locke's early life in Oxford, and then in London with Shaftesbury, brought him into contact with working scientists such as Boyle and Hooke and progressive medical men. So he was imbued with the new empirical spirit of observation and experimentation that Francis Bacon had inspired.

Unlike Descartes, Locke was no isolated genius working in a dark cupboard. His philosophy was more relaxed, open to revision and lively. If there is a single thread running through Locke's philosophy it is that an individual must think for him- or herself and not be seduced by the beliefs of the crowd. His view that 'there is much more falsehood and error amongst men than truth and knowledge' rings true. This notion tied in with the right of an individual to rebel against an abusive government described in Chapter 28. Locke expected the human mind to be active and responsive.

Yet Locke also realized that there are limits to what we can know. When looking at an object, it is impossible to grasp its true 'essence', 'the being of anything whereby it is what it is', and it is vital to recognize this. 'Men extending their enquiries beyond their capacities and letting their thoughts wander into those depths where they can find no sure footing, 'tis no wonder, that they raise questions and multiply disputes, which never coming to any clear resolution... confirm them at last to perfect scepticism.'[16] This is a realistic view, but Locke is emphatically *not* saying that because you cannot reach certainty, you cannot learn something of truth. He provided the analogy of a ship using a long

rope dangling down to warn it of approaching shallows. The rope has a crucial importance for the immediate safety of the ship but it cannot tell us anything about the depths of the ocean, since it is unable to reach them. 'Our business here', states Locke, 'is not to know all things, but those which concern our conduct.' He places himself between the rationalists, who believe that reason can achieve certain knowledge, and the sceptics. By doing so he raised a wide spectrum of philosophical ideas that have absorbed readers ever since.

In Book 1 of the *Essay*, Locke starts with the basics: how a person becomes a knower. Famously, he dismisses innate principles, concepts that we are born with, including the concept of God. If there had been a common inheritance of this kind, then there would be general agreement what these principles were; moreover, they would not be in conflict with what we experience in the real world. Yet the concept of God is perceived differently in different cultures. Descartes was among Locke's targets here. Instead, at birth the mind is a *tabula rasa*, a blank slate. (In contrast, Plato and his followers had believed that humans were born programmed with ideas that could be recovered.) This does not mean that it is completely empty. It has innate capacities for relating to the external world and the relationships it forms are what Locke calls 'ideas'. 'Ideas' are 'whatsoever is the object of understanding when a man thinks'. So if one looks at a tree, the tree itself is not an 'idea'; the 'idea' is rather the tree as it is conceived within the mind of the observer. By eliminating the concept of innate knowledge Locke was confronting those who believed that there were eternal truths embedded in the mind that theologians had the right to elucidate. It was an important breakthrough, a major challenge to the authority of religious leaders.

John Locke in the last year of his life. Godfrey Kneller's portrait (1704) catches something of the otherworldliness of the great philosopher.

In Book 2 of the *Essay*, Locke addresses the question, where do our 'ideas' come from? Locke's answer is dramatically different from that of Descartes. They come from 'experience'. As he puts it:

> Experience: In that, all our Knowledge is founded; and from that it ultimately derives itself. Our Observation employed either about external, sensible Objects; or about the internal Operations of our Minds, perceived and reflected on by ourselves, is that, which supplies our Understandings with all the material of thinking.[17]

The first kind of experience, 'sensation', is apparently straightforward; it refers simply to the objects which we can experience with our senses.

The second, 'reflection', relates to the activity of thinking, which embraces a wide variety of 'internal operations': using our memories, meditating, choosing between alternatives, judging what is true, and so on. There is a distinction between the tree as it might be objectively analysed by scientific instruments (defined by its primary and unchanging qualities) and the tree in the form that our minds perceive it – defined by its secondary qualities such as colour or beauty, which are unique to the perception of the observer. Locke left unresolved the connections that might exist between primary and secondary qualities. Locke's philosophy now becomes more complicated because even the most simple object is more than just a single 'idea'. A tree has a trunk, bark, branches, leaves, flowers and fruit. Once embedded in our minds, we might compare it to other trees we have seen or perhaps a memory of that same tree as a sapling. So we are continuously combining 'ideas' into ever more complex forms. Among the most demanding of Locke's concepts is that of 'substance' or 'substratum', the underlying support that holds true across a variety of 'ideas'.[18]

Locke develops further categories of 'ideas' and looks at the ways in which they can be distinguished from each other. 'Knowledge', he said in a much-quoted statement from Book 4 of the *Essay*, 'seems to me to be nothing but the perception of the connection and agreement, or disagreement and repugnancy of any of our ideas'. So two 'ideas' might be identical or have definable differences. If these differences are obvious, say two contrasting colours, or a difference in size, then these can be grasped 'intuitively'. If they are not at first obvious they can be demonstrated through a proof, as in geometry, for instance. It may not be obvious that the angles of two triangles of different shapes and sizes will add up to 180 degrees but it can be shown through a proof.

The variety of ways in which Locke categorizes 'ideas' leaves much room for discussion. He explores the complexities of the way we think in searching detail. In his conclusion to Book 2 (and even more so in Book 4), Locke has to tie his reflections up into some kind of method through which knowledge can be achieved. There are 'ideas' that are 'clear' in that they can be explained in simple unambiguous language and have some relationship to what can actually be observed. The 'idea' of a unicorn, which can be imagined but does not exist and is therefore 'fantastical', is less clear than the 'idea' of a horse, which can be related to real horses. However, there are many features of a horse (its innermost nature as a living animal, for instance) that might never be grasped and, crucially, Locke accepts this. The duty of the knower remains to try to break down more obscure 'ideas' into clearer, simpler ones. Locke believed that even quite complex 'ideas', such as God, space or infinity, could be broken down in this way. It was inevitable that the intricate analysis of the relationship of the mind and the external world would raise many questions that would challenge psychologists as much as philosophers in the centuries to come.

Locke is particularly innovative when he discusses the nature of personal identity (Book 2, chapter 27). He rejects Augustine's idea that we are burdened with original sin and also Descartes's assertion that we can fall back on ideas that are innate within our soul. Locke was aware that our bodies change over time, as they grow from childhood through adulthood and into old age. What stays constant is our consciousness, our ability to build up experiences. Yet as we go through life, our identity is based not only on our immediate experiences, the tree I am looking at right now, but our memories of all the trees that we have known. Our identity at this moment is made up of the memories we hold in our consciousness, and that links back to the experiences we have had in the past to create our personal identity. The problem arises when we forget the experiences of trees we have seen in the past. Locke argued that these had no place in our identity and he was much criticized for this. One result of Locke's argument that an individual depends heavily on his or her memories is that it then falls to teachers and parents to provide positive memories that will help create the child's future consciousness. In the treatise *Some Thoughts Concerning Education* (1693), Locke would stress the importance of inculcating children with good mental habits. He distrusts learning by rote, abhors corporal punishment and stresses the value of practical learning. Locke's ideas on education would exert an immense influence, not just on Enlightenment thinkers such as Rousseau, but up to the present day.

In Book 3 Locke digresses to examine the nature of language. For students of linguistics this is an absorbing text, full of assertions to argue over. While Locke accepts that words usually refer to a defined object, so that one person using the word 'tree' will use it in such a way as it can be understood by others as describing the same object, he recognizes that the actual words or sounds chosen are arbitrary. In this sense he is a nominalist, one who believes that there are no fixed universal ideas lurking beyond the material world, as Plato had argued. Words have evolved to describe external objects. Yet it would be impossible to have a single word for each 'idea', so there must be a way of creating general terms which refer to groups of objects – trees, for instance. However, there is an intractable problem here, in that it seems impossible to set clear boundaries around the definition of general terms.* Again our understanding of a word might change as one matures. There will always be new resonances to our vocabulary as we grow up and form a more profound understanding of reality. In this sense the meaning of a word may lack stability. Locke was acutely aware of how the meanings of words shift with time, making it inevitable that language is often used without suitable precision and clarity. He criticizes the scholastics for introducing terms that could not be related back to defined 'ideas'. He argues, especially in chapter 10 of Book 3, that special care should be made to use words in a consistent sense and make sure that one's definitions are clearly communicated to others in order to maintain the rigour of the debate. While Locke lays down the standards for serious philosophical work, pioneering the philosophy of language in so doing, his insistence that all language is the result of arbitrary choices makes it hard to achieve consistency. What is important is that he spotted the problem as one that is rooted in the world of everyday discourse.

In order to achieve clear 'ideas', the knower has to organize his or her mind properly. This is among the concerns of Book 4 of *The Essay Concerning Human Understanding* and of another work of Locke's, a short handbook entitled *Of the Conduct of the Understanding*, published posthumously in 1706. As both titles suggest, the key concept here is 'understanding'. Locke's concept of 'understanding' is a difficult one to grasp as it evolved along with the philosopher's own thinking. At one level it is simply 'perception', but it has a greater power than this in that 'understanding' orientates the mind towards being able to think clearly. 'It is, therefore, of the highest concernment that great care should be taken of the understanding, to conduct it right in the search of knowledge and in the judgements it makes.' 'To conduct it right' requires discipline: 'He that will conduct his understanding right must look for [clear ideas] not in the acuteness of invention, nor the authority of writers, but will find them only in the consideration of things themselves.'[19] Locke is here setting out the quest of knowledge as one in which the knower acts for him- or herself, eschewing the opinions of earlier authorities or of those around them.

So what makes up this 'consideration of things'? Locke believed that one must engage with the objects themselves, what he called 'sensitive knowledge' based on experience and observation. This leads straight to the most fundamental problem of all, the reliability of the senses. If 'ideas' are what we hold in the mind about an object outside it – a

* The twentieth-century philosopher Ludwig Wittgenstein would show how difficult it was to use the word 'game' in any coherent way.

tree, for instance – what is the quality of the 'idea' insofar as it provides knowledge about the particular tree that is observed? Locke has to accept that it is very limited, but, rather than end up at a philosophical dead end, he argues that while we may not reach the limits of knowledge, we can learn enough for us to live comfortably. So we can see that a tree may be cut up into wood and the wood burned to give us warmth. He accepts that there is enough evidence to believe in the existence of God and that one can also justify a system of morals based on the New Testament and reasoning about the nature of God's law.[20]

But it is often impossible to gain certainty, so the reasoning mind has to weigh up probabilities; admitting this is an important feature of Locke's philosophy. His defence of probability has a certain charm. 'So in the greatest part of our concernment, God has afforded us only the twilight of Probability, suitable I presume to that state of mediocrity and probationship he has been pleased to place us in here.'[21] Here, sensibly, Locke accepts that we must live within our capacities to understand. There is no overall encompassing system. Descartes would have been furious at such a concession.

Reason is, of course, important to Locke, as it is a capacity of the mind that can sort out ideas. This presupposes, as Locke argues in Book 2, chapter 21 of *The Essay Concerning Human Understanding*, that we know from our own experience that we can decide to do one thing or the other – lift or fail to lift our arm, for instance. It follows that the mind can work out a particular course of action to follow: 'We have opportunity to examine, view and judge, of the good or evil of what we are going to do.'† Locke goes further than simply using reason; 'examining, viewing and judging', he wishes to examine the difficulties in applying reasoning. He is aware, as the sceptics were, that the misuse of language can lead to different and contradictory conclusions. Reasoning is especially important in understanding divine revelation. Locke is prepared to accept that God may have provided revelations but they should never be believed if they conflict with reason. He distrusts those who follow their faith blindly. He also argues that the Bible might reflect the human minds that created it and should not be accepted uncritically as revelation. Blind faith, for Locke, is in the same category as accepting the opinions of the ancients or those of the crowd. This did not stop Locke being a religious man – one of his tracts was *The Reasonableness of Christianity* (1695) – but he stuck to the simplest ex-

† Locke has been classified as a 'compatibilist', in that while he accepts that our actions are determined by pre-existing factors, he believes we are still free to act, not least in the sense of making moral choices.

pression of faith, namely that Christ was the Messiah. He believed that the basis of morality was the threat of divine punishment and that God could act through miracles. He felt that the evidence of the gospels was sufficient to suggest that Jesus had indeed effected miracles. Locke's views entangled him in sterile debates with conservative Christians.

The difficulties of understanding divine revelation led Locke to put forward a rationale for religious toleration, expounded in his *A Letter Concerning Toleration*, written during the turmoil of the Revocation of the Edict of Nantes, and published in 1689.[22] By 1689 Locke had lived in Anglican England, Catholic France and Calvinist Holland so he was well aware that Christianity had split into various mutually intolerant factions. 'Every church is orthodox to itself and erroneous or heretical to others.' He was well read in works that condemned intolerance – his library contained works by Castellio, Episcopius, Spinoza and Bayle. He asked how a state could know what is the correct form of belief and, if it does not, how it can enforce it on others. It was not one of the purposes of a government to enforce religious conformity, especially when it primarily concerned the relationship between God and the believer or solely matters of ritual. 'Every man has an immortal soul, capable of eternal happiness or misery; whose happiness depends on his believing and doing those things which are necessary to the obtaining of God's favour.'[23] In other words, Locke believed in toleration based on the necessity and freedom of a Christian individual to find his or her own salvation. He argued that it was impossible for the state to coerce a mind and that any such coercion would surely lead to social unrest. His tolerance did not extend to Catholics, however, whom he saw as subservient to a foreign power, the pope, nor to atheists, who, not believing in divine punishment or reward, had no foundation for morality. Any expression of religious belief that disturbed the peace, especially when it involved intolerance, must be forbidden. This was a further reason for not extending toleration to the Catholic Church with its record of persecution.*

The Act of Toleration of 1689 was welcomed by Locke as a step forward even if it did not go nearly far enough to satisfy his aspirations. Yet, as Jonathan Israel has pointed out,[24] while Locke has been idealized as an apostle of freedom he was intolerant of many forms of dissent, scepticism and atheism among them. He linked those who

* Astonishingly, in 2015 a manuscript was found among Locke's papers, 'Reasons for tolerating Papists equally with others', which suggests a more nuanced approach. The manuscript dates from 1667–8 and is available online at https://doi.org/10.1017/S0018246X19000207

were in search of salvation with high moral standards and believed that the state was justified in enforcing these. Faced by the overwhelming hostility to full religious toleration from both political and religious authorities, Locke might perhaps be best characterized as a pragmatist so far as religious toleration was concerned.

Newton and Locke are usually portrayed as harbingers of the Age of Enlightenment. The philosopher Gilbert Ryle, scourge of Cartesian dualism, claimed that Locke's *Essay* 'teaches us how to be sensible or reasonable in our adoption, retention and rejection of opinions'.[25] This is often seen as a very English way of doing things, compared to the more abstract philosophy of the continent, but Locke raised philosophical issues that resonated throughout Europe, just as Descartes had done. His was a further challenge to Aristotelian scholasticism.

The contrast between Descartes and Locke is often seen as one between the 'rationalists' and the 'empiricists', but this is probably too rigid. It is not as if Descartes ignored observation or that Locke denied the importance of reason. But there were differences of emphasis: the 'rationalists' were more cautious about the value of the senses and described the universe as if it obeyed a single rational order. They demanded clarity and so were naturally drawn to mathematics, especially geometry, as the discipline that gave them precision and certainty. Both Descartes and Spinoza (see p. 728) valued the axioms of Euclid, logically developing them into propositions that ranged beyond pure mathematics. Locke's tradition of 'empiricism' is normally seen as carried on by the Irish bishop George Berkeley (1685–1753) and the Scot David Hume (1711–76), both of whom lie beyond the scope of this book. The 'rationalists' claim our next subject, Gottfried Wilhelm Leibniz (1646–1716), for their own.[26]

Withdrawing as a child into his academic father's extensive library and reading voraciously from then on, Leibniz is often seen as the best-read philosopher of them all. Although he was well known for starting an immense variety of projects and never finishing them, Leibniz awed his contemporaries by the breadth of his learning and philosophical interests. In the words of Michael E. Moore: 'Historians are bewildered in their attempts to identify the influences on Leibniz for the simple reason he had read everything, from primary Christian theologians to ancient and modern philosophers, likewise investigating Chinese philosophy and on to alchemy, the Rosicrucians and Christian Kabbalism.'[27] Unlike Descartes or Locke, Leibniz's output does not offer a single, dominant work that includes a summing-up of his main ideas. The only full-length book that he ever published was his *Theodicy* of

1710, where he discussed the nature of God and the problem of evil, one of his main concerns. (What appears to be evil, according to Leibniz, is often a means through which God brings about a greater good.) While his most mature work was done in the eighteenth century, an enormous output of pamphlets and letters to his hundreds of correspondents, much of it still unpublished, detail his earlier philosophical views.

Most of Leibniz's life was spenst as a courtier rather than at a university, but he was more receptive of Aristotle's works than were many of his contemporaries (in one project he set out to reconcile Aristotle with Descartes). While some ridiculed him for his subservience to the princes of German states who employed him, often as court librarian, he benefited from their patronage and actually enjoyed a great deal of freedom, notably in the course of diplomatic trips to Paris and London, where he was able to engage with the finest minds of the day. He learned a great deal about mathematics and physics from Christiaan Huygens in Paris in 1672, and in London the following year he so impressed members of the Royal Society with a calculating machine he had developed that they promptly elected him a Fellow.

Leibniz remains famous as a logician, seen by many as the best since Aristotle. In mathematics he was one of the founders of calculus (occasioning a celebrated row with Newton over who was first to discover it; see p. 692) and refined the binary number system. Leibniz developed a philosophical system based on a rationally organized universe. The foundations of his reasoning lay in the principle that any argument containing a contradiction must be false and that there is a principle of sufficient reason 'by virtue of which we consider that we can find no true or existent fact, no true assertion, without there being a sufficient reason why it is thus and not otherwise, although most of these reasons cannot be known to us'. Leibniz was able to accept that finite minds were often unable to comprehend God's plan, but there was never any doubt in his mind that there *was* a plan. This led on to the principle that a rational being will always act for the best and that God, as the perfect rational being, would have only created the best of possible worlds. Leibniz was lampooned as hopelessly naive for this idea by the French writer and philosopher Voltaire in his satire *Candide* (1759), which cites such events as the devastating Lisbon earthquake of 1755 and the Seven Years War of 1756–63 as evidence of the absurdity of the German philosopher's outlook. A profound belief in the benevolence of God's creation was nonetheless central to Leibniz's work.

Unlike Spinoza (see p. 726), Leibniz did not see the world as a unified substance; he believed that it was a harmonious whole of indivisible objects (or 'monads' as he termed them) created by God. One can imagine God as a clockmaker who assembles two clocks that start off exactly at the same time. They can be separate but continue to tick and chime in harmony, neither causing nor influencing the working of the other. Leibniz provides another nice analogy, of listening to the sea – a harmonious sound reaches the listener but the sound of each individual wave can be distinguished. Leibniz was no arrogant isolationist on the model of Hobbes or Descartes. If there is indeed a harmony to the workings of the world, he accepted that others must also have grasped it. He was happy to draw on other traditions of thought, and was delighted to find that the binary system that he believed he had invented had in fact been known to the Chinese. He was attracted by the work of the classical philosophers. As he put it in his *Theodicy*: 'If we were sufficiently informed concerning the opinions of ancient philosophers, we shall find therein more reason than is supposed.'[28] In particular he found support for his rational conception of the universe in the work of the Stoics, who had argued for a cosmos that moved on through a logical sequence towards an ultimate purpose. His mentor here appears to be Chrysippus (*c*.279–*c*.209 BC), one of the founders of the Athenian school of Stoicism.

One of Leibniz's ambitions was to find a way of reducing complex concepts, even one as complex as God, to numbers. Here Pythagoras, famous for his belief that numbers underlay the material reality of the world, was an influence. Leibniz hoped that if one could find a numerical formulation for each concept, it could be transferred across languages and cultures and so rendered comprehensible to all. A further aspect of Leibniz's protean intellect was his engagement with Chinese civilization. He corresponded with Christian missionaries in China, and, having read *Confucius Sinarum Philosophus* (*Confucius, Philosopher of the Chinese*, 1687) – an annotated translation into Latin, by Philippe Couplet and other Jesuit scholars, of several books in the Confucian canon – developed a respect for the Confucian ethical tradition.

Leibniz remained a (Lutheran) Protestant but his most important public work was to attempt a reconciliation between the different Christian traditions. He was committed to using philosophy as a means of underpinning Christian truth in the hope that this would negate the use of coercion by the authorities. While he denounced Spinoza as perfidious, he hoped to refute him rather than condemn him in the way that other conservatives were urging.* He went beyond

* He desperately tried to get access to a copy of Spinoza's as yet unpublished *Ethics* but only found one after Spinoza's death in 1677.

Æt 28 Petit F.

Tel fut l'illustre Bayle, honneur des beaux esprits,
Dont l'élégante plume, en recherches fertile,
Fait douter qui des deux l'emporte en ses écrits,
De l'agréable ou de l'utile!

D.L.M.

L'Estample ce trouve chez J. Rollin fils quay des augustins a S.t Athanase.

a system of simply tolerating differences, as Locke had argued for, towards finding some underlying theological principles on which all could agree. He put forward a plan to bring the European states together in a confederation. Among his other projects, he advocated a public health system, vocational training, even a pension scheme. The enlightened ruler must cultivate philosophy, history, geography and modern languages as well as the science of politics. Scholasticism was to be discarded and practical works encouraged. Leibniz was fascinated by machines and the way they could be used to manipulate natural forces, from the wind for windmills to the tensions in springs for clocks and calculators. There were no limits to his inventive mind.

When Leibniz's full works are published (and one estimate is that at the current rate another 200 years will be needed to release his entire canon), it will be surprising if they do not have an overall connectedness and coherence. That was simply the way his mind worked: 'My principles are such that they can hardly be torn apart from each other. He who knows one well, knows them all.'

The same cannot be said of Leibniz's French contemporary Pierre Bayle (1646–1706).[29] Bayle, like Alberico Gentili, risks being forgotten, his famous *Dictionnaire historique et critique* (*Historical and Critical Dictionary*) of 1697 bypassed by the sophisticated twenty-eight-volume Enlightenment *Encylopédie* (1751–72) of Denis Diderot and his collaborators. Yet in his time there are few thinkers who more represent the turmoil of ideas of the late seventeenth century. 'Turmoil' is appropriate because Bayle, always in the thick of debate, is so busy trying to get to the root of everything in arguments, counter-arguments and his own ripostes to these, that his ulterior motives remain hotly debated.[30]

The French philosopher Pierre Bayle, as portrayed in the frontispiece to a 1740 edition of his *Historical and Critical Dictionary*. The caption praises his 'elegant pen', which is 'fertile in its researches'.

Bayle was born to a Huguenot family in the south of France, converted to Catholicism in the late 1660s for intellectual reasons after his education by the Jesuits, then converted back to Protestantism. This was anathema to the Catholics of Louis XIV's France, of course, and not surprisingly the Calvinists forced him to go to Geneva, partly to confirm his reintegration into his community but also to master Calvinist theology. Distrusted by both sides, he naturally extolled the virtue of living by one's conscience. It was the probability that consciences might err, as – presumably – Bayle believed his own had done when he strayed from his Protestant roots, that he would later use as an argument for religious toleration. He moved back to France in

1674 and taught at a Calvinist academy at Sedan. However, the growing oppression of Protestants saw the academy closed down in 1681. Bayle headed for the Dutch Republic, where he found a post at a French academy, the École Illustre, in Rotterdam. Once again the Republic had provided a haven for freethinkers. Bayle was able to denounce the Aristotelian scholasticism of the Catholic universities and champion Cartesianism.

Bayle's early works were attacks on superstition and intolerance. When the appearance of a comet in 1680 led to claims that this was a message from God, Bayle pointed out the foolishness of a God who would provide portents of such a nature. The existence of an ancient superstition or the belief of a majority in a portent or miracle did not absolve scholars from showing there was no evidence to support it. Bayle's pamphlet on the matter, *Diverse Thoughts on the Occasion of a Comet* (1683), provided – as its title suggests – an exhaustive array of arguments and historical evidence that went way beyond what was needed to prove his point. In another pamphlet, of 1686, he attacked a tradition going back to Augustine that taught that Jesus' words 'Constrain them to come in' (Luke 14:23) could be used as a justification for forced conversion. In practice each Christian church could claim that the words of Jesus referred to their own sect. This could only lead to mutual intolerance and so, as recent history had shown, to the atrocities of the Thirty Years War. The death of both Bayle's father and brother (the latter in prison for refusing to convert to Catholicism) in France as a result of the suppression of Protestantism further confirmed him as a champion of tolerance.

Pierre Bayle's *Dictionary*, the title page of whose 1740 edition is shown here, was a Europe-wide success, and a harbinger of Enlightenment philosophy.

Bayle ranged well beyond Locke in arguing that there could be no rational basis for proclaiming that one faith has greater truth than another, or even that there is one true faith at all. The risk of oppression is so high that there should be tolerance of all beliefs, including atheism. While Locke had argued that atheists should not be tolerated as they lacked a basis for morality, Bayle argued that, on the contrary, atheists offered no threat to society and that there was no reason why a community of atheists should not be well regulated. In effect, he was breaking the link between religion and morality in denying that revelation provided the basis for moral behaviour. Christians could not assume that they possessed a superior morality. Every conscience that diligently sought the truth had an equal right to toleration and this included Jews and Muslims. Bayle's toleration was not inspired by

DICTIONAIRE HISTORIQUE ET CRITIQUE,

PAR

M^R. PIERRE BAYLE.

CINQUIEME EDITION,

REVUE, CORRIGÉE, ET AUGMENTÉE.

AVEC LA VIE DE L'AUTEUR,

PAR MR. DES MAIZEAUX.

TOME PREMIER.

A——B.

A AMSTERDAM, Chez P. BRUNEL, P. HUMBERT, J. WETSTEIN & G. SMITH, F. L'HONORE' & Fils, Z. CHATELAIN, COVENS & MORTIER, PIERRE MORTIER, F. CHANGUION, J. CATUFFE, & H. UYTWERF.
A LEIDE, Chez SAMUEL LUCHTMANS.
A LA HAYE, Chez P. GOSSE, J. NEAULME, A. MOETJENS, G. BLOCK, & A. VAN DOLE.
A UTRECHT, Chez ETIENNE NEAULME.
LIBRAIRES.

M D C C X L.

AVEC PRIVILEGE.

Christian love but rather by the injustice of oppressing the innocent. Even though he was living in Holland, he included Calvinists among the persecutors.

While Bayle proclaimed that he personally remained a fideist, accepting the revelations of God as a matter of faith, his fellow Calvinists in the Rotterdam consistory were outraged. His books, a later judgement said, 'contain many damaging propositions tending against God's word and the whole Christian faith'. Scholarly discussion continues to this day over whether Bayle's fideism was merely a front, and that he was a crypto-radical from the start. Whatever the truth, in 1693 he lost his teaching post. Extracts from his writing were read out and a phrase saying that there was no point in God effecting miracles in his cause because he had nothing to fear from atheism was found particularly offensive.[31] A bitter struggle now ensued between Bayle and his erstwhile friend and colleague from Sedan, the theologian Pierre Jurieu. Jurieu had become increasingly fanatical in defence of orthodox Calvinism and insisted that Bayle was an atheist. Bayle's *Philosophical Commentary* (1686–8), where he advocated religious toleration, had already raised Jurieu's hackles, but the last straw for the latter was the anonymously published *Avis important aux refugiés* (*Important Advice to Refugees*, 1690). Convinced of the identity of its author, Jurieu denounced Bayle as a heretic in a furious counter-attack. Despite the claim of atheism and suspicions that he was faking his commitment, Bayle remained a practising member of his local church in Rotterdam until his death.

In the 1690s Bayle began to conceive the idea of a dictionary. He now had the ambition of correcting not only the errors of organized religion but of the entire intellectual tradition of his time. This was to be a polemical work 'filled with the sins of the Latin world [the learned community] and a heap of the filth of the republic of letters'. It was to concentrate on biographies, especially those of more obscure figures whom Bayle felt had not been given their due. It would offer an accurate account of their lives, a commentary on each and would then digress into any philosophical issue that Bayle considered relevant. A massive work, some 6 million words in length, the *Dictionary* proved an immediate success on publication in the Dutch Republic in 1697, its popularity boosted by the expected invective from Jurieu and its banning in France. In the introduction to his translation of Bayle's *Dictionary*, the late Richard Popkin, a distinguished historian of scepticism, catches its mood: 'A marvelous suite of themes and variations, on such problems as those of cuckoldry, and castration fears, and religious intolerance, and historical accuracy, and of finding certainty in philosophy, science and religion. These themes flash back and forth and interplay through the columns of folio footnotes.'[32] A second edition followed in 1702 containing another 2 million words, including a series of 'Clarifications', in which Bayle answered his critics.

Bayle, and his *Dictionary* in particular, has baffled scholars over the years. He simply cannot stay still but has to go on worrying at every issue. As Paul Hazard puts it in a chapter on Bayle in his *The Crisis of the European Mind, 1680–1715*: 'Constantly, as though by sort of logical obsession, [his philosophy] kept harking back to questions which he could never persuade himself he had satisfactorily settled'.[33] There is a revealing passage in the *Dictionary*, which I have reproduced as the opening quotation to this chapter, where Bayle laments what he sees as the limitations of the use of reason and philosophy as a means of finding truth. As Blaise Pascal knew only too well, one can stand at the edge of a psychological void. The contrast between Bayle and Leibniz, who believed that reason *would* eventually find the underlying truths of human existence, is stark.

So does Bayle deserve to be placed among the sceptics? His biography of Pyrrho of Elis (see p. 482) and the accompanying notes and philosophical discussion in the *Dictionary* is extensive and supportive of scepticism. In contrast to Leibniz, he can find no good reason why God would permit the existence of evil. Another thinker who left his mark on Bayle was the Jewish theologian Moses Maimonides, whose *Guide for the Perplexed* (1190) displayed a similar lack of certainty. Others have pointed to the gently sceptical influence of Montaigne. One can well argue that Bayle had reached the brink of an intellectual precipice, where the thinker teeters in frustration at not being able to pin down anything of certainty.

This position could all too easily have resulted in Bayle being seen as irrelevant; or, in the words of Paul Hazard, 'he might have floated away into that far-off void where actions lose their significance and life its purpose'.[34] Yet the very issues he raised, the problem of morality, religious intolerance, the lack of reason in Christian doctrine, the need for intellectual caution, resonated with his immediate successors at that particular moment in the history of European thought when conservatism was battling with an influx of new thinking. Bayle's greatest champion was Voltaire, who described the *Dictionary* as the 'Arsenal of the Enlightenment'. The mistake of later scholars perhaps is to take Bayle out of his immediate circumstances, in which his own family faced persecution for their beliefs, and to try to relate him to other currents of European thought. One can acknowledge Bayle as a philosopher who showed the frustrations inherent in the search for truth and as an important advocate of religious toleration, but he cannot be fitted into any particular school of thought.

But what cannot be denied is Bayle's powerful sense of moral purpose. It mattered intensely to him that there should be freedom of thought. The English philosopher Anthony Ashley Cooper – grandson of the first earl of Shaftesbury of the same name – who met Bayle in the Netherlands, offered this accolade: 'Almost the only man I ever knew who, professing philosophy, lived truly as a philosopher; with that innocence, virtue, temperance, humility and contempt of the world which might be called exemplary.'[35] Even on the day of his death Bayle was writing replies to opponents.

In one long article in the *Dictionary*, Bayle lambasts a philosopher who had already been dead for twenty years when Bayle was writing. This was 'an impious atheist' whose most important work, *Ethics*, Bayle described as 'a pernicious and detestable book'. So we come to a man who, in the words of Jonathan Israel, 'decisively shaped a tradition of radical thinking which eventually spanned the whole continent, exerted an immense influence over successive generations, and shook western civilization to its foundations'.[36] This is Baruch, later Benedictus, Spinoza (1632–77). Bayle's article remains a focus of academic controversy to this day. Was this *really* an attack on Spinoza, plain and simple, or, by according the Dutch philosopher so much space in the *Dictionary*, was Bayle grudgingly but decisively asserting his central place in the debates of the day?

Spinoza came from a family of Jewish refugees from Catholic Portugal who had settled in Amsterdam some decades before his birth.[37] He received a conventional early education, studying the Torah and the Hebrew scriptures, but through a Gentile teacher, Franciscus van den Enden, a former Jesuit turned doctor who was fascinated by the new sciences, he came under the influence of Descartes and gradually moved away intellectually from his Jewish roots. He knew Hebrew, of course, but he also mastered Latin and his change of name reflected his rejection of his Jewish background. In 1656 he was expelled from his community in a particularly aggressive way, 'an excommunication of altogether exceptional vehemence and severity' which implied an 'open, systematic, premeditated and blatant doctrinal rebellion of a fundamental kind', although the details of his offences are unknown.[38] No Jew was allowed to communicate with him or even to offer him shelter. There was now no turning back for Spinoza. He began to plough his own highly individual philosophical and theological furrow, still studying with van den Enden. He had the immense advantage of being at home with two major theological traditions, Judaism and Christianity.

Like Descartes, Spinoza preferred a quiet life, distant from the controversies that he had provoked. In 1660 he moved from Amsterdam to Rijnsburg, a village near Leiden. He would move again, several times, but he never left the Dutch Republic, spending his final years in The Hague. One report by a visitor to Rijnsburg ran: 'He lives without doing harm to other people and he occupies himself with the construction of telescopes and microscopes.'[39] His personal life was blameless. Spinoza's embrace of the profession of lens-grinding seems to have been prompted as much by scientific interest as by the need to make a living. It makes him a rare case of a modern philosopher with practical skills. The one serious disturbance to Spinoza's placid existence came during the French invasion of 1672, when his friends the de Witt brothers – prominent republican politicians, and in the case of Johan, an accomplished mathematician – were lynched by an Orangist mob in The Hague. According to Leibniz, who visited Spinoza some years later, Spinoza felt impelled to rush out with a placard denouncing the 'barbarians' who had committed the outrage but was prevented from doing so for fear he too would be lynched.

In these years he was dedicated to his writing. The only work that he published under his own name, a critique of Descartes's final work, *The Principles of Philosophy*, appeared in 1663. While Spinoza distanced himself from Descartes, and especially from Descartes's belief in free will, he placed himself in the 'rationalist' school by championing geometry as a model for understanding the material world. This was to govern his approach to philosophy. The two major works for which he is remembered are the *Theological-Political Treatise*, published anonymously, which appeared in 1670, and his more influential *Ethics*, conceived in the 1660s but published only in 1677, shortly after his death. Spinoza's ambition was to carry the message of Descartes's mechanical philosophy into new territory of religion and ethics. If there was one underlying purpose to his work, it was to create a system that would ensure his and his followers' peace of mind. The single force that he felt most threatened this was the conventional view of a punishing God.

The aim of the *Treatise* was to challenge the Bible as the source of divine revelation. Clearly, there is some residual use for the scriptures but Spinoza limited them to the demand that one should love God and one's neighbour. Spinoza railed against the ways that the Bible had been used by the militant clerics of his day. He showed that much of its narrative could not be true, that the words of God proclaimed by the prophets reflected their time and place, and so lacked the universality of relevance that would surely characterize the word of God. There were no grounds for the Jews to claim that they were God's chosen people. The Bible had no accurate information to provide about the material world and there was no reason to give it special status: it was to be examined critically, as with any other work of literature. Not many books were banned in the Dutch Republic but the *Treatise*, whose author was soon known and ostracized, was one of them.

In the *Ethics* Spinoza follows the pattern established by Euclid's *Elements*, of axioms from which irrefutable conclusions can be drawn. His aim was to create a system that was completely transparent, but the reader is often confused by the conceptual leaps. Can Euclidean axioms *really* be used to prove the existence of God? Spinoza introduces the concept of a 'substance' that, by his definition, exists totally independently of any other matter or concept. The essence of this 'substance' is contained in its attributes, 'what the intellect perceives of a substance', and an attribute cannot be separated from its substance. It follows that the same attribute cannot be found in different substances and from this Spinoza reasons that there is only one 'substance' and that that 'substance' is God, who possesses an infinite variety of attributes. This was an extraordinary conclusion, and one which, of course, was not accepted without vigorous counter-arguments from Spinoza's opponents.* It immediately distinguishes Spinoza from those who believe the world is made up of a variety of substances. These included Descartes, who believed that God was the perfect substance, living alongside other lesser substances; and Leibniz, with his God as creator of many substances existing together in harmony. Spinoza's conclusion also destroys the classical idea, adopted by Christianity and the other monotheistic religions, that God is somehow distinct from his creation. This was truly revolutionary. Spinoza argued that God was essentially impersonal; he did not worry about the human condition, and certainly not to the extent of reigning over an afterlife in which he offered rewards or punishment. There was no point in even praying to him.

While Spinoza does not develop a theory of toleration, it follows naturally from his conception of God that any attempt to enforce religious belief is to be condemned. He denounced the churches for failing to uphold justice and charity and for claiming that they alone

* The philosopher who comes closest to this is Parmenides (*c.*500 BC) of Elea, a Greek settlement in southern Italy, who argues in his *On Nature* that everything is one and unchanging and that it is only our senses that convince us otherwise.

held the truth. For Spinoza, their stance damaged the individual's chances of being able to discern the difference between truth and falsehood. Once the power of the churches was removed, people would have a genuine opportunity to express themselves freely. Spinoza's ideal was a society where individuals surrender certain rights in order to have mutual security under the auspices of the state – but not their freedom to think and express their opinions. Spinoza was one of the first to advocate a free press. He is happy to accept people's allegiance to the existing churches, as long as these were not granted any political power by the state. Spinoza's overriding aim is for societies to be at peace, and this is best achieved when there is freedom of speech. Noting the religious antagonisms around him even in tolerant Holland, he argues that attempts to impose religious dogmatism are in fact the main causes of political and social disturbance.

So what can one say about Spinoza's perplexing 'divine substance'? He identifies God with Nature, a stance that would later be called pantheism. This does not get us very far, of course, as much more needs to be said about the relationship. If God does not act as an external creator, he must infuse nature through his own attributes. One attribute is thought; another is extension, the occupation of a space by a material object. These are the only divine attributes that can be grasped by the human mind but they are, of course, attributes of the same substance seen in different ways. As a monist, a believer in the unity of all material things, Spinoza firmly rejects Descartes's dualism. The mind and the body of an individual are united.

Yet individual human beings believe that they are free. This, says Spinoza, is an illusion resulting from a lack of rational thought. Even if one has ensured the freedom of the individual by abolishing the power of the churches, there still has to be a system by which knowledge can be achieved. Otherwise, freedom of speech is ineffective. Spinoza suggests that there are four levels in the acquisition of knowledge. The first level is knowledge picked up by hearsay, perhaps telling a child that those looking after him are his parents. Next is the knowledge built up from personal experience, that a fire burns, for instance. Spinoza calls this 'imagination'. At the next level, we begin to appreciate that what we see may not actually be the reality – and we use reasoning to make the distinction between appearance and reality. At the fourth level, we understand things through their essence. This is the only true knowledge, but Spinoza terms it 'intuition'. 'Intuition' may seem an invalid way of knowing, but as the human mind and body are a single substance, part of the substance that is God/Nature, then perhaps intuition just reflects the realization of this. While at a lower level of knowing an individual believes that he or she can choose or not choose to put a finger in the fire, at the fourth level, one realizes one is locked into the closed system that is God. Within God/Nature there are no external causes; everything exists in a way that could not be otherwise. This brings Spinoza close to the Stoics, who also preached the unity and interlocking nature of all things. Seneca was his favourite among the Stoics.

This recognition that we are in bondage is a key aspect of Spinozan thought, but he does offer us the possibility of liberation. He first recognizes that human beings have the power 'to strive to persevere in being'. This is not an autonomous power but is part of the very essence of existence. It is within our nature to resist being destroyed or diminished. The way out starts with the acceptance that we are subject to our passions. Spinoza reduces these to three: joy, sadness and desire. If we can understand the cause of a passion, sadness at the death of a loved one, for instance, we can control that passion better. However, sadness deflates us (it is a passive emotion) while joy and desire are active emotions that can be used to create understanding of our place within the wider whole that is Nature.

Spinoza does not expect this to be easy as each individual is subject to the forces of nature around them. Yet reasoning will lead to an understanding of one's place within Nature, which demands 'that everyone loves himself, seeks his own advantage, wants what will really lead a man to greater perfection, and absolutely, that everyone should strive to preserve his own being as far as he can'.[40] This may seem to be ethical egoism – everyone in it for themselves – but Spinoza believes that reason will lead each individual towards a society that will be stable and harmonious (and democratic): 'Men who are governed by reason desire for themselves nothing which they do not also desire for the rest of mankind, and consequently are just, faithful and honourable in their conduct.'[41] At his most optimistic he argues that there might not even be the need for an external political authority (how different from Hobbes!). Intellectually, each individual, as part of Nature, will also come to love God, who is reflected in one's own self-love. Of course, God will not respond, so what is achieved is actually a form of serenity through finding harmony within one's pantheistic being. The most important aim of Spinoza's philosophy is the elimination of fear and there is something of Lucretius in the way he derides the fear of death.

While Jonathan Israel argues passionately that the influence of Spinoza has been vastly underrated in recent scholarship, he recognizes that there was immense hostility to him from the authorities, both Jewish and Christian: 'Since his philosophy stood in total contradiction to the tenets of Judaism and all forms of Christianity as well as Cartesianism and the mainstream of the western philosophical tradition since the end of antiquity, it was obvious that his philosophy could only be propagated clandestinely.'[42] Israel has done a fine job in digging out references to Spinoza among the reading classes throughout Europe to show how widely he was studied. He even sees Spinoza as the primary inspiration for the radical ideas that drove the French Revolution whose initial success was, however, thwarted by counter-revolutionaries and dictators such as Robespierre.[43] While I enjoyed Israel's fascinating and provocative volumes, I found it hard to believe that Spinoza's unique philosophy could ever have fomented an actual revolution in thought. His impact appears to be restricted to a later – gentle – influence in literary circles of the Romantic period, when nature moves to the forefront of European consciousness. As the German writer Goethe put it: 'Let me just say I found something in it [the *Ethics*] to calm my emotions and it seemed to open a broad, free, view over the physical and moral world.'[44] When the poet William Wordsworth writes of how the ruins of Tintern Abbey aroused in him feelings of

> A presence that disturbs me with the joy
> Of elevated thoughts; a sense sublime
> Of something far more deeply interfused
> Whose dwelling is the light of setting suns...[45]

this seems pure Spinoza.*

The eighteenth-century Enlightenment is usually seen as the moment when European thought took on new dimensions and challenged the ideas of the past. Yet the seventeenth century, an age of upheaval and religious strife, was also the source of intellectual reactions that were radical in their implications. Crucial was debate, even if it was often bitter and entangled in religious bigotry. I have no hesitations in feeling that the western mind had been further reawakened by the thinkers of this century, but can one come to a balanced conclusion? This is the subject of my last chapter.

---

* Another enthusiast was the earnest young Mary Ann Evans, later known as the novelist George Eliot (1819–80), who translated the *Ethics* and was intrigued by Spinoza's philosophy. A new edition of Eliot's translation (ed. Clare Carlisle) will be published by Princeton University Press in early 2020.

Was There Really 'a Reawakening of the Western Mind'?

'We look back on the savage condition of our ancestors with the triumph of superiority; we are pleased to mark the steps by which we have been raised from rudeness to elegance.'

Thomas Warton, *The History of English Poetry* (1774–81)[1]

In his *The Age of Genius: The Seventeenth Century and the Birth of the Modern Mind*, the philosopher A. C. Grayling claims that 'the seventeenth century in Europe redirected the course of human history by changing humankind's perspective on the universe and itself'.[2] I find this much too sweeping. The last six chapters have made it clear that new ways of thinking emerged in the seventeenth century that have continuing relevance today, but, equally, it would be wrong to neglect the underlying conservatism of society in 1700. The War of the Spanish Succession that broke out when Charles II of Spain died childless in 1700 showed that dynastic ambition remained the driving force of European politics. Political reform, such as it was in eighteenth-century Europe before the French Revolution of 1789, came from above, via the 'enlightened' absolute monarchs, not from below. In a short but brilliant book, *The Hebrew Republic*,[3] Eric Nelson has argued that the study of Old Testament texts led to an obsession with republicanism, but the two foremost republics of the day – those of the Venetians and the Dutch – were in decline after 1700, and Nelson's book neglected the large number of contemporary texts that drew on Old Testament models of kingship. Republicanism in practical politics, would, of course, revive in the Amercian and French revolutions, but here the inspiration came, once again, from classical, not biblical, models. Science had not yet begun to improve the lives of the masses; epidemics continued to cause havoc among populations still cared for by physicians steeped in the texts of Hippocrates and Galen. The vast majority of the population toiled on the land with only a rudimentary awareness of how food production might be increased or made more reliable. Famines remained common.

The universities still relied heavily on classical and theological set texts and at best provided the skills, in languages and logic, which more creative thinkers could use to define their own intellectual pathways. At Cambridge, when Newton arrived at Trinity College in 1661, 'religious duties formed the core of the daily regimen that had changed little since it had been laid down at the college's foundation [1546]'.[4] He, of course, made his own pathway. In Catholic Europe brilliant preachers such as Jacques-Bénigne Bossuet, who lived on until 1704, provided powerful defences of traditional Catholicism, playing on the deeds of the great saints, invoking miracles as the sign that God supported his church, 'watchful guardian of the dogmas committed to her charge… [She] makes no change in them, she adds not, neither does she take away'.[5] Shrines continued to attract thousands and the great monasteries dripped with the vast wealth of the church. I was recently overwhelmed by the eighteenth-century magnificence of the *Certose* (Charterhouses) of San Lorenzo and San Martino near and in Naples whose few monks were required to donate a family estate to support them for life in their Carthusian solitude.

In Protestant Europe the wealth of Christianity was not so extravagantly displayed but toleration of alternatives to the state religion was in short supply. The doctrine of the Trinity was defended with vigour, even if not through reason, and denial was enough to ban one from public life. It was hard not to be conscious of one's own sinfulness – though whether this proved a catalyst for productive living or a brake on intellectual creativity can be debated. Socially, Christianity remained very conservative, not only in family life, for which there could certainly be some justification, but in the maintenance of slavery with the support of biblical precedent. It is often said that Christianity encouraged equality, yet it is hard to find any 'Christian' political system outside a few radical sects where this was recognized. Nowhere did the established churches actively fight for democracy. The authority of God, in whichever denomination one was born into, still inspired a culture of obedience of one class to another.

Yet the eighteenth century was to see a further outburst of critical thinking in the so-called Age of Enlightenment. The Enlightenment is a vast topic encompassing almost every field of human inquiry. It is still rather simplistically presented as a movement committed to reason, and hence 'progress', but it is hard to separate the 'reason' of the Enlightenment from its emotional underpinning. The Enlightenment was essentially a starburst of intellectual fervour that was to be exploited in many different ways by later generations. Fascinating and important as it is for anyone with an interest in the history of European thought, this book would risk losing any coherence if it tried to cover it.

In conclusion, bringing together the many different elements that led to the 'awakening of the western mind' is a challenge. It is important to stress just how bereft Europe was, economically and culturally, after the fall of the Roman empire compared to what it had been before. While at first the church provided a framework within which some form of stability could be maintained, it would never have fostered the revival of the economy. This was rather the result of the tentative traders of northern Italy finding richer pickings among the prosperous Arab states of the eastern Mediterranean and North Africa. It was not only the profits that mattered. Despite being derided in the European sources as little more than pirates, by the late eighth century, the golden age of the Abbasid caliphate, the Arabs had achieved a sophisticated culture that was far ahead of anything known in a stagnant and impoverished

Europe before the thirteenth century. The point is forcibly made by the immense contribution of Arab texts, many of them translated from the original Greek or commentaries on them, that would infuse the learning of the universities. It has even been argued that the university itself was an Arab idea and that Copernicus adopted his astronomy from Arab sources. Traditional narratives of the west feeding on its own resources still underestimate this contribution to recovery.

By 1100 and the time of Abelard, 600 years after the fall of the empire, it is still surprising how few texts were available for him to teach from. It is impossible to overstate the importance of the classical texts for what actually might be termed a 'reawakening'. Their sources were various. Some came via the Arabs, of course; others had been copied in the first millennium, notably by the scribes of Charlemagne; others again came directly from the Byzantine empire that had survived the fall of the western empire (and then even more in the flood of scholars who fled west after the fall of Constantinople in 1453). While Latin was nowhere near as sophisticated and subtle a language for intellectual debate as Greek, it had been spread through the auspices of the church and provided a means by which these texts could be accessed. They were used in many different contexts and as a result they pervade the 'awakening'. The reappearance of Roman law was perhaps the single most important advance, as it established a framework within which traditional areas of conflict could be resolved and new challenges addressed. Roman law accepted private rights and provided a means of making commercial contracts that could be enforced. In practice, even the church accepted the primacy of a classical legal system over a mass of conflicting scriptural and papal injunctions.

Yet in other contexts the classical sources froze new thinking, in that they were accepted uncritically. This was particularly the case in the universities, where the key texts or summaries of them became embedded in the curriculum. The humanists broke free from this straitjacket and were the first to engage in serious scholarly study of the sources themselves. The investigations of the humanists coincided with a moment of renewed confidence in human ability to create. I cannot hide my enthusiasm for the exuberance and vitality of Renaissance Italy, and I have highlighted Brunelleschi's dome in Florence as bringing together ancient sources, confidence, imagination and technological know-how into one triumphant achievement.

The problem of summarizing the impact of the classical sources lies in the way they could provide models for every kind of government, from absolutism on the models of the Roman emperors to republicanism. The priors of Florence each held office for only two months, as Aristotle, writing in his *Politics* some 1,750 years earlier, had told them they should. Even in the seventeenth century, when so much was in flux, many texts were still considered authoritative whether in supporting or undermining conventional views. In medicine, as long as the classical doctrine of the four humours persisted, doctors would continue to drain blood from their ailing patients. When Newton's propensity for mathematics was noted, his first interview with the relevant professor (Isaac Barrow) centred on Euclid's *Elements* of 300 BC. Leibniz and Spinoza also relied heavily on Euclid, suggesting that no more recent mathematician had provided a text to rival it.

Yet with a new emphasis on empirical observation, the inadequacies of Pliny's *Natural History* or Ptolemy's *Geographike* and *Almagest* became glaringly obvious to those observing the natural world and so one sees modern science beginning to emerge. 'Science' was not then a concept as well defined as it is today when there are distinctive scientific disciplines and methods (the word was not used in its modern sense until the 1830s), but no one can deny the intellectual rigour and energy which the 'natural philosophers' of the sixteenth and seventeenth centuries put into attempting to understand the natural world on its own terms. Francis Bacon noted how the European discovery of the New World rendered the ancient authors irrelevant. The wider natural world revealed – and native societies encountered – by European colonization of the Americas was crucial in challenging conventional ideas of 'man' and providing a vast array of new exotic materials that stimulated further thought. As David Wootton argues, perhaps rather sweepingly, in his *The Invention of Science*, the key word was 'discovery'. 'If the discovery of America was a happy accident,' he writes, 'it gave rise to another even more remarkable accident – the discovery of discovery... It is this assumption that there are new discoveries to be made which has transformed the world, for it has made modern science and technology possible.'[6]

The impact of Christianity on the evolution of the western mind needs further consideration. A number of recent texts have placed the influence of Christianity at the core of this evolution. In his *Inventing the Individual: The Origins of Western Liberalism*[7] Larry Siedentop argues that it was within the Christianity of the Middle Ages that the foundations of liberalism are to be found. But this is to ignore the array of ancient texts that allowed debate across the intellectual spectrum. The articulation of different viewpoints and the freedom to debate them is surely at the core of liberalism. While the moment in history when the individual is 'invented' proves elusive, it was not as if individualism was *unknown* in the classical world. One can hardly argue that the dramatists of fifth-century Athens, Aeschylus, Sophocles and Euripides, were not aware of the agonized choices facing figures such as Antigone, Oedipus or Medea. And amid the power struggles of late republican Rome, Cicero's commitment to republicanism and his searching studies of Greek philosophy and ethics can arguably be described as manifestations of 'liberal humanism'. The economy of the Roman empire relied heavily on free enterprise and Roman law protected the rights of Roman citizens. In the Greek cities of the Roman empire, it was the esteem sought by individuals which underpinned their patronage of buildings – the city awarded them statues in return.

If one turns to Christianity, there is no doubt that there were theological constructions of 'the individual' as far back as the letters of the apostle Paul but many other factors encouraged individualism in the Middle Ages, not least economic opportunism and the hunger for political solutions. One of the most important developments in the historiography of medieval Europe has been the recognition of alternative voices. Classical sources, such as Roman law and the philosophical works of Cicero, were crucial ingredients that fuelled the concept of *libertas* in the city-states of northern Italy. Aristotle's *Politics* provided models for oligarchic rule, his *Nicomachean Ethics* a more coherent (and pragmatic) approach to ethics than could be found in the varied texts of the Bible. A tradition of resistance to tyranny came as much from republican Rome as from the gospels. Many areas of intellectual thought, geography and mathematics, for instance, developed with no reference to the scriptures.

Christianity was, in short, only one element of the development of European thought in the Middle Ages. Its impact was weakened by the sheer variety of ways in which it was given expression. Siedentop assumes a consistency in medieval Christianity which was never there and he fails to make the link between the proclamation of doctrine and any ensuing changes in the behaviour and beliefs of the laity. Did a papal decree or the thoughts of someone such as William of Ockham (to whom Siedentop devotes a whole chapter) actually change the direction of western thought? The authority of religious leaders was weakened by incessant claims of their corruption, in particular from voices within the church. In fact, it seemed to be *de rigueur* for prominent intellectuals to decry this corruption, which hardly suggests an institution that inspired respect. The activities of the Roman Curia were suspect in the medieval period and so they continue to be up to the present day. Enough has been said in earlier chapters to show how difficult it was to challenge church doctrine. It becomes very hard to see how, specifically, the medieval church, preoccupied as it was with the protection of its hierarchy, gave birth to what are normally assumed to be the core elements of liberalism.

Siedentop does not extend his text as far as the Reformation and the seventeenth century when, many would contend, western liberalism was born. He assumes that everything was in place for the evolution of liberalism by 1500. Yet one can argue (along with Perez Zagorin, in his *How the Idea of Religious Toleration Came to the West*) that it was specific developments *after* 1500 that gave a new impetus to European thought. The concept of religious toleration, a key element of liberalism, evolved as a *reaction* to Christian authoritarianism and intolerance, as this book has repeatedly asserted. Sebastian Castellio's elaboration of the concept arose from his outrage at the burning of Michael Servetus by the Calvinists for challenging the doctrine of the Trinity. It was the atrocities of the Thirty Years War and Louis XIV's Revocation of the Edict of Nantes that triggered the flight of a mass of religious refugees which impelled seventeenth-century thinkers such as John Locke to formulate philosophies of toleration. There is enough material in my last chapters to show how relentlessly those who thought creatively, even if they still saw themselves as Christians, were assailed by religious conservatives. Every philosopher had to find a place for his own conception of God within any system proposed, but that does not mean that it was God, or the churches founded in his name, that encouraged progressive thinking.

In his wide-ranging study *Dominion: The Making of the Western Mind*[8] (which, unlike Siedentop's work, extends to the present day) Tom Holland argues that 'Christianity may be the most enduring and influential legacy of the ancient world, and its emergence the single most transformative development in Western history'.[9] Holland is a distinguished classicist, so it surprising that he does not give greater importance to the impact of a thousand years of classical civilization which had an immense influence on the evolution of western thought. The two immediate questions that Holland needs to answer to sustain his argument are: 'Which Christianity are we talking about?'; and 'In what ways were religious leaders able to transform thinking?' A major theme of this book has been the wide variety of Christianities that have appeared in western Europe. Although there were attempts – through confession, for instance – to control the minds of the Catholic laity, there is not much evidence that they believed what they were supposed to believe. Furthermore, the mechanisms by which Christian doctrine were transmitted downwards are seldom explored; they are just assumed, by both Siedentop and Holland, to exist. It is as if the mass of the population had no spiritual feelings or allegiances of their own and simply absorbed whatever they were told by the church hierarchies. This is surely to underestimate the power of the human mind to think for itself. Locke is the key philosopher here in his insistence that the mind must actively and independently search for its own knowledge.

In short, Holland, like Siedentop, falls into the trap of believing that Christianity was in some way a coherent entity. The early Christian communities provided systems of care for their members in what was a hostile environment and they survived despite vigorous persecution. Then, in the fourth century, the church compromised with imperial Rome so that the bishops were brought into mainstream society to uphold traditional structures of society rather than 'transforming' them (the argument of my earlier book *The Closing of the Western Mind*). As I showed in my study of medieval relics, *Holy Bones, Holy Dust*, local Christianities centred on relic shrines and the bodies of saints made sure that there were many vibrant centres of spirituality that offered alternative ways of expressing religious feeling. Until the sixteenth century Christians were not even able to read the Bible in their own languages. The mass of alternative devotional texts that were available by the fifteenth century in many vernacular languages (the *Golden Legend* of Jacobus de Varagine is a good example) makes one aware that the scriptures were not the major source for belief. When exploring the fresco cycles of medieval churches, one can distinguish the narratives, such as those illustrating the childhood of the Virgin Mary, that have no scriptural source. Luther, understandably, saw it as his mission to restore the Bible's importance. The Protestant Reformation created many more denominations, each with its distinctive theology and hostility to its competitors. As discussed in Chapter 23, after 1550, the location of your birth defined what kind of Christian you were likely to be. Christianities became territorial and thus, inevitably, bound up with national identity. If one wants to argue, as Holland does, that the emergence of Christianity was 'the single most transformative development in Western history', then a much more nuanced evaluation, rooted in these historical facts, needs to be made.

Christianity also played an ambiguous role in the way the peoples of the Americas were treated when they were 'discovered' by Europeans. What can be seen as the central ethical problem of Christianity, how to deal with those not of the faith, now became critical. It was accepted, as this book has shown, that those left outside needed to be coerced, with different levels of persuasion, into salvation. 'As for these poor Indians,' opined John Eliot, a graduate of Jesus College, Cambridge, in 1631, 'they have no principles of their own nor yet wisdom of their own... and therefore they do most readily yield to any direction for the Lord, so that there will be no such opposition against the rising kingdom of Jesus Christ.'[10] In his recent *In Pursuit of Civility*, the distinguished historian Keith Thomas shows how conflicting notions of 'civilization' both legitimized and criticized imperial missions dedicated to bring a superior way of life to those 'pagans' who were now subservient to European rule.[11] Chapter 22 has shown how this was played out in Spanish America, with both biblical and classical sources providing ammunition for both tolerance or denigration of native cultures. A hierarchy of races became part of standard thinking in the west. It was tragic that in practice economic forces swept aside any philosophical or theological justifications for benign rule and even those who were most committed to tolerance supported the right of missionaries to convert the 'natives' from paganism. By the nineteenth century the British were adopting a high moral tone derived from both Christianity and Virgil's panegyric of Roman imperialism in his *Aeneid* for their civilizing role in India and Africa.

Even if one cannot give unqualified support for the idea that the seventeenth century achieved intellectual or cultural breakthrough, it undoubtedly spawned important new ways of thinking that can be recognized as feeding into the modern world and providing more open and tolerant perspectives. This does not mean that 'progress', however it is defined, is inevitable. While I would not go so far as the philosopher John Gray when he argues that the idea of progress in history is essentially a myth created by the need for meaning,[12] Gray can be welcomed for striking a cautionary note. The issue that weighs on anyone who sees the importance of fostering tolerance, accepting that science has achieved more for the welfare of humanity than institutional religion, and being open to more profound thinking about the human condition, is that these values are still under threat 300 years later. In *The End of History and the Last Man*,[13] Francis Fukuyama was seriously mistaken in assuming that liberal democracy had triumphed after the fall of the Iron Curtain in 1989 and that a high point of civilization had been reached. Every passing year seems to throw further doubt on this assessment. It is all the more vital to learn how painful was the birth of such values and how vulnerable their survival. But it is also right to applaud the cultural riches that they have provided. I do think I am justified in describing the long centuries from the fall of the Roman empire to 1700 as a process, often fitful and haphazard, of an 'awakening of the western mind'.

Appendix I

The *Triumph of Thomas Aquinas* (pages 212–13)

This extraordinary fresco, created a century after Aquinas's death, shows the philosopher associated with every virtue and tradition of learning. Hovering over Aquinas, as the Seven Virtues, are the three theological Virtues, Faith, Hope and Charity, above Temperance, Prudence, Justice and Fortitude. Alongside him are ten biblical figures from the Old and New Testaments. From *left to right* these are Job, David, St Paul (busy writing a letter), Mark, Matthew, John, Luke (with their gospels), Moses, Isaiah and Solomon. Under Aquinas's feet are three heretical figures: Nestorius, who over-emphasized the humanity of Christ, Arius, who championed the subordinate nature of Christ, and Averroes who suggested that secular knowledge was equal to theological knowledge. In the row below Aquinas on the left are shown the Seven Sacred Sciences with their most prestigious proponents. From the left, Justinian sets at the feet of Civil Law. Pope Clement V sits at the feet of Canonical Law and Aristotle at the feet of Philosophy. Holy Scripture is accompanied by Jerome and Theology by the Eastern theologian John of Damascus. Contemplation sits above Dionysius the Areopagite and Preaching above Augustine. In the row below Thomas on the right are the Seven Liberal Arts, again with their proponents. From the Quadrivium, the figure of Arithmetic sits above Pythagoras and Geometry above Euclid. Ptolemy is below Astronomy and Tubal-cain (a blacksmith mentioned in Genesis, here seen striking an anvil for sound) below Music. For the Trivium, an unknown figure is sitting at the feet of Dialectics, while Cicero, of course, represents Rhetoric and Priscian Grammar.

Appendix II

The *studiolo* at Urbino (page 305)

Above the *intarsie* of the *studiolo* at Urbino are the figures of some of those who appealed to the humanists. In this section are shown from *left to right, top row:* Euclid (Greek mathematician), Vittorino da Feltre (fifteenth-century humanist teacher at the court of Mantua), Solon (sixth-century BC Athenian lawgiver), Bartolus di Sassoferrato (medieval lawyer); *bottom row:* Pope Pius II (humanist pope), Cardinal Bessarion (intellectual and conciliator of eastern and western Christianity), Albert the Great (one of the finest medieval 'scientists'), Pope Sixtus IV (patron of the arts, creator of the Sistine chapel and founder of the Capitoline Museums).

Acknowledgements

I suppose that I ought to go back to the early 1960s to acknowledge a Miss Owles of Ipswich Museum for encouraging me to join the excavation of a Roman villa in Suffolk and my father's sharing with me Bernard Berenson's study of Giotto. Both are important moments in my book, the first because the villa's ashes defined the collapse of Roman authority in Britain, this book's starting point, and the second because the frescos of the Arena Chapel in Padua were seen in their time as a new beginning, an awakening, in western art.

However, I shall concentrate on those who have helped me over the past three or four years to bring this book to fruition. I lament the deaths of two close friends, John Rogers and Tony Trayling, whose interests in history, philosophy and theology provided the basis of many conversations. If they had lived the conversations would have continued and I miss them. As the book developed and I began to wonder whether it would come together in any kind of coherent form Stephen Calloway and Susan Owens and, in the US, Stan Prager read much of it, provided suggestions and encouraged me on my way. Stephen and Susan, both retired curators from the Victoria and Albert Museum, also gave suggestions for illustrations. Here I am also grateful to Christopher Lloyd for putting me onto the *Triumph of Thomas Aquinas* in the convent of Santa Maria Novella in Florence.

Paul Cartledge has been an enormous support, not only personally, but as adviser in all things classical. I can always rely on Julian Barker for deep discussions of matters theological from a liberal Anglican perspective. On the problems of religious belief in European history,

I have had many fruitful conversations with Aldo Matteucci and I was delighted that he and his wife Sylvie have joined two of my tours to discuss these issues in person. Anthony Stanton read Abelard for me. Charles Handy wished for even more on Montaigne. René-Oliver Orléan discussed the presentation of the book, especially in his native US market, and my daughter Cordelia advised me on her specialist subject, Latin America. An academic press that turned this book down nevertheless explained why it was doing so through three extensive readers' reports which provided completely differing perspectives on the book but offered many good suggestions for improvement. My agent, Bill Hamilton, worried that this book would be too long to sell to a publisher, but he managed it.

Having been described in one memorable school report as a 'harum-scarum character', I rely heavily on the expertise and care of editors and copy-editors. Richard Milbank at Head of Zeus has been a meticulous editor, not least because we have very similar visions for this book. Richard has saved me from many infelicities and mistakes and his support has been invaluable. Catherine Hanley as copy-editor has done a wonderful job in bringing everything together and spotting inconsistencies many pages apart. Clémence Jacquinet as Production Director has done a marvellous job, not least in assembling and placing so many illustrations and bringing the whole book together in its final form. Isambard Thomas has created a design with all the panache that is needed for such an ambitious survey of European history. Anna Nightingale as assistant editor has cast an eagle eye over the final text. Many thanks to all for achieving such a stunning result. Isobel McLean created an admirably thorough index. Of course any remaining errors in this complex book are my own.

The final volume will assure my wife Lydia that I have not just been sitting around in my study barn for the last three years and that the vital support she has given to keep me going has not been in vain. This book is dedicated to my daughter Cordelia. Its publication comes just at the moment when she takes up her new post as Lecturer in Political Geography at the University of Exeter from where she will be able to continue her Wellcome Trust funded work on women's rights in Latin America. May both our endeavours have a long and fruitful life.

Bibliography

Abramson, Jeffrey, *Minerva's Owl: The Tradition of Western Political Thought* (Cambridge, MA and London: Harvard University Press, 2009).

Abulafia, David, *The Discovery of Mankind: Atlantic Encounters in the Age of Columbus* (New Haven and London: Yale University Press, 2008).
———, *The Great Sea: A Human History of the Mediterranean* (London: Allen Lane/Penguin, 2011).
——— (ed.), *The New Cambridge Medieval History: Volume 5, c.1198–c.1300* (Cambridge: Cambridge University Press, 1999).
——— (ed.), *Italy in the Central Middle Ages, 1000–1330* (Oxford: Oxford University Press, 2004).

Ackerman, James and Phyllis Massar, *Palladio* (London: Pelican Books, 1966).

Adamson, Peter, 'Aristotle in the Arabic Commentary Tradition', pp. 645–664 in Christopher Shields (ed.), *The Oxford Handbook of Aristotle* (Oxford: Oxford University Press, 2012).
———, *A History of Philosophy without any Gaps: Philosophy in the Hellenistic and Roman World* (Oxford: Oxford University Press, 2015).
———, *A History of Philosophy without any Gaps: Philosophy in the Islamic World* (Oxford: Oxford University Press, 2016).
———, *A History of Philosophy without any Gaps: Medieval Philosophy* (Oxford: Oxford University Press, 2019).

Allmand, Christopher (ed.), *The New Cambridge Medieval History: Volume 7, c.1415–c.1500* (Cambridge: Cambridge University Press, 1998).

Angold, Michael, *The Fourth Crusade: Event and Context* (London: Routledge, 2003).

Annas, Julia, *Plato: A Very Short Introduction* (Oxford: Oxford University Press, 2003).

Anstey, Peter (ed.), *British Philosophy in the Seventeenth Century* (Oxford, Oxford University Press, 2013).

Arcais, Francesca Flores d', *Giotto*, 2nd ed. (New York: Abbeville Press, 2016).

Arnold, John H. (ed.), *The Oxford Handbook of Medieval Christianity* (Oxford: Oxford University Press, 2014).

Armstrong, Guyda, (ed.), *The Cambridge Companion to Boccaccio* (Cambridge: Cambridge University Press, 2015).

Asbridge, Thomas, *The Crusades: The War for the Holy Land* (New York and London: Simon and Schuster, 2010).

Attenborough, David, et al., *Amazing Rare Things: The Art of Natural History in the Age of Discovery* (New Haven and London: Yale University Press, 2007).

Bakewell, Sarah, *How to Live: A Life of Montaigne in One Question and Twenty Attempts at an Answer* (London: Chatto and Windus, 2010).

Bala, Arun, *The Dialogue of Civilizations in the Birth of Modern Science* (New York: Palgrave Macmillan, 2006).

Ball, Philip, *Universe of Stone* (London: Bodley Head, 2008).

Barber, Malcolm, *The Two Cities: Medieval Europe, 1050–1320*, 2nd ed. (London: Routledge, 2004).

Barkan, Leonard, *Unearthing the Past: Archaeology and Aesthetics in the Making of Renaissance Culture* (New Haven and London: Yale University Press, 1999).

Barnes, Jonathan, *Aristotle, Past Masters* series (Oxford: Oxford University Press, 1982).
———, *Aristotle: A Very Short Introduction* (Oxford: Oxford University Press, 2001).

Bartlett, Robert, *The Making of Europe, Conquest, Colonization and Cultural Change, 950–1350* (London: Penguin Books, 2003).

Barton, John, *A History of the Bible: The Book and its Faiths* (London: Allen Lane/Penguin, 2019).

Bate, Jonathan, *How the Classics made Shakespeare* (Princeton and Oxford: Princeton University Press, 2019).

Becher, Matthias, *Charlemagne* (New Haven and London: Yale University Press, 2003).

Belting, Hans, *Florence and Baghdad: Renaissance Art and Arab Science* (Cambridge, MA and London: Belknap Press of Harvard University Press, 2011).

Benner, Erica, *Be Like the Fox, Machiavelli's Quest for Freedom* (London: AllenLane/Penguin, 2017).

Bennett, Jim, 'The Mechanical Arts', pp. 673–95 in Katherine Park and Lorraine Daston (eds.), *The Cambridge History of Science: Volume 3, Early Modern Science* (Cambridge: Cambridge University Press, 2006).

Bianchi, Luca, 'Continuity and Change in the Aristotelian Tradition', pp. 49–71 in James Hankins (ed.), *The Cambridge Companion to Renaissance Philosophy* (Cambridge: Cambridge University Press, 2007).

Bischoff, B. (trans. David Ganz), *Latin Palaeography: Antiquity and the Middle Ages* (Cambridge: Cambridge University Press, 1990).

Black, Christopher, *Italian Confraternities in the Sixteenth Century* (Cambridge: Cambridge University Press, 1989).
———, *Church, Religion and Society in Early Modern Italy* (London: Palgrave Macmillan, 2004).
———, *The Italian Inquisition* (New Haven and London: Yale University Press, 2009).

Black, Robert, 'Humanism', pp. 243–77 in Christopher Allmand (ed.), *The New Cambridge Medieval History: Volume 7, c.1415–c.1500* (Cambridge: Cambridge University Press, 1998).
———, 'Education and the Emergence of a Literate Society', pp.18–36, in John M. Najemy (ed.), *Italy in the Age of the Renaissance* (Oxford: Oxford University Press, 2004).

Blair, John, *Building Anglo-Saxon England* (Princeton and Oxford: Princeton University Press, 2018).

Blanning, Tim, *The Pursuit of Glory, Europe 1648–1815* (London: Allen Lane/Penguin, 2007).

Bodiam, Miriam, 'Christianity and Judaism', pp. 483–503, in R. Po-Chia Hsia (ed.), *The Cambridge History of Christianity: Volume 6, Reform and Expansion 1500–1660* (Cambridge: Cambridge University Press, 2007).

Bodnar, Edward (ed. and trans.), *Cyriac of Ancona, Later Travels* (Harvard, MA : The I Tatti Renaissance Library, Harvard University Press, 2003).
———, Charles Mitchell (trans.), Clive Foss (eds.), *Cyriac of Ancona, Life and Early Travels* (Harvard, MA : The I Tatti Renaissance Library, Harvard University Press, 2015).

Bolgar, R. R., *The Classical Heritage and its Beneficiaries from the Carolingian Age to the End of the Renaissance* (new ed., New York: Harper and Row, 1964).

Bosworth, R. J. B., *Whispering City: Rome and its Histories* (New Haven and London: Yale University Press, 2011).

Boucher, David and Paul Kelly (eds.), *Political Thinkers: From Socrates to the Present* (Oxford: Oxford University Press, 2003).

Boulting, William, *Giordano Bruno: His Life, Thought and Martyrdom* (London: Routledge, 2013 reprint; orig. 1914).

Bouwsma, William J., *The Waning of the Renaissance, 1550–1640* (New Haven and London: Yale University Press, 2000).

Braudel, Fernand (trans. Sian Reynolds), *The Mediterranean and the Mediterranean World in the Age of Philip II*, 2 vols (London: Collins, 1972).

Breay, Claire and Joanna Story (eds.), *Anglo-Saxon Kingdoms, Art, Word, War* (London: British Library, 2018).

Brockliss, Laurence, *The University of Oxford: A History* (Oxford: Oxford University Press, 2016).

Brooke, Rosalind, *The Image of St. Francis: Responses to Sainthood in the Thirteenth Century* (Cambridge: Cambridge University Press, 2008).

Brotton, Jerry, *A History of the World in Twelve Maps* (London: Allen Lane/Penguin, 2012).

Brown, Giles, 'The Carolingian Renaissance', pp. 1–51 in Rosamond McKitterick (ed.), *Carolingian Culture; Emulation and Innovation* (Cambridge: Cambridge University Press, 1994).

Brown, Peter, *Augustine of Hippo: A Biography*, rev. ed. (Berkeley: University of California Press, 2000).
———, *Poverty and Leadership in the Later Roman Empire* (Waltham, MA: Brandeis University Press, 2001).

Bruce, Susan (ed.), *Three Early Modern Utopias* (Oxford: Oxford University Press, 1999).

Bryson, Bill (ed.), *Seeing Further: The Story of Science and the Royal Society* (London: Collins, 2010).

Bull, Malcolm, *The Mirror of the Gods: How Renaissance Artists Rediscovered the Pagan Gods* (Oxford: Oxford University Press, 2005).

Burke, Peter, *The Fabrication of Louis XIV* (New Haven and London: Yale University Press, 1992).

Burns, Tony, 'Aristotle', pp. 73–90, in David Boucher and Paul Kelly (eds.), *Political Thinkers: From Socrates to the Present* (Oxford: Oxford University Press, 2003).

Burrow, John, *A History of Histories* (London: Allen Lane, 2007).

Bynum, Caroline Walker, *Christian Materiality: An Essay on Religion in Late Medieval Europe* (New York: Zone Books, 2011).

Campbell, Stephen J. and Michael W. Cole, *A New History of Italian Renaissance Art* (London: Thames and Hudson, 2012).

Cannadine, David, *G. M. Trevelyan: A Life in History* (London: HarperCollins, 1992).

Cantor, Norman, *Inventing the Middle Ages: The Lives, Works and Ideas of the Great Medievalists of the Twentieth Century* (Cambridge: Lutterworth Press, 1991).

Cartledge, Paul, *Democracy : A Life* (Oxford: Oxford University Press, 2016).

Casey, John, *After Lives: A Guide to Heaven, Hell and Purgatory* (Oxford: Oxford University Press, 2009).

Celenza, Christopher, *Machiavelli: A Portrait* (Cambridge, MA., Harvard University Press, 2015).
———, *Petrarch: Everywhere a Wanderer* (London: Reaktion Books, 2017).
———, *The Intellectual World of the Italian Renaissance: Language, Philosophy, and the Search for Meaning* (Cambridge: Cambridge University Press, 2018).

Chadwick, Henry, *East and West: The Making of a Rift in the Church* (Oxford: Oxford University Press, 2003).

Chapman, Hugo and Marzia Faietti, *Fra Angelico to Leonardo: Italian Renaissance Drawings* (London: British Museum Press, 2010).

Charney, Noah and Ingrid Rowland, *The Collector of Lives, Giorgio Vasari and the Invention of Art* (London and New York: W. W. Norton and Co., 2017).

Clanchy, M. T., *Abelard: A Medieval Life* (Oxford: Blackwell Publishing, 1997)
———, *From Memory to Written Record*, 3rd ed. (Hoboken, NJ: John Wiley, 2012).

Clark, Kenneth, *Leonardo da Vinci* (Cambridge: Cambridge University Press, 1939; rev. ed. with Martin Kemp, London: Penguin Books, 1988).

Cohen, Mitchell, *The Politics of Opera: A History from Monteverdi to Mozart* (Princeton and Oxford: Princeton University Press, 2017).

Coldstream, Nicola, *Medieval Architecture*, (Oxford: Oxford University Press, 2002).

Cole, Alison, *Art of the Italian Renaissance Court* (London: Calmann and King, 1995).

Coleman, Edward, 'Cities and Communes', pp. 27–57,in David Abulafia (ed.), *Italy in the Central Middle Ages, 1000–1330* (Oxford: Oxford University Press, 2004).

Colish, Marcia L., *Medieval Foundations of the Western Intellectual Tradition, 400–1400* (New Haven and London: Yale University Press, 1997).

Como, David, *Radical Parliamentarians and the English Civil War* (Oxford: Oxford University Press, 2018).

Cottingham, John, *The Rationalists: A History of Western Philosophy* (Oxford: Oxford University Press, 1988).

Coward, Barry, *The Stuart Age*, 4th ed. (London: Routledge, 2012).

Cox, Virginia, *A Short History of the Italian Renaissance* (I. B. Tauris, 2016).

Creighton, Mandell, *The Church and the Nation: Charges and Addresses* (London: Longman, Green and Co., 1901).

Curran, Brian, *The Egyptian Renaissance: The Afterlife of Ancient Egypt in Early Modern Italy* (Chicago and London: University of Chicago Press, 2007).

Davies, Martin, *Aldus Manutius: Printer and Publisher of Renaissance Venice* (London: British Library, 1995).

Deane, Jennifer, *A History of Medieval Heresy and Inquisition* (Lanham, MD: Rowman and Littlefield, 2011).

Dear, Peter, *Revolutionizing the Sciences: European Knowledge and its Ambitions, 1500–1700*, 2nd ed. (London: Palgrave Macmillan, 2009).

DeGregorio, Scott (ed.), *The Cambridge Companion to Bede* (Cambridge: Cambridge University Press, 2010).

Devlin, Keith, *The Man of Numbers: Fibonacci's Arithmetic Revolution* (London: Bloomsbury, 2011).

Dickens, A. G. and Whitney Jones, *Erasmus the Reformer* (London: Methuen, 2000).

Dinshaw, Minoo, *Outlandish Knight, The Byzantine Life of Steven Runciman* (London: Allen Lane/Penguin, 2016).

Domingo, Rafael and Giovanni Minnucci, 'Alberico Gentili and the Secularization of the Law of Nations', forthcoming in Rafael Domingo and John Witte (eds.), *Christianity and Global Law: An Introduction* (Cambridge: Cambridge University Press, 2020).

Donnelly, John Patrick, 'New Religious Orders for Men', pp. 162–179, in R. Po-Chia Hsia (ed.), *The Cambridge History of Christianity: Volume 6, Reform and Expansion, 1500–1660* (Cambridge: Cambridge University Press, 2007).

Duffy, Eamon, *The Stripping of the Altars* (New Haven and London: Yale University Press, 1992).
———, *The Voices of Morebath: Reformation and Rebellion in an English Village* (New Haven and London: Yale University Press, 2001).
———, *Marking the Hours, English People and their Prayers 1240–1570* (New Haven and London: Yale University Press, 2006).

Eisenstein, Elizabeth, *The Printing Revolution in Early Modern Europe*, 2nd ed. (Cambridge: Cambridge University Press, 2005).

Eire, Carlos, *Reformations, The Early Modern World, 1450–1650* (New Haven and London: Yale University Press, 2016).

Everett, Barbara, *Young Hamlet, Essays on Shakespeare's Tragedies* (Oxford: Clarendon Press, 1989).

Everitt, Anthony, *Cicero: A Turbulent Life* (London: John Murray, 2001).

Faietti, Marzia and Hugo Chapman, *Fra Angelico to Leonardo: Italian Renaissance Drawings* (London: British Museum Press, 2010).

Febvre, Lucien and Henri-Jean Martin, *The Coming of the Book: The Impact of Printing 1450–1800*, 3rd ed. (New York: Verso, 2010).

Feser, Edward, *Aquinas: A Beginner's Guide* (London: Oneworld Publications, 2009).

Fitzgerald, Allan (ed.), *Augustine Through the Ages: An Encyclopedia* (Cambridge: William Eerdmans, 1999).

Flint, Valerie, *The Rise of Magic in Early Modern Europe* (Princeton and Oxford: Princeton University Press, 1991).

Frankopan, Peter, *The Silk Roads, A New History of the World* (London: Bloomsbury, 2015).

Freedberg, David, *The Eye of the Lynx, Galileo, His Friends, and the Beginnings of Modern Natural History* (Chicago and London: Chicago University Press, 2002).

Freeman, Charles, *The Closing of the Western Mind, The Rise of Faith and the Fall of Reason* (London: William Heinemann, 2002).
———, *AD 381* (London: Pimlico, 2009;).
———, *Holy Bones, Holy Dust: How Relics Shaped the History of Medieval Europe* (New Haven and London: Yale University Press, 2012).
———, *Egypt, Greece and Rome: Civilizations of the Ancient Mediterranean*, 3rd ed. (Oxford: Oxford University Press, 2014).
———, 'Historical Introduction' to *Blue Guide Florence*, 11th ed., (London: Somerset Books, 2017).

French, Katherine, 'Localised Faith: Parochial and Domestic Spaces', pp.166–82, in John H. Arnold (ed.), *The Oxford Handbook of Medieval Christianity* (Oxford: Oxford University Press, 2014).

Fried, Joannes (trans. Peter Lewis), *The Middle Ages* (Cambridge, MA and London: Belknap Press of Harvard University Press, 2015).

Fritze, Ronald, *New Worlds, The Great Voyages of Discovery 1400–1600* (Stroud: Sutton Publishing, 2002).

Fukuyama, Francis, *The End of History and the Last Man* (New York: The Free Press, 1993).

Fumaroli, Marc, *The Republic of Letters* (New Haven and London: Yale University Press, 2018).

Ganz, David, 'Book Production in the Carolingian Empire and the Spread of Caroline Miniscule', pp. 786–808, in Rosamond McKitterick (ed.), *The New Cambridge Medieval History: Volume 2, c.700–c.900* (Cambridge: Cambridge University Press, 1995).

Garber, Daniel, 'Physics and Foundations', pp. 19–69, in Katherine Park and Lorraine Daston (eds.), *The Cambridge History of Science: Volume 3, Early Modern Science* (Cambridge: Cambridge University Press, 2006).

Gatti, Hilary, *Essays on Giordano Bruno* (Princeton and Oxford: Princeton University Press, 2011).

Ghosh, Khantir, 'Wycliffites and Lollardy', pp. 443–445, in Miri Rubin and Walter Simons (eds.), *The Cambridge History of Christianity: Volume 4, Christianity in Western Europe c.1100–c.1500* (Cambridge: Cambridge University Press, 2009).

Gilson, Étienne, *History of Christian Philosophy in the Middle Ages* (London: Sheed and Ward, 1955).

Gingerich, Owen, *The Book that Nobody Read: Chasing the Revolutions of Nicolaus Copernicus* (New York: Walker and Son, 2004).

Gittes, Tobias Foster, 'Boccaccio and Humanism', pp. 155–170, in Guyda Armstrong (ed.), *The Cambridge Companion to Boccaccio* (Cambridge: Cambridge University Press, 2015).

Gleick, James, *Isaac Newton* (London and New York: Fourth Estate, 2003).

Goodriaan, Koen, 'Empowerment Through Reading, Writing and Example: The *Devotio Moderna*', pp. 407–19, in Miri Rubin and Walter Simons (eds.) *The Cambridge History of Christianity: Volume 4, Christianity in Western Europe c.1100–c.1500* (Cambridge: Cambridge University Press, 2009).

Gordon, Bruce, *Calvin* (New Haven and London: Yale University Press, 2011).

Gottlieb, Anthony, *The Dream of Enlightenment: The Rise of Modern Philosophy* (London: Allen Lane/Penguin, 2016).

Grafton, Anthony, *Leon Battista Alberti, Master Builder of the Italian Renaissance* (London: Allen Lane/Penguin, 2000).
———, 'Libraries and Lecture Halls', pp. 238–50, in Katharine Park and Lorraine Daston (eds.), *The Cambridge History of Science: Volume 3, Early Modern Science* (Cambridge : Cambridge University Press, 2006).
———, *Worlds made by Words: Scholarship and Community in the Modern West* (Cambridge MA and London: Harvard University Press, 2009).
———, 'Diogenes Laertius: From Inspiration to Annoyance (and Back)', pp. 536–544 in James Miller (ed.), *Lives of the Eminent Philosophers by Diogenes Laertius* (Oxford: Oxford University Press, 2018).

Grafton, Anthony, et al. (eds.), *The Classical Tradition* (Cambridge, MA and London: Belknap Press of Harvard University Press, 2010).

Grant, Edward, *God and Reason in the Middle Ages* (Cambridge: Cambridge University Press, 2001).

Gray, John, *Straw Dogs: Thoughts on Humans and Other Animals* (London: Granta Books, 2002).
———, *Heresies: Against Progress and Other Illusions* (London: Granta Books, 2004).
———, *Seven Types of Atheism* (London: Allen Lane, 2018).
Grayling, A. C., *The Age of Genius: The Seventeenth Century and the Birth of the Modern Mind* (London: Bloomsbury, 2016).

Grazia, Margreta de, *Hamlet without Hamlet* (Cambridge: Cambridge University Press, 2007).

Greenblatt, Stephen, *Renaissance Self-Fashioning: From More to Shakespeare* (Chicago and London: University of Chicago Press, 1980).
———, *Marvellous Possessions: The Wonder of the New World* (Chicago and London: University of Chicago Press, 1991).
———, *The Swerve: How the World Became Modern* (New York: W. W. Norton, 2011, English edition, *The Swerve, How the Renaissance Began*, London: Vintage, 2012).

Greengrass, Mark, *Christendom Destroyed: Europe 1517–1648* (London: Allen Lane/Penguin, 2014).

Gribbin, John, *Science: A History* (London: Allen Lane/Penguin, 2002).

Griffiths, Eric, *If Not Critical* (Oxford: Oxford University Press, 2018).

Guicciardini, Niccolo, *Isaac Newton and Natural Philosophy* (London: Reaktion Books, 2018).

Gunn, Steven, *Henry VII's New Men and the Making of Tudor England* (Oxford: Oxford University Press, 2016).

Hale, John, *The Civilization of Europe in the Renaissance* (London: Harper Perennial, 2005).

Hall, Edith, *Aristotle's Way: How Ancient Wisdom Can Change Your Life* (London: Bodley Head, 2018).

Hamburger, Joseph, *John Stuart Mill on Liberty and Control* (Princeton and Oxford: Princeton University Press, 1999).

Hamel, Christopher de, *Meetings with Remarkable Manuscripts* (London: Allen Lane/Penguin, 2016).

Hanke, Lewis, *Aristotle and the American Indians: A Study of Race Prejudice in the Modern World* (Chicago: Henry Regnery Company, 1959).

Hankins, James, *Plato in the Italian Renaissance*, 2 vols, Columbia Studies in the Classical Tradition (Leiden and New York: E. J. Brill, 1990).
———, 'Rhetoric, History and Ideology: The Civic Panegyrics of Leonardo Bruni', pp. 143–78, in James Hankins (ed.), *Renaissance Civic Humanism: Reappraisals and Reflections* (Cambridge: Cambridge University Press, 2000).
———, *Humanism and Platonism in the Italian Renaissance*, 2 vols (Rome: Edizioni di storia e litteratura 2004).
——— (ed.), *Renaissance Civic Humanism: Reappraisals and Reflections* (Cambridge: Cambridge University Press, 2000).
——— (ed.), *The Cambridge Companion to Renaissance Philosophy* (Cambridge: Cambridge University Press, 2007).

Harper, Kyle, *Slavery in the Late Roman World, AD 275–425* (Cambridge: Cambridge University Press, 2011).

Harries, Jill, *Sidonius Apollinaris and the Fall of Rome, AD 407–485* (Oxford: Clarendon Press, 1994).

Harris, Robin, *Dubrovnik: A History* (London: SAQI, 2003).

Haskell, Francis and Nicholas Penny, *Taste and the Antique: The Lure of Classical Sculpture 1500–1900* (New Haven and London: Yale University Press, 1981).

Haskins, Charles, *The Renaissance of the Twelfth Century* (Harvard MA, and London: Harvard University Press, 1927).

Hawes, James, *The Shortest History of Germany* (London: Old Street Publishing Ltd., 2017).

Hazard, Paul, *The Crisis of the European Mind, 1680–1715*, trans J. Lewis May (New York: New York Review Books Classics, 2013).

Heale, Martin, *The Abbots and Priors of Late Medieval and Reformation England* (Oxford: Oxford University Press, 2016).

Heather, Peter, *The Fall of the Roman Empire: A New History of Rome and the Barbarians* (Oxford: Oxford University Press, 2005).
———, *Empires and Barbarians: Migration, Development and the Birth of Europe* (London: Macmillan, 2009).

Hedley, J. and J. Tomaro (eds.), *San Carlo Borromeo: Catholic Reform and Ecclesiastical Politics in the Second Half of the Sixteenth Century* (Washington, DC: Folger Books, 1988).

Heilbron, J. L., *Galileo* (Oxford: Oxford University Press, 2010).

Helvétius, Anne-Marie and Michael Kaplan, 'Asceticism and its Institutions', pp. 275–98, in Thomas Noble and Julia Smith (eds.), *The Cambridge History of Christianity: Volume 3, Early Medieval Christianities, c.600–1100* (Cambridge: Cambridge University Press, 2008).

Henderson, John, *Piety and Charity in Late Medieval Florence* (Chicago and London: University of Chicago Press, 1994).

Henry, John, *The Scientific Revolution and the Origins of Modern Science*, 3rd ed. (London: Red Globe Press, Macmillan International Higher Education, 2008).

Hill, Christopher, *The World Turned Upside Down, Radical Ideas During the English Revolution* (Harmondsworth, Penguin Books, 1975).
———, *God's Englishman: Oliver Cromwell and the English Revolution* (London: Weidenfeld and Nicolson, 1979).

Hodgkin, Thomas, *The Letters of Cassiodorus* (London: Henry Frowde, 1886).

Hodgson, Peter E., *Theology and Modern Physics* (London: Routledge, 2017).

Hoenen, Maarten and Robert Wisnovsky, 'Philosophy and Theology', pp. 689–706 in Robert Pasnau (ed.), *The Cambridge History of Medieval Philosophy: Volume 2* (Cambridge: Cambridge University Press, 2010).

Hollingsworth, Mary, *The Medici* (London: Head of Zeus, 2017).

Hoskin, Michael (ed.), *The Cambridge Concise History of Astronomy* (Cambridge: Cambridge University Press, 1999).
———,and Gingerich, Owen, 'Medieval Latin Astronomy', pp. 68–93, in Michael Hoskin (ed.), *The Cambridge Concise History of Astronomy* (Cambridge University Press, 1999).

Housley, Norman, *Religious Warfare in Europe, 1400–1536* (Oxford: Oxford University Press, 2002).

Howard, Deborah, *Venice and the East: The Impact of the Islamic World on Venetian Architecture, 1100–1500* (New Haven and London: Yale University Press, 2000).

Hsia, R. Po-Chia, *The World of Catholic Renewal, 1540– 1770*, 2nd ed. (Cambridge: Cambridge University Press, 2005).
——— (ed.), *The Cambridge History of Christianity: Volume 6, Reform and Expansion 1500–1660* (Cambridge: Cambridge University Press, 2007).

Hughes, Kathleen, *The Church in Early Irish Society* (Ithaca, New York: Cornell University Press, 1966).

Humfress, Caroline, 'Law and Legal Practice in the Age of Justinian', pp. 161–84, in Michael Maas (ed.), *The Cambridge Companion to Justinian* (Cambridge: Cambridge University Press, 2005).

Iliffe, Rob, *Priest of Nature: The Religious Worlds of Isaac Newton* (New York: Oxford University Press, 2017).

Ingram, Robert, *Reformation without End: Religion, Politics and the Past in Post-Revolutionary England* (Manchester: Manchester University Press, 2018).

Israel, Jonathan, *The Dutch Republic: Its Rise, Greatness and Fall, 1477–1806* (Oxford: Clarendon Press, 1993).
———, *Radical Enlightenment: Philosophy and the Making of Modernity 1650–1750* (Oxford: Oxford University Press, 2001).
———, *Enlightenment Contested: Philosophy, Modernity, and the Emancipation of Man, 1670–1752* (Oxford: Oxford University Press, 2006).
———, Revolutionary Ideas: *An Intellectual History of the French Revolution from the Rights of Man to Robespierre* (Princeton and Oxford: Princeton University Press, 2015).

Jacobus, Laura, *Giotto and the Arena Chapel: Art, Architecture and Experience* (Turnhout: Brepols/Harvey Miller Publications, 2008).

Jacoff, Rachel (ed.,), *The Cambridge Companion to Dante*, 2nd ed. (Cambridge: Cambridge University Press, 2007).

Jardine, Lisa, *The Curious Life of Robert Hooke, the Man who Measured London* (London: HarperCollins, 2003).

Jenkyns, Richard, *The Victorians and Ancient Greece* (Oxford: Blackwell, 1980).

Jones, Alexander, *A Portable Cosmos: Revealing the Antikythera Mechanism, Scientific Wonder of the Ancient World* (New York: Oxford University Press, 2017).

Jones, Michael (ed.), *The New Cambridge Medieval History: Volume 6, c.1300–c.1415* (Cambridge: Cambridge University Press, 2000).

Jones, Philip, *The Italian City-State: From Commune to Signoria* (Oxford: Clarendon Press, 1997).

Kaminsky, Howard, 'The Great Schism', pp. 674–96 in Michael Jones (ed.), *The New Cambridge Medieval History: Volume 6, c.1300–c.1415* (Cambridge: Cambridge University Press, 2000).

Kaye, Joel, *A History of Balance, 1250–1375* (Cambridge: Cambridge University Press, 2014).

Kelly, Paul and David Boucher (eds.), *Political Thinkers: From Socrates to the Present* (Oxford: Oxford University Press, 2003).

Kemp, Martin, *Leonardo da Vinci: The Marvellous Works of Nature and Man* (Oxford: Oxford University Press, 2006).
———, *Leonardo da Vinci: Experience, Experiment and Design* (London: Victoria and Albert Publications, 2007).
———, *Living with Leonardo: Fifty Years of Sanity and Insanity in the Art World and Beyond* (London: Thames and Hudson, 2018).

Kenny, Anthony, *Medieval Philosophy: A New History of Western Philosophy, Volume 2* (Oxford: Oxford University Press, 2005).
———, *The Rise of Modern Philosophy: A New History of Western Philosophy, Volume 3* (Oxford: Oxford University Press, 2006).

Kenny, Anthony, et al., *Renaissance Thinkers* (Oxford: Oxford University Press, 1993).

King, Ross, *Brunelleschi's Dome: The Story of the Great Cathedral in Florence* (London: Penguin Books, 2000).

Kingdon, Robert, M., 'The Calvinist Reformation in Geneva', pp. 90–103, in R. Po-Chia Hsia (ed.), *The Cambridge History of Christianity: Volume 6, Reform and Expansion 1500–1660* (Cambridge: Cambridge University Press, 2007).

Kishlansky, Mark, *The Penguin History of Britain: A Monarchy Transformed, Britain 1630–1714* (London: Allen Lane/Penguin, 1996).

Knight, Jeremy K., *The End of Antiquity: Archaeology, Society and Religion, AD 235–700* (Stroud: Tempus Publishing, 1999).

Kraye, Jill, 'The Revival of Hellenistic philosophies', pp. 97–112, in James Hankins (ed.), *The Cambridge Companion to Renaissance Philosophy* (Cambridge: Cambridge University Press, 2007).
——— (ed.), *The Cambridge Companion to Renaissance Humanism* (Cambridge: Cambridge University Press, 1994).

Kristeller, Paul Oskar, *Eight Philosophers of the Italian Renaissance* (Stanford, CA: Stanford University Press, 1964).

Laird, Walter Roy, 'Change and Motion', pp. 404–35 in David Lindberg and Michael Shank (eds.), *The Cambridge History of Science: Volume 2, Medieval Science* (Cambridge: Cambridge University Press, 2013).

Lambdin, Laura and Robert Lambdin, *Encyclopedia of Medieval Literature* (Westport, CT: Greenwood Press, 2000).

Lancel, Serge, *St Augustine* (London, SCM Press, 2002).

Landtsheer, Jeanine G. de, 'Michel de Montaigne, Marie De Gournay and Justus Lipsius. Some Overlooked Particulars Preserved at Leiden University Library', pp. 63–78, in Karl A. E. Enenkel and Mark S. Smith (eds.), *Montaigne and the Low Countries (1580–1700)* (Leiden: Brill, 2007).

Lapidge, Michael, *The Anglo-Saxon Library* (Oxford: Oxford University Press, 2006).

Lea, Henry, *A History of Auricular Confession and Indulgences in the Latin Church* (Philadelphia: Lea Brothers, 1896).

Legassie, Shayne Aaron, *The Medieval Invention of Travel* (Chicago and London: Chicago University Press, 2017).

Leroi, Armand, *The Lagoon: How Aristotle Invented Science* (London and New York: Bloomsbury, 2014).

Levi, Anthony, *Renaissance and Reformation: The Intellectual Genesis* (New Haven and London: Yale University Press, 2002).

Lewis-Jones, Hugh (ed.), *The Writer's Map: An Atlas of Imaginary Lands* (London: Thames and Hudson, 2018).

Lindberg, David, *The Beginnings of Western Science*, 2nd ed. (Chicago and London: University of Chicago Press, 2007).
———, 'Science and the Medieval Church', pp. 268–85, in David Lindberg and Michael Shank (eds.), *The Cambridge History of Science: Volume 2, Medieval Science* (Cambridge: Cambridge University Press, 2013).

Lindberg, David and Michael Shank, 'Introduction', pp. 1–26 in David Lindberg and Michael Shank (eds.), *The Cambridge History of Science: Volume 2, Medieval Science* (Cambridge: Cambridge University Press, 2013).

Lindberg, David and Michael Shank (eds.), *The Cambridge History of Science: Volume 2, Medieval Science* (Cambridge: Cambridge University Press, 2013).

Lindberg, David and Katherine Tachau, 'The Science of Light and Color: Seeing and Knowing', pp. 485–511 in David Lindberg and Michael Shank (eds.), *The Cambridge History of Science: Volume 2, Medieval Science* (Cambridge: Cambridge University Press, 2013).

Lloyd, Geoffrey, *Aristotelian Explorations* (Cambridge: Cambridge University Press, 1996).

Long, A. A., *Hellenistic Philosophy* (London: Bloomsbury, 1996).

Lowe, E. J., *Locke* (London: Routledge, 2005).

Lowry, Martin, *The World of Aldus Manutius: Business and Scholarship in Renaissance Venice* (Oxford: Blackwell, 1979).

Luscombe, David, and Jonathan Riley-Smith (eds.), *The New Cambridge Medieval History: Volume 4, c.1024–c.1198, Part 1* (Cambridge: Cambridge University Press, 2004).

Maas, Michael (ed.), *The Cambridge Companion to Justinian* (Cambridge: Cambridge University Press, 2005).

Macadam, Alta, *Blue Guide Florence*, 11th ed. (London: Somerset Books, 2017).

McClelland, J. S., *A History of Western Political Thought* (London: Routledge, 1996).

McCormick, Michael, *The Origins of the European Economy: Communications and Commerce, AD 300–900* (Cambridge: Cambridge University Press, 2001).

MacCulloch, Diarmaid, *Thomas Cranmer* (New Haven and London: Yale University Press, 1996).
———, *Reformation: Europe's House Divided 1490–1700* (London: Allen Lane/Penguin, 2003).
———, *All Things Made New: Writings of the Reformation* (London: Allen Lane/Penguin, 2016).
———, *Thomas Cromwell: A Life* (London: Allen Lane/Penguin, 2018).

McKitterick, Rosamond, *The Carolingians and the Written Word* (Cambridge: Cambridge University Press, 2008).
———, *Charlemagne: The Formation of a European Identity* (Cambridge: Cambridge University Press, 2008).
——— (ed.), *Carolingian Culture: Emulation and Innovation* (Cambridge: Cambridge University Press, 1994).
——— (ed.), *The New Cambridge Medieval History: Volume 2, c.700–c.900* (Cambridge: Cambridge University Press, 1995).

Machamer, Peter, *The Cambridge Companion to Galileo* (Cambridge: Cambridge University Press, 1998).

Machiavelli, Niccolò, *The Prince*, trans and ed., Tim Parks, Oxford Classics (Oxford: Oxford University Press, 2011).

Mackintosh-Smith, Tim, *Arabs: A 3,000 Year History of Peoples, Tribes and Empires* (New Haven and London: Yale University Press, 2019).

Macintyre, Alasdair, *After Virtue* (Notre Dame IN: Notre Dame Press, 1981).

Madigan, Kevin, *Medieval Christianity: A New History* (New Haven and London: Yale University Press, 2015).

Majanlahti, Anthony, *The Families Who Made Rome: A History and a Guide* (London: Chatto and Windus, 2005).

Makdisi, George, *The Rise of Colleges: Institutions of Learning in Islam and the West* (Edinburgh: Edinburgh University Press, 1981).

Malcolm, Noel, *Useful Enemies: Islam and the Ottoman Empire in Western Political Thought, 1450–1750* (Oxford: Oxford University Press, 2019).

Mann, William, E., 'Faith and Reason', pp. 707–19, *The Cambridge History of Medieval Philosophy: Volume 2* (Cambridge: Cambridge University Press, 2010).

Mansel, Philip, *King of the World: The Life of Louis XIV* (London: Allen Lane/Penguin, 2019).

Marenbon, John, 'Carolingian Thought', Chapter Six in Rosamond McKitterick (ed.), *Carolingian Culture: Emulation and Innovation* (Cambridge: Cambridge University Press, 1994).
———, *Medieval Philosophy: An Historical and Philosophical Introduction* (London and New York: Routledge, 2007).
———, *Pagans and Philosophers: The Problem of Paganism from Augustine to Leibniz* (Princeton and Oxford: Princeton University Press, 2015).

Marenbon, John (ed.), *The Cambridge Companion to Boethius* (Cambridge: Cambridge University Press, 2009).

Marshall, John, *John Locke: Toleration and Enlightenment Culture* (Cambridge: Cambridge University Press, 2006).

Marshall, Peter, *Heretics and Believers: A History of the English Reformation* (New Haven and London: Yale University Press, 2017).
———, *Martin Luther and the Invention of the Reformation* (Oxford: Oxford University Press, 2017).
——— (ed.), *The Oxford Illustrated History of the Reformation* (Oxford: Oxford University Press, 2015).

Martinich, A. P., *Hobbes: A Biography* (Cambridge: Cambridge University Press, 1999).

Massar, Phyllis and James Ackerman, *Palladio* (London: Pelican Books, 1966).

Massing, Michael, *Fatal Discord: Erasmus, Luther and the Fight for the Western Mind* (New York: HarperCollins, 2016).

Mattern, Susan, *The Prince of Medicine: Galen in the Roman Empire* (New York: Oxford University Press, 2013).

Maurer, Armand, *Medieval Philosophy*, 2nd ed. (Rome: Pontifical Institute of Medieval Studies, 1982).

Melling, David, *Understanding Plato* (Oxford: Oxford University Press, 1987).

Merton, Robert, *Science, Technology and Society in Seventeenth-Century England* (Bruges: St Catherine Press, 1938, New York: Howard Fertig, 2002).

Miller, James (ed.), *Lives of the Eminent Philosophers by Diogenes Laertius* (Oxford: Oxford University Press, 2018).

Mills, Kenneth, 'The Naturalization of Andean Christianities', pp. 504–35, in R. Po-Chia Hsia (ed.), *The Cambridge History of Christianity: Volume 6, Reform and Expansion 1500–1660* (Cambridge: Cambridge University Press, 2007).

Minnucci, Giovanni and Rafael Domingo, 'Alberico Gentili and the Secularization of the Law of Nations', forthcoming in Rafael Domingo and John Witte (eds.), *Christianity and Global Law: An Introduction* (Cambridge: Cambridge University Press, 2020).

Mokyr, Joel, *The Culture of Growth: The Origins of the Modern Economy* (Princeton and Oxford: Princeton University Press, 2016).

Molland, A. George, 'Mathematics', pp. 512–31 in David Lindberg and Michael Shank (eds.), *The Cambridge History of Science. Volume 2, Medieval Science* (Cambridge: Cambridge University Press, 2013).

Montaigne, Michel de (trans. M. A. Screech), *The Complete Essays*, rev. ed. (London: Penguin Classics, 2003).

Moore, R. I., *The Formation of a Persecuting Society: Authority and Deviance in Western Europe, 950–1250*, rev. ed. (Oxford: Wiley/Blackwell, 2006).

Mout, Nicolette, 'Peace without concord: religious toleration in theory and practice', pp.227–243 in R. Po-Chia Hsia (ed.), *The Cambridge History of Christianity: Volume 6, Reform and Expansion, 1500–1660* (Cambridge: Cambridge University Press, 2007).

Mormando, Franco, *The Preacher's Demons: Bernardino of Siena and the Social Underworld of Early Renaissance Italy* (Chicago and London: University of Chicago Press, 1999).

Murray, Alexander, *Reason and Society in the Middle Ages* (Oxford: Oxford University Press, 1978).

Nadler, Steven, *Spinoza: A Life*, 2nd ed. (Cambridge: Cambridge University Press, 2018).

Najemy, John, 'Dante and Florence', pp. 236–256 in Rachel Jacoff (ed.), *The Cambridge Companion to Dante*, 2nd ed. (Cambridge: Cambridge University Press, 2007).

Najemy, John, *A History of Florence, 1200–1575* (Oxford: Wiley-Blackwell, 2008).

Najemy, John M. (ed.), *Italy in the Age of the Renaissance* (Oxford: Oxford University Press, 2004).

Nauert, Charles, *Humanism and the Culture of Renaissance Europe*, 2nd ed. (Cambridge: Cambridge University Press, 2018).

Nederman, Cary J., 'Marsiglio of Padua', pp. 124 –38, in David Boucher and Paul Kelly (eds.), *Political Thinkers: From Socrates to the Present* (Oxford: Oxford University Press, 2003).

Nelson, Eric, *The Greek Tradition in Republican Thought* (Cambridge: Cambridge University Press, 2000).
———, 'The Problem of the Prince', pp. 319 –77 in James Hankins (ed.), *The Cambridge Companion to Renaissance Philosophy* (Cambridge: Cambridge University Press, 2007).
———, *The Hebrew Republic, Jewish Sources and the Transformation of European Political Thought* (Cambridge MA and London: Harvard University Press, 2010).

Nelson, Janet L., *King and Emperor: A New Life of Charlemagne* (London: Allen Lane/Penguin, 2019).

Nicholl, Charles, *Leonardo da Vinci: The Flights of the Mind* (London: Allen Lane/Penguin, 2004).

Niekerk, Carl, (ed.), *The Radical Enlightenment in Germany: A Cultural Perspective* (Leiden: Brill, 2018).

Noble, Thomas and Julia Smith (eds.), *The Cambridge History of Christianity: Volume 3, Early Medieval Christianities, c.600–1100* (Cambridge: Cambridge University Press, 2008).

Nurminen, Mario, T., *The Mapmakers' World: A Cultural History of the European World Map* (London: Pool of London Press, 2015).

O'Callaghan, Joseph, *Reconquest and Crusade in Medieval Spain* (Philadelphia: University of Pennsylvania Press, 2004).

O'Donnell, James, *Cassiodorus* (Berkeley: University of California Press, 1969).

Ogilvie, Brian W., *The Science of Describing: Natural History in Renaissance Europe* (Chicago and London: University of Chicago Press, 2006).

Oldfield, Paul, *Urban Panegyric and the Transformation of the Medieval City 1100–1300* (Oxford: Oxford University Press, 2019).

O'Malley, John W., *Trent: What Happened at the Council* (Cambridge, MA and London: Belknap Press of Harvard University Press, 2013).
———, *The Jesuits: A History from Ignatius to the Present* (Lanham, MD: Rowman and Littlefield, 2017).

Orchard, Andy, 'Language, Literature and Learning', pp. 33–8 in Claire Breay and Joanna Story (eds.), *Anglo-Saxon Kingdoms, Art, Word, War* (London: British Library, 2018).

Osler, Margaret J., *Reconfiguring the World: Nature, God and Human Understanding from the Middle Ages to Early Modern Europe* (Baltimore, MD: Johns Hopkins University Press, 2010).

Ostler, Nicholas, *Ad Infinitum: A Biography of Latin and the World it Created* (London: Harper Press, 2007).

Ostrow, Steven, *Art and Spirituality in Counter-Reformation Rome: The Sistine and Pauline Chapels in S. Maria Maggiore* (Cambridge: Cambridge University Press, 1996).

Ozment, Steven, *The Age of Reform, 1250–1550: An Intellectual and Religious History of Late Medieval and Reformation Europe* (New Haven and London: Yale University Press, 1980).

Pagden, Anthony, *The Fall of Natural Man: The American Indian and the Origins of Comparative Ethnology* (Cambridge: Cambridge University Press, 1982).
———, *European Encounters with the New World* (New Haven and London: Yale University Press, 1993).

Page, Christopher, *The Christian West and its Singers* (New Haven and London: Yale University Press, 2010).

Park, Katherine and Lorraine Daston, (eds.), *The Cambridge History of Science: Volume 3, Early Modern Science* (Cambridge: Cambridge University Press, 2006.)

Parker, Geoffrey, *The Thirty Years War*, 2nd ed. (London: Routledge, 1997).
———, *Emperor: A New Life of Charles V* (New Haven and London: Yale University Press, 2019).

Partridge, Loren, *The Renaissance in Rome* (London: Weidenfeld and Nicolson, 1996).
———, *Art of Renaissance Florence, 1400–1600* (Berkeley, CA: University of California Press, 2009).

Pasnau, Robert (ed.), *The Cambridge History of Medieval Philosophy, Volumes 1 and 2* (Cambridge: Cambridge University Press, 2010).

Pedersen, Olaf (trans. Richard North), *The First Universities: Studium Generale and the Origins of University Education in Europe* (Cambridge: Cambridge University Press, 1997).

Pennington, K., *The Prince and the Law, 1200–1600: Sovereignty and Rights in the Western Legal Tradition* (Berkeley, CA: University of California Press, 1993).

Pettegree, Andrew, *The Book in the Renaissance* (New Haven and London: Yale University Press, 2010).
———, *Brand Luther* (London: Penguin Books, 2016).

Pettegree, Andrew and Arthur de Weduwen, *The Bookshop of the World: Making and Trading Books in the Dutch Golden Age* (New Haven and London: Yale University Press, 2019).

Phillips, Jonathan, *Holy Warriors: A Modern History of the Crusades* (London: Bodley Head, 2009).

Christophe Picard, *The Sea of the Caliphs: The Mediterranean in the Medieval Islamic World*, trans. Nicholas Elliott (Cambridge MA and London: Belknap Press of Harvard University Press, 2018).

Pincus, Steve, *1688: The First Modern Revolution* (New Haven and London: Yale University Press, 2009).

Pinner, Rebecca, *The Cult of St. Edmund in Medieval East Anglia* (Woodbridge: Boydell Press, 2015).

Popkin, Richard, *The History of Scepticism from Savonarola to Bayle*, rev. ed. (Oxford: Oxford University Press, 2003).

Porter, Roy, *The Greatest Benefit to Mankind: A Medical History of Humanity from Antiquity to the Present* (London: HarperCollins, 2007).

Principe, Lawrence M., *The Scientific Revolution: A Very Short Introduction* (Oxford: Oxford University Press, 2011).

Pullen, Brian, *Rich and Poor in Renaissance Venice* (Cambridge MA and London: Harvard University Press, 1971).

Putallaz, François-Xavier, 'Censorship', pp. 99–113 in *The Cambridge History of Medieval Philosophy: Volume 1* in Robert Pasnau (ed.), *The Cambridge History of Medieval Philosophy: Volume 1* (Cambridge: Cambridge University Press, 2010).

Putnam, Robert, et al., *Making Democracy Work: Civic Traditions in Modern Italy* (Princeton and Oxford: Princeton University Press, 1993).

Rapp, Claudia, *Holy Bishops in Late Antiquity: The Nature of Christian Leadership in an Age of Transition* (Berkeley: University of California Press, 2005).
———, 'Bessarion', pp. 125–6 in Anthony Grafton et al. (eds.), *The Classical Tradition* (Cambridge, MA and London: Belknap Press of Harvard University Press, 2010).

Rée, Jonathan, *Witcraft: The Invention of Philosophy in English* (London: Allen Lane/Penguin Books, 2019).

Regenos, Graydon (ed. and trans.), *The Letters of Lupus of Ferrières* (The Hague, Nijhoff, 1966).

Reynolds, Barbara, *Dante: The Poet, the Political Thinker, the Man* (London and New York: I. B. Tauris, 2006).

Reynolds, L. D. and N. G. Wilson, *Scribes and Scholars: A Guide to the Transmission of Greek and Latin Literature*, 4th ed. (Oxford: Oxford University Press, 2013).

Ridder-Symeons, Hilde de (ed.), *A History of the University in Europe: Volume 1, Universities in the Middle Ages* (Cambridge: Cambridge University Press, 1991).

Riley-Smith, Jonathan, 'The Crusades, 1095–1198', pp. 534–63 in David Luscombe and Jonathan Riley-Smith (eds.), *The New Cambridge Medieval History: Volume 4, c.1024–c.1198, Part 1* (Cambridge: Cambridge University Press, 2004).

Robinson, Ian, *The Papal Reform of the Eleventh Century: Lives of Pope Leo IX and Pope Gregory VII* (Manchester: Manchester University Press, 2004).

Roper, Lyndal, *Martin Luther, Renegade and Prophet* (London: Bodley Head, 2016).

Rowland, Ingrid, 'Raphael's Eminent Philosophers: *The School of Athens* and the Classic Work Almost No One Read', pp. 554–561 in James Miller (ed.), *Lives of the Eminent Philosophers by Diogenes Laertius* (Oxford: Oxford University Press, 2018).

Rowland, Ingrid and Noah Charney, *The Collector of Lives: Giorgio Vasari and the Invention of Art* (London and New York: W. W. Norton and Co., 2017).

Rubin, Miri and Walter Simons (eds.) *The Cambridge History of Christianity: Volume 4, Christianity in Western Europe c.1100–c.1500* (Cambridge: Cambridge University Press, 2009).

Ruggiero, Guido, *The Renaissance in Italy: A Social and Cultural History of the Rinascimento* (Cambridge: Cambridge University Press, 2015).

Ruskin, John, *The Stones of Venice, Volume 2* (London: Smith, Elder and Co., 1853).

Ryan, Alan, *On Politics: A History of Political Thought from Herodotus to the Present* (London: Allen Lane/Penguin, 2012).

Rybczynski, Witold, *The Perfect House: A Journey with Renaissance Master Andrea Palladio* (New York: Scribner, 2002).

Ryle, Gilbert, *Critical Essays, Collected Papers* (London: Routledge, 2009).

Saliba, George, *Islamic Science and the Making of the European Renaissance* (Cambridge MA: MIT Press, 2011).

Santagata, Marco (trans. Richard Dixon), *Dante: The Story of his Life* (Cambridge, MA and London: Belknap Press of Harvard University Press, 2016).

Schama, Simon, *The Embarrassment of Riches: An Interpretation of Dutch Culture in the Golden Age* (London: Collins, 1987).

Shank, Michael and David Lindberg, 'Introduction', in David Lindberg and Michael Shank (eds.), *The Cambridge History of Science: Volume 2, Medieval Science* (Cambridge: Cambridge University Press, 2013).

Shapin, Steven, *The Scientific Revolution* (Chicago and London: University of Chicago Press, 1996).

Shapiro, James, *1599: A Year in the Life of William Shakespeare* (London: Faber and Faber, 2005).

Sharpe, Kevin, *The Personal Rule of Charles I* (New Haven and London: Yale University Press, 1992).

Sharratt, Michael, *Galileo: Decisive Innovator* (Cambridge: Cambridge University Press, 1994).

Shields, Christopher, *The Oxford Handbook of Aristotle* (Oxford: Oxford University Press, 2012).

Siedentop, Larry, *Inventing the Individual: The Origins of Western Liberalism* (London: Allen Lane/Penguin, 2014).

Skinner, Quentin, *The Foundations of Modern Political Thought: Volume 1, The Renaissance* (Cambridge: Cambridge University Press, 1978).

———, 'A Genealogy of the Modern State', pp. 325–70 in Ron Johnston (ed.), *Proceedings of the British Academy, Volume 162, 2008 Lectures* (London: British Academy, 2009).

———, *From Humanism to Hobbes: Studies in Rhetoric and Politics* (Cambridge: Cambridge University Press, 2018).

Slack, Paul, *The Invention of Improvement: Information and Material Progress in Seventeenth-Century England* (Oxford: Oxford University Press, 2015).

Stein, Peter, *Roman Law in European History* (Cambridge: Cambridge University Press, 1999).

Stone, M. W. F. and Robert Wisnovsky, 'Philosophy and Theology', pp. 689–706 in Robert Pasnau (ed.), *The Cambridge History of Medieval Philosophy: Volume 2* (Cambridge: Cambridge University Press, 2010).

Stubblebine, James (ed.), *Giotto: The Arena Chapel Frescos* (New York and London: W. W. Norton, 1996).

Stuurman, Siep, *The Invention of Humanity: Equality and Cultural Difference in World History* (Cambridge MA and London: Harvard University Press, 2017).

Taylor, Charles, *A Secular Age* (Cambridge, MA and London: Belknap Press of Harvard University Press, 2007).

Terpstra, Nicholas, 'Civic Religion', pp. 148–65 in John Arnold (ed.), *The Oxford Handbook of Medieval Christianity* (Oxford: Oxford University Press, 2014).

———, *Religious Refugees in the Early Modern World: An Alternative History of the Reformation* (Cambridge: Cambridge University Press, 2015).

Thomas, Keith, *Man and the Natural World: Changing Attitudes in England 1500–1800* (London: Allen Lane/Penguin, 1983).

———, *In Pursuit of Civility, Manners and Civilization in Early Modern England* (New Haven and London: Yale University Press, 2018).

Thomson, Ian, *Dante's Divine Comedy: A Journey without End* (London: Head of Zeus, 2018).

Thornton, John, *A Cultural History of the Atlantic World, 1250–1820* (Cambridge: Cambridge University Press, 2012).

Thorsteinsson, Runar, *Roman Christianity and Roman Stoicism* (Oxford: Oxford University Press, 2010).

Tinniswood, Adrian, *The Royal Society* (London: Head of Zeus, 2019).

Tremlett, Giles, *Isabella of Castile* (London: Bloomsbury, 2017).

Trevor-Roper, Hugh, *Europe's Physician: The Various Life of Sir Theodore De Mayerne* (New Haven and London: Yale University Press, 2007).

Tuck, Richard, *Hobbes: A Very Short Introduction* (Oxford: Oxford University Press, 1989).

Turner, Denys, *Thomas Aquinas: A Portrait* (New Haven and London: Yale University Press, 2013).

Turner, Frank M., *The Greek Heritage in Victorian Britain* (New Haven and London: Yale University Press, 1981).

Turner, James, *Philology: The Forgotten Origins of the Modern Humanities* (Princeton and Oxford: Princeton University Press, 2014).

Tyerman, Christopher, *How to Plan a Crusade: Reason and Religious War in the High Middle Ages* (London: Allen Lane/Penguin, 2015).
———, *The World of the Crusades: An Illustrated History* (New Haven and London: Yale University Press, 2019).

Van Bueren, Geraldine, 'Take Back Control: A New Commons Charter for the Twenty-First Century is Overdue, 800 Years After the First', *Times Literary Supplement*, 10 March 2017.

Vauchez, André, 'The Religious Orders', in David Abulafia (ed.), pp. 220–55 in *The New Cambridge Medieval History: Volume 5, c.1198–c.1300* (Cambridge: Cambridge University Press, 1999).

Verger, Jacques, 'Schools and Universities', pp. 220–42 in Christopher Allmand (ed.), *The New Cambridge Medieval History: Volume 7, c.1415–c.1500* (Cambridge: Cambridge University Press, 1998).
———, 'The Universities and Scholasticism', pp. 256–78 in David Abulafia (ed.), *The New Cambridge Medieval History: Volume 5, c.1198–c.1300* (Cambridge: Cambridge University Press, 2008).

Vergerio, Claire, *Constructing the Right to War: Alberico Gentili and His Receptions in International Law* (Oxford: Oxford University Research Archive, 2017).

Vollerthun, Ursula, James Richardson (ed.), *The Idea of International Society: Erasmus, Vitoria, Gentili and Grotius* (Cambridge: Cambridge University Press, 2017).

Vout, Caroline, *Classical Art: A Life History from Antiquity to the Present* (Princeton and Oxford: Princeton University Press, 2018).

Walsham, Alexandra, *The Reformation of the Landscape: Religion, Identity, and Memory in Early Modern Britain and Ireland* (Oxford: Oxford University Press, 2011).
———, 'Reformation Legacies', pp. 227–68 in Peter Marshall (ed.), *The Oxford Illustrated History of the Reformation* (Oxford: Oxford University Press, 2015).

Ward-Perkins, Bryan, *The Fall of Rome and the End of Civilization* (Oxford: Oxford University Press, 2006).

Watts, John, *The Making of Polities, 1300–1500* (Cambridge: Cambridge University Press, 2009).

Westgard, Joshua, 'Bede and the Continent in the Carolingian Age and Beyond', pp. 201–15 in Scott DeGregorio (ed.) *The Cambridge Companion to Bede* (Cambridge: Cambridge University Press, 2010).

Wheeler, Catherine and Ben Thomas, *Raphael: The Drawings* (Oxford: Ashmolean Museum, 2017).

White, Eric Marshall, *Editio Princeps: A History of the Gutenberg Bible* (Turnhout: Harvey Miller, 2017).

Wickham, Chris, *The Inheritance of Rome: A History of Europe from 400 to 1000* (London: Allen Lane/Penguin, 2009).
———, *Sleepwalking into a New World: The Emergence of Italian City Communes in the Twelfth Century* (Princeton and Oxford: Princeton University Press, 2015).
———, *Medieval Europe* (New Haven and London: Yale University Press, 2016).

Wilson, Catherine, 'Thomas Hobbes' *Leviathan*', Chapter Twenty-Two in Peter Anstey (ed.), *British Philosophy in the Seventeenth Century* (Oxford: Oxford University Press, 2013).

Wilson, Christopher, *The Gothic Cathedral: The Architecture of the Great Church 1130–1530*, rev. ed. (London: Thames and Hudson, 1992).

Wilson, Peter, *Europe's Tragedy: A New History of the Thirty Years War* (London: Allen Lane/Penguin, 2009).

Wilson-Lee, Edward, *The Catalogue of Shipwrecked Books: Young Columbus and the Search for a Universal Library* (London: William Collins, 2017).

Witt, Ronald, *In the Footsteps of the Ancients: The Origins of Humanism from Lovato to Bruni* (Leiden: Brill, 2000).

Wood, Ian, *The Transformation of the Roman West* (Leeds: ARC Humanities Press, 2018).

Woolhouse, Roger, *Locke: A Biography* (Cambridge: Cambridge University Press, 2007).

Wootton, David, *Galileo; Watcher of the Skies* (New Haven and London: Yale University Press, 2010).
———, *The Invention of Science: A New History of the Scientific Revolution* (London: Penguin Books, 2016).

Wyatt, Michael (ed.), *The Cambridge Companion to the Italian Renaissance* (Cambridge: Cambridge University Press, 2014).

Yates, Frances, *Giordano Bruno and the Hermetic Tradition* (Chicago and London: University of Chicago Press, 1964).

Zagorin, Perez, *How the Idea of Religious Toleration Came to the West* (Princeton and Oxford: Princeton University Press, 2003).

Zutshi, P. N. R., 'The Avignon Papacy', pp. 651–73 in Michael Jones (ed.), *The New Cambridge Medieval History: Volume 6, c.1300–c.1415* (Cambridge: Cambridge University Press, 2000).

Notes

Preface

1 The story is told, with superb illustrations, in Marjo T. Nurminen, *The Mapmakers' World: A Cultural History of the European World Map* (London: Pool of London Press, 2015), pp. 84–92. The story is expanded in my Chapter 17.

2 For the background to this see the outstanding study by Tim Mackintosh-Smith, *Arabs: A 3000 Year History of Peoples, Tribes and Empires* (New Haven, CT, and London: Yale University Press, 2019).

3 Dati's *Sfera-Cosmographia* and its additions are discussed in detail in Nurminen, *The Mapmakers' World*, pp. 122–30.

4 Francis Bacon, *Novum Organum* (1620) Book 1, section 84.

5 A. C. Grayling, *The Age of Genius: The Seventeenth Century and the Birth of the Modern Mind* (London: Bloomsbury, 2016), p. 319.

6 Charles Freeman, *The Closing of the Western Mind: The Rise of Faith and the Fall of Reason* (London: William Heinemann, 2002; New York: Alfred Knopf, 2003).

7 The variety of roles exercised by bishops is well illustrated by Claudia Rapp, *Holy Bishops in Late Antiquity: The Nature of Christian Leadership in an Age of Transition* (Berkeley: University of California Press, 2005). The continuing existence of slavery within a Christianized Roman society is well covered by Kyle Harper in *Slavery in the Late Roman World, AD 275–425* (Cambridge: Cambridge University Press, 2011), especially part 2. For the recognition of 'the poor', see Peter Brown, *Poverty and Leadership in the Later Roman Empire* (Waltham, MA: Brandeis University Press, 2001).

8 Charles Freeman, *AD 381* (New York: Overlook Press, 2009; London: Pimlico, 2009).

9 This issue is explored by Runar Thorsteinsson in his *Roman Christianity and Roman Stoicism* (Oxford: Oxford University Press, 2010). While Stoicism talks of universal human values, Christian ethics contained within them an emphasis on exclusion, not only on earth but permanently in the afterlife, for those who do not make a commitment to Christ.

10 Diarmaid MacCulloch, *Reformation: Europe's House Divided, 1490–1700* (London: Allen Lane/Penguin Books, 2003), p. 671.

Prologue

1 I have provided an overview of this history in my *Egypt, Greece and Rome: Civilizations of the Ancient Mediterranean*, 3rd ed. (Oxford: Oxford University Press, 2014).

2 Siep Stuurman, *The Invention of Humanity: Equality and Cultural Difference in History* (Cambridge, MA, and London: Harvard University Press, 2017), p. 89.

3 'The Antikythera Mechanism was a machine designed to predict celestial phenomena according to the sophisticated astronomical theories current in its day, the sole witness to a lost history of brilliant engineering, a conception of pure genius, one of the great wonders of the ancient world – but it didn't really work very well!' Tony Freeth and Alexander Jones, *The Cosmos in the Antikythera Mechanism*, Institute for the Study of the Ancient World, Paper 4, February 2012. For a full overview see Alexander Jones, *A Portable Cosmos: Revealing the Antikythera Mechanism, Scientific Wonder of the Ancient World* (New York: Oxford University Press, 2017).

1 The Saving of the Texts

1 Rabanus Maurus (*c.*780–856), bishop of Mainz, was a prominent teacher and writer in the Carolingian period. This quotation is to be found in Rosamond McKitterick, *The Carolingians and the Written Word* (Cambridge: Cambridge University Press, 2008), p. 151.

2 A full introduction to Boethius, his life and times can be found in John Marenbon (ed.), *The Cambridge Companion to Boethius* (Cambridge: Cambridge University Press, 2009).

3 There is an English translation of *De nuptiis* in W. Stahl, R. Johnson and E. L. Burge, *Martianus Capella and the Seven Liberal Arts, Volume Two* (New York: Columbia University Press, 1977). The text is discussed in John Marenbon, 'Carolingian Thought', chapter 6 in Rosamond McKitterick (ed.), *Carolingian Culture: Emulation and Innovation* (Cambridge: Cambridge University Press, 1994), pp. 173–4.

4 There is a host of standard introductions to Plato. David Melling's *Understanding Plato* (Oxford: Oxford University Press, 1987) is a readable introduction. Julia Annas's *Plato: A Very Short Introduction* (Oxford: Oxford University Press, 2003) is also recommended.

5 There are 252 references to Plato and the Platonists in Augustine's works, even though he could only read the original texts in Latin translations. See the article 'Plato, Platonism' in Allan Fitzgerald (ed.), *Augustine through the Ages: An Encyclopedia* (Cambridge: William Eerdmans, 1999), pp. 651–3.

6 *The Consolation of Philosophy* is available in many recent editions, including Penguin Classics (1999) and Oxford Classics (2008).

7 A full biography and critique of Cassiodorus's works can be found in James O'Donnell, *Cassiodorus* (Berkeley: University of California Press, 1969), which can also be found online as an e-text (1979) at http://faculty.georgetown.edu/jod/texts/cassbook/toc.html.

8 Thomas Hodgkin, *The Letters of Cassiodorus* (London: Henry Frowde, 1886), p. 58. Also available online at Project Gutenberg at www.gutenberg.org/files/18590/18590-h.htm.

9 See O'Donnell, *Cassiodorus*.

10 This final work of Cassiodorus underlines the purpose of the Vivarium enterprise: the accurate copying of texts. It concludes: 'Farewell, brethren; deign to remember me in your prayers. I have written this brief guide to spelling, and I have prepared copious instructions on the interpretation of scripture. Just as I have sought to separate you from the ranks of the unlearned, so may the heavenly power not allow us to be mixed with evil men in community of punishment' (*De orthographia*, 209.28).

11 *The Etymologies of Isidore of Seville* have been published in a critical edition by Stephen Barney, J. A. Beach, W. J. Lewis and Oliver Berghof (Cambridge: Cambridge University Press, 2006) and I have drawn on their introductory essay for much of the following information.

12 L. D. Reynolds and N. G. Wilson, *Scribes and Scholars: A Guide to the Transmission of Greek and Latin Literature*, 4th ed. (Oxford: Oxford University Press, 2013), p. 85.

13 This was Bishop Braulio, who compiled a list of Isidore's works after his death in 636. Quoted in the introduction of *The Etymologies* (ed. Barney et al.), p. 8, note 10.

14 This point is stressed by John Blair, *Building Anglo-Saxon England* (Princeton, NJ, and Oxford: Princeton University Press, 2018), pp. 131–8. This comprehensive book by an established authority on the subject has received widespread acclaim as the most thorough examination of its subject. In chapter 2, 'Family Stories Charles Might Have Known', of her *King and Emperor: A New Life of Charlemagne* (London: Allen Lane/Penguin, 2019), Janet Nelson touches on the relationship between Charlemagne's forebears and their monastic foundations. See especially the quotations on p. 42.

15 This is recounted in Book 1, chapters 28–32 of *Eusebius: Life of Constantine*, ed. and trans. Averil Cameron and Stuart Hall, in the Clarendon Ancient History Series (Oxford: Clarendon Press, 1999).

16 From Ambrose, *De Fide* (*The Exposition of the Faith*), Book 2, chapter 16. Available online at http://www.newadvent.org/fathers/3404.htm.

17 Quoted in Nelson, *King and Emperor*, p. 86.

18 The quotation comes from Bede in his *Ecclesiastical History*, Book 1, chapter 32. There is a good description of the rituals surrounding Christian kingship (in this case relating to Charlemagne's parents, Pippin and Bertrada) on pp. 70–1 of Nelson, *King and Emperor*.

19 See Anne-Marie Helvétius and Michael Kaplan, 'Asceticism and its Institutions', chapter 13 in Thomas Noble and Julia Smith (eds.), *The Cambridge History of Christianity: Volume 3, Early Medieval Christianities, c.600–1100* (Cambridge: Cambridge University Press, 2008).

20 It is now in the *Biblioteca Laurenziana*, the Medici library in Florence. In 2018, for the first time in 1,300 years, the *Codex* was brought back to England for an exhibition in the British Library in London and it was moving to see this vast compilation. There is an excellent chapter on the *Codex* in Christopher de Hamel's *Meetings with Remarkable Manuscripts* (London: Allen Lane/Penguin Books, 2016), pp. 54–95. On a visit to the Abbazia, Hamel found a relic box which could also be traced back to Northumbria and suggests that they were part of the same intended gift to the pope.

21 A solid and informative introduction to Bede can be found in Scott DeGregorio (ed.), *The Cambridge Companion to Bede* (Cambridge: Cambridge University Press, 2010).

22 Editions of *The Ecclesiastical History of the English People* are widely available, e.g. in Penguin Classics, translated by Leo Sherley-Price (1990), or in Oxford Classics, translated by Bertram Colgrave (2008). This quotation comes from an autobiographical addition at the end of the work.

23 An English translation of the text of the *Letter* is included in J. McClure and R. Collins's translation of the *Ecclesiastical History* (Oxford: Oxford University Press, 1994). Whether it was from his impending death or years of seclusion in monastic life, Bede comes across as deeply distressed.

24 The point and quotation is made in the excellent introduction to Bede's *The Reckoning of Time* in Faith Wallis's translation (Liverpool: Liverpool University Press, 1999), p. lxxxi.

25 The composition of *The Reckoning* is set out in easy stages starting with methods of measuring time and then exploring various calendars and the 'ages of man' up to Bede's day. This is why is it often seen as a teaching manual.

26 David Lindberg, *The Beginnings of Western Science*, 2nd ed. (Chicago and London: University of Chicago Press, 2007), p. 158.

27 John Burrow's *A History of Histories* (London: Allen Lane, 2007) places Bede within the context of his times and explains his superiority to his contemporaries in chapter 15, 'Bede: The English Church and the English People'.

28 There is a good chapter on Bede's influence by Joshua Westgard, 'Bede and the Continent in the Carolingian Age and Beyond', chapter 14 in DeGregorio (ed.), *The Cambridge Companion to Bede*.

29 David Ganz, 'Book Production in the Carolingian Empire and the Spread of Caroline Minuscule', chapter 29 in Rosamond McKitterick (ed.), *The New Cambridge Medieval History: Volume 2* (Cambridge: Cambridge University Press, 1995), p. 797. Uncials, derived from Roman scripts, were ubiquitous in the fourth to eighth centuries for manuscripts. They were written in majuscule, larger (or capital) letters, in contrast to the later Carolingian minuscule, smaller case letters, but were difficult to read out loud as there were no spaces between words.

30 Hamel, *Meetings with Remarkable Manuscripts*, p. 128.

31 From Giles Brown, 'The Carolingian Renaissance', chapter 1 in McKitterick (ed.), *Carolingian Culture*, p. 8.

2 Charlemagne

1 Einhard, *The Life of Charlemagne*, trans. Samuel Epes Turner, chapter 25, available online at https//:sourcebooks.fordham.edu.

2 Biographies of Charlemagne abound. Rosamond McKitterick, *Charlemagne: The Formation of a European Identity* (Cambridge: Cambridge University Press, 2008), is a detailed look at the contemporary sources. This is now joined by the excellent Nelson, *King and Emperor*. Nelson makes a critical assessment of the sources for the period in her introductory chapter. Chris Wickham has two penetrating chapters, 16 and 17, 'The Carolingian Century, 751–887' and 'Intellectuals and Politics' in his authoritative *The Inheritance of Rome: A History of Europe from 400 to 1000* (London: Allen Lane/Penguin, 2009).

3 Quoted in Matthias Becher, *Charlemagne* (New Haven and London: Yale University Press, 2003), p. 60. This brutal policy was announced at a royal assembly in January 775.

4 McKitterick, *Charlemagne*. This is from chapter 1, 'Representations of Charlemagne'.

5 Einhard's biography, together with a later biography by Notker the Stammerer, can be found in a Penguin Classics edition (2008), translated by David Ganz. This comes from Einhard's own preface.

6 Vauchez is quoted, and discussed, in Kevin Madigan, *Medieval Christianity: A New History* (New Haven and London: Yale University Press, 2015), p. 85. Nelson, *King and Emperor*, discusses the arrival of Alcuin at Charlemagne's court, pp. 315–18. The quotation about religion comes from p. 317 as part of a discussion by Nelson of *De rhetorica*. Augustine's *The City of God* was a popular theological text and manuscripts of it were to be found in every well-stocked Christian library of the period.

7 This was the capitulary known as *De litteris colendis* (*On the Cultivation of Letters/Learning*). The English translation is to be found in P. D. King, *Charlemagne: Translated Sources* (Bloomington: Indiana University Press, 1987), pp. 232–3. Quoted in McKitterick, *Charlemagne*, p. 316.

8 McKitterick, *Charlemagne*, p. 315.

9 McKitterick defines *correctio* as yoking the acquisition of knowledge to the exercise of power. McKitterick, ibid., p. 294.

10 The *Admonitio Generalis* is fully explored in Nelson, *King and Emperor*, pp. 258–64.

11 Quoted in McKitterick, *Charlemagne*, p. 316.

12 Chapter 26 of Einhard's biography.

13 See McKitterick, *Charlemagne*, pp. 347–50, which explores the issue. Nelson, *King and Emperor*, discusses the building of the palace at Aachen on pp. 356–9.

14 B. Bischoff, *Latin Palaeography: Antiquity and the Middle Ages*, trans. David Ganz (Cambridge: Cambridge University Press, 1990), p. 208. See the comparative illustrations, p. 61–5.

15 McKitterick, *Charlemagne*, has two good sections: 'The Court Atelier', pp. 350–63, and 'The Royal Library', pp. 363–72, that give full details, with lists, of what is known.

16 In a letter to Einhard of 830, Lupus praises the achievements of Charlemagne in reviving learning, but in general he is more gloomy. 'In these days those who pursue an education are considered a burden to society… Men have consequently shrunk from this noble endeavour, some because they do not receive a suitable reward for their knowledge, others because they fear an unworthy reputation. It is quite apparent to me that knowledge should be sought for its own sake.' *The Letters of Lupus of Ferrières*, trans. Graydon Regenos (The Hague: Martinus Nijhoff, 1966), Letter 1, p. 2.

17 Wickham, *The Inheritance of Rome*, p. 411. Jane Nelson suggests that the court at Aachen initiated the debate between Aristotle and theology that was to be such a feature of the thirteenth century. 'Nothing quite like this had happened for centuries and it would not really recur outside episcopal schools before the High Middle Ages.' Nelson, *King and Emperor*, p. 446. On pp. 447–8, Nelson records a discussion between the scholars on the nature of virtue.

18 There is an excellent discussion of the *Aratea*, with illustrations, in Hamel, *Meetings with Remarkable Manuscripts*, chapter 4, pp. 140–88.

19 See the authoritative Christopher Page, *The Christian West and its Singers* (New Haven and London: Yale University Press, 2010).

20 For discussion of this famous plan see http://www.stgallplan.org/en/index_plan.html.

21 For the library catalogues I have drawn heavily on chapter 5, 'The Organization of Written Knowledge', in McKitterick, *The Carolingians and the Written Word*, pp. 165–210. See also Michael Lapidge, *The Anglo-Saxon Library* (Oxford: Oxford University Press, 2006), that stresses how limited most monastic libraries were in this period.

22 Quoted in Patrick Hughes, *Dictionary of Islam*, reprint of 1885 edition (Canada: Indigo Books, 2004), p. 108.

23 Peter Brown, 'A World Winking with Messages', review article in *The New York Review of Books*, 20 December 2018, p. 53.

24 Andy Orchard, 'Language, Literature and Learning', in Claire Breay and Joanna Story (eds.), *Anglo-Saxon Kingdoms, Art, Word, War* (London: British Library, 2018), pp. 36–7. This was the catalogue to the superb exhibition of Anglo-Saxon manuscripts held at the British Library in 2018.

25 Rosamond McKitterick, 'The Legacy of the Carolingians', chapter 11 in McKitterick (ed.), *Carolingian Culture*, p. 323.

26 Quoted in Nelson, *King and Emperor*, p. 394.

3 Conformity and Diversity

1 St John Cassian (*c.*360–*c.*435), *The Conferences* (New York: Newman Press, 1997), from Book 8. Cassian is revered for having brought eastern monasticism to Europe.

2 Richard Southern, *Western Society and the Church in the Middle Ages* (Harmondsworth: Penguin Books, 1970). This quotation is the opening sentence of chapter 1.

3 See the section on Christian theology in John Marenbon's essay 'Carolingian Thought', in McKitterick (ed.), *Carolingian Culture*, pp. 179–83.

4 See Charles Freeman, *Holy Bones, Holy Dust: How Relics Shaped the History of Medieval Europe* (London and New Haven, CT: Yale University Press, 2012). The degree to which congregations valued their local cults seems underestimated. Shrines provided much of the buzz of medieval society and certainly acted as 'alternative' centres of religious activity.

5 There are valuable essays in the section 'Christianity: Books and Ideas', in Noble and Smith (eds.), *The Cambridge History of Christianity: Volume 3*.

6 See Freeman, *AD 381*, where I describe the process by which Theodosius issued his Trinitarian decree and imposed the doctrine as the orthodox theology of the Catholic Church.

7 There are many biographies of Augustine but that by Peter Brown, *Augustine of Hippo: A Biography*, rev. ed. (Berkeley: University of California Press, 2000), is usually considered the best, notably for Brown's sensitivity to the complexities of Augustine's mind. I have tended to use the translation of *The Confessions* by R. S. Pine-Coffin in the Penguin Classics edition (2002) but there are many others – of varying quality.

8 In his recent *A History of the Bible: The Book and its Faiths* (London: Allen Lane/Penguin, 2019), John Barton devotes little more than a page (pp. 354–6) to Augustine. This suggests that, whatever his massive influence as a theologian, he did little to transform our understanding of the scriptures.

9 Quoted by Garry Wills in 'Reading Augustine's Mind' (book review of *Augustine: Conversions to Confessions* by Robin Lane Fox), *New York Review of Books*, 14 January 2016, p. 71.

10 See Henry Chadwick, *East and West: The Making of a Rift in the Church* (Oxford: Oxford University Press, 2003), p. 27. Nelson, *King and Emperor*, pp. 449–53, relates how the *filioque* dispute flared up during a service at Bethlehem on Christmas Day, 807.

11 'Augustine's *filioque* would in time encourage among Greek theologians a keen distrust of Augustinian theology generally.' Chadwick, *East and West*, p. 28.

12 The crushing of Pelagius, and the Pelagian controversy in general, is well described in Chapter XXVIII, 'Pelagius', in Serge Lancel, *St Augustine* (London, SCM Press, 2002).

13 Steven Ozment, in *The Age of Reform, 1250–1550: An Intellectual and Religious History of Late Medieval and Reformation Europe* (New Haven and London: Yale University Press, 1980), has a good section on this: 'How Man is Saved: Theories of Salvation from Augustine to Gabriel Biel', pp. 22–42.

14 From an article by Fredriksen on Paul in Fitzgerald (ed.), *Augustine through the Ages*, p. 621. The comments on the 'idolatry' shown to Augustine comes from Marenbon, 'Carolingian Thought', pp. 175 and 179.

15 'There is another form of temptation, even more fraught with danger. This is the disease of curiosity [*curiositas*]… It is this which drives us to try and discover the secrets of nature, those secrets which are beyond our understanding, which can avail us nothing and which man should not wish to learn.' Augustine, *The Confessions*, Book 10, section 35. There is an excellent discussion of the various ways in which Augustine used the term *curiositas* by N. Joseph Torchia in Fitzgerald (ed.), *Augustine through the Ages*, pp. 259–61. This is an area where Augustine is heavily influenced by Platonism, in that the natural world is volatile and provides only a semblance of reality compared to the eternal truths above. Therefore, an unnatural interest in the natural world, 'a lust of the eyes' as Augustine puts it, is a deviation from the stability of divine contemplation.

16 'There are eight principal vices that attack humankind. The first is gluttony, which means the voraciousness of the belly; the second is fornication; the third is filargyria, which is avarice or love of money; the fourth is anger; the fifth is sadness; the sixth acedia, which is anxiety or weariness of heart; the seventh is cenodoxia, which is boastfulness or vainglory; and the eighth is pride.' From St John Cassian, 'On the Eight Deadly Sins', in *The Conferences* (New York: Newman Press, 1997), pp. 183–96.

17 Gregory the Great, *Homilies on the Gospels*, preached AD 591–2.

18 Barton, *A History of the Bible*, p. 311.

19 *The Confessions*, trans. R. S. Pine-Coffin, Book 2, chapter 2.

20 Augustine became the first archbishop of Canterbury. It is almost certain that he brought the so-called *Gospels of St Augustine* (now in the Parker Library in Corpus Christi College, Cambridge) from Rome. See chapter 1 of Hamel, *Meetings with Remarkable Manuscripts*.

21 Kathleen Hughes, *The Church in Early Irish Society* (Ithaca, NY: Cornell University Press, 1966), p. 7.

22 Edward Gibbon, *The Decline and Fall of the Roman Empire, Volume 3* (published in 1781), chapter 28.

23 Valerie Flint, *The Rise of Magic in Early Modern Europe* (Princeton, NJ, and Oxford: Princeton University Press, 1991). The 'swallowing up of paganism' comes from Alexander Murray, quoted in Blair, *Building Anglo-Saxon England*, p. 95. For the archaeological evidence, see Knight, *The End of Antiquity*, especially chapter 6, 'The World Turned Upside Down: The Christianisation of the Gallic Countryside', and part 3, 'Towards New Horizons'.

24 Bede, *The Reckoning of Time*, trans. Faith Wallis, pp. 53–4.

25 Chapter 22, 'The Caging of the Peasantry, 800–1000', in Wickham, *The Inheritance of Rome*.

26 See Rebecca Pinner, *The Cult of St. Edmund in Medieval East Anglia* (Woodbridge: Boydell Press, 2015), p. 87. Among St Edmund's [illegible], Pinner shows how 'punitive miracles', in support of the abbey or the dignity of his relics, were used by St Edmund as the protector of his shrine.

27 Charles Taylor, *A Secular Age* (Cambridge, MA, and London: Belknap Press of Harvard University Press, 2007). This is an extraordinarily wide-ranging study of the process of secularization since 1500 by a prominent Canadian philosopher. Chapter 1, 'The Bulwarks of Belief', starts with the question: 'Why was it virtually impossible not to believe in God in, say, 1500 in our Western society, while in 2000 many of us find this not only easy, but even inescapable?' The argument that follows is presented with formidable strength and breadth but I still think that Taylor assumes that the European mind in 1500 was static and conformist – see especially his assessment on pp. 25–6. I hope that my later chapters will show just how fragmented the western mind had become by that date.

4 Authority and Dissent

1 The clauses of the *Dictatus papae* are set out in Madigan, *Medieval Christianity*, pp. 137–8.

2 Article on Rendlesham in *The Historian* (Journal of the UK Historical Association), Issue 139, Autumn 2018.

3 Simony takes its name from Simon Magus in the Acts of the Apostles who offered money to two disciples in the hope that they would enable him to pass on the power of the Holy Spirit.

4 Quoted in Ian Robinson (trans.) in *The Papal Reform of the Eleventh Century: Lives of Pope Leo IX and Pope Gregory VII* (Manchester: Manchester University Press, 2004), p. 14.

5 Madigan, *Medieval Christianity*, has a useful discussion of the *Dictatus* on pp. 134–9, and this is followed by his survey of the Investiture Controversy.

6 Recent accounts of the crusades include Thomas Asbridge, *The Crusades: The War for the Holy Land* (New York and London: Simon and Schuster, 2010), and Jonathan Phillips, *Holy Warriors: A Modern History of the Crusades* (London: Bodley Head, 2009). A different, more analytical, angle on the crusades is taken by Christopher Tyerman, *How to Plan a Crusade: Reason and Religious War in the High Middle Ages* (London: Allen Lane/Penguin, 2015), who has also recently published *The World of the Crusades: An Illustrated History* (New Haven and London: Yale University Press, 2019).

7 Jonathan Riley-Smith, 'The Crusades, 1095–1198', chapter 14 of David Luscombe and Jonathan Riley-Smith (eds.), *The New Cambridge Medieval History: Volume 4, c.1024–c.1198* (Cambridge: Cambridge University Press, 2004), p. 557.

8 For many years this held its own as the definitive history of the crusades, although it is now considered dated. This quotation comes from the closing pages of the third volume. In his fine biography of Steven Runciman, *Outlandish Knight* (London: Allen Lane/Penguin, 2016), Minoo Dinshaw devotes chapter 18 to 'The Trilogy'.

9 Neither side held back in the bitter onslaught they launched on each other. This is Frederick in 1239: 'The bishop of Rome seated in the chair of perverse doctrine, that Pharisee anointed with the oil of pestilence above the rest of his consorts who for his abominable pride is cast down from heaven, endeavours with his power to destroy and to undo all… But, we say, he is that monstrous beast of whom we read [in the Book of Revelation].' Quoted in Johannes Fried, *The Middle Ages*, trans. Peter Lewis (Cambridge, MA, and London: Belknap Press of Harvard University Press, 2015), pp. 280–1.

10 An English translation of *De laude* is available at https://history.hanover.edu/courses/excerpts/344bern2.html. The first three (short) chapters outline the argument. Bernard of Clairvaux will emerge as the main opponent of Abelard in my next chapter.

11 The Fourth Crusade and its aftermath is well explored by Michael Angold, *The Fourth Crusade: Event and Context* (London: Routledge, 2003).

12 This notorious quotation, which is a development of 2 Timothy 2:19, was recorded by the Cistercian monk Caesarius of Heisterbach in his *Dialogus Miraculum* (*c.*1219–23).

13 See the assessment of monastic health in André Vauchez, 'The Religious Orders', chapter 9 in David Abulafia (ed.), *The New Cambridge Medieval History: Volume 5, c.1198–c.1300* (Cambridge: Cambridge University Press, 1999), pp. 220–55.

14 The first quotation is from the Rule of the Franciscans. 'Learning robs many people of their gentle characters and does not allow them to bend their stiff necks to humble tasks… I would wish an educated man first to offer a prayer to me: "Brother, grant me a home far removed from the bustle of the world, in which I can recall my years passed in sorrow, recollecting the distractions of my heart and reshape my soul to better ends."' Quoted in Rosalind Brooke, *The Image of St. Francis: Responses to Sainthood in the Thirteenth Century* (Cambridge: Cambridge University Press, 2008), p. 322. The quotation comes from the earliest *Life* of St Francis by his contemporary, Thomas of Celeno, completed in 1229.

15 It is well covered in Olaf Pedersen, *The First Universities: Studium Generale and the Origins of University Education in Europe*, trans. Richard North (Cambridge: Cambridge University Press, 1997), pp. 176ff.

16 Vauchez, 'The Religious Orders', provides a good summary, pp. 241–55.

17 Assessment by Katherine French on p. 167 of her essay 'Localised Faith: Parochial and Domestic Spaces', in John H. Arnold (ed.), *The Oxford Handbook of Medieval Christianity* (Oxford: Oxford University Press, 2014).

18 Grosseteste is quoted in Jennifer Deane, *A History of Medieval Heresy and Inquisition* (Lanham, MD: Rowman and Littlefield, 2011), p. 95. Leff is quoted in Ozment, *The Age of Reform*, p. 94.

19 Henry Lea, *A History of Auricular Confession and Indulgences in the Latin Church* (Philadelphia, PA: Lea Brothers, 1896), p. 230.

20 Fried, *The Middle Ages*, p. 263.

5 Abelard and the Battle for Reason

1 *The Letters of Abelard and Heloise*, trans. Betty Radice, Penguin Classics edition, 1974; rev. ed., 2003. This is from the revised edition, letter 2, pp. 47–55, p. 52.

2 The best biography of Abelard is that by M. T. Clanchy, *Abelard: A Medieval Life* (Oxford: Blackwell, 1997). The topics discussed in this chapter are well covered in this biography. For assessments of Abelard, see his lover Heloise's adulation above, and those of other contemporaries quoted by Clanchy, pp. 95–6. To Peter the Venerable, abbot of Cluny, who sheltered Abelard in his last days, he was *noster Aristoteles*, 'unequalled, unrivalled, among the logicians who ever were'.

3 Tyerman, *How to Plan a Crusade*.

4 For a study of reason in the Middle Ages, see Edward Grant, *God and Reason in the Middle Ages* (Cambridge: Cambridge University Press, 2001). Grant quotes Anselm on p. 54 as follows: 'For I do not seek to understand, in order that I might believe; but I believe that I may understand. For I believe this too, that unless I believed, I should not understand.' The point about Anselm's claim that he had relied so heavily on Augustine is made by Étienne Gilson, *History of Christian Philosophy in the Middle Ages* (London: Sheed and Ward, 1955), p. 363. I disagree with Grant over his claim in his 'Conclusion' (pp. 356–64) that the reasoning of the Middle Ages was carried on through to the post-Renaissance world. A broader perspective is provided by Alexander Murray, *Reason and Society in the Middle Ages* (Oxford: Oxford University Press, 1978).

5 The background to the medieval curriculum is covered in detail in the opening chapters of Pedersen, *The First Universities*.

6 See Page, *The Christian West and its Singers*.

7 Pedersen, *The First Universities*, p. 106.

8 A survey of what texts became available when is to be found throughout R. R. Bolgar, *The Classical Heritage and its Beneficiaries from the Carolingian Age to the End of the Renaissance* (Cambridge: Cambridge University Press, 1954) with a new edition by Harper and Row, New York, 1964. Specifically for this chapter see chapter 4, 'The Pre Scholastic Age'. Bolgar shows that the enthusiasm over the rediscovery of classical texts was met with opposition from conservatives (Abelard versus Bernard of Clairvaux, for instance) and it was not until the thirteenth century that assimilation of theology and classical philosophy was effected. See my Chapters 7 and 8.

9 Charles Haskins, *The Renaissance of the Twelfth Century* (Cambridge, MA, and London: Harvard University Press, 1927).

10 The question of Abelard's marriage in relationship to his clerical status is discussed by Clanchy, *Abelard*, pp. 45–6.

11 The *Historia calamitatum* is translated by Betty Radice in *The Letters of Abelard and Heloise*, pp. 3–43.

12 From letter 4, p. 68 in the Radice translation.

13 Ibid., letter 2, pp. 51 and 53.

14 Ibid., letter 5, p. 72.

15 For Abelard as a logician, see Clanchy, *Abelard*, chapter 5, 'Logician', pp. 95–118. The quotation from Bolgar, *The Classical Heritage*, is to be found on p. 158. Bolgar stresses how dialectic was seen as a means of counteracting the perceived disintegration of intellectual life.

16 Grant, *God and Reason in the Middle Ages*, p. 54.

17 The issue is given full discussion in John Marenbon, *Pagans and Philosophers: The Problem of Paganism from Augustine to Leibniz* (Princeton, NJ, and Oxford: Princeton University Press, 2015), chapter 5, 'Abelard', pp. 73–94. The quotation from the letter to Heloise is on p. 92.

18 An article on 'Universals' by Mary MacLeod and Eric Rubenstein can be found online in *The Internet Encyclopedia of Philosophy*: https://www.iep.utm.edu/universa.

Abelard's conceptualism is discussed online under 'Metaphysics' in the article on Abelard by Andrew Arlig and Peter King in *The Stanford Encyclopedia of Philosophy*, available online at https://plato.stanford.edu/entries/abelard. See also the article by G. Klima, 'The Medieval Problem of Universals' in the *Stanford Encyclopedia of Philosophy*, available online at https://plato.stanford.edu/entries/universals-medieval.

19 This famous quotation comes from chapter 7 of Tertullian's *De praescriptione haereticorum* (*On the prescription of heretics*).

20 From a Homily of Gregory the Great, often quoted by Thomas Aquinas in his *Summa Theologiae*.

21 The hunting down of Abelard by Bernard of Clairvaux is detailed in Clanchy, *Abelard*, chapter 13, 'Heretic'.

22 This quotation comes from section 8 of the *Dialogue*, ed. and trans. John Marenbon and Giovanni Orlandi, in *Peter Abelard, Collationes* (Oxford: Clarendon Press, 2001), p. 11.

23 Abelard knew this well himself. In his *Theologia* (the book that was burned at Soissons) he wrote: 'For it is not ignorance that makes a heretic, but pride… Professors of dialectic very easily fall into this trap because they think they are so strongly armed with reasons that they are free to defend or attack whatever they like. Their arrogance is so great that nothing is thought beyond comprehension, or incapable of explanation, by their petty reasonings.' Quoted in Clanchy, *Abelard*, p. 302.

24 Abelard, *The Dialogue of a Philosopher with a Jew and a Christian*, ed. and trans. Marenbon and Orlandi, in *Peter Abelard, Collationes*, pp. 1–223.

25 Cary Nederman (ed.), *John of Salisbury: Policraticus* (Cambridge: Cambridge University Press, 1991), p. 176.

26 The point is made by Christopher Celenza in his *The Intellectual World of the Italian Renaissance: Language, Philosophy, and the Search for Meaning* (Cambridge: Cambridge University Press, 2018), pp. 56–7, when he discusses Colluccio Salutati, the erudite chancellor of Florence.

6 The Rebirth of the City-State

1 Quoted in Paul Oldfield, *Urban Panegyric and the Transformation of the Medieval City 1100–1300* (Oxford: Oxford University Press, 2019), p. 4. This panegyric is dependent on classical sources in praise of cities.

2 This famous work was published in 1937 by Alcan in Paris and Nouvelle Société d'éditions in Brussels.

3 Michael McCormick, *The Origins of the European Economy: Communications and Commerce, AD 300–900* (Cambridge: Cambridge University Press, 2001).

4 The quotation comes in the concluding chapter of McCormick, *The Origins of the European Economy*, p. 797. On the slave trade see chapter 9, 'Traders, Slaves and Exiles', pp. 237–77. See also David Abulafia, 'Crossing the Boundaries between Christendom and Islam, 900–1050', part 3, chapter 2 of *The Great Sea: A Human History of the Mediterranean* (London: Allen Lane/Penguin, 2011).

5 Christophe Picard, *The Sea of the Caliphs: The Mediterranean in the Medieval Islamic World*, trans. Nicholas Elliott (Cambridge, MA: Belknap Press of Harvard University Press, 2018). Oddly structured and clumsily translated, this is still a mine of information not easy to find elsewhere. Fernand Braudel's celebrated *The Mediterranean and the Mediterranean World in the Age of Philip II*, trans. Sian Reynolds, appeared in two volumes (London: Collins, 1972).

6 Picard, *The Sea of the Caliphs*, p. 3.

7 John Ruskin, *The Stones of Venice, Volume Two* (London: Smith, Elder and Co., 1853), chapter 4, section 18. There are many subsequent editions of *The Stones*, which was originally published in three volumes, 1851–3.

8 Chris Wickham, *Sleepwalking into a New World: The Emergence of Italian City Communes in the Twelfth Century* (Princeton, NJ, and Oxford: Princeton University Press, 2015). Pisa is dealt with in detail in chapter 3, pp. 67–117. See also Abulafia, *The Great Sea*, part 3, chapter 3, 'The Great Sea-Change 1000–1100'.

9 Wickham, *Sleepwalking into a New World*, pp. 174–6.

10 The code is discussed in Caroline Humfress, 'Law and Legal Practice in the Age of Justinian', chapter 7 in Michael Maas (ed.), *The Cambridge Companion to Justinian* (Cambridge: Cambridge University Press, 2005), pp. 161–84.

11 A comprehensive introduction is to be found in Peter Stein, *Roman Law in European History* (Cambridge: Cambridge University Press, 1999).

12 *De officiis* (*On Duties*), written in 44 BC by Cicero, was an enormously influential text in the Middle Ages and Renaissance, not least because it emphasized the moral obligations of the politician and administrator. This extract is from Book 2:73.

13 For the evolution of the university at Bologna – and Paris and Oxford– see Pedersen, *The First Universities*, especially chapter 5, 'From school to *studium generale*', pp. 122–54.

14 Philip Jones, *The Italian City-State: From Commune to Signoria* (Oxford: Clarendon Press, 1997), is the fullest study of the process by which communes emerged. Sadly, copies are almost unobtainable and the author died before completing the second volume.

15 Quoted in Malcolm Barber, *The Two Cities: Medieval Europe, 1050–1320*, 2nd ed. (London: Routledge, 2004), p. 235, followed by discussion.

16 Peter Stein, *Roman Law in European History*, p. 60. K. Pennington, *The Prince and the Law, 1200–1600: Sovereignty and Rights in the Western Legal Tradition* (Berkeley: University of California Press, 1993), is the key text on the power of the prince versus the rights of his subjects.

17 See Pierre Pellegrin, 'Aristotle's *Politics*', chapter 21 in Christopher Shields (ed.), *The Oxford Handbook of Aristotle* (Oxford: Oxford University Press, 2012), pp. 558–85. See also: chapter 3, 'Aristotle: Politics is not Philosophy', in Alan Ryan, *On Politics: A History of Political Thought from Herodotus to the Present* (London: Allen Lane/Penguin, 2012); chapter 5, 'Aristotle', by Tony Burns in David Boucher and Paul Kelly (eds.), *Political Thinkers: From Socrates to the Present* (Oxford: Oxford University Press, 2003.); 'Aristotle and the Science of Politics', chapter 4 in J. S. McClelland, *A History of Western Political Thought* (London: Routledge, 1996).

18 As Philip Jones puts it: 'A revolutionary new phase opened [after the Peace of Constance]: a phase of enhanced state enterprise, intensified town-planning, and particularly of structural reorientation, a progressive resecularization of urban institutional topography, all centred on the new symbolic feature of the *palazzo pubblico*.' Jones, *The Italian City-State*, pp. 441–2. See also Edward Coleman, 'Cities and Communes', chapter 1 in David Abulafia (ed.), *Italy in the Central Middle Ages, 1000–1330* (Oxford: Oxford University Press, 2004), p. 47.

19 Coleman, 'Cities and Communes', p. 38.

20 Ibid., p. 42.

21 Chris Wickham, *Sleepwalking into a New World*. Wickham has a long section in his chapter on Pisa, pp. 67–117, on the backgrounds of the consuls and he notes the consuls' dependence on trained lawyers. From p. 110: 'Such judicial experts were also evidently committed to the communes, which gave them a status and a career structure which they would not have managed to gain on their own: it was in effect men like these who most clearly represented the commune in its day-to-day activity in the city.'

22 There is a good biography of Fibonacci: Keith Devlin, *The Man of Numbers: Fibonacci's Arithmetic Revolution* (London: Bloomsbury, 2011). I have used it here as my source.

23 The origins of Guelph and Ghibelline lie in Germany when two rival factions were in conflict with each other in the early twelfth century. Guelph is derived from the German Welf, the dynastic title of the dukes of Bavaria, and Ghibelline from the name of a castle of their opponents, the Hohenstaufens. It appears that the names were brought to Italy during the campaigns of Emperor Frederick Barbarossa and by the thirteenth century had attached themselves to rival parties in the northern Italian cities.

24 Quoted in Chris Wickham, *Medieval Europe* (New Haven and London: Yale University Press, 2016), p. 159, in a useful chapter: 'The Ambiguities of Political Reconstruction, 1150–1300', pp. 141–69.

25 Quoted (and discussed) in Fried, *The Middle Ages*, pp. 251–2.

26 Ibid., pp. 297–8.

27 For the Charter of the Forest see Geraldine van Bueren, 'Take Back Control: A New Commons Charter for the Twenty-First Century is Overdue, 800 years After the First', *Times Literary Supplement*, 10 March 2017, pp. 23–5.

28 This statute dates from 1303. It is quoted in Robert Putnam, Robert Leonardi and Raffaella Nanetti, *Making Democracy Work: Civic Traditions in Modern Italy* (Princeton, NJ, and Oxford: Princeton University Press, 1993), p. 125. Putnam et al.'s thesis is that traditions of civic society that go back to the medieval period are still potent today and this explains why northern Italy has been more successful than southern Italy in creating a workable civil society.

7 The Medieval University

1 Pope Honorius III (r.1216–27) had been archdeacon of Bologna. He was a major patron of learning and this bull illustrates his support for the students of law at Bologna at a time when they were in conflict with the citizen body. It acknowledges that Bologna has already achieved fame as a place of learning. Translated from the Latin original by M. Mulchahey in Katherine Jones, Joanna Drell and Frances Andrews (eds.), *Medieval Italy: Texts in Translation* (Philadelphia: University of Pennsylvania Press, 2009), pp. 466–8.

2 An example is the wide-ranging discussion of a group of intellectuals recorded in Plutarch's *On the Face of the Moon*, available online at https://archive.org/stream/plutarchonfacewhooplut/plutarchonfacewhooplut_djvu.txt.

3 See George Makdisi, *The Rise of Colleges: Institutions of Learning in Islam and the West* (Edinburgh: Edinburgh University Press, 1981), especially chapter 4, 'Islam and the Christian West', pp. 224–91.

4 See chapters 16–19 on Avicenna, pp. 113–39, in Peter Adamson, *Philosophy in the Islamic World* (Oxford: Oxford University Press, 2016). Peter Adamson provides an overview of the Arab philosophers' approach to Aristotle in chapter 25, 'Aristotle in the Arabic Commentary Tradition', in Shields (ed.), *The Oxford Handbook of Aristotle*, pp. 645–64.

5 Adamson, *Philosophy in the Islamic World*, p. 114.

6 Ibid., p. 116, with specific reference to Avicenna's work on Aristotle.

7 Ibid., chapters 25 and 26 on Averroes.

8 Quoted in Pedersen, *The First Universities*, p. 280.

9 This fascinating nugget comes from Ian Thomson, *Dante's Divine Comedy: A Journey without End* (London: Head of Zeus, 2018), pp. 74–7.

10 James Hankins, *Plato in the Italian Renaissance* (Leiden: E. J. Brill, 1994), p. 4.

11 Excerpts taken from the introduction to *The Almagest*, trans. G. J. Toomer (Princeton, NJ, and Oxford: Princeton University Press, 1998).

12 For the medical school at Salerno, see Pedersen, *The First Universities*, pp. 122–5.

13 Quoted at p. 257 in Jacques Verger, 'The Universities and Scholasticism', chapter 10 in Abulafia (ed.), *The New Cambridge Medieval History: Volume 5*, pp. 256–78.

14 The *Carmina Burana* is discussed in Hamel, *Meetings with Remarkable Manuscripts*, chapter 8, pp. 330–75. It is now in the Bayerische Staatsbibliotek in Munich.

15 This was in a letter to Abelard from the Canon Fulques de Deuil. It goes on: 'Throngs of young Englishmen would not be frightened by the ocean blocking them with its storms and waves... Far Brittany has sent thee her coarse-grained young fellows to be polished...' and so on through the nationalities of Europe. Quoted in Pedersen, *The First Universities*, p. 132.

16 The university in Bologna is discussed in Pedersen, *The First Universities*, pp. 137–45. Documents relating to the duties of the university officials and booksellers are set out in Jones, Drell and Andrews (eds.), *Medieval Italy*, pp. 466–73.

17 For the university of Paris see Pedersen, *The First Universities*, pp. 145–51.

18 Quoted in ibid., p. 164.

19 Pedersen discusses Oxford in the *The First Universities*, pp. 151–4. A good recent history of the university from its origins in the thirteenth century is Lau rence Brockliss, *The University of Oxford: A History* (Oxford: Oxford University Press, 2016).

20 Pedersen, *The First Universities*, p. 293.

21 See Michael Hoskin and Owen Gingerich, 'Medieval Latin Astronomy', in Michael Hoskin (ed.), *The Cambridge Concise History of Astronomy* (Cambridge: Cambridge University Press, 1999), p. 78. This chapter gives a good overview of medieval astronomy.

22 See David Wootton, *The Invention of Science: A New History of the Scientific Revolution* (London: Penguin Books, 2016), p. 113, for his reference to the derivation of 'high seas'. Chapter 4, 'Planet Earth', pp. 110–59, provides an excellent introduction to this 'two-sphere' hypothesis.

23 Quoted in ibid., p. 188.

24 Quoted in Nicholas Ostler, *Ad Infinitum: A Biography of Latin and the World it Created* (London: Harper Press, 2007), p. 222.

25 Bolgar, *The Classical Heritage*, p. 206.

26 Armand Maurer, *Medieval Philosophy*, 2nd ed. (Rome: Pontifical Institute of Medieval Studies, 1982), p. 90.

27 Quoted in Ostler, *Ad Infinitum*, p. 216, note 23. 'I confess I have been unable to convey in Latin the elegant qualities of the style of this most learned and eloquent man [the author of Pseudo-Dionysius].'

28 Reynolds and Wilson, *Scribes and Scholars*, p. 122.

29 Ostler, *Ad Infinitum*, has an excellent chapter on the problems of translating, not only from Greek but from Arabic: chapter 14, '*Ex oriente lux* – Sources of Higher Learning', pp. 207–30.

30 Grant, *God and Reason in the Middle Ages*, p. 211.

31 Ibid., p. 209.

32 Hilde de Ridder-Symeons (ed.), *A History of the University in Europe: Volume 1, Universities in the Middle Ages* (Cambridge: Cambridge University Press, 1991), p. 382.

33 Lindberg, *The Beginnings of Western Science*, p. 335.

34 From Paracelsus, 'Of the Supreme Mysteries of Nature', quoted by Anthony Grafton in chapter 10, 'Libraries and Lecture Halls', in Katharine Park and Lorraine Daston (eds.), *The Cambridge History of Science: Volume 3, Early Modern Science* (Cambridge: Cambridge University Press, 2006), p. 240.

35 Reynolds and Wilson, *Scribes and Scholars*, p. 119.

36 The issue, and the reasons for increasing external control of the universities, are explored by Jacques Verger in chapter 11, 'Schools, Universities and Society', in Christopher Allmand (ed.), *The New Cambridge Medieval History: Volume 7, c.1415–c.1500* (Cambridge: Cambridge University Press, 1998), pp. 234–8.

37 John Marenbon, *Medieval Philosophy: An Historical and Philosophical Introduction* (London and New York: Routledge, 2007), pp. 349–40. Marenbon goes on to say that 1400 is not the end of a period in philosophy as such; rather, one can characterize the period *c.*200 to *c.*1700 as 'one, long, period'. As we shall see it is scholasticism within university education that the intellectual elites are rejecting.

38 'While lacking a prominent university might not seem an advantage at first glance, in the case of [Florence's] embrace of humanism, it was. The reason is that, though universities were and are productive and efficient centers for preserving the most useful knowledge, they are not always "early adopters" when it comes to embracing new forms of knowledge creation.' Celenza, *The Intellectual World*, p. 47.

39 Verger, 'Schools, Universities and Society', has a good section on the relationship between universities and society in the fifteenth century, pp. 238–42.

8 Medieval Philosophy

1 From the *Summa theologiae*, part 1, question 1, article 2, quoted in Grant, *God and Reason in the Middle Ages*, p. 208.

2 From the opening paragraph in M. W. F. Stone and Robert Wisnovsky, 'Philosophy and Theology', chapter 50 in Robert Pasnau (ed.), *The Cambridge History of Medieval Philosophy: Volume 2* (Cambridge: Cambridge University Press, 2010), pp. 689–706.

3 Standard introductions to medieval philosophy that I have found helpful include: Anthony Kenny, *Medieval Philosophy: A New History of Western Philosophy, Volume 2* (Oxford: Oxford University Press, 2005); Marenbon, *Medieval Philosophy*; Peter Adamson, *A History of Philosophy without any Gaps: Medieval Philosophy* (Oxford: Oxford University Press, 2019); Pasnau (ed.), *The Cambridge History of Medieval Philosophy*; Maurer, *Medieval Philosophy*; Gilson, *History of Christian Philosophy*. I have also used two online sources: *The Stanford Encyclopedia of Philosophy* and the *Internet Encyclopedia of Philosophy*; the essays in the latter are often more accessible than the former.

4 There is a vast literature on Aristotle. A short life by Jonathan Barnes, a major authority on the philosopher, is to be found in the Past Masters series: *Aristotle* (Oxford: Oxford University Press, 1982). Barnes has also contributed the volume on Aristotle in the Oxford University Press 'A Very Short Introduction' series, 2001. I have particularly enjoyed Armand Leroi, *The Lagoon: How Aristotle Invented Science* (London and New York: Bloomsbury, 2014), and, for his lasting relevance, Edith Hall, *Aristotle's Way: How Ancient Wisdom Can Change Your Life* (London: Bodley Head, 2018). Another authority on Aristotle is Geoffrey Lloyd, e.g. *Aristotelian Explorations* (Cambridge: Cambridge University Press, 1996). For a comprehensive overview that includes chapters on Aristotle in the Arabic and Latin worlds, see Shields (ed.), *The Oxford Handbook of Aristotle*.

5 Quoted on p. 10 in Leroi, *The Lagoon*.

6 There is an excellent essay on this in Lloyd, *Aristotelian Explorations*, chapter 3, 'Fuzzy natures?', pp. 67–82.

7 Quoted in Maurer, *Medieval Philosophy*, p. 139. Chapter 11 on St Bonaventure, from which this quotation comes, is recommended.

8 Quoted in Marenbon, *Medieval Philosophy*, pp. 232–3.

9 Quoted in Lindberg, *The Beginnings of Western Science*, p. 241.

10 Ibid., p. 239.

11 Thomas Aquinas is treated fully in all the texts cited in note 3. See also Denys Turner, *Thomas Aquinas: A Portrait* (New Haven and London: Yale University Press, 2013), and a well-received study by the Catholic philosopher Edward Feser, *Aquinas: A Beginner's Guide* (London: Oneworld Publications, 2009). For a full exposition of Aquinas's philosophy the article in *The Internet Encyclopedia of Philosophy* by Christopher Brown from the University of Tennessee at Martin is recommended. I also warmed to the chapter on Aquinas in Maurer's *Medieval Philosophy*, chapter 13.

12 Gilson's apt phrase is to be found in Gilson, *History of Christian Philosophy*, p. 365.

13 Pedersen, *The First Universities*, p. 282.

14 Turner, *Thomas Aquinas*, chapter 3 'The Soul', pp. 70–99; quotation on p. 79.

15 See the discussion on Aquinas's approach to faith and reason in William E. Mann, 'Faith and Reason', chapter 51 in *The Cambridge History of Medieval Philosophy: Volume 2* (Cambridge: Cambridge University Press, 2010), pp. 713–16. The quotation on contemplation comes from the *Summa theologiae*, II.II, q. 180.

16 Pedersen, *The First Universities*, p. 285.

17 Gilson, *History of Christian Philosophy*, p. 408.

18 These are both quoted (pp. 100–1) in François-Xavier Putallaz, chapter 8, 'Censorship', pp. 99–113, in Pasnau (ed.), *The Cambridge History of Medieval Philosophy: Volume 2*. This chapter also has a discussion of the Condemnation of 1277.

19 See Kenny, *Medieval Philosophy*, p. 93.

20 From William of Ockham, *Dialogus*, vol. 1, book 2, chapter 22, translated by John Scott, British Academy, 1999; available online at https://www.thebritishacademy.ac.uk/pubs/dialogus/t1d2b.html.

21 Quoted in Murray, *Reason and Society*, p. 236.

22 Maurer, *Medieval Philosophy*, p. 268.

23 Gilson, *History of Christian Philosophy*, p. 528.

24 Ozment, *The Age of Reform*, chapter 3, 'The Spiritual Traditions'.

25 In his recent book *Out of Our Minds: What We Think and How We Came to Think It* (London: Oneworld, 2019), Felipe Fernandez-Armesto notes: 'Thomas Aquinas was part of what can properly be called a scientific movement – perhaps even a scientific revolution or renaissance – in high-medieval Europe.' Quoted by the philosopher John Gray in a review, *New Statesman*, 21–27 June 2019, p. 43.

26 Quoted from the Apostolic Letter *Lumen Ecclesiae*, chapter 43. Available in English at www.superflumina.org/paulvi_on_stthomas.

27 The philosopher Alasdair Macintyre (born 1929) was heavily influenced by Aristotle's texts on ethics and from there he developed an appreciation that they had found their most effective champion in the works of Aquinas. He eventually converted to Catholicism. His *After Virtue* (1981) is the best-known exposition of his views.

28 Ozment, *The Age of Reform*, p. 13.

9 A Scientific Revival, 1200–1350

1 Quoted in A. George Molland, 'Mathematics', chapter 21 in David Lindberg and Michael Shank (eds.), *The Cambridge History of Science: Volume 2, Medieval Science* (Cambridge: Cambridge University Press, 2013), p. 520. The accolade of Fibonacci as 'the greatest of the medieval mathematicians' by Molland is on the same page. For Fibonacci, see pp. 151–2.

2 For Grosseteste and Roger Bacon, I have made a composite portrayal drawing on many of the same sources on medieval philosophy listed under chapter 8, note 3.

3 Quoted in Robert Pasnau, chapter 26, 'The Latin Aristotle', in Shields (ed.), *The Oxford Handbook of Aristotle*, p. 667.

4 Quoted in David Lindberg and Katherine Tachau, 'The Science of Light and Color, Seeing and Knowing', chapter 20 in Lindberg and Shank (eds.), *The Cambridge History of Science: Volume 2*, p. 498.

5 Bolgar, *The Classical Heritage*, p. 426.

6 Maurer, *Medieval Philosophy*, p. 129.

7 The optical theory of Alhazen, and Grosseteste's and Bacon's development of it, can be found in Lindberg, *The Beginnings of Western Science*, pp. 313–20. See also Lindberg and Tachau, 'The Science of Light', pp. 491–511. There is also a clear description of Alhazen's contribution in Arun Bala, *The Dialogue of Civilizations in the Birth of Modern Science* (New York: Palgrave Macmillan, 2006), chapter 8, 'The Alhazen Optical Revolution'.

8 Bala, *The Dialogue of Civilizations*, chapter 8.

9 Lindberg and Tachau, 'The Science of Light', pp. 499–500.

10 Gilson, *History of Christian Philosophy*, p. 308.

11 Walter Roy Laird, 'Change and Motion', chapter 17 in Lindberg and Shank (eds.), *The Cambridge History of Science: Volume 2*, especially pp. 415–35, covers the main themes.

12 This quotation is found in most standard histories of mathematics, e.g. Peter E. Hodgson, *Theology and Modern Physics* (London: Routledge, 2017), p. xi.

13 For 'Projectile Motion and the Theory of Impetus', see Laird, 'Change and Motion', pp. 421ff.

14 For a summary of Duhem's place in the 'continuity' theory of medieval science, see David Lindberg and Michael Shank, 'Introduction', in Lindberg and Shank (eds.), *The Cambridge History of Science: Volume 2*, pp. 10–12.

15 J. L. Heilbron, *Galileo* (Oxford: Oxford University Press, 2010), provides a glossary of all those 'scientists' from Aristotle and Archimedes onwards who influenced Galileo.

16 Brockliss, *The University of Oxford*, p. 125.

17 See, for an overview, David Lindberg, 'Science and the Medieval Church', chapter 10 in Lindberg and Shank (eds.), *The Cambridge History of Science: Volume 2*, especially pp. 282–5.

18 Jones, *The Italian City-State*, p. 452.

19 Murray, *Reason and Society*, p. 184. Two chapters, 'The Emergence of the Arithmetical Mentality' and 'Men and Mathematics', chart the main developments.

20 For a technological overview of this clock see Francesco Xavier Jufre, *The Astrarium of Giovanni de Dondi. Mechanical Principles*, RACO, 2010, available online at https://www.raco.cat/index.php/ImagoTemporis/article/download/262116/349283.

10 Dante, Marsilius and Boccaccio

1 On Dante there are excellent biographies by Barbara Reynolds, *Dante: The Poet, the Political Thinker, the Man* (London and New York: I. B. Tauris, 2006), and Marco Santagata, *Dante: The Story of his Life*, trans. Richard Dixon (Cambridge, MA, and London: Belknap Press of Harvard University Press, 2016). There is also Rachel Jacoff (ed.,), *The Cambridge Companion to Dante*, 2nd ed. (Cambridge: Cambridge University Press, 2007) – see in particular chapter 14 by John Najemy, 'Dante and Florence'. I particularly enjoyed Thomson, *Dante's Divine Comedy*.

2 The best history of medieval and Renaissance Florence is John M. Najemy, *A History of Florence, 1200–1575* (Oxford: Wiley-Blackwell, 2008). I have written a short historical introduction to Florence in Alta MacAdam's *Blue Guide Florence*, 11th ed. (London: Somerset Books, 2017).

3 The Ordinances are discussed in Najemy, *A History of Florence*, pp. 81–7. The quotation is from p. 83.

4 There is a very good section on the guilds in ibid., pp. 39–44.

5 For schools within the cities, see Jones, *The Italian City-State*, pp. 447–50.

6 Scholars have argued the point citing the flourishing of the vernacular in Icelandic scripts in Old Norse at a time when clerical influence was limited. See M. T. Clanchy, *From Memory to Written Record*, 2nd ed. (Oxford: Wiley-Blackwell, 2009), p. 185. This is an important book, first published in 1979, which argues that the expansion of record-keeping was the catalyst for a growth of literacy.

7 There are many translations of the *Divine Comedy* and critics argue endlessly about which is the best. A recent one by the Australian poet and critic Clive James (London: Picador, 2013) has been well received. Robin Kirkpatrick's translation in Penguin Classics, 2012, has the original on a facing page and [illegible]

8 There are famous illustrations of the *Divine Comedy*. See those by Sandro Botticelli drawn between 1480 and 1495, reproduced in the catalogue by The Royal Academy of Arts, London, for their 2000 exhibition of the drawings. Better known are those by Gustave Doré published in Paris between 1861 (*Inferno*) and 1868 (*Purgatorio* and *Paradiso*) and in many editions since.

9 For an overview, see Reynolds, *Dante*, pp. 329–33.

10 See the chapter on Marsilius by Cary J. Nederman in Boucher and Kelly (eds.), *Political Thinkers*, chapter 8, pp. 124–38. Quentin Skinner, *The Foundations of Modern Political Thought: Volume 1, The Renaissance* (Cambridge: Cambridge University Press, 1978), chapter 3, 'Scholasticism and Liberty' deals with Marsilius's political thought.

11 This is discussed in detail in Joel Kaye, *A History of Balance, 1250–1375* (Cambridge: Cambridge University Press, 2014), chapter 6, 'The New Model of Equilibrium in Medieval Political Thought, Part 1: The *Defensor pacis* of Marsilius of Padua'.

12 Quoted in Skinner, *The Foundations of Modern Political Thought*, p. 55.

13 From Aristotle, *The Politics*, Book 5, chapter 6.

14 *Defensor pacis*, Book 1, 13.6, 8.

15 The case for Boccaccio as a pioneering humanist is made by Tobias Foster Gittes in 'Boccaccio and Humanism' in Guyda Armstrong (ed.), *The Cambridge Companion to Boccaccio* (Cambridge: Cambridge University Press, 2015), pp. 155–70

16 See Laura Lambdin and Robert Lambdin, *Encyclopedia of Medieval Literature* (Westport, CT: Greenwood Press, 2000), p. 62.

17 I have used G. H. McWilliam's translation of *The Decameron* (Penguin Classics, 1972, and revised editions), complete with introduction by the translator.

18 For the *ricordanze* see Najemy, *A History of Florence*, p. 219.

11 The Challenge to the Scholastics

1 This is from the Fifth Story of the Sixth Day, translation G. H. McWilliam. The story involves Giotto and a companion being caught in a storm.

2 Bernard Berenson, *Italian Painters of the Renaissance* (New York: Phaidon, 1952, and several later editions).

3 There is coverage of Giotto in every standard history of Renaissance art, e.g. Stephen J. Campbell and Michael W. Cole, *A New History of Italian Renaissance Art* (London: Thames and Hudson, 2012). For an introduction to Giotto see Francesca Flores d'Arcais, *Giotto*, 2nd ed. (New York: Abbeville Press, 2016). For the Arena Chapel see James Stubblebine (ed.), *Giotto: The Arena Chapel Frescos* (London and New York: W. W. Norton, [illegible] Laura Jacobus, *Giotto and the Arena Chapel: Art, Architecture and Experience* (Turnhout, Belgium: Brepols/Harvey Miller Publications, 2008).

4 This is the famous work, first published in 1550, which established the canon of Renaissance art and is known for its mass of biographical details and anecdotes of the artists whom Vasari selected as the finest of the era. There is now a good study of Vasari by Ingrid Rowland and Noah Charney, *The Collector of Lives: Giorgio Vasari and the Invention of Art* (London and New York: W. W. Norton, 2017).

5 This was a medieval bestseller with full details, sometimes accurate, sometimes fictional, of the lives of the major saints. Renaissance artists often used it as a source book for their depictions of saints. There is a Penguin Classics edition of selections translated by Christopher Stace (1998).

6 Originally published in German in 1860, and in an English translation in 1878, and in subsequent editions (e.g. Penguin Classics, 1990), this is a famous study of the exuberance of the Italian Renaissance.

7 'In painting Cimabue thought he held the field, and now it's Giotto they acclaim – the former only keeps a shadowed fame' (*Purgatory* XI, 94–6).

8 Quoted in Rowland and Charney, *The Collector of Lives*, p. 80.

9 This is a continuation of the quotation from the Fifth Story of the Sixth Day (see note 1 to this chapter).

10 In his *Commentarii* of 1447. There is an Italian edition, L. Bartoli (ed.), *Lorenzo Ghiberti, I Commentarii* (Florence: Guinti Editore, 1998). The unfinished *I Commentarii* is one of the earliest autobiographies of an artist and was quarried by Vasari for his *Lives of the Artists*.

11 See, as general surveys of humanism, Charles Nauert, *Humanism and the Culture of Renaissance Europe*, 2nd ed. (Cambridge: Cambridge University Press, 2018), and Jill Kraye (ed.), *The Cambridge Companion to Renaissance Humanism* (Cambridge: Cambridge University Press, 1994). See also James Turner, *Philology: The Forgotten Origins of the Modern Humanities* (Princeton, NJ, and Oxford: Princeton University Press, 2014), chapter 2, '"A Complete Mastery of Antiquity". Renaissance, Reformation and Beyond'.

12 Ruggiero discusses *virtu* on pp. 16–17 of his *The Renaissance in Italy: A Social and Cultural History of the Rinascimento* (Cambridge: Cambridge University Press, 2015).

13 Probably the best biography of Cicero is by Anthony Everitt, *Cicero: A Turbulent Life* (London: John Murray, 2001).

14 See Ronald Witt, *In the Footsteps of the Ancients: The Origins of Humanism from Lovato to Bruni* (Leiden: Brill, 2000). Witt champions Lovato and Mussato as the first real humanists. See especially chapter 3, 'Padua and the Origins of Humanism', and chapter 4, 'Albertino Mussato and the Second Generation'.

15 For a recent comprehensive biography of Petrarch see Christopher Celenza, *Petrarch: Everywhere a Wanderer* (London: Reaktion Books, 2017). For the ascent of Mount Ventoux see pp. 57–61. The text of the letter is to be found in the Fordham University Medieval Sourcebook, available online at https://sourcebooks.fordham.edu/source/petrarch-ventoux.asp.

16 This quotation is from chapter 8 of the *Confessions*.

17 Quoted in Celenza, *Petrarch*, p. 224.

18 The text of 'On His Own Ignorance' can be found online at https://online.hillsdale.edu/document.doc?id=386. Two versions in Petrarch's own hand survive. In one passage, Petrarch laments the lack of emotion in Aristotle and shows his preference for the Latin authors. 'He [Aristotle] teaches what virtue is. I do not deny that but his lesson lacks the words that sting and set afire and urge towards love of virtue or hatred of vice or, at any rate, does not have enough of such power. He who looks for that will find it in our Latin writers, especially in Cicero and Seneca, and, what may be astonishing to hear, in Horace, a poet somewhat rough in style but most pleasing in his maxims.' There is an extensive discussion of 'On His Own Ignorance' in Celenza, *Petrarch*, pp. 181ff.

19 In a poem, *Italia mia*, written in 1344–5, Petrarch refers to Italy as his 'homeland' and suggests that the peninsula would not be hard to reunite as it had a natural boundary in the north. 'Virtue will take up arms against rage and the fighting shall be short, since the ancient strength in Italian hearts is not dead.' Celenza, *Petrarch*, pp.90ff.

20 Ruggiero, 'Introduction: The End of the World and its Rebirth (*Rinascita*) as the Rinascimento', in *The Renaissance in Italy*, pp. 1–20.

21 Quoted in Witt, *In the Footsteps of the Ancients*, p. 318.

22 This is dealt with in chapter 4, 'The Interior Man', in Celenza, *Petrarch*, especially pp. 108ff.

23 Quoted in ibid., p. 222.

24 Quoted in Robert Black, 'Education and the Emergence of a Literate Society', chapter 1 in John M. Najemy (ed.), *Italy in the Age of the Renaissance* (Oxford: Oxford University Press, 2004), p. 31.

12 Florentine Humanism

1 Translation from Matteo Palmieri, *Vita civile*, ed. G. Belloni (Florence: Sansoni 1982), pp. 43–4. This was an important paean of praise for the revival of knowledge after 800 years of *lunga ignoranza*, 'deep ignorance'. Palmieri uses the word *rinascita*, a rebirth, to describe the process. He demands that citizens should live both public and private lives committed to the republic. See Najemy, *A History of Florence*, pp. 211–15.

2 'In the morning when a large number of bodies were found in the pit, they took some earth and shovelled it down on top of them; and later others were placed on top of them and then another layer of earth, just as one makes lasagne with layers of pasta and cheese.' Marchionne di Coppo Buonaiuti, quoted by Ole Benedictow, 'The Black Death: The Greatest Catastrophe Ever', *History Today*, Volume 55, 3 March 2005.

3 This is covered in 'War Against the Church', pp. 151–5 in Najemy, *A History of Florence*.

4 Quoted in ibid., p.152.

5 'The Ciompi Revolution', ibid., pp. 161–6.

6 Quoted in ibid., p. 165.

7 Quoted in ibid., p. 177. Najemy's description of the hostility to the working classes (from p. 176 onwards) is valuable.

8 Hans Baron, *The Crisis of the Early Italian Renaissance*, rev. ed. (Princeton, NJ, and Oxford: Princeton University Press, 1966). Putnam, Leonardi and Nanetti, *Making Democracy Work*, argue that Renaissance traditions of civic humanism have persisted in northern Italy to this day (in contrast to the cities of the south).

9 Available online at https://www.york.ac.uk/teaching/history/pjpg/bruni.pdf, from which the quotations are taken. On Bruni's rhetoric, see James Hankins, 'Rhetoric, History and Ideology: The Civic Panegyrics of Leonardo Bruni', chapter 5 in James Hankins (ed.), *Renaissance Civic Humanism: Reappraisals and Reflections* (Cambridge: Cambridge University Press, 2000).

10 Quoted in Hankins, 'Rhetoric, History and Ideology', p. 172.

11 This has been translated by James Hankins as *History of the Florentine People*, published by Harvard University Press in their important I Tatti Renaissance Library series; vol. 1, 2001; vol. 2, 2004.

12 'The first modern history' and 'historiographical coup' come from Burrow's *A History of Histories*, p. 285.

13 Lodi Nauta of the University of Groningen, Netherlands, has contributed an excellent article on Valla's works in the online *Stanford Encyclopedia of Philosophy*: https://plato.stanford.edu › entries/lorenzo-valla. See also chapters 8–10 in Celenza, *The Intellectual World*, which largely deal with Valla.

14 Celenza, *The Intellectual World*, pp. 206–10, has a good analysis of Valla's text on the Donation forgery. See also Nelson, *King and Emperor*, for an analysis of the eighth-century background of the Donation at pp. 353–6.

15 Robert Black, 'Humanism', chapter 12 in Allmand (ed.), *The New Cambridge Medieval History: Volume 7*, p. 266.

16 Ruggiero, *The Renaissance in Italy*, deals with these schools, pp. 246–9.

13 The Florentine Renaissance

1 From the prologue of Leon Battista Alberti, *Della pittura*, 'On Painting', trans. John R. Spencer (New Haven and London: Yale University Press, 1970).

2 There are many surveys of Florentine Renaissance art. The subjects of the following pages are covered well with illustrations in [illegible] 'The Cathedral and the City', and chapter 3, '1410–20: Commissioning Art: Standardization, Customization, Emulation', in Campbell and Cole (eds.), *A New History of Renaissance Art*. See also Loren Partridge, *Art of Renaissance Florence, 1400–1600* (Berkeley: University of California Press, 2009).

3 Campbell and Cole (eds.), *A New History of Renaissance Art*, chapter 4, '1420–30: Perspective and its Discontents'. See also Wootton, *The Invention of Science*, pp. 164–72.

4 There is a useful discussion of the use of 'pre-perspective' by Giotto in Hans Belting, *Florence and Baghdad: Renaissance Art and Arab Science* (Cambridge, MA, and London: Belknap Press of Harvard University Press, 2011), pp. 135–45. This book is essentially 'a [comparative] history of the gaze' in two distinct cultures, what can and cannot be looked at.

5 Quoted in ibid., pp. 164–5.

6 There is an excellent discussion of *Della pittura* in Anthony Grafton, *Leon Battista Alberti: Master Builder of the Italian Renaissance* (London: Allen Lane/Penguin, 2000), chapter 4. This quotation comes from p. 123.

7 'Orsanmichele and its Tabernacles', pp. 72–82 in Campbell and Cole (eds.), *A New History of Renaissance Art*.

8 Ibid., pp. 101–3.

9 An excellent history of the Medici is now provided by Mary Hollingsworth, *The Medici* (London: Head of Zeus, 2017). For Giovanni de' Medici, see chapter 3, 'The Fortune'. There is a wealth of detail in Najemy, *A History of Florence*, especially chapter 9, 'Fateful Embrace: The Emergence of the Medici', and chapter 10, 'The Medici and the Ottimati: A Partnership of Conflict, Part One: Cosimo and Piero'.

10 For Cosimo, Hollingsworth, *The Medici*, chapters 4–6 and the chapters in Najemy, *A History of Florence*, as above. There is a good section on the birth of the public library in Celenza, *The Intellectual World*, pp. 231–40.

11 Campbell and Cole (eds.), *A New History of Renaissance Art*, pp. 150–2. This includes a photograph of the courtyard of the Medici Palace where the *David* originally stood.

12 For a full description of the palace as it exists today, see Alta Macadam, *Blue Guide Florence*, pp. 155ff. The humanist historian Flavio Biondi declared in 1450 that the palace was more magnificent than any known from ancient Rome.

13 Grafton, *Leon Battista Alberti*, is excellent throughout.

14 Grafton discusses the way Burckhardt uses the 'autobiography', which is written in the third person but is assumed to be by Alberti himself, in ibid., pp. 14ff.

15 This quotation actually comes from an essay by Grafton in a new edition of *Lives of the Eminent Philosophers by Diogenes Laertius*, ed. James Miller, trans. Pamela Mensch (Oxford: Oxford University Press, 2018). The essay is 'Diogenes Laertius: From Inspiration to Annoyance (and Back)', pp. 546–54. Alberti was one of the first humanists to enthuse about this famous, but untrustworthy, book from the first half of the third century AD that was translated from the Greek into Latin for the first time in the 1430s.

16 The various strategies that Alberti [illegible] impression of supreme mastery are well explored in Grafton, *Leon Battista Alberti*, in his chapter 'Who Was Leon Battista Alberti?', especially pp. 18–29.

17 A point made by David Wootton in his *The Invention of Science*, p. 200.

18 Cennino Cennini was heavily influenced by Giotto. His *Il libro dell'arte* (*A Treatise of Painting*) of *c.*1400 is a mine of information on the practicalities of painting, the preparations of pigments and the different surfaces to which they might be applied. Cennini still sees the artist as essentially a craftsman rather than as a creative genius.

19 This is well covered in chapter 8, 'Alberti on the Art of Building', in Grafton, *Leon Battista Alberti*.

20 I am indebted to Ross King's *Brunelleschi's Dome: The Story of the Great Cathedral in Florence* (London: Penguin Books, 2000), for a superb account of the building of the dome that I have relied on heavily here.

21 On Gothic architecture an excellent introduction, concentrating on Chartres Cathedral, is Philip Ball, *Universe of Stone* (London: Bodley Head, 2008). See also Nicola Coldstream, *Medieval Architecture*, in the Oxford History of Art series (Oxford: Oxford University Press, 2002), and the older, but comprehensive, Christopher Wilson, *The Gothic Cathedral: The Architecture of the Great Church 1130–1530*, rev. ed. (London: Thames and Hudson, 1992).

22 Quoted in Grafton, *Leon Battista Alberti*, p. 72.

23 For the mechanical achievements of Brunelleschi and their aftermath, see Jim Bennett, 'The Mechanical Arts', chapter 27 in Park and Daston (eds.), *The Cambridge History of Science: Volume 3*, especially pp. 677–9.

24 See the assessment in Hollingsworth, *The Medici*, chapter 7, 'The Succession Crisis'.

25 Ibid., chapters 8–9 for Lorenzo. Also Najemy, *A History of Florence*, chapter 12, 'The Medici and the Ottimati: A Partnership of Conflict, Part Two: Lorenzo'.

26 From 'The Oration on the Dignity of Man' (1486), available online at http://web.mnstate.edu/gracyk/courses/web%20publishing/pico_oration.htm. I took the quotation from MacCulloch, *Reformation*, p. 106, where MacCulloch extols the air of optimism before the French invasion of Italy in 1494.

27 The crisis in Lorenzo's finances is dealt with in Hollingsworth, *The Medici*, pp. 185–8. The quotation from Guicciardini comes from ibid., p. 186.

28 *The History of Italy* and *The History of Florence* by Guicciardini can be found translated by Cecil Grayson with an introduction by the Renaissance scholar John Hale in The Great Histories Series (New York: Washington Square Press, 1964). In his *A History of Histories*, Burrow discusses Guicciardini in chapter 18, 'From Civic Chronicle to Humanist History'.

29 Guicciardini, *The History of Florence*, chapter 9.

14 Plato Re-enters the Western Mind

1 Quoted in Celenza, *The Intellectual World*, pp. 244–5.

2 From 'The Logic of the Moral Sciences' (1862) seen as 'one of the founding documents of modern social science'. Mill is arguing here that certain intellectuals can transcend the time they live in to have a lasting influence. See Joseph Hamburger, *John Stuart Mill on Liberty and Control* (Princeton, NJ, and Oxford: Princeton University Press, 1999), p. 32.

3 For Plato in the Middle Ages see James Hankins, 'Plato in the Middle Ages', reprinted in James Hankins, *Humanism and Platonism in the Italian Renaissance* (Rome: Edizioni di storia e litteratura 2004), vol. 2.

4 *Phaedo*, 82 a–b.

5 From 'On His Own Ignorance'. Petrarch was here reacting to a growing feeling that there were more profound issues in philosophy that Aristotle was ignoring and that major figures such as Augustine had praised Plato as the pagan philosopher closest to Christianity. Augustine said, in fact, that if Plato had been born later he would have been a Christian.

6 Quoted in Hankins, *Plato in the Italian Renaissance*, vol. 1, pp. 45–6.

7 It was typical of Plato that he took actual individuals (as with Parmenides above) to represent one side of an argument against Socrates. Gorgias was a Sicilian orator who visited Athens in 427 BC and who was able to defend either side of any argument presented to him. Plato, in contrast, argues, through Socrates, that there were values that existed eternally and could not be subverted.

8 See chapter 41, 'The Councils of Basel and Ferrara/Florence: Pope Eugenius IV', in Chadwick, *East and West*.

9 For the story of this controversy I have relied heavily on the account given by Hankins, *Plato in the Italian Renaissance*, vol. 1, pp. 161–263.

10 There is a good assessment of Bessarion by Claudia Rapp in Anthony Grafton et al. (eds.), *The Classical Tradition* (Cambridge, MA, and London: Belknap Press of Harvard University Press, 2010), pp. 123–5.

11 This comes from a letter to 'a pious Catherine' published in Venice in *c.*1489. Quoted in Martin Lowry, *The World of Aldus Manutius: Business and Scholarship in Renaissance Venice* (Oxford: Blackwell, 1979), p. 57.

12 Again I have relied on Hankins's meticulous survey for Ficino, *Plato in the Italian Renaissance*, vol. 1, pp. 267–359. See also Paul Oskar Kristeller, *Eight Philosophers of the Italian Renaissance* (Stanford, CA: Stanford University Press, 1964), chapter 3, 'Ficino'. There are also two excellent chapters, 12 and 13, on Ficino in Celenza, *The Intellectual World*.

13 Quoted by Hankins, *Plato in the Italian Renaissance*, vol. 1, p. 316.

14 The classic work on this is Frances Yates, *Giordano Bruno and the Hermetic Tradition* (Chicago and London: University of Chicago Press, 1964).

15 Miller (ed.), *Lives of the Eminent Philosophers by Diogenes Laertius*. Book 3 is devoted to Plato. For the *The School of Athens* see the essay by Ingrid Rowland in the same volume: 'Raphael's Eminent Philosophers: *The School of Athens* and the Classic Work Almost No One Read'.

16 Kristeller, *Eight Philosophers of the Italian Renaissance*, p. 52.

17 For Victorian Britain see Frank M. Turner, *The Greek Heritage in Victorian Britain* (New Haven and London: Yale University Press, 1981), and Richard Jenkyns, *The Victorians and Ancient Greece* (Oxford: Blackwell, 1980), chapter 10, 'Plato'.

15 The Printing Press

1 Quoted in Grafton, *Leon Battista Alberti*, p. 330.

2 The topics in this chapter are well covered in Andrew Pettegree, *The Book in the Renaissance* (New Haven and London: Yale University Press, 2010). For this chapter I have also used the classic Lucien Febvre and Henri-Jean Martin, *The Coming of the Book: The Impact of Printing 1450–1800*, 3rd ed. (New York: Verso, 2010), and Elizabeth Eisenstein, *The Printing Revolution in Early Modern Europe*, 2nd ed. (Cambridge: Cambridge University Press, 2005).

3 Pettegree, *The Book in the Renaissance*, pp. 17–19. Hugo Chapman and Marzia Faietti, *Fra Angelico to Leonardo: Italian Renaissance Drawings* (London: British Museum Press, 2010), has a useful section on papermaking, pp. 36–8.

4 For the Gutenberg Bible see Eric Marshall White, *Editio Princeps: A History of the Gutenberg Bible* (Turnhout, Belgium: Harvey Miller, 2017).

5 See Martin Davies, *Aldus Manutius: Printer and Publisher of Renaissance Venice* (London: British Library, 1995).

6 See Edward Wilson-Lee, *The Catalogue of Shipwrecked Books: Young Columbus and the Search for a Universal Library* (London: William Collins, 2017).

7 Owen Gingerich, *The Book that Nobody Read: Chasing the Revolutions of Nicolaus Copernicus* (New York: Walker and Son, 2004; London: Arrow/Penguin Books, 2005).

8 See Bala, *The Dialogue of Civilizations*, chapter 7, 'The Narrow Copernican Revolution', and George Saliba, *Islamic Science and the Making of the European Renaissance* (Cambridge, MA: MIT Press, 2011), chapter 6, 'Islamic Science and Renaissance Europe: The Copernican Connection'.

9 Quoted in Celenza, *The Intellectual World*, p. 230.

16 The Rise of the Laity, 1300–1550

1 Quoted in Christopher Black, *Italian Confraternities in the Sixteenth Century* (Cambridge: Cambridge University Press, 1989), p. 16.

2 John Watts, *The Making of Polities, 1300–1500* (Cambridge: Cambridge University Press, 2009), is a penetrating survey of the process of state formation in this period.

3 The exile is covered in Madigan, *Medieval Christianity*, pp. 374–7. See also P. N. R. Zutshi, 'The Avignon Papacy', chapter 19 in Michael Jones (ed.), *The New Cambridge Medieval History: Volume 6, c.1300–c.1415* (Cambridge: Cambridge University Press, 2000).

4 Euan Cameron, *The European Reformation*, 2nd ed. (Oxford: Oxford University Press, 2012), p. 36.

5 From a letter to friend, available online at the Fordham University Medieval Sourcebook, https://sourcebooks.fordham.edu/source/14Cpetrarch-pope.asp. The rest of the letter continues in much the same vein.

6 Howard Kaminsky, chapter 20, 'The Great Schism', in Jones (ed.), *The New Cambridge Medieval History: Volume 6*. Steven Ozment has a searching examination of the attempts to solve the Schism in *The Age of Reform*, pp. 155–81. See also Madigan, *Medieval Christianity*, pp. 378–83.

7 Ozment, *The Age of Reform*, discusses the theology of Gerson, pp. 73ff.

8 Quoted in ibid., p. 161.

9 See Robin Harris, *Dubrovnik: A History* (London: SAQI, 2003), especially chapter 10, 'Religious Life: Ecclesiastical Organization and Spirituality in Dubrovnik (c.1190–1808)'.

10 The Misericordia is discussed in Nicholas Terpstra, *Religious Refugees in the Early Modern World: An Alternative History of the Reformation* (Cambridge: Cambridge University Press, 2015), pp. 22–6.

11 Cameron, *The European Reformation*, p. 14.

12 For the eloquent Bernardino, see Franco Mormando, *The Preacher's Demons: Bernardino of Siena and the Social Underworld of Early Renaissance Italy* (Chicago and London: University of Chicago Press, 1999).

13 Najemy, *A History of Florence*, pp. 55–6.

14 See Koen Goodriaan, 'Empowerment through Reading, Writing and Example: The *Devotio Moderna*', chapter 26 in Miri Rubin and Walter Simons (eds.), *The Cambridge History of Christianity: Volume 4, Christianity in Western Europe c.1100–c.1500* (Cambridge: Cambridge University Press, 2009).

15 One study of flagellant confraternities in northern Italy found twenty-seven founded in the thirteenth century, ninety-eight in the fourteenth and thirty-two from the fifteenth. Quoted in Brian Pullen, *Rich and Poor in Renaissance Venice* (Cambridge, MA, and London: Harvard University Press, 1971), p. 39. See also John Henderson, *Piety and Charity in Late Medieval Florence* (Chicago and London: University of Chicago Press, 1994).

16 See Nicholas Terpstra, 'Civic Religion', in Arnold (ed.), *The Oxford Handbook of Medieval Christianity*, pp. 148–65.

17 Najemy, *A History of Florence*, pp. 51–4.

18 See Diarmaid MacCulloch, *Thomas Cromwell: A Life* (London: Allen Lane/Penguin, 2018), pp. 31–5. The young Thomas Cromwell was a consultant for the guild.

19 Martin Heale, *The Abbots and Priors of Late Medieval and Reformation England* (Oxford: Oxford University Press, 2016), especially chapters 5 and 6.

20 Eamon Duffy, *Marking the Hours: English People and their Prayers, 1240–1570* (New Haven and London: Yale University Press, 2006).

21 For what follows see Carlos Eire, *Reformations: The Early Modern World, 1450–1650* (New Haven and London: Yale University Press, 2016), chapter 3, 'Reform and Dissent in the Late Middle Ages', which sets Wycliffe and Hus in the wider context of their times. See also Madigan, *Medieval Christianity*, chapter 19 '"Morning Stars" or Heretics? Wyclif, Hus and Followers'. Also chapter 28, 'Wycliffites and Lollardy', by Khantir Ghosh in Rubin and Simons (eds.), *The Cambridge History of Christianity: Volume 4*.

22 A full account of Hus and the Bohemian Wars is given in Norman Housley, *Religious Warfare in Europe, 1400–1536* (Oxford: Oxford University Press, 2002), chapter 2, 'A Crucible of Religious Warfare: Bohemia during the Hussite Wars, 1400–1436'.

23 The story is covered in Giles Tremlett, *Isabella of Castile* (London: Bloomsbury, 2017), especially chapters 24–7. For the background to the *Reconquista* as part of the crusading movement, see Joseph O'Callaghan, *Reconquest and Crusade in Medieval Spain* (Philadelphia: University of Pennsylvania Press, 2004).

24 Terpstra, *Religious Refugees*, p. 2.

25 Detailed in Tremlett, *Isabella of Castile*, chapters 43–4.

26 John Najemy gives an excellent survey of Savonarola's rule in *A History of Florence*, notably pp. 382–400.

27 Parenti (1449–1518) provides one the best accounts of the political turmoil of 1490s Florence in his *Storia Fiorentina* (written in Italian). He had enjoyed a top-class humanist education from Marsilio Ficino, among others.

28 Quoted by Najemy, *A History of Florence*, p. 393.

29 From Savonarola's *Treatise on the Government of Florence*, quoted in Najemy, *A History of Florence*, pp. 393–4.

30 Quoted in Hugh Honour and John Fleming, *A World History of Art*, 3rd ed. (London: Laurence King, 1991), p. 420. There are also later editions of this famous work.

31 This is discussed in Ruggiero, *The Renaissance in Italy*, pp. 565–7.

32 See Rowland and Charney, *The Collector of Lives*.

33 For Erasmus, A. G. Dickens and Whitney Jones, *Erasmus the Reformer* (London: Methuen, 2000); Carlos Eire, *Reformations*, 'Erasmus', pp. 105–113; MacCulloch, *Reformation*, 'Erasmus, Hopes Fulfilled, Fears Stilled?', pp. 97–105; Turner, *Philology*, chapter 2, '"A Complete Mastery of Antiquity". Renaissance, Reformation and Beyond'.

34 From a letter to Erasmus's pupil Robert Fisher, 5 December 1499, letter 118, p. 235 of *Collected Works of Erasmus: Correspondence, 1484–1500* (Toronto: University of Toronto Press, 1974). This is widely quoted elsewhere.

35 Quoted by Eric Nelson, *The Greek Tradition in Republican Thought* (Cambridge: Cambridge University Press, 2000), p. 26. Pace argues that anything of intellectual quality only came to Rome via Greece.

36 The quotation is by MacCulloch, *Reformation*, pp. 100–1, where there is a good overview of these issues.

37 The quotation about the 'newfangled reasoning' comes from a letter Erasmus wrote to Albert of Brandenburg in October 1519, cited by Nicolette Mout, 'Peace without Concord: Religious Toleration in Theory and Practice', chapter 13 (pp. 227–43), in R. Po-Chia Hsia (ed.), *The Cambridge History of Christianity. Volume 6, Reform and Expansion, 1500–1660* (Cambridge: Cambridge University Press, 2007), p. 230. The quotation about scholastic argument is found in Dickens and Jones, *Erasmus the Reformer*, p. 55.

38 Caroline Walker Bynum, *Christian Materiality: An Essay on Religion in Late Medieval Europe* (New York: Zone Books, 2011).

39 Peter Marshall, *Heretics and Believers: A History of the English Reformation* (New Haven and London: Yale University Press, 2017), p. xvii.

17 The Mapping of the New World

1 See Nurminen, *The Mapmakers' World*, pp. 162–4, which deals with the map and includes an illustration of it.

2 See chapter 3, 'Faith: Hereford *Mappamundi*', in Jerry Brotton, *A History of the World in Twelve Maps* (London: Allen Lane/Penguin, 2012).

3 This is brilliantly illustrated with text in 'The Portolan Chart: The Direction, Distance, and Scale in Maps', pp. 60–70 of Nurminen, *The Mapmakers' World*.

4 Ibid., pp. 70–4 with illustrations.

5 See chapter 3, 'Late Medieval European Exploration of the Atlantic and Africa before 1492', in Ronald Fritze, *New Worlds: The Great Voyages of Discovery 1400–1600* (Stroud: Sutton Publishing, 2002).

6 Ibid., 'Christopher Columbus and His Enterprise of the Indies', pp. 98–121.

7 Ibid., 'Vasco da Gama and the Sea-Road to India', pp. 127–41.

8 It is illustrated with commentary in Nurminen, *The Mapmakers' World*, pp. 170–5.

9 Ibid., pp. 160–7, and chapter 5, 'Discovery: Martin Waldseemuller, World Map, 1507', in Brotton, *A History of the World in Twelve Maps*.

10 See Wootton, *The Invention of Science*, chapter 4, for a full survey of this.

11 Brotton, *A History of the World in Twelve Maps*, chapter 7, 'Toleration: Gerard Mercator, World Map, 1569', and 'Gerard Mercator – The Father of Modern Map Projection', in Nurminen, *The Mapmakers' World*, pp. 235–46.

12 From Melanchthon's *Initia doctrinae physicae* (*The Origins of Physics*), quoted in Brotton, *A History of the World in Twelve Maps*, p. 230.

13 Quotation from Brotton, *A History of the World in Twelve Maps*, pp. 235–6, who discusses the cordiform maps in more detail, pp. 235–7.

14 Nurminen, *The Mapmakers' World*, p. 236 for the details as part of an account of Mercator's life.

15 Brotton, *A History of the World in Twelve Maps*, gives an excellent account of the Mercator projection, pp. 247–56.

16 Adam Smith, *The Wealth of Nations* (London: Strahan and Cadell, 1776), Book 4, chapter 7, 'On the Advantages which Europe has Derived from the Discovery of America'.

17 Quoted in Wootton, *The Invention of Science*, p. 81.

18 Leonardo and Vesalius

1 The 'Treatise on Painting' was a series of Leonardo's thoughts on paintings gathered together in the early sixteenth century by one of his pupils, Francesco Melzi, whose original manuscript, the *Codex Urbinas Latinus 1270*, is in the Vatican. As many of Leonardo's original notebooks are lost, it is not clear how accurate a recording of Leonardo's thoughts these are but they reflect his beliefs.

2 Some of Cyriac of Ancona's travels are now recorded in two volumes edited by Edward Bodnar for the I Tatti Renaissance Library. This important publishing initiative is discussed by Anthony Grafton in chapter 7, 'The Universal Language: Splendors and Sorrows of Latin in the Modern World', pp. 137–59, in his *Worlds Made by Words* (Cambridge, MA, and London: Harvard University Press, 2009).

3 Quoted in John Hale, *The Civilization of Europe in the Renaissance* (London: Harper Perennial, 2005), p. 191.

4 See the introductory essay by Hugo Chapman in Chapman and Faietti, *Fra Angelico to Leonardo*, pp. 15–75, for a good survey of fifteenth- and sixteenth-century drawings.

5 Ibid., p. 72.

6 Michelangelo's 'presentation drawings' of the early 1530s for the Roman aristocrat Tommaso de' Cavalieri are seen as the masterpieces here. For Raphael, see Catherine Wheeler and Ben Thomas, *Raphael: The Drawings* (Oxford: Ashmolean Museum, 2017), a catalogue of a wonderful exhibition whose introductory essays have much to say about the art of drawing in this period.

7 Many see the best survey of Leonardo as that by Kenneth Clark, *Leonardo da Vinci* (Cambridge: Cambridge University Press, 1939; rev. ed. with Martin Kemp, Penguin Books, 1988). Charles Nicholl, *Leonardo da Vinci: The Flights of the Mind* (London: Allen Lane/Penguin, 2004), is a readable biography. Martin Kemp is an authority; see his *Leonardo da Vinci: The*

Marvellous Works of Nature and Man (Oxford: Oxford University Press, 2006), and *Leonardo da Vinci: Experience, Experiment and Design* (London: Victoria and Albert Publications, 2007). Martin Kemp's *Living with Leonardo: Fifty Years of Sanity and Insanity in the Art World and Beyond* (London: Thames and Hudson, 2018), is an excellent account of Kemp's adventures in the world of Leonardo studies.

8 Kemp, *Leonardo da Vinci: Experience, Experiment and Design*, p. 3.

9 Quoted in Kemp, *Leonardo da Vinci: Marvellous Works*, p. 111.

10 From 'The Treatise on Painting'; see note 1 to this chapter.

11 Quoted in Kemp, *Living with Leonardo*, p. 40.

12 Quoted by Kemp, *Leonardo da Vinci: Marvellous Works*, p. 270.

13 Ibid., p. 120.

14 Ibid., p. 112.

15 Ibid., pp. 292–3.

16 Leonardo da Vinci, *Notebooks*, ed. Thereza Wells and Martin Kemp (Oxford: Oxford University Press, 2008), quoted on p. 8.

17 This account of Vesalius is largely based on Roy Porter, *The Greatest Benefit to Mankind: A Medical History of Humanity from Antiquity to the Present* (London: HarperCollins, 2007).

18 See Hugh Trevor-Roper's *Europe's Physician: The Various Life of Sir Theodore De Mayerne* (New Haven and London: Yale University Press, 2007).

19 Exploring the Natural World

1 The death of Pliny the Elder is described in a letter by his nephew Pliny the Younger to the historian Tacitus. Letter 6.16, trans. J. B. Firth, available online at http://www.attalus.org/info/pliny.html.

2 The story is well told by Brian W. Ogilvie, *The Science of Describing: Natural History in Renaissance Europe* (Chicago and London: University of Chicago Press, 2006), pp. 121–33. This is an excellent survey of the events and personalities described in this chapter.

3 Ibid., p.127.

4 This was a common feature of the period as interest in the pagan gods recovered. See Malcolm Bull, *The Mirror of the Gods: How Renaissance Artists Rediscovered the Pagan Gods* (Oxford: Oxford University Press, 2005).

5 Robin Lane-Fox, 'The Walls have Pears', *Financial Times*, 1 December 2018.

6 Ogilvie, *The Science of Describing*, pp. 236–40.

7 Quoted in ibid., p. 83. For the Republic of Letters see Grafton, *Worlds Made by Words*, chapter 1, 'A Sketch Map of a Lost Continent: The Republic of Letters'.

8 Clusius is referred to in many parts of Ogilvie, *The Science of Describing*, but pp. 184–6 concentrate on his methods of description.

9 See David Attenborough, et al., *Amazing Rare Things: The Art of Natural History in the Age of Discovery* (New Haven and London: Yale University Press, 2007)

10 Ogilvie, *The Science of* Describing, pp. 186–97.

11 Ibid., p. 211.

20 Imagining Princely Politics

1 From 'The First Book of the Communication of Raphael Hythloday, Concerning the Best State of a Commonwealth' in Susan Bruce (ed.), *Three Early Modern Utopias*, World Classics (Oxford: Oxford University Press, 1999).

2 From *The Prince*, trans. and ed. Tim Parks, Oxford Classics, (Oxford: Oxford University Press, 2011), chapter 14, 'That Which Concerns a Prince on the Subject of War'.

3 Quoted in Eric Nelson, 'The Problem of the Prince', chapter 17 in James Hankins (ed.), *The Cambridge Companion to Renaissance Philosophy* (Cambridge: Cambridge University Press, 2007), p. 32. This essay is relied on for the first part of this chapter.

4 Ruggiero, *The Renaissance in Italy*, pp. 246–8. See also for patronage Alison Cole, *Art of the Italian Renaissance Court* (London: Calmann and King, 1995).

5 I have used the text and introduction to *Utopia* in the Oxford World Classics *Three Early Modern Utopias*, ed. Susan Bruce (Oxford: Oxford University Press, 1999).

6 Dominic Baker-Smith in 'Thomas More', *Stanford Encyclopedia of Philosophy*, available online at https://plato.stanford.edu/entries/thomas-more.

7 *The Writer's Map: An Atlas of Imaginary Lands*, ed. Huw Lewis-Jones (London: Thames and Hudson, 2018), p. 45.

8 Anthony Kenny et al., *Renaissance Thinkers* (Oxford: Oxford University Press, 1993), p. 290.

9 From Susan Bruce's 'Introduction to Utopia' in *Three Early Modern Utopias*, p. xix.

10 Quoted in the preface to Erica Benner, *Be Like the Fox: Machiavelli's Quest for Freedom* (London: Allen Lane/Penguin, 2017), p. xviii.

11 Christopher Celenza, *Machiavelli: A Portrait* (Cambridge, MA, and London: Harvard University Press, 2015), chapter 2, 'Highs and Lows', for his Roman interests, p. 59 for the letter.

12 See Celenza, 'Who Owns Culture? Classicism, Institutions and the Vernacular', chapter 6 in *The Intellectual World.*

13 Skinner, *The Foundations of Modern Political Thought*, p. 125.

14 See Quentin Skinner's essay 'Machiavelli on Misunderstanding Princely *Virtu*' in his *From Humanism to Hobbes: Studies in Rhetoric and Politics* (Cambridge: Cambridge University Press, 2018).

15 Benner, *Be Like the Fox*, p. 251.

16 Celenza, *Machiavelli*, p. 120.

17 Benner, *Be Like the Fox*, p. 272.

18 Mitchell Cohen, *The Politics of Opera: A History from Monteverdi to Mozart* (Princeton, NJ, and Oxford: Princeton University Press, 2017).

19 James Hankins, 'The Significance of Renaissance Philosophy', chapter 18 in Hankins (ed.), *The Cambridge Companion to Renaissance Philosophy*, p. 341.

21 Broadening Horizons

1 Quoted in Leonard Barkan, *Unearthing the Past: Archaeology and Aesthetics in the Making of Renaissance Culture* (New Haven and London: Yale University Press, 1999), chapter 1, p. 3. The letter was written some sixty years after the event but was only published in print in Rome in 1790.

2 See Turner, *Philology*, 'Classical Antiquarianism, Chronology and the Expansion of Antiquity', pp. 50–64.

3 Loren Partridge, *The Renaissance in Rome* (London: Weidenfeld and Nicolson, 1996), as a general introduction.

4 See the discussion on the Laocoön in chapter 1, 'Discoveries', in Barkan, *Unearthing the Past*.

5 Francis Haskell and Nicholas Penny, *Taste and the Antique: The Lure of Classical Sculpture 1500–1900* (New Haven and London: Yale University Press, 1981), p. 10.

6 Ibid., p.8.

7 See ibid., chapter 2, 'The Public and Private Collections of Rome'.

8 Quoted in ibid., p. 12.

9 Ingrid Rowland, 'Raphael's Eminent Philosophers', in Miller (ed.), *Lives of the Eminent Philosophers by Diogenes Laertius*, p. 561.

10 Jill Kraye, 'The Revival of Hellenistic Philosophies', chapter 6 in Hankins (ed.), *The Cambridge Companion to Renaissance Philosophy*. For the original sources a classic introduction is that by A. A. Long, *Hellenistic Philosophy* (London: Bloomsbury, 1996), and Peter Adamson's *A History of Philosophy without Any Gaps: Philosophy in the Hellenistic and Roman World* (Oxford: Oxford University Press, 2015).

11 Luca Bianchi, 'Continuity and Change in the Aristotelian Tradition', chapter 4 in Hankins (ed.), *The Cambridge Companion to Renaissance Philosophy*.

12 Quoted in Kraye, 'The Revival of Hellenistic Philosophies', p. 101.

13 Ibid.

14 Thorsteinsson, *Roman Christianity and Roman Stoicism*, stresses the contrast between these two different ethical traditions.

15 From Montaigne's essay 'On Books', from *The Complete Essays*, trans. M. A. Screech, rev. ed. (London: Penguin Classics, 2003), p. 461.

16 The most recent book on the rediscovery of Lucretius by Stephen Greenblatt was entitled, in its original edition, *The Swerve: How the World became Modern* (New York and London: W. W. Norton, 2011), a vast exaggeration of the influence of Lucretius. The British edition went even further in its subtitle, proclaiming *The Swerve: How the Renaissance Began* (London: Vintage, 2012). The Renaissance was, in fact, largely over by the time Lucretius became accepted. Greenblatt has also been criticized by medieval scholars for his denigration of medieval thought. Nevertheless, *The Swerve* won the author, a distinguished commentator on Shakespeare, a Pulitzer Prize.

17 See Miriam Bodiam, 'Christianity and Judaism', chapter 26 in R. Po-Chia Hsia (ed.), *The Cambridge History of Christianity: Volume 6, Reform and Expansion, 1500–1660*. Also Turner, *Philology*, chapter on '*Philogia Trilingua*, the Bible and History', pp. 39–42.

18 Bodiam, 'Christianity and Judaism', p. 499.

19 Turner, *Philology*, p. 46.

20 See Brian Curran, *The Egyptian Renaissance: The Afterlife of Ancient Egypt in Early Modern Italy* (Chicago and London: University of Chicago Press, 2007).

21 For a concise and authoritative life see James Ackerman and Phyllis Massar, *Palladio* (London: Pelican Books, 1966), and subsequent editions, and the entertaining Witold Rybczynski, *The Perfect House: A Journey with Renaissance Master Andrea Palladio* (New York: Scribner, 2002).

22 Ruggiero, *The Renaissance in Italy*, pp. 538ff., is my source for the following account.

23 The Accademia is well covered by David Freedberg, *The Eye of the Lynx: Galileo, His Friends, and the Beginnings of Modern Natural History* (Chicago and London: Chicago University Press, 2002).

22 Peoples of the 'Newe Founde Worldes'

1 Quoted in Stephen Greenblatt, *Marvellous Possessions: The Wonder of the New World* (Chicago and London: University of Chicago Press, 1991), p. 130.

2 See Nurminen, *The Mapmakers' World*, pp. 282–300, where the maps of Blaeu are analysed in full with superb illustrations.

3 The problems of these sources are exhaustively covered in Shayne Aaron Legassie, *The Medieval Invention of Travel* (Chicago and London: Chicago University Press, 2017).

4 See for an overview, Ronald Fritze, *New Worlds*, chapters 5, 'Comprehending the Americas – Outlining the Coastline for a Way to Asia', and 6, 'Conquests'; David Abulafia, *The Discovery of Mankind: Atlantic Encounters in the Age of Columbus* (New Haven and London: Yale University Press, 2008); Greenblatt, *Marvellous Possessions*; Anthony Pagden, *European Encounters with the New World* (New Haven and London: Yale University Press, 1993); John Thornton, *A Cultural History of the Atlantic World, 1250–1820* (Cambridge: Cambridge University Press, 2012). There is an important chapter on Spanish views of the American Indians in Siep Stuurman, *The Invention of Humanity*, chapter 5, 'The Atlantic Frontier and the Limits of Christian

Equality'. For the view from Spain see Geoffrey Parker, *Emperor: A New Life of Charles V* (New Haven and London: Yale University Press, 2019).

5 See Abulafia, *The Discovery of Mankind*, chapter 19, 'Vespucci's Tabloid Journalism, 1497–1504'.

6 Quoted in Marenbon, *Pagans and Philosophers*, p. 248. See especially 'Pagan Knowledge in the New World', pp. 247–58.

7 For Caminha, see Abulafia, *The Discovery of Mankind*, pp. 268ff.

8 Parker, *Emperor*, chapter 13, 'The Taming of America', p. 346, for Charles's commitment to conversion.

9 See Lewis Hanke, *Aristotle and the American Indians: A Study of Race Prejudice in the Modern World* (Chicago: Henry Regnery Company, 1959), and Anthony Pagden, *The Fall of Natural Man: The American Indian and the Origins of Comparative Ethnology* (Cambridge: Cambridge University Press, 1982).

10 Pagden, *The Fall of Natural Man*, p. 48.

11 For Oviedo, see Pagden, *European Encounters*, especially pp. 17–18 and 56–68.

12 See 'A Compulsory Voluntary Requirement, 1511–20', chapter 22 in Abulafia, *The Discovery of Mankind*.

13 This is well covered in Thornton, *A Cultural History of the Atlantic World*, chapter 3, 'The African Background'.

14 See Marenbon, *Pagans and Philosophers*, p. 251.

15 See Pagden, *The Fall of Natural Man*, chapter 5, 'The Rhetorician and the Theologians: Juan Ginés de Sepúlveda and his Dialogue, *Democrates secundus*'. Also Marenbon, *Pagans and Philosophers*, pp. 250ff.

16 Las Casas is a central figure in these debates and so is covered in the sources mentioned in note 4 to this chapter. See especially Pagden, *European Encounters*, pp. 69–87.

17 Quoted in Keith Thomas, *In Pursuit of Civility: Manners and Civilization in Early Modern England* (New Haven and London: Yale University Press, 2018), p. 250.

18 This is well dealt with by Parker, *Emperor*, 'The New Laws' and 'The Rebellion of Peru', pp. 358–67.

19 An evaluation of Charles's relationship with the Americas can be found in ibid., 'Did Charles Really Care?', pp. 372–5.

20 The debate is discussed in detail in Hanke, *Aristotle and the American Indians*, chapters 4–6.

21 Pagden, *The Fall of Natural Man*, p. 122.

22 Acosta is a key figure for Anthony Pagden – see ibid., chapters 6–7.

23 See Kenneth Mills, 'The Naturalization of Andean Christianities', in Po-Chia Hsia (ed.), *The Cambridge History of Christianity: Volume Six*, p. 504, and Thornton, *A Cultural History of the Atlantic World*, chapter 10, 'Religious Stability and Change'.

24 Bacon, *Novum Organum*, Book 1, section 84.

25 English translation of *De la vicissitude ou varieté des choses en l'univers* (1575) as *The Variety of Things* (1594).

23 The Reformation

1 This tract (*De haereticis an sint persequendi*) was published anonymously in Basle. It was largely a collection of texts from the Church Fathers opposing persecution. For Castellio and his campaign for toleration, see later in this chapter.

2 There is a vast literature on the Reformation. Among the authoritative accounts see MacCulloch, *Reformation*; Cameron, *The European Reformation*; Eire, *Reformations*.

3 A recent biography by Lyndal Roper, *Martin Luther: Renegade and Prophet* (London: Bodley Head, 2016), is especially fine.

4 See Peter Marshall, *Martin Luther and the Invention of the Reformation* (Oxford: Oxford University Press, 2017), for a full discussion.

5 For the Diet and Charles's responses, see Parker, *Emperor*, pp. 116–26.

6 Andrew Pettegree, *Brand Luther* (London: Penguin Books, 2016).

7 Quoted in Michael Massing, *Fatal Discord: Erasmus, Luther and the Fight for the Western Mind* (New York: HarperCollins, 2016), p. 396.

8 Roper, *Martin Luther*, pp. 227–8, 421.

9 Ibid., p. 208.

10 Cameron, *The European Reformation*, chapter 11, 'The Reformers' Message: Scripture', provides an excellent overview.

11 There is a very good exposition of Reformer theology in ibid., chapter 10, 'The Reformers' Message: Salvation'. The Calvin quotation is to be found on p. 149.

12 From Luther's *Defence and Explanation of all the Articles* (1520).

13 This is indeed the concluding sentence of Roper, *Martin Luther*, p. 423.

14 There is an excellent chapter on these issues in Ozment, *The Age of Reform*, chapter 8, 'Humanism and the Reformation'. See also Roper, *Martin Luther*, pp. 285–90 and p. 401, for Luther's condemnation of Erasmus to hell.

15 There was no obvious solution to the issue of predestination: the incompatibility of insisting that God was loving but also able to condemn to eternal suffering those who had not accepted the grace he decided to offer them. Cameron, *The European Reformation*, pp. 155–9, explores some of the issues of what has proved the subject of intensive theological debate over the centuries.

16 Quoted in Marshall, *Martin Luther*, p. 115.

17 For the aftermath of Luther's death see Roper, *Martin Luther*, pp. 406–23.

18 Probably the best biography is that by Bruce Gordon, *Calvin* (New Haven and London: Yale University Press, 2011).

19 This comes in the second book of the *Institutes*, chapter 2, 'Man Now Deprived of Freedom of Will and Miserably Enslaved', section 4.

20 This and other relevant passages in the *Institutes* come from Book 3, chapter 21, 'Of the Eternal Election, By which God has predestined some to salvation and others to destruction', available online at https://web.archive.org/web/20060829234225/http://www.ccel.org/ccel/calvin/institutes.iv.iii.xxii.html.

21 See Robert M. Kingdon, 'The Calvinist Reformation in Geneva', chapter 6 in Po-Chia Hsia (ed.), *The Cambridge History of Christianity: Volume 6*.

22 See Steven Gunn, *Henry VII's New Men and the Making of Tudor England* (Oxford: Oxford University Press, 2016).

23 See Marshall, *Heretics and Believers* (p. 575 for the quoted assessment). This is the best survey of the upheavals. The two key biographies by Diarmaid MacCulloch are his *Thomas Cranmer* (New Haven and London: Yale University Press, 1996), and *Thomas Cromwell: A Life* (London: Allen Lane/Penguin, 2018). Both provide a wealth of background detail.

24 See Eamon Duffy's classic *The Stripping of the Altars* (New Haven and London: Yale University Press, 1992) and *The Voices of Morebath: Reformation and Rebellion in an English Village* (New Haven and London: Yale University Press, 2001).

25 Mandell Creighton's views on the relationship between the Anglican church and the state can be found in two essays, 'The National Church: Its Continuity in Order' and 'The Idea of a National Church', in his *The Church and the Nation: Charges and Addresses* (London: Longman, Green and Co., 1901). So far as I know this quotation comes from one of his letters but the essays contain the same sentiments.

26 I have drawn on chapter 4, 'The First Champion of Religious Toleration, Sebastian Castellio', in Perez Zagorin, *How the Idea of Religious Toleration Came to the West* (Princeton, NJ, and Oxford: Princeton University Press, 2003). The quotation comes from p. 106.

27 MacCulloch, *Reformation*, p. 671.

28 Zagorin, *How the Idea of Toleration Came to the West*, p. 144.

29 Diarmaid MacCulloch, *All Things Made New: Writings on the Reformation* (London: Allen Lane/Penguin, 2016), pp. 7–8, and *Reformation*, pp. 262–3.

30 I recommend the full discussion of these issues by Alexandra Walsham, 'Reformation Legacies', in Peter Marshall (ed.), *The Oxford Illustrated History of the Reformation* (Oxford: Oxford University Press, 2015).

31 Peter Harrison, *The Fall of Man and the Foundations of Science* (Cambridge: Cambridge University Press, 2007).

32 At last we have a full study of Newton's religious beliefs, which were as profound as his interest in mathematics, in Rob Iliffe, *Priest of Nature: The Religious Worlds of Isaac Newton* (New York: Oxford University Press, 2017).

24 Catholic Renewal

1 R. Po-Chia Hsia, *The World of Catholic Renewal, 1540–1770*, 2nd ed. (Cambridge: Cambridge University Press, 2005).

2 The best account is that by John W. O'Malley, *Trent: What Happened at the Council* (Cambridge, MA, and London: Belknap Press of Harvard University Press, 2013). See also chapter 1 of R. Po-Chia Hsia, *The World of Catholic Renewal.*

3 O'Malley, *Trent*, pp. 107–16.

4 See the excellent Anthony Majanlahti, *The Families Who Made Rome: A History and a Guide* (London: Chatto and Windus, 2005).

5 This is well covered in Christopher F. Black, *The Italian Inquisition* (New Haven and London: Yale University Press, 2009), chapter 7, 'Censorship'.

6 Quoted in ibid., pp. 168–9.

7 A good survey of Borromeo's career is J. Hedley and J. Tomaro (eds.), *San Carlo Borromeo: Catholic Reform and Ecclesiastical Politics in the Second Half of the Sixteenth Century* (Washington, DC: Folger Books, 1988).

8 Zagorin, *How the Idea of Toleration Came to the West*, p. 99.

9 John Patrick Donnelly, 'New Religious Orders for Men', chapter 10 in Po-Chia Hsia (ed.), *The Cambridge History of Christianity: Volume 6*, pp. 170–6. John O'Malley has written a short history, *The Jesuits: A History from Ignatius to the Present* (Lanham, MD: Rowman and Littlefield, 2017).

10 A quotation from Donnelly, 'New Religious Orders for Men', p. 174.

11 For these opulent chapels see Steven Ostrow, *Art and Spirituality in Counter-Reformation Rome: The Sistine and Pauline Chapels in S. Maria Maggiore* (Cambridge: Cambridge University Press, 1996).

12 For Bruno see Yates, *Giordano Bruno and the Hermetic Tradition*; the most recent study by an acknowledged authority is Hilary Gatti, *Essays on Giordano Bruno* (Princeton, NJ, and Oxford: Princeton University Press, 2011).

13 This was the view of the prior of a Carmelite monastery in Paris where Bruno was staying in the late 1580s. Quoted in William Boulting, *Giordano Bruno: His Life, Thought and Martyrdom* (original edition 1914; republished by Routledge, 2013), p. 221.

14 From a letter quoted by David Wootton in his *The Invention of Science*, p. 143.

15 Quoted in ibid., p. 144.

16 The honouring of Bruno is well described by R. J. B. Bosworth, *Whispering City: Rome and its Histories* (New Haven and London: Yale University Press, 2011), pp. 107–11.

17 Terpstra, *Religious Refugees*, p. 4. His 'introduction' is particularly valuable.

18 Jonathan Israel, *Enlightenment Contested: Philosophy, Modernity, and the Emancipation of Man, 1670–1752* (Oxford: Oxford University Press, 2006), p. 136.

25 Montaigne and Hamlet

1 M. A. Screech's translation of *The Complete Essays*, with his own introduction, is usually considered the best edition of the essays and will be used here. Sarah Bakewell, *How to Live: A Life of Montaigne in One Question and Twenty Attempts at an Answer* (London: Chatto and Windus, 2010), is a delightful biography.

2 Quoted in Bakewell, *How to Live*, p. 29.

3 Ibid., pp. 36–7.

4 From the essay 'On Drunkenness', II.2 in Screech, *The Complete Essays*; and from the essay 'In Defence of Seneca and Plutarch', II:32 in ibid., respectively.

5 Details of their correspondence are explored in Jeanine G. De Landtsheer, 'Michel de Montaigne, Marie De Gournay and Justus Lipsius. Some Overlooked Particulars Preserved at Leiden University Library', pp. 63–78, in Karl A. E. Enenkel and Mark S. Smith (eds.), *Montaigne and the Low Countries (1580–1700)* (Leiden: Brill, 2007). It is assumed that Montaigne took the initiative in making the contact although of the correspondence only three letters to the philosopher by Lipsius survive. Landtsheer's essay is available online at https://doi.org/10.1163/ej.9789004156326.i-373.10.

6 This encounter is discussed in Stuurman, *The Invention of Humanity*, pp. 247–55.

7 Richard Popkin, *The History of Scepticism from Savonarola to Bayle*, rev. ed. (Oxford: Oxford University Press, 2003), p. 52.

8 Jonathan Bate, *How Classics Made Shakespeare* (Princeton, NJ, and Oxford: Princeton University Press, 2019). Bate discusses the influence of Ovid *passim* but especially p. 11 and pp. 194–203.

9 Barbara Everett, *Young Hamlet: Essays on Shakespeare's Tragedies* (Oxford: Clarendon Press, 1989), p. 30.

10 Eric Griffiths, 'A Rehearsal of Hamlet', chapter 5 in *If not Critical* (Oxford: Oxford University Press, 2018), p. 109.

11 Barbara Everett, 'Hamlet Growing', in *Young Hamlet*, p. 16.

12 Margreta de Grazia, *Hamlet without Hamlet* (Cambridge: Cambridge University Press, 2007), p. 158.

13 James Shapiro, *1599: A Year in the Life of William Shakespeare* (London: Faber and Faber, 2005), p. 328.

14 The issue is raised, for instance, by Jonathan Bate in *How the Classics Made Shakespeare*, pp. 11–12.

15 Hilary Gatti raises the issue in a chapter 'Bruno and Shakespeare: Hamlet' in her *Essays on Giordano Bruno*. Florio was Bruno's closest friend when he was in England, and Gatti finds similarities between the thoughts of Hamlet and those of Bruno, who was undergoing his long trial for heresy in Rome.

26 Absolutist France versus the Dutch Republic

1 Quoted in Mark Greengrass, *Christendom Destroyed: Europe 1517–1648* (London: Allen Lane/Penguin, 2014), pp. 676–7.

2 Quoted in ibid., pp. 395–6.

3 Peter Wilson, *Europe's Tragedy: A New History of the Thirty Years War* (London: Allen Lane/Penguin, 2009), is the most authoritative and comprehensive account of this complex sequence of conflicts and atrocities. The older account by Geoffrey Parker, *The Thirty Years War*, 2nd ed. (London: Routledge, 1997), is more succinct.

4 Philip Mansel details the achievements of Colbert in chapter 7, 'Making France Work', in *King of the World: The Life of Louis XIV* (London: Allen Lane/Penguin, 2019).

5 Ibid., pp. 51 and 111.

6 Ibid., p. 197.

7 Peter Burke's *The Fabrication of Louis XIV* (New Haven and London: Yale University Press, 1992) is an excellent survey of the way Louis presented himself.

8 The point is made by Mansel, *King of the World*, p. 173.

9 This propaganda is well covered by Burke, *The Fabrication of Louis XIV*, chapter 6, 'The Years of Victory', which contains illustrations from contemporary paintings.

10 Mansel, *King of the World*, p. 184.

11 Ibid., pp. 277–8.

12 Ibid., p. 32.

13 Ibid., p. 202.

14 Ibid., p. 232.

15 The comparison is made in ibid., p. 145.

16 Ibid., p. 227.

17 Ibid., chapter 12, 'The King Outdoors', covers the gardens and the other outdoor pursuits of the king.

18 Quoted in ibid., p. 143.

19 Ibid., chapter 16, 'The Huguenot Cataclysm', is excellent, especially on the damage done to the economy and reputation of France.

20 Quoted in John Marshall, *John Locke: Toleration and Enlightenment Culture* (Cambridge: Cambridge University Press, 2006), p. 151.

21 Quoted in Simon Schama, *The Embarrassment of Riches: An Interpretation of Dutch Culture in the Golden Age* (London: Collins, 1987), p. 223. This is a classic study by a master historian. Another fundamental source for the republic is Jonathan Israel, *The Dutch Republic: Its Rise, Greatness and Fall, 1477–1806* (Oxford: Clarendon Press, 1993).

22 Quoted in Schama, *The Embarrassment of Riches*, p. 99.

23 One estimate is that the Dutch had 9,000 trading vessels whereas France had only 500–600. Mansel, *King of the World*, p. 121.

24 For studies of toleration in the republic see chapter 5, 'The Toleration Controversy in the Netherlands', in Zagorin, *How the Idea of Religious Toleration Came to the West*, and Eric Nelson, *The Hebrew Republic: Jewish Sources and the Transformation of European Political Thought* (Cambridge, MA: Harvard University Press, 2010), pp. 97–111.

25 Zagorin, *How the Idea of Religious Toleration Came to the West*, p. 178.

26 Israel, *The Dutch Republic*, p. 676.

27 Britain's Revolutionary Century

1 Quoted in Christopher Hill, *The World Turned Upside Down: Radical Ideas during the English Revolution* (London: Maurice Temple Smith, 1972; Penguin Books, 1975). This quotation is from the Penguin edition, p. 107.

2 Two excellent introductions to this period are Barry Coward, *The Stuart Age*, 4th ed. (London: Routledge, 2012), and Mark Kishlansky, *The Penguin History of Britain: A Monarchy Transformed, Britain 1630–1714* (London: Allen Lane/Penguin, 1996).

3 Quentin Skinner, 'A Genealogy of the Modern State', lecture to the British Academy, has much of interest here. It appears in Ron Johnston (ed.), *Proceedings of the British Academy, Volume 162, 2008 Lectures* (London: British Academy, 2009), pp. 325–70.

4 See 'Rethinking Liberty in the English Revolution', chapter 7 in Skinner, *From Humanism to Hobbes*. Skinner argues that this distinction was crucial when looking at the debates over who exactly was 'a free man'.

5 Quoted in ibid., p. 143.

6 Quoted by Skinner in 'A Genealogy of the Modern State', p. 339.

7 The Declaration can be read in full at https://www.bilderberg.org/land/poor.htm.

8 This comes from 'The Ready and Easy Way to Establish a Free Commonwealth', a tract issued by Milton in February 1660 during the political vacuum before the restoration of the monarchy in May of that year.

9 'This petition for the release of John Lilburne is claimed to be England's first ever all-women petition… Elizabeth Lilburne and Katherine Chidley presented the petition to the House of Commons on 25th April, 1649… MPs reacted intolerantly, telling the women that "it was not for women to petition; they might stay home and wash their dishes… you are desired to go home, and look after your own business, and meddle with your housewifery". One woman replied: "Sir, we have scarce any dishes left us to wash, and those we have not sure to keep." When another MP said it was strange for women to petition Parliament one replied: "It was strange that you cut off the King's head, yet I suppose you will justify it."' This is from an excellent article on Elizabeth Lilburne, available online at www.spartacus-educational.com.

10 Hill, *The World Turned Upside Down*, p. 14.

11 Quoted by Steve Pincus, *1688: The First Modern Revolution* (New Haven and London: Yale University Press, 2009), p. 480. Pincus argues that the Glorious Revolution was in fact more significant than the 'English revolution' of the 1640s.

12 John Rees, *The Leveller Revolution* (London and New York: Verso, 2016), p. 348.

13 David Como, *Radical Parliamentarians and the English Civil War* (Oxford: Oxford University Press, 2018).

14 From *The Adventures of Sir Launcelot Greaves* (1762), chapter 11, 'Description of a Modern Magistrate'.

15 Pincus, *1688*, has a good section on the importance of the coffeehouse, pp. 74–81. The quotations come from pp. 77 and 74.

16 Paul Slack, *The Invention of Improvement: Information and Material Progress in Seventeenth-Century England* (Oxford: Oxford University Press, 2015).

17 The quotation is from Israel, *The Dutch Republic*, p. 850.

18 The key text was Macaulay's *The History of England from the Accession of James the Second*, 1848.

19 Quoted in Pincus, *1688*, p. 480.

20 These are explored in ibid., chapter 5, 'The Ideology of Catholic Modernity', and chapter 6, 'The Practice of Catholic Modernity'.

21 Ibid., p. 483.

22 Ibid. The figures Pincus quotes are 9 per cent of the total in 1660–89 and 10.7 per cent in 1690–1715.

23 This is dealt with at length in Israel, *The Dutch Republic*, part 4, 'The Age of Decline, 1702–1806'.

24 David Cannadine, *G. M. Trevelyan: A Life in History* (London: HarperCollins, 1992), p. 197.

28 Envisaging an Ideal Society

1 For the background to this Treatise see below and Roger Woolhouse, *Locke: A Biography* (Cambridge: Cambridge University Press, 2007), pp. 185–90.

2 Ursula Vollerthun, *The Idea of International Society: Erasmus, Vitoria, Gentili and Grotius*, ed. James Richardson (Cambridge: Cambridge University Press, 2017), has a chapter on Gentili, pp. 106–44. See also Claire Vergerio, *Constructing the Right to War: Alberico Gentili and his Receptions in International Law* (Oxford: Oxford University Research Archive, 2017); Rafael Domingo and Giovanni Minnucci, 'Alberico Gentili and the Secularization of the Law of Nations', in Rafael Domingo and John Witte, Jr (eds.), *Christianity and Global Law: An Introduction* (Cambridge: Cambridge University Press, forthcoming 2020).

3 Quoted in Vollerthun, *The Idea of International Society*, p. 112.

4 Ibid., p. 110.

5 Quoted in Domingo and Minnucci, 'Alberico Gentili', p. 12.

6 Quoted in Vollerthun, *The Idea of International Society*, p. 140.

7 Quoted in ibid., p. 114.

8 Noel Malcolm, *Useful Enemies: Islam and the Ottoman Empire in Western Political Thought, 1450–1750* (Oxford: Oxford University Press, 2019), pp. 125–30 and 247–50.

9 There is a full chapter on Grotius in Vollerthun, *The Idea of International Society*, chapter 5, pp. 145–203. There are also good overviews of Grotius's life, thought and legacy by Jon Miller in the *Routledge Encyclopedia of Philosophy* and by Andrew Blom in the *Internet Encyclopedia of Philosophy*.

10 Quoted in Vollerthun, *The Idea of International Society*, p. 169.

11 There is a good discussion of this aspect of Grotius's philosophy in Stuurman, *The Invention of Humanity*, pp. 268–72.

12 See the discussion of Grotius's view on commerce in Vollerthun, *The Idea of International Society*, pp. 180–5.

13 Vollerthun, for instance, in the chapter cited here concludes (p. 203): 'It has been contended here that the assigning of Grotius to the tradition that bears his name cannot withstand a thorough reading of the texts.'

14 A standard biography is A. P. Martinich, *Hobbes: A Biography* (Cambridge: Cambridge University Press, 1999). For *Leviathan*, see Catherine Wilson, 'Thomas Hobbes' *Leviathan*', chapter 22 in Peter Anstey (ed.), *British Philosophy in the Seventeenth Century* (Oxford: Oxford University Press, 2013). See also Richard Tuck, *Hobbes: A Very Short Introduction* (Oxford: Oxford University Press, 1989).

15 Hobbes's views on religion are well covered by Tuck, *Hobbes*, pp. 83–104.

16 Hobbes's attitudes to women have been the subject of great scholarly contention. He talks of women as 'naturally equal' but many of his works assume a patriarchal society. See section 11 of the article on 'Hobbes's Moral and Political Philosophy' in the *Stanford Encyclopedia of Philosophy* by Sharon Lloyd and Susanne Sreedhar available online at https://plato.stanford.edu/entries/hobbes-moral/#HobWomFam.

17 This is covered in Martinich, *Hobbes*, pp. 143ff.

18 From the Dedicatory Letter to William, earl of Devonshire, in Hobbes's *De Cive* (1642) a tract originally in Latin, with an English translation in 1651, which anticipates many of the ideas in *Leviathan*.

19 Tuck, *Hobbes*, p. 67.

20 Hobbes explores the difficulties in the opening paragraphs of the 'Review and Conclusion' to *Leviathan*.

21 He notes the causes of war as competition for the same resources, distrust of one's fellow human beings and the desire for glory. Martinich, *Hobbes*, p. 145.

22 Wilson, 'Thomas Hobbes' *Leviathan*', p. 530.

23 *Leviathan*, chapter 18.

24 Quoted in Tuck, *Hobbes*, p. 106.

25 Quoted in ibid., p. 107.

26 From 'On the Law of Nature and Nations', Book II.3.15.

27 The quotation deserves to be quoted in full as it suggests an obligation to act positively to bring together a community. 'It is not enough, however, not to have hurt another, or not to have deprived him of the esteem he is owed. These only remove the just cause for hatred. Something good must also be conferred on the other, at least if the minds of men are to be conjoined by a still closer bond. Someone who has not driven me away from himself by some hostile or ungrateful deed has not discharged the debt of sociability, rather, he should furnish something beneficial so that I am glad that others who share my nature also live upon this earth. And, as well, the affinity and kinship established among men by nature must be exercised by means of natural duties.' From Pufendorf's *De jure naturae et gentium* (1672), part 3, pp. 1–3.

28 From Pufendorf's *De officio hominis et civis juxta legem naturalem* (*On the Duty of Man and Citizen According to the Natural Law*; 1673), Book 2, chapter 16.

29 Michael Zuckert, 'Pufendorf: Some Comments on His Intentions and Significance'. Posted on *The Online Library of Liberty*, January 2016, available at https://oll.libertyfund.org/pages/lm-pufendorf#response2.

30 Woolhouse, *Locke*, covers Locke's dissatisfaction with Oxford, pp. 15–20. See especially the comments on the curriculum on p. 18.

31 From the *Second Treatise*, chapter 11.

32 Ibid., chapter 11. This chapter, 'On the Extent of the Legislative Power', is a major statement of Locke's views on the importance of consent.

33 Ibid., chapter 18, 'On Tyranny'.

29 The Astronomers

1 This was an important statement made by Galileo of his views of the relative status of science and the Bible. The full letter can be read at https://sourcebooks.fordham.edu/mod/galileo-tuscany.asp. The background is discussed in Heilbron, *Galileo*, pp. 211–12.

2 Quoted in Coward, *The Stuart Age*, p. 47.

3 The quotation comes from Steven Shapin, *The Scientific Revolution* (Chicago and London: University of Chicago Press, 1996), p. 3. The themes of this paragraph are covered by Katherine Park and Lorraine Daston in their 'Introduction: The Age of the New' to *The Cambridge History of Science: Volume 3*. See also for an overview Lawrence M. Principe, *The Scientific Revolution: A Very Short Introduction* (Oxford: Oxford University Press, 2011).

4 The argument over Copernicus's debt to the Arab astronomers is made in Saliba, *Islamic Science*, chapter 6, 'Islamic Science and Renaissance Europe: The Copernican Connection'. See also Bala, *The Dialogue of Civilizations*, chapter 7, 'The Narrow Copernican Revolution'. Bala also discusses the Indian contribution to Copernicus's mathematics. The quotation about Copernicus and the Maragheh School is cited on p. 83 of Bala and comes from N. M. Swerdlow and O. Neugeberger, *Mathematical Astronomy in Copernicus's* De Revolutionibus (New York: Springer, 1984), p. 295.

5 Gingerich, *The Book That Nobody Read.*

6 This is the calculation of Robert Westman, cited in John Henry, *The Scientific Revolution and the Origins of Modern Science*, 3rd ed. (London: Red Globe Press/ Macmillan International Higher Education, 2008), p. 23.

7 There is a good chapter on this by Jim Bennett, 'The Mechanical Arts', chapter 27 in Park and Daston (eds.), *The Cambridge History of Science: Volume 3*.

8 I have used Heilbron's *Galileo* extensively for this section. See also David Wootton, *Galileo: Watcher of the Skies* (New Haven and London: Yale University Press, 2010), and Michael Sharratt, *Galileo: Decisive Innovator* (Cambridge: Cambridge University Press, 1994).

9 Heilbron, *Galileo*, pp. 246–7.

10 From *The Assayer*, p. 184. As Heilbron, *Galileo*, p. 247, points out, some scholars have seen Galileo taking this idea from Plato's *Timaeus*. Heilbron himself considers that this was a riposte to Tycho Brahe, who, Galileo claimed, did not understand the rudiments of geometry.

11 There is a full description of the debates in Heilbron, *Galileo*, pp. 331–44.

12 Quoted in ibid., p. 340.

13 Quoted in Daniel Garber, 'Physics and Foundations', chapter 2 in Park and Daston (eds.), *The Cambridge History of Science: Volume 3*, p. 62.

14 This quotation comes from the thorough analysis of Gassendi's ideas in the article 'Pierre Gassandi' by Saul Fisher in the online *Stanford Encyclopedia of Philosophy* available at https:// plato.stanford.edu/entries/gassendi/.

15 From Pascal's *Pensées* (1670), trans. W. F. Trotter (1958), quoted in Wootton, *The Invention of Science*, p. 448.

30 An English Scientific Revolution

1 The Accademia del Cimento was founded in Florence in 1657 by followers of Galileo and concentrated on experiments as shown here. The Royal Society adopted many of its ideals by translating its proceedings. The quotation comes from Peter Dear, *Revolutionizing the Sciences: European Knowledge and its Ambitions, 1500–1700*, 2nd ed. (London: Palgrave Macmillan, 2009).

2 *The New Organon*, Book 1, 'Aphorisms Concerning the Interpretation of Nature', aphorism 8.

3 From the first edition of Newton's *Optics* (1704), query 31.

4 From the text of *New Atlantis* in Bruce (ed.), *Three Early Modern Utopias*, pp. 167–8.

5 See the assessment made by Joel Mokyr in *The Culture of Growth: The Origins of the Modern Economy* (Princeton, NJ, and Oxford: Princeton University Press, 2016), chapter 7, 'Francis Bacon, Cultural Entrepreneur', pp. 70–98.

6 There is a useful survey of Boyle's life and achievements in John Gribbin, *Science: A History* (London: Allen Lane/Penguin, 2002), pp. 126–42.

7 See Adrian Tinniswood, *The Royal Society* (London: Head of Zeus, 2019), and Bill Bryson (ed.), *Seeing Further: The Story of Science and the Royal Society* (London: Collins, 2010).

8 David Wootton describes the process in *The Invention of Science*, pp. 383–91.

9 For Hooke, see Lisa Jardine, *The Curious Life of Robert Hooke: The Man who Measured London* (London: HarperCollins, 2003).

10 A recent biography of Newton is Niccolò Guicciardini, *Isaac Newton and Natural Philosophy* (London: Reaktion Books, 2018). Guicciardini's introductory chapter, 'Images of Newton', is especially good at describing the reception of Newton's ideas in his lifetime and beyond. James Gleick, *Isaac Newton* (London and New York: Fourth Estate, 2003), is an excellent introduction to Newton's life. See also chapter 5, 'The Newtonian Revolution', in Gribbin, *Science*.

11 Luckily, his writings on this survive and have recently been explored by Iliffe, *Priest of Nature*.

12 Gribbin, *Science*, pp. 186–7.

13 The letter is quoted in full in Guicciardini, *Isaac Newton*, pp. 224–5.

14 Quoted in Jonathan Rée, *Witcraft: The Invention of Philosophy in English* (London: Allen Lane/Penguin, 2019), p. 97.

15 Robert Merton, *Science, Technology and Society in Seventeenth-Century England* (Bruges: St Catherine Press, 1938). A new edition was published by Harper and Row, New York in 1980.

16 Mokyr, *The Culture of Growth*, chapter 13, 'Puritanism and British Exceptionalism', pp. 247–66.

17 Ibid., p. 238.

18 Wootton, *The Invention of Science*, pp. 454–8.

19 This is explored in ibid., chapter 14, 'Knowledge is Power'.

20 Guicciardini, *Isaac Newton*, pp. 7–21.

31 The Making of the Modern Mind

1 From the entry in Pierre Bayle's *Dictionnaire historique et critique* (*Historical and Critical Dictionary*, 1697). Uriel Acosta or Uriel da Costa (1585–1640) was a Portuguese philosopher who converted from Catholicism to Judaism. He was excommunicated from the community after challenging basic tenets of Judaism and eventually committed suicide. Some see him as a forerunner of Spinoza.

2 Jonathan Israel, *Radical Enlightenment: Philosophy and the Making of Modernity 1650–1750* (Oxford: Oxford University Press, 2001).

3 Ibid., p. 7. The introductory chapter, pp. 3–22, is particularly good at setting out the issues.

4 Ibid., preface, p. xi.

5 Jonathan Israel, *Enlightenment Contested: Philosophy, Modernity and the Emancipation of Man, 1670–1752* (Oxford: Oxford University Press, 2006).

6 Israel, *Radical Enlightenment*, p. 14.

7 Paul Hazard, *La Crise de la conscience européenne* (1938); published in a new English edition, *The Crisis of the European Mind, 1680–1715*, trans J. Lewis May with a preface by Anthony Grafton (New York: New York Review of Books Classics, 2013).

8 Israel, *Radical Enlightenment*, p. 10.

9 Two works used here that cover the main figures of this chapter are Anthony Gottlieb, *The Dream of Enlightenment: The Rise of Modern Philosophy* (London: Allen Lane/Penguin, 2016), and Anthony Kenny, *The Rise of Modern Philosophy: A New History of Western Philosophy, Volume 3* (Oxford: Oxford University Press, 2006).

10 From the *La vie de Monsieur Des Cartes* (1691); *The life of Monsieur Des Cartes containing the history of his philosophy and works: as also the most remarkable things that befell him during the whole course of his life*. Available online at https://quod.lib.umich.edu.

11 I have taken this quotation from 'Descartes' Ontological Argument', an article by Lawrence Dolan in the online *Stanford Encyclopedia of Philosophy*, September 2015. Available at https://plato.stanford.edu/entries/descartes-ontological.

12 The quotation is from 'Meditation, No. 6'.

13 From *Letters on England*, '13. On Mr. Locke'. Available at https://ebooks.adelaide.edu.au/v/voltaire/letters-on-england/chapter13.html.

14 See Woolhouse, *Locke*, where there is a good description of the genesis and development of the *Essay*, pp. 98ff.

15 From the 1876 biography of Locke by H. A. Fox Bourne, quoted in ibid., p. 2.

16 *An Essay Concerning Human Understanding*, Book 1, chapter 1, paragraph 7.

17 Ibid., Book 2, chapter 1.

18 This is explored by E. J. Lowe, *Locke* (London: Routledge, 2005), part 3, 'Substance and Identity'.

19 Quotations taken from *On the Conduct of the Understanding*.

20 This is well covered in Woolhouse, *Locke*, pp. 336–44.

21 *An Essay Concerning Human Understanding*, Book 4, chapter 14, 'On Judgment', section 2.

22 There is an excellent chapter, 'Locke, Bayle and Spinoza: A Contest of Three Toleration Doctrines', chapter 6, in Israel, *Enlightenment Contested*.

23 Ibid., p. 139.

24 Ibid., pp. 141–4.

25 This comes from the chapter on John Locke in vol. 1 of Ryle's *Critical Essays, Collected Papers* (London: Routledge, 2009), p. 159.

26 There is a good chapter on Leibniz, 'Leibniz and the Radical Enlightenment', chapter 26, in Israel, *Radical Enlightenment*. See also John Cottingham, *The Rationalists: A History of Western Philosophy* (Oxford: Oxford University Press, 1988), which has several sections on Leibniz.

27 From Michael E. Moore, *The Sublime Stoicism of Leibniz*, available online at https://www.academia.edu/2493814/The_Sublime_Stoicism_of_Leibniz.

28 Leibniz, *Theodicy*, section 335.

29 See chapter 18, 'Bayle and the "Virtuous Atheist"', in Israel, *Radical Enlightenment*. See also the chapter on Pierre Bayle, chapter 5 in Hazard, *The Crisis of the European Mind*.

30 Paul Hazard's chapter on Pierre Bayle in his *The Crisis of the European Mind* is particularly valuable here.

31 See Israel, *Radical Enlightenment*, pp. 337–8, note 28.

32 From p. xi of the 'Introduction' by Richard Popkin to his translation of 'Selections', from Bayle's *The Historical and Critical Dictionary* (Cambridge, MA: Hackett Publishing Co., 1991).

33 Hazard, *The Crisis of the European Mind*, p. 109.

34 Ibid., p. 112.

35 'Introduction' to Richard Popkin's translation from Bayle's *The Historical and Critical Dictionary*, p. xxi.

36 Quotation from Israel, *Radical Enlightenment*, p. 159.

37 A standard life is by Steven Nadler, *Spinoza, A Life*, 2nd ed. (Cambridge: Cambridge University Press, 2018). Popkin, *A History of Scepticism*, with a chapter 'Spinoza's Scepticism and Anti-Scepticism', was extended in a third edition to include Bayle (Oxford: Oxford University Press, 2003). Spinoza is the central character in part 2 of Israel, *Radical Enlightenment*, 'The Rise of Philosophical Radicalism'.

38 Israel, *Radical Enlightenment*, p. 172.

39 This was the remark of a Dutch traveller who visited Spinoza's village in 1661. It is quoted in Kenny, *The Rise of Modern Philosophy*, p. 63.

40 This is spelled out in part 4 of the *Ethics*, 'Of Human Bondage or the Strength of the Emotions'.

41 Proposition XVIII from part 4 of the *Ethics*.

42 Israel, *Radical Enlightenment*, pp. 162–3.

43 This is the argument of Jonathan Israel in *Revolutionary Ideas: An Intellectual History of the French Revolution from the Rights of Man to Robespierre* (Princeton, NJ, and Oxford: Princeton University Press, 2015).

44 A fuller quotation is provided in Carl Niekerk (ed.), *The Radical Enlightenment in Germany: A Cultural Perspective* (Leiden: Brill, 2018), p. 356. This comes from Goethe's account of his encounter with Spinoza's works while a student at Strasbourg. 'The intellect that has affected me so markedly and was to have such a great influence on my whole way of thinking was Spinoza's. For after I had searched everywhere in vain for a means of cultivating my strange personality, I finally happened upon this man's *Ethics*. I could not possibly give an account of what I read out of this work, or into it. Let me just say, I found something in it to calm my emotions, and it seemed to open a broad, free view over the physical and moral world... I was particularly captivated by the infinite selflessness that radiated from each of his propositions.'

45 This is from William Wordsworth's poem 'Lines Composed a Few Miles above Tintern Abbey, On Revisiting the Banks of the Wye during a Tour, July 13, 1798'. It was first published in *Lyrical Ballads*, by Wordsworth and Samuel Taylor Coleridge, in 1798, a volume considered to be the birth of the English Romantic movement.

32 'A Reawakening of the Western Mind'

1 Thomas Warton, *The History of English Poetry* (1774–81), from the preface to vol. 1 (1774), pp. i–ii.

2 Grayling, *The Age of Genius*. The quotation comes from p. 391.

3 Nelson, *The Hebrew Republic*. Nelson has done an important service in bringing to light influential sources in the Hebrew scriptures supporting republicanism in the seventeenth century.

4 Iliffe, *Priest of Nature*, p. 56.

5 There is an excellent chapter on Bossuet in Paul Hazard, *The Crisis of the European Mind*, chapter 4, 'Bossuet at Bay'. The quotation comes from p. 199.

6 Wootton, *The Invention of Science*, pp. 61–2, from his chapter 3, 'Inventing Discovery'.

7 Larry Siedentop, *Inventing the Individual: The Origins of Western Liberalism* (London: Allen Lane/Penguin, 2014).

8 Tom Holland: *Dominion: The Making of the Western Mind* (New York and London: Little, Brown, 2019).

9 Ibid., from the preface, p. xxv.

10 Quoted in Rée, *Witcraft*, p. 65.

11 Thomas, *In Pursuit of Civility*. See especially chapter 5, 'Exporting Civility', and chapter 6, 'Civilization Reconsidered'.

12 This is a consistent theme in Gray's work, e.g. *Straw Dogs: Thoughts on Humans and Other Animals* (2002), *Heresies: Against Progress and Other Illusions* (2004) and *Seven Types of Atheism* (2018).

13 Francis Fukuyama, *The End of History and the Last Man* (New York: The Free Press, 1992), available online at A29412.0001.001/1:3?rgn=div1;view=fulltext.

Picture credits

ii *Christ Treading the Beasts*, mosaic in the Archbishop's Chapel, Ravenna © José Luiz Bernardes Ribeiro / CC BY-SA 4.0

4–5 A modern copy of the *Tabula Rogeriana*, made by Konrad Miller; Wikimedia Commons

9 The Greek astronomer Claudius Ptolemy; Photo Josse / Bridgeman Images

20–1 Thomas Cole, *Destruction*, from *The Course of Empire*; New-York Historical Society / Wikimedia Commons

34–5 Miniature from *The Consolation of Philosophy*; courtesy of Getty's Open Content Program

39 Cassiodorus, *Codex Amiatinus*; Biblioteca Medicea Laurenziana Firenze, Su concessione del MiBACT

42 Bede, *De Temporum Ratione* (*On the Reckoning of Time*); British Library / Bridgeman Images

53 Albrecht Dürer, *Charlemagne*; German National Museum, Nuremberg / Bridgeman Images

58 Palatine Chapel, Aachen; Takashi Images / Shutterstock

61 Vergilius Vaticanus; Vatican Library / Bridgeman Images

62–3 Gospels of St Augustine; The Parker Library, Corpus Christi College, Cambridge

65 top The Book of Kells, Gospel of Matthew; Granger Historical Picture Archive / Alamy

65 bottom Grandval Bible; British Library / Bridgeman Images

72–3 *The Conversion of Saint Augustine*; Musée Thomas-Henry, Cherbourg / Wikimedia Commons

80 Pilgrims at the shrine of Edward Confessor, from a Life of St Edward the Confessor (MS Ee.3.59) © Cambridge University Library

82–83 The Abbey of Saint Germain-des-Prés, 1687; Wikimedia Commons

93 The Pope in Council, from *Decretum Gratiani*; Chronicle / Alamy Stock Photo

96–7 Siege of Antioch, detail of a medieval miniature from Sébastien Mamerot's *Les Passages d'Outremer*; Adam Bishop / Wikimedia Commons

100–1 The Albigensian Crusade; The History Collection / Alamy Stock Photo

103 Giotto di Bondone, *St Francis Receiving the Stigmata*; Bridgeman Images

104 Pedro Berruguete, *St Dominic de Guzman and the Albigensians*; Museo del Prado / Alamy Stock Photo

114–15 Representation of Heloïse and Abelard; Photo Josse / Bridgeman Images

124 Monument in Père Lachaise cemetery; CC BY 4.0 Wellcome Collection

134 Salerno Cathedral; © Mitzo / Shutterstock Photo

136–7 Venice in 1338; Bettmann / Getty Images

140–141 Pisa central complex; Bogusz Strulak / Shutterstock

144 The *Codex Justinianus*; De Agostini Picture Library / Getty Images

150 Palazzo Pubblico, Siena; Delpixel / Shutterstock

154–5 *The Effects of Good Government in the City*, Ambrogio Lorenzetti; Palazzo Pubblico, Siena / Wikimedia Commons

162–3 *Philosophy Consoling Boethius and Fortune Turning the Wheel*, Master Coëtivy (Henri de Vulcop?); courtesy of Getty's Open Content Program.

167 *Henry of Germany Delivering a Lecture*, Laurentius de Voltolina; The Yorck Project / Wikimedia Commons

175 Ptolemy's *Almagest*; Granger Historical Picture Archive / Alamy Stock Photo

182 *The Dissection*, illustration from *Fasciculus Medicinae* by Johannes de Ketham, 1493 (woodcut); Bridgeman Images

201 Albertus Magnus, *On the Nature of Things* (*De Natura Rerum*); De Agostini / Getty Images

204–5 *Triumph of the Catholic Doctrine Embodied by St Thomas*, Andrea di Bonaiuto di Firenze; De Agostini / Getty Images

221 *Cardinal Nicholas of Rouen*, Tommaso da Modena; The Picture Art Collection / Alamy Stock Photo

222 God the Geometer, *c.*1220–30; Australian National Library / Wikimedia Commons

226 Roger Bacon conducting an experiment, from Michael Maier, *Symbola Aureae* (1617); Science History Images / Alamy Stock Photo

23 Front page of a Latin edition of the *Opticae Thesaurus*; Wikimedia Commons

238–9 *La commedia illumina Firenze* ('The Comedy Illuminating Florence'), Domenico di Michelino; Museo dell'Opera del Duomo / Wikimedia Commons

244–5 *Dante's Inferno*, Gustave Doré; Wikimedia Commons

254–5 Giovanni Toscani, *cassone* front showing a scene from Boccaccio's *Decameron*; from Christie's Old Masters Sale catalogue, 6 July 2017

265 *The Kiss of Judas,* Giotto di Bondone (c.1305); Dennis Hallinan / Alamy Stock Photo

268–9 *The Three Philosophers*, Giorgione; Kunsthistorisches Museum, Vienna / Google Art Project / Wikimedia Commons

272 Simone Martini, frontispiece to Petrarch's *Virgil*; Photo 12 / Alamy Stock Photo

275 Petrarch presenting book to King Louis XII; Photo Josse / Leemage / Getty Images

278 *The Young Cicero Reading*, Vincenzo Foppa; Wallace Collection / Wikimedia Commons

284–5 *View of Florence*, Francesco Rosselli (attrib.); DEA Picture Library / Getty Images

288–9 Ceiling mosaic of the Baptistery, Florence; Ilia Baksheev / Shutterstock

292 Tomb of Leonardo Bruni; Zvonimir Atletic / Shutterstock

296 *Studiolo* in the Ducal Palace of Urbino, detail; Leemage / Getty Images

297 Justus van Gent, portrait series of 'famous men' for the south wall of the *studiolo*; Bridgeman Images

300 Ospedale degli innocenti; Borisb17 / Shutterstock

302 Lorenzo Ghiberti, *Gates of Paradise*; Jasmine K / Shutterstock

304 Masaccio, *Holy Trinity*; Mondadori Portfolio / Getty Images

307 Piero della Francesca, *Polyptych of St Anthony*; Ivan Vdovin / Alamy Stock Photo

317 Ludovico Cardi's drawing of a cross-section of Brunelleschi's dome; Leemage / Getty Images

318 Florence Cathedral (*Duomo di Firenze*); Vladimir Badaev / Shutterstock

330 Fresco painting in the cathedral crypt, Anagni © Ivan Vdovin / Alamy Stock Photo

335 Anonymous miniature showing the rector of the University of Paris and Cardinal Bessarion; Venice, Biblioteca Nazionale Marciana / Wikimedia Commons

338 Hermes Trismegistus, mosaic in Siena Cathedral © Science History Images / Alamy Stock Photo

342–3 Raphael, *The School of Athens*; UniversalImagesGroup / Getty Images

353–4 The Gutenberg Bible © Science History Images / Alamy Stock Photo

357 Aldus Manutius's edition of Pietro Bembo's *De Aetna*; Wikimedia Commons

360 Johannes Regiomontanus: calendar printed in Venice by Erhard Ratdolt, 9 August 1482; by kind permission of the University of Glasgow Library, Archives & Special Collections

364–5 Leonhart Fuchs, *De Historia Stirpium commentarii insignia*, showing Heinrich Füllmaurer and Albertus Meyer at work; Bridgeman Images

371 Palace of the Popes, Avignon; Horst Lieber / Shutterstock

377 Benedetto Bonfigli, *Gonfalone di S. Francesco al Prato* (Misericordia di San Bernardino in Perugia); CC Attribution 3.0 Georges Jansoone (JoJan) / Wikimedia Commons

381–2 Gentile Bellini, *Procession in Piazza San Marco*; Peter Barritt / Alamy Stock Photo

389 Girolamo Savonarola's execution on the Piazza della Signoria, Florence © Heritage Image Partnership Ltd / Alamy Stock Photo

395 Hans Holbein the Younger, *Erasmus*; National Gallery / Wikimedia Commons

404–5 Portolan chart of the Mediterranean Sea; Library of Congress / Wikimedia Commons

406 Marco Polo's caravan in the *Catalan Atlas*; Wikimedia Commons

418–19 World map by Henricus Martellus; CC 0 1.0 British Library / Wikimedia Commons

420–1 Abraham Ortelius's map of the Americas, from *Theatrum Orbis Terrarum*; Marzolino / Shutterstock

429 Leonardo's study of bones; GraphicaArtis / Getty Images

430 Leonardo's study of muscles; GraphicaArtis / Getty Images

434–5 Notes and diagram on optics, from Leonardo's rough book of observations; British Library / Bridgeman Images

437 Andreas Vesalius in *De humani corporis fabrica* ('On the Structure of the Human Body'); with the kind permission of St John's College, Cambridge

438 Skeleton from Vesalius' *De humani corporis fabrica*; Science & Society Picture Library / Getty Images

443 Albrecht Dürer, *The Large Piece of Turf*, 1503; Google Art Project / Wikimedia Commons

446 Loggia of Cupid and Psyche; Villa Farnesina / Wikimedia Commons

449 *Gallopavo* (turkey), from Conrad Gessner's *Historiae Animalium*, Vol. III, 1555; Courtesy of the U.S. National Library of Medicine

450 From Conrad Gessner's *Historia Plantarum*; courtesy of the University Library, Erlangen-Nuremberg

452–3 Arabia and India, from the Atlas Miller, *c.*1519; The Print Collector / Alamy Stock Photo

454 Nicolás Monardes's natural history of the West Indies; from the Historical Collections of the National Library of Medicine

460 Raphael, *Baldassare Castiglione*; Louvre Museum / Wikimedia Commons

463 Frontispiece to *The Courtier of Count Baldessar Castilio*; British Library / Bridgeman Images

464 Plan of the island of Thomas Moore's *Utopia*; Hulton Archive / Stringer / Getty Images

469 Santi di Tito, *Portrait of Niccolò Machiavelli*; Palazzo Vecchio, Florence / Wikimedia Commons

477 *Laocoön and His Sons*; Vatican Museums / Wikimedia Commons

480 Lorenzo Lotto, *Andrea Odoni*; Art Collection 3 / Alamy Stock Photo

486–7 The moving of an Egyptian obelisk to St Peter's Square, in *Speculum Romanae Magnificentiae* (*The Mirror of Roman Magnificence*); Artokoloro / Alamy Stock Photo

489 Athanasius Kircher, *Sphinx Mystagoga;* PR Archive / Alamy Stock Photo

490 Teatro Olimpico, Vicenza; CC Share Alike 4.0 Didier Descouens / Wikimedia Commons

495 Villa Medicea La Petraia, Florence; Wikimedia Commons

501 *Codex Magliabechiano* (folio [illegible]); PR Archive / Alamy Stock Photo

506 Illustration from a Latin translation of *The Destruction of the Indies*, by Bartolomé de Las Casas; Bridgeman Images

510–11 Page from a 1626 copy of the Aztec herbal, *Codex Badianus*; Royal Collection Trust / © Her Majesty Queen Elizabeth II 2020

514–15 Theodoor Galle, *Amerigo Vespucci Rediscovers America*, print series entitled *Nova Reperta* (*New Inventions of Modern Times*), engraved by Jan Collaert I, after Jan van der Straet (Stradanus); The Picture Art Collection / Alamy Stock Photo

517 John White, Secotan village; British Museum / Wikimedia Commons

518 Mission San Xavier del Bac; Frank Kovalchek / Wikimedia Commons

523 Martin Luther and Lucifer; Everett Historical / Shutterstock

524 Destruction of religious icons in Zurich, 1524; Wikimedia Commons

536 Christian Fritzsch, *Michael Servetus*, engraving c. 1740; Wikimedia Commons

539 Frontispiece of the first edition of the Great Bible, 1539; Culture Club / Getty Images

540 J. M. W. Turner, *Tintern Abbey*; Heritage Images / Getty Images

547 Opening session of the Council of Trent by Nicolò Dorigati; DEA / A. Dagli Orti / Getty Images

551 Jesuits in China; Everett Historical / Shutterstock

554 Gesù Church, Rome; Stefano_Valeri / Shutterstock

563 Château de Montaigne; CC Share Alike 3.0 Tom Canac / Wikimedia Commons

565 Frontispiece of Montaigne's copy of *De rerum natura*; DEA Picture Library / Getty Images

568 François Dubois, *The Massacre of St Bartholomew*; © DEA / G. Dagli Orti / Getty Images

573 Frontispiece of Shakespeare's *Hamlet*, Second Quarto, 1604/5; © Classic Image / Alamy Stock Photo

583 Joseph Werner, *Louis XIV as Apollo*, 1662/7; © Château de Versailles, RMN / Jean-Marc Manaï

584 Louis XIV visiting the Royal Academy of Sciences, 1671; The Elisha Whittelsey Collection, The Elisha Whittelsey Fund, 1962 / Wikimedia Commons

588 *Audience Given to the Ambassadors of the King of Siam*; © Bibliothèque nationale de France

594 Bartholomeus van Bassen, *Great Assembly of the States-General in 1651*; The Picture Art Collection / Alamy Stock Photo

598 Library of the University of Leiden, 1610; Wikimedia Commons

601–2 Rembrandt, *The Anatomy Lesson of Dr Nicolaes Tulp*; Mauritshuis / Wikimedia Commons

609 Wenceslaus Hollar, *The Trial of Thomas Wentworth, Earl of Stafford*; © Heritage Images / Getty Images

612 *The Embleme of England's Distractions* (1658); Print Collector / Getty Images

619 *The Triumph of Peace and Liberty over Tyranny*, James Thornhill; Wikimedia Commons

635 Frontispiece of Thomas Hobbes's *Leviathan* (1651); Wikimedia Commons

645 Frontispiece of John Locke's *Two Treatises of Government* (1690); Wikimedia Commons

654 *Nasir al-Din at the Observatory*, fifteenth-century Persian miniature; Roland and Sabrina Michaud / akg-images

657 Frontispiece of Nicolaus Copernicus's *De Revolutionibus Orbium Coelestium* (*On the Revolutions of Heavenly Bodies*); Lebrecht Music & Arts / Alamy Stock Photo

658 Engraving from Tycho Brahe's *Astronomiae instauratae mechanica* (1598); Wikimedia Commons

665 Frontispiece of Johannes Hevelius's *Selenographia* (1647); Wikimedia Commons

666 Frontispiece of Galileo Galilei's *Dialogue Concerning the Two Chief World Systems*; Wikimedia Commons

673 Frontispiece of Thomas Sprat's *The History of the Royal Society of London* © Artokoloro Quint Lox Limited / Alamy Stock Photo

674 Paul van Somer, *Francis Bacon* (1617); Lazienki Palace / Wikimedia Commons

677 Frontispiece of Francis Bacon's *Novum organum scientiarum*, 1645; EC. B1328.620ib, Houghton Library, Harvard University / Wikimedia Commons

680 Boyle's air pump, New Experiments; © CC BY 4.0 Wellcome Collection / Wikimedia Commons

683 Torricelli's barometer experiment, 1644; Science & Society Picture Library / Getty Images

684–5 Robert Hooke, spread from *Micrographia* (1665) © CC BY 4.0 Wellcome Collection

686 Antonie van Leeuwenhoek's *Animalcules*; © CC BY 4.0 Wellcome Collection

691 Frontispiece of Isaac Newton's *Principia Mathematica*, first edition (1687); Wikimedia Commons

701 Frans Hals, *René Descartes* (late 1600s); IanDagnall Computing / Alamy Stock Photo

705 René Descartes, *Meditations* (1641); Bibliothèque Nationale de France / Wikimedia Commons

710 Godfrey Kneller, *John Locke* (1697); Hermitage Museum / Wikimedia Commons

720 Pierre Bayle on the frontispiece of the 1740 edition of his *Dictionnaire Historique et Critique* (*Historical and Critical Dictionary*); Artokoloro / Alamy Stock Photo

723 Frontispiece of Pierre Bayle's *Dictionnaire Historique et Critique*; Wikimedia Commons

Index

Page numbers in **bold** refer to main entries for writers, thinkers and themes; page numbers in *italic* refer to illustrations.

B

C

D

G

H

I

J

M

N

O

Q

R

S

T

U

V

W

X

Y

Z

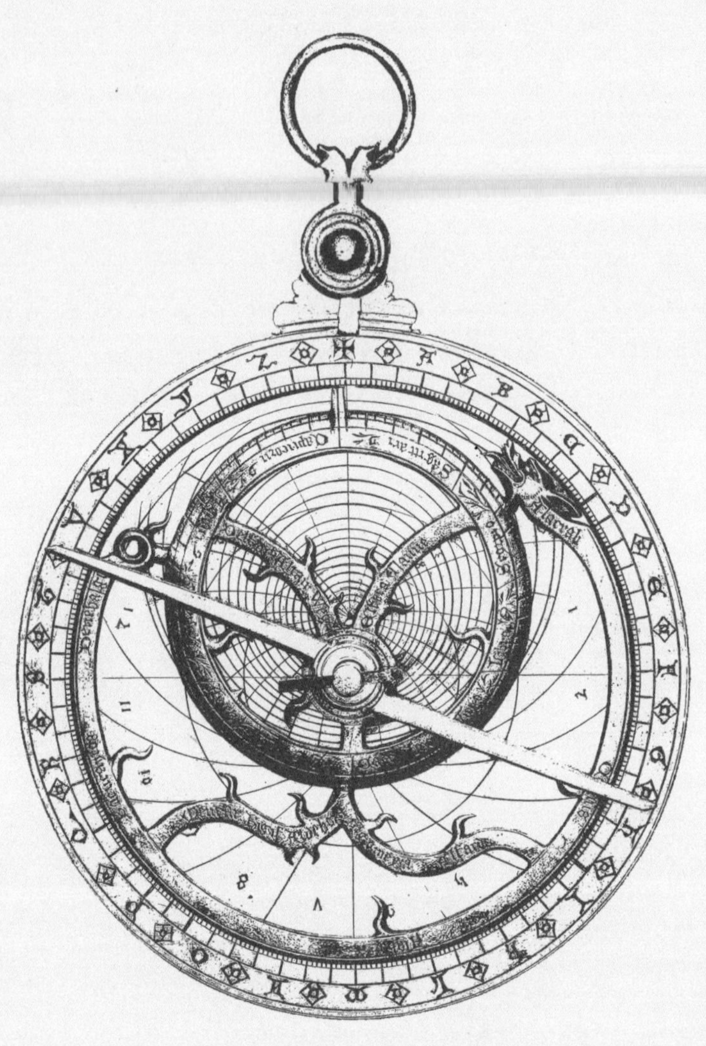